"PRIMITIVISM" IN 20TH CENTURY ART

"PRIMITIVISM" IN 20TH CENTURY ART

Affinity of the Tribal and the Modern

Edited by William Rubin

Volume II

The Museum of Modern Art, New York

"PRIMITIVISM" IN 20TH CENTURY ART
Affinity of the Tribal and the Modern

Published in conjunction with an exhibition of the same title shown at the following museums:

The Museum of Modern Art, New York
Detroit Institute of Arts
Dallas Museum of Art

The exhibition and its national tour are sponsored by Philip Morris Incorporated. Additional support has been provided by the National Endowment for the Arts.

This publication has been made possible by grants from Philip Morris Incorporated and the Eugene McDermott Foundation.

Designed by Steven Schoenfelder
Design assistant: Judy Smilow
Production by Tim McDonough
Production assistants: Ann Lucke and Carlo Pettorali
Typeset by Concept Typographic Services, New York
Printed and bound by Arnoldo Mondadori, Verona, Italy

The Museum of Modern Art
11 West 53 Street
New York, N.Y. 10019

Printed in Italy

CONTENTS

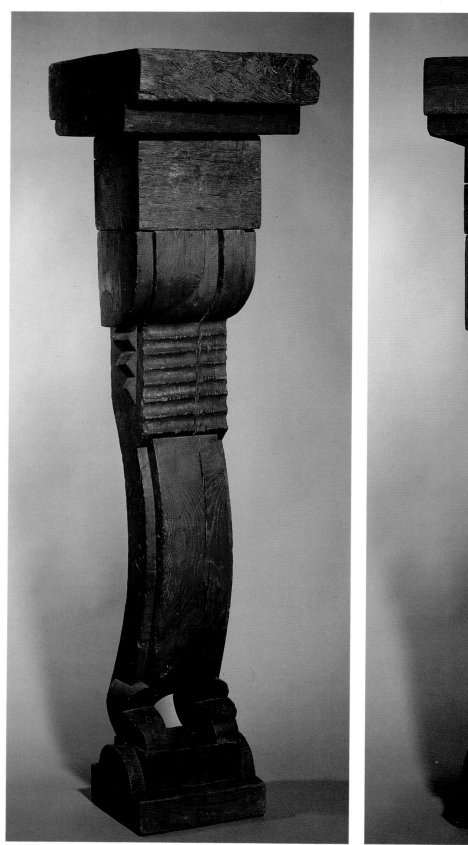

Constantin Brancusi. *Caryatid* (two views). 1914–26. Wood, 65⅝" (166.7 cm) high. Fogg Art Museum, Harvard University, Cambridge; gift. William A. Coolidge, Joseph H. Hazen Foundation, Inc., and Mrs. Max Wasserman; purchase: Francis H. Burr Memorial and Alpheus Hyatt Funds

BRANCUSI

Sidney Geist

Brancusi's primitivism is usually thought to begin with an African influence in a wood carving of 1913, but we may already discern a tendency to a more generalized primitivism in a series of stone carvings he executed during 1907–08. He had rented a ground-floor studio at the end of April 1907 in order to carry out a commission for a funerary monument in Rumania. After completing *The Prayer*, a modeled work, as part of that commission, and then doing several heads in clay, he spent the rest of the year carving, and indeed devoted himself almost exclusively to this practice for the rest of his career.[1]

The stone and marble works of 1907 comprise six heads and busts, five being realistic portrayals of children.[2] Four of the latter display a coarse facture from having been carried out with a "point," a tool usually used for beginning or roughing out a carving. It must have been toward the end of 1907 that he made *Head of a Girl* (p. 346), labeled "Première pierre directe, 190 " (with the year missing).[3] It would seem that this work was followed by *The Kiss* (p. 347), probably begun near the end of the year and completed at the beginning of 1908.[4] The purpose of this recital is to show that once *The Prayer* was out of the way, Brancusi was occupied, during the second half of 1907, in searching for a carving style in a "direct" manner, that he found it in the fresh, confident *Head of a Girl* (the five children's heads have disappeared), and brought it to full artistic realization in *The Kiss*.

It is altogether likely that Brancusi's thoughts took this new direction after his visit to the Gauguin retrospective at the Salon d'Automne, October 6–November 15, 1906.[5] In this large and immensely influential exhibition he would have seen Gauguin's primitivistic carvings in stone and wood, a body of sculpture that cast a spell on a younger generation of artists that included Matisse, Picasso, and Derain. In 1907 Picasso carved *Standing Figure*, wood (p. 259), and "In the spring of 1907," as D.-H. Kahnweiler writes,[6] Derain made *Crouching Man* (p. 215), a compact design in limestone that exemplifies the method of direct carving, or *taille directe*, which had also been Gauguin's. The attraction of this approach—which avoids the copying of a model, whether mechanically or by eye—was precisely its directness, its implied honesty, and the conviction that it produced a new kind of form, one that was essentially "stony." It was also, to be sure, a way of getting around Rodin.

Brancusi, as we have seen, worked throughout most of 1907 on quite realistic carvings rendered with a coarse surface. If he did not catch on to the idea of direct carving as quickly as did Picasso and Derain, it was because he was in tow to his long and thorough academic training in sculpture, a discipline to which neither Picasso nor Derain had been subjected. He finally became aware, as I think, of the significance of *taille directe* with the exhibition of Derain's *Crouching Man* in September 1907, at Kahnweiler's new gallery on Rue Vignon.[7]

The Kiss and *Crouching Man* resemble each other in several ways: they are of comparable size, are carved in limestone of blocky proportions, and are symmetrical in design. Both deal with the nude figure, emphasize the hands, and contain the motif of encircling arms. At the same time, *The Kiss* has clear affinities with Gauguin's primitivizing relief, *Hina and Te Fatou* (p. 203), which had been in the retrospective. Brancusi's *La Sagesse*, 1908,[8] which followed *The Kiss*, is based on a synthesis of figures by Gauguin, the *Breton Eve* and the rather similar old woman at the left of *Where Do We Come From? ...* (p. 180), images which themselves have an ancestry in a Primitive artifact.[9] I am suggesting here that the Primitive influence on Brancusi was no less important for coming secondhand, or for being in the nature of a mystique. The large and varied retrospective of Gauguin's oeuvre, glamorized by the magic of his name and his flight to a supposed Eden, transformed the

Constantin Brancusi. *Head of a Girl*. 1907. Stone. Whereabouts unknown

Fauvist effort and assisted at the creation of two Brancusi figures; it also impelled Derain, Picasso, and Brancusi to undertake direct carving, the most significant development in sculpture in the first decade of this century. Hindsight makes it possible to regard *taille directe*—with its abandonment of the traditional "pointing machine," its return to immediacy of design and execution, its engagement of the stony *matière*—as a product of the primitivizing impulse of the opening of the twentieth century.

While never ceasing to practice *taille directe*, Brancusi developed an ever-increasing control and refinement that mask the directness of his approach and eliminate the primitivistic residues of its beginnings. In 1913 he carved *The First Step* in wood (p. 348), initiating a long series of works in this medium, most of which would be executed in the next ten years. From the first, a new spirit is visible in the form and facture of the wood sculpture: a return to the primitivism of the earliest *taille directe* stone carvings, but governed now by the control gained in the intervening years. But the influences at work on the wood carvings do not operate at second hand;

they reflect a by now long attention to the art of black Africa.

Discussion of the influence of this art on Brancusi has been infrequent, African influence often being taken for granted and just as often ignored. It has been repudiated by one writer as not "important" for two reasons: because of Brancusi's "denial" of African art, and because of a resemblance between Rumanian folk art and African tribal art, a resemblance which unquestionably, in her view, shifts the source of influence on Brancusi from Africa to his native Rumania. But neither the extent of one or the other influence nor the date of Brancusi's "denial" is examined.[10] In any case, this comparison of African and Rumanian native arts does not face the problem of influence raised by specific works of Brancusi.[11] In the earliest extensive examination of these issues, by Katherine Jánszky Michaelsen,[12] the thesis of African influence is supported by several telling comparisons, but is exaggerated to include a classicizing work such as *Sleeping Muse* on the basis of superficial resemblances—what Robert Goldwater used to call "lookalikes." Unfortunately, Goldwater himself has sown some confusion in the matter of Brancusi's Africanism by misreading a key document on the subject: Jacob Epstein's 1940 memoir, *Let There Be Sculpture*. According to Goldwater, "In 1912 [Brancusi] protested to Epstein against [African] influence, and may even have destroyed work which he thought betrayed certain African traits."[13] But a careful reading of Epstein reveals that Brancusi's strictures against African sculpture were made not in 1912, the date of Epstein's first visit to Brancusi's studio, but "twenty years later," when he visited Brancusi again.[14] Of this meeting he writes, "Brancusi, some of whose early work was influenced by African art, now declares categorically that one must not be influenced by African [*sic*], and he even went so far as to destroy works of his that he thought had African influence in it [*sic*]."[15] The "now" in this sentence, written after the visit in the early 1930s, restores the actual sequence of events: Brancusi's interest in African art, first apparent in 1913, his reported destruction of some of his work, and his repudiation of African influence in the early thirties.

The whole issue of Africanism is rejected by Rumanian art historians, who, almost to a man, are inimical to the notion of a Brancusi touched by African art—or indeed subject to any influence except Rumanian folk art and Rodin. But there is nothing in Brancusi's culture or character that would have caused him to shun African or other Primitive art. He had copied casts of classical works in Bucharest, and then, to improve himself, had gone to Paris. Once there, he can be shown to have been observant and eclectic, absorbing features not only from the towering Rodin, but from other contemporary artists, from the many public monuments, and from the museums rich with objects from diverse cultures. His quick intelligence would have led him to sense at once the importance of tribal art, whose discovery, like that of Japanese art some fifty years earlier, was regarded as a revelation by the more adventurous artists. If he did not submit to the direct influence of African art until five years or so after its discovery, it was because he had become involved in what was, for him at least, a revolutionary approach to stone carving.

The First Step, 1913 (p. 348), was Brancusi's first original freestanding figure. Its novel conception obscures the fact that both title and subject—a toddling child—were Salon staples.

Constantin Brancusi. *The Kiss.* 1907–08. Stone, 11" (28 cm) high. Muzeul de Artă, Craiova, Rumania

It exhibits a stylization more radical than that of the third, 1910, version of *The Kiss,*[16] his most abstract work to date, and is, in fact, his first venture in the direction of total formalization, surely learned from African sculpture. Indeed, it is almost certain that a Bambara figure at the Musée de l'Homme (p. 349) was its immediate inspiration. In both works the arms, torso, and head-and-neck have axes that follow the grain of the wood; both have hollowed-out mouths with strongly peaked upper lips, and the heads of both are ovoidal. The Bambara figure has an unstable stance, as though caught in an awkward instant of incipient movement; *The First Step,* of course, portrays the hesitant action announced by the title. Since the Bambara figure was illustrated in a study of African art by Marius de Zayas, published in New York in 1916,[17] we may speculate that de Zayas became aware of the piece because Brancusi pointed it out to him before he left Paris. The two men were acquainted: they attended a garden party at Edward Steichen's place, outside of Paris, in July 1914,[18] and de Zayas later sold several works by Brancusi at the Modern Gallery, New York, of which he was the director.

The First Step was shown in New York early in 1914 at the Gallery of the Photo-Secession, whose director, Alfred Stieglitz, was the center of a circle that included de Zayas. Upon the return of the sculpture to Paris, Brancusi destroyed it, saving only the head—although the torso-and-the-thighs served as the model for *Torso of a Young Man,* c. 1917 . *The First Step* is thus the first known candidate for a work supposedly destroyed by Brancusi because of its African appearance; there is no evidence of any earlier work destroyed for this reason. If *The First Step* owes much to African sculpture, the debt is the more significant for being incurred in a work in which Brancusi engaged a medium new to him: it was *his* first step in wood carving. Once this debt is acknowledged, we must recognize that the form of the whole work and of its component parts achieves a technical perfection, an absolute elegance of design only rarely encountered in Primitive art, and certainly not in the Bambara piece. As Brancusi said much later, when he was tired of having been compared with prehistoric and Primitive sculptors: they did not know "how to work with such precision up to the end as I do now."[19]

Elegantly designed and perfectly finished examples of African sculpture apparently had not yet come to his attention.

The First Step presupposes a long exposure to tribal art and a long gestation in the mind of the sculptor. In 1955 he remembered a visit to the Natural History Museum in Vienna more than fifty years before and, as Muensterberger noted, "immediately recalled some replicas of African rock-paintings and various pieces of tribal art, African...and Oceanic." "The true impact of this art," Brancusi told Muensterberger, "occurred in Paris, possibly first at Apollinaire's [or] at Matisse's studio."[20] In 1909, four years before *The First Step*, Brancusi had met Modigliani, who was an enthusiast of African art. And he soon made the acquaintance, as did Modigliani, of Dr. Paul Alexandre.[21] It is also probable that in 1912 he discussed African sculpture with Jacob Epstein, an admirer of this art since 1902, who much later assembled a large and excellent collection. During Brancusi's visit to London to attend the

Allied Artists Exhibition in July 1913,[22] he would have repaid Epstein's visit of the previous year, and have seen African art with him (as well as Epstein's own work, which was influenced, Epstein's later denials notwithstanding, by African sculpture). It is noteworthy that the manifestation of African influence in *The First Step*, though long in coming, occurred within months of the encounters with Epstein.

The First Step was probably destroyed in 1914, since it is not visible in any later photographs of the studio. If this destruction was carried out because of the figure's African appearance, how is one to account for *Little French Girl*, 1914–18 (p. 351)? For surely this work shows an even clearer African influence than the earlier one. *The First Step* retained, for example, two traditional features that do not occur in *Little French Girl* or indeed in any later work, and whose elimination fostered Brancusi's Africanism: the material continuity of figure and base, and large forms whose axes are not parallel to the

Above: Constantin Brancusi. Head from *The First Step*. 1913. Wood, 10¼" (25.9 cm) high. Musée National d'Art Moderne, Centre National d'Art et de Culture Georges Pompidou, Paris

Left: Constantin Brancusi. *The First Step*. 1913. Wood, c. 44" (111.5 cm) high. Destroyed, except for head

Below: Figure. Bambara. Mali. Wood, 25⅝" (65 cm) high. Musée de l'Homme, Paris

Below right: Constantin Brancusi. Study for *The First Step*. 1913. Crayon, 32⅜ x 15" (82.1 x 38 cm). The Museum of Modern Art, New York; Benjamin Scharps and David Scharps Fund

Constantin Brancusi. *Standing Figure*. 1914. c. 49" (124.5 cm) high. Subsequently reworked as *Little French Girl*

Doll. Bijogo. Bissagos Islands, Guinea-Bissau. Wood and beads, 28″ (71 cm) high. Náprstkovo Muzeum, Prague

Helmet mask. Senufo. Ivory Coast. Wood, 39″ (99 cm) high. Museum Rietberg, Zurich

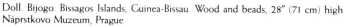

woodgrain. (If the thighs of the destroyed figure of *The First Step* cut diagonally *across* the grain of the wood, in the later *Torso of a Young Man*, based upon it and made from the fork of a tree, they go *along* the grain.) In spite of a general verticality, *The First Step* has a slant to the right, evident especially in its thrusting right leg. This feature too will disappear; henceforth and for decades the carvings (with the exception of *Prodigal Son*) will be, like African figures, fundamentally vertical and symmetrical.

The early roughed-out state (p. 349) of *Little French Girl* (not Brancusi's title)[23] bears a general resemblance to *The First Step*. In the finished work the arms have vanished, and the neck and body have been fused in a tapered spine whose entire length is covered with grooves—Brancusi's economical version of the annulation prevalent in African sculpture. In spite of its few and unusual elements, the figure is touchingly evocative of a little girl in a short skirt, while at the same time being insistently African. The head repeats the cranium, eye, and nose of *The First Step*, and its echo of the latter's Africanism is prolonged by the treatment of the mouth and the serrated hair. And as William Rubin observes, the projecting ear and the ringed neck and torso would have been familiar to Brancusi from Senufo helmet masks, whose helmet tops also

provide a model for the bell-like skirt of Brancusi's figure. Indeed, *Little French Girl*, Rubin notes, has even more similarities to a Bijogo fertility doll in Prague, though it is doubtful that Brancusi could have seen such a doll at that time. No reproductions of this piece were available—and other versions of such dolls are much less in the Brancusi spirit. The arms of Brancusi's figure are absent in a manner surely radical for a European work, but common to some styles from West Africa and Zaire. It is not simply the absence of arms that is African here—they were already famously absent in a number of works by Rodin—but their elimination *by design*, as it were. They are not missing as a result of an actual or implied cutting-off, as in Rodin; there is no proper place to which they might be returned. Also African are the stiff, round legs, pinched into sections like those of the Bijogo fertility figure, with simple shapes at the pedal extremities that permit the sculpture to stand without being fixed to a base. The fact that the image of a girl coincides with the carved object (which contains no allusion to a base or support) allies *Little French Girl* to the Bambara figure as well, and, in fact, to a way of representing the human figure that is pervasive in African sculpture. The figure as an independent object, standing on its own legs, is, at any scale, a magical presence. Brancusi assimilates this magic by giving up the European practice of making the human figure continuous with the setting it inhabits. Material continuity harbors an illusion: that the figure and the ground are different stuffs—flesh and earth, let us say. Brancusi had already rejected this illusion in several versions of *The Kiss*, a broad-bottomed, stable shape; in *Little French Girl* he rejects it in a typically African manner, and will do so henceforth with a thoroughness not always encountered in African sculpture. And while *The Kiss* shows the embrace, the interlace, of two creatures—no less an illusion than foot touching ground—no new image made after 1913 will contain the illusion of two or more things in contact with each other. Beginning in 1914, Brancusi's sculpture shows single iconic objects magically present in our space.

The central element of *Caryatid*, begun 1914 (p. 344), was Brancusi's tallest carving to that date. Its feet rest on—but are not continuous with—the base below, thereby reaffirming the principle of figural independence manifested in *Little French Girl*. Like the latter work, it contains an area of repeated grooving, a typical African feature as we have seen, which occurs again at each side in the more usual form of serration. At the same time, the pervasive African motif of annulation is present in a flattened version on the back of the sculpture. In *Caryatid* the African elements are absorbed into a compact decorative-architectural image in which illustration of the human anatomy has given way to sheer, barely allusive design.

In 1914, Brancusi began the most "African" of his sculptures, *Madame L. R.* (p. 353), which he would not complete until 1918. The piece is radically abstract, standing on a single, central leg. (Although its footing is now separate from the rest and a reconstruction, the work was originally carved in a single block of wood.) While no element imitates any anatomical feature, the whole image has a very feminine character and stance, even apart from the "comb" at the top of the head and the centrally placed concavity at the edge of the lower mass. As in the case of *Little French Girl*, it has no arms, nor can we imagine where they might be attached. Its obviously African air is due in great degree to the head, a cubistic version of the copper-covered Hongwe reliquary figures of Gabon (p. 352), from which Brancusi adopted not only the outer contour, but the central, vertical band and the angular projection at the top, which became his "comb." These reliquary figures—unlike the more familiar ones of the Kota people—have a support that is at right angles to the head, and thus would be read from the front, as Rubin observes, as a single leg. *Madame L. R.*, regardless of its affinities with a subject,[24] is highly conceptual in its design. "Can you imagine an African artist using a model?!" asked Brancusi in 1955[25]—nor did he use one in making this work.

Brancusi carved second versions of *Little French Girl* and *Madame L. R.*; both met the same fate as *The First Step*—disappearance of the body and retention of the head. The destruction of these works, the tampering with others, the lingering for years over still others are signs that for Brancusi the making of images affected by African design was beset with problems. These images, furthermore, yielded very few *series*, whereas he was able to develop many series, some of them long, from the stone carvings.[26]

Unexpectedly, a sculpture in marble, *Princess X* (p. 354), may have been affected by a Primitive work. The sculpture is actually a recarving of a large representational bust of a

Constantin Brancusi. *Little French Girl*. 1914–18. Wood, 49 x 8¾ x 8½" (124.5 x 22.3 x 21.6 cm). The Solomon R. Guggenheim Museum, New York, gift, Estate of Katherine S. Dreier

Reliquary figure (two views). Hongwe. Gabon. Wood, brass, and copper, 20⅞" (53 cm) high. Private collection, Paris

woman with an inclined head, completed—or so it seemed—in 1909. Some time later Brancusi began to work on it again, carving it down or simplifying it.[27] We have noted his visit to London in July 1913; at that time he could have seen a stone pestle from New Guinea (p. 354), recently acquired by the British Museum. With its head-and-neck arching over two prominent breastlike forms, it would surely have drawn Brancusi's attention by its resemblance to his own *Pasarea Maiastra*, 1910 (a marble bird whose head-and-neck are curved over a full breast), and have suggested a stylization for the work in progress, which was not brought to its present state until 1916. Apart from the large design of *Princess X*, the hand which lies alongside its single breast, although unique in the Brancusi oeuvre, has counterparts in African sculpture.

Indecision, radical change, and recombination attend the creation of *Adam and Eve*, 1916–21 (p. 355), a tall structure composed of carved upper and lower parts, with a large block of wood between them. This massive shape accomplishes the miracle of integrating the other two, fashioned in clearly different styles. And indeed they were made at different times and surely on themes unrelated to the original couple. Having made a wedding of these forms, Brancusi would expatiate on the seductiveness of Eve and the responsibilities of Adam. To a

reporter who interviewed him in 1926, he explained the symbolic significance of several formal features of the *Eve* (p. 355)[28]—an exegesis uniquely detailed among his utterances, and as fanciful as other of his explanations.

For who was *Eve* before being linked to *Adam*? In a photograph of 1916 (p. 355) we see her in her debut, a finished sculpture standing, like *Madame L. R.* and the later *Socrates*, on a single leg. Formally, the work is African from domed head to flangelike foot and absent arms. Graphically, it shows a woman of African descent: the full lips are just like those on the marble head of 1920 which Brancusi will call *White Negress*. Thus, a black woman with emphatic lips (mouth) and exposed breasts. Such a literal reading cannot accept a single leg: the long cylinder must be a compressed or sheathed version of the hips and (two) legs. I am supposing, of course, that *Eve* started her career as a sculpture of a black nightclub singer, and that she changed her identity in order to join *Adam*, giving up her supporting cylinder and the lower curve of her breasts. It is too much to think that the pruning of these elements could confer on the remaining parts an Edenic symbolism. This was surely a rationalization after the fact, on a par with the fairy tale Brancusi invented to explain his *Pasarea Maiastra*, and the revision of Greek myth offered in explanation of his *Leda*. Yet it

Constantin Brancusi. *Madame L. R.* (front and rear). 1914–18. Wood, c. 37″ (94 cm) high. Private collection

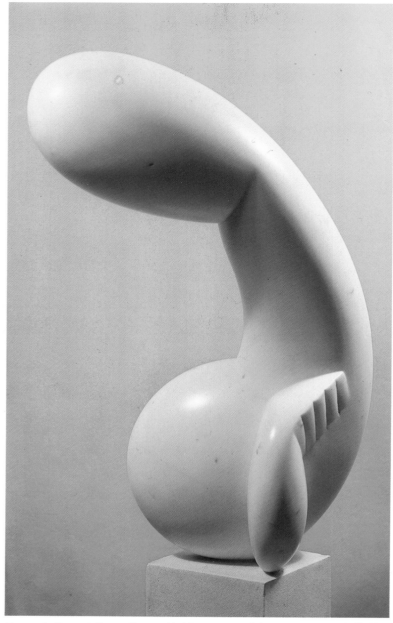

Pestle. Papua New Guinea. Stone, 14¼" (36.3 cm) high. The Trustees of the British Museum, London

Constantin Brancusi. *Princess X.* 1916. Marble, 22 x 11 x 9" (55.9 x 8 x 22.9 cm). Sheldon Memorial Art Gallery, University of Nebraska, Lincoln; gift of Mrs. A. B. Sheldon

was appropriate for Brancusi to design this image of a black singer in the African manner, just as it was fitting later for him to conceive of Eve as black.

As for the *Adam,* it was originally the lower part of a columnar carving of c. 1920, and was separated from it to become the lower half of *Adam and Eve,* thus retaining its formal position while changing, like *Eve,* its symbolic status. The angularities of *Adam,* the grooving at the throat, and the serration below are all distinctly African. At the same time the image calls to mind Epstein's *Sunflower,* 1910 (p. 430), which Brancusi must have known. While *Adam and Eve* and most of the other works in wood are redolent of the modes and motifs of African sculpture, they also demonstrate the sophistication with which Brancusi absorbs the African influence—a sophistication rarely matched by his French and German contemporaries, and strikingly evident in *Endless Column* (p. 358), the most abstract of all his creations.

In 1966 Cecilia Cuțescu-Storck, one of the leading Rumanian painters of the early part of the century and a friend of Brancusi, published a memoir in which she stated that she had seen "the first version" of *Endless Column* and "portions of treetrunks cut obliquely" in Brancusi's studio in 1909.[29] Barbu Brezianu, the Brancusi scholar, accepted this statement at face value, and pointed out besides that a 1911–12 *Portrait of Dr. Paul Alexandre* by Modigliani (p. 356), painted at a time when he was close to Brancusi, contains a motif similar to *Endless Column* running the length of the picture, and that its presence there validates the 1909 date for a *Column.*[30] This analysis labors under two difficulties. The first is chauvinistic: the reluctance to admit any non-Rumanian influence on Brancusi except that of Rodin; a corollary of this attitude is the belief that all influence flows *from* Brancusi, none *to* him, excepting always that of Rodin. The second lies in the fact that Brancusi dates *Endless Column* as of 1918 (correctly);[31] and we can see

Photograph of *Eve* published in unidentified newspaper, New York, February 1926

Constantin Brancusi. *Standing Woman.* 1916. Wood, c. 32″ (81 cm) high. Reworked

Constantin Brancusi. *Carving.* c. 1920. Wood, c. 64″ (162.5 cm) high. Reworked

Right: Constantin Brancusi. *Adam and Eve.* 1916–21. Wood and limestone, 94¼″ (239.4 cm) high. The Solomon R. Guggenheim Museum, New York

Amedeo Modigliani. *Portrait of Dr. Paul Alexandre.* 1911–12. Oil on canvas, 36¼" x 23⅝" (92.1 x 60 cm). Private collection

him approaching it in the few years before this date. Neither the *Column* nor any other wood carving appears in photographs of Brancusi's studio before 1914, nor does the studio, in the few photographs of 1910, look as if it could harbor, beyond camera view, "portions of treetrunks" and a work of the abstraction of *Endless Column*. Let us recall that 1909–10 is the period of *Torso, Woman Looking into a Mirror, Baroness R. F., Sleeping Muse, Narcissus,* and *The Kiss* (Montparnasse Cemetery)—representational carvings in stone and marble that make it impossible to imagine a contemporaneous *Endless Column* in wood. In short, Mme Storck's statement is unacceptable—but not inexplicable. Writing almost sixty years after her first visit to Brancusi's studio, she described it as containing a work which appeared in its first version six years later. In confusing her memories of different visits and possibly different studios, she is like other memorialists of Brancusi's early

years who attribute to the studio on Rue de Montparnasse the contents of the studios in the Impasse Ronsin, often by reference to photographs of the latter.

How are we to account for the motif in Modigliani's portrait? Early in 1968, in answer to my request for any knowledge in the Alexandre family concerning the design, I received a letter from Georges Bréfort with information supplied by his mother, the daughter of Dr. Alexandre, herself unable to write. According to Mme Bréfort: "It is very probable that, to paint the vertical band and the motif on it, Modigliani was inspired by a hanging or drape of Moroccan or African origin which was in the house where Dr. Alexandre was living at the time when Modigliani did his portrait. It is not surprising that Modigliani was pleased by this hanging. We know that he was much taken by "art nègre," and it is very possible that he took advantage of the existence of the hanging to reconcile his

Constantin Brancusi. *Endless Column.* 1918. Wood, c. 83" (210.9 cm) high. Reworked

desire to give the painting this harmony and his taste for African art. We have not been able to find the original hanging, but my mother is quite convinced that it was not a matter of the artist's invention, but of a hanging which actually existed."[32]

In view of Brancusi's friendship with both Modigliani and Dr. Alexandre, we may assume that he knew the hanging from the painting, from visits to the Alexandres, or from both. The motif in the hanging may, therefore, well be the germ of *Endless Column,* which would not be the only instance of Brancusi's projection into depth of a flat design. Although the motif is found in many folk arts, it seldom takes the form we see in Modigliani's painting—that of stacked rhomboids rather than the more usual squares—a form which persists in the *Column.* No claimant for a Rumanian source has been able to find, in the rich lexicon of Rumanian columns, anything

resembling *Endless Column.* Several writers reproduce the top of the same provincial gate post, an unlikely source.[33] Much closer to the character of the *Column* is a small work in marble by Brancusi: the base of *Maiastra,* 1912, clearly serrated, and very possibly suggested by the hanging in the Alexandre house.[34]

There seems to be no doubt that when Brancusi decided to translate the motif to wood a few years later, he intended it to serve as a base. Thus, a 66-inch example of 1915, carved only on two sides in *L'Enfant au monde, groupe mobile,* 1917 (later dispersed), supports a *Cup.* As we can see by the white chalk drawing on a side of the column, Brancusi entertained the idea of piercing it with round holes (and he redrew the circles even after he faceted the flat sides); the column disappeared. Replying to a question about what should be put on the *Column* of 1918, Henri-Pierre Roché wrote to the collector John Quinn,

"[Brancusi] says the column does not need a base till it is put forever in a special place, supporting a special thing..."[35] If the 1918 *Column* began as a base, it *became* a sculpture by a progressive act of imagination. It entered the state of sculpture definitively in 1927 when Brancusi removed the mortise by which it was held in a stone block, and conferred on it that formal independence which is a characteristic of his other sculpture. The piece had gone beyond its origins as a base, beyond the repetitive-decorative, and at 80 inches became a metaphor for the presence of man.

The 20-foot *Endless Column*, set up in 1920 in Edward Steichen's garden in Voulangis, was carved in a treetrunk taken from the garden; it is an emblem of human consciousness in the midst of nature. The 96-foot cast-iron *Column*, 1938, in Tîrgu Jiu, is sometimes claimed to have a funerary function which reinforces its (supposed) derivation from old Rumanian funerary columns. But the *whole emplacement* at Tîrgu Jiu—not its parts—is funerary. Since the *Column* in its several previous versions—those of 1915, 1918, 1920— had never carried intimations of funerary use or meaning, the situation at Tîrgu Jiu was one where a Column of no previously funerary significance joined a Table and a Gate, equally devoid of a funereal past, in a monument to those who had died defending the River Jiu in World War I. In this context the great height of the piece and its setting, a large open space, evoke the symbolism of the *axis mundi*. The *Column* is here a pulsating link between heaven and earth; it transcends the more usual earthbound monument even as the motif itself goes beyond its origins in folk or tribal art.

That motif—in spite of its compressed, symmetrical state in the *Column*—is one of serration or dentation, and it is quintessentially African, appearing in many forms and with varying intensity of repetition in the wood carving of many tribal peoples. Brancusi employs it in a later work in wood that is not otherwise "African"—*The Cock*, 1924, and its bronze and monumental plaster versions. In this work serration has, for the first time, an expressive rather than a decorative function, telling us of the simultaneous stretching and crowing of the barnyard creature. *The Cock* in bronze and its serrated stone base enforce a subtle shift in esthesis as the apprehension of the motif as decoration is followed by—or overlaid with— that of the motif as meaning.

In sum, serration, with its African flavor, is present in the bases of at least ten works, most of them Birds, but including *Exotic Plant* and *Princess X*. It appears in a less insistent form in the large bases of seven versions of *Bird in Space*, and in the bases of works as various as *Chimera* (p. 360), *Sleeping Child*, *The Kiss*, and *Fish*. Among design elements that are distinguishable in Brancusi, serration is surely the most pervasive, serving often in the counterpoint of base and sculpture, of angularity below and fluent curvature above. The cumulative effect of the motif was apparent in the Art Institute of Chicago's installation of the Brancusi retrospective, 1970, where a platform holding several sculptures created the impression of an African throne-room.

Long after Brancusi inveighed against the African influence to Epstein, he employed serration several times and to new purpose in *King of Kings*, late 1930s (p. 361). The tall columnar

Constantin Brancusi. *Endless Column*. 1918. Wood, 80 x 9⅞ x 9⅝ (203.2 x 25.1 x 24.5 cm). The Museum of Modern Art, New York; gift of Mary Sisler

figure seems to be crowned with a circular dentation; in the middle of the sculpture a group of ridges is ranged vertically—like a washboard on its side—while on an adjacent plane a similar group of ridges has the more customary horizontal orientation; and the motif may even be said to take another form in the screwlike design near the bottom. This exhaustive use of the related features of serration and dentation, as well as marked segmentation, imparts an African character to *King of Kings*. Less abstract than this work is the larger than life-size *Caryatid*, early 1940s, an imposing, much simplified version of a theme essayed in 1915. This last carving of Brancusi's to show African influence does so in its verticality, symmetry, and the formal distinction of its parts; in the repeated grooving at the throat; in the unitary, bulging torso; in the "bent-knee" stance; and in the separated legs, each terminating in a foot (or footing) so deep as to permit the tall work to stand safely without need of attachment to a base.

This long catalog of Brancusi's sculpture showing African elements calls for an examination of his claim, reported by Epstein, that he had destroyed some works that betrayed African influence. We can find evidence of only three such destroyed works: *The First Step* and the second versions of both *Little French Girl* and *Madame L. R.* In all three cases the head alone was preserved. In the two latter cases, the first versions were kept entire, still exist, and have been shown here to be strongly influenced by African sculpture. I suspect that the second versions were suppressed because they made no improvement or worthwhile variation on the first, not because

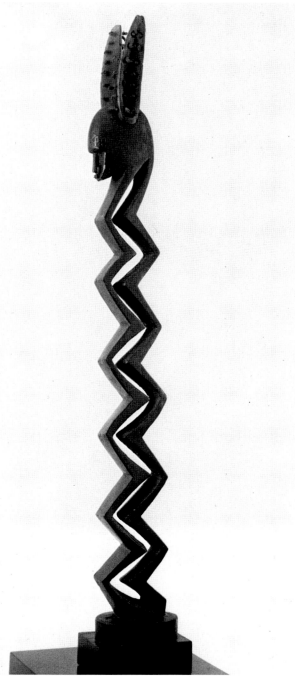

Headdress. Bambara. Mali. Wood. 27¼" (69.2 cm) high. Private collection

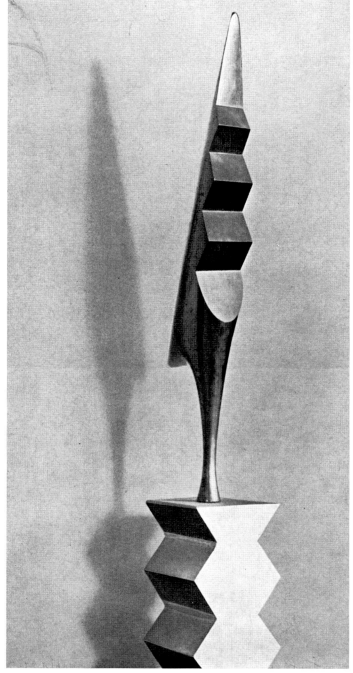

Constantin Brancusi. *The Cock.* 1935. Polished bronze, 40¾" (103.4 cm) high. Musée National d'Art Moderne, Centre National d'Art et de Culture Georges Pompidou, Paris

Helmet mask. Baule. Ivory Coast. Wood, 42⅞" (109 cm) high. Collection Marina Picasso. Formerly collection PABLO PICASSO

Constantin Brancusi. *Chimera*. 1918. Wood, 59¾ x 9¾ x 9¾" (151.8 x 24.8 x 24.8 cm). Philadelphia Museum of Art; The Louise and Walter Arensberg Collection

they showed African influence.[36] In view of the creation of the markedly African initial versions of *Little French Girl* and *Madame L. R.* immediately after *The First Step*, I now think this work was destroyed not because it was African, but because it was not African enough.

The conclusion is inescapable that none of the destructions of which we have knowledge were effected because of manifest African influence. Even if there were destructions of this kind (and I do not believe there were any), they would have been very few, surely insignificant when compared with the important body of work which exists, which reflects a marvelous understanding of African art, and which brilliantly assimilates it.

Why, then, did Brancusi expostulate as he did against the

dangers of African influence? In the 1920s he had become ever more committed to his evolving Bird, a theme which culminated in the white marble *Bird in Space*, 1925, 71 inches high, a version of 1930, 74 inches high, and their shining derivatives in polished bronze. In 1928 he had carved *White Negress* in white marble, and c. 1930 did two monumental versions of *Grand Coq* in plaster (p. 362), and the noble *Column of the Kiss*, a 10-foot structure in smooth white plaster. The luminosity and immateriality of these works is a world away from the particularity, intensity, and actuality of the sculpture in wood. Since Brancusi's efforts were usually generated by clear impulses, the strain of dealing with two tendencies in his work may have become insupportable, the outburst to Epstein occurring at a moment when the arguments for light and space had become imperious. This concern leads him to say, in a conversation in Bucharest in 1939, "I have eliminated holes, which cause shadows."[37] The wood sculpture, with its sharp changes of plane, had especially strong inner shadows, the material itself being dark. Secondly, Brancusi's great pride rebelled against the debt he surely felt toward African sculpture. This was not the first time he had reacted in this way to a powerful influence. After his brief, early Rodinian phase, he had, like other bold sculptors of his generation, turned against the master of Meudon; indeed his espousal of direct carving permitted Brancusi to make what seemed like a clean break from Rodin's influence. Decades later, in 1952, came his statement for the catalog of the exhibition "Hommage à Rodin," in which he admitted the great debt of modern sculpture to the French master. If Brancusi found it necessary to repudiate African art in the early 1930s, he will speak of it later in the warmest terms. His denunciations were heuristic; they helped him to pursue a new line of thought. Long after that pursuit was accomplished, he had the good sense to recant.

Apart from what we deduce from his sculpture, Brancusi's own statements reveal much about his view of African art. And important as his remarks to Jacob Epstein may be, they should not be taken in isolation, as we have already seen.

In July 1923, *The Arts* published an article on Brancusi over the signature M.M.; although based on several discussions with the sculptor in Paris, the article did not claim to be a verbatim report, but a reconstruction of "many conversations." We read: "Christian primitives and Negro savages proceed by faith and instinct; the modern artist proceeds by instinct guided by reason."[38] These statements seem trustworthy since they are consonant with other knowledge of Brancusi, especially his claim that Primitive artists were not able to work with "precision up to the end" as he was able to.

When he came to New York early in 1926 on the occasion of a small exhibition at the Wildenstein Galleries, William Zorach met him and wrote an informative article, also published in *The Arts*, in which he took for granted Brancusi's interest in African art.[39] Dorothy Dudley, writing in *The Dial*, February 1927, took the same point of view—"Brancusi likes Negro art"—and quoted him directly as saying, "There is joy in Negro sculpture." Her interesting account repeatedly quotes the sculptor—who came to New York a second time in 1926 for an important exhibition at the Brummer Gallery— and even touches on the matter of his Rumanian background, but the remark is Dudley's, not Brancusi's.[40] Two years later Benjamin Fondane, a friend and fellow Rumanian whose portrait Brancusi drew, wrote, "He recognizes his brothers only in the primitives, the artists of the Gothic, and the blacks."[41] Within two years we witness a complete reversal in Brancusi's feelings; the inner force of African art that had first attracted him now seemed a danger. To Epstein he said that its influence should be avoided; to others he spoke of "demonic forces."[42] As far as we can tell, Brancusi maintained this attitude for the next twenty years.

Probably in the early 1950s Brancusi declares: "Only the Africans and the Rumanians know how to carve wood."[43] Thus, before he reacknowledges the importance of African art, he links it with another tradition, but, as we see, at the level of craft: "how to carve wood." At the same time, the

Constantin Brancusi. *King of Kings*. Late 1930s. Wood, 9' 10⅛" (300 cm) high. The Solomon R. Guggenheim Museum, New York; gift of the artist

literature records no other mention of Rumanian folk art by Brancusi, except for his criticism of contemporary examples, expressed in conversation with friends in Rumania.[44] For the two parties in his statement are different and unequal: on the one hand, his native tradition, from which he inherited a familiarity with and love of wood as a medium, and on the other, the tribal arts, which in their form and spirit revealed a new universe of artistic possibility.

In 1955 Werner Muensterberger visited Brancusi, who already had a copy of Muensterberger's recent book on tribal art. In their conversations on the subject, Brancusi used the term "'liberation' (of artistic vision), a word he repeated several times with reference to tribal art..."[45] Going beyond this avowal, he remarked, "It is like the air you breathe or the rays of the sun. You forget they are there, but you cannot do without them."[46] These words, spoken near the end of Brancusi's life, give the impression of a mind completely at ease in the universe of African art, as though in a natural medium for the flowering of his thought. After the frank Africanizing of his first wood carvings, it is an essential abstractness that is awakened in him by tribal art. Never again, after *The First Step*, 1913, will Brancusi's sculpture admit the nuanced modeling that is one of the charms of European realism. His every personal fantasy, as well as his use of the partial figure—the legacy of Rodin—will undergo the pressure of the formal. The result is the new *frisson* we recognize in Brancusi— product of the fusion of a local, contemporary humanism with an ancient, other, hieratic rigor.

Constantin Brancusi. *Grand Coq.* 1949. Plaster, 15′ 8⅝″ x 22⅝″ x 39⅜″ (479 x 57.5 x 100 cm). Brancusi Studio, Musée National d'Art Moderne, Centre d'Art et de Culture Georges Pompidou, Paris

Figure. Mama. Nigeria. Wood, 20⅞" (53.1 cm) high. The Art Institute of Chicago; Claire Zeisler Foundation Restricted Gift

Above: Mask. Tsogo. Gabon. Painted wood, 16¾" (42.6 cm) high. The Detroit Institute of Arts; gift of Max J. Pincus

Right: Mask. Chokwe. Zaire or Angola. Wood and fiber, 16⅞" (43 cm) high. Private collection

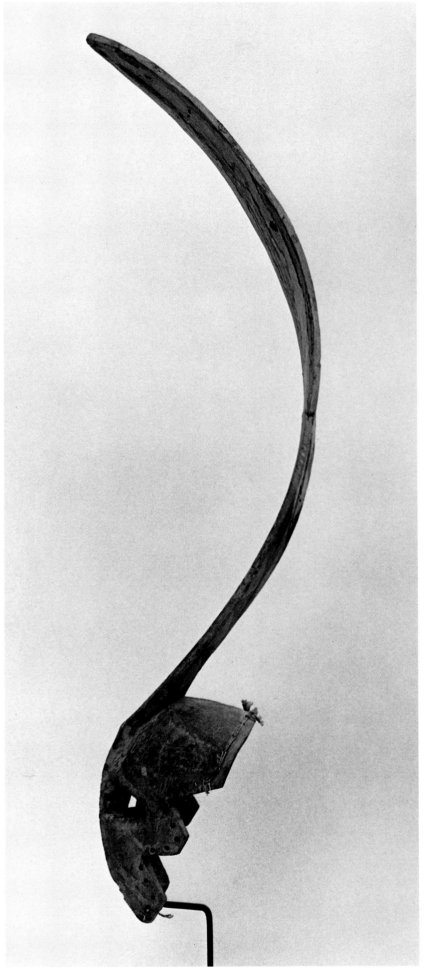

Above: Figure. Lega. Zaire. Wood with paint, 4⅞" (12.4 cm) high.
Collection Marsha and Saul Stanoff

Left: Mask. Mossi. Upper Volta. Wood, 46" (116.9 cm) high.
Collection Elaine Lustig Cohen and Arthur A. Cohen, New York

Figure. Mambila. Cameroon. Wood, 26" (66 cm) high. Collection Bryce Holcombe

NOTES

1. After 1907 Brancusi made occasional studies in clay, which he destroyed; the *Grand Coq* was modeled in clay; a few works were modeled in plaster; the bronzes derived from plaster casts taken from carvings.
2. The five carvings of children are nos. 42, 50, 51, 52, and 53 in Geist 1975 and 1983.
3. *This Quarter*, 1925, illus. no. 42.
4. The date of *The Kiss*, the question of *taille directe*, and related matters in the following three paragraphs are discussed more fully in Geist 1978.
5. John F. Moffitt, "El Beso de Brancusi," *Goya* no. 273, 1983, pp. 296–302, argues that *The Kiss* was influenced by the exhibition of Iberian sculpture that opened at the Louvre in the spring of 1906. This is interesting, but does not satisfactorily account for the appearance of *The Kiss* more than a year and a half later, or the realism of the 1907 carvings of children.
6. Daniel Henry [Kahnweiler], *André Derain* (Leipzig: Klinkhardt and Biermann, 1920), p. 10.
7. See D.-H. Kahnweiler's letter of October 17, 1963, to the author; Brancusi Archive, Library of The Solomon R. Guggenheim Museum.
8. For the change in title from *Wisdom of the Earth*, employed heretofore, see Geist 1976.
9. Wayne Anderson, *Gauguin's Paradise Lost* (New York: Viking, 1971), p. 89 and illus. 57.
10. Edith Balasz, "The Myth of African Negro Art in Brancusi's Sculpture," *Revue roumaine d'histoire de l'art* 14 (1977), pp. 107–124.
11. In the Balasz article, only one Brancusi is reproduced—a drawing. As a result readers cannot estimate the matter of influence. The article labors to demonstrate similarities between African and Rumanian peasant artifacts.
12. Katherine Jánszky Michaelsen, "Brancusi and African Art," *Artforum*, November 1971, pp. 72–77.
13. Robert Goldwater, *Primitivism in Modern Art* (New York: Vintage, 1967), p. 231. Jacob Epstein, *Let There Be Sculpture* (London and New York, 1940), and *Epstein: An Autobiography* (New York: Dutton, 1955).
14. Epstein 1940, p. 223.
15. Ibid., pp. 190–191.
16. *The Kiss*, 1910, is reproduced in Geist 1975 and 1983, no. 59.
17. Marius de Zayas, *African Negro Art: Its Influence on Modern Art* (New York: Modern Gallery, 1916); unnumbered illustrations. The Bambara is listed simply as Upper Volta. The Bambara figure was also reproduced on the cover of a Russian book, from a photograph taken by the author in 1913; Vladimir Markov, *Iskusstvo Negrov* [The Art of the Negroes] (Petrograd: 1919).
18. Agnes E. Meyer, *Out of These Roots: The Autobiography of an American Woman* (Boston: Little, Brown, 1953), p. 105.
19. Geist 1968 and 1983, p. 155.
20. From a letter of April 10, 1983, addressed to the author by Werner Muensterberger, London (see note 32 below), and quoted here with his kind permission. Incidentally, the mention of Matisse is the first unequivocal evidence of relations between him and Brancusi that I have encountered in a Western document. Brancusi, in a conversation of 1939 in Bucharest, said: "In Paris I was a friend of Matisse, of Erik Satie, of Modigliani and—especially—of Guillaume Apollinaire." Petre Pandrea, *Portrete și controverse* (Bucharest: 1945), p. 160. Brancusi also refers to "my friend Picasso," ibid., p. 169.
21. Dr. Alexandre is said to have owned a large group of Baule masks; Jean Laude, *La Peinture française et l'art nègre* (Paris: Klincksieck, 1968), p. 22, note 15. Recent investigation by Jean-Louis Paudrat shows that this was not so.
22. Horace Brodzky, *Henri Gaudier-Brzeska* (London: Faber and Faber, 1933), p. 94.
23. According to Dr. Louise Svendsen, formerly Curator, The Solomon R. Guggenheim Museum, the title was bestowed on the work by James Johnson Sweeney, formerly Director of the museum; personal communication.
24. It is supposed that the work refers to Mme Léone Ricou, a patron of the arts and friend of the sculptor.
25. From the Muensterberger letter, note 20 above.
26. For example, *The Kiss, Sleeping Muse, Mademoiselle Pogany, Torso of a Young Woman, Bird in Space*.
27. Nina Hamnett, *Laughing Torso* (New York: Long and Smith, 1932), pp. 123–24.
28. Reproduced in a New York newspaper, February 1926. I am grateful to Barbu Brezianu, Bucharest, for supplying the illustration.
29. Cecilia Cuțescu-Storck, *O viață dăruită artei* [A life dedicated to art] (Bucharest: Meridiane, 1966), p. 50.
30. Barbu Brezianu, "Note pe marginea articolului 'Brancusi' de Michel Ragon," *Arta plastică*, no. 4, 1966.
31. In the catalog, which he supervised personally, of his exhibition at Brummer Gallery, New York, November 17–December 15, 1926.
32. This letter (as well as Dr. Muensterberger's) will be deposited in the Brancusi Archive, the Library of The Solomon R. Guggenheim Museum. It includes the information that Brancusi was introduced to Dr. Alexandre by the sculptor Maurice Drouard (of whom Modigliani did a portrait), and that the two men had a similar love of nature and took walks together in the woods close to Paris.
33. E.g., Edith Balas, "The Sculpture of Brancusi in the Light of His Rumanian Heritage" (Ph.D. diss., University of Pittsburgh, 1973), pl. 35.
34. The serrated base of another *Maiastra*, 1912 (no. 82 in Geist 1975 and 1983), was made many years after the sculpture. For the early base, see *Maiastra*, 1912 (no. 83 in ibid.).
35. Letter of May 28, 1922; John Quinn Collection, Manuscript Division, New York Public Library.
36. For a photograph of *Little French Girl II*, see Geist 1975 and 1983, no. 123; for a reconstruction of *Madame L. R. II*, see ibid., no. 154.
37. Pandrea 1945, p. 162.
38. M.M., "Constantin Brancusi: A Summary of Many Conversations," *The Arts* 4, no. 1 (July 1923), pp. 15–17.
39. William Zorach, "The Sculpture of Constantin Brancusi," *The Arts* 9, no. 3 (March 1926), pp. 43–50.
40. Dorothy Dudley, "Brancusi," *The Dial* 82 (February 1927), pp. 123–30.
41. Benjamin Fondane, "Brancusi," *Cahiers de l'Etoile* (1929), pp. 708–25.
42. Carola Giedion-Welcker, *Brancusi* (New York: Braziller, 1959), p. 33.
43. Geist 1968 and 1983, p. 149. The remark was reported by Etienne Hajdu at the Brancusi Colloquium, Bucharest, October 13–15, 1967.
44. Pandrea 1945, pp. 155, 157.
45. From the Muensterberger letter, note 20 above.
46. Werner Muensterberger, *Universality of Tribal Art*, Geneva, 1979, p. 15.

REFERENCE LIST

Sidney Geist, *Brancusi: A Study of the Sculpture* (New York: Grossman, 1968).

———*Brancusi: The Sculpture and Drawings* (New York: Abrams, 1975).

———*"La Sagesse or Cuminţenia pămîntului?" Constantin Brancusi* (Duisburg: Wilhelm-Lehmbruck Museum, 1976), pp. 90–99.

———*Brancusi/The Kiss* (New York: Harper and Row, 1978).

———*Brancusi: A Study of the Sculpture* (New York: Hacker, 1983). A revision of the edition of 1968, with catalog brought up to date.

Initiatic posts. Komo. Zaire. Wood. Field photograph by Charles Henault

Max Pechstein. *African Wood Sculpture*. 1919. Oil on canvas. 31¾ x 27½" (80.5 x 69.8 cm). Private collection

GERMAN EXPRESSIONISM

Donald E. Gordon

Over the past half-century art historians have interpreted the relationship between German Expressionism and tribal art in a variety of ways.[1] Robert Goldwater remarked that what fascinated German Expressionists about Primitive art was its "power and immediacy"; the Expressionists' response was direct and emotive, unlike that of Gauguin and the Fauves, which had been more romantic and idealized. These were important observations, yet it is unfortunate that Goldwater chose to define the German attitude by the phrase "emotional primitivism."[2] For the word "emotional" often carries with it connotations of anti-intellectualism or irrationality. There is an implication that Expressionists were atavistic, that they uncritically identified with—or somehow even reverted to—the earlier art of folk or tribe. By 1968 L. D. Ettlinger could even argue, beyond Goldwater, that a leading Expressionist responded not to the Primitive image but to the exotic idea: "He came to his admiration not through an aesthetic experience, but through his reading."[3]

Goldwater's viewpoint has become entrenched in recent years. In 1979 Expressionists were said to seek a "regression" to states of preadult innocence or prehuman animality.[4] And in 1983 the "essence of Expressionism" was attributed to "the belief that there exists a content beyond convention, a reality beyond representation—in short a Nature opposed to Culture." Needless to add, since all language is cultural and since "Expressionism denies its own status as a language," the alleged German belief in unmediated nature is delusional.[5]

Nevertheless, there have been critics who took a contrary view of the notion that Expressionist primitivism was uniformly emotional, regressive, and nature-based. As early as

1920, for example, a friend of Freud pointed out that Expressionist regression was but a *reculer pour mieux sauter*, a tactical withdrawal the better to advance. According to Oskar Pfister, regress was but a "stage of transition" to further progress: "Every step on the road to progress is possible only through the detour of such a regression."[6] And in 1947 Gustav Hartlaub distinguished between a "primary" and a "secondary" Expressionism whereby only the former was unconscious, locally determined, and truly "primitive." Medieval mystics or tribal sculptors were primary "primitives" in this sense, but German Expressionists were of the secondary type, that is, "consciously primitive" or primitivizing "by choice."[7] It follows that in studying archaic or tribal art the modern Germans were choosing a cultural language—a primitivizing language, but a language nonetheless.

Furthermore, there is evidence that Expressionist primitivism *was* aesthetically meaningful as well as culturally oriented. By 1964 historians of modern art and of tribal art could actively collaborate in the search for formal relationships. In their exhibition "The Primordial and the Modern," for example, Leopold Reidemeister and Kurt Krieger demonstrated the "form-relation" between the two kinds of art.[8] And in 1972 in the Munich exhibition "World Cultures and Modern Art," it was conclusively demonstrated, I believe, that the Brücke's response to tribal art was "analytic" as well as "emotional." As Manfred Schneckenburger put it in the catalog to that show, "It would be wrong to reduce their reception of primitive art to a kind of mysticism, without understanding of form." Today we must confirm Schneckenburger's finding that primitivism affected Expressionism in *two* ways: both as life idea and as art idea.[9]

Ernst Ludwig Kirchner. *Girl under Japanese Umbrella.* 1909. Oil on canvas, 36¼ x 31½"
(92 x 80 cm). Kunstsammlung Nordrhein-Westfalen, Düsseldorf

The difference between Expressionism in Germany and
Austria lies, in fact, in the inability of Austrians to identify, as
did the Germans, with a primitivizing ideal. Thus Oskar
Kokoschka responded to tribal art in 1908 by admitting its
emotional immediacy but by insisting on its divergence from
Viennese culture:

[I immediately understood] a Polynesian mask with its incised tattooing,...because I could feel my own facial nerves reacting to cold
and hunger in the same way. For all my sympathy with primitive art,
[however,] it would not have occurred to me to imitate it. I was not a
savage. I would have had to live like them for my imitation to be
genuine. And I had just as much feeling for fossils, stuffed animals,
meteorites, or any documents of a time which is lost forever.[10]

In Germany, by contrast, Expressionists discovered in themselves a kinship with agrarian peoples. It was easy to idealize
such peoples around 1910–11, during Germany's rapid urban-
ization, or again around 1919–20 after a dehumanizing, mechanized war. In city studios artists re-created the imagined
environment of tribal life. And in the countryside the life style
of peasants was appreciated for its own sake. Some artists even
"went native" during summer vacations, living in the nude
with their models and practicing a sexual camaraderie that
paraphrased—so they thought—the supposed instinctual
freedom of tribal life.[11]

As with life style, so with art style: German artists emulated
Primitive example. The prototypes ranged from the flat and
silhouettelike painted reliefs of Palau to the powerful, three-
dimensional forms of Cameroon sculpture. There is a hardy
"look" to much Expressionist art—angular in shape, geometric in detail, stubby in proportion—that is unthinkable
without the Primitive precedent. Vitalism was also important:
Eyes, mouths, breasts, genitalia were all given expressive
prominence. Even in repose the Expressionist face and figure

seem packed with energy. These are all German derivations
from tribal art. One must provisionally assume that at least
some specific Expressionist works derive directly from identifiable tribal sources. Demonstration of such derivations, however, has proved difficult. Reidemeister in 1964 and
Schneckenburger in 1972 each brought together some five or
six dozen works of German Expressionist and tribal art in
impressive shows displaying formal similarities. And in a few
cases, to be sure, exact comparison revealed the influence of
a specific Primitive object on an Expressionist work. Six or
seven such comparisons, including several documented by
the Nolde scholar Martin Urban, will be illustrated once again
in this study.[12]

Yet most of the comparisons put forward in these shows
were inexact or unconvincing. This was mainly because the
actual availability of a given Primitive object to the German
artist before 1910, or even 1920, went unexamined. One
abiding problem is that holdings of German ethnographic
museums were decimated during World War II, as many public
collections of Expressionist art had been a few years before. A
surprising number of such objects, however, have survived in
reproduction, and the majority of the works themselves are
still extant. Studying illustrations of lost objects along with
the surviving ones can shed significant light on the process by
which Expressionists utilized Primitive sources. Furthermore,
when such comparisons are made, the likelihood of selective
or eclectic borrowing must be investigated. Did an Expressionist work take its inspiration from two or more Primitive
models? Did it respond selectively to a distinctive feature, but
not all features, of its precedent? These are the kinds of issues,
unexamined in the literature, that will be explored in this
essay.

In his *Discourse on the Origin of Inequality,* Jean-Jacques Rousseau
saw Primitive man as prerational. His view of evolution
required what Claude Lévi-Strauss has called a "threefold
passage": from nature to culture, from feelings to knowledge,
and from animality to humanity.[13] Yet this gap did not prevent
Rousseau in old age, on one or two brief occasions, from
experiencing a transcendent empathy with the precultural
state. "I feel ecstasies, inexpressible ravishings," he wrote, "to
melt myself, as it were, into the system of beings, to identify
myself with all of nature."[14]

In German-speaking lands a century later, Ferdinand Tönnies established a distinction between natural "community"
and more advanced capitalist "society." Community or
Gemeinschaft was the "folk's" mode of social organization, based
on familial feelings of love, kinship, and neighborhood,
whereas the "educated classes" preferred a society or
Gesellschaft based instead on individualism, contracts, and
commodity values. "Organic" community grew from a consensus of "natural wills"; "mechanical" society yielded objective ties between "rational wills."[15] Tönnies' concepts define
what Lévi-Strauss calls "cultural discontinuity." The Primitive
community evinces a need for wholeness, a respect for nature
and a rejection of historical time, but is meanwhile subject to
exploitation by more competitive colonial societies.[16]

In the Expressionist generation, Georg Simmel wrote most
eloquently on the ills of the depersonalized modern city. Even
more than Tönnies he found urban life alienating: "What

appears in the metropolitan style of life...as dissociation is in reality only one of its elemental forms of socialization"; "under certain circumstances, one nowhere feels as lonely and lost as in the metropolitan crowd."[17] Nevertheless, Simmel insisted—contrary to Tönnies—that art arises at the crossroads of nature and culture. Indeed, Tönnies had discussed creativity and genius under the heading of the common people's "natural will"; art allegedly arose in feelings, "feminine" values, and in community.[18] Yet Simmel observed that art-making required not only raw "life" (nature) but also artistic "form" (culture). The crisis in modern culture rested precisely on the struggle between the two:

Whenever life expresses itself, it desires to express only itself; thus it breaks through any form which would be superimposed on it by some other reality....[Today] the bridge between the past and the future of cultural forms seems to be demolished; we gaze into an abyss of unformed life beneath our feet. But perhaps this formlessness is itself the appropriate form for contemporary life.[19]

Following Tönnies, in sum, Expressionists such as Nolde saw art in relation to the prerational folk community, to the instincts and feelings of natural life, indeed to what Rousseau knew as the "primitive" state of nature.[20] Yet most German artists also knew, with Simmel, that art was a cultural product. In industrial society painting and sculpture could only *evoke* a state of nature; it could never return to it fully.

When the Brücke (Bridge) group was formed in Dresden on June 7, 1905, it took the name *Künstlergruppe* (artists' group), rejecting the more folkish title of *Gemeinschaft* (community).[21] And when the *Brücke Program* of autumn 1906 called for "youth" to oppose "the well-established older forces," it referred not to the youthful innocence of Tönnies' natural community[22] but rather to youth's "glorious power" as championed in 1898 on behalf of the sophisticated Vienna Secession.[23] Even the style of the woodcut *Program*, with elegant letters carved between ruled lines, evokes an image not of nature but of advanced culture.[24]

What is new in the *Brücke Program*, however, is its concluding invitation to every artist "who renders with immediacy and authenticity that which drives him to creation." The stress on "immediacy and authenticity," like Simmel's emphasis on raw "life," reflects that Dionysian or vitalist impulse in art that had earlier been advocated by Friedrich Nietzsche and Walt Whitman. Among the Brücke's founders, Erich Heckel and Karl Schmidt-Rottluff had been reading Nietzsche for several years,[25] while Whitman was Ernst Ludwig Kirchner's favorite author.[26]

The Dionysian impulse was not tied to a truly natural or "primitive" kind of sexuality, however, until certain works of 1909. In *Girl under Japanese Umbrella*, for example, Kirchner poses a seductive nude against a studio screen filled with erotic incident. Here, and in the background of Heckel's contemporary *Girl with Rose*,[27] the screen depicts among other nudes a bending woman upper left exposing her buttocks and, to the right, a male figure with an erection. With these 1909 paintings the Brücke artists convert the *Program*'s vague call for "immediacy" into explicitly erotic subject matter.

The causes for the new eroticism are several. Literary precedents played a role, certainly. The Dresdeners most likely knew Nietzsche's attribution of art's "genesis" to the relation between the mind's idea of "beauty" and the body's

Ernst Ludwig Kirchner. *Bathers in a Room.* 1909, repainted 1920. Oil on canvas, 59½ x 78" (151 x 198 cm). Saarland-Museum, Saarbrücken

Sam and Milli in Dresden Studio. Photograph by Ernst Ludwig Kirchner. 1911. Archive Hans Bollinger and Roman Norbert Ketterer

experience of "sexuality": "Everything perfect and beautiful works as an unconscious reminder of...this aphrodisiac bliss....The demand for art and beauty is an indirect demand for the ecstasies of sexuality communicated to the brain."[28] Equally likely is the precedent of Whitman:

Urge and urge and urge,
Always the procreant urge of the world.
Out of the dimness opposite equals advance, always substance and increase, always sex,
Always a knit of identity, always distinction, always a breed of life.[29]

In addition, it is possible that the arrangement of nude figures on the screen could derive from the poses of bathers at the Moritzburger Lakes from the 1909 summer as recalled by Kirchner in his city studio.[30] Additional Kirchner works from 1909 or 1909–10 indeed depict male and female nudes in sexually suggestive poses, most crudely in a ceramic tile *Love Scene* in which lovers physically arouse one another.[31] Finally there is also, most probably, a tribal art precedent for the screen. Its frieze of figures and its phallic erection resemble those typifying Palau house beams (p. 373)—a source impor-

Erich Heckel. *Girl with Pineapple.* 1910. Oil on canvas, 31½ x 27½″ (80 x 70 cm).
Whereabouts unknown

tant for the Brücke after the spring of 1910 but undoubtedly
seen earlier.

Nevertheless, Kirchner and Heckel took extraordinary
steps to *limit* the primitivizing implications of such a source.
For their very titles stress the "Japanese umbrella" and the
"rose"—emblems of a modern sensibility. The background
screen shows raw "life," but the foreground nudes hold
attributes of civilization. Where crude sex is suggested above,
we find below the parasol of high fashion or the flower of
romantic love. Despite differences, both paintings evoke the
Brücke's ambivalent life style—a style which confronts the
raw with the sophisticated, the natural with the cultured.

The pattern is confirmed in a group of works set in
Kirchner's Dresden studio from the winter of 1909–10 on.[32]
The earliest of these, *Bathers in a Room* from late 1909 (p. 371),
depicts graceful! and artfully posed "bathers" in a stark and
colorfully "primitive" interior. The nudes resemble those of
Matisse's 1906 *Joy of Life:* They stand, recline, eat, or arrange
their hair, all the while evoking a serene and idyllic arcadia.[33]
The interior, however, evokes the appearance of a space in a
tribal house: Tall figures in black silhouette adorn the door-
jambs to one side room while a pair of boldly painted curtains
protect the entrance to another. The curtains have geometric
designs: Each field was bright yellow, was framed in shapes of
black, and contained green and black roundels depicting a
seated king below and coupling lovers above. The bedroom
within, apparently quite small, was also hung with painted
wall-drapes in the course of 1910, drapes once again depicting
couples making love—if now, more scenically, under tropical
trees. Later, in the course of 1911, the black-framed mirror to
the right of *Bathers in a Room* was flanked by a pair of meter-
high logs on which were finally set Kirchner's own wood
sculptures.[34]

Among the Kirchner masterpieces of 1910 that make use of
these pseudotribal curtains and drapes, the most revealing is
the well-known *Standing Nude with Hat,* in Frankfurt.[35] For
after we strip away the identities of this nude as Cranach's 1532
Venus and as Kirchner's girlfriend, the dancer Doris ("Dodo")
Grohse, the image still stands as an icon of high civilization.
From the Cranach prototype the *Standing Nude* takes its sinuous pose and fashionable necklace—augmented now by
earrings and wrist band—while the pink slippers identify
Dodo's calling. Yet the large hat and shaved pubic hair under-
line the model's sophistication: She is in fashion publicly and
privately alike. The wedge-shaped triangle forces a focus on
the pubes—as did Cranach's transparent cloth—and ends by
stressing the refinement of the woman's sex. Thus the graceful
nude undercuts its background of stark shapes and brutish
couplings. By opposing the Primitive with the elegant,
Kirchner once again confronts nature with culture.

Heckel, too, utilized such contrast, but more subtly. In his
1910 *Girl with Pineapple* we see a reprise of Kirchner's theme: a
graceful nude before a Primitive backdrop. But, below, Heckel
also pairs a kneeling girl with a wooden stool Kirchner had
carved after a Cameroon model.[36] The girl's smile mimics that
of the stool's animal support, while the pineapple evokes
nature (as tropical staple) and culture (as European delicacy) at
once. Thus Heckel softens Kirchner's antithesis. The modish
and the exotic are related, not opposed.

There are indeed two different ideas at work within the
Brücke, which naturally led to two different approaches to the
Primitive: nature against culture and nature as culture. The
latter idea was essentially Gauguin's, whose work was shown
in Dresden in September 1910. As a European in Polynesia,
Gauguin had employed native themes within the context of a
high-art style. In a similar manner, Heckel uses an animal
frieze with Primitive ornament as setting for the colorful but
sexually provocative *Nude (Dresden).*[37] Even Kirchner adopted
Heckel's imagery—and Heckel's animal frieze—in several
1910 paintings.[38] Here German girls appear as "primitive" as
their backdrops.

Yet it was another Brücke artist, Max Pechstein, who had
joined the group in 1906 but had moved to Berlin in 1908, who
best built on Gauguin's precedent. In a 1910 color woodcut
entitled *Somaliland Dance,* Pechstein worked with black rather
than white models, yet he depicted them not in a tribal
situation but in the urban milieu of the cabaret stage.[39] Thus
the image is both "primitive" and contemporary. Tribal dance
rhythms and tribal clothing patterns are brilliantly evoked,
yet the alternation of black and white shapes also bespeaks the
artist's peculiarly modern sense of decorative abstraction. Not
unlike Gauguin's models, Pechstein's black dancers and musicians become the vehicle for high culture. And his taste for the
exotic, like Gauguin's, would soon prompt him to travel to the
tropics.

Kirchner, however, who was using Negro models
throughout the 1909–11 years, provided the most radical
variation on this theme.[40] He was subject to those white
myths about blacks that emphasized their instinctual vitality,
not just in musical expression (as in ragtime and jazz) but also
in a fabled sexual prowess. Such fantasies led him first
to photograph the black circus performers Sam and Milli
(p. 371) and then to depict Milli's bulging buttocks and
Sam's enlarged phallus in a 1911 painting called *Negro Couple.*

Ernst Ludwig Kirchner. *Exotic Scene*. Postmarked June 20, 1910. Ink and colored crayon on postcard. Altonaer Museum, Hamburg

Decorated house beam (detail). Palau Islands, Caroline Islands. Painted wood. Published in Eckhart von Sydow, *Die Kunst der Naturvölker und der Vorzeit*, 1923

Decorated house beam (detail). Palau Islands, Caroline Islands. Painted wood, 14" (35.5 cm) high. University Museum, University of Pennsylvania, Philadelphia

Kirchner completed his work with these models by having them strike six erotic poses involving oral and genital intercourse from which as many lithographs were made.[41] Yet he pulled but a few prints from each stone; they were not done, so far as we know, as pornography-for-profit. Instead, his goal must have remained the "immediacy and authenticity" he had advocated in the *Brücke Program* a half decade before. And indeed now, in these late Dresden works, the Expressionist comes closest to fusing instinctual nature with high culture. Both the passionate urgency of the models and the equally avid draftsmanship of the artist-voyeur are recognizable.

A number of carved and painted house beams from the Palau Islands, a German colony at the westernmost edge of Micronesia, provided the first major model for Expressionist primitivism in Germany. Depicting what the museum guide describes as the "frequently singular customs" of the Palau peoples, these beams were displayed in the Anthropological-Ethnographical Museum at the easternmost corner of the Zwinger Gallery in Dresden.[42] They had been installed in 1902[43] and placed in a glass case with mirrors behind so that images on both front and back could be clearly seen.[44] But they had long been known in the West, having first been published in 1881 and having been given three-color illustration in Karl Woermann's 1900 *History of the Art of all Epochs and Peoples*.[45] It is not particularly surprising, then, that architecture students in Dresden early in the century, such as Kirchner, would have had their attention directed to these remarkable works. Kirchner asserted on several occasions that it was he who, in 1903, "in the Dresden Ethnographic Museum...discovered the beams of the Palau Islanders, whose figures displayed exactly the same formal language as my own."[46] Though he could conceivably have "discovered" the beams this early, however, they exercised no direct influence on his work before 1910.[47]

Thus, suggestions that Kirchner's interest in Primitive art began as early as that of the Fauves must be rejected.[48] Early commentators were led astray by Kirchner drawings of late 1909 and 1910, which the artist had later misdated, pushing them forward by as much as six years.[49] Instead, Kirchner's intensive study of works in the Dresden Ethnographic Museum should be dated between March and June of 1910.

On March 31 Kirchner in Dresden wrote to Heckel and Pechstein in Berlin: "The Ethnographic Museum here is open again, only a small part but the famous bronzes from Benin are yet a change and a delight. A few things by the Pueblos from Mexico are still exhibited, and some Negro sculptures."[50] And on June 20, 1910, Kirchner sent a postcard to Heckel in Dangast reporting that "the [house] beam is really beautiful."[51] On the front of this postcard Kirchner drew an *Exotic Scene*, which was taken directly from one of the Palau beams (above). It is noteworthy that Kirchner has not copied the Palau source literally. He schematizes the beam's border of regular triangular shapes into a heavy and continuous zigzag form at the top of the sketch. This zigzag form resembles, in turn, the "talk-lines" employed on some Palau beams (above).[52] Of equal importance is the fact that Kirchner slightly exaggerates the sexual characteristics of the Palau figures. The phallus on the male figure is even larger than in its prototype. And the female figure is so drawn, in a three-quarter back view, that one sees both the broad buttocks and the profile breast, both of which are considerably less pronounced in the Oceanic source.

When analyzed visually, one can see why the Palau figures would have seemed to display, from Kirchner's viewpoint in 1910, "exactly the same formal language as my own." Both Palau frieze and Kirchner drawing are rigorously flat and two-dimensional; a monochromatic and planar "ground" provides the spaceless matrix within which equally flat figures and objects have their being. The figures and objects are set off from this ground, in turn, by a narrow light border: a thick groove incised in the wood beam in one case, a firmly con-

Karl Schmidt-Rottluff. *Two Female Nudes*. Christmas 1911. Painted wood relief, 7⅝ x 11" (19.5 x 27.8 cm). Brücke-Museum, Berlin

toured white surround in the other. It is as if the ground in both works were the mainland, the light surrounds were a continuous body of water, and the figures or objects were the large islands consistently separated from the mainland shore. Since figures nowhere overlap one another, they have no means of suggesting depth.

Historians agree that it is this "Palau style" that informs the primitivistic Brücke work executed at the Moritzburg Lakes during the summer of 1910. In a woodcut like Kirchner's *Bathers Throwing Reeds*,[53] for example, the angular figures with black hair masses are clearly of Palau derivation; even distinctions between female and male depend, as they do in the beams, on little more than a curved haunch or an extended phallus. But it is now the Expressionist's black woodcut contour that takes the place of the Palau beams' white surround; in both cases the figure within and the "ground" without remain essentially flat and two-dimensional. Again, in a summer 1910 painting like Heckel's *Forest Pond* the angular figures are silhouetted against the largely monochromatic ground.[54] Despite some lifelikeness, the figures appear both simplified and awkwardly schematized, in ways not unlike their Micronesian source. A similar "shorthand style" appears in Moritzburg paintings from that same summer by Pechstein.[55] And the style even appears as late as 1912 in the work of the Brücke's last convert, the Berlin-based Otto Mueller, in a *Cover to the 1912 Annual Brücke Portfolio*.[56]

Yet another belated derivation from the Palau house beams occurred in the work of Karl Schmidt-Rottluff from Christmas 1911, after all the Brücke artists had moved from Dresden to Berlin. We see it in Schmidt-Rottluff's painted wood relief of *Two Female Nudes*. The Expressionist's figures here are of an extraordinary three-dimensional complexity. The left-hand woman bends forward and reaches down so that the black trapezoid of her hair approaches the black triangle of her pubic region. And the right-hand woman, four times overlapped by the limbs of her neighbor, is presented seated in a complexly foreshortened pose. Despite all this, Schmidt-Rottluff manages to create out of two torsos and eight limbs a single light orange mass, isolated and flattened within a heavily textured dark blue surround. The surround is, in turn, framed by the outermost field of the relief, painted brown and incised to stress the object's wooden, planklike structure. Since Schmidt-Rottluff's figures are also outlined by grooves

deeply incised in the wood surface, the work captures the flat, angular relief style of the Palau beams in this respect as well.

What happened between the years 1910 and 1911 must not be overlooked. By the latter year Schmidt-Rottluff, in his response to Palau art, created a complex variation on a simplified theme; in this sense, he exemplified Hartlaub's distinction between a primary mode of Primitive expression and the Expressionist's secondary mode of—more or less consciously—"primitivizing" creation. What is more, Schmidt-Rottluff showed how he could select meaningfully from his sources, choosing the strong silhouetting but rejecting the total two-dimensionality of the Palau source. The same is true in other Palau-related works of the Brücke's last year in Dresden.[57]

In a 1911 derivation from an African source, rare this early in the Brücke's production, there is a similar concern for complex, three-dimensional effect. Kirchner's drawing of a *Benin Bronze Sculpture* was copied not from a book illustration, as I had once thought,[58] but from a Benin plaque of a king and attendants in the Dresden Ethnographic Museum itself. Donald Rosenthal, who made this discovery, believes that "Kirchner copied the plaque with painstaking exactness" and that the drawing "may well date from [March 1910] or slightly earlier."[59] Yet close examination of the drawing reveals not only the "hatching" stroke Kirchner first adopted for modeling purposes in 1911[60] but also an unusual divergence from the African work's spatial representation. Indeed, in the Benin plaque the feet of king and attendants are exactly aligned; since the king's feet are larger, they even seem to project further outward—or downward—from the plaque's baseline. But in Kirchner's drawing, by contrast, the attendants walk a step ahead of the king; the two courtiers at the left are even cut off at the ankle by the drawing's bottom edge. As a result, Kirchner's figures leave the plane of the bronze relief and press restlessly forward into our own space. With this new concern in 1911 for three-dimensional space, the 1910 impact of the Palau relief style has finally begun to moderate.

When we shift our attention from Dresden in 1910–11 to the Bavarian capital of Munich in 1911–12, we find a considerably different Expressionist approach to tribal art. Here the key artists are Wassily Kandinsky and Franz Marc, who during these years together published an almanac and organized two art exhibitions under the banner of Der Blaue Reiter; also of interest are the lesser Blaue Reiter artists August Macke and Heinrich Campendonk. For all of them, but especially for Kandinsky and Marc, a unifying literary concept of "the primitive" took precedence over any specific example of Primitive art itself.[61] For the Blaue Reiter, "the primitive" could just as readily signify Archaic court art, folk art, or children's art as it could tribal art. This is why Blaue Reiter primitivism is often discussed, for example, in terms of its debt to folk art.[62]

One purpose of the Blaue Reiter, according to Kandinsky, was to foster the assimilation of *all* expressive art forms. What bothered him most was the seemingly arbitrary separation of the various arts—and "periods" of art history—from one another: "I dreamed of painters and musicians in the front rank" as Blaue Reiter contributors, Kandinsky later wrote. "The harmful separation of one art from another, of 'art' from folk art, children's art, 'ethnography,' the stout walls erected

Ernst Ludwig Kirchner. *Benin Bronze Sculpture.* 1911. Pencil. Kirchner Estate

between what were to my eyes such closely related, often identical phenomena, in a word, synthetic relationships—all this left me no peace."[63] Kandinsky stated that his "ethnographic" interest arose from "the shattering impression made on me by Negro art, which I saw [in 1907] in the Ethnographic Museum in Berlin."[64] Despite this, there is no compelling evidence that tribal art ever directly influenced Kandinsky's style—then or later.

The situation differs significantly with Franz Marc. For the objects in Berlin's Ethnographic Museum had not only a general impact on the artist's aesthetic outlook but in particular a powerful—if momentary—effect on his 1911 style. Marc's letter to Macke of January 14, 1911, speaks for itself:

I spent some very productive time in the Ethnographic Museum in order to study the artistic methods of "primitive peoples."...I was finally caught up, astonished and shocked, by the carvings of the Cameroon people, carvings which can perhaps be surpassed only by the sublime works of the Incas. I find it so self-evident that we should seek the rebirth of our artistic feeling in this cold dawn of artistic intelligence, rather than in cultures that have already gone through a thousand-year cycle like the Japanese or the Italian Renaissance. In this short winter I have already become a completely different person. I think I am gradually really coming to understand what matters for us if we are to call ourselves artists at all: we must become ascetics. Don't be frightened; I mean this only in intellectual matters. We must be brave and give up almost everything which until now was dear and indispensable for us good Central Europeans. Our ideas and ideals must wear a hairshirt. We must nourish them with

Plaque. Court of Benin. Nigeria. Bronze, c. 19⅞" (50.5 cm) high. Staatliche Museum für Völkerkunde, Dresden

Buffalo helmet mask. Bangwa. Cameroon. Painted wood, 29⅛" (74 cm) high. Museum für Völkerkunde, Berlin

Franz Marc. *Donkey Frieze*. 1911. Oil on canvas, 31⅞ x 59⅛" (81 x 150 cm). Collection Frau Ursula Selbach, Lobberich bei Krefeld

Relief. Old Kingdom. Egypt. Limestone, c. 9⅞" (25 cm) high. Rijksmuseum van Oudheden, Leiden

locusts and wild honey, and not with history, if we are to issue forth from the exhaustion of our European bad taste....The goal "to be wished most ardently" is, naturally,...to be brought about by a healthy instinct for color, like that possessed by all primitive peoples. That from this we wish to make "pictures," and not only colorful columns and capitals and straw huts and clay pots, is our advantage, our "Europeanness."[65]

Just as Kirchner had gone on from his 1910 investigation of Gauguin to a 1910–11 analysis of Southeast Asian (Ajanta) painting, so Marc proceeded from his own 1910 study of Gauguin to a 1911 examination of another of Gauguin's sources—namely, Egyptian art. This has been known since Klaus Lankheit published an Egyptian Old Kingdom Donkey Frieze as the source for Marc's 1911 painting with that title.[66] But what Lankheit did not explain was Marc's transformation of the exceedingly low relief in his Egyptian prototype into the remarkable full-bodied and three-dimensional animals of his own painting. I refer not only to the leg positions of Marc's animals—separated in depth by intervening grasses—but also to the fully modeled jaws, bony heads, and pointed ears of the painted donkeys. Moreover, the faces of Marc's animals are fiercer—as it were, more Expressionist—than the Egyptian ones. The eyes have horizontal upper lids rather than rounded ones, while the jaws are partly opened into snarling ellipses

and not primly closed into compressed lines as in the Old Kingdom example. The only explanation for Marc's considered departure from the flattened and understated idiom of his archaic prototype is the intervention in his style of a second, and more truly Primitive, source. As the specific stimulus for this intervention I would propose a painted wood buffalo mask that has been in the collection of Berlin's Ethnographic Museum since 1899,[67] an object which was almost certainly on exhibition in January 1911 and which would have impressed the animal-painter Marc.[68] The Cameroon mask is not only full modeled, but its severe expression and open jaws closely resemble those features of Marc's work.

Marc's association of Egyptian with African art is not unique. For in this he was following the lead of Wilhelm Worringer's 1908 study *Abstraction and Empathy*. Indeed, Worringer's very distinction between the "impulse to imitation" (empathy) and the "art impulse proper" (abstraction) was based on a comparison between popular and court art in Egypt; only the latter, "having arisen in psychic needs, [also] gratifies psychic needs."[69] Moreover, in the nineteenth-century manner, Worringer still reserved the word "primitive" for the pre-Greek arts of Egypt and the Near East and only in passing linked these Primitive arts to the art of "savages" and "Orientals":

We shall then find that the artistic volition of savage peoples, in so far as they possess any at all, then the artistic volition of all primitive epochs of art and, finally, the artistic volition of certain culturally developed Oriental peoples, exhibit this abstract tendency.[70]

Marc was interested not only in Egyptian but also in Mycenaean art, yet his January 1911 letter displays a greater respect for African art than did Worringer a few years earlier.[71] Unlike Worringer, in fact, Marc now calls the Cameroon tribe a "primitive people" and devotes to their work the kind of attention previously devoted to Egypt.

As with the Donkey Frieze, then, tribal sculpture must have exercised a similarly volumetric and expressive influence on other Marc works early in 1911. Certainly this is the case with a Marc painting, *Reclining Dog in the Snow,* executed in the very month (January 1911) in which Marc wrote his ecstatic letter. Based distantly on Gauguin's *Spirit of the Dead Watching* (seen in Munich in August of 1910) and more directly on his own *Reclining Nude among Flowers* (completed in December of 1910), Marc's *Reclining Dog* differs from both its precedents in its angular, fully modeled and volumetric character.[72] Recent research, as yet unpublished, actually identifies Cameroon animal sculptures in the Berlin Ethnographic Museum that might have served Marc as models for the *Reclining Dog in Snow* and for other works of 1911 as well.[73] As in the case of the Donkey Frieze, however, Marc used Cameroon sculpture as a form-giving supplement to other, specifically European, style directions. Indeed, tribal-art sources never permeated Expressionist styles in Munich as they had in Dresden. Moreover, where the Brücke had stressed Primitive eroticism, Marc wanted Expressionists to "become ascetics."

August Macke, as Marc's closest friend, was undoubtedly moved by his colleague's letter of January 1911 to formulate his own response to Primitive art in the course of that year. But the response was limited: several paintings of American Indians which stressed a kind of "Wild West" subject matter.[74] Only in March 1912 did Macke inform Marc that he had acquired a tribal sculpture (Marc responded that he owned one, too);[75] yet there is no perceptible effect on Macke's 1912 work. In fact, Macke treated the subject of Primitive art rather gingerly in his contribution to the Blaue Reiter almanac, an article entitled "Masks." After defining artistic form as "the expression of mysterious powers," Macke described the art forms of "savages" as being as "powerful as the form of thunder."[76] Indeed, Marc's 1911 comparison of European art to African architectural decoration was repeated by Macke in 1912:

What we hang on the wall as a painting is basically similar to the carved and painted pillars in an African hut. The African considers his idol the comprehensible form for an incomprehensible idea, the personification of an abstract concept. For us the painting is the comprehensible form for the obscure, incomprehensible conception of a diseased person, of an animal, of a plant, of the whole magic of nature, of the rhythmical.[77]

Just as these last remarks are highly romantic, so Macke's overall approach to tribal art was quite similar to Kandinsky's notion of "synthetic relationships." For Macke listed not the differences between African, Oceanic, and European art but the ways in which their language was the same: "The cast bronzes of the Negroes from Benin in West Africa (discovered in 1889), the idols from the Easter Islands in the remotest Pacific, the cape of a chieftain from Alaska, and the wooden masks from New Caledonia speak the same powerful language as the chimeras of Notre-Dame and the tombstones in Frankfurt Cathedral."[78] Illustrations of all these works were included in the Blaue Reiter almanac, most in Macke's own article.

Beyond those mentioned by Macke,[79] however, the Blaue Reiter almanac reproduced surprisingly few examples of tribal

Heinrich Campendonk. *The Tiger.* 1916. Woodcut, 10 x 12¾" (25.3 x 32.3 cm). Städtische Galerie im Lenbachhaus, Munich

Plaque. Court of Benin. Nigeria. Bronze, 28⅝" (55 cm) high. Museum für Völkerkunde, Berlin

Above: Emil Nolde. *Still Life of Masks I.* 1911. Oil on canvas, 28¾ x 30½" (73 x 77.5 cm). The Nelson-Atkins Museum of Art, Kansas City, Missouri; gift of The Friends of Art

Left: Emil Nolde. *Canoe Prow.* 1911. Pencil, 11⅞ x 7⅛" (30 x 18 cm). Ada und Emil Nolde Stiftung, Seebüll. After a Solomon Islands canoe prow in the Museum für Völkerkunde, Berlin

art.[80] Perhaps the most interesting of these was a South Borneo ancestor figure illustrated on a page facing Kirchner's 1911 lithograph *Four Dancers*.[80] By this confrontation the almanac editors were obviously suggesting a visual similarity between the features of the Borneo sculpture and those of Kirchner's right-hand girl: In both, the brow arcs are joined to the lines defining a thin vertical nose, while eyes and mouth are all rendered in compressed, pointed ovals. In turn, the similarity once again confirms what Kandinsky called "synthetic relationships," or "closely related, often identical phenomena," and indicates how exactly he and Marc were analyzing the visual material intended for inclusion in *Der Blaue Reiter*.[82] The almanac editors made a number of such illustrative comparisons on facing pages in the 1912 publication, comparisons sometimes overlooked in the layout of later editions.[83]

Emil Nolde. *Trophy Head*. 1911. Pencil and colored chalk, 11⅞ x 7¼"
(30 x 18.2 cm). Ada und Emil Nolde Stiftung, Seebüll

Trophy head. Mundurucú. Brazil. Human head, cotton, and feathers. 6¼" (16 cm) high, excluding
feathers. Museum für Völkerkunde, Berlin

It is not surprising, then, that another member of the Blaue
Reiter, Heinrich Campendonk, should actually "borrow" an
entire image from an African work in the Berlin Ethnographic
Museum. Campendonk's heraldic animal in a 1916 woodcut
was taken directly from a Benin bronze plaque (p. 377).[84] But
Campendonk syncretized other "exotic" sources as well. The
claws of his mythical beast came from Russian folk prints,
while its dotted eyelids and the perforated patterns just to the
right were derived from Egyptian shadow-play figures—all of
which were illustrated in the Blaue Reiter almanac.[85] Yet the
animal as a whole depends on the Benin bronze, from its
irregular clover-shaped spots to its rhythmically striding silhouette. Campendonk's most original touch—aside from the
fusing of tribal and folk art sources—was his placement of a
tree branch in exactly the upward-arching position that the
Benin artist had used for the animal's tail.

Emil Nolde was the last major Expressionist to make a
serious study of tribal art, but last only by a matter of
months. A member of the Dresden Brücke group in
1906–07, Nolde went his own way after that and henceforth spent his winters in Berlin and his summers in Alsen
near the German-Danish border. In the autumn of 1910 and
again from February to April 1911, he resumed contact with
his former Brücke friends when he exhibited alongside
them in the Berlin-based Neue Secession.[86] Then, following a visit to the Belgian painter James Ensor in Ostend early
in 1911,[87] Nolde began to interest himself in both popular
(carnival) and tribal masks; he soon began studying Primitive figure sculpture as well. The best-known product of the
new concern is the 1911 *Still Life of Masks I*.
   The 1911 work, like many of Nolde's ensuing still lifes,
displays a fundamental contradiction, which produces in

Exhibition hall in the Folkwang Museum, Hagen, before 1921

turn a complex expressive effect. The contradiction is between caricature and emotional intensity and the effect is of feelings directed *at* the masks and also emanating *from* them. Caricature is an old story in Nolde's work, finding early outlet in postcards of fantastic mountain faces (the *Matterhorn* as smiling gnome, the *Jungfrau* as veiled "virgin"), which were a popular success in 1897–98. And emotional intensity was the goal of the early religious paintings, such as the 1909 *Last Supper* or *Pentecost* or the 1910 *Christ among the Children*, where the observer is meant to experience the beatitude or fortitude expressed by the painted saints. The combination of caricature and emotional intensity first occurs in *Dance around the Golden Calf* of 1910, a painting in which Nolde both empathizes with Old Testament Jews engaged in orgiastic dance and, simultaneously, caricatures them as decadents and sinners.[88]

In *Still Life of Masks I* the second and third faces are apparently carnival masks: one upside down, the other with a pig snout and upward-streaming hair, presumably as Nolde remembered them from his Ostend visit. Nolde, like Ensor, stresses less the humorous than the brutal aspects of these visages.[89] But Nolde's first and fourth masks can be related directly, through preparatory drawings, to tribal art objects: an ornamental canoe prow from Vella Lavella in the Solomon Islands (p. 378) and a shrunken head of a Yoruna Indian from the Mundurucú of Brazil (p. 379). The head of the Solomon Islands piece is rendered entire: The toothy grin, the slit eyes, and the triangular hair-covering are represented. But the debt to the shrunken head more emphasizes the top half of the visage. The shapes of skull, eyes, nostrils, and covered ears are nearly identical, but the square jaw and screaming mouth are less so.[90]

Less certain is Nolde's debt, in the fifth head, upper right, to a type of Nigerian mask from the Ijo tribe in West Africa (p. 124). Here, too, his borrowing would have been selective, extending to the vertical nose and half-moon eyes with straight upper lids but not to the mask's mouth or overall silhouette. Moreover, while the Oceanic and Peruvian objects had been seen and copied in the Berlin Ethnographic Museum, the Nigerian mask would have been seen on Nolde's 1911 travels. On the journey to Ensor's home in Ostend Nolde stopped in Brussels, Haarlem, and Amsterdam,[91] so he might have stopped as well at famous ethnographic museums in Tervuren, Leiden, or Hamburg—the last two of which possessed examples of the Ijo mask type.[92] It should also be noted that the stern and authoritative expression of this Nigerian mask appears not only in the 1911 *Still Life* but also in Christ's face in the central *Crucifixion* panel of Nolde's nine-part *Life of Christ* from 1911–12.[93]

Considering *Still Life of Masks I* as a whole, it is astounding to recognize visages from Oceania, Europe, South America, and Africa in a single painting. The picture lends itself to display alongside Primitive art objects of many types, and it indeed was displayed in the Folkwang Museum in Hagen around 1920. But Nolde's purpose was less ethnographic than emotive. Here Goldwater's phrase is apt: Nolde's is an "emotional primitivism" in that he employs tribal artifacts to communicate feelings, and in fact uses the physiognomies of tribal objects as a lexicon from which to draw emotive signs. Of course, the lexicon is not "unlocalized" as Goldwater thought: One can readily recognize his tribal sources.[94] Nolde knew his emotional needs so well, in fact, that he could play his sources off against one another: a diabolical grin to the left and, to the right, horrific sightless eyes and an exactly opposed expression of dignified authority. This selective and lexical use of tribal art objects for emotional expression typifies Nolde's approach to primitivism during the prewar years.

This is true even when Nolde chose New World tribal art objects as his models. The 1911 *Exotic Figures I* or *Fetishes*, for example, depicts American Indian Kachinas of the Hopi tribe, one of which, along with a drawing of an elongated wooden pig from an unidentified source, has survived.[95] While Nolde first drew the objects separately, their combination in the painting creates a whimsical caricature of the bourgeois German family: the grim and stolid male, the female with decorative facial ornament, and the domestic dachshund hugging the ground. Here the emotional impact depends on our recognizing tribal forms as being simultaneously like—and unlike—our own. Much the same is true of Nolde's *Exotic Figures II* from the same year, also depicting a Hopi Kachina from Berlin's Ethnographic Museum. Only here the artist has surrounded the richly colored figure with a pair of grimacing heraldic cats, which apparently derive from an Incan textile pattern.[96] In this case, the caricatural quality suggests a nightmarish confrontation between bizarre stalking beasts and an equally bizarre but dignified and self-contained human being. Nolde's overall approach depends upon our assumption of the pathetic fallacy, which leads us to think of wooden figures and other inanimate objects as telling a human tale. The entire approach, like the process of caricature itself, involves both artistic aggression (against the object) and psychic regression (to childlike play).[97]

Nolde's most ambitious attempt to mix non-Western still-

Emil Nolde. *Hopi Kachina*. 1911–12. Pencil and colored chalk, 11⅞ x 7⅛" (30 x 18 cm). Ada und Emil Nolde Stiftung, Seebüll

Emil Nolde. *Exotic Figures II*. 1911. Oil on canvas, 25¾ x 30¾" (65.5 x 78 cm). Ada und Emil Nolde Stiftung, Seebüll

Kachina. Hopi. Arizona. Painted wood, 9½" (24 cm) high. Museum für Völkerkunde, Berlin

Emil Nolde. *The Missionary*. 1912. Oil on canvas, 31⅛ x 25¾" (79 x 65.5 cm). Collection Berthold Glauerdt, Solingen

life objects was *The Missionary* of 1912. It has two Primitive sources: a Yoruba mother and child, now lost,[98] and a Bongo (Northeast Africa) dance mask. The black-frocked "missionary" is actually a Korean roadside idol, nine feet high, made of painted wood. The painting's anecdotal theme is clear. The African woman kneels, in a form of Christian prayer, before the missionary while the disembodied mask, symbolizing her native religion, looks on in horror between them. By teaching the woman to give up her tribal religion in favor of Christianity, the preacher is fostering the extinction of tribal culture. Because of this the missionary is an object of contempt in Nolde's view; he caricatures him as an image based on Oriental folk sculpture. The comic, goblinlike forms of both missionary and

mask contest the woman's soul, but she herself is treated by Nolde with respect and dignity.

Unlike Kirchner and Marc, Nolde initially valued tribal art not for its sculptural potential but for its design quality. When copying even the most cylindrical models, Nolde tended to flatten them into planes. In the Tinu-Hopi Kachina the feet face forward, for example, but in Nolde's *Exotic Figures I* they are flattened sideways; the three-dimensional pig in a preparatory drawing becomes but a dark silhouette in the painting. In *Exotic Figures II* the roundness of the Kachina is given its due, to be sure, but the flatness of the stepped headdress is emphasized in the painting by repeating its dark shape in light tones on the still-life background. And in *The Missionary*, the slight plasticity of

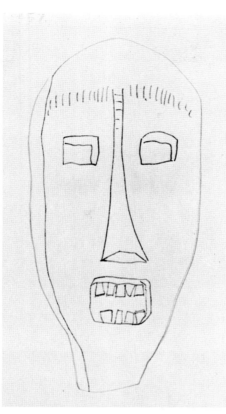

Mask. Bongo. Sudan. Wood, hair, and teeth, 11⅞"
(30 cm) high. Museum für Völkerkunde, Berlin

Emil Nolde. *Bongo Mask.* 1911–12. Pencil, 11 x 8¼" (28 x
21 cm). Ada und Emil Nolde Stiftung, Seebüll

Roadside god. Korea. Painted wood, 9' 6⅝" (291 cm)
high. Museum für Völkerkunde, Berlin

both of Nolde's extant models—the wooden figure from
Korea of a roadside god and the African Bongo mask —
disappears in the painting.

The caricatural or childlike elements introduced into
pictures of 1911–12 dropped away when Nolde actually
visited tribal societies two years later. But his variegated
response to tribal art—both formal and expressive—
remained unchanged. We can see this complexity of
response in his 1912 remarks on Primitive art, cited here in
part:

Not too long ago, the art of only a few periods was deemed
worthy of representation in museums. Then others were added.
… Why then are Indian, Chinese, and Javanese art still considered the province of science and ethnology? And why does the
art of primitive peoples as such receive no appreciation at all?

Why is it that we artists love to see the unsophisticated
artifacts of the primitives?

It is a sign of our times that every piece of pottery or dress or
jewelry, every tool for living has to start with a blueprint.—
Primitive people begin making things with their fingers, with
material in their hands. Their work expresses the pleasure of
making. What we enjoy, probably, is the intense and often
grotesque expression of energy, of life.[99]

Nolde treasured tribal art because he found it "unsophisticated," because it expressed "energy" and "life." But he also
valued this art for the obvious pleasure it seemed to reflect
in the "making" of it, for its sense of material "in the hands."
Thus Nolde identified with the tribal artist as a fellow
craftsman even as he insisted upon his right to depart from
the latter's work in the interest of his own art.

In the autumn of 1911 the Künstlergruppe Brücke moved from
the Saxon capital of Dresden to the national capital of Berlin.
Although Pechstein and Mueller had already resided there for
some years, the move meant a relocation for the others.
Moreover, the Dresden pattern of communal studios was at an
end; several of the artists were married or were living with
their future wives, and each was developing a more personal
style. The *Brücke Program*'s 1906 call for youthful "immediacy"
was clearly less appropriate for men now ranging in age from
twenty-eight (Schmidt-Rottluff) to thirty-eight (Mueller). In
1912 the last Brücke exhibitions took place in Berlin and
Hamburg; in 1913 the group formally disbanded.

No single source of stylistic influence was destined in
1912–13 Berlin to play the role the Palau house beams had

Karl Schmidt-Rottluff. *Four Evangelists: Matthew, Mark, Luke, and John.* 1912. Oil over brass relief, each panel: 16¾ x 13″ (42.5 x 33 cm). Brücke-Museum, Berlin

played in the Dresden style a few years earlier. To be sure, the Berlin Ethnographic Museum displayed a range of Primitive objects unsurpassed in Central Europe. Its variegated strengths—in Oceanic and pre-Columbian, in West and East African objects alike—precluded a too narrow focus for subsequent primitivism. Collecting, too, had become more important. Where Marc and Macke each mentioned owning a single tribal sculpture in March 1912, Heckel's still-life paintings from that year show that he already owned tribal artifacts of Oceanic, East African, and West African provenance (p. 388). And while Schmidt-Rottluff once identified Cameroon sculpture as the Brücke's "major source of inspiration,"[100] his statement is more accurate for his own later style than for that of his friends in the prewar years.

Nevertheless, the earliest primitivist masterpiece to be

created by the Brücke in Berlin derives from an unusual form of Cameroon sculpture. This is Schmidt-Rottluff's relief of early 1912, *Four Evangelists,*[101] whose source is to be found among what the 1911 Berlin *Ethnographic Museum Guide* calls "most remarkable heads covered with skin,"[102] namely, a dance headdress from the Ekoi tribe in northwest Cameroon [103] Though the fragile materials of these heads make it difficult to reconstruct their exact appearance in 1912, the Munich example illustrated here is similar to the one Schmidt-Rottluff saw. On a wooden maquette in the shape of human neck and face was stretched an animal skin—usually antelope—to which was added a fringe of human hair above and, in the mouth, teeth hammered through the skin into the wood support. Most distinctive about the head, in addition to the mouth with flattened lips, were the sightless and misshapen

Headdress. Ekoi. Cameroon. Wood, leather, and mixed media, 9⅛" (23 cm) high. Museum für Völkerkunde, Munich

Matthew and Mark, Pechstein and Kirchner as Luke and John, the Brücke as the evangelists of a new art.[106]

Be that as it may, the specifically "primitive" properties of the 1912 relief are readily apparent. Matthew's almond-shell eyes derive directly from the typically "closed" eyes of the Ekoi facial type (the headdress's left eye in the example illustrated), while John's half-open but sightless triangular eyes derive from the misshapen eyeholes of the Ekoi animal skin (the head's right eye in the present example). Moreover, Mark's flat nose and prominent lips have a Negroid character, again bespeaking the Ekoi type, as do Luke's tuft of forehead hair and even larger lips.

There is nothing quite like the *Four Evangelists* relief elsewhere in Expressionist art, and its peculiar authority depends upon the crude yet spiritual intensity of its African prototype. If one grants the disturbing quality of an art work covered with skin, then in analyzing that work's facial features the Expressionist relief achieves a similarly disturbing, if now more aesthetically considered, forcefulness.

When we turn to Kirchner's approach to Primitive art in 1912, we find less a concern for expressive force than for sculptural form. As early as 1910–11 he had found what he called "body" (*du corps*) in illustrations of cave paintings from Ajanta, India. As he wrote to Henry van de Velde's daughter, Nele: "They are all plane and yet absolute mass and, accordingly, they have absolutely solved the mystery of painting."[107] With the first of his life-size wood sculptures, such as the 1912 *Adam* (p. 387) and related *Eve*, Kirchner had to attack the problem of plane and mass in the volumetric medium of sculpture-in-the-round. He did so by means of an important but previously unnoticed combination of remarkably different principles of Palau and Cameroon form.

The female gable figure from a Palau Men's House in the Hamburg Ethnographic Museum, which Kirchner could have seen on any of several Hamburg visits between 1910 and 1912 (p. 386), shows, once again, the pervasive two-dimensionality of the Palau style.[108] Although the gable figure possesses physical mass, it is actually conceived in planes parallel to the facade plank to which it is attached. Nothing protrudes too far from the figure's surface; details such as breasts or eyes are raised in extremely low relief. In the stylized chest muscles of his *Adam*, for example, Kirchner employs the same kind of low relief plane that the Palau artist had used for the gable figure's pubic triangle; the treatment of the pubic area in the *Eve* derives even more directly from this source. In other respects, however, these Kirchner sculptures are volumetric and therefore relate more to African prototypes. Breasts and phallus break the frontal body plane and thrust forward into space in a manner recalling Cameroon sculpture (p. 394). The same is true of facial features. The heads of *Adam* and *Eve* resemble that of the Palau gable figure in ovoid shape, in the rectilinear form of lips and nose, and in the swelling arc of the brows. But the eyes themselves, particularly *Adam*'s, are volumetric, with even the pupils given three-dimensional articulation in keeping with African precedent.

Another Kirchner wood sculpture, a *Female Figure*, now lost, is visible in a photograph of Kirchner and Erna Schilling in the interior of the artist's studio in Berlin-Wilmersdorf (p. 387). Here the facial features and even the eyes and breasts are carved in low relief, in the Palau manner, and the hands with five identically shaped fingers seem to come directly from the

eyeholes of the animal skin. It is precisely the form of the eyes or the mouth in each of the *Evangelists* panels that demonstrates its derivation from the Ekoi model.

I assume that Schmidt-Rottluff was moved by a particular object of this type in the Berlin Museum and that he responded to it just as selectively as Nolde had to the sources he used. Will Grohmann even finds the *Evangelists* closer to Nolde's Christian works than to Schmidt-Rottluff's own devotional woodcuts of a half-decade later.[104] While avoiding "everything dogmatic," Grohmann notes, Schmidt-Rottluff's motivation was "deep religious feeling"; though omitting the traditional attributes, the heads of the *Four Evangelists* are clearly recognizable as Matthew and Mark above, Luke and John below.[105] To this I would add the likelihood that the artist also had more topical identities in mind: Heckel and himself as

Gable plank with figure. Palau Islands, Caroline Islands. Painted wood, 32⅝" (83 cm) high. Museum für Völkerkunde, Hamburg

Gable figure. Palau Islands, Caroline Islands. Painted wood, 25¾" (65.4 cm) high. The Metropolitan Museum of Art, New York; The Michael C. Rockefeller Memorial Collection, Gift of Nelson A. Rockefeller, and Purchase, Nelson A. Rockefeller Gift

Hamburg gable figure. Nevertheless, the entire construction of arms and legs is remote from the Palau style. Both the shoulders and buttocks are fully rounded, the shoulders thrusting into space even more than the breasts, and the buttocks projecting backward as they do in African carvings. Even the compact mass of head and torso has moved more toward the Cameroon than the Palau type. Kirchner's free-standing sculptures from 1912 thus evince an unusual synthesis of Oceanic and African style characteristics.[109]

Kirchner's wood sculpture became increasingly volumetric and is accordingly African rather than Oceanic in inspiration.[110] It is concerned, as he later wrote, with "the simple primary forms, mainly the cylinder, cone, oval, and sphere." These forms arise not from "mathematical speculation" but from an "instinct for monumentality."[111] But, in addition, such sculpture has erotic and emotional immediacy; it transforms the painted *Negro Couple* from two into three dimensions, from the wall, as it were, into real space. Even the two-level wooden bowl, visible to the right in Kirchner's photograph of his Berlin studio, though based on Cameroon sources, manages to turn the exotic into the utilitarian, art style into life style.

The entire interior of Kirchner's Berlin studio confirmed his wish to use "art as a model for life."[112] Exotic wall-hangings, Japanese umbrellas, a Buddhist reproduction, and even a tablecloth modeled on Coptic textiles furnished the typically Expressionist environment. The "studio primitivism" of the other Brücke artists in Berlin differed only in degree. Heckel's studio, for instance, was even more exotic. In the words of a 1914 visitor: "[Heckel] received us in an attic space which was adorned with colored cloth like a tent. Near the walls stood sculptures carved of wood, female and male figures with large heads and expressive gestures or movements. Hand-carved benches and chairs stood around. Many oil paintings were stored behind colorful, hand-painted drapes...."[113]

By 1912 Heckel had become deeply and directly involved with tribal art. His *Still Life with South Seas Sculpture* (p. 389), dating from that year, depicts a Melanesian carving he apparently owned. It is a small piece which originated in New Ireland (or Neumecklenburg as it was then called).[114] Also from 1912 is Heckel's *Still Life with Mask*, which depicts a woven calabash from the Cameroon Grasslands and an East African mask that has survived (p. 388).[115] In addition, a 1913 painting called *Girl Playing the Lute* shows Heckel's fiancée playing an instrument sent to her by Heckel's brother Manfred, then living in Africa,[116] who was undoubtedly the source of many of Heckel's tribal pieces.

Manfred's accounts of Africa would also have sparked Heckel's interest in going there. He expressed the hope "to go to Africa in order finally to find a 'savage' life, people in a natural environment," which was a theme he was "always seeking for his painting";[117] a friend characterized his wanderlust as a "longing for a return to primordial nature

Ernst Ludwig Kirchner. *Adam.* 1912. Wood, stained and burned, 66¾ x 11⅞ x 12¼" (169.6 x 30 x 31 cm). Staatsgalerie Stuttgart

Ernst Ludwig Kirchner. *Male Nude Figure.* c. 1911. Wood, stained, burned, and painted, 13¾" (35 cm) high. Staatsgalerie Stuttgart

Interior of Studio, Berlin-Wilmersdorf. Photograph by Ernst Ludwig Kirchner. 1912. Archive Hans Bollinger and Roman Norbert Ketterer

Erich Heckel. *Still Life with Mask.* 1912. Oil on canvas, 27⅛ x 24¾" (69 x 63 cm). Saarland-Museum, Saarbrücken

Mask. East Africa. Wood, 8¼" (21 cm) high. Collection Erich Heckel Estate, Hemmenhofen

[Urnatur]."[118] Such sentiments help explain the symbolic function of Primitive sculpture, or of the human figure rendered as Primitive sculpture, in the 1913 paintings *Convalescent Woman* and *Glassy Day.*[119]

By 1913 the other Brücke artists were exploring tribal art sources as well. For his *Still Life with Negro Sculpture* in Cologne (p. 391) and certain related paintings,[120] Schmidt-Rottluff used a few Cameroon pipe bowls of the type illustrated below (p. 391). And Pechstein's 1913 *Still Life in Gray* (p. 390) depicts a seat he carved after a Cameroon chief's stool then in Berlin's Ethnographic Museum,[121] another example of which is illustrated here (p. 391).[122] Although the Pechstein painting exploits the affinity between Cubism and Primitive art, the fragmentation of fruit and drapery nevertheless mimics Cameroon geometry.

By the time Expressionist artists actually journeyed to faraway tribal settlements, the Primitive way of life they had so long admired was fast disappearing. Perhaps for this reason the results of these voyages were artistically disappointing. The artists were reduced to writing travelogues and drawing tourist sketches as they saw the native culture receding before their eyes. Disappointment was inevitable; "primordial nature" (*Urnatur*) was revealed as a romantic fantasy of the white man, who was in fact bringing indigenous culture to a close.

When Nolde arrived in New Guinea in 1914, after travels across Russia, China, Japan, and the Philippines, he was outspoken in his praise of the natives and his criticism of the white colonialists:

We live at a time when all primitive conditions and peoples are perishing; everything is being discovered and Europeanized. Not a single small region of primordial nature [*Urnatur*] with its original

inhabitants remains intact. In twenty years all will be lost. In three hundred years researchers and scholars will rack their brains, toil and dig in order gropingly to conceive of the precious thing that we had, the primary spiritual values which we destroy today so frivolously and shamelessly.

Primordial peoples live in their nature, are one with it and a part of the entire universe. Sometimes I have the feeling that only they are still real people, while we are like malformed puppets—artificial and full of darkness.

I paint and draw and try to hold on to a bit of primordial being. Some things might well be successful, too. But I believe anyway that my paintings and watercolors of primitives are so true and sharp that it is impossible to hang them in perfumed drawing rooms.

I know of no other painters beside Gauguin and myself who created something permanent out of the endless abundance of life in primordial nature.[123]

The praise of *Urnatur* and *Urmenschen* was resumed two months later:

The natives are a marvelous folk, to the extent that they are not already spoiled through contact with white culture. Only a few times did we have the chance to meet primordial peoples in their villages, but how beautiful it was....

Of course the natives here eat human flesh....But are we so-called cultivated people really much better than the people here? A few people are killed here in feuds while thousands die in Europe in wars. And are not corrupt city people much lower and dirtier in their daily and nightly contraceptions and abortion of fetuses than nature's people here who bear many children to be strong, to be sure that the neighboring tribe does not have more men than they.[124]

Not all natives were praised; those corrupted by colonial life were as bad as their white employers:

All that matters is the law of the stronger. Everything works for economic advantage, and so a special, uniquely beautiful world is lost forever. Natives in the European villages are insufferable, mendacious, infected, and clothed in rags and tinsel of the most wretched kind. And so they return to their own villages, spreading the worst side effects of the white man's culture. But say nothing please, shh! No white man is supposed to see this. Whoever sees it, close your eyes nicely now: "economic profit" transcends any reservations. We live in an evil time, when the white race puts the inhabitants of the whole earth to its own use![125]

Nolde's comparison of himself with Gauguin is presumptuous and cannot be sustained. Such Nolde watercolors as *Natives in a Boat* are hauntingly beautiful, but they were virtually the only product of the New Guinea stay; no major oils were accomplished there. That these "passionate" works could be prompted by "exotic scenery" is hardly reason to travel halfway around the globe![126] Yet Nolde's travels did bear belated fruit. The exotic art and artifacts he collected were to be used, at home, for still-life paintings. The 1915 *Still Life with South Seas Sculpture* (p. 392), for example, contrasts an Uli figure from New Ireland with a porcelain of two women which Nolde acquired in Russia. The content of the *Still Life* seems to reverse that of *The Missionary* of 1912 (p. 382). The Melanesian fetish dominates its composition as the Korean idol did before, but the terrible image of authority is now tribal and admirable in every respect, whereas the conversing women, fundamentally unserious, are European![127]

Max Pechstein resided not in New Guinea but in the as yet unspoiled island group of Palau. As he wrote in his *Recollec-*

Erich Heckel. *Still Life with South Seas Sculpture.* 1912. Oil on canvas, 27⅝ x 19¾" (70 x 50 cm). Whereabouts unknown

Mask. Nomoi Islands, Caroline Islands. Painted wood, 24½" (62.2 cm) high. Rautenstrauch-Joest Museum, Cologne

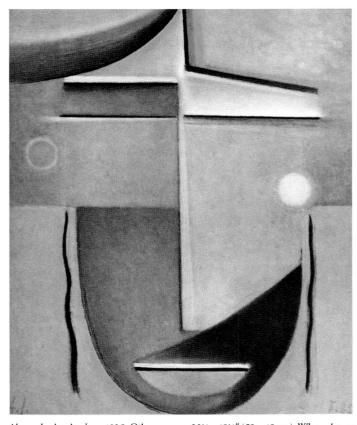

Alexey Jawlensky. *Love.* 1925. Oil on canvas, 23¼ x 19¼" (59 x 49 cm). Whereabouts unknown

Max Pechstein. *Still Life in Gray.* 1913. Oil on canvas. Formerly collection Dr. Karl Lilienfield, Berlin; whereabouts unknown

tions, he planned, "now that I had found this paradise," to stay.[128] Still, like Nolde, Pechstein brought his European wife along on his tropical journey, so his fantasies of Primitive life must have been much different from Gauguin's. And, again like Nolde, he rapidly learned the evils of colonialism. When he first met the Palau governor, in fact, the official "made me swear, for God's sake not to destroy the Palau people itself or its nature-based customs through any kind of European nul-

lity." The final irony of the 1914 visit is that it was cut short by the outbreak of war in Europe. In October Pechstein was interned by the Japanese: "My dream was over."

Pechstein's diary for the few months he spent on the islands reads like a travelogue. He arrived with forty cases of belongings, made an oven for baking bread and, with the help of natives, constructed a sailboat and a new roof for the settlement house. He saw a tribal dance and then visited a nearby island and its native king before finally deciding to build his own house on an uninhabited island given to him.

Throughout the diary, Pechstein expresses an extraordinary empathy with the natives:

Since I myself grew up among simple people amidst nature, I readily came to terms with the abundance of new impressions. I didn't have to change my attitude that much....Out of the deepest feeling of community I could approach the South Sea islanders as a brother. From the outset I was familiar with the management of simple handicrafts, just as I had sailed, fished, and woven nets with the people of Nidden and Monterosso al Mare. So here it was also easy to learn to steer a canoe through the coral reef. I felt the most wonderful unity around me, and I breathed it in with an unbounded feeling of happiness.

When Pechstein happened to leave a wood sculpture he was carving, a Palau youth continued the work. The German artist

Chief's stool. Western Grasslands, Cameroon. Wood, 28¾" (73 cm) high. Staatliches Museum für Völkerkunde, Dresden

[The natives'] lodgings are wooden houses with high, pointed roof-ridges. And on these houses I now saw in everyday use, in the setting for which they were made, the carved and painted beams which once in Dresden had set my creativity flowing and which had then prompted the wish, now fulfilled, to see them on the spot. I saw the primitive ornamentation, the decoration of the huts which grew out of the simplest human need for beauty. I saw the artifice with which

Karl Schmidt-Rottluff. *Still Life with Negro Sculpture*. 1913. Oil on canvas, 28¾ x 25¾" (73 x 65.5 cm). Museum Ludwig, Cologne

Pipe bowls. Grasslands, Cameroon. Terra cotta, 9½" (24 cm) high (largest). Museum für Völkerkunde, Munich

saw that he had "spoiled nothing" and so let him proceed with it.

Only one painting, a few watercolors, and a number of brush drawings are known from Pechstein's Palau stay.[129] *Men's House under Palms* (p. 394) is typical of the last in providing a rapid sketch of native activity. Indeed, the drawing depicts the very type of structure from which a group of house beams in Dresden, Hamburg, and other museums had come:

these primordial folk decorated their bodies in order to rejoice in nature's sovereign changes on their own bellies and to bear witness to the sense of beauty and the passion for structure. I saw the carved idols which had impressed upon them in trembling piety and awe before the incomprehensible powers of nature their hopes and their terrors, their fear and their submissiveness before unavoidable fate![130]

Even after his return to Germany in 1915 and his release from

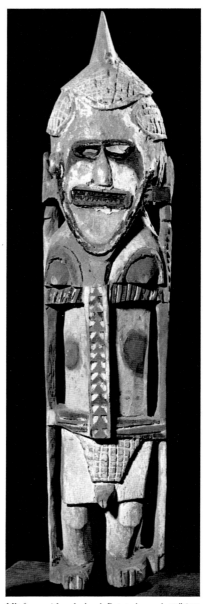

Uli figure. New Ireland. Painted wood, 39″ (99 cm) high. Ada und Emil Nolde Stiftung, Seebüll

Emil Nolde. *Still Life with South Seas Sculpture*. 1915. Oil on canvas, 34⅞ x 29″ (88.5 x 73.5 cm). Ada und Emil Nolde Stiftung, Seebüll

military service in 1917, Pechstein's imagination remained fired by his Palau memories, as reflected in the scarification patterns of his own sculptures (p. 398). A 1917 painting of a *Palau Carver of Idols* is a virtually ethnographic document in which we see a native, adz in hand, studying the features of another native before completing his larger-than-life sculpture.

This painting, and such other 1917 oils as *Palau Triptych, Head of a Palau Islander,* or *Palau Dancers,*[131] are known tò us

only through photographs, as is a large frieze that Pechstein once used to decorate his Berlin studio.[132] While these works seem accurate depictions of Palau life, there is one anachronism. In a behind-the-scenes view *In the Woman's House, Palau,* also from 1917, Pechstein unaccountably introduces into a Micronesian hut a chief's stool modeled on one from Africa.[133] There are also other paintings from 1917, including closely related *Still Lifes* in Mannheim and Saarbrücken, in which the depicted pseudotribal sculpture is based on Cameroon rather than Palau sources, sources presumably available in Berlin's own Ethnographic Museum.[134] In the years immediately following World War I, such mixtures of Oceanic and African sources would continue.

One of the most important interactions between German Expressionism and tribal art occurred in the wartime development of Karl Schmidt-Rottluff. In a series of what Grohmann calls "architectural figures and heads" Schmidt-Rottluff analyzed the formal structures of West African sculpture and adopted it to his own work.[135] At first he wavered between "squat" and "attenuated" proportions. A torso in a 1913 woodcut, *Woman with Her Hair Down*, is actually wider than it is high, while in the 1915 painting *Girl before a Mirror*, the trunk, limbs, and nose of the figure are elongated.[136] Nevertheless, both of these manners, and indeed both of these works, arguably derive from a Ngumba (Cameroon Fang) reliquary figure, which at once lengthened and compressed body parts; the reliquary figure has been in Berlin's Ethnographic Museum since 1896.[137]

The rounded shoulders and the squared-off fingers and feet of the figure in the woodcut recall the Cameroon prototype; in the painting it is the pointed breasts, the arm extended at a right angle, and especially the geometric "fit" of the short neck into the wide shoulders and of the cylindrical torso into the spherical thighs. I stress the structural "fit" because this is the key to Schmidt-Rottluff's wartime borrowing from African art. It is structural principle that fundamentally interests him, rather than the attenuation of form which characterizes much Bambara work. Certainly the Bambara ancestor figure proposed by Schneckenburger cannot have been Schmidt-Rottluff's source: Its neck and breasts are too long and its face is devoid of features.[138] Furthermore, it is the Fang figure that has the ovoid triangular head used in 1915 for the *Girl before a Mirror*. It is not surprising that Schmidt-Rottluff should later utilize this head shape, and particularly its oval projecting mouth, in a 1919 woodcut of *Christ and Nicodemus*.[139]

Yet between these direct borrowings from the Berlin museum piece, the artist's career as a painter was totally interrupted. From May 1915 to December 1918, while in an army battalion stationed in Poland, he made no paintings at all; there were only eight wood sculptures and a handful of woodcuts.[140] These, however, are the very works that demonstrate Schmidt-Rottluff's fascination with the volumetric structure of Cameroon sculpture.

How did a soldier on the Eastern front gain access, then, to African tribal art? He of course remembered pieces studied earlier in Berlin, and he might have visited the Ethnographic Museum during an occasional leave back home. But there was no need for such a visit if Schmidt-Rottluff had bought—as I believe he had—a copy of Carl Einstein's *Negerplastik* of 1915. This was the first book on the topic published anywhere in Europe by a member of the cultural avant-garde.[141] It would not have mattered to Schmidt-Rottluff, of course, that the book's 111 illustrations were without geographic identification or even museum location; he would have known the major tribal styles already, and some objects were in fact from the Berlin Ethnographic Museum.[142] Moreover, as Einstein him-

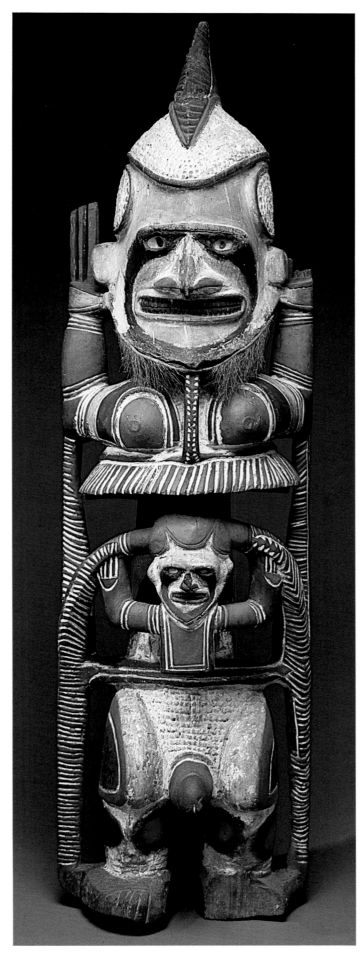

Uli figure. New Ireland. Painted wood, 59⅞" (152 cm) high. Hamburgisches Museum für Völkerkunde.

Figure. Ngumba. Cameroon. Painted wood, 17⅜″ (44 cm) high. Museum für Völkerkunde, Berlin

self argued, "One collects Negro art as art"; "more certain than any possible knowledge of an ethnographic kind, etc., is the fact of African sculpture [itself]!"[143]

By 1917, in any event, Schmidt-Rottluff was almost certainly studying some of the objects depicted in Einstein's illustrations. For in that wartime year, despite his military duties, the artist began a series of inventive variations on the theme of West African sculpture. Typical is the *Three Kings* woodcut in its relation to a Fang reliquary head which was illustrated in both front and profile view in Einstein's *Negerplastik*. The triangular faces and round necks in *Three Kings* probably derive from either this source or the Ngumba figure already discussed. But where the vertical noses, stiff brows, and targetlike eyes resemble the remembered Ngumba piece from Berlin (its eyes are of sheet brass), the pleated

hair on the right, all the mouths, and the "ski-jump" nose on the left more likely derive from the Fang head illustrated in Einstein.

The Fang head, like several other sculptures in Einstein,[144] introduces a facial feature that involves yet another structural commonplace of West African carving: what Hans Himmelheber calls the "concave face."[145] Not only does this African tendency violate the European preference for "round cheeks" and the "arched forehead," but the trait is rare in Western art: As examples, Himmelheber reproduces a drawing by Dürer, a painting by Picasso, and a woodcut by Schmidt-Rottluff.[146] We need look no further than Schmidt-Rottluff's *Blue-Red Head (Fear)* (p. 396), in fact, to see the principle of facial concavity pushed to an unusual extreme. The 1917 sculpture seems to derive both from the Ngumba figure (the hollowed-out open mouth) and the Fang head of the Einstein illustrations (the tubular chin), although its protruding circular eyes and overall silhouette show affinities to features of other Fang heads as well. The result is a memorable image appropriately subtitled *Fear*, but one that recalls less a specific emotion than a general formal principle of physiognomic articulation.[147]

Not all of Schmidt-Rottluff's wartime sculptures have identifiable tribal sources. For example, both Reidemeister and Schneckenburger have seen the 1917 *Green Head* as deriving from yet another Fang piece with brass eyes in the Berlin Ethnographic Museum.[148] Yet such a derivation makes partial sense only in profile view; the two-stage nose and mouthless chin in the Expressionist carving have no analogue in the African work. More to the point, the Fang piece did not enter the Berlin Museum until 1947, and so was almost certainly unavailable to Schmidt-Rottluff three decades earlier.[149]

Nevertheless, another Schmidt-Rottluff work from the same group, a 1917 sculpture entitled simply *Head*, can be directly related to a Luba figure illustrated (although incorrectly identified) in Einstein's *Negerplastik*: a female figure from Zaire, then available in Berlin's Ethnographic Museum but lost during World War II (p. 396).[150] The overall head mass, the shell-like eyes, and the triangular nose are similar in both works. Only the open mouth departs here, as in Schmidt-Rottluff's *Blue-Red Head*, from the model in Einstein.

There is yet another Schmidt-Rottluff derivation from an

Max Pechstein. *Men's House under Palms.* 1914. Ink, 7⅞ x 10⅜″ (20 x 26.5 cm). Neue Nationalgalerie, Berlin

Above: Reliquary head. Fang. Gabon. Wood. Published in Carl Einstein, *Negerplastik*, 1915

Left: Karl Schmidt-Rottluff. *Three Kings*. 1917. Woodcut, comp. 19⁹⁄₁₆ x 15⅜" (49.7 x 39.1 cm). The Museum of Modern Art, New York; purchase

Einstein illustration. The woodcut known as *Apostle*, of 1918, would seem to come directly from a Teke piece (p. 397) reproduced in Einstein. The angular hairline with rounded ear, the finely striped temple and cheek, and especially the projections of mouth and beard from receding chin are similar in both cases.[151] Only the eyes diverge from the Einstein illustration. They, in turn, may well derive from another Teke piece, this time a female fetish figure, featured in the Berlin Ethnographic Museum guide.[152] Since Schmidt-Rottluff ignored both the sex and the squat head shape of the Berlin piece, however, we may be sure that he received his primary stimulus from Einstein's book. Nevertheless, the 1918 *Apostle*, like a similarly bearded *St. Francis* in a 1919 woodcut,[153] was probably created in Berlin after the artist's release from service.

Tribal sculpture, writes Einstein in *Negerplastik*, is characterized by its "religious" purpose and its "cubic space perception."[154] These are both also tendencies of Schmidt-Rottluff's wartime production. In responding to Primitive art he could vary body proportions and facial features almost at will, but he was consistently true to a Primitive work's volumetric logic and structural articulation.

With the armistice in November 1918, Expressionism became popular in Germany. The movement dominated the stage, and painters took the lead in major cultural organizations. This was Expressionism's "second wave,"[155] intense but short-lived, in part because of the deaths of Marc and Macke and the absence of Kandinsky (living in Russia) and Kirchner (living in Switzerland). In mid-1919 the Versailles Treaty stripped Germany of, among other things, its African and Oceanic colonies. By 1920 critics despaired of further Expressionist progress, while the artists, who were approaching their forties, were ambivalent about German art's chances for renewal. Late Expressionist borrowings from Primitive art continued, of course, but such derivations were often tinged with modishness or irony.

After the war Pechstein began to collect examples of tribal art and in 1919 executed numerous wood sculptures.[156] Pechstein's *Quarter-Moon* bust was probably influenced by Schmidt-Rottluff's *Blue-Red Head* of 1917;[157] both heads taper to an elongated, projecting chin with a circular, hollowed-out mouth. But the geometric emphasis is more volumetric in the Schmidt-Rottluff, more surface-oriented in the Pechstein. It is not just that Pechstein's piece displays Oceanic linearity rather

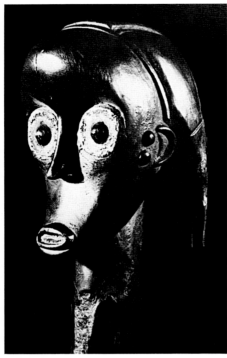

Above: Reliquary head (detail). Fang. Gabon. Wood, 17" (43.2 cm) high. Private collection

Left: Karl Schmidt-Rottluff. *Blue-Red Head (Fear).* 1917. Painted wood, 11⅞" (30 cm) high. Brücke-Museum, Berlin

Right: Karl Schmidt-Rottluff. *Head.* 1917. Wood. Destroyed

Far right: Figure (detail). Luba. Zaire. Wood and fiber, 15" (38 cm) high, overall. Whereabouts unknown (formerly in the collection of the Museum für Völkerkunde, Berlin). Published in Carl Einstein, *Negerplastik,* 1915

Above: Figure (detail). Teke. People's Republic of the Congo. Wood and mixed media. Published in Carl Einstein, *Negerplastik*, 1915

Left: Karl Schmidt-Rottluff. *Apostle*. 1918. Woodcut, 19⅝ x 15¾" (50 x 40 cm). Brücke-Museum, Berlin; gift of the artist

than African mass.[158] *Quarter-Moon* is also the work of a painter not much used to sculpture. Double-square patterns on the hair and deeply incised arcs for brow and beard show Pechstein's preference for two-dimensional design.

Pechstein's tendency to two-dimensionalize is even more apparent in comparing a lost wood sculpture with its probable source, a Luba (Zaire) female figure with a necklace (p. 398). The Luba piece has been in Berlin's Ethnographic Museum since 1904[159] and would seem to have influenced the facial features, the necklace, and even the arched arms of the Pechstein image. But the Pechstein work is in relief; the artist flattens the breasts downward and the buttock sideways compared to the African sculpture in the round. Moreover, the Expressionist regularizes scarification patterns all over the face and body, while the Zaire artist has placed them more randomly across the belly.[160]

The best sculpture in this 1919 series of lost Pechstein carvings is the piece called *Moon* (p. 399). It marks a breakthrough into carving in the round; compared to the *Quarter-Moon* the very title evokes its full-bodied, spherical appearance. And *Moon* is considerably more volumetric than the Zaire figure from the Ngombe tribe (p. 399) that was presum-

ably its source, a piece that entered the Berlin ethnographic collection in 1885.[161] Angular incisions edging the face form a few straight lines in the Ngombe piece but create a wholly circular frame in the Pechstein. Similarly, breasts and lower torso are larger and more spherical in the Expressionist than in the African example, though the flat shoulder plane and protruding navel are similar in both works. Despite all this, however, Pechstein has not yielded his interest in surface decoration one bit. There are diamond patterns in the hair, chevrons on the torso and zigzag side stripes on the limbs and hands. Especially owing to the stripes, Pechstein arrives at a fashionably ornamental style—quite advanced for Germany in 1919—that might be called Tribal Art Deco.

In the woodcut medium, too, Pechstein's late Expressionism leaned heavily on Primitive models. Thus the 1920 *Portfolio Cover* to a cycle of 1919 woodcuts does partly depict "some magic statuette from the Cameroon area," as Orrel Reed has suggested.[162] We can tentatively identify this statuette as another Ngumba figure, in the Berlin Ethnographic Museum since 1896.[163] The brass eyes, the bared teeth, and the fusion of pointed breasts with spread-eagled arms all evoke similar features in the Pechstein woodcut. Yet there is probably

Max Pechstein. Sculpture. 1919. Wood. Whereabouts unknown

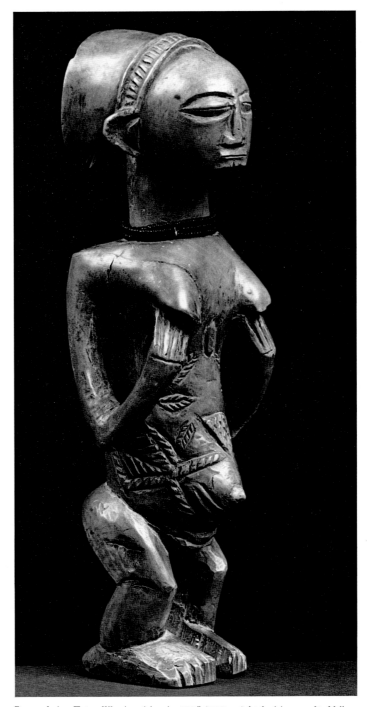

Figure. Luba. Zaire. Wood and beads; 10⅞" (27.5 cm) high. Museum für Völkerkunde, Berlin

another, equally important source as well, a source with which we are already familiar. The zigzag lines at either side of the head do not really resemble the evenly spaced chevron designs of the *Moon* sculpture done the previous year. Instead, they radiate toward the ears like the "talk-lines" on a Palau house beam that Kirchner had sketched on a 1910 postcard (p. 373). And indeed, according to unpublished research findings, the zigzag lines, the earrings, and even the head's perfectly oval shape are all belated evocations of Palau iconography.[164] Pechstein's 1920 *Portfolio Cover* is an effective fusion of African and Oceanic elements.

In contrast to Pechstein, Schmidt-Rottluff continued to explore the religious dimension of tribal art. In 1919 individual woodcuts like *Christ and Nicodemus* and *St. Francis* followed "missionary art" in combining African forms with Christian content.[165] But a painting of 1920 used tribal art for a more universal spiritual statement. In *Conversation about Death*, in which the man's expression has been called one of "anxious questioning,"[166] his irregular face with its bald pate, flat nose and elongated lips seems to be influenced by a Sumatran coffin figure in Berlin's Ethnographic Museum, illustrated a few years later in Eckart von Sydow's authoritative survey of tribal art.[167] It is typical of Schmidt-Rottluff to employ a Primitive fetish in an otherwise bold and colorful painting to raise universal questions about death and afterlife.

More satirical is Paul Klee's 1919 *Portrait of the Artist*, intended, I believe, to be in the guise of a Polynesian cult figure. The multiple lines around eyes and mouth are similar in both cases, as are shoulders, fingers, and squared-off skull, but the Klee stops at the waist, while the large head of the Polynesian piece is matched by a large phallus.[168] It must have amused Klee to identify with an exotic masterpiece of the Ethnographic Museum in Munich, where he lived, especially one with such prominently displayed sex. But the amusement was clearly at Klee's own expense. The German artist-intellectual viewed the instinctual tie between tribal culture and modern man with considerable irony.

Perhaps only Kirchner, living in self-imposed exile in rural Switzerland, achieved something of a "primitive" life style such as others had longed for. During the fall and winter of 1919–20 he carved his own furniture for his rude mountain shack and, in so doing, could not help comparing himself to tribal sculptors, observing, though, "how much further the Negros were in this kind of carving."[169] While making a pine chair, stained with oxblood, for example, Kirchner apparently remembered a Cameroon chief's stool both he and Pechstein had seen in Berlin before the war.[170] But where Pechstein had copied the bottom register, Kirchner recapitulated the top. On the back of the chair he carved a large crouching woman whose open legs mimic those of the remembered male figure from the Cameroon stool top; above, he joined the arms of a man and a woman in just the same V shape the African sculptor had used to create additional support. With the Swiss Alps outside his window, and furniture intended for a woman he would never dignify with the bourgeois title of "wife," Kirchner saw his carving as but an extension of rude nature itself.[171]

"How much further the Negroes were...." Once again we encounter an Expressionist's admiration for tribal artists, just as Nolde a few years earlier had described only natives as "real people." Such admiration also extended from *Urmensch* to *Urnatur*; thus Heckel had once hoped to reside in Africa in order to inhabit primordial nature. Nevertheless, Kirchner, who for two decades experienced a form of *Urnatur* in the Alps, managed to fuse it with modern culture. As early as 1909–10 he had ranged nature and culture against each other; now, even isolated in Switzerland, he would adopt vanguard abstraction. Thus the Expressionist was engaged in a very particular kind of enterprise. He was conducting a dialogue between *Urnatur* and modern art, a dialectic between primordial nature and advanced culture.

German Expressionists did not place nature ahead of culture, then, or somehow prefer raw nature to their own culture. Instead, they saw nature holistically as the origin of the culture of their time. They were heirs to a romantic tradition whereby life prefigured art both vitally and structurally. The guiding principle was art's fidelity to the "inner truth" of nature.[172]

What Expressionists added to this romantic tradition, however, was an understanding of *consciousness* as the link between nature and art. For them the issue was how the mind translated instinct—the mainspring of nature—into art as the high achievement of culture. Expressionists faced the issue as Nietzsche had, by demonstrating a tie between the primitive and the modern mind, between the "savage" storyteller and

Figure. Ngombe. Zaire. Painted wood, 24¾" (63 cm) high. Museum für Völkerkunde, Berlin

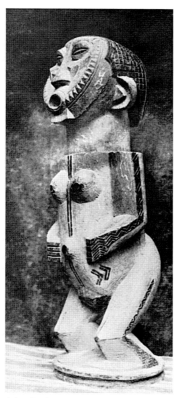

Max Pechstein. *Moon.* 1919. Painted wood. Whereabouts unknown

Ernst Ludwig Kirchner. *Chair.* 1920. Wood stained with oxblood, 31½" (80 cm) high. Brücke-Museum, Berlin

the modern artist-dreamer:

I hold, that as man now still reasons in dreams, so man reasoned also *when awake* through thousands of years; the first cause which occurred to the mind…was sufficient and stood for truth. (Thus, according to travellers' tales, savages still do to this very day.) This ancient element in human nature still manifests itself in our dreams, for it is the foundation upon which the higher reason has developed and still develops in every individual; the dream carries us back into remote conditions of human culture, and provides a ready means of understanding them better.…From these circumstances we may gather *how lately* the more acute logical thinking, the strict discrimination of cause and effect, has been developed, when our faculties of reasoning and understanding *still* involuntarily hark back to those primitive forms of deduction.…The poet, too, and the artist assign causes for their moods and conditions which are by no means the true ones; in this way they recall an older humanity and can assist us to the understanding of it.[173]

By what Nietzsche called, in another passage, "the logic of dreams," the modern artist could reassert a unity between the unconscious and the conscious mind, or between what he also called "dream and culture."

Nietzsche's variables, it will be noted, were three in number: Primitive thought, modern thought, and the artist's dream, which mediates between them. In the year 1919 Kirchner elaborated this triad by equating the Primitive with raw life experience, the modern with discerning or loving intellect, and the dream with culture-creating vision. The result was an aesthetic credo that embodies the Expressionist dialectic between primitive and modern thought:

Threefold is the grand secret of art: dream, life, and discerning love. Dream gives vision, vision brings experience, which is formed into a work of art through the loving intellect.[174]

Max Beckmann. *Early Men (Primeval Landscape)*. c. 1947. Gouache and mixed media on paper mounted on board, 19⅝ x 25⅜" (49.8 x 64.5 cm). Private collection

NOTES

1. This study is indebted to Leopold Reidemeister, pioneer in Expressionist scholarship, whose two decades of publications have proved indispensable to all research in the field. In formulating my ideas, I also profited from conversations with George A. Corbin, Charles W. Haxthausen, William S. Rubin, and Roy Sieber, and from suggestions made by students in graduate seminars on "Expressionism and Primitivism" at Columbia University in the spring of 1982 and at the University of Pittsburgh in the winter of 1983.

2. Robert M. Goldwater, *Primitivism in Modern Painting* (New York and London: Harper and Brothers, 1938), chap. 4, esp. pp. 87–90.

3. L. D. Ettlinger, "German Expressionism and Primitive Art," *The Burlington Magazine*, April 1968, p. 195.

4. Frederick S. Levine, *The Apocalyptic Vision: The Art of Franz Marc as German Expressionism* (New York: Harper and Row, 1979), pp. 3–5, 104 note.

5. Hal Foster, "The Expressive Fallacy," *Art in America*, January 1983, pp. 80–81.

6. Oskar Pfister, *Expressionism in Art: Its Psychological and Biological Basis* (1920), trans. B. Low and M. A. Muegge (New York: Dutton, 1923), p. 195; cf. p. 166. See also the distinction between an "ego overwhelmed by regression" in pathology and a "regression in the service of the ego" in creativity, Ernst Kris, *Psychoanalytic Explorations in Art* (New York: Schocken, 1967), p. 177.

7. Gustav F. Hartlaub, *Die Graphik des Expressionismus in Deutschland* (Stuttgart: G. Hatje, 1947), pp. 9–10; cf. Lothar-Günther Buchheim, *Die Künstlergemeinschaft Brücke* (Feldafing: Buchheim, 1956), pp. 12–13.

8. Leopold Reidemeister, in the catalog *Das Ursprüngliche und die Moderne* (Berlin: Akademie der Künste, 1964), n.p.

9. Manfred Schneckenburger, "Bemerkungen zur 'Brücke' und zur 'primitiven' Kunst," in the catalog *Weltkulturen und moderne Kunst* (Munich: Haus der Kunst, 1972), pp. 456–74, esp. 457–58.

10. Oskar Kokoschka, *My Life*, trans. David Britt (New York: Macmillan, 1974), p. 20. For Kokoschka, see also Goldwater, *Primitivism*, p. 100, note 1.

11. Robert Louis Stevenson and Paul Gauguin portrayed the sexual mores among South Seas peoples as free and permissive. Margaret Mead's famous confirmation of this assumption in her 1928 *Coming of Age in Samoa* has now been questioned in Derek Freeman, *Margaret Mead and Samoa: The Making and Unmaking of an Anthropological Myth* (Cambridge, Mass.: Harvard University Press, 1983).

12. Reidemeister, *Das Ursprüngliche*, nos. 99 and 100 (Heckel); 123 and 125, 129 and 130, 131 and 133 (Nolde). Schneckenburger, *Weltkulturen*, nos. 1777 and 1769 (Schmidt-Rottluff); 1778 and 1793 (Kirchner). The Nolde comparisons, published by Reidemeister and later by Schneckenburger (nos. 1812–23), were presented more exhaustively in Martin Urban, *Emil Nolde: Masken and Figuren* (Bielefeld: Kunsthalle, 1971), nos. 6 and 6a, 5 and 5b, 15 and 15a.

13. J.-J. Rousseau, *Discourse on the Origin of Inequality*; cf. Claude Lévi-Strauss, *Structural Anthropology* (New York: Basic Books, 1976), vol. 2, p. 37.

14. Rousseau, *Les Rêveries*, Seventh Walk; Lévi-Strauss, *Structural Anthropology*, vol. 2, pp. 42–43. In the *Confessions* Rousseau even discovers the depersonalizing effect of empathy; cf. Lévi-Strauss, p. 39, "I am not 'me,' but the weakest, the most humble of 'others.'"

15. Ferdinand Tönnies, *Community and Society* (East Lansing: Michigan State University Press, 1957), parts 1, 2; the book first appeared in 1887.

16. Lévi-Strauss, *Structural Anthropology*, vol. 2, pp. 312–17.

17. Georg Simmel, "The Metropolis and Mental Life" (1903), *The Sociology of George Simmel*, ed. K. H. Wolff (Glencoe: Free Press, 1950), pp. 416, 418; cf. Lévi-Strauss, *Structural Anthropology*, vol. 2, p. 284: "This segregation of man outside the natural environment . . . , his being forced by modern forms of urban life to live almost entirely inside an artifice, constitutes a major threat to the mental health of the species."

18. Tönnies, *Community and Society*, p. 154.

19. Georg Simmel, *The Conflict in Modern Culture and Other Essays*, trans. K. P. Etzkorn (New York: Teachers College Press, 1968), pp. 17, 25; cf. 12. The title essay first appeared in 1914.

20. Cf. Lévi-Strauss, *Structural Anthropology*, vol. 2, p. 278: "The future of art—if it has one—requires . . . a getting in touch with nature again, in its raw state, which is, strictly speaking, impossible. . . ."

21. Georg Reinhardt, "Die frühe 'Brücke': Beiträge zur Geschichte und zum Werk der Dresdener Künstlergruppe 'Brücke' der Jahre 1905 bis 1908," *Brücke-Archiv*, no. 9/10, 1977–78, pp. 23–24. Note that Buchheim gave a different impression in titling his study *Die Künstlergemeinschaft Brücke*. The false title was picked up by Hans Konrad Roethel, *Modern German Painting* (New York: Reynal, [1958]), p. 7.

22. Tönnies, *Community and Society*, pp. 156–57. Rather than the Brücke, it was the *Wandervögel* youth movement that reflected the notion of innocent *Gemeinschaft*; see Walter Laqueur, *Young Germany: A History of the German Youth Movement* (New York: Basic Books, 1962).

23. Reinhardt, "Die frühe 'Brücke,'" pp. 85–87. It should also be noted that the *Program's* Darwinist references to "faith in evolution" and to a youth cohort "which carries the future" are incompatible with a truly regressive—and folkish—rejection of history.

24. The *Brücke Program* has been widely reproduced, most conveniently in Peter Selz, *German Expressionist Painting* (Berkeley: University of California Press, 1957), p. 95.

25. Reinhardt, "Die frühe 'Brücke,'" pp. 28–31.

26. E. L. Kirchner, "Letter of April 17, 1937," *Ernst Ludwig Kirchner* (New York: Curt Valentin Gallery, 1952), n.p.

27. Paul Vogt, *Erich Heckel* (Recklinghausen: Aurel Bongers, 1965), no. 1909/7.

28. Friedrich Nietzsche, *The Will to Power*, trans. Walter Kaufmann and R. J. Hollingdale (New York: Vintage, 1968), p. 424. The first edition appeared in 1901—the title page is transcribed here on p. xxvii—and not in 1906 as stated in Reinhardt, "Die frühe 'Brücke,'" p. 28.

29. Walt Whitman, *Leaves of Grass* (1855), facsimile ed. (Portland, Maine: T. B. Mosher and W. F. Gable, 1942), p. 17. The most popular German edition at the time was Johannes Schlaf's translation, *Grashalme* (Leipzig: P. Reclam, jun., 1907).

30. See, e.g., *Moritzburg Bathing Group* where a foreground female bares her buttocks and where males above have prominent genitals, in Donald E. Gordon, *Ernst Ludwig Kirchner* (Cambridge, Mass.: Harvard University Press, 1968), no. 94. Reinhardt's redating of this painting to 1910 ("Die frühe 'Brücke,'" p. 173, note 378) is stylistically unconvincing.

31. See, e.g., the catalog *Ernst Ludwig Kirchner 1880–1938* (Berlin: Nationalgalerie, 1979–80), nos. 55–60; the *Love Scene* is no. 62.

32. See esp. the group of drawings from 1910 and 1911 reproduced and analyzed in the catalog *Kirchner 1880–1938*, nos. 100–05.

33. The single male to the right was painted out when Kirchner refurbished the canvas around 1920, though the head was unaccountably left; cf. Will Grohmann, *Das Werk Ernst Ludwig Kirchners* (Munich: Kurt Wolff, 1926), pl. 19.

34. For photographs of the curtains and wall-drapes, see the catalog *Kirchner 1880–1938*, p. 18, figs. 7, 8; for drawings, ibid., nos. 104, 105.

35. The Frankfurt *Standing Nude* is in Gordon, *Ernst Ludwig Kirchner*, no. 163. From 1910, compare the Stockholm *Marcella*, the Minneapolis *Seated Fränzi*, and the Bremen *Reclining Negress* and, from 1911, the Los Angeles *Two Women* (Gordon, nos. 113, 123, 58 verso, 189).

36. For the stool, see a postcard dated December 24, 1910, in Gerhard Schack, ed., *Postkarten an Gustav Schiefler* (Hamburg: Christians, 1976), no. 21, and a photograph in Karlheinz Gabler, *E. L. Kirchner Dokumente: Fotos, Schriften, Briefe* (Aschaffenburg: Museum, 1980), p. 139. For its possible Cameroon prototype, see a wooden stool of the Bali tribe, which entered the Berlin Ethnographic Museum in 1897, illustrated in Kurt Krieger, *Westafrikanische Plastik III* (Berlin: Museum für Völkerkunde, 1969), pl. 8, p. 13. Kirchner visited Berlin several times in 1910.

37. Vogt, *Erich Heckel*, no. 1910/3.

38. See Gordon, *Ernst Ludwig Kirchner*, nos. 155, 156, and 157 from 1910. The animal frieze turns up as the border of a tablecloth in Heckel's studio in 1912: see Vogt, *Erich Heckel*, no. 1912/46.

39. Illustrated in the catalog *Brücke* (Cornell University Andrew Dickson White Museum of Art, 1970), no. 79.

40. Gordon, *Ernst Ludwig Kirchner*, nos. 74 (1909), 58 verso (1910), 185–87 (1911).

41. Annemarie and Wolf-Dieter Dube, *E. L. Kirchner: Das graphische Werk*, 2 vols. (Munich: Prestel-Verlag, 1967), lithographs nos. 185–90. See also Gabler, *E. L. Kirchner Dokumente*, pp. 70–71.

42. *Führer durch die Königlichen Sammlungen zu Dresden*, 11th ed. (Dresden: Albanussche Buchdruckerei, 1912), p. 88; cf. plan, p. 56.

43. Donald E. Gordon, "Kirchner in Dresden," *The Art Bulletin*, September–December 1966, p. 355 and note 115.

44. *Führer . . . zu Dresden*, p. 88.

45. Karl Woermann, *Geschichte der Kunst aller Zeiten und Völker* (Leipzig and Wien: Bibliographisches Institut, 1900), vol. 1, opp. p. 56; the Woermann illustration was reproduced in Ettlinger, "Primitive Art," fig. 42. For the 1881 reference, see Eckart von Sydow, *Die Kunst der Naturvölker und die Vorzeit* (Berlin: Propyläen, 1923), pl. 237 and p. 510. Sara Gregg, in my Pittsburgh seminar, first recognized the importance of the von Sydow source.

46. Kirchner, "Die Arbeit E. L. Kirchners" (1925–26), in Eberhard W. Kornfeld, *Ernst Ludwig Kirchner: Nachzeichnung seines Lebens* (Bern: Kornfeld, 1979), p. 333. The year 1903 is also mentioned in a diary entry of 1925: Lothar Grisebach, *E. L. Kirchners Davoser Tagebuch* (Cologne: M. DuMont Schauberg, 1968), p. 84. The discovery of the Palau beams, along with "feather cloaks of South Sea peoples," is mentioned but not dated in a 1916 letter to Botho Graef: Lothar Grisebach, ed., *Maler des Expressionismus im Briefwechsel mit Eberhard Grisebach* (Hamburg: Christian Wegner, 1962), p. 53. "Oceanic beam carvings" are mentioned in the context of events of 1906 in Kirchner's 1913 *Chronik der Brücke*, trans. in Selz, *German Expressionist Painting*, p. 320.

47. Hans Bolliger, "Die Biographie Ernst Ludwig Kirchners," in the catalog *Ernst Ludwig Kirchner* (Dusseldorf: Kunsthalle, 1960), n.p.

48. Cf. Alfred H. Barr, Jr., *German Painting and Sculpture* (New York: Museum of Modern Art, 1931), p. 10.

49. Cf. Will Grohmann, *Zeichnungen von E. L. Kirchner* (Dresden: Arnold, 1925), esp. nos. 7, 9, 10. See also Wilhelm F. Arntz, *Paula Modersohn und die Maler der 'Brücke'* (Bern: Kunsthalle, 1948), p. 13: "Schon aus dem Jahre 1904 kennen wir Zeichnungen Kirchners nach afrikanischen und Südsee-Skulpturen. . . ."

50. Reidemeister, *Das Ursprüngliche*, no. 92, where Kirchner's ink sketch of an African sculpture from this letter is illustrated. Although the exact African source for this sketch has not been identified, it was undoubtedly Cameroon and may have been a female variant of a wooden male figure, 52 cm high, acquired by the Dresden museum in 1909 (inv. no. 24229).

51. Gerd Wietek, ed., *Bemalte Postkarten und Briefe deutscher Künstler* (Hamburg: Altonäer Museum, 1962), no. 214. The word *Balken* ("beam") is here transcribed as *Balkon* ("balcony"), an error missed in my "Kirchner in Dresden," p. 354, but corrected in Reinhardt, "Die frühe 'Brücke,'" p. 174, note 381.

52. Reinhardt, "Die frühe 'Brücke,'" fig. 65, p. 91, has pointed out Kirchner's interest in such "talk-lines" but was not aware that the zigzag form of the 1910 drawing was, in the first instance, an analogue for the triangular shapes of the Palau beam's decorative border. For further discussion of Palau beam iconography, see DeVerne Reed Smith, "The Palauan Storyboards: From Traditional Architecture to Airport Art," *Expedition*, Fall 1975, pp. 2–17, esp. pp. 5 f., 11 f. Kathryn Kramer of my Columbia seminar first brought the latter article to my attention.

53. Dube, *Kirchner: Das graphische Werk*, woodcut no. 160.

54. Vogt, *Erich Heckel*, no. 1910/11.

55. See, e.g., Pechstein's 1910 *Three Bathers at the Pond* illustrated in Reinhardt, "Die frühe 'Brücke,'" fig. 62a, p. 88. For the "shorthand style" and its summer 1910 impact, see also Schneckenburger, *Weltkulturen*, no. 1777, p. 463.

56. Lothar-Günther Buchheim, *Otto Mueller, Leben und Werk; mit einem Werkverzeichnis der Graphik Otto Muellers von Florian Karsch* (Feldafing: Buchheim, 1963), Karsch no. 5.

57. For example, in Kirchner's 1910 *Fränzi in Carved Chair* (Gordon, *Ernst Ludwig Kirchner*, no. 122), the back of the depicted chair is modeled on the Palau relief style, with a pink body and face surrounded by a black body-edge and large hair mass, all rigorously two-dimensional. Yet Kirchner undercuts the two-dimensional effect by placing Fränzi's naturalistic mass *before* the flat chair and by creating color tensions between foreground and background. For another view of Kirchner's carved chair, see Heckel's postcard from December 16, 1910, in Schack, *Postkarten an Gustav Schiefler*, no. 44.

58. Gordon, "Kirchner in Dresden," p. 357, n. 134. Benin art employs a court style, but Expressionists did not distinguish it from tribal art.

59. Donald A. Rosenthal, "Two Motifs from Early Africa in Works by Ernst Ludwig Kirchner," *Abhandlungen und Berichte des Staatlichen Museums für Völkerkunde Dresden*, vol. 35 (Berlin: Akademie, 1976), pp. 169–71, esp. p. 170; Rosenthal bases his dating on Kirchner's mention of Benin bronzes in his letter of March 31, 1910. I am grateful to Sara Gregg for bringing this article to my attention.

60. Gordon, "Kirchner in Dresden," p. 358, note 135.

61. Cf. note 17 above.

62. See Goldwater, *Primitivism* (1938), pp. 102–16, and esp. the slightly revised edition, *Primitivism in Modern Art* (New York: Vintage, 1967), pp. 125–42. Cf. Ludwig Grote, "Expressionismus und Volkskunst," *Zeitschrift für Volkskunde*, no. 2, 1959, pp. 24–31, and Ursula Glatzel, "Zur Bedeutung der Volkskunst beim Blauen Reiter" (Ph.D. diss., Ludwigs-Maximilians-Universität, Munich, 1976), esp. pp. 187–242.

63. Wassily Kandinsky, "Der blaue Reiter (Rückblick)," *Das Kunstblatt*, 1930, as trans. in *Kandinsky: Complete Writings on Art*, ed. Kenneth C. Lindsay and Peter Vergo (Boston: G. K. Hall, 1982), vol. 2, p. 746.

64. Kandinsky, loc. cit. For the 1907 date, see Gold-

65. August Macke and Franz Marc, *Briefwechsel* (Cologne: M. DuMont Schauberg, 1964), pp. 39–41.

66. Klaus Lankheit, *Franz Marc: Sein Leben und seine Kunst* (Cologne: DuMont, 1976), figs. 22, 23.

67. Kurt Krieger and Gerdt Kutscher, *Westafrikanische Masken*, 2d ed. (Berlin: Museum für Völkerkunde, 1967), p. 56, no. 84 (fig. 36).

68. Cameroon masks "in the form of oxheads" were on display: *Führer durch das Museum für Völkerkunde* (Berlin: Georg Reimer, 1911), p. 70.

69. Wilhelm Worringer, *Abstraction and Empathy: A Contribution to the Psychology of Style*, trans. Michael Bullock (New York: International Universities Press, 1963), p. 12.

70. Worringer, *Abstraction and Empathy*, p. 15. The "dread of space" found typical of abstract art is then identified specifically with "Egyptian architecture," op. cit., p. 137, n. 8.

71. For the debt of Marc's 1911 *Yellow Cow* to a Mycenaean gold cup from Vaphio, see Lankheit, *Franz Marc*, p. 78.

72. For the relation between the Gauguin and the two Marcs, see Donald E. Gordon, "Content by Contradiction," *Art in America*, December 1982, pp. 76–89.

73. Alfred Vondermuhll, "Franz Marc and Primitive Art" (master's thesis, Institute of Fine Arts, New York, 1982).

74. Gustav Vriesen, *August Macke*, 2d ed. (Stuttgart: W. Kohlhammer, 1957), nos. 53, *Indianer im Zelt;* 260, *Indianer,* and 273, *Reitende Indianer beim Zelt.*

75. Macke and Marc, *Briefwechsel*, pp. 111, 114.

76. August Macke, "Masks," in *The Blaue Reiter Almanach*, ed. Wassily Kandinsky and Franz Marc, doc. ed. Klaus Lankheit (New York: Viking, 1974), pp. 82–89, esp. 85.

77. Macke, "Masks," p. 88.

78. Macke, "Masks," p. 89. Comparison of Medieval and tribal art works was prompted by the similar usages in Wilhelm Worringer's 1910 *Form Problems of the Gothic* (New York: G. E. Stechert, 1920).

79. Accompanying the Macke article are illustrations captioned "Brazilian" (p. 83), "Easter Islands" (p. 84), "Cameroons" (p. 85), "Mexico" and "New Caledonia" (both p. 87), "Alaska" (p. 88). A Benin plaque appears on p. 129 (facing a German sculpture from Frankfurt Cathedral, p. 128), while a Ceylonese dance mask (p. 215) is described by Macke (p. 89) in these words: "The mask of the disease demon from Ceylon is the gesture of horror of a primitive race."

80. These are a stilt captioned "Marquesas Islands" (p. 96) and a Fang mask from Gabon miscaptioned "Chinese (?) Mask" (p. 190). For the piece captioned "South Borneo" (p. 63), see the ensuing discussion.

81. Dube, *Kirchner: Das graphische Werk*, lithograph no. 168.

82. Kirchner did not know the South Borneo sculpture, of course, but he did know the not unrelated hardwood sculptures from Palau that served as models for his own sculptures from 1912.

83. See, for example, the comparison between the horses in Heckel's 1910 *Circus* lithograph and those in a Russian folk print, juxtaposed in Kandinsky and Marc, *The Blaue Reiter Almanach*, pp. 117 and 118.

84. Campendonk's use of this Benin plaque was first suggested by Sara Gregg in my Pittsburgh seminar.

85. For the Russian folk prints, see Kandinsky and Marc, *The Blaue Reiter Almanach*, pp. 118 and 216; for the shadow-play figures, see pp. 194 and 201.

86. Nolde did not participate in the first Neue Secession show of May 1910 but did in the next ones, Donald E. Gordon, *Modern Art Exhibitions 1900–1916* (Munich: Prestel, 1974), vol. 2, pp. 398, 430, 461.

87. Peter Selz, *Emil Nolde* (New York: Museum of

Modern Art, 1963), p. 32. Nolde himself gives the year 1911 (*Jahre der Kämpfe* [Berlin: Rembrandt, 1934], pp. 161 ff.), but Martin Urban dates the visit in early 1910, *Emil Nolde: Masken und Figuren*, p. [4].

88. Cf. Gordon, "Content by Contradiction," pp. 81–83, where the contradiction in *Dance around the Golden Calf* is given a Nietzschean explanation.

89. The pig-snout nose and garish lips of Nolde's third mask resemble the similar features on two foreground masks to the left in Ensor's 1890 *Intrigue*, now in the Musée Royal des Beaux-Arts, Antwerp.

90. The Solomon Islands object and the Peruvian head were first reproduced, along with Nolde's drawings of them, in Reidemeister and Krieger, *Das Ursprüngliche*, nos. 137 f., but were not there related to the *Still Life of Masks*. The relationship was communicated to me by Dr. Martin Urban.

91. Nolde, *Jahre der Kämpfe*, pp. 162–63.

92. There was a Nigerian piece in Leiden "completely similar" to the one illustrated here from Hamburg: L. Frobenius, *Die Masken und Geheimbünde Afrikas* (Halle: Ehrhardt Karras, 1898), fig. 69 and p. 20.

93. In a communication of August 30, 1983, Dr. Martin Urban maintains the distinction between masks that Nolde copied in extant "study drawings" and those other "more or less free inventions" for which no drawing copies exist. Nevertheless, even in the invented masks Urban would not rule out a distant "dependence on visual precedent," such as the Nigerian mask proposed here.

94. Cf. Goldwater, *Primitivism*, p. 90.

95. The 1911 oil, the Kachina doll, and three Nolde preparatory drawings are illustrated in Urban, *Emil Nolde: Masken und Figuren*, figs. 2–2d.

96. Schneckenburger, *Weltkulturen*, no. 1821.

97. Kris, *Psychoanalytic Explorations in Art*, pp. 180, 197–99.

98. Nolde's drawing of the Yoruba sculpture is illustrated in Reidemeister and Krieger, *Das Ursprüngliche*, no. 130.

99. Nolde, *Jahre der Kämpfe*, pp. 172–73, as trans. in Herschel B. Chipp, *Theories of Modern Art* (Berkeley: University of California Press, 1968), pp. 150–51.

100. Gordon, "Kirchner in Dresden," p. 354, note 116.

101. The date is certain because the relief was intended for the chapel of the Cologne Sonderbund show, which opened May 1912; Will Grohmann, *Karl Schmidt-Rottluff* (Stuttgart: Kohlhammer, 1956), p. 159.

102. *Führer durch das Museum für Völkerkunde*, p. 70; their functions as rank insignia and as dance headdress were also mentioned by the guide.

103. For the attribution of this type of object to the Ekoi tribe and for illustration of a similar example, see Hans Himmelheber, *Negerkunst und Negerkünstler* (Braunschweig: Klinkhardt and Biermann, 1960), p. 279.

104. Also following the Nolde parallel, Leopold Reidemeister suggests German Gothic inspiration for the relief, Reidemeister, "Die Vier Evangelisten von Karl Schmidt-Rottluff," *Brücke-Archiv*, no. 8, 1975–76, pp. 13–16.

105. Grohmann, *Karl Schmidt-Rottluff*, p. 159.

106. Compare the heads in *Four Evangelists* to those in Pechstein's 1909 *Poster for the Brücke Exhibition at Emil Richter's, Dresden*.

107. E. L. Kirchner, *Briefe an Nele* (Munich: Piper, 1961), pp. 20–21.

108. The Palau piece was acquired in 1909; I am grateful to Prof. J. Zwernemann of the Hamburg Museum für Völkerkunde for this information.

109. The lost *Female Figure* is depicted next to Erna in a 1912 painting, Gordon no. 268; in a 1912 pencil drawing illustrated in the catalog *Ernst Ludwig Kirchner 1880–1938*, no. 136; and in a 1912 woodcut mistitled by Kirchner *Woman with Negro Sculp-*

ture, Dube no. 205. Wolfgang Henze has now proposed that the piece is not by Kirchner at all, but is "a large African sculpture [which Kirchner kept] in his studio". Henze, "Kirchner," in the catalog *German Expressionist Sculpture* (Los Angeles County Museum of Art, 1983–84), p. 115 and note 9. Arguing against this interpretation, in addition to the Palau-like flatness of some features, is the very scale of the piece, which apparently exceeds one meter in height; African figure sculptures this large are extremely rare.

110. Joseph Masheck, "Raw Art: 'Primitive' Authenticity and German Expressionism," *Res* 4, Autumn 1982, p. 104, notes the "zigzagging of a carved Melanesian work" in a 1911 Kirchner woodcut without, however, mentioning the volumetric— and African—belly and buttocks of the adjacent nude. Throughout, Masheck minimizes the sculptural properties of both Primitive and Expressionist work in favor of pre-Expressionist sources focusing on ornament in art or the notion of "flatness" in art theory.

111. L. de Marsalle (pseud. E. L. Kirchner), "Ueber die plastischen Arbeiten von E. L. Kirchner," *Der Cicerone* 14, 1925, pp. 695–701.

112. The phrase is Erika Billeter's; see her "Kunst als Lebensentwurf," in the catalog *Kirchner 1880–1938*, pp. 16–25. Cf. my "Ernst Ludwig Kirchner: By Instinct Possessed," *Art in America*, November 1980, pp. 80–95, esp. 90 f.

113. Eberhard Grisebach, letter of January 8, 1914, in L. Grisebach, *Maler des Expressionismus*, p. 39. For studio views of 1912 and 1913, see Heckel watercolors illustrated in Leopold Reidemeister, *Künstler der Brücke in Berlin* (Berlin: Brücke Museum, 1972), nos. 111 and 112.

114. See the Neumecklenburg ancestor figures in Wilhelm Hausenstein, *Barbaren und Klassiker* (Munich: Piper, 1922), figs. 6 and 7.

115. See the calabashes in von Sydow, *Die Kunst der Naturvölker*, pls. IV and 124.

116. Leopold Reidemeister, *Museums Discovered: The Brücke Museum* (Fort Lee, N.J.: Penshurst, 1981), p. 124.

117. Hans Platte, "Erich Heckel: Bilder aus dem Alstertal," *Schriften des Kunstvereins in Hamburg*, 1, 1964, introduction; Platte's source was Frau Luise Schiefler.

118. Grisebach, *Maler des Expressionismus*, letter of January 8, 1914, p. 39.

119. Vogt, *Erich Heckel*, nos. 1913/3 and 1913/31.

120. *Still Life with Vases* in the Busch-Reisinger Museum, Harvard University; *Stilleben mit Stranddisteln* in the Bremen Kunsthalle.

121. Pechstein's stool reappears in a lost painting of 1917, *In the Woman's House, Palau*; Kirchner recalled the lost Berlin original in his own chair of 1920.

122. The stool illustrated here was only acquired by the Dresden Ethnographic Museum in 1914, too late to influence Brücke artists; for the date I am grateful for information provided in 1964 by Dr. S. Wolf, the museum's director. The bottom register of the Dresden piece, however, does closely resemble Pechstein's.

123. Emil Nolde, *Briefe aus den Jahren 1894–1926*, ed. Max Sauerlandt (Berlin: Furche, 1927), p. 98 f. Also cited in Reidemeister, *Das Ursprüngliche*, after no. 149.

124. Nolde, *Jahre der Kämpfe*, pp. 240–41.

125. Ibid., p. 242.

126. Schneckenburger, *Weltkulturen*, p. 473.

127. While Uli figures are hermaphroditic, with breasts and phallus, Nolde's example was predominantly masculine: Urban, *Emile Nolde: Masken und Figuren*, no. 15a. This fact invalidates an interpretation offered in Charles Wentinck, *Modern and Primitive Art* (Oxford: Phaidon, 1979), p. 11b, namely that "the bisexuality of the Uli is split between the man and woman" upper right, also misidentified as "two lovers." Wentinck is also in error in believing that Nolde's Uli figure came from a Dutch collection.

128. Max Pechstein, *Erinnerungen*, ed. L. Reidemeister (Wiesbaden: Limes, 1960), p. 77. See pp. 54, 91, 78, and 67 for the Pechstein quotations cited below in this and the two following paragraphs.

129. Catalog, *Der junge Pechstein* (Berlin: Hochschule für bildende Künste, 1959), n.p.; Pechstein, *Erinnerungen*, passim; Max Osborn, *Max Pechstein* (Berlin: Propyläen, 1922), passim.

130. Pechstein, *Erinnerungen*, pp. 77–78.

131. Osborn, *Max Pechstein*, pp. 86–89, 97, 118.

132. Reidemeister, *Das Ursprüngliche*, n.p. (two photographs). Ettlinger, "Primitive Art," p. 196, considers the studio frieze "little more than a free copy" of the house beams seen in Dresden, but it is closer to Pechstein's own Palau paintings.

133. I owe this observation to Kathryn Kramer, a student in my 1982 seminar at Columbia University.

134. The Mannheim *Still Life* is larger, about 110 x 70 cm, but has been misdated "about 1913" in Roethel, *Modern German Painting*, p. 17. The Saarbrücken painting measuring 78 x 70.5 cm is dated 1917 but mistitled *Still Life with African Sculpture and Lupines* in Reidemeister, *Das Ursprüngliche*, no. 121. The sculpture, though African in inspiration, tapers into a rectangular base that can only have been carved by Pechstein.

135. Grohmann, *Karl Schmidt-Rottluff*, p. 75.

136. For the woodcut, see Gerhard Wietek, *Schmidt-Rottluff Graphik* (Munich: Karl Thiemig, 1971), no. 72. The painting is in the Neue Nationalgalerie, Berlin.

137. Kurt Krieger, *Westafrikanische Plastik I*, 2d ed. (Berlin: Museum für Völkerkunde, 1978), p. 83, no. 194, called *ngulu melan*. The 1911 *Führer durch das Museum für Völkerkunde*, p. 69, mentions "von den Ngumba die Ahnenfiguren (Ngule malang)" in case 34b. (Ngumbe are a Cameroon subtribe of the Fang.)

138. Schneckenburger, *Weltkulturen*, no. 1780. It should also be noted that the Bambara piece is in a Paris private collection; nothing like it is known in pre–1914 Berlin.

139. Wietek, *Schmidt-Rottluff Graphik*, no. 128. The latter similarity was first noted by Christa Paula in my Pittsburgh seminar.

140. Grohmann, *Karl Schmidt-Rottluff*, p. 85.

141. Carl Einstein, *Negerplastik* (Leipzig: Verlag der Weissen Bücher, 1915). Einstein was a novelist before he turned to art criticism.

142. See, e.g., p. 396 below, illustrated in Einstein's 1915 book, no. 76, but also illustrated and located in the Berlin Ethnographic Museum in Carl Einstein, *Afrikanische Plastik* (Berlin: Ernst Wasmuth, 1922), no. 27. Of some fifty-six objects illustrated in the 1922 source, twenty-one were in the Berlin Museum and most of the others in private collections.

143. Einstein, *Negerplastik*, pp. vi, vii.

144. Einstein, *Negerplastik*, nos. 14–15, 20, 31.

145. Hans Himmelheber, "The Concave Face in African Art," *African Arts*, Spring 1971, pp. 52–55. Jonathan Kuhn in my Columbia seminar brought this article to my attention.

146. The *Schmidt-Rottluff Woodcut* is compared to a Guro heddle pulley, but the Guro head in Einstein (nos. 14–15) seems the likely source.

147. Schneckenburger, *Weltkulturen*, no. 1783, mentions Guro masks as parallel to the *Bluish-Red Head*, but he finds a "mimetic emphasis" in mouth and eyes that is not African at all. For the work's subtitle and its meaning, see Reidemeister, *The Brücke Museum*, p. 156.

148. Reidemeister, *Das Ursprüngliche*, nos. 86, 88; Schneckenburger, *Weltkulturen*, nos. 1785, 1789.

149. Krieger, *Westafrikanische Plastik I*, p. 84, no. 198.

150. Einstein, *Negerplastik*, no. 76, and Einstein, *Afrikanische Plastik*, no. 27. The carving's loss after 1940 was kindly verified by Dr. Angelika Rumpf of the Berlin Ethnographic Museum in a recent letter.

151. For this comparison I am again grateful to Jonathan Kuhn of my Columbia seminar.

152. Krieger, *Westafrikanische Plastik I*, p. 108, no. 265 (ill. 222), acquired in 1886. "The row of Bateke fetishes...are noteworthy," according to *Führer durch das Museum für Völkerkunde*, p. 67.

153. Catalog, *Karl Schmidt-Rottluff: Das graphische Werk zum 90. Geburtstag des Künstlers* (Berlin: Brücke Museum, 1974), no. 145, pl. 56.

154. Einstein, *Negerplastik*, pp. 13 f., 17 f.

155. Victor H. Miesel, ed., *Voices of German Expressionism* (Englewood Cliffs: Prentice-Hall, 1970), p. 7.

156. Osborn, *Max Pechstein's*, p. 157, illustrates his painting *Surrounded by Masks* from 1920. Still lifes of tribal objects are also known.

157. Osborn, *Max Pechstein*, p. 235. Schmidt-Rottluff's close friendship with Pechstein began in the summer of 1913 when, "on the trail of Max Pechstein, [Schmidt-Rottluff] was in Nidden on the Kurische Nehrung. He lived there in the cottage of the same fisherman with whom Pechstein had lived in 1909" (Reidemeister, *The Brücke Museum*, p. 130).

158. The *Quarter-Moon* may be compared with the ornamental linear bands across the face of a Solomon Islands ship prow.

159. Krieger, *Westafrikanische Plastik I*, p. 115, no. 286.

160. As will be recalled, Pechstein in 1914 already associated scarification with the Palau islanders' "sense of beauty" and "passion for structure," *Erinnerungen*, p. 78, as cited above. But his arrangement of scarification patterns into neatly subdivided stripes may well derive from West African masks, specifically from the one illustrated in Einstein, *Negerplastik*, no. 91.

161. Krieger, *Westafrikanische Plastik I*, p. 132, no. 327. Patricia Tanner of my Pittsburgh seminar first made this comparison.

162. Orrel P. Reed, Jr., *German Expressionist Art: The Robert Gore Rifkind Collection* (Los Angeles: University of California, 1977), p. 97, no. 151.

163. Krieger, *Westafrikanische Plastik I*, p. 81, no. 191. Kathryn Kramer of my Columbia seminar first pointed out this source.

164. Kathryn Kramer's report on Pechstein's sources is being prepared for publication.

165. For discussion of these woodcuts, see previous section.

166. Grohmann, *Karl Schmidt-Rottluff*, p. 93.

167. Von Sydow, *Die Kunst der Naturvölker*, pl. 252; the 1923 book, in the Propyläen Kunstgeschichte series, was dedicated to Schmidt-Rottluff. Sara Gregg in my Pittsburgh seminar made this connection.

168. The cult figure I have in mind is illustrated in Hausenstein, *Barbaren und Klassiker*, pl. 39. Klee's drawing appears in G. di San Lazzaro, *Klee* (New York: Praeger, 1957), p. 31, and there is given to the "Passadena [sic] Art Institute, California." However, Dr. Jürgen Glaesemer of the Paul-Klee Stiftung, Bern, informs me that the drawing's location remains unknown.

169. Grisebach, *Kirchner's Davoser Tagebuch*, p. 70.

170. Schneckenburger, *Weltkulturen*, nos. 1827, 1828, compares Kirchner's chair with a Cameroon stool in Hamburg's Ethnographic Museum (no. 5323:1), not realizing that the stool did not enter the Hamburg collection until 1953. For the acquisition date I am grateful to Prof. J. Zwernemann of the museum.

171. Lucius Grisebach, in the catalog *Kirchner 1880–1938*, p. 257, notes that Kirchner's efforts to furnish his house "are not to be separated from his longing for a harmonious relationship with [Erna Schilling]."

172. Sixten Ringbom, "Paul Klee and the Inner Truth to Nature," *Arts*, September 1977, pp. 112–17.

173. Friedrich Nietzsche, *Human All-too-Human*, trans. Helen Zimmern (New York: Macmillan, 1909), vol. 1, pp. 24–27. The German edition appeared in 1878.

174. The catalog, *Ernst Ludwig Kirchner* (Frankfurt: Galerie L. Schames, 1919), n.p.

Carlo Carrà. *Composition with Female Figure.* 1915. Tempera on cardboard, 16⅛ x 12¼" (41 x 31 cm). The Pushkin Museum, Moscow

ITALIAN PAINTING

Ezio Bassani

The crisis in modern art of 1906–07, in which the "discovery" of tribal art played such a crucial role, seems not to have touched the Italian art scene, where artists remained faithful to the nineteenth century. Even the Impressionist vogue, when it arrived, had already assumed a much more subdued form. The various Secession styles of the *fin de siècle* and the turn of the century pointed to other, sometimes exotic, experiences, and pointillism achieved widespread currency as a leveler of international differences. Several years would pass before artists became aware of the significance of the revolutionary "discovery" of so-called "art nègre" by a few of the Futurists, who for professional reasons had been in touch with Parisian circles.

Umberto Boccioni and Carlo Carrà were in the French capital in November of 1911 to prepare the exhibition of Futurist painting to be held the following year at the Bernheim-Jeune gallery. They returned to Paris in February of 1912, together with Luigi Russolo and F. T. Marinetti, to attend that exhibition. On display, together with the works of Boccioni, Carrà, and Russolo, were those of Gino Severini, who had been living for some time in Paris, having married the daughter of the poet Paul Fort.

It was Severini and Modigliani, also working in Paris at that time, who encouraged contacts between their Italian colleagues and such exponents of the French avant-garde as Picasso, Braque, Gris, Vlaminck, Derain, Matisse, Brancusi, Kahnweiler, Paul Guillaume, and Guillaume Apollinaire. Apollinaire, however, according to the testimony of Fernande Olivier, had already met Marinetti in 1910 and had embarked on what would be a brief but intense association with the Futurists. This friendship led to his publication, in June 1913, of the manifesto *Antitradition futuriste*, which the poet wrote at a table of the Lapérouse restaurant "while savoring a delicious goose," as Marinetti himself records it.[1] But this friendship was to be short-lived and in the very same year (1913) was rocked by fierce polemics.

While several of the French artists, writers, and art dealers mentioned above were among the discoverers of "art nègre," they were all in any case caught up in the "Negrophilia" rage of those years, as other sections of this volume will clearly show. Hence, Italian artists did not lack for opportunities to come into contact with works by African and Oceanic sculptors. Such works were hardly well known and of course not in vogue in Italy at the time, but they remained at the center of art debate in France.

In the writings of the Futurists, the "discovery" of tribal art is recorded in a rather summary and jarring manner. Boccioni judged it to be a necessary and fateful event. In the Florentine review *Lacerba*, he wrote in 1913: "Gauguin's journey to Tahiti, and the appearance of Central African fetishes in the ateliers of our Montmartre friends, are a historical inevitability in the destiny of the European sensibility, much like the invasion of a barbaric race into the organism of a people in decadence."[2]

The following year Carrà, in the heat of the Futurist polemic against the Cubists, wrote in the same review that this embracing of the lessons of extra-European artists was "a gross error and unwitting fraud into which the major artists of contemporary France had fallen,...mistakes attributable to the fallacy of thinking that they could artificially create for

Carlo Carrà. *Portrait of Russolo.* 1913? Ink, 10⅝ x 7⅛" (27 x 18 cm). Private collection, Florence

Mask. Fang. Gabon. Painted wood, 27⅝" (70 cm) high. Musée de l'Homme, Paris

themselves an innocence and a modern sensibility by turning to the remote center of Africa to find ready-made the inspirations and archaic motifs for their plastic constructions, which, for whatever reason, were then supposed to respond, through a kind of cultural suggestion, to the aesthetic needs of our very modern sensibility."[3]

In 1921, in *Valori Plastici* (in a portrait of Derain), Carrà's comments on the "Africanist practices" of artists at that time take on a particularly vicious tone:

...all of this so-called "Negrism" that has been introduced into painting in the last few years is of no aesthetic importance whatsoever. Like other idiotic aberrations of our times such as Dadaism, "Negrism" is a passing lie invented by snobs. "Negrism," like "Fauvism," shows its origins to be literary, and like the earlier movement, it will inevitably last but a short time.

France especially has a tradition of literature on exoticism in painting, which goes back even further than Baudelaire's time. The root of these atavistic and morbid aberrations, call them what you will, is eclecticism, the same abominable eclecticism so dear to the good French blockheads of the last century....I include "Negrism" together with "Cubism" among the myriad forms of salon gymnastics.[4]

A more reactionary opinion would be hard to imagine.

On the other hand, Ardegno Soffici, a Tuscan artist and writer with close ties to the Futurists (and coeditor, with Giovanni Papini, of *Lacerba*), gives a totally contrary appraisal in his essay *Cubismo e futurismo*, written in 1914. Soffici had been

living on and off in Paris since 1900, taking an active part in the intellectual life there and acting as a bridge with the Italian cultural scene.[5] Here is the passage in which he describes the formal and conceptual role that African art played in the Cubist revolution:

Picasso..., once he came to understand and love this great, naive art, which is at once simple and expressive, coarse and refined, immediately knew how to glean its essential virtues, which lie in a realistic interpretation of nature through the distortion of its appearance according to a secret, lyric necessity, thereby intensifying its subjectivity; from this point on, [Picasso] worked at translating natural forms into his art by transforming and distorting them—not, however, in the general manner in which his teachers had done, but by learning something from the particular example of each—that is, by following the movements of his own modern soul.[6]

The sculpture and paintings of Boccioni and Soffici, who both clearly recognized the role played by African sculpture in the evolution of modern Western art, nevertheless show no evident borrowings from it. It is, on the other hand, most surprising to find traces of *Negrismo* precisely in the work of Carrà, who had expressed such a disdainful and uncompromising opinion on the subject. The contradiction between public proclamation and private artistic practice can only be attributed to the difference in dates and the strategies of his attempt to assert the primacy of Futurism over Cubism.

A thorough knowledge of the works of African and Oceanic art present in Paris during the second decade of the century, along with an examination of the chronology of Carrà's artistic production, would seem to support the supposition, if not the absolute certainty, that Carrà did not remain untouched in the period from 1911 to 1916 by the impact of tribal art on European culture, and that he examined more than once the sculptures from Africa in particular. Carrà went to Paris for the first time in 1899, drawn by the prospect of working as a decorator in the pavilions under preparation for the Universal Exposition of 1900. In his free time he visited the city's museums and, much to his delight, discovered the Impressionists. The ethnographic collections at the Musée du Trocadéro, on the other hand, left him absolutely cold. In fact, he later wrote in his autobiography: "As for the museums, aside from the Louvre, the Petit-Palais, and the Luxembourg, I saw the Trocadéro, which seemed to me rather dreary and of little interest."[7]

Carlo Carrà. *Portrait of Boccioni*. 1913. Ink, 10⅝ x 7½" (27 x 19 cm). Private collection, Reggio Emilia

Luigi Russolo. *Self-Portrait*. 1913. Engraving, 3¾ x 3⅛" (9.5 x 8 cm). Collection Marco Costantini, Laveno

It is rather interesting to note that both Vlaminck and Derain, who would later figure among the discoverers of tribal art, also had negative initial reactions to it. Doubtless they too, like Carrà, were not yet mature enough to grasp the significance of non-Western art. Vlaminck himself states that after having "explored the Musée du Trocadéro in every direction and on several occasions," neither he nor his friend Derain had seen "among the objects on display, anything but what are commonly called barbaric fetishes and ethnographic curiosities."[8]

It was during his second stay in Paris in 1911, and to an even greater extent during his later sojourns in 1912 and 1914, that Carrà, by now mature and flexible as a result of his Futurist experiences, allowed himself to be touched in a positive manner (though he denies it in his writings) by African sculpture. In fact, after 1911 certain elements traceable to African art begin to appear in his work.[9]

The *Portrait of Russolo*, dated 1913, is to my mind clearly derived from the most common type of Fang mask from Gabon, which is made from a wooden panel, often quite large (up to a meter high), slightly curved, and usually painted white. The oval shape of the face is stretched lengthwise and comes to a point at the chin; the elongated, pointed nose is a continuation of the eyebrow arches, which separate the concave from the convex part of the face, the latter being limited to the forehead; the eyes are rendered by two points in relief at the center of each eye-socket. These same elements may be

Mask. Fang. Gabon. Painted wood, 18⅞" (48 cm) high. Musée National d'Art Moderne, Centre National d'Art et de Culture Georges Pompidou, Paris. Formerly collections MAURICE DE VLAMINCK, ANDRÉ DERAIN

Carlo Carrà. *Head of a Young Girl.* 1911 or later. Pencil and charcoal, 5½ x 3½" (14 x 9 cm). Private collection, Milan

found, if we ignore the hair, the beard, and the moustaches, in the *Portrait of Russolo*, whose features were actually quite regular. Moreover, the nose is fashioned according to a model the Cubists had already derived from African sculpture, that is, the "slice of Brie" nose.

This drawing was published in the April 1914 issue of *Lacerba* on page 127, which followed an advertisement for a "Concerto di Intonarumori Futuristi" (Concert of Futurist Noise-Sounds) at the Teatro Dal Verme in Milan, to be conducted by Russolo himself. A very similar portrait of Russolo, this one by Soffici, was published on page 126, beneath the advertisement; it was later used by Severini in his collage *La Ciociara*, which also bears the date 1914.

Two nearly identical portraits of Boccioni by Carrà, one from 1913 (p. 407) and the other from 1916, show a simplification of forms that is less extreme but of the same character (especially the large, semiconical nose) as that in Picasso's *Head of a Woman* of 1909, which is also indebted to African sculpture, although the particular ethnographic source—if indeed there was but one—remains unknown. On the other hand, a 1914 portrait of Guillaume Apollinaire, who himself almost certainly figured among those to introduce Carrà to tribal art, totally lacks any reference to such art.

The pencil and charcoal drawing *Head of a Young Girl* clearly calls to mind the Fang Mask that first belonged to Vlaminck and then to Derain.[10] It is believed, however, that the date of this drawing was added some time after its execution, and that it should be dated at least some time after 1911; in other words, after Carrà's second trip to Paris. In this instance as well, the African object in question came from Gabon. Its surface shows a lightly modulated, slight curvature, its color is a matte white that seems to absorb light, and its nose is in the shape of a pyramid cut lengthwise.

The "slice of Brie" nose and the concomitant simplification of the face's features, to the point where it is transformed into a mask, also characterize many of Carrà's works in subsequent years, such as *Woman, Woman's Figure, Woman's Bust,* all of 1914; the temperas *The Ballerina of San Martino, Clown,* and the drawing *Head of a Gentleman* (seen from the front), all of 1915; two drawings for the *Head of a Gentleman,* the series of drawings *Feminine Head, Head of a Girl, Head of a Woman, Head of a Boy, Boxeur,* and the large oil painting *The Romantics* with all its related preparatory studies.

For the 1914 drawing *Head of a Girl,* the model used was quite possibly a Baule mask or figure from the Ivory Coast, from which the painter seems to have borrowed the essential

Carlo Carrà. *The Romantics*. 1916. Oil on canvas, 59⅛ x 63¾" (150 x 162 cm). Private collection, Turin

Carlo Carrà. *Head of a Boy*. 1916. Watercolor, 7⅝ x 5¾" (19.3 x 14.5 cm). Private collection, Milan

facial elements: the regular oval shape, the lenticular eyes, the narrow but not overly elongated nose which here too continues the clearly delineated lines of the eyebrow arches. Several masks with these same characteristics figured in the collection of Paul Guillaume.

The two portraits of Remy de Gourmont from 1914 and 1916 (p. 410), which are nearly identical beyond their resemblance to their model, clearly remind one of the Teke figures of Stanley Pool (p. 410), both in the general shape of the head and neck and in certain details such as the nose and ears (the latter visible in the 1916 drawing) and especially the flat, trapezoidal beard placed immediately beneath the lower lip. A Teke figure, incidentally, can be seen in the famous photograph of Apollinaire's "cabinet de travail" (p. 312).

The figure in Carrà's tempera *Composition with Female Figure*, 1915, now in the Pushkin Museum in Moscow (p. 404), shows a striking similarity to a small Lega sculpture from Zaire that was also part of Paul Guillaume's collection (p. 411). The little ivory figure's monumental structure, powerful neck, the veritable column bearing its egg-shaped head, the rectangular nose, the coffee-bean eyes, all can be found in almost identical form, placement, and proportion in the painting now in Moscow. The Lega sculpture seems to have served as a point

Carlo Carrà. *Portrait of Remy de Gourmont*. 1916. Pencil, 12 x 7½" (30.4 x 19 cm). Carrà Collection, Milan

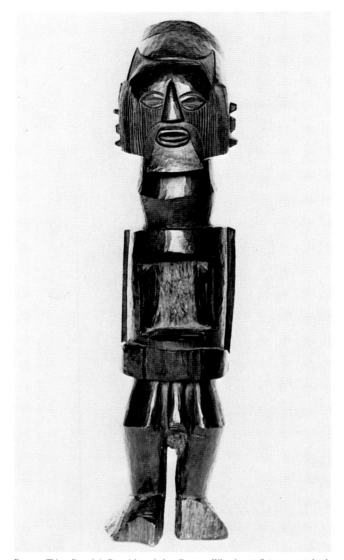

Figure. Teke. People's Republic of the Congo. Wood, 14¾" (37.5 cm) high. Collection Louise and Michel Leiris, Paris

of reference for Carrà in other works as well: The head and neck of the female figure in *The Star* (1916; in the Zaffino Collection in Reggio Calabria) and in the preparatory drawings seem modeled on the above-described figure.

The round faces in these latter works and those in the three drawings of the series *The Violinist*, 1914–15 (p. 413), prefigure the solution adopted for the little girl in *Antigrazioso* (p. 412). In this work, the body of a wooden puppet supports a massive spherical head with accentuated eye-sockets, coffee-bean eyes, and a rectangular nose, all of which, along with the orange-brown color, calls to mind a number of other ivory sculptures of the same Lega population (compare, for example, the famous head formerly in the Ratton Collection in Paris, p. 413).

Characteristic elements of African sculpture can also be found in other works of Carrà, sometimes merely in the execution of a detail: a woman's breasts, stiff, cylindrical arms, fingers represented as rectangular parallelepipeds without any joints and all joined together. Good examples of these may be seen in the hands of the woman in *Nude* (1914), or in the hair of the *Child Prodigy*, where the effect is achieved by alternating areas of light and dark in a manner quite similar to

the undulations of the wood in the elaborate hair-styling of Baule masks and figures.

Carrà's experience of African art was not, however, limited only to the appropriation of a new vocabulary of forms. It seems he probed even further into African sculpture in his search for a rhythmical balance between stasis and movement, in an effort to free essential structures by removing all particular and anecdotal elements.

African sculpture clearly served as a stimulus to Carrà's creation of those compact forms, characterized by a strong simplicity, whose culmination is the *Antigrazioso*, which marks his break from a widespread tradition of false elegance as well as from the vitalistic-mechanistic schemas of Futurism. This break was not a brief flash but the start of a process of serious critical and self-critical reconsideration. It marked a period of growth during the years 1915–20, which followed his encounters with Apollinaire, with the works of Picasso, Derain, and Cézanne ("the Masaccio of our time," in Carrà's words), and with the works of countless anonymous artists of Black Africa and Oceania.

The influence of these works, though obstinately denied by Carrà, was most probably what led, by way of a kind of unconfessed, internal fermentation, to his rediscovery of the purified, fundamental forms of Giotto and Masaccio. The most convincing results of this rediscovery are, to my mind, *I Dioscuri* and *The House of Love* of 1922. In the latter painting, the woman's rounded figure, smooth as varnished wood, seems in its calm and in the discreet positioning of the arms to call to mind the wooden figures of Easter Island, some of which Carrà probably saw at Paul Guillaume's house in Paris. This suggestion appears to be anticipated and corroborated in many of the drawings from 1920 and 1921.

In the same pre–World War I period two other young Italian artists, Giorgio de Chirico and his brother Alberto Savinio (at the time primarily a musician), arrived in Paris and, perhaps through the mediation of Soffici, developed even stronger ties with French avant-garde circles than those established by the Futurists. Not only was the two brothers' association with Apollinaire very close,[11] but Paul Guillaume was de Chirico's Parisian dealer as well as the go-between in the artist's relationship with Marius de Zayas, the Mexican painter who in 1916 published a study in New York with the farsighted title *African Negro Art: Its Influence on Modern Art*. In the advertisements for Paul Guillaume's gallery, which list the names of the artists with works available (including de Chirico), there is always some mention of "African sculpture of the first order."

Thus the opportunity for de Chirico to see and handle works of "art nègre" and to discuss them with others presented itself almost daily, and indeed was almost unavoidable. Yet de Chirico carefully avoided the subject in his writings. Savinio, on the other hand, admitted his fascination when he wrote a piece on African art to be delivered at a conference. He remembers all this in his *Souvenirs*: "In 1913, Paul Guillaume founded the Société des Mélanophiles, with offices on Rue Navarin in Paris. About that time I wrote a lecture on African sculpture for the Société des Mélanophiles, which was recorded on a Pathé disk and given in New York several days later over a gramophone."[12] Unfortunately, this brief reference is all we have of the experience. Despite extensive research, I have so far been unable to locate the text, clearly of great historical interest since it was one of the earliest, if not the very first, critical discussion of this subject. The occasion in New York at which the record was heard was probably the private opening of the African art exhibition in November 1914 (hence a year later than the date recorded by Savinio) in the Alfred Stieglitz Gallery in New York, with sculptures sent from Paris from Paul Guillaume. It may also be of use here to note that the same gallery showed works of de Chirico that had been sent with the shipment of African sculptures,[13] and that Stieglitz's periodical, *291*, published musical compositions and theoretical texts by Savinio.

In the paintings of the two brothers, however, it seems impossible to detect any echo of tribal art, despite all the exposure the two had to exponents of the trend. The same may be said also of Soffici, Boccioni, Severini, and Russolo. Thus the influence of African art on Carrà's work remains an isolated case.

The cultural climate in Italy in the years that followed did not tend to favor the spread of interest in non-Western art. Italy had no colonies, and hence there was no market in African and Oceanic art that might have fostered the growth

Carlo Carrà. *Composition with Female Figure*. 1915. Tempera on cardboard, 16⅛ x 12¼" (41 x 31 cm.) The Pushkin Museum, Moscow. For color reproduction see page 404

Head. Lega. Zaire. Ivory, 2¾" (7 cm) high. Private collection

Carlo Carrà. *Antigrazioso.* 1916. Oil on canvas, 26⅜ x 20½" (67 x 52 cm). Private collection, Milan

of specialized collections. For my part, I know of no private collections of such art in Italy in the first quarter of the century.

According to Paul Guillaume, "The most active and intelligent individuals championing the cause of African art" in Italy were two foreigners living in Rome: Edward Keeling, "a charming dilettante," and Gerald Tyrwhitt (later Lord Berners), a young diplomatic attaché at the British Embassy and a musician as well.[14] Gabriele d'Annunzio, prince of Italian poets, dismissed African art as but a literary vogue. Leon Kochnitzky records this in a conversation he had with the poet in 1920: "You see," said d'Annunzio, "when you talk to me of Negro statues and African masks, I cannot help thinking of the Japanophile manias of the Goncourts. Every epoch has its literary pastimes. Exoticism and carnivals help one to escape the dreariness of reality, to flee the tedium of everyday life."[15]

For the "XIIIth International Exposition of Art of the City of Venice" (the present "Biennale") in 1922, the archaeologist Carlo Anti and the ethnologist Aldobrandino Mochi mounted an exhibition of thirty-three African sculptures, mostly from the Congo, which belonged to the Ethnographic Museum of Rome (named in 1925 the L. Pigorini Museum, after its founder) and to the Museum of Anthropology and Ethnography of Florence.[16] The critics' reaction was for the most part indifferent, cursory, and derisory. Even Anti, the show's organizer, wrote in a 1921 study on *African Sculpture* that he saw in it "only the manifestation of a primitive stage, with all the childishness and simplicity of all the primitive arts." Carrà, who devoted four long articles in *Il Convegno* to the Venice exhibition, makes no mention whatsoever of the African art exhibit.[17]

Such apparent neglect and even outright negation did not,

Left: Head. Lega. Zaire. Ivory, 5⅛" (13 cm) high. Collection Mr. and Mrs. Alain de Monbrison, Paris

Below: Carlo Carrà. *The Violinist.* 1914–15. Pencil, 16⅛ x 10⅝" (41 x 27 cm). Collection Società Reale Mutua di Assicurazioni, Turin

however, bring an end to the processes set in motion in Italy by the "discovery" of non-Western art. It would be more correct to say that such stimuli continued to exert their influence on Italian art in an underground fashion, like a Karst river, and then reemerged on a large scale after World War II.

In 1961 Corrado Cagli wrote that with the discoveries of the avant-garde

a boundless terrain was opened up to painters and poets. By now it seems clear that the stylistic complexity of modern painting, as compared with that of the past, which was bound to Greco-Roman and Renaissance canons, derives precisely from an acquired knowledge of primitive cultures and folk traditions. All such cultures— from the Aruntas to the Aztecs, from the Nuraghics to the Mayas, from the cave dwellers to the Etruscans—have eventually flowed into our modern time just as tributaries ultimately converge toward a great river.[18]

In the many-faceted creations of this Roman artist (and in those of so many others, such as Mirko), as in the symbolic course of the "great river," forms and solutions proper to African, Oceanic, Indonesian, and pre-Columbian art have forcefully found their place, not as eclectic references but as intimately reworked and assimilated parts.

But such considerations belong to the history of our own time, which has yet to be written. It is a history of Western men freed (once and for all, we hope) from the arrogance of believing themselves the world's prime movers.

—Translated from the Italian by Stephen Sartarelli

NOTES

1. F. T. Marinetti, *Una sensibilità italiana nata in Egitto*, ed. L. De Maria (Milan, 1969), pp. 288–89. On the connection between the Futurists and the French avant-garde, see also the catalog *Apollinaire e l'Avanguardia* (Rome: Galleria Nazionale d'Arte Moderna, 1980).

2. Umberto Boccioni, "Fondamento plastico della scultura e pittura futuriste," *Lacerba* 1, no. 6 (March 15, 1913), p. 51.

3. Carlo Carrà, "Vita moderna e arte popolare," *Lacerba* 2, no. 11 (June 1, 1914), p. 167.

4. Carlo Carrà, "André Derain," *Valori Plastici* 3, no. 3 (March 1921), pp. 67–68. According to Carrà, Derain was the first to use African forms: "It was none other than Derain who created the two sins Fauvism and Cubism by echoing in his art the paradoxical lines of African statues" ("Parere intorno a Matisse," in *Pittura metafisica* [Florence, 1919]).

5. See M. Richter, *La formazione francese di Ardegno Soffici, 1900–1914* (Milano, 1969).

6. Ardegno Soffici, *Cubismo e Futurismo* (Florence, 1914), p. 14.

7. Carlo Carrà, *La mia vita* (Rome, 1943), p. 41.

8. M. Vlaminck, *Portrait avant-décès* (Paris, 1943), pp. 106–07.

9. The works are drawn from the catalog *Carrà—Disegni*, Franco Russoli and Massimo Carrà (Bologna, 1977).

10. See E. Bassani, "La maschera bianca di Vlaminck e di Derain," *Africa* 34, no. 3 (Rome, September 1979), pp. 286–94.

11. M. Fagiolo, *Giorgio de Chirico—Il tempo di Apollinaire—Paris 1911–1915* (Rome, 1981).

12. Alberto Savinio, *Souvenirs* (Rome, 1945), p. 150, note 11.

13. M. Fagiolo, op. cit., p. 113.

14. P. Guillaume, "Une Esthétique nouvelle—L'Art Nègre," *Les Arts à Paris*, no. 4, May 15, 1919, p. 4.

15. L. Kochnitzky, "Influence de la plastique nègre sur l'art contemporain," *Synthèses*, no. 121, June 1956, p. 293.

16. The African works of art are listed in the exhibition catalog on pp. 41–44.

17. Carlo Carrà, "L'arte mondiale alla XIII Biennale di Venezia," *Il Convegno* 3, May 1922, pp. 211–20; June 1922, pp. 287–96; July 1922, pp. 406–14; August 1922, pp. 444–53. In this same exposition Carrà's *I Dioscuri* and *The House of Love* were exhibited. The two paintings were the occasion for a violent attack by E. Thovez in the *Gazzetta del Popolo* (May 5, 1922) with the headline "The Monsters: Modigliani, Cézanne, Carrà," giving an indication of the cultural mood of Italy at the time.

18. Cited in C. L. Ragghianti, *La fondazione Cagli per Firenze*, 1979, p. 21.

Crocodile mask. Dogon. Mali. Wood, 25" (63.5 cm) high. Collection Nina and Gordon Bunshaft, New York

Helmet mask. Baule. Ivory Coast. Wood, 34¾" (88.3 cm) high. The Metropolitan Museum of Art, New York; The Michael C. Rockefeller Memorial Collection, gift of Mr. and Mrs. Ben Heller

Figure. Bamileke. Cameroon. Wood, 20¼″ (51.4 cm) high. Collection Pierre Matisse. Formerly collection HENRI MATISSE

Figure. Bangwa. Cameroon. Wood, 31⅞″ (81 cm) high. Private collection

Jacob Epstein. *The Rock Drill*. 1913–14. Bronze, 28 x 26" (71 x 76 cm). The Museum of Modern Art, New York; Mrs. Simon Guggenheim Fund

PARIS AND LONDON
MODIGLIANI, LIPCHITZ, EPSTEIN AND GAUDIER-BRZESKA

Alan G. Wilkinson

Modigliani, like Gauguin, is still far better known for his painting than for his sculpture, and yet contemporary accounts by his friends attest that Modigliani had a deep-seated and abiding ambition to become a sculptor. The dealer Adolphe Basler stated: "Sculpture was his only ideal and he put high hopes in it."[1] The English painter Nina Hamnet, who saw Modigliani frequently in Paris, wrote in her memoires: "He always regarded sculpture as his real *métier*..."[2] When his mother wrote to him in Paris, she addressed him as "Amedeo Modigliani, sculpteur."[3] And yet during his brief and tragic life as an artist, he devoted only five or six years, from about 1909 to 1915, to realizing these ambitions.

Both as a painter and a sculptor, Modigliani was essentially a portraitist. The subject of twenty-three of his twenty-five surviving carvings is the human head. It is in these sculptures and numerous related drawings, rather than in his paintings, that we find Modigliani's subtle assimilation of African tribal art. The almost total lack of documentary evidence makes it difficult, if not impossible, to establish a chronology of his carvings, and the same lack of documentation makes it difficult to discuss Modigliani's debt to tribal art in specific terms. We do not know, for example, when he first became aware of African sculpture, nor do we know how extensive his knowledge was. Yet there can be no doubt that African art was one of the major influences in the formation of the distinctive, highly personal style of Modigliani's elongated stone heads.

Amedeo Modigliani was born in Livorno, Italy, on July 12, 1884. Despite his later reputation in Paris as a bohemian artist par excellence, he never forgot his bourgeois and Jewish background, often introducing himself, "Je suis Modigliani—juif." In 1898 he began studying drawing and painting in Livorno. His more formal academic training began in 1902 when he enrolled at the Accademia di Belle Arti in Florence. The following year he studied at the Istituto di Belle Arti in Venice.

Modigliani arrived in Paris in late 1905 or early 1906 and settled in Montmartre, Rue Caulaincourt, not far from Picasso's studio in the Bateau-Lavoir. The few paintings that have survived from Modigliani's first three years in Paris reflect the influence of Toulouse-Lautrec and the brooding melancholy of Picasso's Blue Period portraits. The work of Cézanne, however, was the most decisive formative influence on Modigliani's development as a painter, so obviously manifest in *The Beggar*, executed during his trip to Italy in the summer and autumn of 1909.

Sometime during the first six months of 1909 Modigliani moved to Montparnasse, to a studio at 14 Cité Falguière. He asked his friend and patron Dr. Paul Alexandre to introduce him to his neighbor Brancusi. The importance of this meeting and the ensuing friendship with Brancusi cannot be overestimated. If Modigliani had lacked the direction or will to devote his energies to sculpture, the example of Brancusi and his work provided the necessary stimulus. The two artists must have met before Modigliani left for Italy in the summer of 1909, for Brancusi visited Modigliani in Livorno, where the latter did a portrait drawing inscribed "Brancusi" and "Livorno." Modigliani may have begun sculpting before his trip home to Livorno and may also have done some carving while he was there. Again, lack of documentary evidence makes it impossible to assign specific carvings to 1909. It is generally agreed

Amedeo Modigliani. *Head.* c. 1911. Stone, 35 x 5 x 13¾" (88.7 x 12.5 x 35 cm). The Trustees of the Tate Gallery, London

that when he arrived back in Paris in the fall of 1909, Modigliani concentrated on sculpture and related drawings.

The sculpture of Modigliani and that of his mentor Brancusi do not share the close stylistic affinities that often occur in the work of artists living and working in close proximity: Picasso and Braque between 1909 and 1913; Moore and Hepworth in the late 1920s and early 1930s. Brancusi's early stone carvings certainly influenced Modigliani, but more important was the "moral" example of the Rumanian, a sculptor who retained his individuality and remained fiercely independent of current movements of the avant-garde in Paris. Modigliani, in his dedication to working exclusively in stone, single-mindedly followed Brancusi's dictum "Direct carving is the true path toward sculpture,"[4] whereas Brancusi himself, by 1913–14, was sculpting in various materials—stone, wood, plaster, and had a number of his works cast in bronze. But it must be remembered that when the two artists met in 1909, almost all Brancusi's sculptures of the previous two years were carved in stone or marble. Modigliani, like Brancusi, Epstein, and Gaudier-Brzeska, turned to direct carving and tribal sources as a way of escaping the overpowering influence of Rodin. Lipchitz has recorded of his friend, "Modigliani, like some others at the time, was very taken with the notion that sculpture was sick, that it had become very sick with Rodin and his influence. There was too much modeling in clay, too much 'mud.' The only way to save sculpture was to begin carving again, directly in stone. We had many very heated discussions about this...but Modigliani could not be budged."[5] In 1909 Modigliani could not have found a sculptor more dedicated to direct carving than Brancusi. In addition, Brancusi's interest in tribal art undoubtedly offered Modigliani an alternative to the Greco-Roman Renaissance tradition.

The features of several of Brancusi's early stone carvings were almost certainly the initial stimulus for Modigliani's nineteen elongated stone heads. Significantly, the earliest work that must have impressed Modigliani was Brancusi's 1907 stone *Head of a Girl* (p. 346), which the latter described as the "first direct stone." As Sidney Geist has written: "Surely this was a head Modigliani saw in 1909, when his friendship with Brancusi began."[6] Apart from the asymmetry of Brancusi's carving, the other features—the smooth face, elongated nose, small mouth, and the textured, incised treatment of the hair—anticipate to a remarkable degree Modigliani's series of heads. Whereas in Brancusi's 1907 *Head of a Girl* the nose is somewhat flat and the cheeks concave, his 1910 carving *Baroness R. F.* (p. 421), with its long, thin, projecting nose, is even more convincingly a source for Modigliani's elongated stone heads.

The twenty-five stone carvings generally accepted as authentic works by Modigliani do not represent his total sculptural oeuvre. We will never know how many carvings he executed, nor how many were lost or destroyed. Of the surviving sculptures, there are twenty-three heads, a standing female figure, and a caryatid (p. 422). An accurate chronology of these works cannot be established. However, four of the heads were photographed in the studio of the painter Cardoso in 1911, providing conclusive evidence that they were executed between 1909 and 1911. Strangely, Ambrogio Ceroni assigns all twenty-five carvings to the years 1911–13, despite general agreement among Modigliani scholars that he concentrated on sculpture between 1909 and 1915 or 1916.[7]

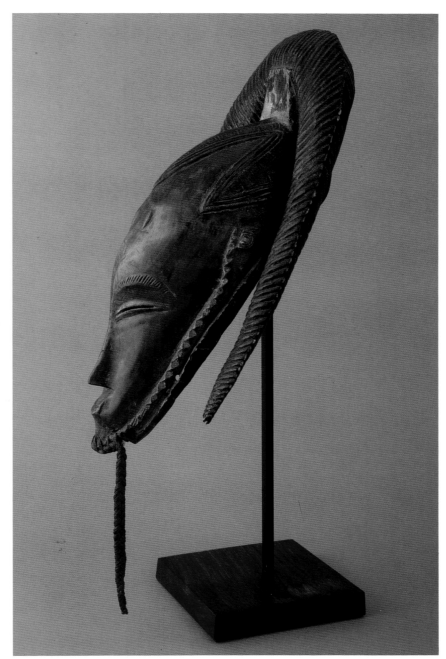

Mask. Guro. Ivory Coast. Wood, 16½" (42 cm) high. Private collection

Modigliani's stone heads made a considerable impact on a number of artists who visited his studio. Years later, Lipchitz recalled his visit in 1912 to the studio and made the important observation that the stone heads were intended to be seen together, and as a group produced a unique effect:

I see him as if it were today, stooping over those heads, explaining to me that he had conceived all of them as an ensemble. It seems to me that these heads were exhibited later the same year in the Salon d'Automne, arranged in step-wise fashion, like tubes of an organ, to produce the special music he wanted.[8]

Modigliani's stone heads, the products of a totally personal vision, have such a powerful, enigmatic presence that once seen, they are not easily forgotten. The English portrait painter Augustus John, who also visited Modigliani in 1912, saw the heads in terms of portraiture. The two heads John acquired must have been among the first carvings Modigliani sold. John wrote:

The stone heads affected me strangely. For some days afterwards I found myself under the hallucination of meeting people in the street who might have posed for them, and that without myself resorting to the Indian Herb![9]

The most haunting account is Epstein's description of the squalor and exoticism of Modigliani's studio:

His studio at that time [1912] was a miserable hole within a courtyard, and here he lived and worked. It was then filled with nine or ten of those long heads which were suggested by African masks, and one figure. They were carved in stone; at night he would place candles on the top of each one and the effect was that of a primitive temple.[10]

Upon Epstein's return to London in late 1912, it was the use of tribal sources by artists such as Modigliani that inspired him to embark on his own drawings and carvings, so clearly indebted to African and Oceanic art.

Although it is not known when Modigliani first became aware

Above: Mask. Marka. Mali. Wood, 14½" (36.8 cm) high. Private collection

Left: Amedeo Modigliani. *Head.* c. 1915. Limestone, 22¼ x 5 x 14¾" (56.5 x 12.7 x 37.4 cm). The Museum of Modern Art, New York; gift of Abby Aldrich Rockefeller in memory of Mrs. Cornelius J. Sullivan

of tribal sculpture, he had met Picasso before 1909 and must have been aware of his interest in African and Oceanic art, and may have seen works of tribal art he had collected. Modigliani's friendship with Lipchitz and Brancusi was another link with tribal sculpture. According to Alfred Werner, Modigliani saw examples of African sculpture at Joseph Brummer's gallery and also in the collection of the painter Frank Burty Haviland.[11] One can assume that if by 1909 Modigliani "talked endlessly of Negro art,"[12] he would have visited the Trocadéro, although no reference to such a visit exists.

Most scholars have suggested that, unlike Picasso, Brancusi, and Epstein, whose painting and sculpture were influenced by a variety of tribal styles, Modigliani relied on a single regional style in African art: Baule dance masks from the Ivory Coast and some work from neighboring peoples. In discussing Modigliani's stone heads, Robert Goldwater wrote:

It is evident enough that in a number of his heads he is following the example of the Baulé style (and especially its masks) in the elongated oval of the head with narrow chin, the almond eyes, the sharply defined drawn-out rectilinear volume of the nose that, like the tiny lozenge-shaped mouth, hardly interrupts the smoothly rounded curve of cheeks and chin. The neck cylinder is African too, but its regional source is less easy to locate.[13]

Yet the subtle way in which Modigliani assimilated and transformed his sources makes it difficult to suggest a specific tribal style as the only source of inspiration. Although the similarities between his stone heads and Baule dance masks are striking, it must be remembered that Fang and Yaure masks also share some of the stylistic features of the Baule style. Indeed, the thin nose and even more pronounced elongation of the head in the Fang (p. 406) and Marka masks are far closer to the proportions of Modigliani's stone heads than is the Baule dance mask mentioned above, closer, indeed, to the exquisitely stylized if somewhat less elongated Guro masks (p. 419). In all probability Modigliani worked from his memory of African art he had seen, thus keeping his distance from his sources. If a carving such as *Head* (p. 418) was indeed inspired by Baule dance masks, Modigliani radically altered the oval shape of these masks and created a thin, axlike head that has no stylistic precedent in these African prototypes (except in certain Guro masks). Given Modigliani's limited subject matter, it is extraordinary how each of the stone heads attains its own character. This is explained in part by the fact that Modigliani was also influenced by several nontribal sources. Goldwater has remarked on the similarities between the treatment of the hair in some of Modigliani's heads and Archaic Greek sculpture, and also observed that their pinched smiles are reminiscent of Archaic Greek Kore figures or the more sensuous features of Khmer sculpture.[14]

The only known works that Modigliani almost certainly based directly on examples of African sculpture are three sketchbook drawings, one of which is illustrated below. The positioning of the eyes close to the top of the elongated nose, the small mouth, and the inner line that defines the right ear and gives the head a sense of depth clearly indicate that this drawing was based on a Baule mask. Whereas in many of the numerous preparatory drawings for the stone heads, and in the sculptures themselves, the influence of Baule dance masks is well assimilated and blended with other influences, in this sketch we have concrete evidence of Modigliani's special interest in the elegant, refined carvings from the Ivory Coast.

Only one of Modigliani's stone caryatids has survived (p. 422), although judging by the gouaches, drawings, and water-colors of the period, this was one of the artist's favorite sculpture subjects. Just as the stone heads were conceived as a series (seven

were shown at the 1912 Salon d'Automne as *Têtes, ensemble décoratif*), Modigliani likewise envisaged, but never realized, the caryatids as a group, which he referred to as *colonnes de tendresse*. In most of Modigliani's drawings of caryatids, the faces, though less elongated than in the stone heads, still retain features distantly related to Baule masks. Just as Modigliani integrated a number of disparate sources in his stone heads, the caryatids appear to me to relate to both tribal and European art. The stone *Caryatid* in The Museum of Modern Art has been compared to Luba stools (p. 423), and in certain respects there are similarities, though it is almost impossible to imagine that Modigliani could have seen Luba material in Paris at that time. In Modigliani's carving, the way in which the figure is compressed between the flat lintel at the top, supported by upraised arms, and the bottom of the sculpture is certainly reminiscent of the tribal works in question. But in this carving and in all the related drawings, the bodies have a contrapposto, twisting pose which is totally foreign to the frontal symmetry of the Luba standing and kneeling figures, indeed, to the caryatids of other African peoples as well. There is also no African influence in the full, sensuous, rounded forms of the figure in Modigliani's *Caryatid*. The pose, European rather than African in inspiration, recalls such well-known sculptures as the marble *Crouching Aphrodite* (Roman copy of a Hellenistic bronze of c. 275 B.C.) in Copenhagen and the marble *Myrtilos, Oinomaos's Charioteer* of 470–75 B.C. in the Olympia Museum, Greece. In both ancient carvings, the figures are kneeling on the right leg, with the left leg raised. This positioning of the legs occurs in Modigliani's *Caryatid* and in many of his drawings of the same subject.

Contrary to the generally accepted view that African sculpture was Modigliani's main source of inspiration, Edith Balas argues that his "main" stylistic source was the ancient art of

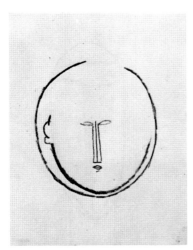

Above: Amedeo Modigliani. *Page from a Sketchbook.* 1914–15. Red crayon, 13¼ x 10⅜" (33.8 x 26.4 cm). Kunstmuseum, Basel, Kupferstichkabinett

Right: Mask. Baule. Ivory Coast. Painted wood, 20¼" (51.4 cm) high. Indiana University Art Museum, Bloomington

Far right: Constantin Brancusi. *Baroness R.F.* 1910. Stone. Private collection

Egypt.[15] She quotes from the memoirs of the Russian poet Anna Akhmatova, who in 1911 was the sculptor's neighbor at 14 Cité Falguière:

In 1911 Modigliani was madly in love with Egypt. He took me to the Egyptian section of the Louvre; he assured me that everything else— *tout le reste*—was unworthy of attention. He drew my head in the headdress of an Egyptian princess and in that of a dancer.[16]

While Balas's arguments read persuasively, they are supported by very selective examples of Modigliani's drawings and sculptures. She relates the breast and abdomen of the stone *Standing Nude* (Modigliani's only surviving carving apart from *Caryatid* to represent the entire figure) to Egyptian art and compares a number of drawings to examples of Egyptian art in the Louvre.

Given the limited repertoire of Modigliani's sculpture, it is not surprising that his work, although it deeply impressed artists such as Epstein, Lipchitz, and Augustus John, had relatively little influence on his contemporaries. We can, however, point to a number of works by other artists that relate to Modigliani's stone heads. In Lipchitz's 1913–14 bronze *Mother and Child* (p. 424) the thin nose and elongated head of the mother were undoubtedly

Amedeo Modigliani. *Standing Nude.* c. 1911–12. Stone, 63″ (160 cm) high. Australian National Gallery, Canberra

Amedeo Modigliani. *Caryatid.* c. 1914. Limestone, 36¼″ (92.1 cm) high, at base 16⅜ x 16⅞″ (41.6 x 42.9 cm). The Museum of Modern Art, New York; Mrs. Simon Guggenheim Fund

influenced by the proportions of Modigliani's heads. In Epstein's *Mother and Child* of 1913 (p. 438) the head of the mother is related to Fang sculpture rather than to Baule masks, which were Modigliani's source of inspiration. Nevertheless, Epstein may well have been inspired by his friend's work, which he had seen in Paris the previous year.

It is generally agreed that Modigliani abandoned sculpture and returned to painting about 1914 or 1915, though his daughter maintained that he continued sculpting until 1916.[17] Various reasons have been given as to why Modigliani gave up sculpture: ill health, the physical effort involved in carving, and the difficulty of obtaining stone during the war. But unquestionably the six or seven years he devoted to sculpture were to influence the style of his portraits of 1915–20. The most striking example is the c. 1915 oil *Lola de Valence*, which is far more a re-creation in two dimensions of his stone carvings, such as the Tate Gallery's *Head* (p. 418), than it is a representational portrait of his model. In many of his later portraits he leaves the eyes blank, a feature found in many of the carvings. This gives the paintings an aloofness, a kind of distancing from the model, that echoes the mysterious character of the sculptures.

Of all the major artists of his generation who responded to Primitive art, Modigliani was the least experimental and daring. The demonic power, the often overt sexuality, the extraordinary formal variety, and the inner logic often totally divorced from the representational considerations found in the European tradition, these were the characteristics of tribal art that had such a liberating and far-reaching influence on the work of Picasso, Brancusi, Epstein, and Moore. But just as Modigliani in his paintings consciously retained his independence from the work of Picasso and the avant-garde, so in his assimilation of the Primitive he kept his distance from his sources.

Perhaps his attraction to the Baule style can in part be accounted for by the fact that these tribal masks are said often to represent secular portraits of living persons. Modigliani will long be remembered as a portraitist, particularly for his paintings of his friends, patrons, and fellow artists: Picasso, Brancusi, Lipchitz, Apollinaire, Frank Burty Haviland, Rivera, Laurens, and Guillaume. As Lipchitz remarked, Modigliani could never forget his interest in people: "This is why Modigliani, though he admired African Negro and other primitive arts as much as any of us, was never profoundly influenced by them—any more than Cubism. He took from them certain stylistic traits, but was hardly affected by their spirit."[18]

The work of Jacques Lipchitz is characterized by extraordinary stylistic and iconographic diversity. His early bronzes (1910–11) were unadventurous portraits and figure studies in the tradition of Maillol and Despiau. But these were soon followed, in 1913–14, by radically different work that reflected his growing interest in tribal art and other non-European sources. Lipchitz's major contribution to the history of twentieth-century sculpture was unquestionably his Cubist bronzes and carvings of 1915–22; in contrast to the unemotional purity and abstract character of Lipchitz's Cubist work, his later sculptures, which often depict biblical and Jewish subjects, impress us as having a tortured and Baroque intensity.

In his early years, when tribal art was one of several major influences on his sculptures, Lipchitz kept a deliberate distance from his sources. Gauguin, Picasso, Brancusi, the German

Stool. Luba. Zaire. Wood, 8¼" (21 cm) high. Musée Royal de l'Afrique Centrale, Tervuren, Belgium

Expressionists, Epstein, and later Moore and Giacometti reacted to Primitive sculpture in ways that appear more direct and immediate. Lipchitz, by contrast, described his contact with these works merely as "encounters,"[19] and showed little inclination to extrapolate specific styles. In the introduction to the 1960 exhibition catalog *The Lipchitz Collection*, he asserted, "I was not exactly looking for a direct influence or a source of inspiration, but only to enlighten and enrich my creative spirit."[20]

Indeed, Lipchitz's borrowings from tribal art are so well assimilated that we can rarely identify a tribal style, let alone a specific African or Oceanic carving, as the likely source of inspiration or point of departure for one of his few primitivist sculptures. Moreover, there is little documentation of what specific works of tribal art he saw during his formative years, 1909–14. In a number of sculptures completed between 1913 and 1926 the intimation of tribal influences is often overshadowed by the more dominant impact of Cubism, and of the work of his friends Brancusi and Modigliani. In his few published comments about the influence of tribal art on this work, Lipchitz tends either to express dissatisfaction with a work because it has too much tribal influence, or to minimize the influence. He describes laconically and in the most general terms certain of his sculptures as reflecting his interest in African art or merely showing a resemblance. For example, he thought his 1913–14 *Mother and Child* interesting but "never found it entirely satisfactory, because of the specifically Negro quality of the figures and particularly of the heads." He goes on to add, "Although I had been collecting African sculpture (whenever I had any money) ever since I first came to Paris [1909], there are few of my works in which I feel a definite influence from Negro art."[21]

Jacques Lipchitz. *Mother and Child*. 1913–14. Bronze, 22½″ (57.1 cm) high. Private collection

Jacques Lipchitz. *Mother and Children*. 1914–15. Bronze, 27¾″ (70.5 cm) high. Private collection

Lipchitz was eighteen when he arrived in Paris in October 1909 from his native Lithuania. Unlike other foreign artists who settled in Paris—Picasso, Brancusi, Archipenko, and Modigliani—he had no previous academic training. In 1909–10 Lipchitz was enrolled at the Ecole de Beaux-Arts and also attended sculpture classes at the Académie Julian and drawing classes at the Académie Colarossi. He was at first not at all responsive to the work of Impressionist and Post-Impressionist artists. In his early months in Paris, a friend took him to Vollard's gallery. Years later, Lipchitz recalled:

I can still feel the sour taste with which the paintings of Renoir left me, and the complete blindness I experienced in front of *The Struggle of Jacob and the Angel* by Gauguin. Later, every time I saw this painting again, I was astonished at how I could have failed to see what it represents. How raw I was when I first came to Paris![22]

The few surviving works from Lipchitz's first two years in Paris, such as the 1910 *Seated Nude* and the 1911 bronze portrait *The Poet and Painter Cesare Sofianopulo*, reflect the tradition of Rodin and his followers rather than the contemporary carvings and bronzes by Picasso, Matisse, Brancusi, and Modigliani. But within two years Lipchitz had turned his back on the nineteenth century and quickly assimilated contemporary developments in the work of sculptors such as Archipenko, Brancusi, Boccioni, and Modigliani, as well as the Cubist work of Picasso.

According to Lipchitz, he became interested in tribal art in 1909, the year he arrived in Paris, although its influence on his sculpture was not manifest until 1913–14. In the catalog introduction to the exhibition of "The Lipchitz Collection" at The Museum of Primitive Art, New York, he wrote that he began collecting African tribal art in 1909, three or four years before he met Picasso, Brancusi, and Modigliani. He also admitted some early ignorance of what he was acquiring:

You will find at this exhibition, among other sculptures, a wooden painted Dahomey cup which I bought fifty-one years ago [1909]. I was sure it was Egyptian. It was only a year and a half later, while visiting the Trocadéro Museum, that I learned that it was negro. And so, by myself I discovered negro art, of which I soon became very fond.[23]

The year 1913 was crucial and transitional in Lipchitz's development. His friend Diego Rivera introduced him to Picasso; he had already gotten to know Brancusi and Modigliani. In the previous year Lipchitz had exhibited at the same Salon d'Automne where Modigliani showed seven of his stone heads inspired by Baule masks. In 1912 or 1913 Lipchitz moved into a studio next door to Brancusi. The sculptures of 1913, which the artist has described as "my proto-cubist phase,"[24] clearly reflect the abrupt change in direction of his work which was undoubtedly stimulated by his contact with Picasso, Modigliani, and Brancusi. In transitional works such as the *Dancer* of 1913, the calm, almost Maillolesque naturalism of *Pregnant Woman* of the previous year has been replaced by more angular, simplified forms, particularly in the flat planes of the torso.

One of the first sculptures to reflect the very generalized influence of African art is the bronze *Mother and Child*, which the artist said may have been made before his trip to Spain in late 1913 or early 1914. Mention has already been made of Lipchitz's dissatisfaction with this work because of its putatively specific African quality. The flat, triangular right breast has any number of prototypes in African art. But whereas the artist described the heads as African, they seem to me to relate more to Brancusi and Modigliani. In the drawing for *Mother and Child* the similarities

with the work of these artists are even more striking. The thin face and elongated nose and neck of the mother seem like a paraphrase of Modigliani's Baule-inspired stone heads, while the round, simplified head of the child is closely related to Brancusi's numerous sculptures of this subject, such as the 1911 marble *Prometheus*.

Still, in a sculpture such as *Mother and Child*, the question of influences is indeed a complex one, and to restrict the discussion to tribal and contemporary sources leaves us with an incomplete understanding of the genius of the work. In my opinion *Mother and Child* owes far more to Egyptian art (considered "primitive" in the early years of this century) than it does to tribal art and to the sculpture of Brancusi and Modigliani. The head of the mother, shown in profile but with the right eye depicted frontally, clearly derives from Egyptian art. Her long neck and thin arms, the way in which the left leg projects almost horizontally from the body, and the almost vertical position of this leg from the knee to the foot must have been inspired by Egyptian sculpture, such as the Eighteenth Dynasty limestone relief of King Akhenaten holding Princess Merytaten, in the Egyptian Museum, Berlin. Furthermore, the heads of the mother and child, although formally indebted to the sculpture of Modigliani and Brancusi respectively, relate to the proximity of heads in the Egyptian relief. It seems strange that Lipchitz, while openly acknowledging his debt to Egyptian art in his 1914 bronze *Girl with Braid*, made no mention of it in his discussion of *Mother and Child*. Given the dominant Egyptian rather than African influence on the latter sculpture, his dissatisfaction with it should have stemmed not from its "specifically Negro quality" but from its Egyptian characteristics.

Lipchitz did not have the same reservations about the *Mother and Children* of 1914–15 that he had about the slightly earlier *Mother and Child*.

Of the works of this period, it is one I particularly like. It is of interest to me for a number of different reasons, which I understood only years later in retrospect. There is first of all the mother-and-child theme, deriving from my feeling for my own mother—a theme, as I said, to which I have returned again and again. There is the absolute frontality of the group, very different from the circular movement of the *Woman with Serpent* or the *Dancer*. There may be some reflection of my interest in African art in this frontality, but I think that the idea developed unconsciously from some recollection of a Russian Byzantine icon of the Madonna and Child.[25]

As always, Lipchitz's reference to African art is generalized and he is reluctant to acknowledge affinities between *Mother and Children* and tribal art. Deborah A. Stott, however, has challenged the artist's denial of African influence.

Another ingredient in the style of *Mother and Children* must have been the joint influence of Brancusi and African wood carvings. Lipchitz denied any such influence, yet the vertical organization, angular carved surface, stick-like arms and even the bent-knee pose recall both Brancusi's early wood sculptures, such as *The First Step*, made in 1913, and *Little French Girl* of 1914, and their probable African prototypes. There is also a Dogon type of group in which one figure carries another on his shoulders, strikingly like Lipchitz's composition, while in another common type of Ba Luba carving, a figure holds up a chief's stool with arms outstretched to the side and up, as Lipchitz's figure does.[26]

Tempting as it is to speculate on these possible affinities, Stott provides no evidence as to where Lipchitz could have seen Luba sculpture this early; we do know that he subsequently admired

Jacques Lipchitz. *Detachable Figure.* 1915. Painted wood, 33¾ x 8⅞ x 6″ (85.7 x 22.5 x 15.2 cm). Collection Yulla Lipchitz, New York

Figure. Kambe. Kenya. Wood, 44¼″ (112.4 cm) high. The Detroit Institute of Arts; Eleanor Clay Ford Fund for African Art and collected Dogon carvings.[27]

In *Mother and Children* the head of the mother and that of the child held aloft recall the work of Modigliani and Brancusi respectively. And although *Mother and Children* and Epstein's drawing *Totem* of c. 1913 (p. 433) were undoubtedly made independently, they are impressively similar in the way in which the figures are locked together in a vertical structure, with, in each case, the child held above the mother's head.

It is important to stress again that for Lipchitz, as for Modigliani, tribal art was not the only non-European source to which he looked for inspiration. Lipchitz's debt to Egyptian art is again, and this time by his own admission, clearly evident in his 1914 bronze *Girl with Braid* (and is even more direct in the preparatory drawing of the same year, *Girl with Braided Hair,* in The Museum of Modern Art, New York).[28] In writing about this sculpture years later, Lipchitz was far more forthright about its formal rapports to Egyptian art than he was in his comments about the relationship of his work to tribal art:

I was also very conscious of the examples of Egyptian and archaic Greek sculpture. In my desire to move away from the classical and Renaissance tradition in which I had been trained, it was natural that I should look to these more ancient cultures, which also had a particular relevance to the findings of the early years of the twentieth century....The Egyptians and archaic Greeks also used the multiple points of view that the cubists had adopted....In the *Girl with Braid* I even turned the head in profile and depicted the eyes in full face in the Egyptian manner. Thus, it is possible to see the many different roots of my cubism.[29]

If the suddenness with which in 1915 Lipchitz adopted the Cubist idiom in his sculpture is somewhat surprising (see Introduction, pp. 51–53), it must be remembered that the sculptor had at his disposal, in the work of Picasso, Braque, and later Gris, a ready-made vocabulary with which to begin. While almost all Lipchitz's Cubist sculptures and reliefs made between 1915 and 1925 relate iconographically and stylistically to the work of these three artists, a few sculptures appear to have very generalized affinities with tribal art. The direct influence, however, of Primitive art all but disappeared from Lipchitz's work of this period. And again, as with the bronzes of 1913–14, any tribal affinities cannot be traced to precise sources. The proportions of the 1915 wood *Detachable Figure*—the way in which the head, long neck, and torso rise vertically above the two carved blocks, attached to the squat legs—have remarkably close stylistic affinities to the Kambe stele in the Detroit Institute of Arts. But Lipchitz never mentioned tribal art in his descriptions of his Cubist work of 1915–25. Rather, he insisted that contemporary sources were the key to the development of his work of this period. "Certainly I was influenced in my ideas by cubist painting which had preceded me, particularly that of Picasso," Lipchitz wrote. "When artists are living and working as closely together as we were in those years, they are all obviously influenced in some degree by one another; they all derive motifs from one another."[30] He did not consider this a matter of imitation: "We were all working with a common language and exploring the vocabulary of that language together."[31]

The 1922 *Seated Man* (p. 51) was, Lipchitz wrote, "a major departure for me, composed as it is from simplified rectangular masses....But now the entire form is solidly cubic in the literal sense rather than traditionally cubist, with the figure frontalized diagonally on the square base, the vertical masses pulled together by the curving, enclosing arms."[32] Nevertheless the

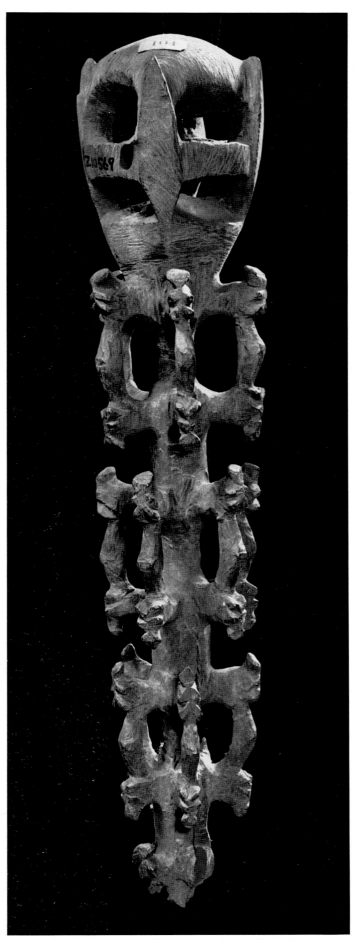

Staff god. Mauke, Cook Islands. Wood, 9" (23 cm) high. Cambridge University Museum of Archaeology and Anthropology, Cambridge, England

Jacques Lipchitz. *Figure*. 1926–30. Bronze, 7′ 1¼″ x 38⅝″ (216.6 x 98.1 cm). The Museum of Modern Art, New York; Van Gogh Purchase Fund

sculpture does have affinities to tribal art, if not to a specific source. The curved arms and incised fingers occur in numerous styles, from Marquesan Tikis to Fang reliquary figures, while the simplified blocklike structure recalls the more geometrical Dogon figures (pp. 50, 273).

Lipchitz's work radically changed direction in 1926 when he executed the first of what he calls his "transparents." This new direction moved, he wrote, from the solid, simplified forms in works such as *Seated Man* of 1922 to "playing with space, with a kind of open, lyrical construction that was a revelation to me."[33]

In one of the sculptures related to the transparents, the 1926 *Study for Figure,* the maquette on which the large 1926–30 *Figure* (left) was based, Lipchitz returned to echoes of tribal art. This maquette had itself evolved from a small bronze sculpture of 1926, *Ploumanach,* named after the resort on the Brittany coast that Lipchitz visited during the summer of that year. He had been intrigued by the rock formations offshore—by the way in which large stones balanced and swayed on other stones which had been eroded by water. This delicate equilibrium is captured in *Ploumanach* from which two maquettes for *Figure* evolved. In the first of these, the reclining figure in relief was retained in the upper portion of the sculpture. Then, as Lipchitz wrote:

I must have begun to see this as a primitive totem, for in the next sketch I transformed the upper part into a head with an indication of staring eyes. This was the genesis of the great *Figure,* 1926–1930, a work that summarized many of my ideas dating back to 1915. Specifically, it pulled together those different directions of massive, material frontality and of aerial openness in which I had been working during the 1920s. It is also very clearly a subject sculpture, an image with a specific and rather frightening personality[34]

Again, Lipchitz seems determined to minimize the influence of tribal art. "Although the *Figure* has been associated with African sculpture and the resemblance is apparent, it is now evident to me that it emerged, step by step, from findings I made in my cubist and postcubist sculpture over the previous fifteen years."

Of all Lipchitz's sculptures that reflect the influence of tribal art, *Figure,* with the hypnotic, staring eyes, comes closest to the demonic presence found in Picasso's work of 1907–08. Possibly the projecting, cylindrical eyes of the *Figure* derive from Grebo masks from the Ivory Coast. Picasso owned such masks (pp. 20, 305), and Lipchitz would almost certainly have seen them. Both the proportions of the *Figure* and the symmetrical, transparent interlocking loops between the head and the base are remarkably close to the Cook Islands staff god in the Cambridge University Museum of Archaeology and Anthropology (p. 427). Also, the frontality of Lipchitz's *Figure* and the way in which the outlines of the body are composed of a series of rhythmic arabesques alternating hollowed-out spaces with solids are distinctly reminiscent of certain New Guinea figure carvings (p. 46).

Lipchitz's debt to tribal art was, as was also the case with Epstein, short-lived. His comments minimizing the influence of African art on his work should be seen less as a denial than as honest self-appraisal. Although tribal art did not have a lasting impact on Lipchitz's sculpture, he described his interest in collecting it as a lifelong "passion."[35] The 1960 exhibit of Lipchitz's collection—from Africa, Oceania, and the Americas[36]—at The Museum of Primitive Art in New York was a fitting tribute to one of the most important artist/collectors of the twentieth century.

Male and female heads. Baga. Guinea. Wood, 17⅞" (45.2 cm) high. Collection Yulla Lipchitz, New York. Formerly collection JACQUES LIPCHITZ

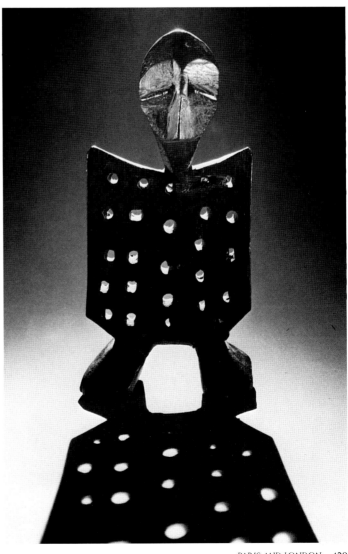

Right: Figure. Lega. Zaire. Wood and fiber, 9¾" (24.8 cm) high. Collection Yulla Lipchitz, New York. Formerly collection JACQUES LIPCHITZ

Jacob Epstein. *Sunflower,* c. 1912–13. Stone, 23" (58.5 cm) high. National Gallery of Victoria, Melbourne; courtesy of the Council of Trustees

Reliquary head. Fang. Gabon. Wood, 22⅞" (58.1 cm). Private collection. Formerly collection JACOB EPSTEIN

In 1902, when the American-born sculptor Jacob Epstein arrived in Paris for the first time, he was twenty-two and had already trained for several years at the Art Students League in New York. Epstein stayed in Paris for three years. He studied at the Ecole de Beaux-Arts and at the Académie Julian, modeling from life and drawing from casts of Michelangelo's sculpture. But he developed a contempt for academic teaching: "The academy was the same as all academies. You know the depressing pseudo-Greek work that wins medals and distinctions and sends its creators to Rome."[37] During these years in Paris he saw the work of Gauguin and van Gogh, which offered him a clear alternative to the teaching of the art schools. In his autobiography he records those sculptures in Paris museums that most impressed him. These were not the classical Greek or the Italian Renaissance but tribal sculpture, prehistoric carvings, and Archaic Greek art.

Visits to the Louvre opened my eyes. The great storehouse of painting and sculpture held me for days on end.... In my prowlings through the Louvre, I discovered works which were not at all famous then, but have since come into their own—early Greek work, Cyclades sculpture, the bust known as the Lady of Elche, and the limestone bust of Akenaton. And at the Trocadero was a mass of primitive sculpture none too well assembled (as our British Museum collection is still).[38]

If indeed Epstein visited the Trocadéro during his first year in Paris, he became aware of tribal art some three years before

Vlaminck, Derain, and Matisse did. Epstein recalled having seen a private collection of tribal art during these first years in Paris, but in all probability this encounter took place only in 1912: "Paul Guillaume had just commenced his collection of African sculpture, which was not yet popular, and had only been discovered by a few artists and writers."[39] Unlike Picasso and Moore, whose painting and sculpture were influenced by Primitive art soon after they discovered it, a decade passed before Epstein's work was to reflect affinities with African and Oceanic art.

In 1905 Epstein resolved to settle in England. He moved to London and found a studio in Camden Town. If, as he wrote, he had any lingering doubts about his decision to leave Paris, "a visit to the British Museum settled the matter for me."[40] In Paris, Epstein has said, it was in the Louvre where he found his real inspiration; in London it was at the British Museum. He recalled:

My aim was to perfect myself in modelling, drawing and carving, and it was at this period I visited the British Museum, and whenever I had done a new piece of work I compared it mentally with what I had seen at the Museum. These rich collections are rarely visited by sculptors. You could pass whole days there and never come across a sculptor.... Fancy a dramatist or poet willingly eschewing Shakespeare and the Elizabethans, or a composer of music deliberately avoiding Bach and Beethoven! Early on, about 1910, I was tremendously interested in the Elgin Marbles and Greek sculpture, and later in the Egyptian rooms and the vast and wonderful collections from Polynesia and Africa.[41]

In retrospect it seems strange that Epstein did not include

Assyrian art among the sculpture he admired in the British Museum. His second commission, obtained shortly after he had completed his notorious Strand statues of 1908 for the British Medical Association building, was to carve a large tomb for Oscar Wilde to be erected in the Père Lachaise Cemetery in Paris. This was almost certainly Epstein's first sculpture to show the direct influence of non-European art. Although, as the artist wrote, "Wilde's enthusiastic admirers would have liked a Greek youth standing by a broken column,"[42] he decided to make a complete break with European precedents and based the tomb's horizontal winged figure (completed in 1911) on one of the Assyrian colossal human-headed winged bulls in the British Museum. The tomb is the earliest example in Epstein's work of his divergence from the Greco-Roman tradition. Like the Strand statues, the Wilde tomb was carved in stone, the choice of material no doubt dictated in part by the Assyrian prototype in the British Museum. Also, the preparatory drawing for the tomb (c. 1910)[43] in its overt sexuality—the phallic shape of the sphinx whispering into the ear of the poet, the couple at lower right embracing, their tongues locked together forming a sinuous line, and beside them the smaller of the two figures fondling the other's breasts—anticipates Epstein's highly personal interpretations of tribal art in his drawings and sculpture of 1913.

Epstein spent the summer and autumn of 1912 in Paris supervising the installation of the Oscar Wilde memorial. During these crucial months his renewed interest in tribal art, which was to have a profound if short-lived influence on his work of

1913–14, must have been sparked both by the collections and the primitivism in the sculpture and paintings of those artists he met for the first time in the French capital, among them Picasso, Ortiz de Zarate, Brancusi, and Modigliani. Epstein associated most often with Modigliani. "I saw him for a period of six months daily," wrote Epstein, "and we thought of finding a shed on the Butte de Montmartre where we would work together in the open air, and spent a day hunting around for vacant grass plots for huts, but without result."[44] He visited Modigliani's studio at the time when the Italian was concentrating on sculpture and related drawings inspired by Baule masks and saw the long stone heads influenced by this style of Primitive art. Epstein also visited Brancusi's studio and almost certainly saw works such as *The Kiss* of 1907, the marble *Sleeping Muse* of 1910, and the marble *Prometheus* of 1911. He was aware of Brancusi's attitude toward tribal art. "African sculpture, no doubt, influenced Brancusi, but to me he exclaimed against its influence. One must not imitate Africans, he often said."[45] It was Epstein's contact with these artists that precipitated a radical change in his sculpture. The 1912 visit was followed by a brief burst of creativity during which (until 1915) he produced an extraordinarily original body of work influenced by tribal art.

Epstein produced little sculpture during these months in Paris. He found that the continual interruptions made it difficult to concentrate on his work: "I remember that when I had taken a studio and started carving, no sooner had I got started than my neighbour, who lived below, complained of my hammering."[46]

Reliquary figure. Kota. Gabon. Wood and copper, 8⅞" (22.5 cm) high. Private collection, Paris

Headdress, Janus-faced. Yoruba. Nigeria. Wood, 24" (61 cm) high. The Metropolitan Museum of Art, New York; Fletcher and Rogers Fund

Jacob Epstein. *Birth.* 1913. Stone, 12 x 10½" (30.6 x 26.6 cm). Art Gallery of Ontario, Toronto; purchase

In the autumn of 1912 he decided to leave Paris for good and return to England.

...I rented a bungalow on the Sussex coast at the solitary place called Pett Level, where I could look out to sea and carve away to my heart's content without troubling a soul. It was here I carved the "Venus," the three groups of doves, the two flenite carvings and the marble "Mother and Child..."[47]

According to the sculptor, the Pett Level period lasted for three years, during which time he produced a group of drawings, carvings, and *The Rock Drill,* which are not only the most primitivistic works of his career but also, in retrospect, the most important. They include two carvings in flenite; *Birth; Mother and Child;* two marble Venuses; three carvings of doves (p. 435); and the plaster *Rock Drill,* later cast in bronze (p. 416).

Although no documentary proof exists that *Sunflower* (p. 430) was executed as early as 1910, it has been assigned this date ever since it was first reproduced.[48] If in fact this date is correct, it is the earliest example (and an isolated one) of the influence of tribal art in Epstein's work. Goldwater has written that the influence of Fang sculpture

is already to be found in *Sunflower* (1910), with its long neck, oval face, single curved line of nose and eyebrow, and small, withdrawn mouth. If in deference to the subject the petal-like surrounding mass is more jagged than in the *bieri* heads, it nevertheless frames the face in much the same way.[49]

The features of the face of Epstein's *Sunflower* contradict several of Goldwater's observations. The incised eyes are more self-contained than continuous with the nose, and there is no mouth at all. Nevertheless, his reference to Fang sculpture is relevant. According to John Donne, Epstein acquired his first work of African art from Paul Guillaume, probably during his visit to Paris in 1912.[50] Lady Epstein told William Fagg that the first piece he bought was a half-length Fang sculpture, cut off at the waist.[51]

Suspension hook. Iatmul. East Sepik Province, Papua New Guinea. Wood, 25½" (64.8 cm) high. The Metropolitan Museum of Art, New York; The Michael C. Rockefeller Memorial Collection, Purchase, Nelson A. Rockefeller Gift

This information suggests that *Sunflower* might in fact date from late 1912, after Epstein's return from Paris, or early 1913; certainly there is a close relationship between *Sunflower* and such Fang reliquary heads as the exquisite one from Epstein's own collection reproduced on page 430.

The double halos of pointed, petallike forms surrounding the head in *Sunflower* are features found in a number of tribal styles from both Africa and the Pacific Islands: a Yoruba Janus headdress (p. 431); a double-faced Baule mask; a mask of Elema, Gulf of Papua (all in The Metropolitan Museum of Art). Also of interest in this regard is an unusual type of Kota reliquary head (p. 431). Hence the difficulty in linking this aspect of *Sunflower* to a specific tribal style. That Epstein again used the petal motif around the head at the top of the center drawing in his *Study for The Rock Drill* of c. 1913 (p. 440), and more forcefully in the study

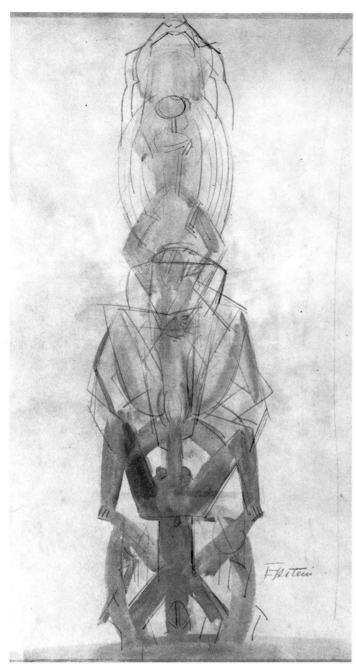

Jacob Epstein. *Totem*. c. 1913. Pencil and wash, 22⅞ x 16⅜" (58.1 x 41.6 cm). The Trustees of the Tate Gallery, London

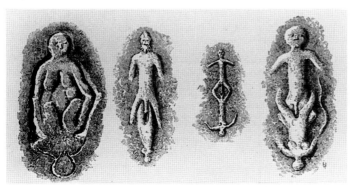

Relief carvings in priests' dwellings, village of Kani Kombole. Drawing by H. Hazler after earlier drawings by Leo Frobenius and Fritz Nansen. Published in Leo Frobenius, *Das Unbekannte Afrika*, 1923

to the drawing's right, also suggests that *Sunflower* may have been done about the same time, and not as early as 1910.

Almost without exception, Epstein's drawings and sculpture of 1913–14 focus obsessively on themes of sexuality: copulation, pregnancy, and birth. The extraordinary frankness of Epstein's treatment of sexual and erotic imagery has no precedent in early twentieth-century art. It does, however, bear witness to his familiarity with tribal sculpture, which typically is replete with such themes. Many of Epstein's sculptures and drawings suggest that the frankly sexual character of certain forms of tribal art provided Epstein with formal prototypes which he adapted and transformed in realizing his own personal preoccupation with these subjects. Epstein defended the candid treatment of this subject in tribal art as the natural iconography of Primitive ritual.

Primitive work when it expresses the principle of sex, does it in a manner which cannot be offensive. First, because it is frankly sexual and, moreover, is part of an attitude which can only be termed ritualistic. Those African statues which are double-sexed are undoubtedly ritual works, embodying the sexual principle in life, and are in no way offensive.[52]

The little-known stone carving *Birth* can almost certainly be assigned to the year 1913 on the basis of its close relationship to the drawing *Birth* (signed and dated). *Birth*, in its contour, its relief carving, the splayed legs of the mother, and the proportions of the child at the moment of delivery, is remarkably close to the British Museum's Sierra Leone soapstone slab with human figures carved in relief.[53] If in fact Epstein had seen this work or one like it, he borrowed certain features, the splayed legs of the figure at left and the child at center, and rearranged these elements. A more plausible source is to be found in Oceanic art, in which the birth theme is more frequently represented than it is in African art. The explicit treatment of this subject is well illustrated in the Sepik River suspension hook, showing an ancestor figure giving birth to a catfish.

Images of copulation are treated explicitly in two of Epstein's most important and intriguing drawings of c. 1913, *Totem* and his *Study for The Rock Drill* (p. 440). In *Totem*, the totemic composition is created by the interlocking forms of three figures. The man stands on his head while penetrating the woman who holds a child high over her head—an extraordinary balancing act. This drawing may possibly be related to the original illustrations—later reproduced in Leo Frobenius's *Das Unbekannte Afrika* (Munich, 1923)—of Dogon relief carvings from priests' dwellings in the village of Kani Kombole.[54] These sketches, by H. Hazler, were based on earlier drawings by Frobenius or Fritz Nansen made during a 1908 German expedition. Although we have no concrete evidence that Epstein had, in fact, seen these drawings, the similarities between them and *Totem* are so close as to suggest that the resemblances are not fortuitous. In *Totem*, the positioning of the male and female figures and their thin rectangular torsos are closely related to the center right copulating figures in the drawing of the Dogon reliefs, while the child held above the woman's head may derive from the upper figure of the right-hand image. Oceanic art should be mentioned as another possible source for *Totem*. The raised splayed legs of the woman have much in common with features of some carvings from Papua New Guinea such as the suspension hook mentioned above. Yet *Totem*, for all its similarities to tribal art, is, in the angular, simplified geometric forms of the bodies, and the nondescript additional complex linear grids and curved lines, styl-

Jacob Epstein. *Female Figure*. 1913. Flenite, 24″ (60.9 cm) high. The Minneapolis Institute of Arts; gift of Messrs. Samuel H. Maslon, Charles H. Bell, Francis D. Butler, John Cowles, Bruce B. Dayton, and anonymous donor

Figure. Tahiti, Society Islands. Wood, 20⅞″ (53 cm) high. The Trustees of the British Museum, London

istically related to Cubism and Epstein's association with Vorticist artists such as Wyndham Lewis.

The two carvings in flenite, shown in Epstein's December 1913 exhibition in London at the Twenty-One Gallery, are *Female Figure* of 1913 and *Female Figure in Flenite* (Tate Gallery, London) of the same year, both executed at Pett Level. The subject matter of both carvings is a pregnant woman about to give birth. Epstein went beyond the external signs of the advanced state of pregnancy, so explicit in these two carvings, in his 1913 drawing for *Female Figure in Flenite*,[55] depicting the mother looking down at her enormous, swollen belly, exposing a sort of X-ray view of the child in the womb, with its head down ready for birth. In this study the elongated neck and torso and the arbitrary positioning of the breasts anticipate Picasso's sexually charged, extremely distorted, and at times grotesque drawings of bathers, executed at Cannes during the summer of 1927. In Epstein's drawing, the dynamic arched forms encircling the figure may be a symbolic representation of the open vagina at the moment of birth. The child, centrally placed in this composition, is the vortex, as

Wyndham Lewis defined it: "At the heart of the whirlpool is a great silent place where all the energy is concentrated. And there, at the point of concentration, is the Vorticist."[56]

Two of Epstein's friends, Gaudier-Brzeska and T. E. Hulme, the philosopher, poet, and critic, associated the flenite carvings with Oceanic art. Gaudier, who visited Epstein's studio on October 7, 1913, wrote the following day: "He's doing most extraordinary statues, absolute copies of Polynesian work with Brancusi-like noses."[57] He must have been referring to the two flenite carvings. In view of Epstein's later statement that it would be absurd for a European artist to try to produce surrogate African idols, he would not have taken kindly to having his work described as "absolute copies." Yet in the flenite *Female Figure* the shape of the head, the sharp edge of the chin and jowl, and the deep, diagonal recess carved out beneath the face and neck are in fact remarkably close to the head of the Tahitian standing male figure in the British Museum, which may well have been the direct source of inspiration.[58] The proportions and position of the arms, resting on the swollen belly, also strongly echo the features of the Tahitian carving. Another possible tribal source for Epstein's *Female Figure* is the Rurutu Islands standing figure in the form of a man, one of the best-known Oceanic sculptures in the British Museum (p. 331). In this carving, although the surface includes numerous small projecting figures, the form of the head and the shape and position of the arms are quite similar to the Tahitian standing male figure.

When the flenite works were shown in Epstein's 1913 exhibition, they were, like the Strand statues of 1908 and the Oscar Wilde tomb of 1910–11, mocked and bitterly attacked in the press. T. E. Hulme, in his review in *The New Age* of December 25, 1913, wrote a response in which he justified the way the modern Western artist borrows from non-European traditions. Hulme analyzed the problem in a typically philosophic way. Answering the criticism that Epstein's flenite carvings were deliberate imitations of Easter Island sculpture, Hulme stated:

This seems to me to depend on a misconception of the nature of the formulae. Man remaining constant, there are certain broad ways in which certain emotions must, and will always naturally, be expressed, and these we must call formulae. They constitute a constant and permanent alphabet. The thing to notice is that the use of these broad formulae has nothing to do with the possession of or lack of individuality in the artist.…The point is, that, given the same emotion, the same broad formula comes naturally to the hands of any people in any century.

I have wandered into this bypath merely to find therein an illustration which will help us to understand the repugnance of the critic to the "Carvings in Flenite." It is, says the critic, "rude savagery, flouting respectable tradition-vague memories of dark ages as distant from modern feeling as the loves of the Martians." Modern feeling be damned! As if it was not the business of every honest man at the present moment to clean the world of these sloppy dregs of the Renaissance.[59]

The critics had totally misunderstood that for Epstein, as for Gauguin and the generation of Picasso, the magical and formal qualities of Primitive art were a newly discovered stimulus and fulfillment of modern artists' needs to find inspiration in the rich and varied sculptural traditions of non-European and tribal cultures.

In his three carvings of doves, done at Pett Level, Epstein's obsession with copulation and phallic imagery continued unabated. During his visit to Paris in 1912 he may well have seen Brancusi's marble *Three Penguins* (Philadelphia Museum of Art),

probably carved in 1912, and been inspired by their interlocking forms. In turn, Gaudier's 1914 carving *Birds Erect* may have been influenced by Epstein's carvings of doves. It is possible that Epstein found in tribal art the inspiration for his dove carvings. Again we are faced with what may simply be astonishing, merely fortuitous resemblances between works from different cultures and periods. Yet in *Doves* the symmetrical way in which the smaller dove is mounted on top of the larger bird is remarkably close to a Torres Strait carving of a pair of mating turtles acquired by the British Museum in 1886. Although, as is so often the case, we have no documentary evidence that Epstein actually saw the Torres Strait sculpture, both the stylistic and iconographic similarities between the works suggest that this Oceanic carving could possibly have served as at least the source of inspiration for Epstein's *Doves*.

One of Epstein's best-known sculptures from the Pett Level period is the 1913 marble *Mother and Child* (p. 438). Like Lipchitz's bronze *Mother and Child* of 1913–14 (p. 424), the simplified head of the child, whose only features are the incised lines representing the nose and eyes or forehead, may again reflect the influence of Brancusi—his studies of children, in particular the 1911 marble *Prometheus* (Philadelphia Museum of Art), which remained in the artist's studio until it was bought in 1919 by the great American collector John Quinn. The slightly concave head of the mother suggests a relation with several African tribal styles, possibly Senufo, but more likely Fang. As mentioned earlier, Lady Epstein told William Fagg that the first work of Primitive art her husband purchased was a Fang carving. He also owned the famous Fang reliquary head (p. 439) now in The Metropolitan Museum of Art.

The largest carvings done at Pett Level were the two marble Venuses. According to the records at the Yale University Art Gallery, where one is exhibited (the other is in the Baltimore Museum of Art), the second, more elongated Venus was begun at Pett Level but not completed until 1917. The themes of these works are pregnancy and copulation. The subject is a classical one, relating to the triumph of Venus, in which the goddess of love is enthroned in her chariot drawn by doves or swans. But in Epstein's African-inspired interpretation, Venus is shown standing on copulating doves. In the preparatory drawing (1914–15) for the second marble Venus, the pointed, pendulous breasts certainly derive from tribal art (any number of possible Primitive

Jacob Epstein. *Doves.* c. 1913. Marble, 25½" (65 cm) long. The Trustees of the Tate Gallery, London

Pair of turtles. Yam-Tutu Island, Torres Strait, Papua New Guinea. Wood, 3⅝" (9 cm) high. The Trustees of the British Museum, London

Above: Reliquary figure (two views). Fang. Gabon. Wood, 27½″ (69.8 cm) high. Private collection. Formerly collection JACOB EPSTEIN

Opposite: Seated figure. Dogon. Mali. Wood, 27⅛″ (69 cm) high. Private collection. Formerly collection JACOB EPSTEIN

Jacob Epstein. *Mother and Child*. 1913. Marble, 17¼ x 17" (43.8 x 43.1 cm). The Museum of Modern Art, New York; gift of A. Conger Goodyear

sources) rather than the classical tradition. William Fagg has compared the S-shaped curve of the body to a Dogon cult figure in the Musée de l'Homme, Paris.[60] In describing the two Venuses, Goldwater has suggested:

The contours of the blunt faces, even though featureless, are once more reminiscent of Fang sculpture, as is the exaggerated length of the necks, while the heavy legs, so flexed that the figure seems half-kneeling, are, as in Gaudier's *Imp*, derived from African practice. African wood sculpture, from the Sudan to the Congo, quite generally employs this disproportionate emphasis on legs and feet, and other modern sculptors have been attracted by it because it unifies and solidifies the figure's total mass.[61]

The Rock Drill of 1913–14 (p. 416), unquestionably Epstein's most important sculpture, was completed at the end of the brief period during which his art was deeply influenced by tribal sculpture. The artist described the sculpture as follows:

It was in the experimental pre-war days of 1913 that I was fired to do the rock drill, and my ardour for machinery (short-lived) expended itself upon the purchase of an actual drill, second-hand, and upon this I made and mounted a machine-like robot, visored, menacing, and

Monkey (detail). Baule. Ivory Coast. Wood, 28½" (72.5 cm) high. Musée Africain, Lyons

Reliquary head. Fang. Gabon. Wood, 18¼" (46.5 cm) high. The Metropolitan Museum of Art, New York; The Michael C. Rockefeller Memorial Collection, bequest of Nelson A. Rockefeller. Formerly collection JACOB EPSTEIN

Above: Jacob Epstein. *The Rock Drill* (detail). 1913–14. Bronze, 28 x 26" (71 x 66 cm). The Museum of Modern Art, New York; Mrs. Simon Guggenheim Fund

Right: Kono mask. Bambara. Mali. 28½" (72.5 cm) high. Musée Picasso, Paris. Formerly collection PABLO PICASSO

carrying within itself its progeny, protectively ensconced. Here is the armed, sinister figure of to-day and to-morrow. No humanity, only the terrible Frankenstein's monster we have made ourselves into. I exhibited this work complete in plaster at the London Group, and I remember Gaudier-Brzeska was very enthusiastic about it when he visited my studio in 1913 with Ezra Pound to view it[62]

Richard Cork sees *The Rock Drill*, quite wrongly, I think, as signaling Epstein's "final rejection of primitive examples in favour of a more original and challenging alternative."[63] Goldwater too minimizes the African influence in *The Rock Drill*: "Epstein's most vorticist production, [it] shows no primitive affinities, unless it is in the animal-mask suggestion of the covered face."[64] The latter is hardly insignificant, however. William Rubin has underlined the affinity of Epstein's head not only with welder's masks but with certain Baule monkey heads and with a Bambara Kono mask in Picasso's collection which Epstein may possibly have seen. This notwithstanding, beginning with *The Rock Drill*, Epstein adopted for a brief time the iconography of the machine age, following perhaps the suggestion of his friend T. E. Hulme, who urged the formation of "a new geometrical and monumental art making use of mechanical forms."[65]

The numerous preparatory drawings for *The Rock Drill* confirm that Epstein had not in fact rid himself entirely of the influences of tribal art. There are more drawings for this sculpture than for any other of Epstein's sculptures of the period. These drawings reveal the genesis and complex transformation of the ideas for the sculpture, some of which are closely related to earlier primitivistic works such as the drawing *Totem* and the stone *Sunflower*. One, probably the first, of the preparatory drawings for *The Rock Drill* (p. 440) is an intermediary link between the primitivism of Epstein's earlier work and the mechanical forms that characterize *The Rock Drill*. The large study in the right half of the drawing shows an almost totally abstract figure above the vertical drill. The drill and figure are surrounded with pointed forms (as is the head at the top of the central study), which are closely related to those in the *Sunflower* carving. The central sketch represents a vertical, copulating couple, the male at the bottom, the female

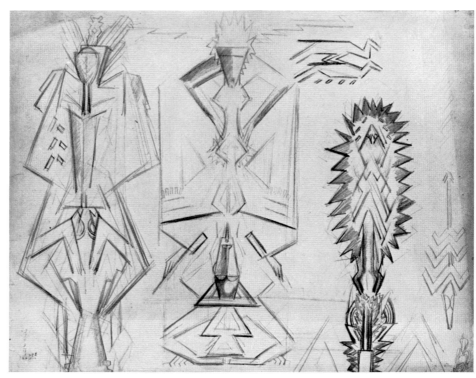

Spatula (detail). Trobriand Islands, Milne Bay Province, Papua New Guinea. Wood with lime, 14" (36 cm) high, overall. Private collection

Jacob Epstein. *Study for The Rock Drill.* c. 1913. Pencil and red and blue crayon, 18 x 23" (45.7 x 58.4 cm). Anthony d'Offay Gallery, London

Figure. Tabwa. Zaire. Wood, 24⅜" (62 cm) high. Private collection. Formerly collection JACOB EPSTEIN

above, as in the *Totem* drawing, but with a mechanical, phallic, drill-like form about to penetrate the large triangular female sex. At least in these early stages in the evolution of *The Rock Drill,* Epstein has again used the theme of copulation, but now represented by both human and machine forms. In this drawing it is as if Epstein were trying, but without success, to free himself from tribal sources in favor of the machine-age aesthetic that Hulme had suggested. The triangular head of the woman at the top of the central sketch in this study prefigures fairly closely the form of the head in *The Rock Drill,* but the man's head below is obviously indebted to African art. Senufo and/or Baule monkey masks were the probable source. The shape of the head is reminiscent of Senufo masks, such as a dance mask formerly in the collection of Charles Ratton.[66] The shape of the nose and nostrils, and the goatee, are extremely close to those in a Baule dance mask from the same collection once owned by Ratton[67]

In two subsequent drawings showing the full-length figure of a man holding the drill,[68] the sexuality remains in the potent phallic image of the drill itself, but in these studies Epstein has, apart from the head, purged himself of tribal influences—the drill and the penis seem almost synonymous in Epstein's mind.

Perhaps another feature of *The Rock Drill* sculpture itself may be traced to a Primitive source. The sculpture's exposed yet protected fetal form may be Epstein's own invention, but it may possibly be related to tribal sculpture, such as a Trobriand Islands (Melanesia) wood spatula showing a child encircled by the limbs of the parent.

Epstein's drawing *Study for Man and Woman* has been dated 1913–15 on the evidence that it might have been a study for a

never-completed sculpture called *Man and Woman,* mentioned in a telegram of June 25, 1916, from Epstein's wife to John Quinn.[69] Also, given the extraordinarily large, grotesque penis, it is tempting to relate this drawing to the central composition in Epstein's c. 1913 study for *The Rock Drill* in which the drill—a surrogate for the penis—has similarly exaggerated proportions. There are, however, several convincing reasons for believing that *Study for Man and Woman* was executed much later. To begin with, its fully worked watercolor technique is more akin to Epstein's later works than it is to the drawings from the *Rock Drill* period. But far more important is its relationship to the Madagascar grave post that Epstein is known to have acquired sometime after 1923 or 1924.[70] In Epstein's drawing, certain of the features are his own invention, such as the head of the man, closely related to the masklike head in *The Rock Drill,* the angular torsos, and the enormous male and female sex. However, the rigid, symmetrical legs of each figure, and the way in which the man at left and the woman at right stand side by side on a base, are so closely related to the position of the man and woman on the Madagascar grave post as to suggest that Epstein executed this drawing after he had acquired this tribal work. With the exception of the influence of Primitive art on a few later works—*Genesis* (1930), *Woman Possessed* (1932), *Primeval God* (1933), *Ecce Homo* (1934), and *Adam* (1938)—for the rest of his working life Epstein was engaged primarily in large figurative sculpture and in portraiture, modeling in clay in the tradition of Rodin many of the most famous people of his day.

Epstein had worked during this period as a solitary artist. He borrowed from Cubism, Vorticism, and tribal art, but was never

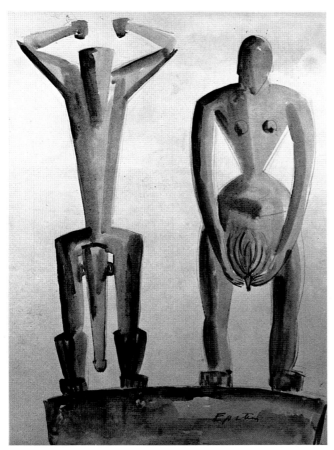

Jacob Epstein. *Study for Man and Woman.* 1913–15 [here dated 1920s]. Pencil and wash, 24¼ x 16¼" (61.6 x 41.3 cm). The Trustees of the British Museum, London

Funerary post figures. Madagascar. Wood, 39¾" (101 cm) high. Private collection. Formerly collection JACOB EPSTEIN

formally allied in a doctrinaire way with any groups or movements. Epstein's drawings and sculpture of 1913–14 have an overt and often violent sexuality that sets them apart from the work of the other major artists who borrowed from African and Oceanic art in the early years of the century. It would seem that only Gaudier shared some of Epstein's obsessive eroticism during these years, as is described below.

Years after he created his primitivist works, Epstein expounded on the characteristics of tribal art as well as on its influence on his own work. Regarding the sculptural qualities of African art, Epstein said:

To start with, in looking at negro sculpture one must realize that it is not something absolutely and entirely apart, cut off from all other art. It is governed by the same considerations that govern all sculpture. In every good school of sculpture there are certain values quite apart from any interest in the object represented.[71]

From a formal point of view, Epstein stated that "the chief features of negro art are its simplification and directness, the union of naturalism and design, and its striking architectural qualities."[72] He pointed out that although African art "is not turned out to a definite pattern laid down by tribal custom…the artist is certainly bound to a certain extent, in the same manner as the Renaissance artist was in depicting a holy family."[73] Although we may not know the names of the carvers, "the finest examples of African art are the works of highly individualised artists, with an outlook and a technique all their own. I can pick out pieces in my own collection that I am convinced are the work of one particular artist."[74]

Epstein was also aware of the religious and ceremonial functions of tribal art. "As fetishes their importance is religious or, at any rate, magical. They were used to impress, terrify and impart to the beholders a state of mind bordering on, or actually, hallucinatory."[75]

In his writings Epstein discusses at some length the problematic question of how to understand the influence of tribal art on his work:

I am influenced by African sculpture in the same manner that all primitive work must influence the artist. African work has certain important lessons to teach that go to the root of all sculpture. I have tried to absorb those lessons without working in the African idiom. It would indeed be absurd for a European artist in these days to produce African idols, and like all imitation it would be insincere.[76]

As Epstein points out, the sensibility of the European artist absorbs and transforms influences, thereby re-creating works uniquely his own:

The word "influence," as I understand it, means more than a mere surface study, it means a full comprehension of both mind and technique, that go to the composition of a work, and a translation of that, according to the personality of the artist. A complete re-creation in fact through a new mind.[77]

In the history of twentieth-century British sculpture, Epstein, and to a lesser extent Gaudier-Brzeska, were the pioneering figures. Both Moore and Caro were well aware of Epstein's importance as a sculptor. In a tribute published in the *Sunday Times* (August 23, 1959) Moore wrote of Epstein: "…he took the

Fetish figure. Kugni. People's Republic of the Congo. Wood and iron, 19" (49 cm) high. Collection Max Granick. Formerly collection JACOB EPSTEIN

brickbats, he took the insults, he faced the howls of derision with which artists since Rembrandt have learned to become familiar. And as far as sculpture in this century is concerned, he took them first."

As important as Epstein's primitivist works are, they have been in some sense overshadowed by the fame of his collection of Primitive art. Over the years he assembled one of the finest and most comprehensive collections not only of African, Oceanic, and Northwest Coast art, but also of sculpture from many other cultures and civilizations—Mexico, Peru, Egypt, Greece, Rome, and China. In 1960 tribute was paid to the importance of this collection in The Art Council of Great Britain's exhibition "The Epstein Collection of Tribal and Exotic Sculpture," with a catalog introduction by William Fagg. Included in this exhibition were a Fang head (p. 430), a Tabwa figure (p. 440), and probably a New Zealand hei-tiki of the type illustrated on page 446.[78] At present Mr. M. D. McLeod, Keeper, Museum of Mankind, London, and Professor Ezio Bassani are working on a catalog of the Epstein collection, which since the sculptor's death has been widely dispersed.

William Fagg's account of Epstein at home with his collection offers a sort of epigram on Epstein's own experience with the process of creating sculpture: "From that repository he would bring down a few pieces of an evening and spend hours in silent contemplation or animated discussion of them, considering always the sculptural problems with which the artist confronted himself, or was confronted by tradition, and the solutions which he found for them."[79]

"The modern sculptor," wrote Henri Gaudier-Brzeska, "is a man

who works with instinct as his inspiring force. His work is emotional. The shape of a leg, or the curve of an eyebrow, etc., etc., have to him no significance whatsoever; light voluptuous modelling is to him insipid—what he feels he does so intensely and his work is nothing more nor less than the abstraction of this intense feeling, with the result that sterile men of Auceps' kind are frightened at the production. That this sculpture has no relation to classic Greek, but that it is continuing the tradition of the barbaric peoples of the earth (for whom we have sympathy and admiration) I hope to have made clear.[80]

This impassioned account of the role and allegiances of the modern sculptor was made by an artist who in a very short period made a significant contribution to the primitivism of early twentieth-century sculpture. Gaudier-Brzeska's statement deals with the central issues that concerned him as well as his contemporaries Epstein, Brancusi, Modigliani, and in the 1920s Moore: the rejection of the classical ideal of beauty; the freedom to create sculpture based on intense feelings and not to strive for anatomical accuracy; the dismissal of modeling in favor of direct carving; and identification with the emotional power of tribal art.

Henri Gaudier was born at Saint-Jean-de-Braye, near Orléans, on October 4, 1891. According to his friend Horace Brodsky, he "inherited his gift for carving from his father...a wood carver and carpenter by trade; and it is interesting to record that his forefathers carved some of the figures on Chartres Cathedral. He was proud to think that he had sprung from a family of stone and wood carvers."[81] Gaudier had spent some time in England between 1906 and 1908, studying business at Bristol and later working in the offices of a coal importer in Cardiff. Family and personal problems arising from his relationship with a Polish woman twenty years his senior, Sophie Brzeska (whose surname

he added to his own), and the fact that Gaudier was due to begin (against his will) military service resulted in his decision to leave Paris in late 1910 or early 1911 and move to England, where he remained until the autumn of 1914. Thus he turned his back on the French capital when it was still the home of the artists who most influenced him—Rodin and Maillol—and those whom he would come to admire—Modigliani, Brancusi, and Archipenko. It was for the most part left to his English friend Epstein, who visited Paris in 1912, to inform Gaudier of the developments of the avant-garde in his native country.

His admiration for Rodin is reflected in a number of Gaudier's early works; sculptures such as *Head of an Idiot* and *Wrestler*, both of 1912, were undoubtedly inspired by the great French sculptor. Just as Brancusi was aware of the stifling effect of so powerful a personality as Rodin—"Nothing can grow in the shadow of the great trees"[82]—so Gaudier, too, despite his praise, was wary of the danger of trying to compete. As he wrote on January 1, 1910:

We will never see a greater sculptor than Rodin, who has exhausted himself trying to surpass Phidias....Rodin is for France what Michelangelo was for Florence, he will have imitators but never rivals....these men by their monstrous personality bleed a nation to death and leave others only the alternatives of imitation or veneration.[83]

Maillol's calm, full nudes were another formative influence on the young Gaudier, reflected in sculptures such as his stone *Sepulchral Figure* in the Tate Gallery. Ezra Pound, Gaudier's great friend and memoirist, recorded Gaudier's subsequent rejection of the two French sculptors:

Gaudier himself refers somewhere to "the usual Rodin-Maillol mixture." The Rodin admixture he had purged from his system when he quit doing representative busts of Frank Harris and Col. Smithers. Maillol I think went next.[84]

The romantic, exotic personality of Gauguin, as well as his work, had an impact on Gaudier, though he does not mention him in his writings. Gaudier's friend Brodsky, however, describes a painting perhaps inspired by the Polynesian canvases of the French painter:

On my next visit I noticed that he had commenced to paint an imaginative tropical landscape, hot in colour, with a dull red sky and exotic palm-like trees, all very Gauguinesque. This also displeased him and was later abandoned, and the canvas was covered with a thin coat of plaster. On this Brzeska carved two wrestling figures.[85]

Gaudier must have been aware of the work of Gauguin, for he was in London during those crucial years when Fry and others introduced the British public to the art of Gauguin as well as of Manet, Cézanne, van Gogh, Redon, Seurat, Matisse, and Picasso. Apart from the painting described by Brodsky, Gaudier's work does not appear in any way to have been directly influenced by Gauguin. But Gaudier seems in some way to have emulated Gauguin's personality by yearning for a tropical paradise and reveling in assuming the guise of a savage. "He was continually talking 'savage' and 'barbaric,'" according to Brodsky, "and gloated over the free and erotic life of the South Seas."[86] During his short-lived and turbulent friendship with the critic Middleton Murry and the New Zealand–born writer Katherine Mansfield, they "talked of going to live together on a Pacific island."[87] Brodsky also records Gaudier's rather theatrical primitivistic notions:

He would want to pierce his nose with a stick some four inches long and hang bells on it like a South Sea Islander. He would wish for earrings long and quaint, and he actually carved a large green stone charm in the manner of the Maoris [p. 446]. This he wore suspended from his neck. This design has been used, embossed on the cover of Pound's book.[88]

Epstein, whom Gaudier met in London in June 1912, interested him in working directly in stone. The first work by Epstein

Henri Gaudier-Brzeska. *Two Men with a Bowl.* 1914. Bronze, 12" (30.5 cm) high. Kettle's Yard, University of Cambridge

that Gaudier saw was the Assyrian-inspired stone tomb of Oscar Wilde, which he sketched in a letter to Dr. Uhlemayr, dated June 18, 1912.

A Russian [sic] sculptor Jacob Epstein also works here—he has just finished a tomb (sarcophagus) for Oscar Wilde in Paris. The thing will be erected at the Père Lachaise cemetery next July. I saw it in the studio last Sunday—Oscar Wilde is flying slowly into space, his eyes shut. The whole work is treated—strongly, filled with insuperable movement and delicate feeling, in the expression and the medium—a piece of sculpture that will live for ever, only the total effect seems to be too small[89]

Later, Epstein was to maintain that following this first visit Gaudier "took to carving after admiring work he saw in my studio."[90]

Epstein also fueled Gaudier's interest in Primitive art, as did Gaudier's visits to the British Museum. In his letter to Sophie of November 28, 1912 (written before he had seen Epstein's primitivistic carvings of 1913), he reveals himself in transition, trying to resolve his admiration for tribal art with the achievements of European sculpture from the Greeks to Rodin:

This afternoon I went to the British Museum. I looked particularly at all the primitive statues—negro, yellow, red, and the white races, Gothic and Greek, and I am glad to say I was at last convinced of a thing which for a long time bothered me. I had never felt sure whether the very conventional form of the primitives, which gives only an enormous sensation of serene joy or exaggerated sorrow—always with a large movement, synthetized and directed towards one end—had not a comprehension more true, more one with nature: in other words, ampler and bigger, than modern sculpture...up to Rodin and the French of to-day. Having very carefully studied the two aspects, at the moment I think not![91]

At this early stage in his development, though, he found that "primitive sculpture seen in large quantities bores me, whereas modern European sculpture seen in the same quantity interests me infinitely."[92] In Gaudier's sculpture of early 1913, works such as *Female Torso, Mermaid, The Wrestler,* and *The Dancer,* he clearly had not broken away from the Rodinesque tradition.

Undoubtedly the example of Epstein's primitivistic carvings of 1913 hastened the liberation of Gaudier from the Greco-Roman tradition and from the influence of Rodin and Maillol. On October 8, 1913, Gaudier wrote to Sophie that on the previous day he had visited Epstein, whom he described as "doing most extraordinary statues, absolute copies of Polynesian work with Brancusi-like noses," most likely referring to Epstein's two flenite carvings.[93] Now stimulated by Epstein's borrowings from tribal art, Gaudier began, probably in late 1913 or early 1914, to create his own works inspired by the art of Africa and the Pacific Islands. At last Gaudier was no longer concerned with comparing the disparate European and Primitive traditions and saw his own work, and that of other modern sculptors, as "continuing the tradition of the barbaric peoples of the earth."[94]

Gaudier, in addition, was now exclusively committed to direct carving. He expressed his esteem for this method in a review of the 1914 exhibition of the Allied Artists' Association held in Holland Park Hall, London:[95]

The sculpture I admire is the work of master craftsmen. Every inch of the surface is won at the point of the chisel—every stroke of the hammer is a physical and mental effort. No more arbitrary translations of a design in any material. They are fully aware of the different qualities and possibilities of woods, stones, and metals. Epstein, whom I consider the foremost in the small number of good sculptors in Europe, lays particular stress on this. Brancusi's greatest pride is his consciousness of being an accomplished workman.[96]

Gaudier's sculpture of late 1913 and 1914 relates both to Vorticism and tribal art. Carvings such as *Birds Erect* (Museum of Modern Art, New York) and *Stags* (Art Institute of Chicago) are deeply faceted, Vorticist works, realizing in three-dimension some of his ideas about sculpture, published in the Rebel Art Centre magazine *Blast* (April 1914): "Sculptural feeling is the appreciation of masses in relation. Sculptural ability is the defining of these masses by planes."[97]

In the c. 1913 *Red Stone Dancer* (Tate Gallery), the arrangement of forms, particularly the way in which the head, with the triangle in the center, creates a sort of vortex, has little in common with tribal art. But in 1914 Pound equated this carving and Epstein's two flenite sculptures with the magical power of witch doctors. The poet identifies with these artists: "We who are the heirs of the witch-doctor and the voodoo, we artists who have been so long the despised are about to take over control."[98]

Gaudier's marble *Seated Woman* of 1914 (Musée National d'Art Moderne) combines European and Primitive characteristics. The

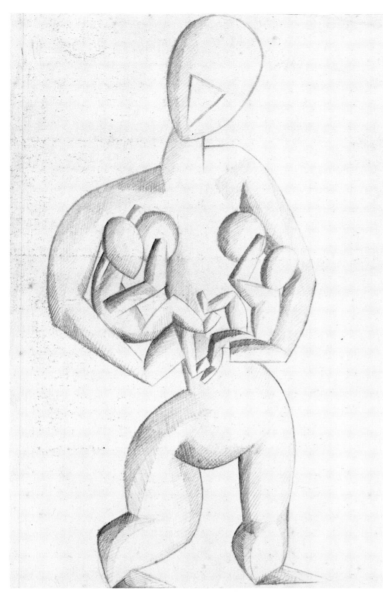

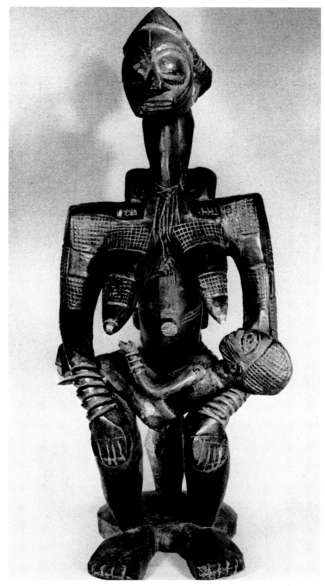

Henri Gaudier-Brzeska. *Caritas*. 1914. Pencil, 18 x 12⅛" (45.7 x 30.8 cm). Kettle's Yard, University of Cambridge

Mother and children. Afo. Nigeria. Wood, 27½" (69.9 cm) high. The Horniman Museum, London

pose and the heavy limbs of the figure are reminiscent of Modigliani's only surviving stone *Caryatid* (p. 422) and of his numerous drawings and watercolors of this subject. The masklike face may well be indebted to tribal or Primitive art, but the asymmetrical pose is clearly in the European tradition.

Those works showing patent affinities to tribal art adhere less rigidly to the sculptural principles of Cubism and Vorticism. *Two Men with a Bowl* of 1914, one of Gaudier's most obviously primitivistic works, was almost certainly inspired by Oceanic art, by such carvings, one would presume, as Hawaiian bowls held by human figures at each end. Another of Gaudier's works recalls several tribal styles of African art: the 1914 drawing *Caritas*, of a mother suckling two children. Both in subject matter and style, particularly in details such as the shape of the feet and the two infants and the positioning of their hands, this drawing was almost certainly inspired either by an Afo mother-and-child carving, such as the well-known example in the Horniman Museum, London, or by some Yoruba sculpture of the subject. In the case of the alabaster carving *The Imp* of 1914 (Tate Gallery), it is difficult to suggest a specific tribal source. In discussing this work Robert Goldwater has suggested that "the oval curves of the

short bent legs whose heaviness pulls down the figure's whole mass is probably influenced by African proportions."[99]

Two small works of 1914 were directly inspired by Oceanic art, which had a greater impact on Gaudier than African sculpture had. The *Doorknocker* of 1914, originally fashioned directly in brass, is one of the few works by Gaudier that can be related to a specific style of tribal art—the Maori jade ornaments (hei-tiki) from New Zealand (p. 446). The four holes in the lower half of *Doorknocker* correspond to the openings found in the New Zealand ornaments. Gaudier gave a disingenuous description of this very figurative and sexual sculpture:

The door-knocker is an instance of an abstract design serving to amplify the value of an object as such. No more cupids riding mermaids, garlands, curtains—stuck anywhere. The technique is unusual—the object is not cast but carved direct out of solid brass.[100]

Indeed, it is not a cupid nor a mermaid, but neither is the *Doorknocker* simply an "abstract design." Gaudier has transformed the single figure represented in New Zealand Tikis into an erotic image. The drawing (c. 1914) for *Doorknocker* (Kettle's Yard, University of Cambridge) makes explicit what in the brass

Henri Gaudier-Brzeska. *Doorknocker.* 1914. Bronze (variant of the original brass), 6⅞" (17.5 cm) high. Musée National d'Art Moderne, Centre National d'Art et de Culture Georges Pompidou, Paris

Ornament (hei-tiki). Maori. New Zealand. Jade and wax, 8½" (21.6 cm) high. The Trustees of the British Museum, London

sculpture is less obvious.[101] The drawing clearly represents a female figure with upraised arms, with the head hanging down between the two breasts. She is sitting or balancing cross-legged, about to be penetrated by an enormous, erect male penis. Could Gaudier have seen Epstein's tribal-inspired *Totem* drawing of c. 1913 (p. 433), which also represents a copulating couple, with the male upside down beneath the female? The central composition in Epstein's c. 1913 preparatory drawing *Study for Rock Drill* (p. 440) is also closely related in subject matter to *Doorknocker*. It seems highly improbable that the sexual themes in Epstein's work of 1913, treated with such frankness, did not influence Gaudier's *Doorknocker* and *Hieratic Head of Ezra Pound* (p. 448). In contrast to the artist's innocuous published account of the design of the *Doorknocker*, in private conversation, according to Brodsky, he would

tell me that so-and-so wanted a watch-charm, a door-knocker, or a paper-weight—something "phallic," to use their words. About this time the word "phallic" was very popular and commonly used as a part of the art jargon of the day. Brzeska would cut a piece of brass for them that would look more like a masonic charm than anything else. He would tell them that it was symbolic of fecundity or virility, or whatever erotic nonsense he had in his head at the time. That was what they wanted. They would believe that it was something highly improper and take it away satisfied...[102]

The influence of hei-tiki ornament is also evident in Gaudier's green stone *Charm*, where the pieced forms of the Maori neck pendants merge with facial features, particularly with the slanted eyes, reminiscent of New Guinea figurative sculpture, such as hunting-charm carvings.

Gaudier's 1914 marble *Hieratic Head of Ezra Pound* (p. 448) is undoubtedly the most powerful and potent sculpture created during the artist's brief career. The poet has left a detailed account of the progress of the work. The bust was begun, wrote

Pound, in 1914, "after the winter had loosened its grip."[103]

Gaudier, Pound recalled, could not afford large pieces of marble.

He had intended doing the bust in plaster, a most detestable medium, to which I had naturally objected. I therefore purchased the stone beforehand, not having any idea of the amount of hard work I was letting him in for. There were two solid months of sheer cutting, or perhaps that counts spare days for reforging the worn-out chisels.[104]

Brodsky wrote of the Pound head that "its purpose and beginnings were entirely pornographic. Both the sculptor and the sitter had decided upon that. Brzeska informed me of the fact that it was to be a phallus."[105] When Brodsky met Pound one evening in Piccadilly Circus, Pound told him that Gaudier was working on a marble carving of the poet. "Yes," Pound declared, "Brzeska is immortalising me in a phallic column!"[106] Gaudier completed this most ambitious carving in a remarkably short time. By May 1914 the work was on display at the Whitechapel Art Gallery.

The marble *Hieratic Head of Ezra Pound* is probably Gaudier's only sculpture that can be linked not merely to a tribal style but to a specific Primitive work—the enormous Easter Island figure Hoa-Haka-Nana-la (p. 448), acquired by the British Museum in 1869. As Cork has pointed out:

Gaudier could not fail to have been impressed by such irrefutable proof of the power of prehistoric art, and his marble *Head* shows that he kept the Easter Island figure securely in the back of his mind as he disposed the various sections of his carving into their unpredictable format.[107]

Gaudier extrapolated the symmetrical features of the Easter Island carving, retaining its massiveness and vertical thrust. In the head of Pound, the nose is slightly tilted to one side, with the flat plane on the right side deeper than the one on the left. Only the upper lip is defined, by a flat plane at center and with downward-

Henri Gaudier-Brzeska. *Charm*. 1914. Stone, 4" (10.2 cm) high. Private collection

Hunting charm. East Sepik Province, Papua New Guinea. Wood, 6½" (16.5 cm) high. Private collection

Henri Gaudier-Brzeska. *Hieratic Head of Ezra Pound*. 1914. Marble, 36" (91.4 cm) high. Private collection

Figure. Easter Island. Stone, 8'4⅜" (255 cm) high. The Trustees of the British Museum, London

curving, deeply cut incisions on either side. Above the menacing horizontal eyes (the photograph of Gaudier at work during the initial stages shows the eyes drawn on the marble, as diagonal and almond-shaped),[108] the irregular, bulging mass of hair contrasts with the smooth, far less dramatic forehead of the Easter Island carving. Seen in isolation, the section of the head of Pound above the eyes is an exercise in the Vorticist aesthetic found in works such as Gaudier's 1914 *Birds Erect.*

Another work, Gaudier's carving *Portrait of Ezra Pound*, which represents the entire figure, is one of his few sculptures in wood. Like the much larger marble *Hieratic Head*, it was probably also inspired by the Easter Island carving in the British Museum, but contains some echoes of African art as well. In this wood sculpture the head is simplified into a series of flat, angular planes. The area of the rib cage has been hollowed out, and beneath it the projecting form suggests a navel. The upward-pointing form

at the bottom, the same shape as the goatee in the marble sculpture, has phallic implications.

In the autumn of 1914 Gaudier left for France to join the army. His career as a sculptor was all but over. He did a few sculptures and drawings in the trenches, using what materials he could find. Gaudier-Brzeska was killed in action at Neuville-Saint-Vaast on June 5, 1915. His death and that of Duchamp-Villon in 1918 were the greatest losses to modern sculpture from World War I.

Despite the publication in 1916 in New York and London of *Gaudier-Brzeska: A Memoir* by Pound, and despite the fact that as distinguished a collector as John Quinn had acquired a number of his most important carvings, neither Gaudier's work nor his writings have, until recently, received the recognition they deserve. With Epstein, he was responsible for the emergence of British sculpture from a provincial academic tradition into the mainstream of modern European art.

Henri Gaudier-Brzeska. *Portrait of Ezra Pound*. 1914. Wood, 28¾" (73 cm) high, base 1½ x 6¾ x 6¾" (3.8 x 7.2 x 7.2 cm). Yale University Art Gallery, New Haven, Director's Fund purchase

NOTES

1. Alfred Werner, *Modigliani the Sculptor* (New York: Golden Griffin, 1962), p. xix.
2. Ibid.
3. Edinburgh International Festival, *Modigliani* (London: Arts Council of Great Britain, 1963), p. 6.
4. Sidney Geist, *Brancusi/The Kiss* (New York: Harper and Row, 1978), p. 9.
5. Werner, *Modigliani the Sculptor*, p. xxiii.
6. Sidney Geist, *Brancusi: A Study of the Sculpture* (London: Studio Vista, 1968), p. 28.
7. Ambrogio Ceroni, *Amedeo Modigliani: Dessins et Sculptures* (Milan: Edizioni del Milione, 1965), pp. 23–26.
8. Werner, *Modigliani the Sculptor*, p. xxiii.
9. *Augustus John: Autobiography*, with intro. by Michael Holroyd (London: Jonathan Cape, 1975), p. 148.
10. Jacob Epstein, *An Autobiography* (London: Art Treasures Book Club, 1963), pp. 46–47.
11. Werner, *Modigliani the Sculptor*, p. xxiv.
12. Robert Goldwater, *Primitivism in Modern Art* (New York: Vintage, 1967), p. 236.
13. Ibid.
14. Ibid.
15. Edith Balas, "The Art of Egypt as Modigliani's Stylistic Source," *Gazette des Beaux-Arts* 97 (Février, 1981), p. 87.
16. Ibid.
17. Musée d'Art Moderne de la Ville de Paris, *Amedeo Modigliani 1884–1920* (Paris, 1981), p. 81.
18. Lipchitz as quoted by Pierre Sichel, *Modigliani* (New York: Dutton, 1967), p. 210.
19. Jacques Lipchitz, in his introduction to the catalog *The Lipchitz [Jacques, Yulla, and Lolya] Collection* (New York: The Museum of Primitive Art, 1960), p. 5.
20. Ibid., p. 7.
21. Jacques Lipchitz with H. H. Arnason, *My Life in Sculpture* (New York: Viking, 1972), pp. 19–20.
22. Lipchitz, *The Lipchitz Collection*, p. 6.
23. Ibid., p. 7.
24. Lipchitz, *My Life in Sculpture*, p. 11.
25. Ibid., p. 16.
26. Deborah A. Stott, *Jacques Lipchitz and Cubism* (New York and London: Garland, 1978), p. 109.
27. *The Lipchitz Collection*, p. 8, nos. 1–3.
28. See Alan G. Wilkinson, *Gauguin to Moore: Primitivism in Modern Sculpture* (Toronto: Art Gallery of Ontario, 1981). The sculpture is illustrated on p. 214, the drawing on p. 215.
29. Lipchitz, *My Life in Sculpture*, p. 25.
30. Ibid., p. 40.
31. Ibid.
32. Ibid., p. 70.
33. Ibid., p. 86.
34. Ibid., pp. 89–90.
35. Lipchitz, *The Lipchitz Collection*, p. 6.
36. For his lively appreciation of similarities between remote art expressions, see *The Lipchitz Collection*, p. 7.
37. Arnold L. Haskell, *The Sculptor Speaks*. Jacob Epstein to Arnold Haskell (London: William Heinemann, 1931), p. 14.
38. Jacob Epstein, *An Autobiography* (London: Art Treasures Book Club, 1963) p. 12.
39. Haskell, *The Sculptor Speaks*, p. 15.
40. Epstein, *An Autobiography*, p. 18.
41. Ibid., pp. 19–20.
42. Haskell, *The Sculptor Speaks*, p. 19.
43. This drawing, the Oscar Wilde tomb, and the Assyrian human-headed winged bull are illustrated in Wilkinson, *Gauguin to Moore*, pp. 170–71.
44. Epstein, *An Autobiography*, p. 46.
45. Ibid., p. 49. See above, Geist, p. 346.
46. Ibid.
47. Ibid.
48. Richard Cork, *Jacob Epstein: The Rock Drill Period* (London: Anthony d'Offay, 1973), p. 13, note 10.
49. Goldwater, *Primitivism in Modern Art*, p. 239.
50. I am grateful to Miss Hermione Waterfield for her help and for discussing this matter with Mr. John Donne and for relaying the information to me.
51. William Fagg, in conversation with the author.
52. Epstein, *An Autobiography*, pp. 191–92.
53. This Sierra Leone carving was not acquired by the British Museum until the 1920s.
54. Frobenius, p. 163. William Fagg has for many years greatly assisted the author in tracing affinities between tribal and modern art, and in some cases direct sources for modern works. He suggested that I consult Frobenius's book.
55. See Wilkinson, *Gauguin to Moore*, p. 175, illus.
56. Ibid., p. 174.
57. H. S. Ede, *Savage Messiah* (London: William Heinemann, 1931), p. 247.
58. I am deeply indebted to Barbara and Murray Frum for their interest in primitivism in modern art and for many productive discussions with them. Dr. Frum pointed out to the author the close stylistic affinities between Epstein's flenite *Female Figure* and the Tahitian standing male figure.
59. Epstein, *An Autobiography*, p. 64.
60. William Fagg, in conversation with the author. See Eliot Elisofon and William Fagg, *The Sculpture of Africa* (New York: Hacker, 1978), p. 31, no. 11 (illustrated).
61. Goldwater, *Primitivism in Modern Art*, pp. 240 and 242.
62. Epstein, *An Autobiography*, p. 56.
63. Cork, *Jacob Epstein*, p. 9.
64. Goldwater, *Primitivism in Modern Art*, p. 240.
65. Cork, *Jacob Epstein*, p. 9.
66. Elisofon and Fagg, *The Sculpture of Africa*, p. 90, no. 111.
67. Ibid., p. 98, no. 122.
68. Cork, *Jacob Epstein*, pp. 45 and 47, illustrated.
69. Ibid., p. 14, note 23.
70. I am indebted to Mr. M. D. McLeod for his suggestion that Epstein's *Study for Man and Woman* was based on the Madagascar grave post.
71. Haskell, *The Sculptor Speaks*, p. 89.
72. Ibid., p. 90.
73. Ibid., pp. 89–90.
74. Ibid., p. 90.
75. Epstein, *An Autobiography*, p. 188.
76. Haskell, *The Sculptor Speaks*, p. 94.
77. Ibid., p. 96.
78. Mr. M. D. McLeod kindly sent the author photographs of works formerly in Epstein's collection.
79. William Fagg, in his introduction to the exhibition catalog *The Epstein Collection of Tribal and Exotic Sculpture* (London: The Arts Council of Great Britain, 1960), unpaginated.
80. Gaudier quoted in Ezra Pound, *Gaudier Brzeska: A Memoir* (London: John Lane—The Bodley Head; New York: John Lane Co., 1916), p. 35.
81. Horace Brodsky, *Henri Gaudier-Brzeska 1891–1915* (London: Faber and Faber, 1931), p. 21.
82. Geist, *Brancusi: A Study of the Sculpture*, p. 2.
83. Roger Cole, *Burning to Speak: The Life and Art of Henri Gaudier Brzeska* (Oxford: Phaidon, 1968), p. 12.
84. Pound, *A Memoir*, p. 90.
85. Brodsky, *Gaudier-Brzeska*, pp. 31–32.
86. Brodsky, *Gaudier-Brzeska*, p. 56.
87. Ede, *Savage Messiah*, p. 141.
88. Brodsky, *Gaudier-Brzeska*, p. 56.
89. Cole, *Burning to Speak*, p. 21.
90. Ibid., p. 22.
91. Ede, *Savage Messiah*, pp. 212–13.
92. Ibid., p. 213.
93. Ede, *Savage Messiah*, p. 247.
94. Pound, *A Memoir*, p. 35.
95. *The Egoist*, 16 March 1914.
96. Pound, *A Memoir*, p. 26.
97. Pound, *A Memoir*, p. 9.
98. Richard Cork, *Henri Gaudier and Ezra Pound: A Friendship* (London: Anthony d'Offay, 1982), p. 9.
99. Goldwater, *Primitivism in Modern Art*, p. 240.
100. Cole, *Burning to Speak*, p. 133.
101. See Wilkinson, *Gauguin to Moore*, p. 186, illustrated.
102. Brodsky, *Gaudier-Brzeska*, p. 90.
103. Pound, *A Memoir*, p. 50.
104. Ibid.
105. Brodsky, *Gaudier-Brzeska*, pp. 58–59.
106. Ibid., p. 62.
107. Cork, *Gaudier and Pound*, p. 11. Gaudier made a number of preparatory sketches which, although they are among his finest drawings, do not reflect the features of the tribal source so obvious in the carving itself.
108. Ibid., facing p. 9.

Stool. Wute. Cameroon. Wood, 20⅞" (53 cm) long. Museum für Völkerkunde, Berlin.

Mask. Kete. Zaire. Wood, 24¾″ (63 cm) high. Collection J. W. MESTACH, Brussels

Marsden Hartley. *Indian Composition*. 1914. Oil on canvas, 47⅛ x 47″ (120 x 119.3 cm). Vassar College Art Gallery, Poughkeepsie, New York; gift of Paul Rosenfeld

AMERICAN ART

Gail Levin

Primitivism in American art began under the aegis of the European avant-garde, but it soon merged with certain American aspirations and assumed a distinctive character. American artists became interested in various tribal arts because of the novel stylistic and symbolic suggestions they found in the artifacts of exotic cultures. Some Americans focused on African art for its diverse formal and evocative qualities. Others looked to the abstract motifs and the characteristic themes of American Indian art which, considered together, offered American modernists an answer to nationalistic critics' demands for both an American style and a native American subject matter.

When Max Weber left New York to study in Paris in September 1905, he had already been encouraged to look at non-Western art by his progressive teacher Arthur Wesley Dow, with whom he first studied at the Pratt Institute in Brooklyn in 1899–1900. Dow had been the protégé of Ernest Fenollosa, a scholar and curator of Japanese art at the Museum of Fine Arts in Boston. Earlier Dow had studied in Paris himself and had painted in Pont-Aven, where he came into contact with Gauguin during the summer of 1886.[1] Dow not only taught a new language of art based on Japanese aesthetics; he also suggested to students that they "bring into play the primitive springs of thought, impulse and action that exist in every human being" and thus put themselves *"en rapport* with the primitive state of mind."[2] Dow's so-called "natural method" drew upon the experiences of the ethnologist Frank Hamilton Cushing, who had lived with the Zuni Indians of New Mexico for five years. Combining scientific and mystical points of view, Cushing believed there was a vast consistency of artistic expression linking Oriental, Occidental, and Primitive cultures.[3] Dow's teaching was the perfect background for the new stimuli the young Weber would encounter in Paris.

When he studied at the Académie Julian in Paris, Weber confronted a rigid, conservative teacher in the person of Jean-Paul Laurens. But he soon met fellow students who introduced him to the advanced circles of Gertrude and Leo Stein and the Delaunay family. The Steins' Saturday evening salons offered Weber a chance to meet and mingle with vanguard artists and writers and to become acquainted with the Steins' growing art collection. Weber saw his first Cézanne at the Steins' apartment, which he must have visited soon after his arrival, and he recalled the "superb Japanese prints" there as well as the "lengthy and involved discussions," led by Leo, "on the most recent developments and trends in art."[4] Robert Delaunay invited Weber to salons held by his mother, and it was at one of these gatherings, in October 1907, that he met Henri Rousseau after a Sunday visit to the Salon d'Automne, in which both artists had exhibited work. Weber accompanied Rousseau on his walk home, soon visited his studio, and began a very close friendship with the older artist.[5]

By February 1906 Weber had left the Académie Julian and begun to work from the model without instruction at the Académie Colarossi and at the Académie de la Grande Chaumière, where Matisse sometimes came to draw. Hans Purrmann, a young German painter and a friend from the Académie Julian, knew Matisse well and suggested to Weber that they form a class to study with him. The class began in early January 1908, and Weber stayed through July. Weber probably first came to know African sculpture through Matisse, who had then been collecting it for almost two years, and he was influenced by Matisse's bold colors, flattened

Figure. Yaka. Zaire. Wood, 10¼" (26 cm) high. Collection Joy S. Weber, New York. Formerly collection MAX WEBER

Max Weber. *Congo Statuette* (also known as *African Sculpture*). 1910. Gouache on board, 13½ x 10½" (34.2 x 26.7 cm). Private collection, New York

spaces, and experimental style.[6]

Weber met Picasso at the Steins' in October 1908, and on the visit to Picasso's studio that followed, when he discovered their shared passion for Henri Rousseau's work, he must have become aware of Picasso's enthusiasm for African and other Primitive sculpture.[7] Several weeks later, after Picasso visited his studio, Weber accompanied him to Rousseau's. Weber claimed that not long afterward he introduced Rousseau to Joseph Brummer, who shortly became Rousseau's dealer and champion.[8] Weber had known Brummer first as a young Hungarian émigré sculptor at La Grande Chaumière and, subsequently, as a dealer in Japanese prints, a student in the Matisse class in 1908, and a dealer in African art (first out of his studio on the Rue Falguière and later out of a small shop on the Boulevard Raspail). Weber later recalled that Brummer kept "two little landscape sketches by Rousseau standing on a shelf beside two or three excellent Congo statuettes."[9] Picasso, Brummer, Weber, and others admired both in Rousseau's paintings and in African art a similar directness, simplicity, sincerity, and power of expression. Weber described Rousseau as "a real 'Primitive' living in our time."[10]

When Weber returned to New York in 1909, he brought with him several examples of Rousseau's work, a keepsake (Rousseau's cane)—and his admonitions about painting. He probably also brought with him the Yaka figure from Zaire— possibly purchased from or through Brummer—which he included in a still life of 1910 that he exhibited under two titles, *Congo Statuette* and *African Sculpture*.[11] Weber generated inter-

est in Rousseau and Primitive art among New York artists, particularly those in the Stieglitz circle. At the death of Rousseau, Weber prompted Stieglitz to do a memorial show at the gallery "291" of the paintings and drawings he had brought back from Paris; it took place from November 18 to December 8, 1910.

Weber had also begun writing essays and poems about Primitive art, some of which were published by Stieglitz in *Camera Work*. The July 1910 issue, for example, contains two such essays. In "The Fourth Dimension from a Plastic Point of View," Weber observed that "a Tanagra, Egyptian, or Congo statuette often gives the impression of a colossal statue, while a poor, mediocre piece of [large] sculpture appears to be the size of a pinhead, for it is devoid of this boundless sense of space or grandeur."[12] In another essay Weber insisted that he had "seen Chinese dolls, Hopi Kachina images, and also Indian quilts and baskets, and other works of savages, much finer in color than the works of the modern painter-colorists."[13]

Years later Weber recalled his visits to the Museum of Natural History in New York, where he had gained an "ever increasing understanding of the art of the primitives and the art of the Western continent." It was, in fact, in that museum that he "began to write...free verse."[14] His first poem, inspired by a pre-Columbian sculpture and called "To Xochipilli, Lord of Flowers," was published in *Camera Work* in January 1911.[15] This was followed by the publication of his book *Cubist Poems* in London in 1914, with a foreword by Alvin

Langdon Coburn, who wrote of Weber: "...best of all he likes to study the art of primitive peoples, the sculptures of Egypt and Assyria, the great simple things that have come down to us in stone from the past."[16] One of the poems, "Bampense Kasai," was written about an African mask, "crudely shaped and moulded," which Weber revered:

> In the crudest geometric form,
> Thy savage maker makes an art
> at once untrifling big and powerful.[17]

It is this power in the art of the Primitives that Weber sought to re-create in his painting *Interior with Women* of c. 1917. The composition reflects both Weber's fondness for Primitive sculpture and his knowledge of the ways in which Picasso and others had already absorbed it. The head of the figure on the far right with its angular mouth, for example, owes its form not only to African masks, but probably also to the head of the lower right figure in Picasso's *Les Demoiselles d'Avignon* (p. 264). The flat decorative area in the upper left corner suggests, however, the influence of Weber's former teacher, Matisse. Weber's synthesis contains a variety of elements adapted from Cubism, among them the stippling on the left-hand figure, reminiscent of many of Picasso's Cubist works of 1913–18, an area of simulated wood graining above the figure on the left, and repeated wavy lines such as Picasso used as a sign for hair. More than any other American, Weber was moved by Picasso's assimilation of Primitive sculpture in his painting. Yet Weber's own dynamic arrangement of forms is very different from Picasso's in its rhythmic qualities.

In 1926, Weber published *Primitives: Poems and Woodcuts*, a book intended "to preserve the feeling of adoration" he experienced before tribal sculptures in the Museum of Natural History.[18] In addition to a reprinting of "Bampense Kasai," *Primitives* included poems such as "Congo Form" and "The Totem Pole Man." The unmodeled woodcuts accompanying them were simplified forms evoking the power rather than the formal vocabulary of Primitive sculpture (p. 456).

By the time Marsden Hartley arrived in Paris in April 1912, Stieglitz had already given him two exhibitions at "291." Although he was acquainted with Weber's primitivistic paintings and his writings in *Camera Work*, Hartley had not yet

Max Weber. *Interior with Women*. c. 1917. Oil on canvas, 18¼ x 23½" (46.3 x 59.7 cm). Forum Gallery, New York

Max Weber. Untitled. Woodcut, 4¼ x 2" (10.8 x 5.1 cm). Published in *Primitives: Poems and Woodcuts*. New York: The Spiral Press, 1926. Forum Gallery, New York

himself explored Primitive art. In July 1912, Hartley wrote to Stieglitz that he was impressed with this new direction in modern art upon reading an article in the magazine *Rhythm*, which claimed Kandinsky was no less than one of Gauguin's disciples, calling him a "neo-primitive" because of a technique that the author found "reminiscent of primitive and savage art."[19]

It was probably the combined effect of this article, the influence of the sculptor Jacob Epstein, whom Hartley had just met in Paris, and familiarity with the Blaue Reiter almanac that prompted Hartley to frequent the Trocadéro Museum. His reaction to the art he saw there was immediate: "Yes," he confirmed in a letter to Stieglitz, "we can find the real thing at [the] Trocadero. These people had no mean ambition. They created out of spiritual necessity."[20] Hartley's use of the phrase "spiritual necessity" reflects his growing interest in Kandinsky's treatise *Über das Geistige in der Kunst*, which he had purchased along with the Blaue Reiter almanac at Clovis Sagot's art gallery.[21]

Hartley's increasing enthusiasm for tribal art had already begun to affect his work. "One can no longer remain the same

Marsden Hartley. *Indian Pottery (Jar and Idol)*. 1912. Oil on canvas, 19¾ x 19¾" (50.2 x 50.2 cm). The Gerald Peters Gallery, Santa Fe

in the presence of these mighty children who get so close to the universal idea," he wrote to Stieglitz.[22] Hartley first experimented with the Primitive by including tribal objects in his still lifes. His *Indian Pottery (Jar and Idol)* of 1912 contains an Acoma Indian pot bearing an image of a bird and a wooden figure resembling the carved sculptures of the Kwakiutl.[23] Yet it also suggests a comparison with Gabriele Münter's *Still Life with St. George* of 1911, which was reproduced in *Der Blaue Reiter*. Like Münter, Hartley arranged a random group of Primitive art objects on a tabletop in a shallow space indicated by a painterly ground. Hartley's simple illustration of American Indian objects and motifs soon evolved into a much more original pictorial synthesis as he absorbed them into his own complex configurations.

In January 1913, Hartley followed his impulse to "meet Kandinsky and size up the Blaue Reiter group" by traveling to Germany, where he met Kandinsky, Münter, and Franz Marc in Munich.[24] Then, in May 1913, Hartley moved to Berlin for an extended stay. But his funds were depleted by October, forcing him to return to New York to raise money in order to live abroad. In pressuring a reluctant Hartley to return to New York, Stieglitz had reminded him of his American roots: "Your European trip was made possible through American cash. . . . Now I don't see any reason why an American should be called upon to give you additional cash without seeing what you have done."[25]

Stieglitz had himself earlier recognized the American Indian as the native New World "exotic" when he included Gertrude Käsebier's photograph *The Red Man* in the first issue of *Camera Work* in January 1903 and later published a discussion of Käsebier's sympathetic attitude to her Indian subject in the *Camera Work* of October 1907.[26] Less than three years later, Weber's praise of American Indian and other Primitive art appeared in *Camera Work*. Among the many artists, writers, and patrons in the Stieglitz circle who eventually focused for a time on the American Indian were Man Ray, Arthur Dove, John Marin, Paul Rosenfeld, William Carlos Williams, and Mabel Dodge.[27] Dove's *Indian Spring* of 1923, for example, contains abstract forms evoking tepees; his interest in Primitive art had been encouraged by Stieglitz, who gave him a copy of the Blaue Reiter almanac in 1913. Marin painted watercolors of Indians, such as *Dance of the Pueblo Indians* and *Dance of the San Domingo Indians* in Taos, New Mexico, in 1929.

Hartley returned to Berlin via London and Paris, arriving by the end of April 1914. After his return, perhaps as a result of his trip home to America, he began a series of abstract paintings based on the theme of the American Indian. He called the series his "Amerika" paintings, using the German spelling.

The American Indian was, to be sure, of great interest in Germany, where, by the end of the nineteenth century, several major collections of American Indian art had been established. German writers from Goethe to novelist Karl May fueled the German fascination with the Indian.[28] More immediate to Hartley's concerns, however, was the fact that August Macke, one of the contributors to the Blaue Reiter almanac, had painted American Indian themes as early as 1910. Macke's interest in the American Indian was also evident in his almanac essay, "Masks," in which he cited "the war paint of Indians" and "the cape of a chieftain from Alaska," the latter illustrated by an example from the Museum für Völkerkunde in

Arthur Dove. *Indian Spring.* 1923. Oil on canvas, 18 x 22" (45.7 x 55.9 cm) The Lane Collection, Leominster, Massachusetts

August Macke. *Mounted Red Indians.* 1911. Oil on wood, 10⅜ x 13⅞" (26.5 x 35.5 cm). Städtische Galerie im Lenbachhaus, Munich

Munich.[29] Hartley was acquainted with Macke and had seen his work well before he began his own paintings with American Indian themes. In 1913, Hartley had seen Bernhard Koehler's collection, which included Macke's *Mounted Red Indians* of 1911. Yet Hartley's Indian-theme paintings are much more abstract and emblematic than those by Macke.

The flat, symmetrical, frontal arrangement and some of the forms (such as mandorlas and wavy lines between two straight lines) in Hartley's Amerika paintings reflect his enthusiasm for Bavarian *Hinterglasbilder*, which he knew from *Der Blaue Reiter*, Kandinsky's personal collection, and the six examples he acquired for himself.[30] Hartley found other forms and motifs, however, in the vast collection of American Indian art at the Museum für Völkerkunde in Berlin. In 1914, the North American collection of this museum included nearly thirty thousand examples, virtually all of which were on exhibition in crowded glass cases.[31] Hartley not only found a vocabulary of new forms in this material but discovered that some of his favorite emblematic motifs had in fact been used by various

Marsden Hartley. *Indian Fantasy*. 1914. Oil on canvas, 47 x 39½″ (119.4 x 100.3 cm). North Carolina Museum of Art, Raleigh; Purchased with Funds from the State of North Carolina

Sio Hemis Kachina. Hopi. Arizona. Painted wood and feathers, 17⅝" (44.8 cm) high. Museum für Völkerkunde, Berlin

Indian tribes. These included eight-pointed stars and the Iron Cross.[32]

Indian Fantasy of 1914 utilizes shapes and motifs from both Bavarian glass paintings and American Indian art in the Völkerkunde collection. The color scheme of this painting, emphasizing red, yellow, and green over a black ground with white details, corresponds to that of an important Sio Hemis Kachina in the Museum, an object from which Hartley also adapted the central arch of the headdress or tableta, the eight-pointed stars enclosed in circles, and the stick figures from each side of the arch, which he placed on a mandorla inside the front tepee. Several tepees were on exhibit in Berlin, and Hartley's canoes with abstract designs probably derive from Chippewa miniatures in that same collection (p. 460). More-

over, the large bird at the top of *Indian Fantasy* recalls a monumental wooden eagle from Vancouver then in the Berlin Museum (p. 460), although the fringelike wing feathers in the Hartley image also suggest an Indian chieftain's cape from Alaska reproduced in *Der Blaue Reiter*.[33] In combining motifs from a wide variety of Indian tribes, Hartley allowed free play to his fantasy, combining motifs that would never have been seen together (such as Plains Indians' tepees and Pueblo pottery).

Hartley's attraction to the abstract character of Indian motifs is also evident in *Indian Composition* of 1914 (p. 452). This painting incorporates various patterns and designs from Plains Indian tribes' beadwork, which is well represented in Berlin. A Comanche infant carrier that juxtaposes a circular

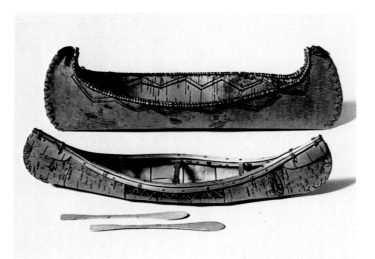

Canoe models. Chippewa. Great Lakes region. Wood and bark; above: 15½″ (39.5 cm) long; below: 16½″ (42.5 cm) long. Museum für Völkerkunde, Berlin

Eagle. Vancouver Island, British Columbia. Painted wood. Formerly collection Museum für Völkerkunde, Berlin. Whereabouts unknown

Marsden Hartley. *American Indian Symbols.* 1914. Oil on canvas, 37 x 37″ (94 x 94 cm). Collection John J. Brady, Jr., Des Moines

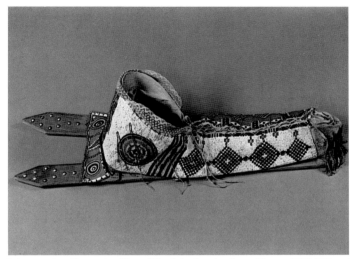

Infant carrier. Comanche. Texas. Wood, leather, beads, and brass, 41⅜" (105 cm) long. Museum für Völkerkunde, Berlin

Moccasin (detail). Crow. Montana or Wyoming. Leather and beads, 10⅝" (27 cm) long, overall. Museum für Völkerkunde, Berlin

medallion next to vertical lines and a cluster of squares may have suggested to Hartley the organization of *Indian Composition*. The shieldlike medallions also reflect Hartley's familiarity with Plains Indians' motifs; the cross within concentric circles on the lower left of Hartley's painting is found frequently on beaded objects, such as a moccasin from the Crow tribe. Once again, however, Hartley included an eight-pointed star and a stick figure on a mandorla within a tepee, recalling the motifs of Hopi Kachinas. He also included white shapes (on the central red disk), which are Hopi symbols for small corn plants, and white branchlike symbols for larger corn plants (on a blue disk on the lower right medallion). Hartley utilized these same Hopi symbols for corn plants in a series of charcoal drawings based on Indian motifs, including *Berlin Symbols No. 6* or *Primitive Art No. 2*.

American Indian Symbols, another 1914 painting of Hartley's Amerika series, also contains forms adapted from the Sio Hemis Kachina, including the eight-pointed stars enclosed in circles and the centralized cross under the arch of the head-dress. The abstract vertical band with a checkerboard pattern along the right side of this painting is probably indebted to such motifs in the beadwork of Plains Indians. Although Hartley abandoned the American Indian theme with the declaration of World War I, he maintained his love of the bold abstract patterns and shapes he had found in Indian art and used them once again in his subsequent series of symbolic German military pictures, which he referred to as "war motives."[34]

Hartley saw the Indian as "the peaceable and unobtrusive citizen" and as exemplary of the nobility of mankind. Frustrated by the war, Hartley wished he were an Indian and told Stieglitz he wanted to emulate them by painting his face with their symbols and going West, facing the sun forever.[35] Some five years after Hartley had painted his Indian themes in Germany, he wrote an article called "Red Man Ceremonials: An American Plea for American Esthetics," which illuminates his continuing interest in the Indian. Writing during a stay in Santa Fe, New Mexico, Hartley apparently worried that he had been excessively influenced by the European avant-garde.

Accordingly, he urged his compatriots to consider Indian art and to create their own native style:

A National esthetic consciousness is a sadly needed element in American life. We are not nearly so original as we fool ourselves into thinking....We have the excellent encouragement of redman esthetics to establish ourselves firmly with an esthetic consciousness of our own.[36]

In a later essay, Hartley called the Indian "one of the essential decorators of the world" and praised particularly the totem poles and the prayer robes of the Indians of Alaska.[37] He also campaigned for Indian art, but admitted that it was not easy to understand the aesthetics of the Indian, as "with all primitives, who invest regimes and modes of expression for themselves according to their own specific psychological needs."[38]

Despite his later resolve never again "to allow any primitive motive to influence [his] work,"[39] Man Ray had gone through an enthusiastic phase of interest in Primitive art. In an unpublished comment in 1957, Man Ray volunteered that he had exhibited "a series of compositions inspired by forms in primitive sculpture" in his one-man show at the Daniel Gallery in 1915.[40] He noted, however, that "primitive sources of inspiration lasted only from 1913 to 1915." It was during this period that Man Ray became familiar with the work of Max Weber, whom he knew at the Modern School of the Ferrer Center where he studied life drawing.[41] Man Ray, who described the sketches of a young girl he drew there as looking "like primitive sculpture," would certainly have been familiar with Weber's continuing interest in tribal art.[42]

One of Man Ray's paintings, *Totem*, of 1914 (p. 462), reveals this interest in Primitive art. It is a brightly colored image of a mysterious monumental head and bust that dramatically dominates its rocky setting. Surrounded by a frieze of small figures, mostly in a crouching position, the large primitivist totem contains a rolling pastoral landscape superimposed on its chest. *Totem* may have been immediately inspired by Man Ray's camping trip to New York's Harriman State Park in the

Man Ray. *Totem*. 1914. Oil on canvas, 35¾ x 24⅛" (90.9 x 61.6 cm). Galleria Il Fauno, Turin

Figure (War God). Zuni. New Mexico. Wood, 30"(76.2 cm) high. The Brooklyn Museum, New York

autumn of 1914 in the company of his wife (the poet Adon Lacroix), poet Alison Hartpence, and others. Man Ray recalled that in a conversation with Hartpence on the trip, he had announced his intention to produce a series of imaginary landscapes before renouncing painting from nature and turning "more and more to man-made sources."[43] A transitional work, *Totem* is both *d'après nature* and from a man-made object, probably a pastiche of such American Indian wood carvings as Zuni War Gods and Northwest Coast Indian totems, such as could be seen at the Brooklyn Museum and the Museum of Natural History. Like the Zuni sculpture, Man Ray's *Totem* features a long neck, a square chin, and a simplified geometric face with a long nose and linear eyes.

Thus Man Ray was fully aware of the vogue of primitivism and not untouched by it—as was the case with everyone in the circle of "291." Man Ray recalled, for example, seeing an African exhibit at "291."[44] The show he saw, which took place in November 1914, was one of the first occasions when African sculpture was exhibited in America as art. It was arranged by Stieglitz with the help of Marius de Zayas. The latter was a witty and sophisticated Mexican-born artist who had shown his caricatures at "291" in 1909, 1910, and 1913. De Zayas had studied art in Europe and had come to know Picasso

in Paris; he collected tribal art and dabbled in dealing. As early as April 1911, he had written to Stieglitz urging him to present an exhibition of African sculpture at "291," explaining that it had had an important influence on the development of modern art in Paris, particularly "among the revolutionists."[45] Stieglitz's exhibition included eighteen sculptures obtained by de Zayas from Paul Guillaume in Paris and shown "in a setting of crude and violent color" designed by Edward Steichen.[46]

On the way to New York from Paris in October 1911, de Zayas stopped off in London, where he visited the ethnographical collection at the British Museum. He recalled being impressed by an object from Pukapuka, or Danger Island, in the Pacific (p. 464):

It impressed me particularly because it reminded me of the physical appearance of Stieglitz. I say "physical" because the resemblance was also spiritual. The object, said the catalogue, was built as a trap for catching souls. The portrait was complete, and it caught my soul, because from it I derived a theory of abstract caricature.... I had previously made a caricature of Stieglitz with the caption "L'Accoucheur d'idées." The two caricatures expressed my understanding of Stieglitz's mission: to catch souls and to be the midwife who brings out new ideas to the world.[47]

De Zayas adapted the basic concept of circular forms along

Exhibition of African sculpture at "291," New York, November–December 1914. Published in *Camera Work*, October 1916

"African Savages the First Futurists," notice for the African sculpture exhibition at Stieglitz's "291," from *The World* (magazine section), January 24, 1915

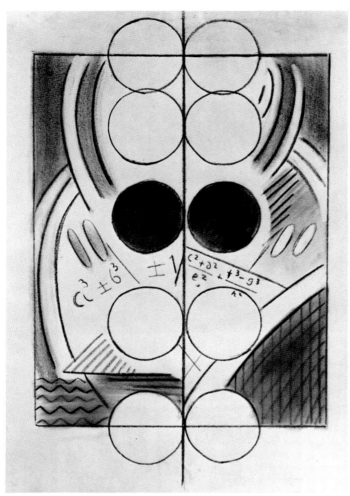

Marius de Zayas. *Alfred Stieglitz.* c. 1912. Charcoal, 24¼ x 18⅜" (61.6 x 46.5 cm). The Metropolitan Museum of Art, New York; The Alfred Stieglitz Collection

Soul-catcher. Pukapuka, Cook Islands. Fiber, c. 40" (101.5 cm) high, variable. The Trustees of the British Museum, London. Reproduced in color, page 70

William Zorach. *The Young Boy.* 1921. Wood, 22½" (57.1 cm) high. Whitney Museum of American Art, New York; Promised 50th Anniversary Gift of Mr. and Mrs. Tessim Zorach

a central axis from the Primitive soul-catcher, recalling Stieglitz's appearance with his wire-rimmed glasses. Stieglitz, de Zayas realized, was not only America's foremost crusader for modern art, but also, as a photographer, a "soul catcher," according to the Primitive notion that a camera image captures a person's soul.

In fact Stieglitz's pioneering African show had been anticipated by an exhibition in Robert Coady's Washington Square Gallery; the latter had contained some examples of African art and had taken place shortly before the "291" show of November 1914.[48] Coady, who also exhibited European modern art, the work of American Negro children, and South Seas sculpture, crusaded for the recognition of the black contribution to American culture. In 1916–17, Coady published a magazine called *The Soil,* which served as a platform for his eccentric opinions regarding modern art in America. In *The Soil,* he juxtaposed reproductions of Primitive sculpture and photographs of industrial machinery and contemporary urban vistas, accompanying these incongruous pairings with typically iconoclastic statements.

About the same time, in October 1915, de Zayas, along with Paul Haviland, Francis Picabia, and Agnes Meyer, opened the Modern Gallery as an extension of Stieglitz's efforts. They showed modern art and photography along with examples of Primitive art, explaining their desire "to illustrate the relationship between these things and the art of today."[49] In *Camera Work* of October 1916, de Zayas published an essay called "Modern Art in Connection with Negro Art," and in that same year also published the book *African Negro Art: Its Influence on Modern Art.*[50] Here he argues that African art "has re-awakened in us the feeling for abstract form, it has brought into our art the means to express our purely sensorial feelings in regard to form, or to find new form in our ideas."[51] De Zayas also wrote the introduction to Charles Sheeler's folio book of photographs, *African Negro Wood Sculpture,* published in 1918, which illustrated works from the Modern Gallery—where important patrons of modern art, including John Quinn, Agnes Meyer, and Walter Arensberg, had purchased Primitive sculptures.[52]

Many of the early American modernist sculptors were influenced by Primitive and other non-Western art, particularly by African sculpture. Like the tribal artists—and unlike most sculptors since the Renaissance—most of them chose to work as direct carvers. As early as 1907, Robert Laurent had been taken by Frank Burty Haviland to visit Picasso's studio, where he later claimed to have seen African sculpture and not unre-

John Storrs. *Architectural Form.* c. 1923. Stone, 19¾ x 3¼ x 3" (50.2 x 8.2 x 7.6 cm). Robert Schoelkopf Gallery, New York

Headdress. Hopi. Arizona. Painted wood, fiber, and feathers, 24" (61 cm) high. Field Museum of Natural History, Chicago

lated work by Picasso himself.[53] After returning to America in 1910, Laurent began to carve wood reliefs influenced not only by Primitive art and Picasso but by carvings by Gauguin and Maillol that he had seen in Paris. About the same time, Max Weber modeled some tiny primitivist figures influenced more by his teacher Matisse's sculpture than by tribal works. William Zorach, who began to sculpt in 1917, purchased a copy of Sheeler's folio book of African sculpture and incorporated aspects of two Fang figures in his depiction of his son Tessim as *The Young Boy* of 1921; his enthusiasm for Primitive sculpture then prompted him to carve three works in mahogany brought back from Africa by a sea captain in Provincetown, Massachusetts.[54]

John Storrs found in American Indian art forms that he could utilize in his most abstract work, such as *Architectural Form* of about 1923. Storrs divided his time between France and America, and his interest in Indian art was probably enhanced by his friendship with Marsden Hartley, who visited him in France at his château near Orléans in 1921. Storrs subsequently visited Chicago's Field Museum of Natural History, and himself collected Navaho blankets, Indian ceramics, and other decorative objects. He saw in the geometric shapes, the zigzag and other motifs of Indian art, much that he was able to assimilate into his sculpture. *Architectural Form* has, for example, been compared to a Hopi headdress that has the same jagged step-motif and sense of vertical energy.[55] Storrs's interest in American Indian art corresponds to the association of his style with the Art Deco movement, which was much influenced by North American Indian as well as pre-Columbian art.[56]

Like Storrs, Alexander Calder divided his time between France and America. Calder may have become interested in non-Western and Primitive sculpture through José de Creeft, one of the first people he came to know after his arrival in Paris in 1926.[57] During 1928 and 1929, Calder experimented with carving primitivist figures in wood such as *African Head* and a *Female Figure* (p. 466).[58] This last figure was made in 1929 "as the mate for a South Pacific wood carving" in the Porcellian Club at Harvard, where Calder's friend Paul Nitze had been a member.[59] With distorted facial features, rigid posture, and pendulous breasts, she suggests Oceanic sculptures. Calder's primitivist figures, however, are related to earlier works by José de Creeft both in his choice of ebony or other exotic wood and in the forms themselves.

George L. K. Morris, who first painted American Indian imagery in 1929, encountered primitivism while studying in the spring of that year with Fernand Léger and Amédée Ozenfant in Paris at the Académie Moderne. Yet as early as 1928, while an undergraduate at Yale, Morris wrote of the need for a national tradition in American art: "...the only remote past this country knows is one of forest and Indians, and all the artist's material he must deliberately create."[60] The

Alexander Calder. *African Head.* 1928. Stained wood, 15⅛ x 5 x 7⅛" (38.4 x 12.7 x 18.1 cm). The Metropolitan Museum of Art, New York; gift of Charles Oppenheim, Jr.

Right: Alexander Calder. *Female Figure.* 1929. Wood, 25" (63.5 cm) high. Private collection

Jan Matulka. *Hopi Snake Dance, Number I.* 1917–18. Crayon, watercolor, and pencil, 15 x 12" (38.1 x 30.5 cm). Whitney Museum of American Art, New York; gift of Gertrude W. Dennis

following fall, Morris began to study at the Art Students League, where two of his teachers, John Sloan and Jan Matulka, had earlier developed an interest in the American Indian as subject matter for their painting. Matulka, a Czech immigrant who had traveled in New Mexico and Arizona, painted and sketched Hopi Indian dancers in 1917–18.[61] Sloan visited Santa Fe regularly from 1919 and developed an intense interest in Indian art and culture which affected many of his subsequent paintings. He helped organize the great Exposition of Indian Tribal Arts held at the Grand Central Art Galleries in New York in 1931–32, which treated the objects as art rather than as ethnological artifacts.

Morris's first painting with an Indian theme, *Battle of Indians No. 1*, painted in Lenox, Massachusetts, during the summer of 1929 just after his return from Paris, is more in Henri Rousseau's style than Léger's. After a second stint with Léger that fall, Morris began to assimilate his Cubism more fully. *Battle of Indians No. 2* of 1933 (p. 468) contains a more abstract, flat configuration not unlike Léger's work, but suggesting the forms of Kachinas.[62] Morris admired Léger's primitivism, as in the decor for *The Creation of the World*, calling him "the real primitive, the adventurer who draws upon his new horizon rather than on the talk of art."[63] He continued to explore the Indian theme in paintings of the thirties and early forties[64] and also constructed abstract collages utilizing birch bark, such as *Indians Fighting* of 1935, which contains fragments of bow and arrow images (p. 468). Traveling to Santa Fe, visiting pueblos and sketching interesting Indian motifs, Morris sought to take the best of native American art and the European idea of primitivism and forge a new artistic expression. "If an authentic American culture is to arise," insisted Morris, "we must go back to a beginning."[65]

Interest in Primitive art in America was fostered by several important publications of the twenties and thirties. In 1926, *Primitive Negro Sculpture* by Paul Guillaume and Thomas Munro was published with illustrations of works in the collection of the Barnes Foundation. Guillaume, the Paris dealer who had provided Marius de Zayas with works for the African sculpture exhibition at "291" in 1914, and Munro, a professor of modern art at the University of Pennsylvania gave consideration to African art's "relation to contemporary art" and saw it as offering a "compromise between representation and design."[66] Anthropologist Franz Boas's influential *Primitive Art*, first published in America in 1928, took issue with the then prevailing attitude that Primitive man's mental capacity was lower than that of Western man.[67] Boas, who endeavored to explain Primitive styles, focused on the art of Northwest Coast Indians; his book generated much interest in their art.

The book most influential in stimulating artists' interest in Primitive art was John Graham's *System and Dialectics of Art*, published in New York and Paris in 1937.[68] Graham, a painter who fled Russia in 1920, lived for a short time in Paris, where he met Eluard, Breton, and Picasso, among others. He kept in touch with many of his French friends during frequent transAtlantic visits after emigrating to America in November 1920. In time, Graham made friends with many of the younger artists, including Jackson Pollock, David Smith, Dorothy Dehner, Barnett Newman, Richard Pousette-Dart, and Adolph Gottlieb, all of whom developed some interest in tribal art. By the late twenties, Graham had already assembled a collection of African sculpture, which he enthusiastically

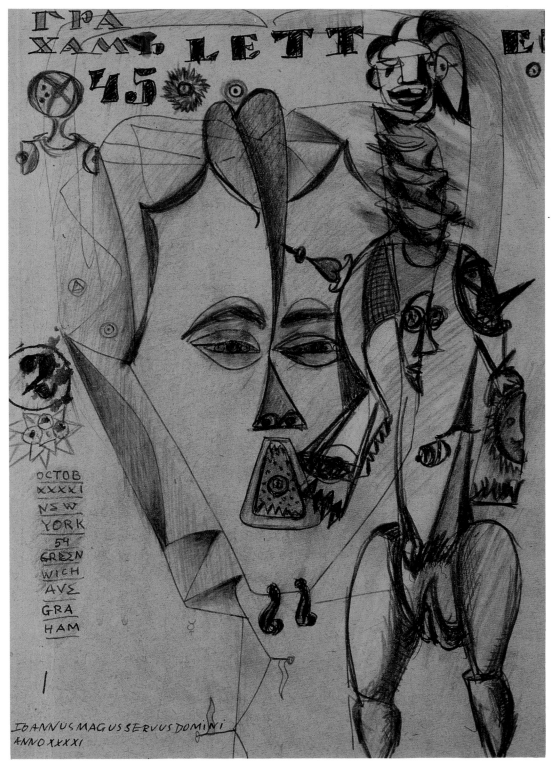

John Graham. Untitled. 1941. Ink, waterolor, pencil, and colored crayon, 12 x 9" (30.5 x 22.8 cm). Allan Stone Gallery, New York

showed to artist friends who visited his New York home and exhibited at the Dudensing Gallery in 1930. His intense involvement with Primitive art, which preceded The Museum of Modern Art's 1935 exhibition "African Negro Art," in combination with his connections in the Paris vanguard establishment, made him an important catalyst during the formative years of many artists later called Abstract Expressionists.

Acting also as a dealer, Graham purchased African sculp-ture for the noted collector Frank Crowninshield, and in the early thirties, at Graham's suggestion, Crowinshield arranged for David Smith to make bases to display his collection of African pieces. Dorothy Dehner recalled that on a trip to Paris in 1935, Graham took her and David Smith to four exhibitions of African art on the day of their arrival.[69] That same year Adolph Gottlieb bought several examples of African sculpture from Paris dealers recommended by Graham.[70]

George L. K. Morris. *Battle of Indians No. 2*. 1933. Oil on canvas, 28 x 64″ (71.1 x 162.6 cm). Estate of the artist

Graham's attitude toward tribal art was more sociologically and anthropologically enlightened than many of its early admirers. "Primitive art," he stated, "is a highly developed art *as a result of a great civilization based on principles different from those of the white man's civilization.*"[71] Elsewhere Graham, who described African art as "singularly perfect in its plastic and emotional form," saw the tribal artists as the direct precursors of abstraction: "African artists were never seduced by the desire to imitate or compete with nature, as they had, more than a thousand years before, travelled the long road from realism and exact representation to abstraction—a journey which we ourselves are only just ending."[72] Graham's significant role in encouraging interest in Primitive art during the twenties and thirties was complex. He dealt with Primitive art as a collector, dealer, writer, and artist. A 1941 drawing of his (p. 467), for example, demonstrates his fascination with both an African figure and a mask. For Graham, Primitive art was a rich new point of departure, and the enthusiasm he shared with so many others had a lasting impact.

For many American artists, the Indian, the African, and even, by extension, the black American became symbols of an earlier, less corrupt age. The directness and simplicity of the Primitive art they created was perceived by modernist visual artists as a valid path to a more honest and less decadent means of expression—the "universal idea" about which Hartley had written to Stieglitz. Kandinsky, in his treatise *The Art of Spiritual Harmony*, published in English in 1914, had written of the modern artist's sympathy with "the Primitives" because of the mutual desire "to express in their work only internal truths, renouncing in consequence all consideration of external form."[73] Marius de Zayas maintained that rather than naturalistic representation in art, and even mechanical representation through photography, "Negro art has made us discover the possibility of giving plastic expression to the sensation produced by the outer life, and consequently also, the possibility of finding new forms to express our inner life."[74]

George L. K. Morris. *Indians Fighting*. 1935. Watercolor, torn-paper and birch-bark collage, 17⅜ x 13″ (44.2 x 33 cm). Meredith Long & Co., Houston

Kandinsky also noted: "The nightmare of materialism, which has turned the life of the universe into an evil, useless game, is not yet past; it holds the awakening soul still in its grip."[75] It was in part this struggle to counteract the growing sense of alienation and sterility in modern society that led so many American artists to investigate the Primitive.

NOTES

1. For information on Dow, see Frederick C. Moffatt, *Arthur Wesley Dow (1857–1922)* (Washington, D.C.: National Collection of Fine Arts, Smithsonian Institution Press, 1977). For information on Fenollosa, see Lawrence W. Chisolm, *Fenollosa: The Far East and American Culture* (New Haven: Yale University Press, 1963).

2. Quoted from an account of the 1902 session of the Ipswich Summer School of Art by Sylvester Baxter, "Handicraft and Its Extension at Ipswich," *Handicraft* 1 (February 1903), pp. 253–54.

3. Moffatt, *Dow*, pp. 93–95. See also Frank Hamilton Cushing, *My Adventures in Zuni*, reprinted from *The Century Illustrated Monthly Magazine*, 1882–83 (Santa Fe: Peripatetic Press, 1941). Baxter, "Handicraft," discussed Cushing and his impact on Dow: "Cushing had this faculty of assuming the primitive attitude towards life and art.... By scrutinizing and studying an object of primitive handicraft he would follow by most intricate trails back into the past the indications thus given, learning just the processes by which it was made, and then, in reproducing it just as its makers wrought it, he would learn the equivalent of written volumes about an ancient and long-vanished people."

4. Max Weber, interviews by Carol S. Gruber, January–March 1958, the Oral History Collection of Columbia University, pp. 73–74. Leo Stein had already acquired his first Cézanne by the time Weber arrived in Paris. Stein's trip to Japan in 1895 had begun his interest in Japanese prints. In my research on Weber, I am especially grateful to Joy Weber, the artist's daughter, for invaluable help. Bella Fishko of the Forum Gallery also deserves my sincere thanks.

5. Max Weber, "Rousseau As I Knew Him," September 7, 1942, unpublished manuscript, artist's file, Whitney Museum of American Art, New York, pp. 1–2: "'Here,' I said to myself, 'is a man, an artist, a poet whose friendship and advice I must cultivate and cherish.'" For an excellent analysis of the relationship of these two artists, see Sandra E. Leonard, *Henri Rousseau and Max Weber* (New York: Richard L. Feigen, 1970).

6. Alfred H. Barr, Jr., *Matisse: His Art and His Public* (New York: Museum of Modern Art, 1951), p. 139. Max Weber, "The Matisse Class," unpublished manuscript read before Matisse Symposium, Museum of Modern Art, November 19, 1951, p. 13, MoMA Archives, reported that Matisse occasionally took his students to his studio and showed them, among other things, his collection of African Negro sculpture: "Matisse was very proud of his small but very choice collection of African Negro sculpture, and this was before Negro sculpture overwhelmed, if not conquered, the art of the continent. He would take a figurine in his hands, and point out to us the authentic and instinctive sculpturesque qualities, such as the marvelous workmanship, the unique sense of proportion, the supple palpitating fullness of form and equilibrium in them." Patrick Henry Bruce, another American student of Matisse, also developed an interest in African art and eventually amassed a large collection of it. Henri-Pierre Roché recalled Bruce's "Negro objects" and noted that "he was beginning to collect Negro statuettes and instruments, including surprising stone pestles, for women's hands, that were directly erotic." Quoted in William C. Agee and Barbara Rose, *Patrick Henry Bruce: American Modernist* (New York: Museum of Modern Art, 1979), p. 223.

7. Weber, "Rousseau As I Knew Him," pp. 21–22. In November Picasso showed Weber Rousseau's *Portrait of a Woman*, which he had just bought in a secondhand shop.

8. Ibid., pp. 23–24.

9. Ibid., pp. 24–25. Weber noted: "The art of the African Negro was destined to exert the most powerful influence upon the modern art movement, and collecting examples of Negro sculpture became the passionate hobby of art students and collectors alike, not only in Paris but all over the world."

10. Max Weber, "A loaned collection of some lithographs by Manet, Cézanne, Renoir and Toulouse-Lautrec; a few drawings by Rodin; and smaller paintings and drawings by Henri Rousseau," "291," November 18 to December, 1910. Weber's preface was reprinted in *Camera Work* 33 (January 1911), in "Photo-Secession Notes," p. 46.

11. Percy North, *Max Weber: American Modern* (New York: The Jewish Museum, 1982), p. 28. North suggests that in 1910 Weber "introduced primitive figurines into two notable gouaches [also *Mexican Statuette*] as a means of dramatizing the distinctions between two- and three-dimensional media." Weber first exhibited this work as *Congo Statuette* at his one-man show at "291" in January 1911.

12. Max Weber, "The Fourth Dimension from a Plastic Point of View," *Camera Work* 31 (July 1910), p. 25.

13. Max Weber, "Chinese Dolls and Modern Colorists," *Camera Work* 31 (July 1910), p. 51.

14. Weber, Oral History, p. 94.

15. Max Weber, "To Xochipilli, Lord of Flowers," *Camera Work* 33 (January 1911), p. 34.

16. Max Weber, *Cubist Poems* (London: Elkin Mathews, 1914).

17. Ibid., p. 14.

18. "Woodcuts and Poems by Max Weber," The Art Students League News, October 15, 1948, p. 2. Max Weber, *Primitives: Poems and Woodcuts* (New York: Spiral Press, 1926).

19. Marsden Hartley to Alfred Stieglitz, July 1912, The Alfred Stieglitz Archives, Beinecke Rare Book and Manuscript Library, Yale University, New Haven, Connecticut (hereafter cited as Yale). M. T. H. Sadler, "After Gauguin," *Rhythm, Art, Music, Literature* 1 (Spring 1912), pp. 23–24. For a discussion of the influence of Kandinsky on Hartley, see Gail Levin, "Marsden Hartley, Kandinsky, and Der Blaue Reiter," *Arts Magazine*, November 1977, pp. 156–60.

20. Hartley to Stieglitz, October 9, 1912, Yale.

21. Hartley sent a second copy of the almanac to Stieglitz and repeatedly stressed its importance. See undated postcard from Hartley to Stieglitz, early September 1912, and postcard of September 27, 1912, Yale.

22. Hartley to Stieglitz, September 1, 1912, Yale.

23. For a similar Acoma pot, see Larry Frank and Francis H. Harlow, *Historic Pottery of the Pueblo Indians, 1600–1880* (Boston: New York Graphic Society, 1974), plate 14, Trios Polychrome Storage Jar, c. 1860. See Paul S. Wingert, *American Indian Sculpture* (New York: Hacker Art Books, 1976), plate 1a, for a similar Kwakiutl figure.

24. Hartley to Stieglitz, letter of mid-November 1912; details of this meeting on January 24, 1913, are recorded in a postcard and in an eighteen-page letter that Hartley sent to Stieglitz in early February after his return to Paris (Yale).

25. Stieglitz to Hartley, October 20, 1913, Yale.

26. *Camera Work* 1 (January 1903), p. 14. For a discussion of this work, see Nancy Corson Carter, "The Inner Circle: Portraits in Alfred Stieglitz's *Camera Work*" (Ph.D. diss., University of Iowa, 1972), pp. 101–17. Joseph T. Keiley, "Gertrude Käsebier," *Camera Work* 20 (October 1907), p. 27, commented on Käsebier's sincerity resulting from her impressions of Indians formed during her childhood in Colorado.

27. Paul Rosenfeld, a critic, noted that "the poor Indian" had, until recent times, been the only American to have developed a "feeling for the earth," and he celebrated the Indian's dances and rituals which put him "in harmony with nature"; see Paul Rosenfeld, *Port of New York* (Urbana: University of Illinois, 1961), p. 94. William Carlos Williams's *In the American Grain* tells how Daniel Boone came to understand the necessity "to be *Himself* in a new world, Indianlike. If the land were to be possessed it must be as the Indian possessed it ... the flower of his world" (New York: New Directions, 1925, pp. 137–38). Mabel Dodge, bohemian hostess to leading writers and artists, led the way to Taos, New Mexico, where she eventually married Tony Luhan, an American Indian, as her fourth and last husband. She then lobbied for various Indian issues through the Bureau of Indian Affairs; see Emily Hahn, *Mabel: A Biography of Mabel Dodge Luhan* (Boston: Houghton Mifflin, 1977), pp. 209–10.

28. This point was well elaborated upon by Ann Tempkin in "Marsden Hartley's America: 1914 Indian Compositions," a paper delivered at the Sixth Annual Whitney Symposium on American Art, April 25, 1983, Whitney Museum of American Art, New York. I had previously submitted my own photographs and conclusions about the Indian art Hartley saw in Berlin (as described in this essay) to the editor of this book. Tempkin's findings concurred with my own only on Plains Indian art. She ignored the equally significant influence of the Hopi Kachinas on Hartley. We agree in general that Plains motifs were important for Hartley; however, the specific examples that I propose are entirely drawn from the collection of the Museum für Völkerkunde that Hartley saw on exhibition in Berlin in 1914.

29. August Macke, "Masks," in *Der Blaue Reiter*, edited by Wassily Kandinsky and Franz Marc, reprinted as *The Blaue Reiter Almanac* documentary edition edited by Klaus Lankheit (New York: Viking Press, 1974), pp. 83–89.

30. Hartley to Stieglitz, October 31, 1913, Yale, quoted in Levin, "Marsden Hartley, Kandinsky, and Der Blaue Reiter," p. 160. For a discussion of the broader context of Kandinsky's influence on Hartley, see Sandra Gail Levin, "Wassily Kandinsky and the American Avant-garde, 1912–1950" (Ph.D. diss., Rutgers University, 1976), pp. 79–140.

31. Over six thousand objects were lost or destroyed during World War II. I am extremely grateful to Dr. Horst Hartmann of the Museum für Völkerkunde for this information and for his expert guidance in my research on the Berlin Collection of North American Indian Art.

32. Hartley would have seen these eight-pointed stars on an anonymous European religious painting reproduced in *Der Blaue Reiter*, p. 167. Hartley, in a letter to Stieglitz, August 1913 (Yale), referred to the eight-pointed star that he saw "everywhere in Berlin...all the kings wore it over their heart—the soldier on the forehead." Arnold Rönnebeck in a letter to Duncan Phillips dated after 1943 (Yale), referred to Hartley's interest in the Iron Cross given to Rönnebeck and his cousin, Karl von Freyburg, for distinguished wartime service.

33. This wooden sculpture was lost or destroyed during World War II. *Der Blaue Reiter*, documentary edition, p. 88.

34. Hartley to Stieglitz, November 3, 1914, Yale. Hartley's last works influenced by Primitive art are abstract paintings from 1925 based on African textiles. (Reproduced as plates 17 A and B in *Marsden Hartley 1877–1943*, C. W. Post Art Gallery, Greenvale, Long Island, November 6–December 14, 1977.)

35. Hartley to Stieglitz, November 12, 1914 (misdated 1913), Yale.

36. Marsden Hartley, "Red Man Ceremonials: An American Plea for American Esthetics," *Art and Archaeology* 9, January 1920, p. 14. For a discussion of the influence of European modern art on Hartley, see Gail Levin, "Marsden Hartley and the European Avant-Garde," *Arts Magazine* 54, September 1979, pp. 158–63.

37. Marsden Hartley, "The Red Man," in *Adventures in the Arts* (New York: Boni and Liveright, 1921), p. 20. Here Hartley referred to the chieftain's cape from Alaska, probably Tlingit (Chilcat) tribe, reproduced in *Der Blaue Reiter*.

38. Ibid., p. 26. Hartley's writings about Indian art

Opposite: Kifwebe mask. Luba. Zaire. Painted wood and mixed media, 17¼″ (43.8 cm) high. Seattle Art Museum; Katherine White Collection

Above: Alexander Calder. *Moonlight in a Gust of Wind* (detail). 1966. Color lithograph, 18¾ x 25⅝″ (47.5 x 65 cm). Private collection, New York

Right: Alexander Calder. *Head with Earrings*. 1950. India ink, 22½ x 15½″ (57.1 x 39.4 cm). Perls Galleries, New York

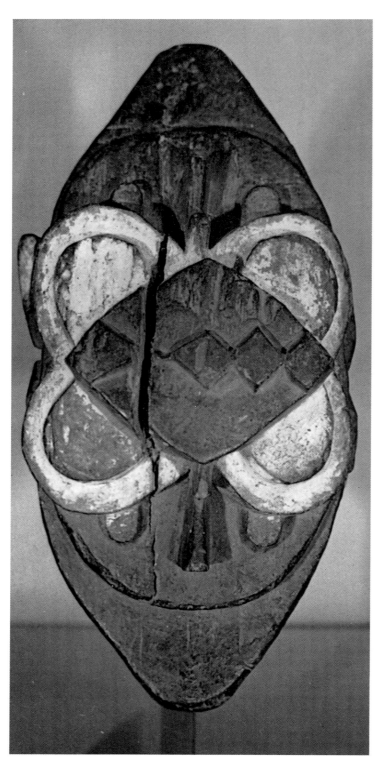

Mask (two views). Igbo. Nigeria. Painted wood, 15" (38.1 cm) high. Collection Mr. and Mrs. Joseph Herman, London

must have had considerable influence. See also Marsden Hartley, "Tribal Esthetics," *The Dial*, November 16, 1918, p. 6.

39. Man Ray, *Self-Portrait* (Boston: Little, Brown, 1963), p. 75. The time described in this memoir was about 1917, when he took up painting with an airbrush. My discussions of Man Ray with Francis Naumann have contributed to this interpretation.

40. This and the following quotation are from a questionnaire Man Ray completed about his painting *Five Figures* (1914) at the time it was acquired by The Whitney Museum of American Art, March 23, 1957.

41. Paul Avrich, *The Modern School Movement: Anarchism and Education in the United States* (Princeton: Princeton University Press, 1980), p. 155. Avrich states that Weber began to frequent the Ferrer Center in 1912 after having been introduced to it by Robert Henri. In June 1913, Weber was the speaker at the third anniversary dinner of the Ferrer Center. His poetry and woodcuts were published in *The Modern School* magazine. Man Ray, *Self-Portrait*, pp. 21–25, recounts his participation in evening life-classes and in the social scene at the Ferrer Center during this same period.

42. Man Ray, *Self-Portrait*, p. 23.

43. Ibid., p. 54.

44. Ibid., pp. 74–75, and p. 18 for his recollection of seeing African art at "291," and pp. 74–75 for his admission that he attempted to persude his wife to wear a leopard skin by arguing that as "primitive and savage art was influencing moderns in all countries; to wear this would make her look more original."

45. De Zayas to Stieglitz, April 21, 1911. Yale.

46. Quoted in William Innes Homer, *Alfred Stieglitz and the American Avant-Garde* (Boston: New York Graphic Society, 1977), pp. 198–99. *Camera Work* 48 (October 1916), p. 13, reprinted Charles H. Caffin's account from the *New York American* quoting the organizers that "this is the first time in the history of exhibitions that Negro statuary has been shown from the point of view of art." For de Zayas's own account of this and other African art exhibitions in New York, see Marius de Zayas, "How, When, and Why Modern Art Came to New York," introduction and notes by Francis M. Naumann, *Arts Magazine* 54, April 1980, pp. 109–12. I wish to thank Francis Naumann for his helpful suggestions pertaining to de Zayas and Primitive art. De Zayas explained, p. 109, that he met Paul Guillaume through Guillaume Apollinaire, whom he had earlier met through Picabia.

47. De Zayas, "How, When, and Why," p. 114. For a thorough analysis of de Zayas's caricatures and their important impact on Picabia and others, see Willard Bohn, "The Abstract Vision of Marius de Zayas," *The Art Bulletin* 62, September 1980, pp. 434–52. My discussion of de Zayas's adaptation of the Pukapuka soul-catcher that follows is based on Bohn's analysis.

48. Coady had met Max Weber in Paris, and through him, Henri Rousseau. He also knew the Steins. See Judith K. Zilczer, "Robert J. Coady, Forgotten Spokesman for Avant-Garde Culture in America," *American Art Review* 2 (1975), pp. 77–89. Coady showed African sculpture in his gallery as early as the spring of 1914.

49. Original announcement circular for the opening of the Modern Gallery, 500 Fifth Avenue, on October 7, 1915, reprinted in *Camera Work* 48 (October 1916), p. 63, as "'291' and the Modern Gallery." Important exhibitions of African art were held at the Modern Gallery in 1916 and in 1918; for reviews, see de Zayas, "How, When, and Why," pp. 110–12.

50. Marius de Zayas, "Modern Art in Connection with Negro Art," *Camera Work* 48 (October 1916), p. 7. Marius de Zayas, *African Negro Art: Its Influence on Modern Art* (New York: Modern Gallery, 1916). For a discussion of the development of de Zayas's ideas on African art, see Judith Zilczer, "Primitivism and

New York Dada," *Arts Magazine* 51, May 1977, pp. 140–42. De Zayas, who viewed Africans as intellectually inferior, childlike savages, was not aware of more accurate anthropological opinions.

51. De Zayas, *African Negro Art*, p. 41.

52. Sheeler published only twenty-two copies of this book, but it was owned by several artists, including Weber and Zorach. B. L. Reid, *The Man From New York: John Quinn and His Friends* (New York: Oxford University Press, 1968), p. 556–57. For example, by 1922, Quinn's "interest in Oriental, African, and Polynesian art and artifacts continued, but mainly among the ancestors of the modern." In June 1922 Quinn bought an African Primitive torso with a stone base for $875 from Marius de Zayas. For Primitive art in the Arensberg Collection, see Francis Naumann, "Walter Conrad Arensberg: Poet, Patron, and Participant in the New York Avant-garde, 1915–20," *Philadelphia Museum of Art Bulletin* 76, Spring 1980, pp. 8–10, which reproduces Sheeler's photographs of the interior of the Arensberg apartment in New York, c. 1918, showing African and Aztec sculpture. Naumann noted of Arensberg, p. 10: "On opposite ends of the mantlepiece, for example, he placed Brancusi's *Prodigal Son* and an African figure, suggesting not only a comparison of material—both being wooden carvings mounted on gray stone bases—but also their tendencies toward a common abstraction of form. It was from de Zayas in 1915 that Arensberg purchased his first Pre-Columbian sculpture."

53. Roberta K. Tarbell, "Sculpture in America before the Armory Show: Transition to Modern," in *Vanguard American Sculpture, 1913–1939* (New Brunswick, N.J.: Rutgers University Art Gallery, 1979), p. 4. See also chap. 4, pp. 45–46, Roberta K. Tarbell, "Direct Carving," for a survey of these American sculptors. There is reason to doubt the accuracy of Laurent's recollections. See Peter V. Moak, "Robert Laurent (1890–1970)," in *The Robert Laurent Memorial Exhibition* (Durham: University of New Hampshire, 1972), p. 15, who notes that Burty introduced Laurent to Picasso in 1906 and that he admired Rose Period paintings. While it is possible that Laurent did correctly recall seeing African sculpture at Picasso's in 1907 (as Tarbell states) before he left for Italy, he later admitted he had invented the much-publicized story that he studied in Rome with a wood carver named Giuseppe Doratori. Rosamund Frost, "Laurent: Frames to Figures, Brittany to Brooklyn," *Art News*, April 1–14, 1941, p. 10, states that Laurent met Picasso in 1905 and admired the work of the Blue Period.

54. Tarbell, "Direct Carving," pp. 51–52. See William Zorach, *Art Is My Life: An Autobiography* (Cleveland: World Publishing Co., 1967), p. 66. "I was interested in primitive art. When we first came to New York I had seen the sculpture of the Aztecs and the Mayans and the carving of the Eskimos in the Museum of Natural History. At '291,' Stieglitz's gallery, I saw De Zayas' exhibition of African sculpture. It had an extraordinary magic and spiritual quality that is unequaled.... Charles Sheeler made a marvelous set of photographs of this sculpture. I could at least have them through Sheeler's book. It cost fifty dollars. I could barely scrape the money together but I bought the book." Zorach recalled incorrectly that he had sculpted Tessim in the African mahogany. Paul S. Wingert, *The Sculpture of William Zorach* (New York: Pitman, 1938), p. 20, mentions that *Young Boy* was carved in Provincetown from maplewood that Zorach brought back from California and discusses his interest in African sculpture and its influence on his work. Zorach carved the three works in mahogany in 1922.

55. See Jeffrey Wechsler, "Machine Aesthetics and Art Deco," in *Vanguard American Sculpture, 1913–1939*, p. 102, who cites Noel Frackman's findings in her unpublished study "John Storrs and the Origins of Art Deco," qualifying paper, Institute of Fine Arts,

New York University, 1975, p. 32.

56. Bevis Hillier, *The World of Art Deco* (New York: E. P. Dutton, 1971), pp. 28–32.

57. Alexander Calder, *Calder: An Autobiography with Pictures* (Boston: Beacon Press, 1966), p. 80. José de Creeft sculpted an abstract limestone carving, *Voyage to Africa* in 1927; see plates 261–62 in Jules Campos, *José de Creeft* (New York: Kennedy Graphics/Da Capo Press, 1972).

58. Calder started carving in 1926 before he went to Paris, but the earliest carved works seem to have been inspired by American folk art rather than Primitive sculpture. I am grateful to Joan M. Marter for sharing with me her excellent research on early Calder. See Joan M. Marter, "Interaction of American Sculptors with European Modernists: Alexander Calder and Isamu Noguchi," in *Vanguard American Sculpture, 1913–1939*, pp. 106–7; Joan M. Marter, "Alexander Calder, the Formative Years" (Ph.D. diss., University of Delaware, 1974).

59. Calder, *Autobiography*, pp. 107–8.

60. George L. K. Morris, "Contemporary Writers, British and Americans," *The Yale Literary Magazine* 93 (March 1928), pp. 103–15, quoted in Melinda A. Lorenz, *George L. K. Morris: Artist and Critic* (Ann Arbor: UMI Research Press, 1982), p. 5.

61. Matulka also collected African and other Primitive masks, which he included in his still-life compositions during the early 1930s. See *Jan Matulka 1890–1972* (Washington, D.C.: Smithsonian Institution Press, 1980), pp. 66–67 and 72.

62. Lorenz, *George L. K. Morris*, p. 13.

63. George L. K. Morris, "Fernand Léger versus Cubism," *Bulletin of the Museum of Modern Art* 1, October 1935, p. 7.

64. For an excellent analysis of some of these, especially *Indians Hunting No. 4*, see Nicolai Cikovsky, Jr., "Notes and Footnotes on a Painting by George L. K. Morris," *University of New Mexico Art Museum Bulletin* 10, 1976–77, p. 6.

65. Morris quoted in Lorenz, *George L. K. Morris*, p. 11.

66. Paul Guillaume and Thomas Munro, *Primitive Negro Sculpture* (New York: Harcourt, Brace, 1926), p. 133. Guillaume's role in promoting African art was discussed by Clive Bell in an essay, "Negro Sculpture," reprinted in Clive Bell, *Since Cézanne* (New York: Harcourt, Brace, 1922), pp. 113–21. Bell also mentioned the impact of African sculpture on modern French artists.

67. Franz Boas, *Primitive Art* (Cambridge, Mass.: Harvard University Press, 1928). Boas had earlier expressed enthusiasm for the art of Northwest Coast Indians in "Representative Art of Primitive People," in *Holmes Anniversary Volume* (Washington, D.C.: Bryan Press, 1916). For a group of artists who became fascinated with Northwest Coast Indian art during the 1940s, see Ann Gibson, "Painting outside the Paradigm: Indian Space," *Arts Magazine* 57, February 1983, pp. 98–104.

68. John Graham, *Systems and Dialectics of Art* (New York: Delphic Studios, 1937); reprint edition, *John Graham's System and Dialectics of Art*, with introduction by Marcia Epstein Allentuck (Baltimore: Johns Hopkins Press, 1971).

69. Ibid., foreword by Dorothy Dehner, pp. xviii–xix.

70. Mary Davis MacNaughton, "Adolph Gottlieb: His Life and Art," in *Adolph Gottlieb: A Retrospective* (New York: The Arts Publisher, 1981), p. 20.

71. Graham, *System and Dialectics*, p. 116. Italics are my own.

72. John Graham, preface to *Exhibition of Sculptures of Old African Civilizations*, Jacques Seligmann Gallery, New York, 1936, quoted in Allentuck, *John Graham's System and Dialectics of Art*, p. 76.

73. Wassily Kandinsky, *The Art of Spiritual Harmony*, trans. Michael Sadlier (London and Boston: Constable, 1914), p. 1. For a discussion of the important influence of Kandinsky's ideas in America, see Levin, "Wassily Kandinsky and the American Avant-garde, 1912–1950."

74. De Zayas, "How, When, and Why," p. 109.

75. Kandinsky, *The Art of Spiritual Harmony*, p. 2.

Fernand Léger. *Bird.* (Costume design for *The Creation of the World.*) 1923. Watercolor, 13⅜ x 9″ (34 x 22.7 cm). Dansmuseet, Stockholm

LEGER
"THE CREATION OF THE WORLD"

Laura Rosenstock

Parisian society after World War I manifested a growing fascination with both African and black American art and culture, the two tending to be confused in the popular mind. The appeal of African sculpture and American Negro jazz and dancing influenced a variety of levels of Parisian culture, including entertainment, fashion, and interior design.

The extent of these preoccupations is perhaps best exemplified by the Ballets Suédois's 1923 production of *The Creation of the World*. The decor and costumes by Fernand Léger were developed from the artist's drawings after African art; the scenario by Blaise Cendrars was based on African myths; the choreography by Jean Börlin involved him in research into the ethnography of African civilizations; and the music by Darius Milhaud was inspired by the jazz the composer had recently heard in New York. It would be, wrote Léger, "the only possible ballet nègre in the entire world," one that would "remain as a model of the genre."[1]

At the time of *The Creation of the World*, the burgeoning vogue of black culture was reaching its apex in Paris. "Art nègre" had been of interest to vanguard artists in Paris since 1906. But it was virtually unknown to the public until after World War I. Before 1919 there were only a few scattered gallery exhibitions containing African sculpture. Then in May 1919, an exhibition of Primitive art entitled Première Exposition d'Art Nègre et d'Art Océanien was organized by Paul Guillaume at the Galerie Devambez in Paris. Guillaume also arranged a "Fête Nègre" in conjunction with it.[2] While the claim that it was the "first" such show was not quite accurate, this exhibition propelled African art toward the larger audience it soon found. Numerous colonial expositions would further augment this interest. In addition, several writers have associated African art's sudden popularity in Paris in the twenties with the presence of Senegalese and Zouave troops that had been brought to France to fight in World War I.[3] Whatever the immediate catalysts were for this trend, it was certainly a reflection of a widespread desire for fresh new art forms that would be more direct, natural, and unrestrained than those of prewar culture.

Vanguard activities in performance, theater, and ballet provided the types of new experiences the public was seeking. From 1917 to 1926 the participation of modern painters in theater and ballet design was greater than at any other time before or since; theater had become the main preoccupation of the day. "There has never been an epoch as frantic for spectacle as ours. The rush of masses toward the screen or the stage is an unending phenomenon," wrote Léger.[4] During this period, theater more than any other art form was responsible for introducing the avant-garde movements to a wide public. Just as Picasso's decor for *Parade* had exposed popular audiences to certain Cubist ideas, so theater familiarized the public with Dada and, later, with Surrealism, movements particularly oriented toward the popularization of Primitive culture.

The Dadaists, and to a lesser extent the Futurists, had looked for inspiration to the sounds and the dance of tribal societies, Africa in particular. "African Nights" were organized at the Cabaret Voltaire in Zurich in 1916 with Richard Huelsenbeck chanting his "authentic" Negro poems (each ending in shouts of "Umba, umba") to the accompaniment of a tom-tom. Huelsenbeck describes these evenings: "Together we created a wonderful Negro singsong with clappers,

475

Above: Paul Colin. *La Revue nègre at the Théâtre des Champs-Elysées*. 1926. Color lithograph, 61 x 46½" (155 x 118 cm). Musée de la Publicité, Paris

Left: Photograph of "The Great Savage," a life-size marionette designed by Fortunato Depero for his and Gilbert Clavel's ballet, *Plastic Dances*, 1918

wooden mallets, and many primitive instruments...our Cubist dances with masks by Janco (p. 537) and homemade costumes of colored cardboard and tinsel."[5] Hugo Ball prepared a soirée at the Galerie Dada: "I am rehearsing a new dance with five Laban-ladies as negresses in long black caftans and face masks."[6] Tristan Tzara, the main force behind the Dada interest in Africa (he published some forty "African poems,"[7] wrote articles comparing Primitive and Western art, and lectured on African sculpture) interspersed pseudo-African words such as "Dschilolu Mgabati Bailunda" or "Soco Bgai Affahou" in his 1916 play *La Première Aventure céleste de M. Antipyrine*.

It was not surprising that Dada primitivism usually took the form of "African" sounds and rhythms, since such performance was an aural as much as a visual expression. There were, however, isolated instances of African-inspired plastic efforts in both the Dada and Futurist movements. Fortunato Depero and Gilbert Clavel's *Plastic Dances*, presented in Rome in 1918 at the Teatro dei Piccoli, revolved around Depero's "The Great Savage," a wood figure taller than a man which, like African sculpture, displayed (in Depero's parody) such accouterments as a headcrest, staff, nose ring, and protruding navel. Marcel Janco's drawing of two Negro figures likewise recalls African art (p. 536).

While Dada and its publications remained virtually unknown in Paris until 1919, an "African" setting for the

Parisian theater had, nevertheless, already been established in Apollinaire's *Les Mamelles de Tirésias*, performed in June 1917, in which one actor was cast as "the people of Zanzibar." This mute character was supplied with a selection of noisemakers.

Black American culture also became popular at this time as a result of the arrival in Paris of waves of Americans who in the 1920s constituted the largest group of foreigners in the city. While American ragtime and cakewalk music had first become known in Europe around 1900 (John Philip Sousa himself played this music in Paris in 1903), the widespread vogue for American black culture—its revues, entertainers, and jazz—became a phenomenon only after the war.

Jazz had been introduced to Europe partly through American soliders stationed there during the war, by radio broadcasts, and by Dixieland albums recorded in 1917 by the U.S. Victor company. Louis Mitchell's orchestra, featuring Sidney Bechet, was the first black jazz band to arrive and remain in Europe, and it was followed in 1917 by the appearance of other black jazz musicians. By 1918 black American orchestras were playing at the Casino de Paris and at parties and numerous social events. Possibly the first private soirée to feature American jazz occurred at the home of Etienne de Beaumont in August 1918. The entertainment, described as a "great Negro fête," included a performance of Francis Poulenc's *Rhapsodie nègre*, as well as jazz played by American Negro soldiers. Many more jazz bands followed in 1919, and in 1921 the Théâtre des

Champs-Elysées presented The Most Famous American Southern Syncopated Orchestra, which performed a varied program featuring spirituals and jazz drumming demonstrations.

The rage culminated in the stardom of Josephine Baker. As recounted in her autobiography, it was Fernand Léger who had suggested to Rolf de Maré that he bring a black troupe from New York to Paris. De Maré was director/manager of the Théâtre des Champs-Elysées, which functioned as an opera-and-music hall following the disbanding of the Ballets Suédois in 1925. *La Revue nègre*, produced by Caroline Dudley, was consequently brought from America and opened in Paris in October 1925. It introduced Josephine Baker, who virtually overnight became a European legend.[8] Artists responded to new black fashions and personally feted Baker. Paul Colin depicted *La Revue nègre* in his posters; Alexander Calder's first fully realized all-wire sculpture is probably a 1926 figure of Josephine Baker.[9]

This enthusiasm for black culture was reflected in film as well. The film *Princess Tam-Tam* (1935) starred Josephine Baker cast as an African native girl who comes to Paris where she is passed off as a "princess" and becomes the toast of fashionable Paris. Even earlier, Jean Renoir's silent fantasy/satire *Charleston*, made in 1927, imagined a black African (portrayed by Johnny Hudgins, star of *La Revue nègre*) coming to Europe in the year 2028 when European civilization had died and encountering a white "aborigine" (Catherine Hessling) dancing the Charleston. Society party scenes in films such as Marcel L'Herbier's *L'Inhumaine* (1923) had commonly depicted black actors as the featured entertainers.

Vanguard artists reflected in their creative efforts their own captivation with black American culture, especially jazz. In New York in 1913, Picabia painted *Negro Song I* and *II* after reportedly hearing Negro songs in a restaurant. Gleizes painted his *Jazz* in New York in 1915, and Cocteau wrote to him there in 1918 to ask him to send some examples of "Negro ragtimes" from New York.[10] The expatriate American painter Gerald Murphy had the latest jazz records sent to him regularly while living in France. In their home on the Riviera, Murphy and his wife entertained friends by singing American Negro folk songs and spirituals, including some unpublished songs they had discovered in libraries.

The first treatment of jazz in serious French music was Erik Satie's score for the 1917 Ballets Russes production of *Parade*,

Set of *The Creation of the World.* Decor and costumes by Fernand Léger. Photograph. 1923. Dansmuseet, Stockholm

Fernand Léger. Study for *The Creation of the World.* c. 1922. Gouache, 11¼ x 17½" (28.5 x 44.5 cm). Private collection

which is animated by jazz rhythms and music hall tunes. His borrowings from jazz are particularly pronounced in the music entitled "Steamship Rag" ("Ragtime du paquebot"), which accompanied the dance of the character called the "Little American Girl" while she mimed the actions of catching a train, driving a car, swimming, acting in a movie, and foiling a bank robbery. At one point, this character imitated Charlie Chaplin's walk set to a passage of syncopated melody and rhythm.[11]

Stravinsky, too, was influenced by the new sound. He had received some ragtime sheet music from the composer Ernest Ansermet during World War I and included a tango, waltz, and ragtime in his score for *Histoire du soldat* in 1918. His *Ragtime*, composed that same year, attempted to raise popular dance music to the status of concert music. And his *Piano Rag Music*, composed in 1919, after Stravinsky had finally heard live jazz bands, conveyed his interest in the rhythmic principles and improvisational nature of jazz.

In Paris after World War I some young composers gathered around Satie, reportedly giving performances among the African sculptures in Paul Guillaume's gallery.[12] Jean Cocteau, who wrote admiringly of American jazz in his 1918 pamphlet *Le Coq et l'harlequin*, was their poet-publicist. These composers—Georges Auric, Louis Durey, Arthur Honegger, Francis Poulenc, Germaine Tailleferre, and Darius Milhaud—were later baptized "Les Six" by the critic Henri Collet. According to Milhaud, Satie was their mascot.

Beginning in February 1921 Cocteau and Les Six frequented

the Bar Gaya, where the pianist Jean Wiener played jazz with the black American saxophonist Vance Lowry. There, and at its later incarnation, the nightclub known as Le Boeuf sur le Toit, Cocteau, Milhaud, and Picabia would take turns as jazz drummers. Although Milhaud had previously been fascinated by similar rhythms he encountered in Brazil in 1917–18,[13] his first significant exposure to jazz came in London in 1920 when Billy Arnold and his New York band played there. In 1922 Milhaud heard Paul Whiteman's orchestra while visiting New York and was taken to hear New Orleans jazz in Harlem, where the music, he said, "was absolutely different from anything I had ever heard before."[14]

Although "primitive," that is, traditional African society and contemporary black American life constituted very different cultures, Europeans of the 1920s frequently confused them; in their naive understanding of black culture they viewed the two as essentially one and the same. The writer and diplomat Paul Morand, on visiting New York (after having traveled to Timbuktu the year before), described Harlem as a "miniature Africa." The film *Charleston* includes both an African character and jazz music accompanying the Charleston. Paul Poiret, the couturier, argued, "Jazz is not American, it is Negro." And Milhaud wrote, "This authentic music had its roots in the darkest corners of the Negro soul, the vestigial traces of Africa."[15]

The fact that certain aspects of African music appeared in the roots of jazz occasioned much of this confusion and obscured the contemporary urban American context that was

FERNAND
LÉGER

Figure. Senufo. Ivory Coast. Wood. Published in Marius de Zayas, *African Negro Art:
Its Influence on Modern Art*, 1916

Fernand Léger. Costume design for *The Creation of the World*. 1922–23.
Gouache and ink, 12 x 8" (30.5 x 20.3 cm). Collection Kay Hillman,
New York

Figure. Chokwe. Angola. Wood,
16½" (42 cm) high. The Pushkin
Museum, Moscow. Published in Carl
Einstein, *Negerplastik*, 1915

the proper home of the jazz idiom. It is widely accepted that
the syncopated rhythms of Africa continued to be identifiable
in jazz even though in jazz they were combined with French
and American popular music, folk songs, military march beat,
and dance music. Many scholars of jazz have written on the
close connection between this new musical form and its
African sources and have noted that the solos played in
Harlem have the same rhythm and expression found in contemporary Congo tom-tom ceremonies.[16] Robert Goffin
insists there is no doubt as to the survival in jazz of the African
tradition and believes the role of the jazz drummer may be
traced back in a direct line to African tom-tom beaters. "At the
base of jazz, then," he asserts, "we find African rhythmic
expression."[17] Marshall Stearns describes the similarity of jazz
rhythm to West African rhythm, detecting the survival in
jazz, albeit diluted, of elements of Dahomey music, including
its complicated rhythms, call-and-response pattern, the blue
note and blues scale, drumming, and use of the so-called
"falsetto break."[18]

There are, nevertheless, clear and substantial differences
between American jazz and African music. Scholars have
observed that unlike jazz, African drumming does not break
down into a structured rhythm, nor does African music have a
developed native harmony. Furthermore, the elements that
give jazz its distinct tonal system and form are European,
placing it firmly within the orbit of Western music.[19]

Whatever relationship may exist between African drumming and jazz, between African dance and the cakewalk or

Jean Börlin wearing an African mask in his dance, *Sculpture nègre*. Photograph. 1920. Dansmuseet, Stockholm

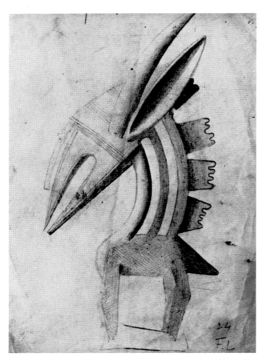

Fernand Léger. Study of a Bambara antelope headdress for *The Creation of the World*. c. 1922. Pencil, 11 x 8¾" (28 x 22 cm). Estate of the artist

Antelope headdress. Bambara. Mali. Wood. Published in Marius de Zayas, *African Negro Art: Its Influence on Modern Art*, 1916

Fernand Léger. *Bird.* (Costume design for *The Creation of the World*.) 1923. Watercolor, 13⅜ x 9" (34 x 22.7 cm). Dansmuseet, Stockholm. Reproduced in color, page 474

Charleston, lies outside the scope of this study. It suffices that for French society in the 1920s, the general public as well as the intellectual, black Africa and black America were inextricably linked and frequently presented together, with black American culture treated generally as an extension of African tribal life.

The confusion and intermixing of the two cultures is evident in the Ballets Suédois's production of *The Creation of the World*, first performed October 25, 1923, at the Théâtre des Champs-Elysées (p. 477). The Ballets Suédois had been founded by Rolf de Maré[20] in Paris in October 1920. The company ventured into experimental dance and theatrical spectacle, sometimes incorporating jazz rhythms, as in the music of Les Six for Cocteau's 1921 production of *Les Mariés de la Tour Eiffel* or that of Cole Porter for *Within the Quota*.[21]

The scenario for *The Creation of the World* was written by Blaise Cendrars, who in 1921 had published *L'Anthologie nègre*, a compilation and translation of African literature. Cendrars admired African literature for its beauty and power and considered Africa one of the richest poetic and philological sources. He developed the story for *The Creation of the World* from African creation myths; animals, insects, birds, and finally man and woman emerge from a shapeless mass in the presence of the three giant deities of creation.

Jean Börlin, the company's choreographer and principal dancer, had wanted to create a "ballet nègre" ever since 1919.[22] In 1920 he performed a solo dance called *Sculpture nègre* at the Comédie des Champs-Elysées (p. 479). For *The Creation of the World*, Börlin researched the ethnography of African civilizations in libraries and museums and, according to André Levinson, was especially impressed by West African dancing on stilts and on all fours, which he adapted to his choreography[23]

Milhaud in turn had wanted since 1922 to adapt the jazz style and write music in the "chamber" scale of the bands in Harlem. "At last in *La Création du Monde* I had the opportunity I had been waiting for to use those elements of jazz to which I had devoted so much study. I adopted the same orchestra as used in Harlem, seventeen solo instruments, and I made wholesale use of the jazz style to convey a purely classical feeling."[24] The score Milhaud composed for the ballet reflects these adaptations in its fugue on a jazz theme and its "blues" sections.

The extent, however, of Milhaud's assimilation of jazz in his ballet score has been debated. Some critics stress the basic dissimilarity between jazz and any form of symphonic music and state that while modern compositions such as Milhaud's have included various rhythms that may have been suggested by jazz, they "do not involve the essentials of the jazz language,"[25] particularly with regard to improvisation.

The drop curtain, decor, and costumes for *The Creation of the World* were designed by Léger, who began his drawings for the ballet by studying and directly copying reproductions of African sculpture.[26] As noted by Jean Laude, Léger's drawings are often almost tracings from Carl Einstein's *Negerplastik* and Marius de Zayas's *African Negro Art: Its Influence on Modern Art*. For example, Léger's pencil study of a Bambara antelope headdress illustrated in de Zayas's book is transformed into a costume design for a brightly plumed bird.

Sketches for the drop curtain show three heads inspired by African sculpture. The decor consisted of three figures representing gods; these were actually free-standing cutouts, movable and meant to be carried about (p. 477). They may have been inspired by Andrée Parr's life-size cutout silhouettes of jazz musicians that flanked the set of an earlier (1921) Ballets Suédois production, *L'Homme et son désir*. Indeed, Léger and the other collaborators of *The Creation of the World* were pho-

Above: Fernand Léger. Study for decor for *The Creation of the World*. 1923. India ink and gouache, 16⅝ x 22⅝ (42.7 x 57.5 cm). Collection Bob Guccione and Kathy Keeton, New York

Below left: Fernand Léger. Study for *The Creation of the World*. 1922. Pencil, 8¼ x 10⅝" (21 x 27 cm). The Museum of Modern Art, New York; gift of John Pratt

Below right: Helmet mask. Baule. Ivory Coast. Wood. Published in Carl Einstein, *Negerplastik*, 1915

The authors of *The Creation of the World*. From left to right: Darius Milhaud, Blaise Cendrars, Jean Börlin, Rolf de Maré, Fernand Léger (and Maurice Raynal). Elements of the decor by Andrée Parr for *L'Homme et son désir* appear in the background. Photograph. Dansmuseet, Stockholm

tographed backstage sitting amongst Parr's figures (above).[27] While Léger's early sketches for the decor were illusionistically modeled, the final result, composed of flat interlocked shapes, was nonsculptural and colored rust, brown, ocher, white, black, and blue. A series of planes—wings and top cloths—bearing geometric or landscape patterns (possibly related to decoration found on African pottery)[28] encompassed a backcloth painted to suggest mountains and clouds. The cloud section of this rear plane could also move.

The costumes were designed for a multitude of characters: messengers (of the gods) on stilts, whose interlocking patterns and colors related them to the deities; characters with outsize masks; figures composed of flat black shapes (p. 479); brightly colored animals (red, blue, green, and yellow) with appended arms, tails, and beaks; a man and a woman in black padded leotards. The surface patterning of the costumes was meant to recall scarification marks and other characteristic patterns of African sculpture.

Léger's costume designs reflected his decor, particularly in their colors and flattened patterning. As a result, the characters lost their individual identity and became extensions of the overall set design. During the performance the scenery was made to participate in the activity of the characters as the costumed dancers actually shifted the decor while performing on stage, further blurring the differences between the characters and setting. As the ballet opened, the crowding and fusion of decor and figures suggested the reign of chaos, then slowly the decor was moved apart, the clouds floated up, and order was initiated.

The Creation of the World, with its story of primeval creation set in an African context, mirrored both the popular desire for societal rebirth—for new sources of energy— that followed the war, and a widespread belief that the Egyptian/Archaic Greek roots of Western art had originated in black Africa (p. 243). Léger hoped to invest his gods with the sense of mystery and exoticism such a theme required. Indeed, Milhaud observed, "Léger wanted to adapt primitive Negro art and paint the drop-curtain and the scenery with African divinities

expressive of power and darkness. He was never satisfied that his sketches were terrifying enough."[29]

Although Léger's decor for *The Creation of the World* was inspired by African sculpture, he was not substantially influenced by Primitive art before or after his work on this ballet. Even for this ballet, the inspiration Léger derived from African art was quite different from that experienced by Picasso and other artists who generally valued Primitive art for its formal and magical properties and absorbed these traits into their own work. Any real interest Léger had in Primitive art depended less on its structure than on what he took to be its spontaneous, vigorous qualities—in effect, the same qualities that had interested the Dadaists. It was this vitality that had attracted Léger to jazz and to black revues as well.

Léger articulated his artistic concerns in a series of early 1920s essays dealing with modern spectacle, the dynamism of daily urban life, and the technology of the new mechanized world. Attracted by the energy and mobility of circuses, cabarets, music and dance halls, which he attended with Börlin and de Maré, he hoped to convey a similar vitality and rhythmic contrast in his work. In the collection of his essays published as *Functions of Painting* he stresses these components again and again but mentions the African context of *The Creation of the World* just once.

For Léger, the African theme of *The Creation of the World* was basically another point of departure from which to express his preoccupations with dynamism and spectacle. Léger thoroughly animated the stage with lighting that continually dimmed and brightened, with the constantly mobile set, and the abstract patterning of the costumes which obscured the human form. He had even hoped to employ in the ballet a complicated apparatus that would have used gas to inflate skins representing flowers, trees, and animals, thereby allowing them to fly up into the air. This project was abandoned, however, because the sound of the gas would have drowned out the music.

Summarizing the purpose of his stage designs, Léger wrote: "Man becomes a mechanism like everything else; instead of being the end, as he formerly was, he becomes a means....If I destroy the human scale, if my scenery moves around, I obtain the maximum effect. I obtain a whole on the stage that is totally different from the atmosphere of the auditorium."[30] Léger's primary focus in *The Creation of the World* was the integration of the performer with the setting and the transmutation of the dancer into a mechanized, dehumanized element. Viewed in this manner, Léger's mechanistic structure ironically contrasts with the popular, albeit false, notion of Africa as a spontaneous, uninhibited society.

To suit the popular taste, the reality of African art in productions such as *The Creation of the World* had to be modified and made less disturbing. In a slightly different context, it has been noted that "*La Création du Monde* smoothed away the rawness of primitive art. Its primitivism was, in a sense, classicized, so that primitive stood for archetypal."[31] Hence, Milhaud acknowledged he transformed jazz "to convey a purely classical feeling," and Léger simplified and flattened his earliest African designs for the ballet into more decorative forms. As Léger affirmed:

In ballet, I thought only in terms of the decorative, of simple surfaces covered with flat colors. I did that for *Skating Rink* and for *The Creation of the World.* In collaboration with Darius Milhaud and Blaise Cendrars, I created an African drama. Everything was transposed in it. As a point of departure, I used African sculpture from the classical period; as documents, the original dances. Under the aegis of three Negro gods twenty-six feet tall, one witnessed the birth of men, plants, and animals.[32]

By 1925 this stereotypical reduction of African art permeated a wide range of fashion and style, including interior decoration. Indeed, the couturier Paul Poiret even used an African mask to advertise his 1930 autobiography *En Habillant l'époque,*[33] and the collection of African ivory bracelets that socialite-intellectual Nancy Cunard wore on her arms from wrist to elbow became famous. Moreover, Art Deco, which had reached its apogee when the "International Exhibition of Modern Decorative and Industrial Arts" was held at the Grand Palais in June 1925, also absorbed the shapes of African art. The two movements frequently shared similar geometric qualities and simplicity of form. Art Deco sculptors Jean Lambert-Rucki (p. 507) and Gustave Miklos derived their sculpted heads of human figures from African masks but made

them more palatable to European collectors through a softening and smoothing of form and expression as well as chic stylization. Art Deco designers incorporated African patterns in their rugs and fabrics and employed Primitive motifs in their jewelry and silverwork. Art Deco furniture, too, was inspired by Africa, as witness the seats derived from ceremonial stools.

The utilization of African forms in the Art Deco movement lent a sense of the dramatic to interior design, suggesting the theatrical foundation that had originally popularized these forms.[34] As we have seen, the public's great interest in African and, by extension, black American culture was due in large part to their extrapolation in theater and ballet during those years. At first vanguard theater was marked by Dada spontaneity and excess; primitivism (among other devices) was a means of provocation. In time, as vanguard artists increasingly offered themselves in the service of fashion and were co-opted by the cultural establishment, Léger's simplified type of primitivism became accessible and acceptable as a decorative idiom.[35] It was in this assimilated mode that primitivism entered the cultural mainstream.

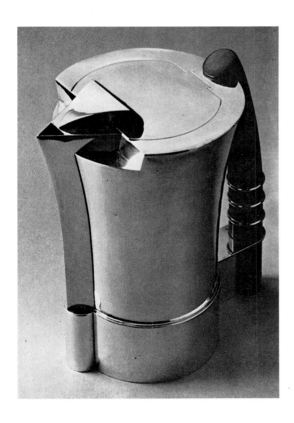

Above left: Jean Puiforcat. Pitcher. 1929–30. Silver and ebony, 9½ x 6¾" (24 x 17 cm). Collection N. Manoukian, Paris

Above right: Marcel Coard. Stool. Wood, 18⅛ x 19¾ x 65" (46 x 50 x 165 cm). Private collection

Right: Jean Lambert-Rucki. *Project for a Necklace or Bracelet.* 1936–37. India ink, gouache, gold and silver ink, 2⅞ x 9⅞" (7.3 x 25 cm). Musée des Arts Décoratifs, Paris

NOTES

I would like to thank Judith Cousins, Diane Farynyk, Beatrice Kernan, and Bernice Rose of The Museum of Modern Art for their generous assistance in the work on this essay.

1. Fernand Léger, letter to Rolf de Maré, September 12, 1922, Dansmuseet, Stockholm. Cited and translated by Melissa A. McQuillan, *Painters and the Ballet, 1917–26: An Aspect of the Relationship between Art and Theatre*, Ph.D. diss., New York University, Institute of Fine Arts, 1979, p. 615.
2. According to Guillaume Apollinaire, "M. Paul Guillaume is preparing a choreographic spectacle for next season that, he says, will be a sensation. He himself will perform some dances whose attitudes, movements, and gestures are inspired by his contemplation of African fetishes." "News and Views of Literature and the Arts," *L'Europe Nouvelle*, July 20, 1918; reprinted in *Apollinaire on Art: Essays and Reviews 1902–1918 by Guillaume Apollinaire*, ed. Leroy C. Breunig, trans. Susan Suleiman (New York: Viking, 1972), p. 472.
3. Francis Steegmuller, *Cocteau* (Boston: Little, Brown, 1970), p. 171.
4. "The Spectacle: Light, Color, Moving Image, Object-Spectacle," *Bulletin de l'Effort Moderne*, 1924; reprinted in *Functions of Painting by Fernand Léger*, ed. Edward F. Fry, trans. Alexandra Anderson (New York: Viking, 1973), p. 37. Cocteau stated that "Everyone is preoccupied with theatre..."; Jean Cocteau, "Entre Picasso et Radiguet," *Carte Blanche*, April 7, 1919; cited in McQuillan, *Painters and the Ballet*, p. 364.
5. Richard Huelsenbeck, 1918. Cited in Henning Rischbieter, *Art and the Stage in the 20th Century* (Greenwich, Conn.: New York Graphic Society, 1968), p. 164.
6. Hugo Ball. Cited in RoseLee Goldberg, *Performance: Live Art 1909 to the Present* (New York: Abrams, 1979), p. 42.
7. Annabelle Henkin Melzer, "Dada Performance at the Cabaret Voltaire," *Artforum*, Nov. 1973, p. 76.
8. For a description of Josephine Baker's opening night at the Théâtre des Champs-Elysées see Janet Flanner, *Paris Was Yesterday, 1925–1939* (New York: Viking, 1972), pp. xx–xxi.
9. H. H. Arnason, *Calder* (Princeton: Van Nostrand, 1966), p. 17. See also David Bourdon, *Calder* (New York: Macmillan, 1980), p. 29.
10. Cocteau, letter to Albert Gleizes, January 30, 1918, reprinted in Steegmuller, *Cocteau*, p. 201.
11. For a description of the role of this character see Steegmuller, *Cocteau*, p. 185. The characters in *Parade* included French and American Managers and a horse (played by two dancers) whose head was inspired by African masks (p. 319). A Negro equestrian dummy was originally envisioned "riding" this horse, but was lost during rehearsal. The two Managers and the Negro formed the components of the French twentieth-century music hall. McQuillan, *Painters and the Ballet*, p. 418.
12. Steegmuller, *Cocteau*, p. 201.
13. Upon his return to Paris from South America, Milhaud assembled some popular Brazilian rhythms—tangos, sambas, etc.—into a piece entitled *Le Boeuf sur le toit* (1919), the name of a Brazilian carnival song. Cocteau invented a scenario to accompany the music, and the ensuing ballet was performed February 1920.
14. Darius Milhaud, *Notes without Music* (New York: Knopf, 1953), p. 136.
15. Milhaud, ibid., p. 137. This tendency to ascribe African qualities to other cultures was not limited to its extension to American black society. Another instance of the confusion between different artistic sources should be noted. In 1910 Stravinsky had envisioned a Russian pagan rite. That would be the basis for *Le Sacre du printemps*, performed at the Théâtre des Champs-Elysées, May 29, 1913. Stravinsky's collaborator and the creator of the visual embodiment of this story was Nicolas Roerich, the painter and archaeologist of ancient Slavonic tribes. The music, while not actually of traditional Russian origin except for the solo bassoon melody in the introduction to Part One, which is borrowed from Lithuanian folk music, does sound folklike in character and did rely on Russian themes and melodies. Yet it is frequently and incorrectly described in terms of Primitive African rhythms. George Antheil, the American pianist and composer, wrote: "Since Wagner, music has had two gigantic blood transfusions; first the Slavic and then the Negro. Two epochal dates in the latter are the 'Ritual of Spring' of Stravinsky with its revolutionary primitivism in 1913 and the arrival in 1917 of the first Negro jazz band in Paris." Cited in Alain Locke, *The Negro and His Music* (New York: Arno, 1969 reprint of 1936 edition), p. 109. One author observes, "After Stravinsky had introduced its most primitive African rhythms in *Sacre du printemps* (1913)..."; Roger Shattuck, *The Banquet Years* (New York: Vintage/Random, 1968), p. 155.
16. A similar relationship has been ascribed to dance. "The forerunners of sambas and rhumbas are African dances"; Claus Raab, "Latin American Dances" in the catalog *World Cultures and Modern Art* (Munich: F. Bruckmann KG, 1972), p. 330. In the 1930s Katherine Dunham's dances, composites from several Caribbean dance themes, would impress viewers with their similarity to contemporary Nigerian dances. See *Katherine Dunham: Her Dancers, Singers, Musicians*, ed. Richard Buckle (London: Ballet Publications, 1949), p. 23. Ragtime, too, contained the rudiments of African rhythmic combinations, and it has been pointed out that while ragtime players were gathering in Chicago in the 1890s, "the Dahomeans were startling World's Fair [World's Columbian Exposition, Chicago] visitors in 1893 with the original African form of the same rhythms"; Rudi Blesh and Harriet Janis, *They All Played Ragtime* (New York: Knopf, 1950), p. 149; cited in Leonard Feather, *The Book of Jazz* (New York: Dell, 1976), p. 25.
17. Robert Goffin, *Jazz from the Congo to the Metropolitan*, trans. Walter Schapp and Leonard G. Feather (Garden City: Doubleday, Doran, 1944), p. 14.
18. Marshall W. Stearns, *The Story of Jazz* (London: Oxford University Press, 1978), pp. 3–15.
19. For a discussion of these differences see Barry Ulanov, *A History of Jazz in America* (New York: Viking, 1952), pp. 11–12; cited in Feather, *The Book of Jazz*, pp. 25–26. See also André Hodeir, *Jazz: Its Evolution and Essence*, trans. David Noakes (New York: Grove Press, 1979), pp. 40–44.
20. Rolf de Maré traveled to Africa and collected African art.
21. *Within the Quota* was devoted to an American theme and set to music by an American composer. The sets and costumes were designed by Gerald Murphy, and the characters included "The Colored Gentleman" who did a vaudeville dance and "The Jazz Baby" who danced a shimmy. *Within the Quota* premiered with *The Creation of the World* on October 25, 1923.
22. *Les Ballets Suédois dans l'art contemporain* (Paris: Editions du Trianon, 1931), p. 67.
23. André Levinson, "La Création du Monde," *Comoedia*, October 28, 1923; cited in Elisabeth Blondel, *Fernand Léger et les arts du spectacle*, Ph.D. diss., Université de Paris, 1969, p. 45. I am grateful to Judi Freeman and Judith Cousins for informing me of this thesis.
24. Milhaud, *Notes without Music*, pp. 148–49.
25. Wilder Hobson, *American Jazz Music* (New York: Da Capo, 1976), pp. 82–83. See also Hodeir, *Jazz: Its Evolution and Essence*, pp. 260–63, and Claus Raab, "Difficulties in the Fusion of Jazz and Symphonic Music," *World Cultures and Modern Art*, p. 322. Milhaud and other European musicians, such as Stravinsky, who experimented with jazz elements in their music did not continue utilizing them for long. On a 1926 trip to the United States Milhaud lost his enthusiasm for jazz upon finding how popular jazz (and Harlem) had become. See John Willett, *Art and Politics in the Weimar Period: The New Sobriety, 1917–1933* (New York: Pantheon, 1978), pp. 159–60, and Milhaud, *Notes without Music*, p. 192.
26. Lois Sacks, "Fernand Léger and the Ballets Suédois," *Apollo*, June 1970, p. 465.
27. McQuillan, *Painters and the Ballet*, p. 290. Milhaud wrote the music for the ballet *L'Homme et son désir* while in Europe. I am indebted to McQuillan's thesis (pp. 614–29) for much of the following description of *The Creation of the World*.
28. Blondel, *Fernand Léger et les arts du spectacle*, p. 46.
29. Milhaud, *Notes without Music*, p. 148.
30. "The Ballet-Spectacle, the Object-Spectacle," *Bulletin de l'Effort Moderne*, 1925; reprinted in *Functions of Painting by Fernand Léger*, p. 72.
31. McQuillan, *Painters and the Ballet*, p. 614.
32. "The Machine Aesthetic: Geometric Order and Truth," *Propos d'artistes*, 1925; reprinted in *Functions of Painting by Fernand Léger*, p. 63.
33. Jean Laude, *The Arts of Black Africa*, trans. Jean Decock (Berkeley: University of California Press, 1971), p. 20. It is of some interest that Poiret writes in this autobiography: "In New York, I asked twenty times over, in every class of society, for the address of an ethnographic museum, which no one was able to tell me. I discovered it right on top of Broadway, and I found nobody there." Paul Poiret, *My First Fifty Years*, trans. Stephen Haden Guest (London: Gollancz, 1931), pp. 266–67.
34. Theater and ballet not only helped introduce African art forms to the public but also triggered the Art Deco style in 1909 by the designs and colors of the Ballets Russes in Paris.
35. For further discussion regarding the decline in the 1920s of the Parisian avant-garde and its absorption into the cultural establishment, see Willett, *Art and Politics in the Weimar Period*, pp. 168–71. See also McQuillan, *Painters and the Ballet*, pp. 373–77.

Mask. Kuba. Zaire. Painted wood and fiber, 21¼" (54 cm) high. Museum für Völkerkunde, Berlin

Paul Klee. *Actor's Mask*. 1924. Oil on canvas mounted on board, 14½ x 13⅜" (36.7 x 33.8 cm). The Museum of Modern Art, New York; The Sidney and Harriet Janis Collection

PAUL KLEE

Jean Laude

aul Klee expressed his thoughts about his involvement with primitivism in two noteworthy statements. In 1912, while already associated with Kandinsky and the Blaue Reiter group, he wrote to a Swiss colleague: "I should like to pacify those troubled spirits who to their puzzlement looked in vain [at the Galerie Tannhauser exhibition] for echoes of old Museum favorites such as El Greco. The fact is that primitivistic innovations are still taking place in art, of the sort that one might find in ethnographic collections or, quite simply, in one's own home, in the nursery."[1] Subsequently, in a conversation with Lothar Schreyer that Schreyer later consigned to paper, Klee said: "Children, the insane, and primitive peoples all still have—or have rediscovered—the power to see. Both what they see and the forms that they derive from this are for me reconfirmations of the most valuable kind. For when we look at something we all see the same thing, though each sees it from a different angle—the same thing, both as a whole and in all its details, beyond all the planets, not the product of a delirious imagination, but a real thing."[2] These two quotations become all the more interesting as we see that the first was written during the period in which Klee became acquainted with the Blaue Reiter almanac, in which children's drawings and Primitive art had been reproduced, and that the second dates from the period in which Lothar Schreyer was teaching at the Weimar Bauhaus (1921–23), when the question of primitivism was no longer a matter of much debate.

These two declarations were made at least ten years apart, and in this period Klee's art underwent some profound transformations. It is therefore not irrelevant to point out that in the first, the emphasis falls on the words "primitivistic innova-

tions," and that in the second, the key phrases are "the power to see" and "reconfirmations of the most valuable kind." Klee's Weimar declaration also stresses a theme that around 1930 would become a commonplace in artistic debate and criticism: namely, the now discredited grouping, within a single aesthetic category, of Primitive art, the creations of the insane, and children's drawings. The association of Primitive art with children's art had earlier been made by S. Levinstein, who juxtaposed them in his *Kinderzeichnungen bis zum 14 Lebensjahre*, published in 1904 in Leipzig. Klee also owned a copy of the book by H. Prinzhorn *Bildnerei des Geisteskranken*, published in Berlin in 1922, which indicates that his conversation with Lothar Schreyer must have taken place, at the earliest, during the same year.

In a study devoted to masks and marionettes in the work of Klee, Calliope Rigopoulu observes that in *Actor's Mask*, 1924, "Robert J. Goldwater...thinks he can discern a Congolese influence. James Pierce Smith, on the other hand, finds it closer to the masks of Oceania. Margaret Plant sees the influence of Hokusai, and especially that of [his work] *The Ghost of the Lantern*, derived from his *100 Stories*, which was reproduced in the book by Wilhelm Michel, *Das Teuflische und Groteske in der Kunst*, which Paul Klee was acquainted with."[3] From this arises the delicate question of the limits of any comparative study. If three writers not known for offhandedness can ascribe the same painting to three different sources, it is because the point is not to find a single possible influence or traceable borrowing; it is also because these possible sources all show certain similarities to each other and because only their common characteristics, such as they appear in the *Actor's Mask*, are of any relevance.

A few points should be emphasized here. Klee never copied the object or work that he might have seen, had access to, or owned a reproduction of. At the moment of painting or drawing, he did not have the work before him. Rather, he formed a mental image of it—an image thereby transformed into the terms of a precise problem (of form and/or content) which he would then resolve within the general problematics running through all of his work. Klee became aware of this fact early on, by 1908 in fact, and quickly set about extrapolating its practical and theoretical consequences: "Just as man has a skeleton, muscles and skin, so does a painting. One may speak of a painting's anatomy. A painting having as its subject 'a nude man' should not draw its representation from the human anatomy, but from the anatomy of painting. One begins by constructing a framework for the painting that one is about to build. The degree to which one strays from this plan, that is the optional part."[4]

Moreover the difficulty of locating any specific source in a work of Paul Klee lies in the fact that when he situated his work with respect to a work by another artist, he limited his initial reference to a single aspect, which he considered apart from a complex whole. In other words, he borrowed only what seemed to him at that very moment to instigate, make possible, or reconfirm his own process. The result is that the source becomes part of a new vision in which it no longer bears the same significance as in its original context but serves its purpose through the transitions and advances that it makes possible, through the growth of the conception with which it is now imbued and of which it is now but a moment nourishing the whole. In Klee, theory relies on method, not on a preestablished system. It is informed by the practice that precedes it and from which it is inferred. But theory is also part of the mental and cultural environment, and is born at the very center of this milieu of association and exchange.

One can correctly say that Klee was familiar with Primitive works of art (in the broad meaning of the term current at the turn of the century), including nonclassical and non-European art. As early as 1906, Klee had seen specimens of such work when he visited the Ethnographic Museum of Berlin. He surely saw, in addition, those works used as illustrations in the Blaue Reiter almanac, and he also owned a copy of the Levinstein book. Moreover, he had probably seen the images reproduced in Hermann Bahr's *Expressionismus* (Munich, 1916). In another respect, in his writings as well as in those of his friends of the Blaue Reiter, primitivism is defined as both a return to origins and the beginning of a new "spiritual era." It therefore is embraced more as an *Idea* in the Goethian sense, a kind of *analogon* of the *Urplantz* in the *Metamorphosis of Plants*, than as a specific repertory of forms from which the artist may draw, and of which a limited number enjoy a privileged status because they conform to an exclusively formal set of concerns.

Another aspect of Klee's art that deserves emphasis is the very particular relationship between its form and content. This relationship is not, at all events, worked out in the same manner as in Picasso, Braque, Matisse, or even Robert Delaunay, to whom Klee probably felt for a brief period a certain kinship. It is reinforced through the mediation of the *Stimmung* (mood) and is related to Novalis's notion of the

Paul Klee. *Room Perspective with Inhabitants.* 1921. Watercolor over oil transfer drawing on paper mounted on cardboard, 19⅛ x 12½" (48.5 x 31.7 cm). Paul Klee-Stiftung, Kunstmuseum Bern

"magical I," or else to the similar notions of the "cryptogram of the ineffable" and the "hieroglyph of lived experience,"[5] as formulated by Ivanov, notions Klee had occasion to become familiar with, either through Kandinsky personally or his writings. It should also be pointed out that by 1905 Klee had already employed the methods of Ernst Mach and had related his strong feelings about them to Carl Einstein, who in turn derived from them certain guiding principles of *Negerplastik* and his interpretations of the work of Picasso, Braque, and Gris. The interdependence, as defined by Mach, between the interior world of the subject and the exterior sheds light on Klee's relationship to nature after 1905: It explains his refusal to imitate nature and must be understood in the light of what Bahr intended when, using Goethe's idea of "experience as the mediator between subject and object," he described Impressionism as representing only the "most-of-the-object" while denying the "most-of-the-subject" and Expressionism as acknowledging only the "most-of-the-subject" at the expense of the "most-of-the-object."[6] However, as far as Klee is concerned, the "most-of-the-subject" must not be taken as an exaltation of the ego, but rather as a predisposition, an attunement, to receiving the manifest or latent events that arise or take shape in the external world. Here once again emerge the problematics of the "sign" through which, according to Bahr, modern man, in living in a historically intolerable situation, comes to resemble "primitive" man. Here the *Weltschmerz* of the Decadents takes on a new meaning.

These elements, revolving as they do around the notion of primitivism, and being the products of both Klee's own thought and the debates of the time, allow us to focus on a number of principles by which we may conduct formal analyses, suggesting directions in which to proceed and providing a sound base for eventual comparisons. Not that primitivism comprises the entire scope of the painter's work and theory. It is, however, an integral part of this whole: His works—as Klee, in tune with the ideas of his time, pointed out—emphasize the power to see (and hence to make visible) and reconfirm the direction of his own pursuits. These are the key points of his 1922 conversation with Lothar Schreyer.

From a very general perspective, one may say that Klee's paintings, drawings, and engravings tend to enclose their surface, above all by means of the line. As for the problem of two-dimensional representation in the picture plane, here again Klee does not confront it in the same manner—nor is his background the same—as Picasso, Braque, or Delaunay. For Picasso and Braque pictorial space emerges as the end of a gradual, methodical procedure, which constitutes the pictorial act; this space is won through a process—in the case of their primitivism, through the study of the masks and figure sculpture of sub-Saharan African—that exhausts all available means: for example, the study of the reaction of solids to light, the desire ideally to preserve local color, the deliberate use of Cézannian "passage," the ambition to establish a "poetics of the object." For his part, Robert Delaunay (whose work Klee followed closely before his trip to Tunisia) wanted to create "new media," since in his opinion, Cézanne had already "broken the fruit-dish." Klee's development, at least in his formative years, was of an entirely different stamp, as it came out of different experiences and was involved with different concerns.

It must once again be emphasized that Klee's style evolved from an engraving technique where the linear element—

which the Jugendstil had already favored in its systematization of the arabesque—dominates, together with floral arabesques. Consequently, his respect for the picture surface can only be seen as resulting from a set of practices wholly different from those followed by the painters working in Paris. In closely examining, as his genetic theory suggests, the development of Klee's art, we find the painter consistently attentive—despite the "Tunisian revelation" that we now know was long in formation[7]—to the properties of line, of which he would do a methodical study in his 1925 *Pedagogical Sketches*. Out of the forty-three sections that make up this work, only the final three are devoted to questions of color, and these come at the end of an exploration of "movement," which linearity supposedly carries forward, and of which the arrow is said to be an ideogram. The work concludes in the following fashion: "We have come to the sphere of the colors of the spectrum, to the chromatic ethos, where all arrows are superfluous. For now our concern is no longer 'towards yonder,' but 'everywhere' and thus 'yonder' as well."[8]

Here, two elements should be taken into consideration to help in the understanding of technical problems. They figure as well in the elaboration of the concept of artistic labor as genesis. First, through his discovery of painting on glass (*Hinterglasmalerei*), which he came upon in 1906—hence before Vassily Kandinsky and Gabriel Munter—Klee developed a method that he describes repeatedly in his *Journal*.[9] Second, the children's drawings that he studied, but from which he eventually wanted to distance himself when his own production came to be compared and likened to them, led him into other experiments with spatial illusion (*Room Perspective with Inhabitants*, 1921) and with the foreshortening of figures and a general economy of means, toward the pure sign (*Animal Catching a Scent*, 1930). The latter work, incidentally, may relate to objects such as the Bukoba (Tanzania) cow of forged iron from the Linden Museum collection at Stuttgart.[10]

"Folk art," like children's drawings, is characterized by a respect for the surface that excludes all recourse to either

Paul Klee. *Animal Catching a Scent.* 1930. Watercolor and india ink on paper mounted on cardboard, 12⅝ x 18⅞" (31.9 x 47.8 cm). Paul Klee-Stiftung, Kunstmuseum Bern

Animal figure. Kingdom of Karagwe. Bukoba, Tanzania. Iron, 7⅞" (20 cm) high. Linden-Museum Stuttgart

A Chin woman of Padaung, Burma, wearing neck rings. Published in Victoria Ebin, *The Body Decorated*, 1979

Kifwebe mask. Luba. Zaire. Painted wood, 13¾" (35 cm) high. Collection Gustave and Franyo Schindler, New York

Incised shell. Collingwood Bay, Northern Province, Papua New Guinea. Shell, 3⅛" (8 cm) high. The Trustees of the Australian Museum, Sydney

LAUDE

linear or aerial perspective. In another connection, certain of the *Hinterglasmalerei* reproduced in the Blaue Reiter almanac are composed of a juxtaposition of separate elements disassociated from the whole. In *The Trinity or Christ's Five Wounds*,[11] the glasspainter composed his work around the radiant heart, girded by the crown of thorns and topped by a cross at whose foot are two open wings. The connections holding the parts together are not of a logical nature, as in classical European painting. And although they undeniably achieve a coherent effect by presenting a formal order, theirs is also and above all a symbolic order, even in their arrangement on the surface. We may find a similar strategy at work in a series of Klee's works of the years 1920 to 1940.

When Paul Klee says to Lothar Schreyer that children and Primitive people possess, to the highest degree, the power to see, he means their ability to make visible through the object represented not a transcendent reality but that which passes freely between interior and exterior, of which the *Stimmung* is at once a sign and a signal. Before going any further—and in order to go further—we must situate and confront this issue. If indeed it sends us back to the question of the similarities that one may find between Klee's method and the workings of mystical thought, it should also spur us to examine some of the consequences as to form. For the progress of meanings can occur only if the elements bearing this meaning are easily detachable from the objects or figures with which they form a whole and can migrate as it were into other wholes; that is, if they are able to form new objects or figures in the same manner as when their coherence manifested a natural order: in other words, if they are, in themselves, unities whose signifi-

Paul Klee. *Picture Album.* 1937. Gouache on unprimed canvas, 23⅜ x 22¼" (59.3 x 56.5 cm). The Phillips Collection, Washington, D.C.

cance depends upon a set of combinations. Those works showing an influence of tribal art and even of folk art—though in the latter the symbolic force is weaker or very attenuated—are made up precisely of aggregates of simple signs, which when isolated are relatively neutral but when combined activate each other.

Consequently, the element in Primitive art that reconfirmed Paul Klee in his own proceeding was not so much its visible structure or its architectural character as it was its ability to create simple, nonimitative signs which are sub-stitutes for, rather than abstractions drawn from, an external reality. For this reason, any connections of Klee's work with this or that piece from black Africa, Oceania, or native America can only be established on the level of specific borrowings or an organization of signifying unities on a surface, an organization of which only the modalities are retained.

It is necessary to resituate Klee's interest in all these matters, not only regarding primitivism in general but regarding specific aspects of tribal art in the history of his own painting. For, as far as the body of his works we know authorizes us to judge, we can say that it was precisely not (with rare exceptions) at the time of the Blaue Reiter, when vanguard attention was consciously focused on non-European art, but from the 1920s until his death that Klee drew upon the repertory of signs of various Primitive cultures and was able to understand and absorb the principles of their pictorial organization.

It would be useful here to mention briefly the status of the sign in the work of Paul Klee. It is complex. He sets up the sign as at once transitive and intransitive. As intransitive, it is first of all a pure, nondelineating orthography, a trace or mark acting on the surface where it is placed or on the plane that it helps to constitute. As transitive, it is the sign of something: It is sometimes a pictogram, sometimes even an ideogram. And, in a precircumscribed body of work, it can only be examined once the semantic transformations of which it is the object have been situated within the iconographic whole of which it is part. A single sign may bear different meanings in different works.

After Klee's Tunisian voyage, his work tends, though only in certain series, to situate itself at the exact boundary between the visible and the legible without, however, crossing over to one side or another. After this trip, Klee began to see inscriptions of "Arabic" characters everywhere, whether in Tunis itself, in Saint-Germain, or in Kairouan. He probably did at some point see Nabeul pottery or *azulejos*.[12] During this period touristic demand had not yet completely directed pottery and ceramic production almost exclusively toward exotic subject matter (camel, palm tree, etc.) at the expense of traditional motifs, which were more "abstract." Moreover, these *azulejos*, and perhaps Bedouin rugs as well as those attributed to Kairouan, possibly led Klee to conceive several of his works as arrangements of rough squares, some inscribed with different kinds of signs. All these arts—*azulejos*, rugs, and calligraphy—which caught Klee's attention are arts concerned with surface as well as sign.

As for the *azulejos*, it may help us to judge their influence on the painter by noting that toward the middle part of his sojourn in Tunisia, Klee began to partition the interior of his surfaces into irregular quadrilaterals and mixed tones (and thus to distance himself from Delaunay's system), which are furnished with abbreviated signs.[13] This formal thematics then branched out into several other series, such as those of the "architectures" and the "magical squares" of the 1920s. Klee continued in this vein, with variations, until around 1938, when he began to combine this style at times with an iconography of Eastern inspiration.[14] The Bedouin and so-called Kairouan rugs probably attracted Klee's attention all the more

Paul Klee. *Oriental–Sweet.* 1938. Oil on panel, 20 x 19⅝" (50.8 x 49.8 cm). Private collection

because of the large 1910 exposition of Islamic art held in Munich, an event that excited a great deal of interest in all of Europe and to which all the major publications, as well as artistic and specialized journals, gave extensive coverage.[15] It is unlikely that the painter would not have gone to see it, as he was already, according to Will Grohmann, attracted to the Near East and its culture even before his trip to Tunisia. Rugs, and by extension, brocaded fabric, and even Primitive tapa cloths, reconfirmed the artist's concern for the surface. They also provided him with examples rather than models of a particular treatment of the plane surface where the field is partitioned into closed sectors by at times irregular squares of varying size and color and also by inscribed rectangles with parallel sides.

In as much as the primitivism of the beginning of the century involved new sources brought together in an Imaginary Museum as it were, sources made up of disparate, dissimilar works whose only common features are the fact that they were neither classical nor Occidental, can we say that this syndrome was a central fact of modern art? Or was primitivism but a stage in a larger pursuit which went beyond it in all respects, though making use of it as a justifying pretext in order to effect a rupture all the more radical?

Here a particular Klee watercolor demands attention, not only because it exemplifies the painter's method, but precisely because it implements a method (but no more than this) analogous to that found in certain works of tribal art. It is entitled *Ventriloquist* and bears the enigmatic subtitle *Caller in the Moor* (p. 494). It dates from 1923, the Weimar Bauhaus period, and was done near the time of the publication of "Wege des Naturstudiums."[16]

It is a complex work in that in it Klee combines two approaches whose specific orientations are radically contradictory. The "background" is made up of rectangles arranged according to horizontal stripes of equal lengths but differing widths, with hues that are varied but equally distinguished according to their import. This approach sets the tone for a whole series of works that begins with certain Tunisian watercolors,[17] continues through the "painting-poems,"[18] and develops into the "architectures"[19] and those pages that, if they were not titled, could pass for "abstract."[20] It would be incorrect to connect this approach exclusively to the structurally oriented work that was being done at the Bauhaus. Beyond the fact that this approach emerges progressively after 1914, it also involves a musical conception, in its stafflike ruling of the rectangles and its polyphonic arrangement of tones and values: greens, reds, and violets.

Against this cross-ruled background is placed, in pen and ink, a human figure of transparent appearance, presented, however, in definitely clearer tones than the rest (pale, luminous greens and pinks); this figure may show certain similarities to the general aspect of children's drawings, but its outline is highly precise and authoritative. The head is in the shape of a bell or helmet and appears distantly related to the masks used in the initiation rites of Mende girls in Guinea and Sierra Leone. As for the belly, it consists of an unspecific form of curved shape on which are depicted, around the navel, five imaginary animals, also transparent. This manner of motif would recur in a series of works until 1939 (p. 495).[21]

Mask. Shira-Punu. Gabon. Painted wood, 13⅜" (34 cm) high. Bernisches Historisches Museum, Bern

But now let us examine more closely an important detail of this work. The animal forms on the figure's belly are transparent, like the rectangles that set the order of the background. This bears a curious similarity to the so-called X-ray compositions found among the tree-bark paintings in Arnhem Land in Northern Australia (p. 495), as well as among certain pieces by the Tlingit peoples of Canada and in Oceanic art. There is, however, a major difference. Whereas in the bark paintings a fetus, intestines, and backbone are depicted according to some notion of realism—that is, the insides of a living organism are presented such as they are imagined to be in reality—in Paul Klee's work we are shown monstrous imaginary beings that are supposed to speak through the ventriloquist. In the same way, in a lithograph of the same period, *The Man in Love* (p. 495), the lover's brain is inhabited by the spread-legged body of his beloved, erotically penetrated. In this way, Paul Klee uses the X-ray method essentially to give substance to phantasms. Hence between the tribal use and his use of the technique there is an analogy of purpose—to show what is not visible to the human eye; but what is shown demonstrates in the first case a knowledge of anatomy, and in the second, a personal imagery or obsession.

Though the tone, techniques, and media are totally different, the young girl in the 1922 *The Man in Love*, is, like the *Ventriloquist* of 1923, the victim of monsters that haunt and subjugate her. What is worthy of note here is that both works—the first through a borrowed form, the second through the transposition of a method of representation—are directly related to non-Western art. It was ostensibly for

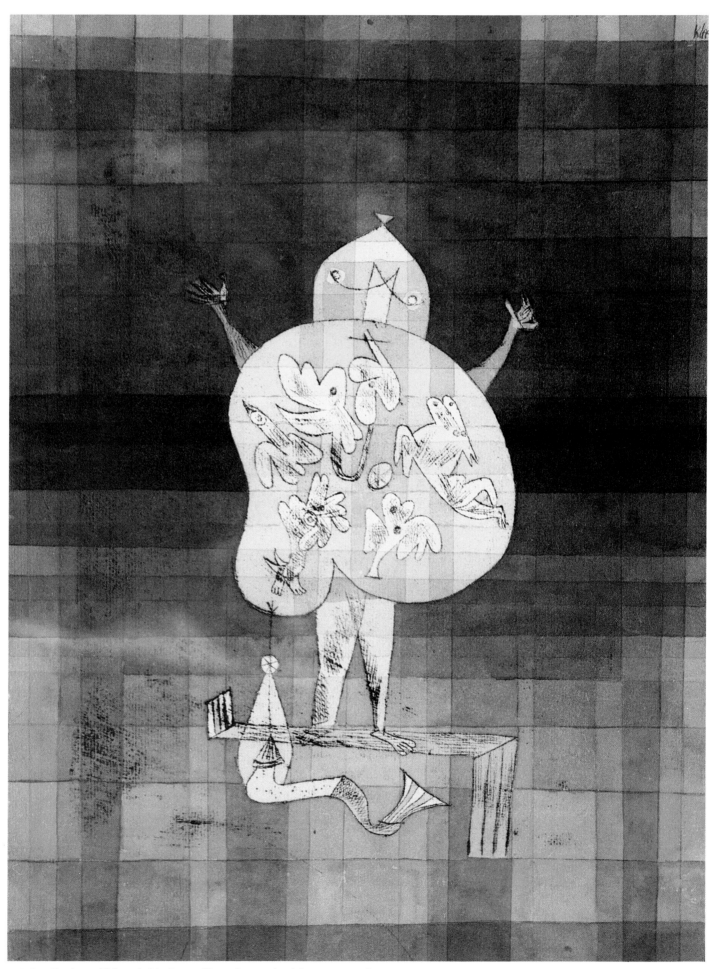

Paul Klee. *Ventriloquist (Caller in the Moor)*. 1923. Watercolor on colored sheet, 15⅜ x 11⅜" (39 x 28.9 cm). Collection Heinz Berggruen, Geneva

Painting. Aborigine. Australia. Painted bark, 19¾" (50 cm) high. Museum für Völkerkunde, Basel

"magical" purposes, in as much as these can be illuminated by psychoanalysis, that Klee made these sallies outside the West. Of course the references in his work to exotic arts can be explained on purely formal and pictorial levels which are themselves justified by a conception of form as genesis; but they should be approached from the perspective of the connotations that they might produce in the work into which they are integrated. This would seem to accord them the significance of archetypes. In other words, the role of possible borrowings must be evaluated on two levels: first, that of an elementary sign sundered from its original signification; and then the signification that the new context will confer upon it, or discover within it. However, the elementary nature characterizing a sign or a form borrowed from a nonclassical, non-

Above: Paul Klee. *The Torso and Its Own (by the Full Moon).* 1939. Water-based paint, waxed, on burlap with a plaster ground, 25¾ x 19⅞" (65.5 x 50.5 cm). Paul Klee-Stiftung, Kunstmuseum Bern

Right: Paul Klee. *The Man in Love.* 1923. Lithograph, 10⅞ x 7½" (27.5 x 19 cm). Collection Carl Djerassi, Stanford

Paul Klee. *Pastorale.* 1927. Tempera on canvas mounted on wood, 27¼ x 20⅝" (69.3 x 52.4 cm). The Museum of Modern Art, New York; Abby Aldrich Rockefeller Fund and exchange

Western work (and whose origin is not easily discernible because of this very elementariness) itself functions as a sign, a sign of primitiveness, of primordiality. This primordiality is both that which gives the artist his psychic qualities as well as that which is ascribed to cultures that do not embrace representation as a mode of communication but admit of an interpenetration between the interior world and the exterior.

Once again we find ourselves faced with the prickly problem of locating a specific "exotic" source borrowed and used by Klee in his work. This source might, for example, have etched itself into the artist's consciousness several years before being used. In this case it reemerges transformed by the unconscious workings of the memory and by the new formal and iconographic context into which the borrowed element will be placed and then integrated. In addition, by this time the element might demonstrate a sense of the elementary that

could have been undifferentiatingly abstracted from numerous objects remote from each other in both time and space. Thus the source cannot be determined with satisfactory precision, as there are no records that might bear witness to it. Finally, and perhaps most important, Klee does not demand of nonclassical, non-Western art a systematization of form that would make locale recognizable in syntactical structure: As he confided to Schreyer, Klee seeks in such art a reconfirmation. On the other hand, and depending on the imaginative exigencies of the work in question, he appropriates and broadens a vocabulary of forms and signs that he adapts to fit his objective at that moment.

But it is important not to make hasty generalizations or extend a priori to all of Klee's output this method of incorporating borrowed forms and signs. For it would seem that in numerous cases the artist found more than reconfirmation in

Above: Mask. Bwa. Upper Volta. Painted wood, 15⅛" (38.5 cm) high. Private collection. Formerly collection TRISTAN TZARA

Above right: Decorated cloth. Bambara. Mali. Dyed cotton. Published in Henri Clouzot, *Tissus nègres*, n.d.

Right: Decorated cloth. Bambara. Mali. Dyed cotton. Published in Henri Clouzot, *Tissus nègres*, n.d.

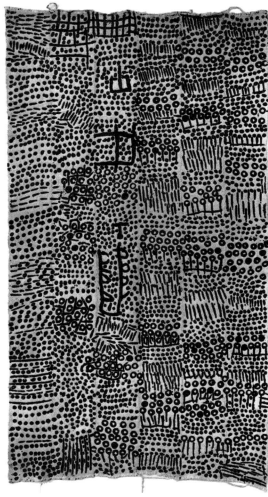

exotic art and that his concerns at times took their shape according to certain types of objects. But to return momentarily to a previous consideration: Formal analysis can be heuristically effective only when adapted to its object. If we are to prevent it from becoming reductive, we must invent or discover the procedures by which formal analysis will be conducted for each work; and in order to invent these procedures we must bring ourselves as close as possible to the pictorial, graphic, or iconographic project in question, the better to assess its relationship to its environment and its time. Thanks to Mathilde Klee, some of the artist's pages and notebooks from his grammar school days have been preserved, and these mark the evolution of her brother's artistic production from early childhood until adolescence.

In one of these notebooks, from 1897, Klee took some notes on a poem by Goethe, "Harzreise in Winter," and drew

Reliquary figure. Kota. Gabon. Wood, copper, brass, and iron, 21¼" (54 cm) high. Collection Philippe and Maryse Dodier, Avranches, France

clusters of heads—frontals and profiles—in the margins of the page. Curiously, though, there is no connection, illustrative or otherwise, between these rather elaborate drawings and the text being studied.[22] Rather than caricatures, these drawings, which were probably executed half-consciously while he distractedly listened to the teacher, fall more into the category of "grotesques," of which many of his works, even late ones, present examples. At least two of these heads, situated at the bottom of the cluster filling the upper left-hand part of the page, merit some attention. One of them shows

some similarities to certain so-called twisted-mouth masks of the Iroquois and Eskimos (p. 96), as well as to Swiss folk masks used in local festivals or during Carnival; the other head reminds one a bit of certain Tlingit and Haida masks. A third face, situated above the head with the twisted mouth, has some of the features of molded skulls (p. 34) and even of Melanesian masks.

Although to my knowledge he makes no mention of it in his *Journal*, his correspondence, or his "theoretical" or pedagogical writings, we can be certain that Klee frequented the

1913 89 götzen

Paul Klee. *Idols*. 1913. Pen and ink, 5 x 4″ (12.7 x 10.2 cm). Collection Joshua and Leda Natkin, West Redding, Connecticut

Bernisches Historisches Museum and visited its ethnographic section. There he must have seen objects that served as sources for some of his drawings and helped lay the ground for the elaboration of his concept of primitivism. Moreover, of the "exotic" objects presented in the Blaue Reiter almanac, five came from the Bern collection (p. 493) and most of the others from the Staatliches Museum für Völkerkunde, Munich.[23] This leads one to believe that Klee had a hand in the choice of the Blaue Reiter illustrations, selecting pieces belonging to the collection of the Bern museum, with Vassily Kandinsky and Franz Marc working to include the pieces from the Munich collections that had caught their interest.[24] If he visited the Berlin Museum für Völkerkunde in 1906, it is because he had been inspired to do so by the exotic works he had discovered as an adolescent in Bern. In another connection, Klee for a time collected bows and arrows from black Africa, according to Ladislas Segy, as cited by J. S. Pierce,[25] and he apparently kept a few African masks in his Munich studio between 1906 and 1914. But Segy says nothing of their origin or their nature.[26]

Paul Klee. *Drawing of a Relief with Exotic Imaginary Animal.* 1897. Pen and ink, 2 x 1⅞" (5 x 4.6 cm). Paul Klee-Stiftung, Kunstmuseum Bern

Paul Klee. *Drawing of a Relief with Exotic Figure.* 1897. Pen and ink, 3⅝ x 1⅞" (9 x 4.6 cm). Paul Klee-Stiftung, Kunstmuseum Bern

One could object, and rightly so, that the heads sketched in the margins of Klee's school notebook were drawn mechanically, so to speak; that they do not result from any specific artistic intention; and that, for this reason, their degree of relevance to the issue under discussion here is questionable. Nevertheless, they would seem to bear witness to the fact that Klee had knowledge at that time of non-Western art. More importantly, they direct us toward the manner in which the adolescent first perceived exotic works of art. Evidence of his frequenting the Bern museum at an early age would settle this matter once and for all. Jürgen Glaesemer recently brought to my attention a number of drawings from the same year, among them *Drawing of a Relief with Exotic Imaginary Animal* and *Drawing of a Relief with Exotic Figure.* Klee himself named the two works "Drawings of reliefs," which would make them imitations or drawings in the manner of objects he may have seen at the Bern museum.

Of course these sketches are but juvenilia. And it would be incorrect to try to draw too much from them. In fact, through his early, precocious exposure to non-Western, nonclassical art, Klee became oriented toward imaginative drawing, or at least, to temper the assertion a bit, felt reassured in this orientation. Moreover, through the slant of satirical drawing and caricature, he felt capable of breaking away from the ideal art that early on seemed to him no longer in step with its time.[27] His movement away from the classical Occident was clearly not the only aspect of this break. But it played an equally important role, though now stripped of all satirical character, in informing certain aspects of an imaginative approach which would be brought progressively into play after 1903.

But this break should not be seen as occurring only on the level of formal systems. When Klee deemed ideal art as henceforth outdated, he was not unaware of being in step with the nihilism that, as an astute reader of Nietzsche, he saw as a dominant feature of his epoch, the very thought of which was a source of anxiety for Kandinsky and Franz Marc. Now, though, like his two friends, he believed in the necessity of the emergence of a new man, and though he made his own the great lines of the Bauhaus utopia (to which the final paragraphs of the Conference of Jena bear witness), his positions—compared with those of his friends and later his colleagues at Weimar and Dessau—were no less original for all this. He had distanced himself from the mysticism of Kandinsky and Marc and the sociologism of the Bauhaus through an innovative use of caricature and satirical drawing, through a classical culture of the most solid sort, and through readings that were always positive and critical.

From this perspective, primitivism in Paul Klee takes on two different connotations which nonetheless never cease to intersect. On the one hand, it bespeaks a new beginning initiated and nurtured by artists. On the other hand, as a notion as well as a phenomenon manifest in dissimilar works attributed to it, primitivism appears central to Paul Klee's development. Inseparable from the idea of genesis, it does not distinguish itself as the proponent of a different model with which to replace the Classical one: Primitivism carries within itself the future, the endless variations and transformations to which all models are subject.

—Translated from the French by Stephen Sartarelli

NOTES

As an expert in both tribal and modern art, who had given doctoral-level seminars in the work of Klee at the University of Paris, Jean Laude was a logical choice as author for this chapter. He became seriously ill during the period when it was to be written and died some months after sending us a lengthy manuscript obviously intended as a book on Klee. With Laude's accord, his friend Pierre Daix edited this text down to the references concerning primitive art. He was able to consult the author, then in the hospital.

Inasmuch as Laude was prevented by his ill health from confronting certain questions, and made few references to particular works, we have taken the liberty of adding some visual material to his chapter beyond that indicated in his text. This includes a juxtaposition of Klee's *Idol* with a Kota reliquary figure, a comparison made in *Paul Klee and Primitive Art* by James Smith Pierce (New York and London, 1976).

1. P. Klee, *Journal* (Paris, 1959) p. 300.
2. L. Schreyer, *Erinnerungen an Sturn und Bauhaus* (Munich, 1956).
3. C. Rigopoulu, "Masques et marionettes chez Paul Klee," (Master's thesis under the direction of Fannette Roche, Université de Paris, 1981) p. 23.
4. P. Klee, *Journal*, p. 300.
5. Cf. C. W. Haxthausen, "Klees künstlerisches Verhältnis zu Kandinsky während der Münchner Jahre," in *Paul Klee: Das Frühwerk, 1883–1922* (Munich, 1979).
6. H. Bahr, *Expressionismus* (Munich, 1916), p. 45.
7. Cf. Regula Suter-Raeber, "Der Durchbruch zur Farbe und zum abstrakten Bild," in *Paul Klee: Das Frühwerk*, pp. 131–65; and *Die Tunisreise (Klee, Macke, Moilliet)*, ed. Ernst-Gerhard Güse (Stuttgart, 1982).
8. P. Klee, *Pädagogisches Skizzenbuch* (Munich, 1925). I shall quote from the translation of P. H. Gonthier, in P. Klee, *Théorie de l'art moderne* (Paris, 1964), p. 143.
9. P. Klee, *Journal*, pp. 197–99. Actually, by 1902 he had developed a technique similar to that of glass painting; ibid., pp. 136, 180, 188.
10. O. K. Werkmeister analyzed the relationships between Klee's work and children's art in "The Issue of Childhood in the Art of Paul Klee," *Arts Magazine*, September 1977, pp. 138–51.
11. Reproduced in the Blaue Reiter almanac, ed. Paris, Klincksieck, 1981, p. 256.
12. August Macke, who together with Louis Moilliet accompanied Klee, left a testimony of Klee's interest in the local pottery in *Marchand et cruches*, 1914. Here one may note as well the division of the surface's interior into squares in the manner of a Bedouin rug. Cf. Ernst-Gerhard Güse, "Raum und Fläche—Europa und der Orient zu August Mackes Tunis Aquarellen," in *Die Tunisreise*, ed. Güse, p. 144.
13. I shall give only two examples: *Hammamet Motif* (1914/48), and *Southern Gardens* (1914/108), reproduced in Güse, ed., *Die Tunisreise*, pp. 192 and 193.
14. Cf. specifically *Legends of the Nile* (1937/U15) (pastel), reproduced in *Paul Klee par lui-même et par son fils Felix Klee* (Paris, 1963), third plate after p. 56.
15. "Meisterwerken mohammedischer Kunst," Munich, May–October 1910. In the first volume of the catalog, forty-six rugs of various origins are reproduced.
16. P. Klee, "Wege des Naturstudiums," in *Staatliches Bauhaus im Weimar 1919–1923* (Weimar, 1923).
17. Notably in *Red and White Domes* (1914/45), Kunstsammlung Nordrhein-Westfalen, Düsseldorf, reproduced in Güse, ed., *Die Tunisreise*, p. 73; and *On a Hammamet Motif* (1914/57), Kunstmuseum, Basel, reproduced in *Paul Klee: Das Frühwerk*, p. 403, no. 337.
18. Notably in *Hoch und strahlend steht der Mond* (1916/20), Galerie Beyeler, Basel, reproduced in *Paul Klee: Das Frühwerk*, p. 456, no. 337.
19. The "architectures" begin in 1919 with *Herbstlicher Ort* (1921/104), private coll., reproduced in *Paul Klee: Das Frühwerk*, p. 534, no. 449, continue through *Orange-violett grüne Stufung, orange Wergehend–Grün-violett gegen Orange (liegend)* (1922/71), reproduced in *50 Werken von Paul Klee* (Bern: Kornfelf und Klipstein sale catalog, June 11–13, 1975), no. 479, and lead up to *Drei Türme* (1923), Felix Klee coll., Bern, reproduced in *Paul Klee* (St-Paul-de-Vence, Maeght Foundation, July–September 1977), p. 77, no. 55, and to *Architektur* (1923), Hermann Rupf coll., Bern, reproduced in Will Grohmann, *Paul Klee* (Cologne, 1966), p. 201.
20. Notably *Freundlicher Blick* (1923/54), reproduced in *Klee*, catalog of the exposition (Paris: K. Flinker, March–May 1974), no. 20; *Alte Klang* (1925/36), Kunstmuseum, Basel, reproduced in *Paul Klee* catalog (Paris: M.N.A.M., November 1969–February 1979), no. 73; *Harmonie der nordlichen Flora* (1927/58), reproduced in *Paul Klee, Opere 1900–1949, dalla collezione Felix Klee*, op. cit., p. 115, no. 78.
21. For lack of a better term I call this series "organic" because of the indeterminate nature of its forms, which float in an undifferentiated space. The series begins with a treatment of trees in *Park am See, ohne Hauser* (1920/119), reproduced in *Paul Klee, Opere*, p. 94, no. 41. Marie Bonaparte wrote in 1933: "Here, psychoanalytic theory sheds some light in showing us just how old *magic* is; what I am referring to is the moment of human ontogenic and phylogenic evolution in which magic becomes dominant" ("La Pensée magique chez le primitif," *Revue française de psychanalyse* VII, 1 (1934), p. 13.
22. Reproduced in Grohmann, *Paul Klee*, p. 34. I verified this absence of relationship in Goethe, *Poésies*, trans. M. Betz (Paris, 1949); the poem is on pp. 68–71.
23. That is, the Dayak sculpture (South Borneo); three Balinese polychrome statuettes and the Shira-Punu mask (p. 493) of Gabon, in the Blaue Reiter almanac, p. 87, fig. 13, p. 136, figs. 46 and 47, p. 148, no. 54, p. 247, fig. 114. The error in the caption, which attributes the Gabonese mask to China, is significant in that it is indicative of all the attention given to China around 1912.
24. An interesting research project that should be conducted in this area would be to make an inventory of what remains of the Blaue Reiter archives and to consult the registers of the Berne and Munich museums, which is probably where the photographs were acquired and possibly where the rights of reproduction were obtained. The reproduced works were most likely selected from a larger body of works which it would be essential to know in order to determine the exotic works accessible to Klee, Kandinsky, and Marc.
25. Cf. Klee's notes for his course at the Bauhaus, April 3, 1922, published by J. Spliller in *Das Bildnerische Denken*, p. 409. Cited by Pierce, *Paul Klee and Primitive Art* (New York and London, 1976), p. 35.
26. L. Segy, *African Sculpture Speaks* (New York, 1952), p. 127. Quoted by Pierce, *Klee and Primitive Art*, p. 35.
27. Cf. sup. Christian Geelhaar recounts Klee's intellectual awakening during a trip to Italy: "In Genoa, Rome, Naples and Florence 'a segment of history came back to life,' and yet [the artist] became painfully aware 'that the notion of an ideal in the domain of the Fine Arts is totally out of date.' A great perplexity took hold of him, which he attempted to defeat through satire and caricature." And he adds that it was in this frame of mind that the young Klee executed, upon his return, between 1903 and 1905, a series of engravings entitled "Inventions: which is what they indeed are in the true sense of the word—independent of any natural, immediate model" (Klee, *Dessins* [Paris, 1975], p. 12). I should add that at the time Rome, Florence, Naples, and to a lesser extent Genoa, had in their ethnographic museums important collections of Oceanic art. But Paul Klee did not visit them.

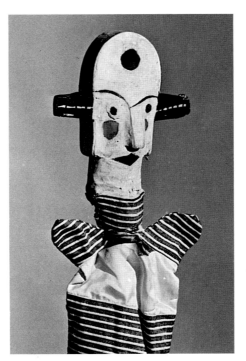

Paul Klee. Hand puppet. *Big-eared Clown*. 1925. Wood, plaster, and paint, 7⅞ x 6¼ x 2⅜" (20 x 16 x 6 cm). Private collection, Bern

Paul Klee. Hand puppet. *White-haired Eskimo*. 1924. Wood, plaster, paint, and horseshoe, 5⅞ x 3¼ x 2⅜" (15 x 8 x 6 cm). Private collection, Bern

Alberto Giacometti. *Invisible Object.* 1934. Bronze (cast 1935), 60⅝ x 12¾ x 11″ (154 x 32.4 x 28 cm). Albright-Knox Art Gallery, Buffalo, Edmund Hayes Fund

GIACOMETTI

Rosalind Krauss

To describe Alberto Giacometti's *Invisible Object* (opposite and p. 504) as "a young girl with knees half-bent as though offering herself to the beholder (a pose suggested to the sculptor by the attitude once assumed by a little girl in his native land)" is to participate in the work of rewriting his beginnings that Giacometti himself started in the 1940s. But this cooperation on the part of Michel Leiris, as he wrote the text for the sculptor's 1951 exhibition catalog, placing *Invisible Object* in the service of a simple transparency to the observable world, is an expression of the ruptures and realignments that were transforming postwar Paris.[1] For this description is a slap in the face of André Breton.

Who can forget the magisterial example through which Breton opens the world of *L'Amour fou* onto the strange but impressive workings of objective chance? Giacometti and Breton go to the flea market, where each one is "claimed" by a seemingly useless object that each is impelled, as though against his will, to buy. Giacometti's purchase was a sharply angled, warriorlike mask (p. 504), for which neither he nor Breton could determine the exact, original use.[2] However, the point of the example was not the object's initial but its ultimate destination. This, according to Breton's account, was in the service of resolving the conflicts paralyzing Giacometti as he attempted to bring parts of *Invisible Object* into focus. The head, particularly, had resisted integration with the rest of the work, and it was to this problem that the mask seemed to address itself. "The purpose of the mask's intervention," wrote Breton, "seemed to be to help Giacometti overcome his indecision in this regard. We should note that here the finding of the object strictly serves the same function as that of a

dream, in that it frees the individual from paralyzing emotional scruples, comforts him, and makes him understand that the obstacle he thought was insurmountable has been cleared."[3] In Breton's account, then, the world of real objects has nothing to do with an art of mimesis; the objects are in no sense models for the sculptor's work. The world is instead a great reserve against which to trace the workings of the unconscious, the litmus paper that makes it possible to read the corrosiveness of desire. Without the mask, the dream, it is claimed, Giacometti could no more have finished *Invisible Object* than Breton could, without his own *trouvaille* from the market, have entered the written world of *L'Amour fou*.

The little Swiss girl of Giacometti's later recollection, and Leiris's account, has nothing to do with this key example of the marvelous and objective chance. By serving as a direct, real-world model for a work of art, the little Swiss girl withdraws *Invisible Object* from the orbit of Surrealism and places it in the postwar realm of Giacometti's studio as he notoriously strained, month after month, through trial and retrial, to catch the likeness of the model posed in front of him.[4] Setting the work in a new context, in relation to a new group of friends and allies like Sartre and Genet, Leiris's account draws it closer to the problematic of *The Phenomenology of Perception* and further from that of *Les Vases communicants*.[5]

This achronicity is, of course, unacceptable to the historian, and thus Reinhold Hohl, the leading scholar of Giacometti's work, does not even mention the memory of the Swiss child in discussing this masterpiece of the sculptor's prewar career. But then Breton's story is, for Hohl, equally suspect. "Contrary to Breton's account," he begins, "that a mysterious object found at the flea market (it was, in fact, the

Iron Mask. Photograph by Man Ray published in André Breton, *L'Amour fou,* Paris, 1937

prototype for an iron protection mask designed by the French Medical Corps in the First World War) had helped the artist to find his forms, Giacometti had borrowed the stylized human shapes from a Solomon Islands *Seated Statue of a Deceased Woman* [page opposite] which he had seen at the Ethnological Museum in Basel, and had combined them with other elements of Oceanic art, such as the bird-like demon of death."[6]

Despite the certainty of his tone, Hohl's evidence for this connection is both scant and indirect. In 1963 Giacometti had spoken to an interviewer about a reconstructed Oceanic house installed in the Basel Museum.[7] Since the Solomon Islands figure had been set up in the same gallery early in the 1930s, Hohl could at least assume Giacometti's knowledge of the object.[8] The detail that lends the greatest credence to Hohl's claim is the schematic, railinglike support for the half-seated figure, a construction that is entirely characteristic of this type of South Seas statue and is not commonly found elsewhere.[9] Since part of the power of the pose of Giacometti's sculpture comes from the enigmatic relation between the half-kneeling posture and the structural elements that seem to contain it—a flat plate against the shins in the front of the figure and the peculiar scaffolding behind it—and since this construction is not "natural" to a model posed in a studio, there has always been the probability that its source was to be found in another work of art. Because of the railing, because of the posture, because of the forward jut of the head and the articulation of the breasts, the Solomon Islands statue of Hohl's nomination would seem a logical candidate.[10]

Of course, behind Hohl's very assertion of this statue as the source of *Invisible Object* there is a whole reservoir of knowledge about the role of Primitive art in the sculptor's work in the years leading up to 1934. Primitivism had been central to Giacometti's early success in freeing himself not only from the classical sculptural tradition but also from the Cubist constructions that had appeared in the early 1920s as the only logical alternative. Giacometti's work matured as a function of its ability to invent in very close relation to Primitive sources, so that just two years after leaving Bourdelle's studio he was able to execute a figure on a major scale that was "his own" by virtue of belonging, quite profoundly, to African tribal art.

That figure, the life-sized *Spoon Woman* (p. 509), was executed in late 1926 or early 1927. In its development beyond

Alberto Giacometti. *Invisible Object (Hands Holding the Void).* 1934. Plaster, 61½" (156.2 cm) high. Yale University Art Gallery, New Haven; anonymous gift. Formerly collection MATTA. Photograph by Dora Maar published in André Breton, *L'Amour fou,* Paris, 1937

Above: Figure. Santa Cruz, Solomon Islands. Wood, hair, and shell inlay, 14½" (37 cm) high. The Trustees of the British Museum, London

Left: Figure. Kopar. East Sepik Province, Papua New Guinea. Painted wood, 63⅜" (161 cm) high. Museum Rietberg, Zurich; von der Heydt Collection

Far left: Figure. Bougainville, Solomon Islands. Painted wood, 69" (175 cm) high. Museum für Völkerkunde, Basel

Alberto Giacometti. *The Couple.* 1926. Bronze, 23¾" (60.1 cm) high. Collection Sylvia and Joseph Slifka

the work that immediately preceded it, *The Couple*, one can see something of Giacometti's intuitions about the way to function sculpturally in relation to Primitive art.[11] Representing Giacometti's first response to African sources, *The Couple* had entered this domain by way of the modish "style nègre" that was extremely widespread by the early 1920s. The sketches published, for example, by Léger in a 1924 issue of *L'Esprit nouveau* as "personnages" for *The Creation of the World* manifest the same generalized, overall shapes—trapezoidal, oval—to express the body as a whole as does *The Couple* and use the same types of ornamental detail to indicate anatomy. The kind

of detail that both Giacometti and Léger exploit comes, for example, from the scarification patterns found on African masks, which the two artists then employ as a way to express anatomical forms (as in the hands in *The Couple*) decoratively. Within the logic of this style, this tribalizing detail is graphically applied to a simplified, planar background. The shapes of that ground might in turn be borrowed from African art (thus there is a possible relation between the general shape of the male figure in *The Couple* and the kind of tribal shields that had also attracted Picasso's attention), and even the figural combinations, as in *The Couple*, might correspond to authentic

Fernand Léger. Sketch for *The Creation of the World* published in *L'Esprit nouveau*, no. 18 (1924)

African types, in this case the oft-used "primal couple" found in Dogon and Baga traditions (pp. 50, 429). But what these applications of random and transformed detail produce is a generalized character of the Afro-Primitive in the absence of any specific sculptural source.

The stylizing attitude that allows for the resultant playful recombination and transmutation of the original examples unites these performances by Giacometti and Léger to the wider field of what could be called Black Deco. Within this context sculptors like Miklos and Lambert-Rucki were producing stylized "African" masks and figurative sculptures by 1925. And the designer Pierre Legrain was conceiving elegant furniture for clients such as Jacques Doucet modeled on seats and stools from tribal Africa. The varied and contradictory suggestions in the Giacometti literature about the ethnographically exact "source" for *The Couple*[12] attest to the success of Black Deco in creating the experience of what Roland Barthes might call Africanity, without preserving much of the structural integrity of the models. It is this stylizing attitude toward the Primitive source that *The Couple* participates in but *Spoon Woman* renounces.

Moving toward a much deeper level of structural assimilation of African carved objects, *Spoon Woman* acknowledges the metaphor frequently put in place by Dan grain spoons (p. 508), in which the bowl of the implement is likened to the lower part of the female, seen as a receptacle, or pouch, or cavity.[13] These spoons—many of which were "abstract" in character—were quite commonplace in the years before 1927. Six spoons from Paul Guillaume's collection were included in the massive exhibition of African and Oceanic art at the Musée des Arts Décoratifs in the winter of 1923–24.[14] By taking the metaphor and inverting it, so that "a spoon is like a woman" becomes "a woman is like a spoon," Giacometti was able to intensify the idea and to make it universal by generalizing the forms of the sometimes rather naturalistic African carvings toward a more prismatic abstraction. In forcing on the Dan model the image of the woman who is almost nothing but womb, Giacometti assimilated the formal elegance of the African object to the more brutish conception of Stone Age fertility Venuses.[15]

With this celebration of the primal function of woman seen through a primitivized formal logic, Giacometti had assumed the aggressive anti-Western stance of the visual avant-garde, given verbal form, for example, by Georges Henri Rivière, soon to be the assistant director of the Trocadéro, when Rivière published a panegyric to archaeology, "parricidal

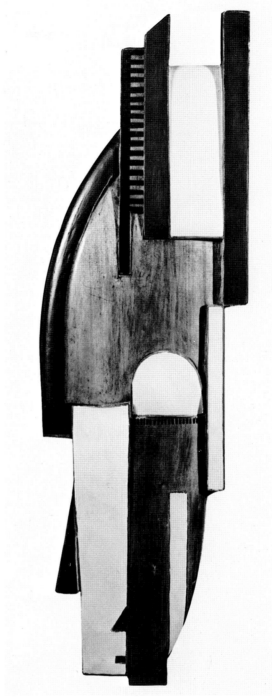

Jean Lambert-Rucki. *Mask.* Wood. Private collection

daughter of humanism," in the initial volume of *Cahiers d'art*.[16] Opening with the bald statement that the miracle of Greek art had run its course, Rivière went on to say that if Louis Aragon and Jean Lurçat were now to go to Spain, unlike their fathers, their most urgent goal would not be the Prado but the caves of Altamira. *Spoon Woman*, contemporary with this statement, is also its confirmation.

But *Spoon Woman* is something else as well. It is what another wing of the intellectual vanguard would view as "soft" primitivism, a primitivism gone formal and therefore gutless. Indeed, to associate *Spoon Woman* with *Cahiers d'art* is to place it within the context of a formalizing conception of the Primitive that we hear, for example, behind the praise that Chris-

Left: Spoon. Dan. Ivory Coast or Liberia. Wood, 20½" (52.1 cm) high. Indiana University Art Museum, Bloomington

Right: Spoon. Dan. Ivory Coast or Liberia. Wood, 17¾" (45 cm) high. Private collection

Far right: Spoon. Wobe. Ivory Coast. Wood, 11¾" (30 cm) high. Musée de l'Homme, Paris

tian Zervos bestowed on Brancusi, calling him the most successful sculptor of the postwar period. Since the great influx of black culture, Zervos wrote in 1929, "Brancusi has explored all the vistas that the Negroes have opened up to him, and which…permitted him to achieve pure form."[17] *Spoon Woman* participates in both the sense of scale and the quality of formal reduction that Giacometti doubtlessly achieved through knowledge of Brancusi's work.

One year before Giacometti made this sculpture, Paul Guillaume published a book that represented the extreme of the movement to "aestheticize" Primitive art.[18] *Primitive Negro Sculpture*, conceived under the aegis of Albert Barnes, written at the Barnes Foundation, and published in English, acknowledges as its only real precedent an analysis of the formal structure of African art by Roger Fry.[19] Because of Guillaume's prominence in the art world, the book would undoubtedly have been well known in Paris even before its translation into French, and it may, indeed, have been one of its illustrations that reinforced Giacometti's conception of the woman/ spoon.

Maintaining that every work of African art can be understood as the solution to a formal problem, *Primitive Negro Sculpture* presents each of its objects as "a rhythmic, varied sequence of some theme in mass, line, or surface," describing the way the geometrically conceived elements are first articulated and then unified by the plastic genius of the Primitive sculptor. But what is insisted upon throughout the text is the continuous presence of a will to art, an aesthetic drive that is understood to be originary or primal. Preceding all ideas, religious or otherwise, this instinct is the joint possession of

children of all races as well as those "children" of the human race: tribal men and women. It is thus the Western child's creative play with paints, and clay, and crayons, that provides access to the processes that drive Primitive art. In concluding with the certainty that "it is not hard to imagine, then, the continuous development of negro art out of the free, naive play of the aesthetic impulse," Guillaume joins the aestheticizing interests of the art world to the most euphoric position of developmental psychology as that was being enunciated in the late 1920s. He places himself in accord with the psychologist G. H. Luquet.[20]

It was undoubtedly Luquet's conviction that the art of children and the art of tribal man form a single category, one that in turn contests the values of "civilized" art, that interested Georges Bataille in his book and drew him to review it in the magazine *Documents*.[21] But Bataille's sharp divergence from Luquet's benign view of the forces at work behind the development of Primitive figuration gives voice to the attack launched by this wing of the radical avant-garde on the art-for-art's-sake view of primitivism. Since, as I will argue, Bataille's attitude had a great deal to do with shaping Giacometti's ultimate conception and use of Primitive material, it is worth attending to Bataille's criticism of Luquet.

Luquet presents the child as having *no* initial figurative intentions but rather as taking pure pleasure in manifesting his own presence by dragging his dirty fingers along walls or covering white sheets of paper with scrawls. Having made

Alberto Giacometti. *Spoon Woman*. 1926–27. Bronze, 56⅞ x 20 x 6⅞" (144.4 x 50.8 x 17.5 cm). Collection Mr. and Mrs. Burton Tremaine, Meriden, Connecticut

these marks, the child later begins to invest parts of them with representational value. With this "reading" of the lines he has made, the child is eventually able to repeat the images voluntarily. Since the basis of the interpretation is enormously schematic, what is involved is the connection of a mark with the idea of an object, a process that has to do with conception and not with resemblance. For this reason Luquet calls Primitive figuration *intellectual realism*, reserving the term *visual realism* for the Western adult's preoccupation with mimesis.

Needless to say, Luquet's presentation of the development of prehistoric cave painting follows the same schema as that of the present-day child: random marking changes gradually to intentional patterning, which in turn gives rise to a figurative reading. Resemblance to external objects having been first "recognized" within the nonfigurative patterns, it can be elaborated and perfected over time.

In Luquet's program, then, an absolute freedom and pleasure initiates the impulse to draw, and it is this instinct, not the desire to render reality, that is primal. On top of this foundation a procedure is gradually built for adjusting the mark to the conditions of representation, and within this a "system" of figuration develops with consistent characteristics over the entire domain of Primitive art, whether that be graffiti, the drawings of children, aborigines, or peasants. Characteristics like the profiles of faces endowed with two eyes and two ears, or the rendering of houses and bodies as transparent in order to display their contents, or the free combination of plan and elevation are what remain unchanged through the practice of "intellectual realism." In Luquet's scheme, knowledge is thus generously added to pleasure.

Of course the chronology of prehistoric art does not support Luquet's cheerful progressivism. The caves of Lascaux with their astonishing naturalism precede the much cruder renderings of later periods. Yet if Bataille draws his reader's attention to this obvious flaw in Luquet's scheme, it is not for reasons of historical accuracy but in order to assert something that had already become a staple of his thinking throughout his editorship of *Documents* and would continue beyond. For what Bataille points to is the unequal mode of representation, within the same period, of animals and men. "The reindeer, the bison, or the horses," Bataille attests, "are represented with such perfect detail, that if we were able to see as scrupulously faithful images of the men themselves, the strangest period of the avatars of humanity would immediately cease being the most inaccessible. But the drawings and sculptures that are charged with representing the Aurignacians themselves are almost all *informe* and much less human than those that represent the animals; others, like the Hottentot Venus, are ignoble caricatures of the human form. This opposition is the same in the Magdalenian period."[22]

It is because "this crude and distorting art has been reserved for the human figure" that Bataille insists on its willfulness, on its status as a kind of primal vandalism wrought on the images of men. Indeed, it is destructiveness that Bataille wishes to substitute for Luquet's serene view of the pleasure principle at work at the origin of the impulse to draw. The child's marking on walls, his scrawls on paper, all proceed from a wish to destroy or mutilate the support. In each subsequent stage of the development charted by Luquet, Bataille sees the enactment of new desire to alter and deform what is there before the subject: "Art, since it is incontestably art, proceeds in this way

by successive destructions. Thus insofar as it liberates instincts, these are sadistic."[23]

The term that Bataille finds to generalize the phenomenon of sadism in both children's art and that of the caves is *alteration*, and this word, in the precision of its ambivalence, is characteristic of Bataille. For alteration derives from the Latin *alter*, which, by encompassing equally a change of state and a change (or advancement) of time, contains the divergent significations of *devolution* and *evolution*. Bataille points out that alteration describes the decomposition of cadavers as well as "the passage to a perfectly heterogeneous state corresponding to . . . the *tout autre*, that is, the sacred, realized for example by a ghost."[24] Alteration—which figures forth the primal impulse of man's self-representation—thus becomes a concept that simultaneously leads downward and upward: like *altus* and *sacer*, the double-directed, primal concepts that interested Freud. The primal, or originary, is therefore irresolvably diffuse—fractured by an irremediable duality at the root of things that was, in his closeness to Nietzsche's thought, dear to Bataille. In its confounding of the logic that maintains terms like high and low or base and sacred as polar opposites, this play on the contradictory allows one to perceive the truth that Bataille never tired of demonstrating: that violence has historically been lodged at the heart of the sacred; that to be genuine, the very thought of the creative must simultaneously be an experience of death; and that it is impossible for any moment of true intensity to exist apart from a cruelty that is equally extreme.[25]

Bataille is perfectly aware that the civilized Westerner might wish to maintain himself in a state of ignorance about the presence of violence within ancient religious practice, so that he either does not notice or does not reflect upon the significance of the deformed anthropoids that appear in the cave, or so that he aestheticizes the whole of African art. In the very first essay he wrote on Primitive civilization he remarked this resistance on the part of scholars to acknowledge what is hideous and cruel in the depiction of the gods of certain peoples. The text, included in a collection of ethnological essays occasioned by the first major exhibition of pre-Columbian art in Paris (1928), was called "L'Amérique disparue," and in it Bataille (assuming the earlier tradition that included pre-Columbian culture within the notion of the Primitive) tried to understand the reality behind the representation of the Aztec gods, depicted as caricatural, monstrous, and deformed.[26] Although his knowledge of pre-Columbian culture was still rather superficial, his analysis proved to be extremely prescient, according to the ethnologist Alfred Métraux as he looked back on this early performance of Bataille's.[27] For what Bataille could read into these images was the presence of malign and dissembling gods, trickster gods to whom was dedicated a religious fervor in which pitiless cruelty combined with black humor to create a culture of delirium: "Doubtless, a bloodier eccentricity was never conceived by human madness: crimes continually committed in broad sunlight for the sole satisfaction of god-ridden nightmares, of terrifying ghosts! The priests' cannibalistic repasts, the ceremonies with cadavers and rivers of blood—more than one historical happening evokes the stunning debaucheries described by the illustrious Marquis de Sade."[28] Broadening the reference from Mexico to de Sade was characteristic of the intellectual field of 1920s ethnological thinking, particularly

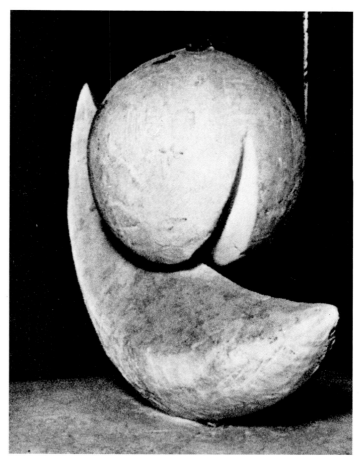

Alberto Giacometti. *Suspended Ball*. 1930–31. Plaster and metal, 24 x 14¼ x 13½" (61 x 36.2 x 34.3 cm). The Alberto Giacometti Foundation, Kunstmuseum, Basel

Alberto Giacometti. *Suspended Ball* (detail). 1930–31. Plaster and metal, 24 x 14¼ x 13½" (61 x 36.2 x 34.3 cm). The Alberto Giacometti Foundation, Kunstmuseum, Basel

in the circle of Marcel Mauss. Mauss's seminar on Primitive religions placed special stress on the violent performance of the sacred in Africa, Oceania, and the Americas. This was to affect not only Bataille's thought but also that of Michel Leiris, as a work like *Les Rites de possessions des Ethiopiens de Goudar et ses aspects théâtraux* demonstrates.

But in speaking of the insatiable thirst for blood of the Aztecs, of their sacrificial practices in which the living victim's heart was cut out of his body and held up, still palpitating, by the priest at the altar, Bataille stresses the "astonishingly joyous character of these horrors." As in the case of the concept of alteration, the practice of sacrifice by the Aztecs allows the double condition of the sacred to be experienced. "Mexico was not only the most streaming of the human slaughterhouses," Bataille writes in comparing Aztec culture with that of the Incas, which he found bureaucratic and dour, "it was also a rich city, a veritable Venice of canals and bridges, of decorated temples and beautiful flower gardens over all."[29] It was a culture of blood that bred both flowers and flies.

If Giacometti had begun in 1926 and 1927 with a conception of Primitive art inscribed on the Luquet side of the ledger, he had moved by 1930, the year "L'Amérique disparue" was published, to that of Bataille's. For in the intervening years, Giacometti had been assimilated into the group that made up *Documents*.

In 1928, the year after he finished *Spoon Woman*, Giacometti

showed his work for the first time. He exhibited two of the plaquelike heads and figures he had made that year, objects that carried the blank frontality of *Spoon Woman* to a new simplicity and elegance. In accordance with the direction implied in his aestheticized primitivism, preclassical objects now became his models for abstracting and reducing his form. The presence of these models in his practice was immediately apparent to the viewers of this work. In one of the earliest commentaries on Giacometti's sculpture, Zervos spoke of its connection to Cycladic art.[30]

On the basis of these two exhibited objects, André Masson asked to meet Giacometti. Thereupon began the sculptor's initiation into the group that included Masson, Desnos, Artaud, Queneau, Leiris, and Bataille, the group that was known as the dissident Surrealists, for whom the intellectual center was *Documents*. Since three of the editors of *Documents* were Bataille, who was deeply committed to the development of ethnographic theory as it was being formulated at the Ecole des Hautes Etudes in the seminars of Marcel Mauss,[31] Michel Leiris, who had become an ethnologist by 1931, and Carl Einstein, who had published his study of Primitive sculpture by 1915, the commitment of the magazine to this subject is obvious. Giacometti's close and lasting friendship with Leiris brought with it an association with the details and theories not only of ethnography but of the uses to which it was being put by the *Documents* group.[32] In 1930, at the end of his initiation into *Documents*, Giacometti made *Suspended Ball*. A sculpture that was to cause a sensation among the orthodox Surrealists, giving Giacometti instant access to Breton and Dali, a sculpture that set off the whole Surrealist vogue for creating erotically charged objects, it was nonetheless a work that had much less to do with Surrealism than it did with Bataille.[33]

Maurice Nadeau remembers the reactions originally triggered by *Suspended Ball*: "Everyone who saw this object functioning experienced a strong but indefinable sexual emotion relating to unconscious desires. This emotion was in no sense one of satisfaction, but one of disturbance, like that imparted by the irritating awareness of failure."[34] An erotic machine, *Suspended Ball* is, then, like Duchamp's *Large Glass*, an apparatus for the disconnection of the sexes, the nonfulfillment of desire. But *Suspended Ball* is more explicitly sadistic than *The Bride Stripped Bare*. For the sliding action that visibly relates the sculpture's grooved sphere to its wedge-shaped partner not only suggests the act of caressing but that of cutting: recapitulating, for example, the stunning gesture from the opening of the 1928 film *Un Chien andalou*, as a razor slices through an opened eye.[35]

In this double gesture in which love and violence are simultaneously incarnated, one can locate a fundamental ambiguity with regard to the sexual identity of the elements of Giacometti's sculpture. The wedge, acted upon by the ball, is in one reading its feminine partner; in another, distended and sharp, it is the phallic instrument of aggression against the ball's vulnerable roundness: It is not only the razor from *Un Chien andalou* but the bull's horn from Bataille's *L'Histoire de l'oeil*, which penetrates the matador, killing him by ripping out his eye.[36]

And the wedge is possibly a third substitute for the phallus, joined in yet another way to the universe of sacred violence that had, by 1930, become the shared interest of Giacometti and Bataille. The wedge is shaped like the palmette stones of the ancient Mexican ballgame—wedge-shaped elements that were thought to have been worn for protection by the nearly naked participants in a game in which the ball could only be kept in play by being hit with the knees and buttocks and in which the very names used for the game stressed the instrumentality of the buttocks (for example, from Molina's 1571 Nahua dictionary we have "*ollama*: to play ball with the buttocks," and "*olli*: certain gum of medicinal trees of which they make balls which they play with their buttocks").[37] Like

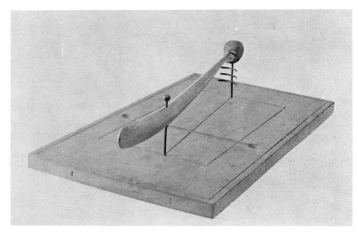

Alberto Giacometti. *Point to the Eye*. 1932. Wood and metal, 4¾ x 24 x 14" (12.2 x 61 x 35.6 cm). Musée National d'Art Moderne, Centre National d'Art et de Culture Georges Pompidou, Paris

everything else in the Mexico Bataille admired, the ancient ballgame was a combination of exuberance and cruelty, with accounts of bloody wounds caused by the ball and deaths of the players on the courts. With its use of the buttocks as a principal instrument of play, the game had a further homoerotic overtone. If, as I am suggesting, the Mexican ballgame was a component in the formation of *Suspended Ball*—opening as the work does onto Giacometti's immediately subsequent investigation of sculpture itself as a ball court, or playing field, or gameboard, as in *Point to the Eye*, *Circuit* (p. 529), and *No More Play* (*On ne joue plus*)—then a "third sex" must be added to the cycle of indeterminacy of the work's sexual signifiers.

Giacometti's early sculpture had already demonstrated an interest in pre-Columbian art, along with that of Africa and the Cyclades. Jacques Dupin, whose study was completed during the sculptor's lifetime, reports that Giacometti's early "exotic" sources were from Africa, Oceania, and Mexico.[38] Two works that bear obvious witness to this early Mexican connection are the *Crouching Man* of 1926 and a possibly even earlier plaster, *Head* (p. 514). A third sculpture that permits a reading of more than an aesthetic relationship to Mexico, but rather a Bataille-like experience of the ethos of Aztec culture, is *The Hour of the Traces* of 1930 (p. 514). It is the imagery of "L'Amérique disparue" and the other reports of Aztec culture published in *Documents*—the full series of which Giacometti carefully guarded his entire lifetime[39]—that provides a possible reading of *The Hour of the Traces* as the ecstatic image of human sacrifice. For the figure at the top of the work, whose rictus is either that of extreme ecstasy or pain (or as Bataille would have it, both), appears posed on an altar below which swings the form of a disembodied heart.[40]

The Hour of the Traces immediately preceded *Suspended Ball*. The two sculptures are structurally connected by virtue of their shared play with a pendant element swung from a cagelike support. Within the universe of ideas associated at that moment to Aztec culture, the sculptures may be thematically connected as well. But without any doubt they are both assimilable to Giacometti's fully elaborated accounts of his own thoughts of sadism and violence. Although first published in Breton's magazine, a text like "Hier, sables mouvants," with its fantasy of rape ("the whole forest rang with their cries and groans") and slaughter, has little to do with the

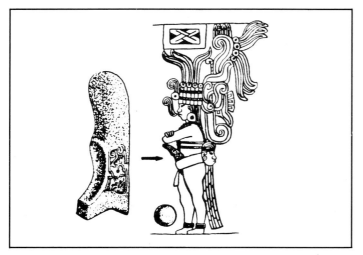

Ball-game player. Vega de Aparicio, Veracruz, Mexico. Drawing adapted from a stone sculpture in the Museo Nacional de Antropologia, Mexico City. Published in Stephan F. and Suzanne de Borhegyi, *The Rubber Ball Game of Ancient America*, 1963

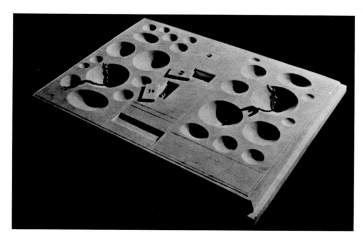

Alberto Giacometti. *No More Play* (*On ne joue plus*). 1933. Marble, wood, and bronze, 2 x 15¾ x 11⅞" (5 x 40 x 30 cm). Collection Mrs. Julien Levy, Bridgewater, Conn.

Gameboard. Gio. Liberia. Wood, 22" (55.8 cm) long. Peabody Museum of Archaeology and Ethnology, Harvard University, Cambridge

notions of convulsive beauty authorized by Surrealism.[41] Its relationship is to Georges Bataille, whose own writing and preoccupations seem to have given Giacometti permission to express these fantasies of brutality. Like his lifetime attachment to Bataille's magazine, Giacometti's writing about violence—as in his essay on Jacques Callot or his text "Le Rêve, le Sphinx et le mort de T."—continued well beyond the 1930s and his repudiation of Surrealism. In both their structure and imagery these texts often call Bataille to mind.[42]

I said before that *alteration* functions as a Bataillian concept because of the primal contradiction that operates its relation to meaning, such that the signifier oscillates constantly between two poles. This same kind of oscillation of meaning—or for the complexity involved the more accurate term might be *migration*—is what is put into play by *Suspended Ball*. For though the work is structured as a binary opposition, with male and female juxtaposed and contrasted, the value of each of these terms does not remain fixed. Each element can be read as the symbol of either the masculine or feminine sex (and for the ball, in addition to an interpretation as testicles, there are the additional possible semantic values of buttocks and eye, neither of these determined by gender). The identification of either form within any given reading of the work is possible only in opposition to its mate; and these readings circulate through a constantly shifting theater of relationships, cycling through the metaphoric statement of heterosexual connection into the domains of transgressive sexuality—masturbatory, homosexual, sadistic—and back again. (The transgression contained in the sculpture's signifying gesture—it should be noted—sets it apart simultaneously from Breton's adamant rejection of the sexually perverse, and the rather anodyne, formal *jeux d'esprit* of Picasso's transformations of the human body in the late 1920s, with which *Suspended Ball* is often compared.[43]) In its continual movement, its constant "alteration," this play of meaning is thus the enactment in the symbolic realm of the literal motion of the work's pendular action.

Although the alter(n)ation of *Suspended Ball* is constant, it is nonetheless regulated in a way that is entirely structured by the possibilities of metaphorical expansion of its two elements—wedge and sphere—and the oscillations of their sexual values. In this erotic play within a structurally closed

system, the sculpture participates in the demonic logic of Bataille's *L'Histoire de l'oeil*. In Bataille's work, which, as Roland Barthes points out, is literally the story of an object—the eye—and what happens to it (and not to the novel's characters), a condition of migration is established in which the object is, as it were, "declined" through various verbal states. As a globular element, the eye is transformed through a series of metaphors by means of which, at any given point in the narrative, other globular objects are substituted for it: eggs, testicles, the sun. As an object containing fluid, the eye simultaneously gives rise to a secondary series related to the first: yolk, tears, urine, sperm. The two metaphoric series thus establish a system of combination by which terms can interact to produce a near infinity of images. The sun, metaphorized as eye and yolk, can be described as "flaccid luminosity" and can give rise to the phrase "the urinary liquefaction of the sky." Yet it is more correct to characterize the two metaphorical series as two chains of signifiers, "because for each one it is obvious that any term is never anything but the signifier of a neighboring term."[44] And if, as one part of one chain connects to that of the other, this *combinatoire* is a machine for the production of images, it is essential to note that because of the logical constraints regulating the chains, there is nothing Surrealist in these "encounters"; they are not meetings by chance.

The structure of these metaphoric substitutions thus produces not only the course of the erotic action of the narrative but the verbal fabric through which the *récit* is woven. And it is important to compare this aspect of *L'Histoire de l'oeil* to the action of *Suspended Ball*. For, conceived as the action of metaphor, the story of the eye is not the story of a literal eye. Deprived of a point of origin in the real world, a moment that would be anterior to the metaphorical transformations, conferring on them both their point of departure and their sense, the story thus has no privileged term. As Barthes says of the work's structure, "The paradigm has no beginning anywhere." Because the eye's sexual identity remains perfectly ambiguous (a round phallicism), the narrative does not have a single sexual fantasy hidden within its depths that would provide its ultimate meaning. "We are left no other possibility than to reflect on a perfectly spherical metaphor within *L'Histoire de l'oeil*: each of its terms is always the signifier of another term

Alberto Giacometti. *Head*. c. 1925. Plaster, 11¼ x 11¾ x 2¾" (28.5 x 29.5 x 7.2 cm).
Musée National d'Art Moderne, Centre National d'Art et de Culture Georges
Pompidou, Paris

(and no term is ever a simple signified), without the relay ever being able to be halted."[45]

This round phallicism, this collapse of distinction between what is properly masculine and what is properly feminine, this obliteration of difference is for logic what perversions are for eroticism: it is transgressive. As Bataille explains in his "Dictionary entry" in *Documents* for the word *informe*, philosophy's task is to make sure that everything *has* its proper form, its defined boundaries, its limits. But certain words, and *informe* is one of them, have a contrary mission. Their task is to declassify, to strip away the "mathematical frockcoats" that philosophy drapes over everything. Because by opening onto formlessness, to the collapse of difference, *informe* "comes down to saying that the world is something like a spider or a glob of spit [*crachat*]."[46] *Informe* denotes what alteration produces, the reduction of meaning or value, not by contradiction—which would be dialectical—but by putrefaction: the puncturing of the limits around the term, the reduction to the sameness of the cadaver, which is transgressive. Round phallicism is a destruction of meaning/being. This is not to say that the objects and images of *L'Histoire de l'oeil* or *Suspended Ball* literally have no form by resembling spittle, but rather that the work they do is to collapse difference. They are machines for doing this.

Bataille's "Dictionary" was dedicated to revealing the jobs that words do.[47] His magazine *Documents*, within which it was housed, also had a "job," and part of this was to use ethnographic data to transgress the neat boundaries of the art world with its categories based on *form*. This is the "hard" use of primitivism, as opposed to what I referred to as the "soft" or "aestheticized" view of it. It certainly cannot limit itself to borrowing this or that shape from the repertory of Primitive objects the way even art school students (particularly within the decorative arts) were being encouraged to do during the 1920s.[48] Instead, it uses the "primitive" in an expanded sense (although with close attention to ethnographic detail) to embed art in a network that, in its philosophical dimension, is violently anti-idealist and antihumanist. Bataille ends his article "Primitive Art" by invoking the modern art he respects, art that "rather quickly presented a process of decomposition and destruction, which has been no less painful to most people than would have been the sight of the decomposition and destruction of a cadaver."[49] "Intellectual realism"—Luquet's aestheticizing, cognitively constructive category, which itself owes much to the early defense of Cubist painting[50]—will no more address the conditions of this "rotting painting," Bataille insists, than it can address the whole of sculpture in general. When it comes Bataille's turn in *Documents* to think about Picasso's work, he does so under the rubric "Soleil pourri."[51]

It is only through this expanded conception of the "job" that primitivism performed for the dissident Surrealists that we can understand the brilliance of a sculpture like *Suspended Ball* or judge the claims about the "source" of *Invisible Object*. For the elaborate network of the Primitive that had been developed by the early 1930s tends to provide a sculpture like *Invisible Object* with many interconnected references, thus supporting not only Hohl's assertions about the work but Breton's and Leiris's as well and opening onto still further conditions that generated the sculpture.

Alberto Giacometti. *The Hour of the Traces*. 1930. Wood, plaster, and metal. Whereabouts unknown

Alberto Giacometti. *Head.* 1934. Plaster. Whereabouts unknown

Carnival mask. Photograph by Jacques-André Boiffard published in Georges Limbour, "Eschyle, le carnaval et les civilisés," *Documents* 2, no. 2 (1930)

If we start with Leiris's report about the little Swiss girl, which in the context of this moment of Giacometti's art is certainly the most questionable of referents, we see that in fact it fits into the circumstances surrounding the development of the work. Breton reports that the first stage of the head, the one ultimately replaced by the mask from the flea market, was flat and undefined, although the conception of the eyes as large wheels—the right one intact, the left one broken—continued through the first and second versions.[52] There is a plaster from 1934, a time just prior to the making of *Invisible Object*, that fits Breton's description and was undoubtedly the sketch for the initial idea of the figure's head (above). Where the final version is crystalline and defined, the plaster sketch is flabby and almost formless, but what connects the two conceptions (beyond the wheellike eyes) is their being masks.[53] The plaster head is clearly copied from one of the carnival masks photographed by Jacques-André Boiffard and reproduced in *Documents* to accompany Georges Limbour's text "Eschyle, le carnaval et les civilisés."[54]

The setting for Limbour's meditation on this subject is a chaotic general store in which the author watches a little girl shyly pick up a carnival mask of a bearded man, and, trying it on, transform herself into a kind of Lolita by lasciviously running her tongue along the lips of the papier-mâché face. The vivid description of this "Salomé of the streets" may well be the vehicle of association with the little Swiss girl.

The rest of Limbour's article also rewards attention. Speaking first of the conception of death into which the grimacing masks of Greek tragedy froze the mobility of the human face, Limbour then turns to Primitive masks. For the *Documents* group as well as for the orthodox Surrealists, the preferred domain of Primitive art was no longer that of Africa, which was considered too rational, too formalist, but that of Oceania, and it is to this that Limbour refers.[55] In a passage that is representative of the angrily anticolonialist feeling of both groups, Limbour castigates the violation of these territories by the white man, who substitutes his "missionaries of Lent, his papier-mâché Jesuits" for the incredible force of the Melanesian conception of the mask.[56] And in an image that is

Protection of Men. Photograph published in "Aboutissements de la mécanique," *Variétés,* January 1930

right out of Bataille's conception of the *soleil pourri*, he speaks of the faces carved onto the great poles stuck into the earth, "staring straight into the sun."[57] Having raped the South Seas to send its sacred objects back to the art markets and Trocadéros of "civilization," the West has also developed its own masks, ones, Limbour writes, that are worthy of Aeschylus. These, of course, are the gas masks that alone are authentic to our times. "Because if religion, the cult of the dead, and the festivals of Dionysos turned the mask into a sacred, ritual ornament among the various ancient peoples, we too have our own religion, our own societal games, and consequently our own masks. Only the general standardization of our age requires that we all wear the same one."

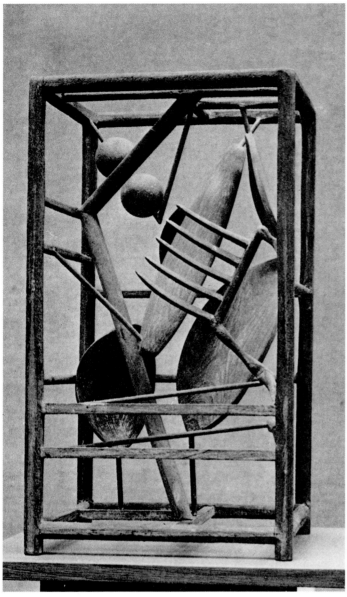

Alberto Giacometti. *Cage.* 1931. Wood, 19¼" (49 cm) high. Moderna Museet, Stockholm

Malanggan figure (detail). New Ireland. Painted wood, 69⅛" (175.6 cm) high, overall. Collection Dorothea Tanning, New York. Formerly collection MAX ERNST

The image of the gas mask, which substitutes for the "humanity" of the face a horrific image of the brutality of industrialized war, had become extremely widespread among the 1920s avant-garde. A suite of photographs in *Variétés* showing not only wearers of gas masks but of other kinds of mechanical devices attested to this fascination for what modern imagination had created to replace the head of man (p. 515).[58] As with all the mechanical candidates, but with extraordinary force in the case of the gas mask, this substitute calls to mind not higher stages in the evolution of the species, but much, much lower ones, because the wearer of the gas mask looks like nothing so much as an insect.

The man with the insect head is *informe,* altered. What should be the sign of his highest faculties—his mind, his spirit—has become lowly, like the crushed spider, or the earthworm. The man with the insect head is, like the deformed anthropoids of the caves, *acéphale,* a transgressive thought of the human.[59] The term is, of course, Bataille's, and

in his work it functioned as a kind of password used to enter the conceptual theater within which humanity displays the richness of its contradictory condition. For *acéphale* opens onto the experience of man's verticality—his elevation in both its biological and moral significance—as a negation: a development toward the primitive, an ascendance downward. As will be shown, this conceptual inversion would also play a structural role in the redefinition of sculpture that Giacometti explored in these years. But for Giacometti, as well as for many of his fellow artists, its most obvious impact was thematic.

Within the imaginative circuit of the period being considered, the man with the insect head is also the *woman* with the insect head: the praying mantis. The symbol of a collapse of the distinction between life—or procreation—and death, the praying mantis fascinated the vanguard of *Variétés, Documents,* and *Minotaure* because of one detail: the female of the species was known to eat its partner after, or even during, copulation.

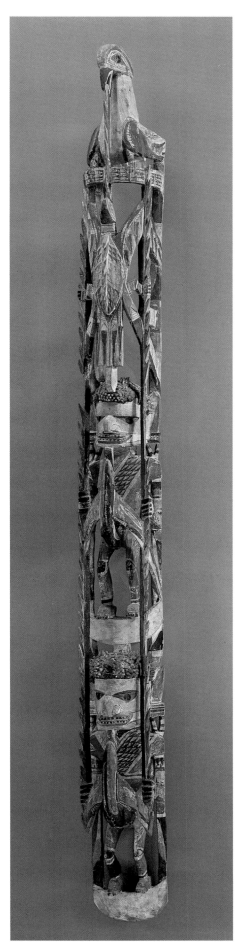

Malanggan figure. New Ireland. Painted wood, 69⅛"
(175.6 cm) high. Collection Dorothea Tanning,
New York. Formerly collection MAX ERNST

Malanggan figure. New Ireland. Painted wood, 52¾" (134 cm) high. Musée National des Arts
Africains et Océaniens, Paris

Max Ernst. Collage from *Une Semaine de bonté*. 1934. Fifth book. Element: Darkness. Example: Easter Island

Alberto Giacometti. *Three Figures in a Field*. 1930. Destroyed

Because of the strongly anthropomorphic character of this insect, its mating habits seemed extremely portentous to the Surrealists. Roger Caillois's essay on the mantis, published in *Minotaure* in 1934, which became the basis of his later studies of the function of myth and the ambiguity of the sacred, reported that Breton, Eluard, and Dali all kept large collections of these insects, in cages.[60]

Caillois's essay released a swarm of praying mantises onto the surfaces of Surrealist painting.[61] But even before 1934 the insect had appeared in Giacometti's work as well as Ernst's. Giacometti's 1930 *Woman, Head, Tree* depicts the woman as a mantis and seems to have introduced the production of the two *Cages* (p. 516) of the following year. In both of these an abstracted image of the mantis is at work within the nightmarish confines of the sculpture, attacking its masculine partner, which is represented by a simple sphere, or cranium.[62] With these *Cages*, the mantis appears as well to have been influenced by the extreme formal disjunction considered to be the major visual characteristic of Oceanic art, giving it its power and its savage poetry. Several of the Malanggans from New Ireland that could have been known to Giacometti at this time are highly suggestive as a possible source for the idea of a disjointed, caged figure (p. 517).[63] And in the analysis of Melanesian motifs that Carl Einstein published in the 1920s, the Malanggan's structure, conceived as a cranium contained within a scaffolding of bones that is the Primitive reconception of the skeleton, is even more suggestive for an iconological reading of the *Cages*.[64]

After this it was Ernst who took up the theme of the mantis, and in his production of *Une Semaine de bonté*, published in 1934, one finds the image embedded within a whole oeuvre dedicated to the conditions of the *acéphale*. [65] In one chapter of this collage novel in which the human (male) head is replaced by everything from worms to birds to lions, the actors are depicted with the heads of the great Easter Island statues, and juxtaposed to one such figure looking at itself in a mirror is a mantis in the act of consuming her mate.[66]

The rapport between Giacometti and Ernst during the early 1930s resulted in Ernst's visit to the Giacometti family's summer home at Maloja in 1934, where with Giacometti's help Ernst made a series of sculptures by slightly reworking and etching large stones that the two men dragged from a moraine (p. 29). The figures Ernst chose to represent on these sculptures were both the birds from the Easter Island cults and the Papuan bird from New Guinea with which Ernst identified and which he used as his alter ego Loplop.[67] Much of the sculpture that Ernst went on to make in the following years shows the effects of this visit. His *Lunar Asparagus* (1935, p. 564), for example, is obviously indebted to *Three Figures in a Field*, a work resonant with Primitive associations and which Giacometti had set up in 1930 in the Swiss countryside.[68] But the interest obviously ran both ways, as Giacometti's *Project for a Passageway* (1930–31) indicates with its closeness to images like Ernst's *Anatomy of a Bride* or *La Belle Jardinière*.

Thus Ernst's association in *Une Semaine de bonté* of the mantis with the context of Oceania and the site of the Papuan spirit bird provides yet one more aspect of the many factors that determined the conception of *Invisible Object*, with its own inclusion of a bird's head reminiscent of Loplop's. It establishes a conceptual site within which to see how the logic of *Invisible Object* works to combine the Solomon Islands spirit of the

Alberto Giacometti. *Head/Landscape.* 1930–31. Plaster, 9½ x 27½" (24.1 x 69.8 cm). Whereabouts unknown

Child's coffin. Nouméa, New Caledonia. Wood and fiber, 15¾" (40 cm) high. Musée de l'Homme, Paris

Village of Goulfé, Cameroon. Published in André Gide, "Architectures nègres," *Cahiers d'art,* no. 7–8, 1927

dead with the mythic/biological purveyor of death supplied by the form of the mantis. In Breton's story of the substitution of one version of the work's head by another, the constant factor now appears to be the idea of the head as a mask, and the figure, therefore, as *acéphale.* As the mask itself becomes increasingly cruel of aspect, it more and more closely resembles the pointed shape of the mantis's face, with its huge staring eyes.[69] Giacometti's attraction to the flea-market mask was indeed, as Freud would have said, overdetermined.

One wing of Giacometti scholarship is extremely focused on the psycho-biographical underpinnings of his art.[70] To what has been said about the factors contributing to *Invisible Object,* this interpretive strategy would undoubtedly add a hallucinatory maternal presence hovering behind the Sol-

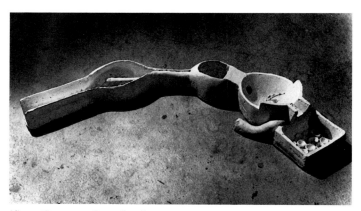

Alberto Giacometti. *Project for a Passageway.* 1930–31. Plaster, 6 x 50 x 17" (15.2 x 127 x 43.2 cm). The Alberto Giacometti Foundation, Kunsthaus, Zurich

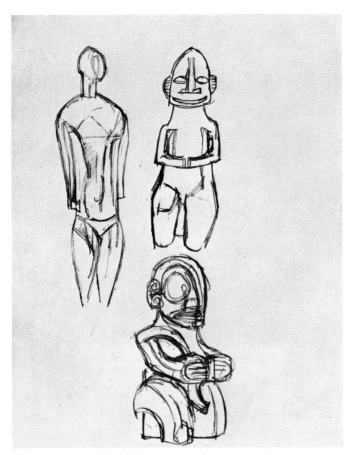

Alberto Giacometti. *Tribal Sculptures.* c. 1929. Pen, 10⅝ x 8¼" (27 x 21 cm).
Private collection, Paris

omon Islands spirit of the dead. Dressed in black, the woman whom Giacometti rapes and slaughters in his adolescent fantasies is the same woman who enters the *Palace at 4 A.M.* to disrupt its erotic idyll. The great proscriber of his sexuality, she is Annetta Stampa Giacometti.[71] It is possible to trace the way this maternal force was simultaneously associated with the ideas of death that haunt his work and its equally strong focus on pregnancy and birth. Giacometti was obsessed with the idea of the rock that bears fruit, or, as Arp had written, "The stones are full of entrails. Bravo. Bravo."[72] Interesting as that territory might be to explore, it is tangential to the subject of this study, although in what follows, with its concern with death and the monument, the additional testimony of this personal, biographic motivation is certainly not unwelcome.

Any artist's work can be seen from either of two, possibly conflicting, perspectives. One of these looks at the oeuvre from within the totality of the individual. The other regards it, far more impersonally, within a historical dimension, which is to say, comparatively, in relation to the work of others and the collective development of a given medium. Often these two perspectives overlap. The shape of Mondrian's career, for example, in its search for the Neo-Plastic elements of painting, coincides with his position at the forefront of the general development of abstraction within twentieth-century art.

In Giacometti's case this is not so. Giacometti's sculpture

Figure. Nukuoro, Caroline Islands. Wood, 19⅝" (50 cm) high. Rautenstrauch-Joest Museum, Cologne

Figure. Marquesas Islands. Wood, 13¾" (35 cm) high. Museum für Völkerkunde, Berlin

Figure. Marquesas Islands. Wood, 13¼" (33.5 cm) high. Etnografiska Museet, Stockholm

viewed from the perspective of his individual oeuvre is over-whelmingly that of the monument: the single, vertical figure, raised commemoratively in space, hieratic, immobile, tall. From *Spoon Woman*, to *Invisible Object*, to any of the 1950s standing figures, we can follow the trajectory of this concern, using it to bestow a conceptual unity on Giacometti's art. But from the point of view of the history of sculpture—an imper-sonal and far less sympathetic measure—Giacometti's entire production of the vertical monument is less interesting, that is, less totally innovative, than the work he made in the years 1930–33; for that intervening work is horizontal.

The formal innovation of those sculptures, almost wholly unprepared for by anything else in the history of the medium, was their ninety-degree turn of the axis of the monument to fold its vertical dimension onto the horizontality of the earth. In objects like *Project for a Square, Head/Landscape* (p. 519), and the extraordinary gameboard sculptures like *Circuit* and *On ne joue plus*, the work itself is simply and directly conceived of as a base. We could challenge the innovative character of this invention by saying that Degas, with his *Bather* (c. 1886), had already dispensed with the intermediary of a base and placed a sculpture directly on the ground, or by saying that already, in the 1910s, Brancusi had canceled the distinction between sculpture and base. Yet we would then be missing the point of the profound originality of Giacometti's move. For Degas's *Bather*, like Giacometti's own *Woman with Her Throat Cut* (1932), conceives of the sculpture *without* a base and therefore as a figure seen from above; but it does not understand the work *as* a base. And although Brancusi often thinks this absolute fusion, his base/sculptures, unlike Giacometti's, remain vertical. Brancusi's works continue to house the object within the domain created by the primal opposition between what is not artistically determined—the ground—and what is—the sculpture. The very axis of verticality declares the separateness of sculpture's representational field and the world of actuality, and this dimension is traditionally introduced by the uprightness of a pedestal, which lifts the work above the ground and removes it from the space of the real. Like a picture frame, the pedestal closes off the virtual field of representation from the actual space around it.

But if the picture is somehow *only* its frame, then this distinction is not so easy, and the representation begins to fuse with its literal surroundings. This was the transformation of the sculptural that Giacometti put in place between 1930 and 1933. The rotation of the axis onto the horizontal plane was further specified by the contents of the work as the "lowering" of the object, thereby joining it simultaneously to the ground and to the real—to the actuality of space and the literalness of motion in real time. From the perspective of the history of modern sculpture, this is the inaugural act of Giacometti's art, with implications for much of what would take place in the rethinking of sculpture after World War II. And it is precisely within this theater of operations that Giacometti's relationship to tribal art and the primitive is once again encountered.

The earliest of these sculptures is *Project for a Passageway* (1930–31, p. 519), an object both close to Ernst's "anatomies" and determined by the ethnographic metaphor of the body as a cluster of African clay huts (p. 519).[73] Giacometti's alternate name for this work—*The Labyrinth*—reinforces the rela-tionship of its conception to the world of the primitive.[74] For in the thinking of the early 1930s, with its obsession with the

Alberto Giacometti. *Nimba Mask and Women.* c. 1956. Pen, 11½ x 8¼" (29.2 x 21 cm). Private collection, Paris

Minotaur, the labyrinth was set in primal opposition to classi-cal architecture's connotations of lucidity and the domination of space. In the grip of the labyrinth, it is man who is dominated, disoriented, lost.[75]

With the second of these horizontal sculptures the issue of *rotation* of the axis becomes more perspicuous. *Head/Landscape* (1930–31) was initially called *Fall of a Body onto a Diagram*, and it is this notion of the body's fall that verbally acknowledges what the sculpture visually performs.[76] The structural princi-ple of *Head/Landscape* depends on the metaphorical relation between the two things operated through the spatial device of anamorphosis: Rotated onto the horizontal plane, the face resembles a landscape. This precise relationship was spelled out in a display of "paranoid critical" thinking by Salvador Dali when he "read" a photograph of African natives sitting in front of their huts as a Picasso head, a (mis)reading that resulted, he explained, from his disorientation with regard to the pho-tograph. In Dali's presentation the image is then, like *Head/ Landscape*, rotated ninety degrees.[77] But Giacometti's sculpture is less like a head in rotation than it is like a mask or flat covering of some sort. And the landscape that is its alternate reading does not seem like the neutral terrain of Dali's example but rather resembles a necropolis, its rectangular openings suggesting a tomb.[78] (This combination of tomb and ne-cropolis would be made more precise by the coffins sunk into the ground of *On ne joue plus* of the following year.)

Various African masks photographed and published lying down may have played a role in suggesting the morphology of *Head/Landscape*.[79] But the object that weaves together most of the threads of association suggested by the work's meta-phorical play, the object that could well have been a source, is the lid of a child's coffin from New Caledonia in the Musée de

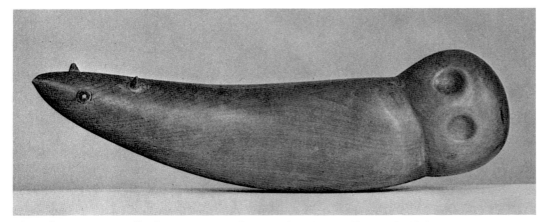

Fish. Easter Island. Wood, 6¾" (17.2 cm) long. Formerly Museum für Völkerkunde, Berlin. Whereabouts unknown

Alberto Giacometti. *Disagreeable Object.* 1931. Wood, 19" (48.3 cm) long. Private collection, New York

Ear ornament. Marquesas Islands. Ivory, 3½" (9 cm) high. Private collection. Formerly collection TRISTAN TZARA

Alberto Giacometti. *Disagreeable Object to Be Disposed Of.* 1931. Wood, 8½" (21.6 cm) long. Private collection, London

l'Homme (p. 519). This object figured in the copious illustrations of the 1929 *Cahiers d'art* special issue on Oceania, an issue that Giacometti possessed and from which he made many copy-drawings. Giacometti had constantly insisted that his frequent drawing after other works of art was most often done from illustrations rather than in front of the things themselves.[80] The example (p. 520) of his early drawings of Oceanic objects bears this out, for they are practically all taken from the same published source.[81] This resource, at the time the largest easily accessible repertory of Oceanic images (containing, moreover, many representatives of the Surrealists' collections: Breton, Aragon, Tzara), may have suggested other types of relationship to Giacometti besides the head/landscape of the coffin lid of the magazine's figure 122. The Easter Island fish of figure 180 (above) could have operated behind the development of the phallically conceived *Disagreeable Objects* (1931), and the tusklike earring owned by Tzara, figure 169, is strongly related to the same series's

Disagreeable Object to Be Disposed Of.[82] Further, the bird/woman statue of figure 46 resembles one of the two personages that inhabit the necropolis of *On ne joue plus*; and, as has been suggested above with regard to the object owned by Max Ernst, the various Malanggan, particularly the one belonging to Louis Aragon (figure 65), contain the idea of sculptural scaffolding one finds in Giacometti's repeated use of the cage.

Given the almost exclusive identification of the Surrealists with Oceania, the upsurge of these sources among the range of Primitive images fueling Giacometti's imagination at this time might be used to reinforce the general characterization of this period of his work (1930–32) as his "Surrealist epoch."[83] However, Giacometti's connection with the orthodox Surrealists did not really begin in 1930. *Suspended Ball*, the object that excited their attention, was not exhibited until the end of that year. It is not to the Surrealist conceptual domain, to its fascination with the aleatory, with games of chance and the *objet trouvé*, that we should look for the matrix of ideas that operate in Giacometti's conception of sculpture's rotated axis: the horizontal gameboard, movement in real time, the sculpture as base, the base as necropolis. The year this all began was 1930, and at that time Giacometti was still connected with *Documents*. The preoccupation with real time that enters his work with *Suspended Ball* and *The Hour of the Traces* opens onto a consideration of real space; and real space is defined by sculpture that has become nothing but its base, a vertical that is rotated into "baseness." This very operation was made continually by Bataille as he developed the concept of *"basesse"*—a low, or base, materialism—in *Documents*.[84]

In the anatomical geography of Bataille's thought the vertical axis symbolizes man's pretentions toward the elevated, the spiritual, the ideal; his claim that the uprightness separating him biologically from the bestial distinguishes him ethically as well. Bataille, of course, does not believe in this distinction and insists on the presence—behind the repressive assumptions of verticality—of lowness as the real source of libidinal energy. Lowness here is both an axis and a direction, the horizontality of the mud of the real. If feet are highly charged objects, Bataille insists in "Le Gros Orteil," it is because, simultaneously the focus of disgust and eros, they are the part of the body that is mired in the ground. "A return to reality implies no new acceptance whatever, but it means that we are basely seduced, without symbolic substitutions and up to the point of crying out, in staring, eyes wide open: staring thus in front of a big toe."[85]

In the "Dictionary" entry *Bouche* this opposition between the vertical and horizontal axes is developed specifically through the operation of rotation. The mental axis is the one connecting eyes and mouth, issuing in language, the expressive function that heralds the human. The biological axis on the other hand connects mouth to anus—locating the alimentary functions of ingestion and excretion. To lower the mental, or spiritual, axis onto the biological one is to think about the real transformation of articulate sounds into bestial ones at the moments of man's greatest pain or pleasure and to see these in their true operation as excretory. The summit of the body is thus given an opening that has nothing to do with the ideational, but is rather a hole resembling the anus. In *Documents* this text was illustrated by a full-page photograph by Boiffard of a mouth, wide open, wet with saliva.[86]

This idea of a hole at the top of man's head—one that

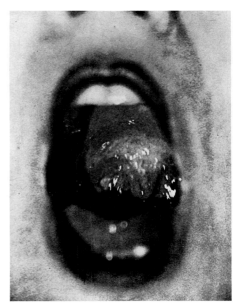

Above left: Jacques-André Boiffard. Untitled photograph. c. 1930. 3¼ x 10⅞" (8.2 x 27.7 cm). Private collection

Above right: Photograph by Jacques-André Boiffard published in Georges Bataille, "Bouche," *Documents* 2, no. 5 (1930)

Man Ray. Photograph. Published in *Minotaure*, no. 7 (1935)

functions to de-idealize, de-rationalize, dis-equilibrate—led Bataille to try to construct the mytho-anatomical legend of the pineal eye. This gland at the summit of the human structure Bataille conceives of as a blind spot. The very opposite of Descartes's belief that the pineal eye was the organ connecting the soul to the body, Bataille's notion of the gland's function is that it propels man upward, attracting him toward the empyrean—representative of all that is lofty—impelling him, however, to stare straight into the sun, becoming as a result crazed and blind.[87] The obsession with the sun promoted by the pineal (blind) eye is, then, another instance of the collapse of the vertical into the horizontal, as man in his disorientation literally and symbolically loses his head.[88] The image of the man with the hole at the top of his cranium—another form of the *acéphale*—connects in this way to the experience of the labyrinth, the space of implosion, as the distinction is blurred between inside and outside, beginning and end.

The blinding, crazing sun is the *soleil pourri* at which the

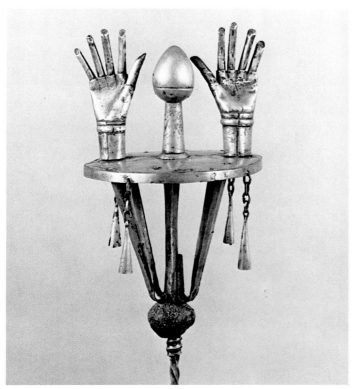

Staff (detail). Fon. People's Republic of Benin (formerly Dahomey). Silver, 46" (117 cm) high, overall. Collection Charles Ratton, Paris

Alberto Giacometti. *Table*. 1933. Bronze, 56¼" (142.9 cm) high. Musée National d'Art Moderne, Centre National d'Art et de Culture Georges Pompidou, Paris

Easter Island idols stare and to which Bataille consecrated his essay on Picasso's "rotting art." But then, for Bataille, the entire problematic of modern painting subtends his conception of the beginnings of art as the representation of sacrifice, the symbolic correlative of the mutilation of the human body. The space of this mutilation is initially the cave or grotto of the prehistoric painters, the first occupants of the labyrinth. There art begins, but not with an act of self-duplication, as the relationship of painting's origins with the myth of Narcissus would have it. Painting is born with man's refusal to reproduce himself, and out of an act of self-mutilation.[89]

This set of connections between painting, a fascination with the sun, and the mutilation of the body in an act of sacrificial madness is spelled out in Bataille's essay "La Mutilation sacrificielle et l'oreille coupée de Vincent van Gogh." Needless to say, for Bataille, van Gogh's is not an aberrant gesture but is entirely representative of art's essential, archaic function. As one scholar of Bataille's work explains, "Self-mutilation demands to be thought of as an act, in fact, *the* pictorial act *par excellence*. Because painting is nothing if it doesn't strike at the architecture of the human body; this architecture which, precisely, is not simple because it implies self-mutilation."[90] The Minotaur, not Narcissus, presides over the birth of an art in which representation represents alteration.

One after another, Giacometti's gameboard, horizontal sculptures enact the marriage of the field of representation with the condition of the base, the ground, the earth. This rotation of the axis onto the dimension of the physical is the shift of direction of the *acéphale*. But these rotated works share with the theme of the headless man and the labyrinth another aspect. For, with one exception, all of them carry the further signification of death. *On ne joue plus* conceives of the "sculp-

ture" as a game, its board cratered with semicircular hollows modeled on the African pebble game *i* (p. 513),[91] but into its center are sunk two tiny coffins, their lids askew. The literal space of the board on which pieces can be moved in real time fuses with the image of the necropolis.

As one of the meanings of *représentation* the Littré dictionary lists the pall-covered coffinlike frame used in commemorative religious services. Representation, a stand-in for the dead, is thus conceptually suspended between the symbolic and the real decay of matter—the precise condition of alteration. Bataille's notion of a "base materialism" operates in this very middle ground between the literal and the symbolic, for it conceives the entire field of social relationships as wholly structured by the conditions of representation, which is to say, language. But language is thought of as a directionless maze in which, for example, the sacred is the function of the very conditions of the word itself: *sacer*, like *altus*, pointing in two directions, toward the blessed and the damned. Classical philosophy wishes to repress this duality and reconstruct a language in which each element has a specific value, and only one. It wants to build vertical monuments to cover over the necropolis where meaning burrows into the dirt of decay, contamination, death. The space of this linguistic necropolis, in which language both forms and represents the real desires of the *acéphale*, is the labyrinth.

The gameboard of *On ne joue plus* is not a readymade; its horizontality is not the unmodulated topple of the snow-shovel of Duchamp's *In Advance of a Broken Arm*. The gameboard, with its little pieces, is a representation in which the symbolic is made a function of the base, the base in Bataille's sense (*basesse*), a concept far from Surrealist poetics, forged instead out of a vision of the primitive.

In 1935 Giacometti's art changed abruptly. He began to

work from life, with models who posed in the studio, instead of making sculptures—as he later said of his work of the early 1930s—that "used to come to me complete in my mind."[92] The break this precipitated with the Surrealists left Giacometti violently hostile. He declared that "everything he had made up to that time had been masturbation and that he had no other goal but to render a human head."[93] As part of this repudiation he is also reported to have denied his connection to Primitive art, saying that if he had taken anything from objects of this type, it was simply because "art nègre" was modish during his early career.[94]

What Giacometti was rejecting was not simply Surrealism or a related connection to tribal art. At a deeper, structural level, he renounced the horizontal and everything it meant: both a dimension within which to rethink the formal concerns of sculpture and a matrix through which human anatomy was "altered." From 1935 on, he devoted himself to vertical sculpture. Having made this decision, he left behind those two concerns that had worked together to generate the brilliance of his work of the early 1930s: the base and the primitive.

Right: Alberto Giacometti. *Three Eyes–Two Arms*. 1931–32. Marble, 14⅝" (37 cm) high. Private collection, Paris

Below: Doll. Mossi. Upper Volta. Wood, 15¾" (40 cm) high. Private collection, Belgium

Figure. Mbole. Zaire. Wood, 36⅝″ (94 cm) high. Collection Jacques Blanckaert, Brussels

Figure. Zulu. Republic of South Africa. Wood, 24⅜″ (62 cm) high. The Trustees of the British Museum, London

Alberto Giacometti. *Man.* 1929. Bronze, 15¾ x 11⅞ x 3¾″ (39.9 x 30 x 9.5 cm). Collection Ruth and Frank Stanton

NOTES

1. Michel Leiris, "Pierres pour un Alberto Giacometti," in *Brisées* (Paris: Mercure de France, 1966), p. 149.

2. André Breton, *L'Amour fou* (Paris: Gallimard, 1937), pp. 40–57. This was originally published as "L'Equation de l'objet," *Documents* 3, 4, 1 (June 1934), pp. 17–24.

3. Breton, "L'Equation," p. 20.

4. One of these sitters wrote a detailed account of this process, observing that "inasmuch as it was then expressed in the particular acts of painting and posing, there were elements of the sado-masochistic in our relationship... [although] it would have been difficult to determine exactly what acts were sadistic and/or masochistic on whose side and why" (James Lord, *A Giacometti Portrait* [New York: Museum of Modern Art, 1965], p. 36).

5. See Simone de Beauvoir, *La Force de l'âge* (Paris: Gallimard, 1960), pp. 409–503.

6. Reinhold Hohl, *Alberto Giacometti* (New York: Solomon Guggenheim Museum, 1974), p. 22. See also Hohl, *Alberto Giacometti* (London: Thames and Hudson, 1972), p. 298, note 15.

7. Jean Clay, *Visages de l'art moderne* (Paris: Editions Rencontre, 1969), p. 160.

8. The statue came to the museum from the 1929–30 expedition of Felix Speiser and was published in 1933 in *Führer durch das Museum für Völkerkunde Basel, Salomonen* as fig. 11 (*Totenstatue, Bougainville*), p. 21. In 1930 the art of the Solomon Islands was the focus of an essay in *Documents* that dealt with both the visual and religious significance of its production. See Louis Clarke, "L'Art des Iles Salomon," *Documents* 2, no. 5 (1930).

9. See for example the Solomon Islands *duka* figure in the British Museum, 1944, Oc.2.1177 (p. 505).

10. Hohl published the Solomon Islands figure in his 1972 monograph (p. 291, fig. 30) without the "railing" although this structural support appeared in the 1933 publication of the Basel Ethnological Museum. (Subsequent to this publication of the figure the support bars were lost.) Instead, Hohl postulates the influence of Egyptian statuary for the architectural elements of *Invisible Object* (Hohl, 1972, p. 300, n. 34). William Rubin has suggested Sepik River spirit figures as another possible source for the structure behind the woman's body in Giacometti's sculpture. One of these (p. 505), now in the Rietberg Museum (RMe 104), was in that part of the Van der Heydt collection deposited in the Musée de l'Homme in 1933 and placed on display. It could therefore have been seen by Giacometti. (I owe this information to Philippe Peltier, who has generously shared with me his knowledge of the disposition of the great collections of Oceanic art of this period.) However, the presence of a vertical structure that either flanks the body or appears to contain it is also to be found in New Ireland Malanggans, an Oceanic type admired and collected by the Surrealists (see p. 54). But neither the Sepik River nor the New Ireland sculptures relate morphologically to the smooth-surfaced, generalized anatomical style of *Invisible Object*. Evan Maurer suggests the presence of the Caroline Islands figural type on the basis of stylistic similarity and because one of Giacometti's drawings after Oceanic objects represents such a figure. See Maurer, "In Quest of the Myth: An Investigation of the Relationships between Surrealism and Primitivism" (Ph.D. diss., University of Pennsylvania, 1974), p. 318. The Caroline Islands figural type, however, does not assume the bent-knee position that is so forceful in *Invisible Object*, nor is it supported by any structural adjunct.

   A precedent for the stylization of the body of *Invisible Object* and its enigmatic gesture has been brought forward from within modern sculptural practice. This is Georg Kolbe's 1921 *Assunta*, with

the elongated Virgin's hands held in a peculiar gesture of prayer. See Jeffrey Spalding, *Max Ernst from the Collection of Mr. and Mrs. Jimmy Ernst*, Glenbow Museum, Calgary, Alberta, Canada, 1979, p. 12. Aside from the lack of information about whether Giacometti could have known this work, this suggestion is weakened by the remoteness in theme between the two sculptures, Giacometti's primitivized subject being very far from ideas of conventional Christian doctrine.

11. *Spoon Woman* is conventionally assigned to 1926 except in Hohl's monograph, where, for reasons not argued, it is dated 1927, and in Michael Brenson, "The Early Work of Alberto Giacometti: 1925–1935" (Ph.D. diss., The Johns Hopkins University, 1974), p. 225. In following Hohl's and Brenson's dating, I am proposing the greater stylistic maturity, accomplishment, and thus later date of *Spoon Woman* precisely on the basis of Giacometti's developing relationship to Primitive sources.

12. For the female half of *The Couple*, Maurer suggests a Hongwe reliquary figure and Cowling proposes Makonde body shields; see Maurer, op. cit., p. 316; and Elizabeth Nesbitt Cowling, "The Primitive Sources of Surrealism" (M.A. thesis, London, The Courtauld Institute, 1970), p. 46. These seem unconvincing on the basis of conceptual and morphological comparison. But however unpersuasive the specific "source" might be, the suggestions put forward by these authors attest to their experience of the Africanizing character of the figures in *The Couple*. It is this quality, in turn, that makes suggestions of a neolithic source for the work, put forward by other scholars, somewhat dubious. There is a strong compositional (but not conceptual) resemblance between the female figure of *The Couple* and one of the menhir figures from Saint-Sernan-sur-Rance, a work included in the illustrations of the Carnac Museum catalog of 1927. This connection was first suggested by Stephanie Poley ("Alberto Giacomettis Umsetzung Archaischer Gestaltungsformen in Seinem Werke Zwischen 1925 und 1935," *Jahrbuch der Hamburger Kunstsammlungen* 22 [1977], p. 177) and later by Alan Wilkinson (*Gauguin to Moore, Primitivism in Modern Sculpture* [Art Gallery of Toronto, 1981], p. 222). There are other examples of the effect of prehistoric images and objects on Giacometti's work, most obviously in the 1931 sculpture *Caress*, where the stenciled hands of the cave painters—themselves having become almost a symbol of Modernism, as their emblematic appearance on the cover of Ozenfant's *Foundations of Modern Art* (1931) attests—undoubtedly suggested the splayed hand etched onto the sculpture's surface. But in *The Couple* the prehistoric image, if it indeed functioned as a suggestion for the composition, has been converted into an evident "style nègre."

13. The Dan source was first suggested by Jean Laude, *La Peinture Française (1905–1914) et l'art nègre* (Paris: Klincksieck, 1968), p. 13. Michael Brenson suggests the influence of a Bakota funerary statue which Giacometti had borrowed from the painter-sculptor Serge Brignoni in the years 1926–30 (op. cit., pp. 56–57). In a conversation with William Rubin (January 1984), Brignoni added the information that he had actually sold the Bakota figure to Giacometti and that he was of the opinion that it had affected the form of the female half of *The Couple*. This opinion is supported by the evidence of a now-lost plaster figure which forms a transition between the Léger-inspired, Cubist works of 1925–26 and *The Couple* (indeed, Diego Giacometti has confirmed that the lost plaster immediately preceded *The Couple*). Combining the ovoid shape of Kota statuary with a plaquelike, rectangular plane to create the body of the figure, this rather architectural conception of the human form could as well betray knowledge of and interest in the kind of anthropomorphic locks that were the product of

West African tribes and figured in collections of Bambara and Dogon material, among others.

Alberto Giacometti. *Woman*. c. 1926–27. Plaster. Destroyed

14. The "Exposition de l'art indigène des colonies d'Afrique et d'Océanie," Musée des Arts Decoratifs (November 1923–January 27, 1924), was organized by André Level. Among the collections drawn upon for the exhibition were those of Félix Fénéon, André Lhote, Patrick Henry Bruce, Paul Guillaume, and of course the Trocadéro. Guillaume contributed seventy-nine objects, of which six were spoons listed as "Côte d'Ivoire." Jean-Louis Paudrat believes that these must have included Dan objects. Two other spoon/women that Giacometti could have seen were: the Lega spoon in Carl Einstein, *La Sculpture africaine* (Paris: Editions Crès, 1922), pl. 42; and the utensil illustrated in pl. 3 of Paul Guillaume and Thomas Munro, *Primitive Negro Sculpture* (New York: Harcourt, Brace, 1926). The French edition of this book appeared in 1929.

15. See the copy Giacometti made of the Venus von Laussel, published in Luigi Carluccio, *A Sketchbook of Interpretive Drawings* (New York: Abrams, 1968), pl. 2. It is difficult to date these drawings, but this page also contains the sketch idea for Giacometti's *Three Figures Outdoors* of 1929.

16. Georges Henri Rivière, "Archéologismes," *Cahiers d'art* 7 (1926), p. 177.

17. Christian Zervos, "Notes sur la sculpture contemporaine," *Cahiers d'art* 10 (1929), p. 465.

18. Guillaume and Munro, op. cit.

19. Roger Fry, "Negro Sculpture," *Vision and Design* (New York: Brentano's, 1920).

20. As one of many examples of the aestheticizing discourse that analyzed Primitive art as just one moment of the collective representation of art-in-general and thus of the aesthetic impulse common to all humanity, see A. Ozenfant, *Foundations of Modern Art: The Ice Age to 1931* (New York: Brewer, Warren and Putnam, 1931). French publication, 1928.

21. G. H. Luquet, *L'Art primitif* (Paris: Gaston Doin, 1930). For Bataille's review, see "L'Art primitif," *Documents* 2, no. 7 (1930), pp. 389–97. Collected in Georges Bataille, *Oeuvres complètes* (Paris: Gallimard, 1970), vol. 1, pp. 247–54.

22. *Oeuvres complètes*, vol. 1, p. 251. *Informe* translates as "unformed," although Bataille intends the word to undo the Aristotelian distinction between form and matter.

23. *Oeuvres complètes*, vol. 1, p. 253.

24. *Ibid.*, p. 251. This notion of the double sense of the root word of a given concept takes into account Freud's interest in this kind of etymological study in which precisely *altus* and *sacer* are used as examples. See Freud's "Antithetical Sense of Primal Words," published in 1910 in the *Jahrbuch für psycho-analytisches und psychopathologisches Forschungen*, vol. 1, as a review of Karl Abel's *Gegensinn der Urworte.* For Bataille's knowledge of this text, see Denis Hollier, *La Prise de la concorde* (Paris: Gallimard, 1974), p. 240.

25. Obviously Bataille was dependent upon the ethnological data available to him at the time, from which he made his own particular selection in order to support his own critique of philosophy. For a discussion of Bataille's connection to ethnography in the 1920s and 1930s, see Alfred Métraux, "Rencontre avec les ethnologues," *Critique* 195–6 (1963), p. 677–84.

26. In Jean Babelon, *L'Art précolumbien* (Paris: Editions Beaux-Arts, 1930). This collection of essays was to accompany the 1928 *Exposition de l'art de l'Amerique* in the Pavillon de Marsan and included texts by Alfred Métraux and Paul Rivet, among others. That pre-Columbian art was seen at the time as occupying a field continuous with that of Africa and Oceania is evident, for example, in the text "L'Art nègre," which Zervos wrote to introduce a special issue of *Cahiers d'art* (no. 7–8, 1927). He speaks of "the attachment of our generation for *art nègre*," specifying, "That is what was produced twenty years ago with Negro sculpture, it is what is produced right now with Melanesian and pre-Columbian art" (p. 230). On this same subject Breton wrote, "The very particular interest that painters at the beginning of the twentieth century had for African art, today it is American art from before the conquest that, along with Oceanic art, exercises an elective influence on artists" (Breton, *Mexique*, [Paris: Renous and Colle, 1939], preface). The Breton and Eluard collections auctioned in 1931 were devoted to pre-Columbian art to almost as great an extent as to Oceanic objects. The 1936 exhibition of Surrealist objects at the Charles Ratton Gallery included American objects along with those of Oceania; the catalog specifies these American works as Eskimo, Peruvian, and pre-Columbian.

27. Métraux, *op. cit.*

28. Bataille, *Oeuvres complètes*, vol. 1, p. 152.

29. Ibid., p. 157.

30. Zervos, "Notes sur la sculpture contemporaine," p. 472.

31. For an account of the way Bataille's thought was shaped by Mauss, see Métraux, *op. cit.* Another discussion of this relationship is James Clifford's "On Ethnographic Surrealism," *Comparative Studies in Society and History* (October 1981), pp. 543–64.

32. Hohl insists on Giacometti's knowledge and employment of the kind of precise ethnographic information about the contexts of tribal art that would have come to him easily through his connection with Leiris (Hohl, 1972, p. 79). In an interview with the author (February 24, 1983), Leiris supplied no detailed information but agreed that Giacometti was present at discussions concerning ethnography held by the *Documents* group.

33. Along with Miró and Arp, Giacometti exhibited in the autumn of 1930 at the Galerie Pierre. Georges Sadoul recalls, "In late 1930 I was introduced to Alberto Giacometti, who had just been taken into the Surrealist group.... In 1930 he gave Surrealism a new impulse with his kinetic objects. He started the fashion for Surrealist objects with symbolic or erotic overtones, and it became the duty of every self-respecting Surrealist to make them" (cited in Hohl, 1972, p. 249). The date of Dali's "Objets à fonctionnement symbolique," *Le Surréalisme au service de la révolution* 3 (1931), 16–17, demonstrates this later attempt to absorb Giacometti's innovative work into the heart of the Surrealist movement.

34. Maurice Nadeau, *Histoire du Surréalisme* (Paris: Seuil, 1945), p. 176.

35. Bataille's article "L'Oeil," *Documents* 1, no. 4 (1929)—the same issue that carried the first essay on Giacometti's work (Michel Leiris, "Alberto Giacometti," pp. 209–10)—opens with a discussion of this image and lists the various screenings of *Un Chien andalou* as the places where the image had been reproduced. Not only does Bataille's concentration on the theme of the eye carry forward his own preoccupations from *L'Histoire de l'oeil*, but through Marcel Griaule's article on the evil eye and its significance in primitive belief systems published in this number as well, the link is once more forged between ethnographic analysis and modern thematic interests.

36. In his article "La Pointe à l'oeil d'Alberto Giacometti," *Cahiers du Musée National d'Art Moderne* 11 (1983), pp. 64–100, Jean Clair argues for the direct connection between Bataille's eroticized, phallic conception of the eye, as found in both *L'Histoire de l'oeil* and the *Documents* material, and Giacometti's sculpture *Point to the Eye.* His discussion of this work turns, in part, on Bataille's notion of vision objectified at the limiting condition of the disembodied eye.

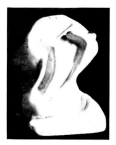
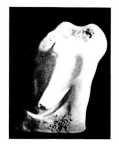

Jean Arp. *Head.* 1929. Plaster. Published in *Variétés*, June 1929, special issue: *Le Surréalisme en 1929*

37. Whatever our present state of ethnographic knowledge of the ballgame, in the 1930s its level was represented by the kind of account one finds in Frans Blom, "The Maya Ball-Game Pok-Ta-Pok," *Middle American Papers* (Tulane University: 1932), in which the dictionary entries for the names of the game were published. It was on material such as this that Bataille depended. The relation between the ballgame and death is strengthened by the carved relief panel from the ballcourt at El Tajin, Veracruz, which depicts a sacrificial scene on the ballcourt.

38. Jacques Dupin, *Alberto Giacometti* (Paris: Maeght, 1962), p. 88.

39. Jacques Dupin told this author that when he began work on his monograph on Giacometti, the sculptor lent him his own carefully protected, full set of *Documents* to work from. For one of the *Documents* articles on this subject, illustrated by codex representations of the victims and the places of sacrifice, see Roger Hervé, "Sacrifices humains du Centre-Amérique," *Documents* 2, no. 4 (1930).

40. *Cahiers d'art* 10 (1929), p. 456, reproduces a photograph of an Aztec pyramid topped by an altar whose structure suggests that of *The Hour of the Traces* (p. 514).

41. Alberto Giacometti, "Hier, sables mouvants," *Le Surréalisme au service de la révolution* 5 (1933).

42. Alberto Giacometti, "A propos de Jacques Callot," *Labyrinthe* 7 (April 15, 1945), p. 3. This essay relates the fascination with horror and destruction on the part of Callot, Goya, and Géricault: "For these artists there is a frenetic desire for destruction in every realm, up to that of human consciousness itself." In a thought that is obviously close to Bataille, Giacometti concludes that in order to understand this, one would have to speak "on the one hand of the pleasure in destruction that one finds in children, of their cruelty... and on the other hand of the subject-matter of art." "Le Rêve, le Sphinx et la mort de T.," *Labyrinthe* 22–23 (December 15, 1946), pp. 12–13. Not only does the story of the spider, in the dream recounted in this text, recall Bataille's theme of the *informe*, but the description of T's head, rendered hideously objective by death, is pure Bataille. Become "an object, a little measurable, insignificant box," the head is seen as a rotting cadaver, "miserable debris to be thrown away," into the mouth of which, to Giacometti's horror, a fly enters.

43. Hohl declares, for example, "The cones and spheres of Picasso's series of *Projects for a Monument* ...must certainly have coauthored the forms in Giacometti's *Suspended Ball*" (Hohl, 1972, p. 81).

44. Roland Barthes, "La Métaphore de l'oeil," *Critique* 195–96 (1963), p. 772. My discussion of the structure of metaphor in Bataille's novel follows that of Barthes.

45. Ibid., p. 773.

46. "Informe" was Bataille's entry in the "Dictionnaire" of *Documents* 1, no. 7 (1929).

47. For a discussion of Bataille's "Dictionary" within the context of the various avant-garde dictionaries, see Denis Hollier, *op. cit.*, pp. 59–65.

48. For example, a four-volume series of photographic reproductions was published specifically for the instruction of arts and design students under the

Pyramid. Aztec. Castillo de Teayo, Mexico. Published in *Cahiers d'art*, no. 10, 1929

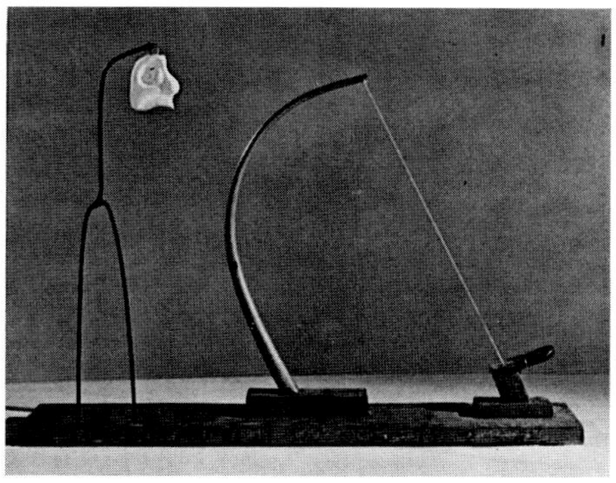

Alberto Giacometti. *Flower in Danger.* 1933. Wood, metal, and plaster, 21⅞ x 30¾ x 7⅛" (55.7 x 78.1 x 18.1 cm). The Alberto Giacometti Foundation, Kunsthaus, Zurich

Alberto Giacometti. *Circuit.* 1931. Wood, 2 x 18½ x 18½" (5 x 47 x 47 cm). Henriette Gomès, Paris

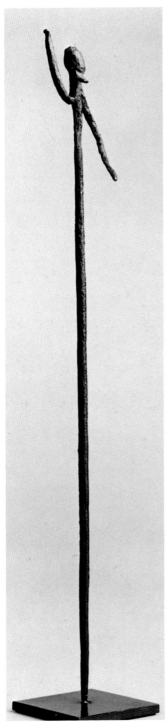

Staff. Dogon. Mali. Iron, 18¾" (47.6 cm) high. Collection Lester Wunderman, New York

Rhythm pounder. Bambara. Mali. Wood, 42½" (108 cm) high. Collection Maude and René Garcia, Paris

Staff. Mbuun. Zaire. Wood and metal, 33" (83.8 cm) high. Collection Erle Loran, Berkeley

Figure. Kulango. Ivory Coast. Wood, 18" (45.7 cm) high. Friede Collection, New York

Figure. Mumuye. Nigeria. Wood, 47½" (120.7 cm) high. Private collection

Funeral pole. Konso. Ethiopia. Wood, 6' 10⅞" (213 cm) high. Private collection, Paris

Figure. Namshi. Cameroon. Wood, 14¼″ (36.9 cm) high. Private collection

title *La Décoration primitive* (Paris: Editeur Calavas, 1922). The volumes were equally devoted to African, Oceanic, and pre-Columbian objects, both sculptures and textiles.

49. Bataille, *Oeuvres complètes*, vol. 1, p. 253.

50. For example, Apollinaire insists in *Les Peintres cubistes* (Paris, 1913) that Cubism "is not an art of imitation, but an art of conception." Or, in Léger's essay "Les Origines de la peinture et sa valeur représentative" (*Montjoie!* 8 [May 1913], p. 7), he concentrates on the difference between "visual realism" and a "realism of conception."

51. This appeared in the special issue on Picasso, *Documents* 2, no. 3 (1930).

52. Breton, "L'Equation," p. 20.

53. The year before making the plaster mask/sketch for *Invisible Object*, Giacometti executed another "mask" in plaster: the deformed head of *Flower in Danger* (1933, p. 529). This sculpture, with its images of incipient decapitation of the flower/head, is like a little machine for the production of the *acéphale*. It is possible that a plaster head by Arp, published in the special issue on Surrealism in *Variétés* (June 1929), contributed to the notion of the head as a mask in the process of decomposition.

54. *Documents*, 2, no. 2 (1930), pp. 97–102.

55. See texts by Evan Maurer and Philippe Peltier in this volume.

56. In 1931 Louis Aragon organized an anticolonialist exhibition in a meeting hall in the Rue de la Grange-Batelière to protest the official Exposition Coloniale. Giacometti's contribution consisted of political cartoon drawings. Two photographs of the room set up by Aragon, Eluard, and Tanguy for the exhibition "La Vérité sur les colonies" appear in *Le Surréalisme au service de la révolution* 4 (December 1931).

57. "Soleil pourri" concentrates on the Mithraic cult and the spasmodic practices incited by looking into the sun. This theme was elaborated in the series of texts entitled "L'Oeil pinéal"; see note 87, inf.

58. "Aboutissements de la mécanique," *Variétés* 2, no. 9 (January 1930).

59. Bataille's concentration on the *acéphale* led, in 1936, to the creation of a journal of that name for which Masson designed the cover. One of his early treatments of the representation of man in ancient culture as *acéphale* was his text "Le Bas Matérialisme et la gnose," *Documents*, 2 no. 1 (1930), pp. 1–8. Leo Frobenius deals with this theme in "Bêtes hommes ou dieux," *Cahiers d'art* 10 (1929).

60. Roger Caillois, "La Mante religieuse," *Minotaure* 1, no. 5 (May 1934), p. 25. See also "La Nature et l'amour," *Variétés* 2, no. 2 (June 1929).

61. William Pressly, "The Praying Mantis in Surrealist Art," *Art Bulletin* 55, December 1973, pp. 600–15.

62. Hohl traces the use of the sphere as the metonymic representation of the male in the works of these years (Hohl, 1972, pp. 81–82).

63. These are D 62.2.10 of the Musée des Arts Africains et Océaniens, formerly in the collection of M. Girardin; and the important Malanggan in the collection of Max Ernst (p. 517).

64. Carl Einstein, "Sculptures mélanésiennes," *L'Amour de l'art* 8 (1926), p. 256.

65. Ernst's *Femme 100 Têtes* (1929) was nominally dedicated to this theme even though it does not directly illustrate it.

66. *Une Semaine de bonté*, p. 168.

67. See Maurer's discussion, p. 560, inf. Although Ernst's extensive collection of Oceanic art contained other things as well, it specialized in objects of the Papuan Gulf (New Guinea), according to the research of Philippe Peltier.

68. Now destroyed, the work was published in *Minotaure* 3–4 (1933), p. 40. There is an obvious resemblance between these stakelike personnages driven directly into the ground and the tribal wooden posts totemically carved and set into the earth at the entrance to villages or houses, to protect a given area, that were widely known at this time.

69. Giacometti spoke of his attraction to Oceanic sculpture in terms of the exaggeration of the eyes: "New Hebrides sculpture is true, and more than true, because it has a gaze. It's not the imitation of an eye, it's purely and simply a gaze. All the rest is a prop for the gaze." Georges Charbonnier, *Le Monologue du peintre* (Paris: Julliard, 1959), p. 166.

70. This is true not only of Hohl's monograph, but also of the approach taken by Yves Bonnefoy, who is preparing a major study of the artist. See "Etudes comparées de la fonction poétique," in *Annuaire du Collège de France*, 1982, pp. 643–53.

71. Giacometti, "Le Palais de quatre heures," *Minotaure* 3–4 (1933), p. 46.

72. This is the epigram for the chapter in *Une Semaine de bonté* that contains the Easter Island section. Giacometti's text, "Hier, sables mouvants," begins with his account of the large rock into which he would crawl as a child, remaining there for hours.

73. See André Gide, "Architectures nègres," *Cahiers d'art* 7–8 (1927), particularly the image on p. 265.

74. *Die Sammlung der Alberto Giacometti-Stiftung* (Zurich: Kunsthaus, 1971), p. 94.

75. It was Bataille who contributed the name for the review *Minotaure*, in 1933.

76. In Zervos's "Quelques notes sur les sculptures de Giacometti," *Cahiers d'art*, 8–10 (1932), pp. 337–42, the work, which bore the written inscription "la vie continue," was published with the title *Chute d'un corps sur un graphique*. Later, in picturing his art of these years, Giacometti labeled this now-lost sculpture *Paysage–Tête couchée*. See "Lettre à Pierre Matisse," in *Alberto Giacometti* (New York: Pierre Matisse Gallery, 1948). Carola Giedion-Welcker, who knew Giacometti, published an Etruscan votive bronze from the museum in Piacenza as the possible inspiration for *Project for a Square* (in Giedion-Welcker, *Contemporary Sculpture* [New York: Wittenborn, 1969]). Hohl suggests that this ancient object was more likely related to *Chute d'un corps sur un graphique* and is the source of this name (Hohl, 1972, p. 299, n. 29).

77. Salvador Dali, "Communication: visage paranoïaque," *Le Surréalisme au service de la révolution* 3 (December 1931), p. 40.

78. See Hohl, 1972, p. 82.

79. Cf. the special issue on "art nègre" of *La Nervie* 9–10 (1926), fig. 9.

80. Alberto Giacometti, "Notes sur les copies," *L'Ephémère* 1 (1966), pp. 104–08. Diego Giacometti confirmed to this author that the drawings of Oceanic objects reproduced in Carluccio (op. cit.) were copied from the 1929 issue of *Cahiers d'art*.

81. Carluccio, op. cit., pl. 5 shows three sculptures from the Basel Museum: figs. 104, 105, and 114 in the 1929 *Cahiers d'art*. Pl. 6 represents Easter Island statues, figs. 188 and 187 in *Cahiers d'art*. Carluccio pl. 8 shows two New Guinea objects copied from figs. 43 and 41 respectively. Pl. 9 displays copies of figs. 2, 153, and 157 from the *Cahiers d'art*. The late drawings in Carluccio after Primitive sources were, in accordance with Giacometti's post–1930s commitment to working from life, probably made in direct contact with the objects.

82. There is also the probable influence of the extremely phallic *casse-têtes* from New Caledonia, Fiji, and Easter Island, many examples of which had been in the Musée de l'Homme since the end of the nineteenth century (p. 564).

83. Hohl, 1972, p. 81.

84. Bataille, "Le Bas Matérialisme et la gnose."

85. Bataille, "Le Gros Orteil," *Documents* 1, no. 6 (1929), p. 302.

86. In a 1926 drawing of a nude (below), Giacometti depicts this axial rotation by conflating the mouth and genitals. This relationship is the formal idea as well behind the female figure in *The Couple* of the same year and is a common motif in African art.

87. The five texts on the pineal eye were written between 1927 and 1930. Never published, they are collected in the *Oeuvres complètes*, vol. 2, pp. 13–50.

88. See "Soleil pourri," where Bataille speaks of "un être anthropomorphe *dépourvu de tête*" (p. 174). Hollier discusses this notion of the change of axis, op. cit., pp. 137–54.

89. In "La Mutilation sacrificielle et l'oreille coupée de Vincent van Gogh," *Documents* 2, no. 8 (1930), Bataille attacks, for example, Luquet's acceptance of the "folded-finger" hypothesis to explain the cave paintings in which stenciled hands are recorded with missing fingers (*Oeuvres complètes*, vol. 1, p. 267). A motif of great fascination, the stenciled hand is used in *Caress* (1930).

90. Hollier, op. cit., p. 148.

91. Hohl mentions Benin wooden gameboards Giacometti might have seen at the Charles Ratton Gallery that could have served as a model for this work (Hohl, 1972, p. 299, n. 27). M. Ratton, however, says that no Benin objects of this type exist. Instead, one has only to turn to the wooden gameboards for *i* (p. 513), which are still being produced today. The surfaces for this game were

The game of *i*. Dogon. Mali. Published in Marcel Griaule, *Jeux dogons*, 1938

often improvised: hollowed out of the earth or in stone. Marcel Griaule's study shows such a board in stone (Griaule, *Jeux dogons*, Paris, 1938, fig. 95).

92. James Lord, op. cit., p. 48. See Giacometti's account in "Le Palais de quatres heures," op. cit.

93. Marcel Jean, *Histoire de la peinture surréaliste* (Paris: Seuil, 1959), p. 227.

94. In the late 1930s Giacometti is reported to have said this to Greta Knutson, then the wife of Tristan Tzara, for whom he sat for a portrait (as told to the author by Knutson's daughter-in-law, Madame Tzara).

Alberto Giacometti. *Nude*. 1926. Ink, 7 x 5" (17.8 x 12.7 cm). Private collection

Wifredo Lam. *The Jungle*. 1943. Gouache on paper mounted on canvas, 7'10¼" x 7'6½" (239.4 x 229.9 cm). The Museum of Modern Art, New York; Inter-American Fund

DADA AND SURREALISM

Evan Maurer

Press announcement, 2nd February, 1916:
Cabaret Voltaire. Under this name a group of young artists and writers has formed with the object of becoming a centre for artistic entertainment. The Cabaret Voltaire will be run on the principle of daily meetings where visiting artists will perform their music and poetry. The young artists of Zurich are invited to bring along their ideas and contributions.[1]

It is ironic that this innocuous announcement heralded the European launching of the revolutionary international art phenomenon the "Voltairists" would call Dada. Anticipated by Marcel Duchamp and some New York artists, the spirited activities of Dada challenged and extended the literary and visual arts in Europe and America for eight years, from the beginning of World War I through the early 1920s. "Dada's only programme," wrote Hans Richter, "was to have no programme...and, at that moment in history, it was just this that gave the movement its explosive power to unfold *in all directions*, free of aesthetic or social constraints. This absolute freedom from preconceptions was," Richter continued, "something quite new in the history of art. The frailty of human nature guaranteed that such a paradisical situation could not last."[2] Then in 1924, the Parisian contingent, under the leadership of André Breton, proclaimed its allegiance to Surrealism, and, in accordance with related but different ideals, continued the impassioned commitment to the cause of artistic, political, and social change that had first brought the group together.

Dada as so named was conceived by an assortment of German, French, and Rumanian writers and artists who had come to Zurich at the beginning of World War I. Although there was a simultaneous and independent development of a similar nature taking place in New York, we must look to the Swiss group in order to study its more active involvement with primitivism and Primitive art.[3] It is significant that Dada developed in Zurich, the cosmopolitan intellectual center of Switzerland, which stood as a neutral haven in the very midst of global carnage that would irrevocably change the course of political and social history. Dada's acute sense of the absurd and its insistence on artistic and social freedom were engendered by the bourgeois societies responsible for a war that consumed the lives of men at a rate beyond comprehension. Hugo Ball, the original "impresario" of Dada events, expressed his colleagues' attitude of cynical revolt against the establishment when he wrote:

It is not possible for this degraded time to make us pay our respect. What's supposed to be so respectable about them? Their cannons? Our drums drown them out. Their idealism? It has long become a subject of derision....the grandiose butcher festivals and the cannibalistic heroisms? Our voluntary madness, our enthusiasm for illusion will put them to shame.[4]

The first two years of the war had led to a deadly pattern of attrition among armies of millions of men who were blowing one another apart with seemingly endless artillery duels along the front line slashing across Europe. On February 21, 1916, just weeks after the opening of the Dadaist's Cabaret Voltaire, the German armies attacked the heavily fortified positions around the small city of Verdun in a calculated effort to force the French into the largest concentration of artillery ever assembled and to decimate them by drawing their reserves

Marcel Janco. *Cabaret Voltaire*. 1916. Oil on canvas. Whereabouts unknown

an elementary art that would, we thought, save mankind from the furious folly of these times. We aspired to a new order that might restore the balance between heaven and hell."[8]

As was somewhat the case in the Montmartre of the turn of the century, the central focus of early Dada activity in Zurich was to be found in the cabaret, where the social atmosphere of food and drink, noise and conversation, provided a lively context for the performances, exhibitions, and the launching of broadsides and publications. The excitement and drama of the Dada evenings were marked by a riotous mixture of nonsense poems, sound poems, recitations in various languages, piano playing, drums, jazz. African music and poems, African-inspired masks, screams and laughter, pantomimes, and insults were all offered with straightforward seriousness in a calculated effort to activate and involve the audience.

The sole pictorial record of those first Dada soirees is Marcel Janco's painting *Cabaret Voltaire* of 1916, which not only captures the excitement and action described by Richter but also provides clear evidence of Zurich Dada's involvement with primitivism. On the wall behind the platform an oversized face mask leers menacingly at the audience, one of the many masks made for these performances by Janco, a young Rumanian who had come to Zurich to study architecture. According to the accounts left by the Dadaists themselves, Janco's masks were an important element in their presentations. Although Janco produced them out of a variety of crude, common materials, their impact was disturbing and emphatic. In a 1948 statement about Janco, Arp wrote: "I haven't forgotten the masks you used to make for our Dada demonstrations. They were terrifying, most of them daubed

into the deathtrap. The growing horror of Verdun lasted for ten months, during which, in an area of about three and a half miles, the combined German and French losses were estimated to be as high as 420,000 killed and 800,000 gassed or wounded.[5]

The tensions caused by this extraordinary and senseless tragedy had a strong effect on the people of Zurich, especially the young artists and writers who had congregated there from countries throughout Europe. The psychological and emotional effect of the war among the civilians in this neutral enclave was more immediate than one might expect. The proximity of the fighting brought the noise of battle to the very outskirts of the city; as Marcel Janco recalled, just a few kilometers beyond Zurich one could hear the cannon.[6] Jean Arp, the Dada and Surrealist artist and poet, also commented on the physical imminence of the conflict when he wrote: "In Zurich in 1915, losing interest in the slaughterhouses of the World War, we turned to the Fine Arts. While the thunder of the batteries rumbled in the distance, we pasted, we recited, we versified, we sang with all our soul."[7]

The Dadaists' rejection of the inevitably linked aesthetics and social values of the established order led them to Primitive art as well as to related areas such as folk art, naive art, and children's art. All these were considered to be expressions of elemental feelings and ideas unspoiled by traditional Western values and utilizing alternative artistic means. Jean Arp was responding to these issues when he said that during the beginning of the Dada movement in Zurich "we searched for

Marcel Janco. *Invitation to a Dada Evening*. 1916. Charcoal, 28¾ x 21⅝" (73 x 55 cm). Kunsthaus, Zurich, Graphische Sammlung

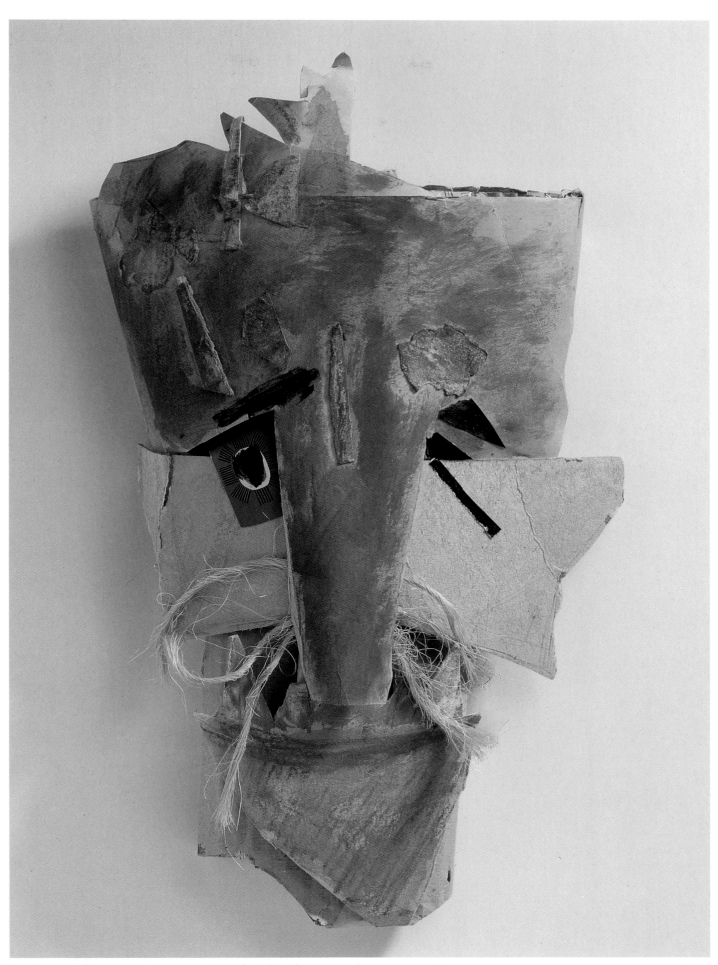

Marcel Janco. *Mask.* 1919. Paper, cardboard, twine, gouache, and pastel, 17¾ x 8⅝ x 2″ (45 x 22 x 5 cm). Musée National d'Art Moderne, Centre National d'Art et de Culture Georges Pompidou, Paris

called "Negro Masks" by his fellow Dadaists, "Negro" in this context being applied equally to the art of Africa and Oceania.[11] While Janco's masks never specifically copied a known African or Oceanic prototype, his colleagues immediately associated them with what they perceived to be the inherent spiritual power of Primitive art. For Hans Richter this evocative force was embodied by "the abstract Negro masks of Janco, which carried the audience from the primeval language of the new poems into the primeval forests of the artistic imagination."[12]

For Janco, Primitive art was one of several inspirational influences from nontraditional sources that were direct and free in the forms and manner they utilized to represent the world. In a recent interview, the artist stated that "we not only thought of primitive art as the real art, but we also regarded the art of childhood as a real art. We even came to the idea of exhibiting the art of the insane."[13] A profound interest in these three areas—in the art of the Primitive, the child, and the insane—would later become a major aspect of the literature and art of Surrealism.

Like the Primitive masks that were their general inspiration, Janco's masks were made to be worn by dancers who performed to music. When an African dancer dons a mask for a

Hannah Höch. *The Sweet One* from the series From an Ethnographical Museum 1926. Collage, 11⅞ x 6⅛" (30 x 15.5 cm). Collection Eva-Maria and Heinrich Rössner, Backnang, Germany

with bloody red. Out of cardboard, paper, horsehair, wire and cloth..."[9] Janco's choice of nontraditional, impermanent materials was also related to the Dadaists' understanding of art in Primitive societies, especially those in Oceania. In describing his own collages, Jean Arp compared his work to that of the artists of the South Seas: "Instead of cutting the paper, I tore it up with my hands, I made use of objects I found on the beach, and I composed natural collages and reliefs. I thus acted like the Oceanians, who never worry about the permanence of their materials when making masks, and use perishable materials like sea shells, blood, and feathers."[10]

Although there is no documentary evidence of the inclusion of or direct reference to actual African or Oceanic masks in these performances, Janco's masks were most frequently

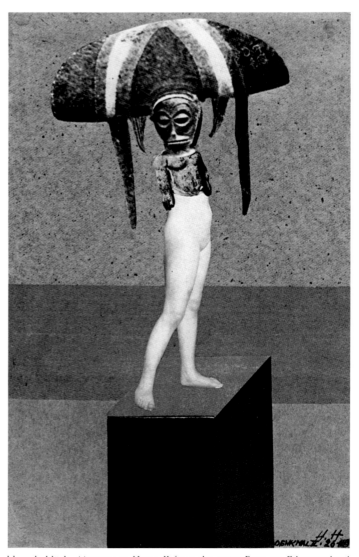

Hannah Höch. *Monument to Vanity II* from the series From an Ethnographical Museum. 1926. Collage, 10¼ x 6⅝" (25.8 x 16.7 cm). Collection Eva-Maria and Heinrich Rössner, Backnang, Germany

sacred ritual he also becomes the vehicle of the spirit the mask represents. The mask is therefore a significant element in the process of the transformation of the individual's consciousness from the human to the mythic. Hugo Ball, founder of the Cabaret Voltaire, understood this and was fascinated by the manner in which Janco's masks affected the actions of the performers who wore them. He wrote:

We were all there when Janco arrived with the masks, and each of us put one on. The effect was strange. Not only did each mask seem to demand the appropriate costume; it also called for a quite specific set of gestures, melodramatic and even close to madness.... The dynamism of the masks was irresistible. In one moment we became aware of the great importance of such masks in mime and drama. The masks simply demanded that their wearers should start up a tragico-absurd dance....What fascinated us about these masks is that they represent...characters and emotions that are larger than life.[14]

In addition to his masks, Janco produced a powerful drawing for a poster directly inspired by an African sculptural aesthetic. *Invitation to a Dada Evening* (p. 536) shows a frontal seated figure and a standing figure seen from the back. Both bodies are made up of large black planes that abstract and simplify legs, arms, and torso in a way characteristic of the

Man Ray. *Noire et blanche.* 1926. Silver print on tissue, 8⅝ x 10⅞"(21.9 x 27.7 cm). Zabriskie Gallery, New York

style and surface color of African figurative sculpture. The head of the seated figure is also abstracted into planes with emphasis on the large oval mouth with bared teeth, a prominent nose, large triangular eyes, and an elaborate peaked hairdo. This facial type is very similar to that produced by the sculptors of the Cameroons, especially the Bangwa. It is not entirely certain that Janco knew the strong tradition of Cameroon sculpture, but these powerful figurative statues and masks were available to the interested public in ethnological museums, particularly in Germany, and in publications.[15]

Direct references to the Dadaists' interest in public collections of tribal art were made in a series of photocollages by Hannah Höch, entitled From an Ethnographical Museum. Collages such as *The Sweet One* and *Monument to Vanity II*, both 1926, satirize traditional European ideals of beauty by combining photographs of African sculpture with drawn and painted elements of human bodies. The specific ethnographic museum to which the series title refers cannot be determined, because Höch moved from Berlin to Holland the year these collages were made. However, the African images she used are recognizable as a Chokwe (Zaire) sculpture in the *Monument to Vanity II* and a mask in a Gabonese style, perhaps Sogo, in *The Sweet One.*

Man Ray. *Sculpture by Itself I.* 1918. Iron, wood, and cork, 17 x 7⅜ x 7½" (43 x 18.5 x 19 cm). Westfälisches Landesmuseum für Kunst und Kulturgeschichte, Münster

Man Ray was another Dadaist whose work has affinities to Primitive art. His 1918 *Sculpture by Itself I* is a minimal figural abstraction that generally recalls Primitive styles such as the reductive aesthetic of Dogon masks.[16] In 1921 he moved from the United States to Paris, where he was active with the Dadaists who would soon form the nucleus of the Surrealist movement. During this period the reigning style of Art Deco fostered chic renditions of Primitive forms. Man Ray's photograph *Noire et blanche,* 1926, is an elegant yet eerie comment on Art Deco's use of "l'art nègre." The model's disembodied masklike face is contrasted to a Baule-style mask with the overrefined proportions and highly polished surface that would seem to indicate its being one of the many commercially produced African objects popular at the time.

Another important primitivist aspect of Zurich Dada was

Headdress crest. Senufo. Mali. Wood, 23⅝" (60 cm) high. Collection Pierre Harter, Paris

an interest in African figural sculpture, poetry, and so-called "chants nègres," African-inspired songs accompanied by drums. The greatest exponent of this aspect of the Dadaists' interest in the Primitive was Janco's fellow Rumanian Tristan Tzara, who later would also play an important role in the Dada experience in Paris.

Tzara, one of Zurich Dada's most active members, was the Dada personality most interested in African and Oceanic art and in concepts of primitivism; he also seems to have been the only member of the Zurich group actually to have owned African sculpture at that time. Emmy Hennings, who with Hugo Ball was one of the founders of the Cabaret Voltaire, told of a 1917 Galerie Dada exhibition built around what she described as a very beautiful and expensive African sculpture

owned by Tzara. The sculpture was so artistically powerful that it maintained its presence in a room hung with paintings by Kandinsky, Feininger, Klee, and Campendonk.[17]

In that same year Tzara published a note on African and Oceanic art, which was followed by articles on Oceanic and pre-Columbian art in 1929.[18] The short piece, "Note sur l'art nègre," appeared in *SIC*, the Futurist-oriented Parisian art magazine.[19] In this brief essay Tzara emphasized the need for a new way of representing objects so that they would be freed from the limitations of traditional definitions and associations. Art must go beyond the mere surface representation and slavish limitation of nature's exterior forms to express their true, essential inner qualities. As an illustration of this concept Tzara used the analogy of two brothers, one representing the bleak and limited reliance on past forms, the other enjoying the artistic freedom and creative energy of the Primitive. The Primitive sculptor was not bound by Western canons of proportion; he was—the Dadaists mistakenly thought—without any conventional restraints and therefore created sculptures that grew from an organic process of free associations. This served as an exemplary definition of Dada and Surrealist process.

Tzara was strongly attracted to Primitive art not only for formal reasons but because he perceived it as an art that expressed an integrated view of life. In "Note sur l'art nègre" he stated the then commonly held view that the arts of tribal cultures were prime examples of human creativity in its earliest and purest form. Tzara felt that during this powerful elemental stage art also reflected the integral relationships of things in nature and the associative power of forms to suggest other images, emotions, or ideas based on the principle of universal correspondences. It is particularly significant that in this early statement Tzara mentions the creative powers of the mouth as well as the hand. This reflects his own activity as a poet and established yet another tie between Dada and primitivism in the area of the literary and performing arts.

"Negro" music, dance, and poetry are frequently listed as major elements of the Zurich Dada performances. Accompanied by the incessant drumming of Richard Huelsenbeck, who was obsessed with African music, Tzara and others recited their own African-inspired songs. Later in his career Tzara explained the interest Dada had in the elemental qualities of the Primitive arts and their fundamental social necessity as expressions of both the conscious and the unconscious creative powers.

…the art of primitive peoples was an integral part of their social and religious functions and appeared as the very expression of their life. DADA, which advocated "dadist spontaneity" meant to make of poetry a way of life much more than the incidental expression of intelligence and will. For DADA, art was one of the forms, common to all men, of that poetic activity whose profound roots mingle with the primitive structure of affective life. DADA tried to put that theory into practice, joining African Negro and Oceanic art with mental life and with its immediate expression…by organizing NEGRO SOIREES of improvised dance and music. It was for dada a matter of recapturing in the depths of consciousness the exalting sources of the function of Poetry.[20]

For Tzara this "primitive poetry" was a true artistic expression of life because it was used in the service of all its activities. In his "Note sur la poésie nègre" of 1918 Tzara summarized this point of view by declaring that "one creates an organism when the elements are close to life. Poetry lives at first for the functions of dance, religion, music, and work."[21]

In his enthusiastic involvement with the Primitive, Tzara also produced versions of Oceanic chants for the magazine *Dada*, chants that served as examples of "primitive art" and as comparative models for what some writers refer to as Dada's "pseudo-African" language.[22] All three of these "poèmes nègres" were versions of totemic myths from the oral traditions of the aboriginal tribes of Australia.[23] The chants reflect Dada's interest in the Primitive not only in terms of elemental forms but because of its profound concerns with the mythic as a principal preoccupation of art making. Dada sought a philosophical and artistic alternative to traditional European modes, which Dada considered to be psychologically and aesthetically limiting. Primitivism offered Dada a positive model, one that would later also serve the Surrealist movement.

Surrealism was created in the early 1920s by a group of French writers and poets who, as members of the Dada movement, had been searching for a new way of confronting a social and artistic environment that was stifling and repugnant to them. In their quest for a fresh approach to life, for a new world view, the Surrealists could draw upon a strong and well-established avant-garde tradition that put a premium on change. The Surrealists were intent on developing an entire philosophy of life as well as of art, and their interests, which were at first primarily literary, involved an intimate contact not only with contemporary trends in the verbal and visual arts, but with psychology, anthropology, philosophy, and politics. This somewhat eclectic intellectual background exposed them to wide and often disparate influences that had varied effects on their development. Many of these influences followed from a direct interest in the Primitive, while others contained ideas about elemental forms of human consciousness that reflected attitudes and concepts similar to those understood to be at the foundation of Primitive experience.

Three of the most important elements of Surrealist philosophy are a conviction that the dream is a valid and integral part of life experience, a belief in the creative power of the unconscious, and an acceptance of the universal need for myth, which arises from a common factor of human mentality and unites the peoples of all civilizations. From the inception of the movement, the Surrealists studied the ideas and creations of past thinkers and artists for inspiration and historical support in the formulation and justification of their own philosophy.

In their search for precedents, the Surrealists were attracted not only to Primitive objects but to the world view of Primitive man, a subject that had been studied increasingly throughout the nineteenth and early twentieth centuries by a variety of ethnographers, anthropologists, psychologists, and philosophers. As it was described by the scholars who investigated it, the Primitive mentality directly embodied those very qualities the Surrealists were desperately trying to integrate into their own lives and art. We can demonstrate the essence of this European intellectual explanation of the Primitive, which formed the background of the Surrealists' theoretical interests, by considering the writings of four principal representative figures with whose work the Surrealists were famil-

Figure. San Cristobal, Solomon Islands. Painted wood and feathers, 28½" (72.4 cm) high. The Trustees of the British Museum, London

iar: Sir James Frazer, Lucien Lévy-Bruhl, Sigmund Freud, and Henri Bergson.

Frazer believed in the existence of a common human mentality that reveals itself in the similar ways in which people from various geographic locations, cultures, and time periods conceptualize and express their relationship to the world in which they live. *The Golden Bough*, which was very popular among the Surrealists, is a huge cultural sourcebook in which a number of basic themes in human thought are illustrated with thousands of examples from the myths and legends of the ancient world, the Orient, European folk culture, the Primitive cultures in Africa, Oceania, and the Americas.

One of Frazer's greatest contributions to the study of the Primitive mind was his investigation of the function of the

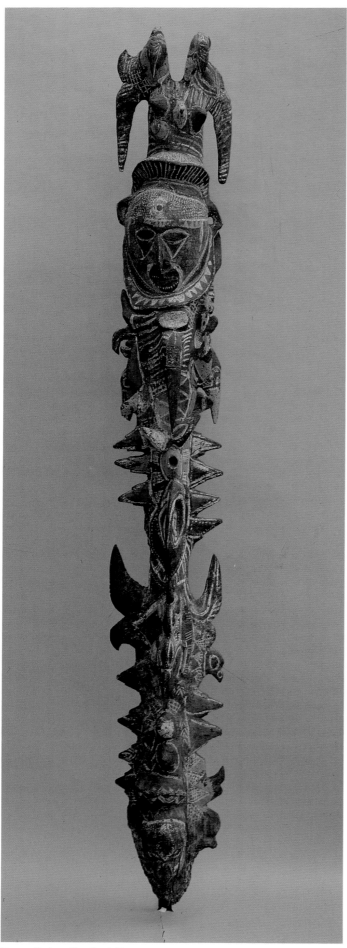

Figure. Abelam. East Sepik Province, Papua New Guinea. Painted wood, 10' (305 cm) high. Friede Collection, New York

dream. Through many intriguing and often charming accounts, *The Golden Bough* demonstrated Primitive man's implicit belief that his dreams were an integral and essential part of his everyday life, and that these experiences of the mind and spirit were just as important in influencing his behavior as those events and thoughts that activated his waking hours. Moreover, he cited numerous examples proving that the dream life of Primitive man was regarded as conveying a higher level of truth than the experiences of his waking consciousness. In one example from the Gran Chaco tribe he related that "the Indians are firmly convinced of the truth of what they relate [about dreams]; for these wonderful adventures are simply their dreams, which they do not distinguish from waking realities."[24]

In *The Golden Bough* Frazer also showed that in Primitive cultures people regarded themselves as existing in a universe in which every object and force in nature was motivated by a soul or spirit that had a value equal to their own. Such a world view by necessity brought these people into a much closer relationship with their environment, because they regarded the objects, flora, and fauna with which they lived as possessing a spirit power capable of the same type of action and reaction as that which provided the life force of their own being. Thus, the successful person in a Primitive culture maintains a harmonious relationship with the forces of nature, unlike the modern Westerner who tends to view man as superior to nature and therefore separates himself from it both physically and psychologically. Frazer's investigation into the dualistic structure of the Primitive world view and the functional importance of the dream was a major step in the development of the European awareness and understanding of Primitive culture.

During the first three decades of the twentieth century, French scholars developed a strong tradition of anthropological research. One of the founders of this movement was Lucien Lévy-Bruhl, who enjoyed widespread popularity and was especially influential among the Surrealists. In his two major publications, *Les Fonctions mentales dans les sociétés inférieures* of 1910 and *La mentalité primitive* of 1922, Lévy-Bruhl attempted to define the basic differences between the ways in which individuals from Primitive and contemporary Western cultures viewed the world and structured their relationships to it. His main thesis was that Primitive man organized the world on a dualistic principle which gave great value to the mystical, spiritual forces that animate all things and give impetus to all causal motivation. Like Frazer and others who published on the subject, Lévy-Bruhl also maintained that the dream was the most important meeting place of physical reality and the more elusive causal spirit entities.[25] However, while claiming the dream state to be the most overt medium of rapport between man and the spirits, Lévy-Bruhl asserted that one of the principal characteristics of Primitive society was that its members felt themselves to be in a state of uninterrupted communication between material, temporal reality and the realms of the spirits.[26] Lévy-Bruhl's theories were therefore particularly attractive to the Surrealists, who were trying to develop the ability to use the dream and the unconscious mind as a means of illuminating conscious experience and enriching the creative process.

In his investigations of Primitive perception and cognition, Lévy-Bruhl emphasized the importance of totemism—the system whereby a certain social unit identifies itself with some natural element, plant, or animal and recognizes it as its leading spirit and guardian. Although the individual unit identifies with only one particular natural element, it is aware that the other animals, plants, and natural forces in the world are related in the same mystical way to other groups. The resulting shared recognition underlies what Lévy-Bruhl called the process of collective representation. He explained that

to the "primitive" who belongs to a totemistic community, every animal, every plant, every object indeed, such as the sun, moon, stars, forms part of a totem.... Even in communities where this form does not exist the collective representation of certain animals (possibly of all if our records were complete) is mystic in character.[27]

The totemic role of spiritually viable plant and animal forms as described by Lévy-Bruhl will be shown to be of great importance in the work of Surrealist artists, especially that of André Masson and Max Ernst.

The relationship between Lévy-Bruhl's theory of the Primitive world view and the interests of the Surrealists was first discussed in 1945 by Jules Monnerot in *La Poésie moderne et le sacré*, where the author emphasized the dream and the myth as the most important shared elements of primitivism and Surrealism. Monnerot's work is particularly relevant because it was highly acclaimed by André Breton, who wrote that it gave "excellent evidence of the affinities of Surealist thought and that of the Indians."[28]

The individual who had the most profound influence on the development of Surealism's ideological links with primitivism was Sigmund Freud. *The Interpretation of Dreams*, published in 1905, brought to the field of modern psychoanalysis the belief in the validity of dream phenomena discussed here in relation to the Primitive mind. Freud postulated that all hidden feelings and emotions that man could not face in his waking consciousness appeared in some disguised, metaphoric form during the dream period; the key to his oneirocritical theories was thus the coupling of the processes of free association with the interpretation of dream symbols. These two methods were of great importance to the Surrealists, whose preoccupation with dreams and dream symbolism was based on their desire to incorporate the resources of the unconscious into works of art in order to give them the deeply suggestive and consciousness-expanding power of the actual dream experience.

Freud's *Totem and Taboo* of 1913 also had a major effect on many of the Surrealists and their interest in and understanding of the Primitive. In this study Freud attempted to bridge the gap between social anthropology, folklore, and psychology in order to deduce the original meaning of totemism from the recognizable vestiges of it remaining in childhood in Western culture. Accordingly, the book tried to establish a relationship between the Primitive mind and certain psychological elements still evident in Western society in order to better understand each of them. Freud's preface to *Totem and Taboo* asserted that men still live today who are close in psychological structure to the earliest humans, the "first primitives."

There are men still living who, as we believe, stand very near to primitive man, far nearer than we do, and whom we therefore regard as his direct heirs and representatives. Such is our view of those whom we describe as savages...and their mental life must have a particular interest for us if we are right in seeing in it a well-preserved

Openwork board. Sawos. East Sepik Province, Papua New Guinea. Painted wood, 6'10" (208.3 cm) high. Collection Milton and Frieda Rosenthal

Lime spatula with flying fox. Trobriand Islands, Milne Bay Province, Papua New Guinea. Wood, 10¼" (26 cm) high. Friede Collection, New York

In a chapter of *Totem and Taboo* entitled "Animism, Magic and the Omnipotence of Thoughts," Freud discussed the role of art in relation to human psychology:

In only a single field of our civilization has the omnipotence of thoughts been retained, and that is in the field of art. Only in art does it still happen that a man who is consumed by desires performs something resembling the accomplishment of those desires.... People speak with justice of the "magic of art" and compare artists with magicians. But the comparison is perhaps more significant than it claims to be. There can be no doubt that art did not begin as art for art's sake. It worked originally in the service of impulses which are for the most part extinct today. And among them we may suspect many magical purposes.[30]

That this image of the artist as magician, which had been utilized in the previous century by Baudelaire and Mallarmé, was especially fitting for the Surrealist artist will be seen in our discussion of the work of Max Ernst and Wifredo Lam. In the chapter of *Totem and Taboo* entitled "The Return of Totemism in Childhood," Freud found within his theory of the Oedipus complex an explanation for the phenomenon of the totemic clan. This concept established a distinct parallel between the Primitive mind and certain mental states in modern man. The ramifications of the theory will be shown to have exerted a great influence on the work of Ernst, who was very familiar with Freud's writings from the years when he studied psychology at the University of Bonn before World War I.

Henri Bergson was exploring the unconscious and the dream during the same period Lévy-Bruhl and Freud were publishing. He based many of his constructs on the primacy of intuition in the human mental process. This concept had been advanced by a great variety of nineteenth-century thinkers who influenced the Symbolists and now was equally inspiring to the Surrealists in their search for a creative alternative to the limited rationalism of traditional Western society. Bergson's philosophy, which was entirely familiar to the Surrealists, posited a dualistic world in which the powers of reason and the abstract intellect are foreign to the *élan vital*, the creative life force which is guided by intuition. Just as Primitive man sees his world as a spatial and temporal amalgam of spirit and matter, so Bergson viewed the essential character of the upward movement of life and evolution as one in which time and space interpenetrate in a great surging mass of eternal change that is the very rhythm of life itself. *La durée*, this state of undifferentiated duration where the spirit of the life impulse is free to move, is quite close to the European conception of the Primitive mind in which past, present, and future exist in a state of constant communication. In this respect, Surrealist artists and people from Primitive societies as described by the scholars discussed here might be seen as the embodiment of Bergson's influential philosophy of life force moving in the positive direction.

During the early years of Surrealism there was a parallel growth of interest in Primitive art on the part of galleries and magazines as well as among the individual members of the Surrealist group itself. Of the many authors who wrote about it then, the poet Guillaume Apollinaire had the most direct tie to the Surrealists. As early as 1912, Apollinaire had mentioned the Primitive arts of Oceania and Africa in his poem "Zone." Here he describes an individual who sees little value in the

picture of an early age of our own development. If that supposition is correct, a comparison between the psychology of primitive peoples, as it is taught by social anthropology, and the psychology of neurotics, as it has been revealed by psychoanalysis, will be bound to show numerous points of agreement and will throw new light upon familiar facts in both sciences.[29]

Using frequent references to the ideas of Frazer and Lévy-Bruhl, as well as to those of other well-known ethnographers, Freud acknowledged the dualistic world view of the Primitive, expressing it in terms of people, or body-soul, and things, or object-spirit. He also wrote that causation in Primitive society is attributed to spirit forces, and, following Frazer in *The Golden Bough*, placed heavy emphasis on the power of homeopathic magic, or the Primitive's belief in the power of mental forces to affect the world. Freud called this power the "omnipotence of thought."

Mask. Sulka. New Britain. Painted pith, wood, and feathers, 47¼" (120 cm) high. Übersee-Museum, Bremen

Installation view of "Exhibition of Surrealist Objects," Galerie Charles Ratton, Paris, 1936

traditional forms of Western culture; after a day of thoughtful searching, "you travel home towards Auteuil on foot to sleep among your fetishes from Oceania and Guinea, they are Christs of other forms, of other faiths, they are the lesser Christs of obscure expectations."[31] Apollinaire's interest in Primitive objects and the beliefs of the cultures from which they came were confirmed in his preface to the book *Sculptures nègres*, which was published in 1917 by the Parisian art dealer Paul Guillaume, and in April of the same year, Apollinaire wrote an article on "Fetishist Sculpture of the Black Races," which was destined to reach a wider audience in the popular *Mercure de France*.

During Surrealism's early Paris years, the number of books and articles devoted to Primitive culture and art multiplied. For example, in 1919—when the Devambez Gallery organized one of Paris's first exhibitions of African and Oceanic art—André Clouzot and René Level published *L'Art nègre et l'art océanien*. This trend continued the next year with the appearance of the article "Opinions sur l'art nègre" in the review *Action*, featuring statements by Picasso, Gris, Lipchitz, Cocteau, and others.[32] The growing popularity of Primitive art and its attendant primitivism was also reflected in the increasing publication of Primitive material in the art magazines of the late 1920s and 1930s, particularly *Documents, Cahiers d'art, La Révolution surréaliste*, and *Minotaure*.[33]

While this growing interest in the Primitive was being demonstrated in the scholarly and literary fields, many members of the Surrealist group were themselves actively collecting Primitive art. We have already noted that Tzara owned African sculpture when he was in Zurich. After moving to Paris late in 1919, he continued his interest in collecting—which was now to be shared by many of his colleagues. Two outstanding early collections were those of Breton and Paul Eluard. The Surrealists' preference for Oceanic, American Indian, and Eskimo art over that of Africa is reflected in the relative numbers of objects from each area that are listed in the auction catalog of their combined collections when, in response to extremely hard financial times, they were offered for sale at the Hôtel Drouot in July of 1931. Out of a total of 312 items there were 30 from Africa, 134 from Oceania, 124 from the Americas, 14 from Malaysia, and 7 "Divers."[34] The Breton-Eluard sale was one of the most important Primitive art

auctions held in Paris between the two wars, and its scope is an indication of a much-increased availability of material, and the variety and range of the Surrealists' interests.

Primitive art was also included in various exhibitions organized by the Surrealists themselves. The first of these was the opening exhibition of the Galerie Surréaliste in Paris on March 16, 1926, which featured the work of Man Ray and a selection of Oceanic objects from the collections of Breton, Eluard, Louis Aragon, and others. Another major event of this kind was the 1936 "Exhibition of Surrealist Objects," held between May 22 and 29 at the gallery of Charles Ratton, the noted Parisian Primitive art dealer. Amid the incredible mélange of items displayed was a large selection of pieces from the Primitive cultures of Oceania and America. These were placed side by side with natural objects, interpreted objects, and objects made by Surrealist artists and poets.[35] The same pattern was followed on a larger scale when the "International Surrealist Exhibition" was organized in London in 1936 by a group of English artists with the support of Breton, Eluard, and Man Ray. The exhibition consisted of over four hundred paintings, sculptures, and objects, including a large number of pieces from Africa, Oceania, and the Americas.[36] Most of the objects in both exhibitions were borrowed from the collections of individual Surrealists.

Primitive society found the answers to the questions of life in the spirit world and the realm of the dream. The Surrealists, in studying Primitive arts and cultures, followed a similar path. It has been recognized that in Primitive societies the relationship between art and the creative process is closely influenced by magic, a subject that provides another affinity between the Surrealist and the Primitive. For the latter, the magical quality of the object depends on its role as an embodiment of power. In Surrealist philosophy, the ability of an object to evoke mental images and, through them, powerful emotions is its measure of the "marvelous." Breton sought a way by which the contemporary artist might create forms that would have the same degree of psychic power and associative meaning as the objects of the Primitive artist-magician. It is, therefore, in his role as artist that the Surrealist comes closest to Primitive culture, for it is in art, both literary and visual, that the Surrealist best realizes his aspirations and goals.

In his role of *l'homme révolté*, Breton was much like Lautréamont's Maldoror, a character whom he admired and sought to emulate by turning his whole life into a search for new ways in which to relate to the world. This search led both Lautréamont's Maldoror and Breton to a state of being that involved a closer contact and spiritual union with the fundamental elements of the world, in a manner that both ascribed to Primitive man.

It is not surprising [wrote Clifford Browder] that Breton developed an early interest in primitive art...and that he visited American Indian reservations and witnessed Haitian voodoo ceremonies providing living proof of the survival among savages of the very state of mind that Surrealism would cultivate. Insofar as they had escaped the "contamination" of Christianity, primitive societies for Breton offered the spectacle of man in harmony with nature, giving uninhibited expression to the exuberant desires repressed by Western culture. Consequently, hope for the latter lay not in the anthropological study of such societies, but in the recreation of their modes of experience. It was by exercising this bold imagination and systematic credulity common to the child and the savage alike that one recovered the lost paradise of the *surréel*.[37]

Mask. Baining. New Britain. Painted bark cloth, cane frame, 39" (99 cm) high. Hamburgisches Museum für Völkerkunde

Breton prized Oceanic and American Indian art for the provocative juxtapositions of sculptural plasticity and two-dimensional decorativeness with which they expressed natural and spiritual metaphors, and he felt that they provided him with a model for the evocative imagery he was seeking in his poetry. "You see what justification these objects have for the Surrealist vision, even what new flights they have ready for us," he said of his collection. "This Eskimo mask features a swan which guides the hunter in the spring.... In the crenellated headdress [of the Hopi Kachina] you find the clouds on

Above: André Masson. *Apollo and Daphne*. 1933. Oil on canvas, 35 x 45⅝" (88.9 x 115.9 cm). Private collection

Right: André Masson. *The Legend of Corn*. 1943. Tempera on wood, 19¾ x 24" (50 x 61 cm). Private collection

the mountain; in the center of this small checkerboard a little ear of corn; a rainbow around the mouth; in the vertical striations of the dress, the rain falling in the valley."[38]

The evocation of the physical environment of Primitive cultures was also used by Breton as a theme in many of his works. The strange and enticing scenes of wild, untrammeled nature play a major role in *Martinique charmeuse de serpents*, written in 1948 with Masson. In 1937 Breton published *L'Amour fou*, in which he described exotic plants and settings which were for him the embodiment of the marvelous incongruities and mysterious wonders that only nature,

unaffected by modern artifice, can produce. The nature he exalts is a timeless one, set in Oceania and with roots deep in a primordial past—a nature that transcends man and yet can lead him beyond the barriers and limitations of obvious daily realities. Breton saw in these primordial and evocative natural settings "a dream world" (*un pays de rêve*)[39] where the restrictions of society were broken and where there existed a state of natural harmony allowing man to exercise the deep, inborn desires of the dream and the unconscious.

Breton's long and highly developed involvement with the art and life of Primitive cultures culminated in *L'Art magique* of

1957. A lengthy, discursive, and unfortunately often disconnected book, it did not add much new information to recorded knowledge of the connection between Surrealism and primitivism, but it did serve to demonstrate Breton's strong feeling for and grasp of the many phases and types of Primitive art as they apply to theories of magic. It also elucidated the ways in which Breton related Primitive art forms to the images used by the magicians, occultists, and alchemists of European history, thus establishing yet another link between the Western and Primitive cultures.

Like Breton, André Masson was involved with primitivism on an intellectual as well as artistic level. In 1943 Masson produced a painting reflecting those transcultural ties between classical and tribal myths which, from the 1920s on, were such a major influence on his development. Entitled *The Legend of Corn*, 1943, the painting treats an Iroquois Indian legend concerning the mythical relationship between the Corn Goddess and the Sun. Masson's source for the myth was Frazer's *Golden Bough*,[40] though its attraction for him lay partly in its almost exact duplication of the classical legend of Apollo and Daphne, a theme he had depicted in 1933. It is significant that Masson painted *The Legend of Corn* when he was living in the United States, as if the proximity to the land of the Indian legend gave him the necessary inspiration to produce the work, which in composition is quite similar to the earlier painting of the classical myth.[41] In both pictures the movement is from left to right as the sun god pursues the unwilling female, who looks back in terror as she flees toward the edge of the canvas. Both myths follow the same basic pattern of desire, conflict, chase, appeal, and a transformation which results in the bonding of anthropomorphic entities with the vegetal forms of either laurel or corn. The appeal of both myths for Masson lay in their statement of the human potential for physical unity with other aspects of nature. They imply that not only do plants and trees, earth and rocks, have a motivating spirit whose source and power is similar to that possessed by man, but that people themselves have a physical kinship with the elements of nature and a potential for corporeal transformation, which the process of metamorphosis symbolizes and reveals.

The Legend of Corn is the one work most often selected to illustrate Masson's interest in Primitive mythology. There are, however, other myths and tales from the world of Primitive cultures with which Masson was familiar and which helped to provide an impetus for his many images of human-plant metamorphosis. We need only turn to Masson's favorite source of Primitive mythology, *The Golden Bough*, to find a series of references dealing with the symbolic and ritualized change of human into plant. In a section entitled "Human representations of tree-spirits," Frazer prefaced a list of examples with this statement:

The representation of the tree—or vegetation—spirit by a tree, bough, or flower is sometimes entirely dropped, while the representation of him by a living person remains. In this case the representative character of the person is generally marked by dressing him or her in leaves or flowers...[42]

We shall demonstrate the relevance of this concept for Masson's work after taking note of two other important sources for

his images of human-plant metamorphosis. These involved actual objects of Primitive art and the literature dealing with them.

Scholarship on Primitive art since the beginning of the twentieth century has acknowledged the fact that the Primitive cultures that produced magico-religious images regarded them in a conceptual context entirely different from that which Europe had traditionally applied to its own artistic production. In a Primitive culture, the masks, statues, and other objects that are part of their artistic heritage are seen not as primarily commemorative or aesthetic objects, but rather as embodiments of spirit entities which, during times of ritual, carry an enormous and immediate charge of spiritual power.[43] This concept applies in a special way to the ceremonial masks and costumes that play such an important role in the spiritual and artistic life of these societies. During the religious ritual, the person who dons the mask in order to represent a specific spirit entity loses for that time his individual identity and becomes the spirit itself; in the Primitive view, man thus has the capacity to be temporarily transformed into some other spirit, whether of an ancestor, animal, or tree. The transformation is visual as well as psychological, for the mask costume usually totally alters the appearance of the ritual participant. A good example of this can be seen in the fiber costumes of the Asmat from Irian Jaya, which, while hiding the figure of the wearer, maintain enough general delineation of the head, face, and arms that this object of rattan, sennit, and other natural materials becomes a haunting image of the mythical tree-person come to life.

Mask and dance costume. Asmat. Irian Jaya (formerly Netherlands New Guinea). Painted wood, rattan, fiber, and mixed media, 67" (170 cm) high. The Metropolitan Museum of Art, New York; The Michael C. Rockefeller Memorial Collection, gift of Nelson A. Rockefeller and Mrs. Mary C. Rockefeller

André Masson. *Sur les rives de l'ennui*. 1938. Pen and ink from *Mythologies*, 1946

Masson's most consistent use of the image of the anthropomorphized tree can be found in his drawings from the late 1930s and early 1940s, most particularly in *Mythologies* of 1938, published in 1946, a collection of drawings devoted to his exploration of myth. In the chapter entitled "Mythology of Nature," seven out of the fifteen drawings depict woman-tree images. *Sur les rives de l'ennui* is a representative example, in which the voluptuous bodies of the women in the foreground also evidence distinct arboreal features. The tree trunks are torsos, branches and twigs form arms and fingers, legs and toes, the hair is a mass of leaves. Masson

achieves a true amalgam of plant and human forms by using each element in such an integrated, dual capacity that the image is ultimately definable neither as one nor the other.

One could also cite the widely accepted image of Mother Nature as perpetuating the ancient idea that women are the symbolic source of reproductive power in the world. Frazer thought this aspect of early religion so important that in his publication of 1926, *The Worship of Nature*, he devoted six chapters to the examination of earth worship among cultures ranging from Aryan peoples of antiquity to African and various American Indian tribes.[44] These chapters included numerous anecdotes concerning the role of the female divinity who represents the earth as the mother and giver of sustenance to all, since many of these Primitive cultures believed the earth to be the central element in the continuation of the life cycle. In one illustration of this point Frazer quoted a primary source as saying that "the Indians consider the earth as their universal mother. They believe that they were created within its bosom, where for a long time they had their abode, before they came to live on its surface."[45]

The strong belief in a sustaining earth mother among Primitive cultures throughout the world was noted by both Frazer and Lévy-Bruhl. Masson adopted this ancient and Primitive concept of woman as idol with her promise of eternal fertility, utilizing it as one of the central elements of his symbolic representations. Masson's use of this theme is found in many works, one of the most effective of which is *The Earth* of 1939, in which sand was mixed with the paint. The figure of the woman representing the earth is clearly recognizable. Her

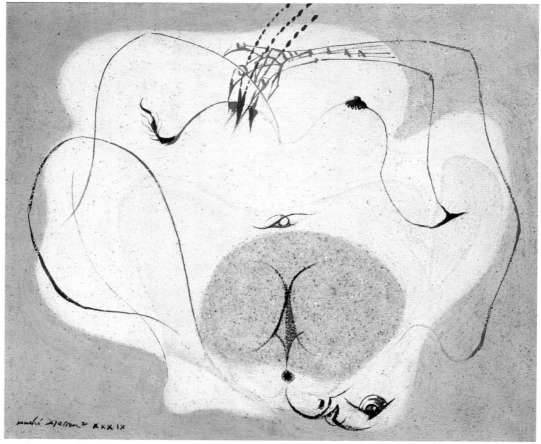

André Masson. *The Earth*. 1939. Sand and oil on wood, 17 x 20⅞" (43.2 x 53 cm). Musée National d'Art Moderne, Centre National d'Art et de Culture Georges Pompidou, Paris

large breasts in the upper half of the canvas are balanced by the exposed genitalia, emphasized by a circular area of darker colored sand. The right arm of the figure reaches over the torso and with a curiously clawlike hand squeezes milk from the left breast—an additional symbol of her life-giving capacities. Masson's use of a natural element such as sand as the medium of his technical process evokes the underlying idea of woman as an embodiment of the earth itself, a concept also frequently found in Primitive beliefs.[46]

Throughout the long years of his awareness of Primitive art, Masson had always been able to maintain a certain intellectual detachment and objective honesty about the cultural and aesthetic qualities for which he felt such a creative attraction. He has acknowledged that a gap will always exist between Western man's appreciation of the Primitive arts and his ability to decipher and comprehend them in the ways they are understood by the cultures that produced them.[47] In *Le Plaisir de peindre* Masson warned against the dangers of "comparing a work painted in Paris to the work of a native of the New Hebrides with whom...we have nothing in common in the area of art, metaphysics, or way of life."[48] It is because of such factors that Western man, while able to appreciate the plastic values and, to some extent, the expressive intent of Primitive art, cannot hope to grasp all the inherent, deeply intuitive, and emotional meanings that operate on the planes of magic and the spiritual. However, this very strangeness and ambiguity may well be one of the principal attractions that these art forms have for Western society.

The Surrealists' predilection for the arts of Oceanic cultures above those of Africa has already been mentioned. Commenting on the emergence of Oceanic art in Paris during the 1920s, Masson asserted that the Surrealists' interest in it was aesthetic rather than anthropological, that they "discovered this art for the artists, not for the ethnographers but for the world of culture."[49] In the process of defining exactly what constituted the aesthetic attraction of Oceanic art, Masson acknowledged the vastness of the territories and the divergence of the cultural groups that inhabit them, mentioning not only general island clusters such as Polynesia but also New Zealand, New Guinea, the Marquesas, the Bismarck Archipelago, and Australia.[50] But while recognizing their diversity, he also identified a stylistic imperative that characterized many types of Oceanic art and differentiated them from the major African forms. As an illustration of his observation Masson cited the anthropomorphic sculptures made by the Maori of New Zealand, which he found particularly effective because of "the entangling of the body—the visceral coalescence that is not found in African art."[51]

As is the case with most artists who borrow forms or themes from Primitive sources, there are few one-to-one visual relationships between Masson's work and any specific example of Primitive art. Rather, the process of his incorporation of tribal forms or styles into his own oeuvre is analogous to the phenomenon of learning the vocabulary of a new language, but using its words or images within a personal syntactical structure. The indirect effects of Primitive influence can be seen in Masson's work from the 1930s and 1940s, including his three important books of drawings—*Mythologies, Anatomy of My Universe,* and *Nocturnal Notebook*—as well as other drawings, prints, and paintings.

In 1935 Masson produced two paintings that are visual

André Masson. *Dawn at Montserrat.* 1935. Oil on canvas, 20 x 26" (50.8 x 66 cm). Snite Museum of Art, University of Notre Dame; extended loan from Dr. Roy H. Stern

Easter Island. Pen-and-ink drawing attributed to Pierre Loti. 1872

summations of his philosophy of cosmic unity: *The Landscape of Wonders* and *Dawn at Montserrat.* In these works, earth, air, fire, and water are represented in a cataclysmic landscape animated by a furious, elemental sense of movement. Astral bodies whirl and spin through the skies while the earth rends itself with a volcanic eruption signaling a moment of creation. The sense of genesis in *Dawn at Montserrat* is also a testimony to Masson's involvement with primitivism and represents one of his few direct borrowings from specific works of Primitive art. Set in the landscape are images of the enigmatic stone figures of Easter Island, which Masson knew both from publications and from the example that is still on display at the Musée de l'Homme in Paris. It is appropriate that he chose this most famous and inexplicable type of large-scale Polynesian sculpture to act as silent witness in his primal landscape; for these figures, placed as they are in reality on the island's slopes overlooking the Pacific, are imbued with a sense of timeless mystery. In *Dawn at Montserrat* these giant Primitive figures represent humanity as it was and as it will be, both an integral element and a conscious observer of the world's spiritual, creative force.

Max Ernst. *Elephant of the Celebes*. 1921. Oil on canvas, 49¼ x 42½" (125.1 x 107.9 cm) The Trustees of the Tate Gallery, London

Corn bin. Konkombwa. Ghana or Togo. Published in Roland Penrose, *Max Ernst's Celebes*, 1972

The power to create hallucinations is the power to exalt existence. It can be argued this constitutes a form of madness, but I think that Max Ernst accepts this as part of the task of the artist.... In this sense Max Ernst is a primitive man, even if he doesn't live in a primitive society.[52]

This statement by Matta characterizes the way many of Max Ernst's fellow Surrealists have associated him with the mentality of Primitive societies and with its art-making processes. Ernst's long and active career, which began before World War I and continued until his death in 1976, was marked by a deep intellectual and aesthetic interest in the Primitive. While a student of psychology and philosophy at the University of Bonn from 1909 until 1914, he combined his reading of authors such as Hegel, Nietzsche, and Freud with Frazer (*The Golden Bough*) and with that of the German ethnographer Wilhelm Wundt.[53] Ernst's involvement with ethnology continued through his university years and beyond as he added the studies by Lévy-Bruhl, Claude Lévi-Strauss, later a good friend, and others to his store of knowledge of the subject. He also began early on to visit the many excellent collections of tribal art accessible to him in the German ethnographic museums and began reading books on the subject. What he learned about Primitive cultures was a major influence on him, and its effects can be clearly seen both in his writings and his art. Roland Penrose has shown that as early as 1921 Ernst used the image of an African corn bin he found in an English anthropological journal as the model for his *Elephant of the Celebes*.[54] Two years later he again turned to an anthropological source for the image of the tattooed figure in his *La Belle Jardinière*, which is clearly based on studies of Marquesan personal adornment.

As one of the founding members of the Surrealist movement, Ernst developed a complex self-image which he described succinctly in his most famous essay, *Beyond Painting*, first published in 1936. *Beyond Painting* is divided into three main sections, the third of which, entitled "Instantaneous Identity," presents Ernst's most telling descriptions of his appropriation of the Primitive world view.

Like Breton and Masson, and in common with their predecessors back to Gauguin, Ernst felt that the Surrealist artist must regain the mythic, spiritual harmony with nature that was lost in the development of Christianity, Western rationalism, and technology. Nature in all its forms became the central motif of his work, and it was in relation to his feelings about nature that he defined his ties to the Primitive. In "Instantaneous Identity" he wrote of himself in the third person as follows:

Regarding "nature" for example, one may discern in him two attitudes, in appearance irreconcilable: that of the god Pan and the man Papou who possesses all the mysteries and realizes the playful pleasure in his union with her ("He marries nature, he pursues the nymph Echo," they say) and that of a conscious and organized Prometheus, thief of fire who, guided by thought, persecutes her with an implacable hatred and grossly injures her. "This monster is pleased only by the antipodes of the landscape," they repeat. And a teasing little girl adds: "He is a brain and a vegetable at the same time."[55]

Ernst defined the first half of his dual relationship with "nature" in terms of two figures who represent the traditions of classical mythology and of Primitive man, for like Masson, Ernst perceived both as sources of inspiration and identification. His fascination with mythology stemmed from a recognition of the West's urgent need for a new and relevant system of beliefs, a point he emphasized when, after describing the cultural influences on his childhood, he expressed the hope that "one day some elements of a new mythology will spring out of this drama."[56]

Pan is a classical Arcadian god of forests and shepherds, a many-faceted and complex figure whose physical attributes mark him as a combination of man and animal, who was, moreover, held to possess the power of inspiration and prophesy.[57] When Ernst also identified himself with "Papou," as a complement to the god Pan, he was using the French word for "Papuan." The art of the Papuan Gulf region had been one of his favorite styles,[58] and "the man Papou" is clearly intended to represent tribal man in general. Ernst saw him as living in a harmonious relationship with nature and keeping intact the mythic structures that establish and define this relationship. Thus, the Papuan parallels the deity Pan in that he too "possesses all the mysteries and realizes the playful pleasure in his union with her ('He marries nature, he pursues the nymph Echo,' they say)."[59] The Primitive aspect that Ernst saw in himself, then, not only enabled him to live in harmony with nature, but helped him explore all her mysteries and appropriate the secrets of her creative powers.

In both classical and tribal mythology, animals and their anthropomorphized variants appear as symbols of both the spiritual forces of nature and man's mystical relationship to these forces. These types of images appear throughout Max Ernst's oeuvre—a bizarre menagerie of insects, fish, animals, and fantastic hybrids that constitute his personal bestiary.

The bird, however, is by far his favorite and most frequently represented creature, and in his intimate association with birds we find Ernst's most significant association with the Primitive.

In 1948 Ernst wrote an autobiographical fantasy, which begins by characterizing his birth in avian terms: "The 2nd of April (1891) at 9:45 a.m. Max Ernst had his first contact with the sensible world, when he came out of the egg which his mother had laid in an eagle's nest and which the bird had brooded over for seven years."[60] Birds continued to be vital symbols in his childhood. In the same document he described the death of his pet bird, whose corpse he found the next morning at the very moment his father announced the birth of a new sister. "The *perturbation*," Ernst recalled, "was so enormous that he fainted."

In his imagination he connected both events and charged the baby with extinction of the bird's life. A series of mystical crises, fits of hysteria, exaltations, and depressions followed. A dangerous confusion between birds and humans became encrusted in his mind and asserted itself in his drawings and paintings...and even later Max identified himself voluntarily with *Loplop, the Superior of the Birds.*[61]

As Ernst's friend and biographer Patrick Waldberg understood, the bird had become his "totem."[62] What Ernst recounted is indeed a classic example of the totemic relationship discussed by Frazer, Wundt, and Lévy-Bruhl, among others, as one of the fundamental elements of Primitive culture. But perhaps the most influential source that Ernst had read on the subject was Freud's 1913 *Totem and Taboo*, a title that Ernst himself adopted for a 1941 painting in which bird and female forms appear against a background reminiscent of

Max Ernst. *La Belle Jardinière*. 1923. Oil on canvas. Presumed destroyed

A Marquesas Islander with full body tattooing. Drawing. 1804. Published in Captain A. J. von Krusenstern, *Voyage around the World*, London, 1913

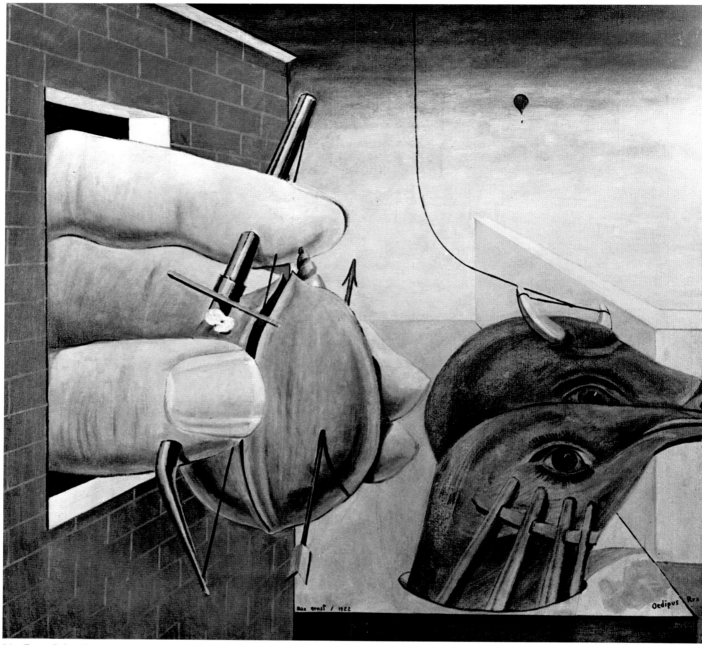

Max Ernst. *Oedipus Rex.* 1922. Oil on canvas, 35 x 45¾" (88.9 x 116.2 cm). Private collection

clustered Northwest Coast totem poles. In Freud's texts there were descriptions of the totemic relationship that exactly corresponded to Ernst's identification with birds. Freud demonstrated that as a rule the totem was not only a clan animal with whom individuals identify, but also "their guardian spirit and helper, which sends them oracles."[63]

Freud's major purpose was to trace the origin of the Oedipus complex through the totemism of Primitive cultures. From both biographical sources and Ernst's own writings it is clear that he had very strong Oedipal attitudes, despising his father but sustaining close emotional ties with his mother.[64] His attempt to express these feelings artistically in the light of Freud's theories resulted in one of his most intriguing paintings, *Oedipus Rex,* of 1921, which also marked his first major use of the totemic image of the bird.[65]

Oedipus Rex, perhaps Ernst's last major work prior to his

taking up residence in Paris in the summer of 1922, has a spatial theater and mysterious imagery clearly indebted to Giorgio de Chirico. On the right, two bird heads project through round holes in the pavement. On the left, the fingers of an enormous (left) hand emerge through a window set into a red brick wall. The fingers hold a very large partially opened nut, similar in shape to a walnut, which is pierced by an arrow. The thumb and forefinger of the hand are also pierced, in this case by two halves of a mechanical instrument which, because of the string that connects the ends, looks much like a bow. Finally, the ensemble is completed by a form emerging from behind the nut and pressing against the flesh of the forefinger, a form whose spiral shape is reminiscent of some sort of snail shell, or perhaps the end of a large screw. The setting consists only of the uncluttered ground plane, the blank wall and window, clear sky, and a distant balloon.

Basing our interpretation on Freud's text and Ernst's auto-biographical account, we might identify the two birds as the artist's parents—the smaller confined or "imprisoned" one with the more graceful head and feminine eye symbolizing his mother, and the larger horned one his father. The partially opened nutshell suggests the female sex, just as the arrow that pierces it is an obvious phallic symbol. The thumb and fore-finger that hold the nut are also pierced by a metal implement and a hornlike object, which are joined by a taut string, creating a bow form to complement the arrow and thereby establishing a relationship between this set of forms and the similar arrangement of the male bird's horns. As the birds represent the totem, the pierced hand and nutshell stand for the desires and restrictions of the taboo.[66] Thus, in *Oedipus Rex* Ernst utilizes Freud's theories of the relationship between the Oedipus complex and totemism to create a very personal expression of his own mingled feelings about his parents and sense of totemic identification with the bird. This interpretation is also borne out by his 1934 collage novel *Une Semaine de bonté*, in which Ernst used bird-headed humans as the central image for the Wednesday series that is devoted to Oedipus. The example here shows two of the bird-headed creatures, above which a large hand holding a sharp implement can be seen coming through an open window—a direct reference to the *Oedipus Rex* painting done twelve years earlier.

Ernst's famous frottage series, Histoire Naturelle of 1925, included four images whose subjects are large centrally placed birds. The most striking of these, *The Origin of the Pendulum* (p. 560), bears a close resemblance to depictions of birds with outstretched wings often found in North American Indian art. His inspiration for this form could have been any of the many painted thunderbird images from either the Northwest Coast tribes or those of the Plains Indians. A beautiful example of the latter type is a Sioux warrior's shield (p. 560) whose energized lines of power emanating from the bird's wings are very close to Ernst's composition and to the two tree forms with wavy grain patterns that stand behind his similarly posed bird. The comparison is particularly relevant for Ernst because the shield served as a form of personal totem for the Plains warrior.

Ernst's 1927 series of monuments to birds led to a new avian image based both on his personal identification with birds and on the childhood conflation of it he had experienced on the death of his pet bird and the birth of his sister. The result, the "dangerous confusion between birds and humans" about which he had spoken, is manifest in *After Us, Motherhood* (p. 557), where the bird's wings and tail take on the appearance of human arms and legs. The central image is that of a seated anthropomorphic bird clutching a smaller bird to its breast, suggestive both of Ernst's metaphorical birth from an egg in the eagle's nest and the birth of the baby sister whose advent he associated with the extinction of the pet bird's life.

In *Max Ernst: Loplop*, Werner Spies presented a valuable account of the artist's complicated association with bird imagery. However, an additional intriguing visual source for Ernst's anthropomorphic birds can be found in the art of the Polynesian culture of Easter Island, which had a significant influence on many aspects of his work. Indeed, the measure of the esteem in which Easter Island was held by the Surrealists can be judged by the huge size of this tiny island in the "Surrealist Map of the World," published in *Variétés* in 1929 (p. 556). Since

its discovery by a Dutch expedition on Easter day, 1722, Easter Island and its art have been a source of great fascination for Western scholars, collectors, and artists. The bibliography on the island and its culture is extensive and includes at least sixty-five items that appeared between 1900 and 1927.[67] Max Ernst was greatly attracted by the Easter Island culture, and, as it will be seen, its art provided a source for much of his imagery in various mediums.[68]

Max Ernst. Collage from *Une Semaine de bonté*. 1934. Fourth book: Wednesday. Element: Blood. Example: Oedipus

The principal deity of Easter Island was a god named MakeMake, who was represented by figures that have both avian and human characteristics (p. 556). MakeMake was associated with the sooty tern, a seabird which, along with its eggs, was a major source of food for the islanders. Each spring the man who swam out to their nesting places on the small rock islands just off shore and brought back the season's first egg was regarded as the reincarnation of the god—an important ceremonial role he held for one year.[69] Images of MakeMake were carved in and on stone and wood as well as painted on stone. Along with the famous giant figures and heads of stone, they were the most widely popularized art objects from that culture. It is among these images that we find the principal visual source for Ernst's anthropomorphic birds.

Ernst's first adaptation of the Easter Island avian forms can be observed in the round, puffed-out bodies of the floating

Dorsal ornament. Easter Island. Wood, 3¾" (9.5 cm) high. Congregazione di SS. Cuore, Rome

Bird-Man figure. Easter Island. Wood, 13" (33 cm) high. American Museum of Natural History, New York, Department of Anthropology

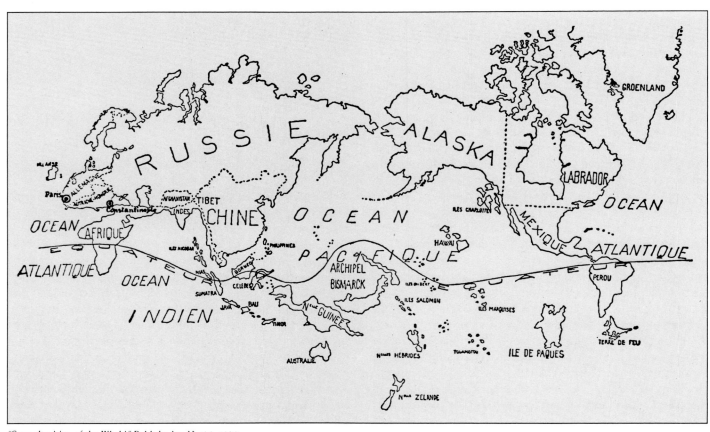

"Surrealist Map of the World." Published in *Variétés*, 1929

Max Ernst. *After Us, Motherhood.* 1927. Oil on canvas, 55¾ x 45⅛" (141.6 x 114.9 cm). Kunstsammlung Nordrhein-Westfalen, Düsseldorf

birds in his Monument to the Birds series, which bear a strong resemblance to the carved wood dorsal ornaments representing similar birds from Easter Island (page left). The full segmented body as well as the features of the head, eye, and beak of the sculpture is echoed in the two main birds that dominate the largest painting of Ernst's series (p. 558). His anthropomorphic bird images appeared soon after and are fully recognizable in *After Us, Motherhood,* whose individual features and compositional relationship closely recall the groups of similar images carved and painted on the rocks of Orongo on Easter Island (pp. 558, 559).

One of the most interesting phases in Ernst's use of the anthropomorphized bird occurred in the 1930s. In *Nature at Dawn* of 1936 (p. 559), the bird-headed human is shown in profile bending forward at the waist in a jungle setting, with large arms bent at the elbow and oversized gesticulating hands.[70] This posture (and body type) was used for many paintings and is clearly related to the anthropomorphic bird images from Easter Island, such as shown in photographs of carvings on the rocks published in Paris just one year before *Nature at Dawn* was executed.

We have noted that a chief aspect of the Easter Island bird

Max Ernst. *Monument to the Birds.* 1927. Oil on canvas, 64 x 51¼″ (162.5 x 30.2 cm). Private collection

cult was the finding and bringing back of the first tern's egg of the new season. A fascinating specimen illustrating this theme is an egg-shaped stone (p. 28) on which is engraved and painted the familiar crouched figure of the bird-headed god holding another egg in his hand. The stone was discovered in 1914 and first published and illustrated in 1919 in a book about Easter Island that was available to Ernst in either Germany or Paris.[71] Beginning in 1927, Ernst produced a series of large egg-shaped compositions filled with round, stylized birds and anthropomorphic bird figures, which are quite close to the Easter Island image. Then in 1929 Ernst painted a series of eight works sharing the title *The Interior of Sight: The Egg* (p.

Right and opposite right: Petroglyphs of Bird-Men on the cliffs of Orongo, Easter Island

Max Ernst. *Nature at Dawn*. 1936. Oil on canvas, 9⅜ x 13¾" (23.8 x 34.9 cm). Städelsches Kunstinstitut, Frankfurt am Main

560), each of which featured a large egg-shaped oval field filled with a variety of curvilinear bird forms. Ernst added a further Easter Island reference in four of the series by placing one or two smaller eggs in or around the birds' mouths (p. 560). Ernst again drew upon this Easter Island object in 1934 when he carved and painted a group of granite river-stone sculptures during a summer spent with Alberto Giacometti in Maloja, Switzerland. While several of these oval stones are decorated with abstracted birds, the sculpture entitled *Oval Bird* (p. 29) is the closest Ernst came to re-creating the exact

forms of the Easter Island image, for in the shape and proportions of the egglike stone and the single bird-human figure the two objects are almost identical. Ernst avoided a direct imitation by omitting the bent leg and foot and by substituting a small bird form for the egg. But while certain details of the image have been altered, the two sculptures have close affinities in all the most essential features of form and spirit.

Still another example of the direct influence of Easter Island art on Ernst's work appears in the 1934 collage novel *Une Semaine de bonté*. The novel is organized into sections representing the days of the week. Thursday has two themes, the first of which is entitled "Le Rire du coq," featuring rooster heads attached to men's bodies similar to the Easter Island bird-human forms. The second theme is "L'Ile de Pâques" (Easter Island), a section containing nine collages whose central figures are fitted with heads of the type for which Easter Island is famous. Reproductions of these monumental stone sculptures (p. 561) were published in many sources, and actual examples were in public museums, such as the one that has been on view at the Trocadéro (Musée de l'Homme) in Paris since 1930. Profiles of these Easter Island heads were used frequently in the series, as, for example, in the collage featuring the "Easter Island Man" and a voluptuous woman (p. 561). In 1935 Ernst again utilized an image from Easter Island in his enigmatic sculptural group *Lunar Asparagus* (p. 564), to the extent that the tall, attenuated "asparagus" topped with

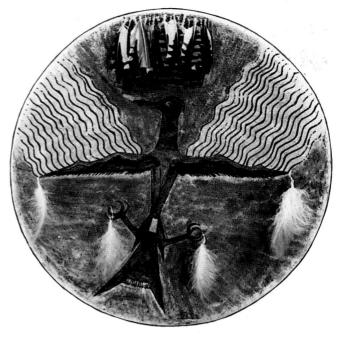

Above: Shield. Sioux. Dakotas or Minnesota. Painted leather and feathers, 17¾" (45 cm) high. Denver Art Museum, gift of C. W. Douglas

Left: Max Ernst. *The Origin of the Pendulum.* 1925. Frottage and pencil, 16½ x 10¼" (42 x 26 cm). Cabinet des Estampes de Strasbourg

abstract anthropomorphic heads were inspired by the very similar forms of Easter Island clubs, some of them with almost human heads, which are of the same proportions and sometimes rather similar heights (p. 564).

That Ernst continued to find Easter Island imagery stimulating is witnessed by his illustrated book *Maximiliana,* published in 1964 (p. 565).[72] This is a compilation of etchings, collages, calligraphy, with minimal text, dedicated to the life of Wilhelm Leberecht Temple (1821–89), an amateur astronomer who discovered a previously unknown asteroid which he named Maximiliana. A large proportion of Ernst's book consists of a strange form of picture-writing which the artist developed for this publication. This marvelous but meaningless cursive script was derived from an equally interesting form of Easter Island picture-writing that was engraved on wooden plaques (p. 189). While Ernst's forms are less precise than the Primitive pictographs, they share a similar style in the drawing and linear arrangement.

We have already noted that in *Beyond Painting* Ernst acknowledged identification with a Melanesian Oceanic culture, that of the Papuan Gulf region of New Guinea. By the early 1960s, his collection of sculpture from this area had expanded to include over twenty-five examples, a majority of which were "cut-out" figures made of flat sections of wood

Right: Max Ernst. *The Interior of Sight: The Egg.* 1929. Oil on canvas, 30⅜ x 31¼" (77.2 x 79.4 cm). Menil Foundation Collection, Houston

Max Ernst. Collage from *Une Semaine de bonté*. 1934. Fifth book. Element: Darkness. Example: Easter Island

Head. Easter Island. Stone. Published in Stéphen Chauvet, *L'Ile de Pâques et ses mystères*, 1935

carved in shallow relief and painted. In an example from Ernst's collection (p. 565) we can see that these figures are marked by a strongly expressed outline and by interior linear detailing that schematically delineates facial features, bones, ribs, and internal organs.

Such Papuan Gulf figures, which held a particularly strong attraction for Ernst as a collector, seem also to have served as a generalized source for almost fifty figure paintings that he produced in 1927, including the series entitled The Horde. Typical examples from this series (p. 566) have figural outlines and interior linear patterns obtained through "grattage." Like the Papuan figures, the figures in Ernst's Hordes are frontally oriented and exhibit a similar variety of poses and head and body shapes. Their clear outlines and system of interior delineation have direct visual affinities to the Papuan artist's use of line to indicate details of anatomy. Ernst also used heavy overpainting which lessens the effect of the automatic line but emphasizes the effect of shallow relief that is equally characteristic of the Papuan bas-relief figures. In all the Horde paintings, however, Ernst sought to capture the mysterious and frightening quality of the Papuan images, utilizing their wraithlike, attenuated, and dismembered forms to create his own similarly haunting and menacing phantoms.

Like so many Europeans, Ernst was fascinated by North American Indians, which he first encountered as a child in the

immensely popular novels of Karl May. Although Ernst subsequently utilized native American imagery from the Plains and the Northwest Coast, his greatest interest was in that of the Hopi and Zuni of the Southwest. Breton was the first to relate Ernst's work to these Pueblo deïties when he referred to the "dolls of New Mexico" in his 1927 essay on Ernst: the Kachina "dolls" of the Hopi and Zuni Indians. These small-scale painted wood carvings of deities are actually children's instructional objects representing the over 200 Kachinas, or supernatural beings, in the Hopi and Zuni religious firmament. They are carved in the likeness of Kachina dancers: the specific costumes identifying individual Kachina spirits as they appear in the structured cycle of ceremonial dances held during eight months of the year.

After emigrating to America in 1941, Ernst was able to assemble a large collection of Kachina figures, many of which are visible in a photograph of the artist taken by James Thrall Soby in New York in 1942 (p. 566). This new accessibility of Hopi and Zuni material may also have played an inspirational role in the sculptures created in 1944. The major piece, *The King Playing with the Queen* (p. 568), is an image referring to chess, the subject of an exhibition at the Julien Levy Gallery. The main figure's rectangular head, surmounted by a pair of curving horns, resembles configurations exemplified by the Zuni Buffalo Kachina that Ernst holds in the Soby photograph (p. 569).[73] Of course, Ernst continued to be interested in other forms of tribal art in this period, and the same work shows an

Max Ernst. Photograph by Arnold Newman. 1942

Kachina. Zuni. Arizona or New Mexico. Painted wood and mixed media, 32″ (81.3 cm) high. Collection Mr. and Mrs. Kelley Rollings, Tucson. Formerly collection MAX ERNST

affinity, as Rubin has pointed out, to anthropomorphic Mossi whistles from Africa (p. 569). Other interesting affinities of his work to African art can be clearly seen in his *Woman of Tours* of 1960 (p. 567) and typical Ashanti terra-cotta heads, as well as in the intriguing comparison of his painting *Head of a Man,* 1947 (p. 570), and a similarly abstract Kono mask (p. 571) made by the Bambara of Mali, another example of which was in his collection.

Following his marriage to the painter Dorothea Tanning in 1946, Ernst bought property in the town of Sedona, Arizona, where he and Dorothea lived until 1953 in a house they built themselves. While Ernst had traveled in the Southwest before,[74] this was the first time he had actually lived in close proximity to the Indians he so admired. "The Indians," remarked John Russell, "were one of the things that most attracted Max Ernst to Arizona....The tenacity of the Hopi Indians in keeping to their ancient customs and refusing to be corrupted by money was one of the grandest things that Max Ernst found in Arizona."[75] Waldberg, too, emphasized the importance of Ernst's move to Arizona, noting that Ernst's art, "like that of the Hopi, Navaho, and Apache Indians who were his neighbors for more than ten years, is neither realistic nor abstract, but emblematic.

With few exceptions, he never tried to capture the appearance of the human being (nor, for that matter, of things). Throughout his

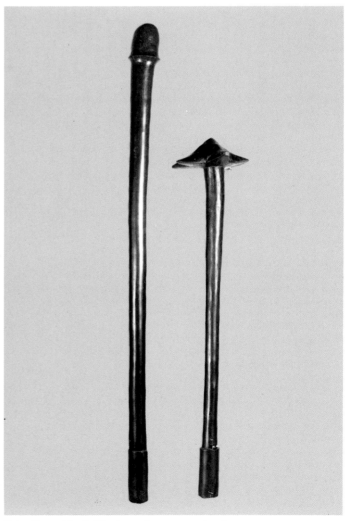

Max Ernst. *Lunar Asparagus.* 1935. Plaster, 65¼" (165.7 cm) high. The Museum of Modern Art, New York; purchase

Clubs. Easter Island. Wood, 33½" (85 cm) and 25" (63.7 cm) high. Musée de l'Homme, Paris

work, man is represented by some substitute, either an imaginary form, or a mark, usually by a bird, but often, too, by a schematized figure whose head may be a rectangle, a triangle or a disk. In a similar manner, the Indians use simple geometric forms in their paintings, figurines and masks. Here the head may be a circle, there a square and elsewhere a triangle, while the ornamental motifs surrounding it—quadrille patterns, wavy lines and parallel bands—may symbolize the sea, the clouds, the days or the seasons. Thus forms do not represent appearances, but ideas.[76]

While Ernst created many horned *personnages* during the 1940s that reveal the influence of Kachinas, their full effect on his imagery can be seen best in *Capricorn* of 1948, his most imposing sculpture (p. 572). *Capricorn* consists of a seated horned figure holding a staff in his right hand, a fish-tailed creature in his left, and an animal on his lap. At his side is an armless female whose joined legs are covered with the scale-like pattern of a fish. Lucy Lippard has called this group "a 'family portrait' of Ernst, his wife Dorothea, and their two long-haired Tibetan dogs.... It is in essence a guardian group, with the barbaric dignity intrinsic to this role."[77] Lippard also pointed out that the ancient symbol of Capricorn was associated with metamorphosis and rebirth, Primitive beliefs that reflected Ernst's sentiments about his new life in the Arizona environment. The horned mask of the seated figure is clearly related to Kachinas like the large example standing at the left foreground of the photograph of Ernst with his Kachina collection (p. 566). The headdress of the female form in *Capricorn* is also related to Kachinas, specifically to single-horned types such as the Zuni Rain Priest of the North. The heads of the two small animals also echo Kachina forms, and given Lippard's interpretation of them as the Ernsts' two dogs, it should be noted that one of the latter was actually named Kachina.[78] Kachinas also frequently hold large staffs in their hands, and in the Hopi culture a staff is often the representation of spiritual power and authority.[79] Thus the gesture of *Capricorn's* main figure presents yet another instance of Ernst's art reflecting a favorite Primitive culture, the Pueblo Indians.[80]

Ernst's sculpture, like some of his earlier paintings, is also indebted to the totem images of the Northwest Coast peoples, whose art he was able to purchase from sources in New York such as Julius Carlebach and the Heye Foundation (p. 572), which afforded exciting collecting opportunities that were not available in Europe. The most direct example of this is *The Spirit of the Bastille* of 1960 (p. 573), in which the artist employed the type of standing bird figure in accordance with the Northwest Coast usage, that is, perched on the top of a tall pole. This can be seen in a Tlingit totem pole (p. 573), whose summit figure of a bird with outstretched wings provides clear evidence of Ernst's model. Ernst also actually incorporated Western images of Plains Indians into his early collage novel *La Femme 100 Têtes* of 1929 (p. 572), where he used engravings of Sun Dance participants in a manner that parallels his absorption of Easter Island heads into the collages of *Une Semaine de bonté*.

Of course, Ernst's sculptures reveal the influence of other tribal cultures as well. A form he used commonly in works from the 1940s through the 1960s is characterized by a round head with round eyes and mouth, found in *Moonmad* of 1944 and many examples, such as *Head*, from the Miniature Mask series of 1959 (p. 574). These elegantly abstracted faces are close to Eskimo "finger" masks of the same form as well as to a small Eskimo bone maskette that was part of Ernst's private collection (p. 574). Another work from this period with striking affinities to Eskimo art is Ernst's *Gay Dogs* of 1958 (p. 574), which, as Rubin has noticed, is quite similar to the

Max Ernst. Page from *Maximiliana*. Paris, 1964. New York Public Library

Figure. Era River, Gulf Province, Papua New Guinea. Painted wood, 21¼" (54 cm) high. Collection Dorothea Tanning, New York. Formerly collection MAX ERNST

Max Ernst. *The Horde*. 1927. Oil on canvas, 18 x 21¾" (45.7 x 55.2 cm). Collection Dr. Henry Roland, Woking, England

Eskimo mask seen at the far right in a photograph of Breton's collection (p. 578).

In his biography of Ernst, Waldberg described the artist as a shaman, "invocator of hidden spirits, agent of heavy secrets."[81] The shaman has been a subject of great scholarly interest since the 1880s, and specifically a great deal of information was published in German and French during the first three decades of this century.[82] Lévy-Bruhl, for example, mentioned shamans as examples of Primitive clairvoyance,[83] as interpreters of dreams,[84] and as embodiments of supernatural powers,[85] while Frazer in his *Golden Bough* related anecdotes that also reveal the shaman to be a magical image-maker who carves human figurines.[86] In an interview with the author, Ernst acknowledged his longtime interest in shamanism and his familiarity with its literature, which was summarized in Eliade's great study published in 1951.[87] Essentially the shaman is a healer and seer able to act effectively because of his ability to communicate with elements of the spirit world. The initiatory requirements for the shaman spec-

Max Ernst with his Kachina collection. Photograph by James Thrall Soby. 1942. Collection Arthur A. and Elaine Cohen, New York

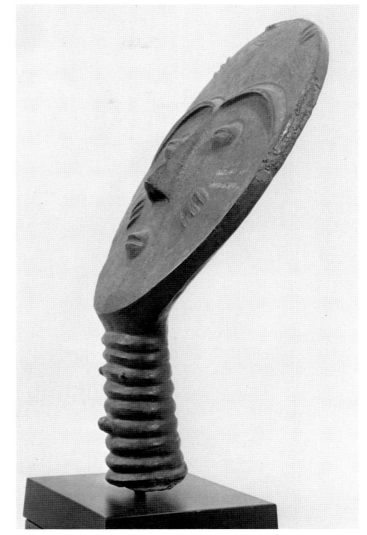

Max Ernst. *Woman of Tours.* 1960. Bronze, 10¼" (26 cm) high. Collection Dorothea Tanning, New York

Head. Asante. Ghana. Terra-cotta, 19½" (49.5 cm) high. Private collection

ify particulars that Ernst re-created in his own autobiographical statements. Eliade writes:

However selected, a shaman is not recognized as such until after he has received two kinds of teaching: (1) ecstatic (dreams, trances, etc.) and (2) traditional (shamanic techniques, names and functions of the spirits, mythology and genealogy of the clan, secret language, etc.). This twofold course of instruction, given by the spirits and the old master shamans, is equivalent to an initiation.[88]

As cited earlier, in the opening lines of his autobiographical statement Ernst wrote: "The 2nd of April (1891) at 9:45 a.m. Max Ernst had his first contact with the sensible world, when he came out of the egg which his mother had laid in an eagle's nest and which the bird had brooded over for seven years."[89] This concept of a human born from an egg hatched by a bird can be found throughout shamanic literature. As Eliade claimed, "We may also note the motif of the giant bird that hatches shamans in the branches of the World Tree; it has wide application in North Asian mythologies, especially in shamanic mythology."[90] Ernst's naming the eagle as the bird that hatched his egg is another important indication of his identification with the shaman. Eliade stated:

We must also consider the mythological relations that exist between the eagle and the shaman. The eagle, it will be remembered, is held

to be the father of the first shaman, plays a considerable role in the shaman's initiation, and, finally, is at the center of a mythical complex that includes the World Tree and the shaman's ecstatic journey.[91]

Ernst also alluded to shamanism by his use of the number seven to denote the years the eagle brooded on the nest from which he was born, seven being a significant factor in many shamanic rites.[92]

The autobiography continued to recount the most important events of Ernst's childhood as he described his "first contact with hallucination. Measles...a fever-vision provoked by an imitation-mahogany panel opposite his bed, the grooves of the wood taking successively the aspect of an eye, a nose, a bird's head, *a menacing nightingale*, a spinning top and so on."[93] In his study of shamanic initiation, Eliade wrote that "usually sickness, dreams, and ecstasies in themselves constitute an initiation; that is, they transform the profane, pre-'choice' individual into a technician of the sacred."[94] In fact, it was his susceptibility to such "'sickness,' attacks, dreams, and hallucinations that determine a shaman's career in a very short time."[95] It is significant that Ernst's first hallucinating experience involved the ability, common to both shamans and artists, to perceive ordinary objects in a transformative

Max Ernst. *The King Playing with the Queen.* 1944. Bronze (cast 1954, from original plaster), 38½″ (97.8 cm) high, at base 18¾ x 20½″ (47.7 x 52.1 cm). The Museum of Modern Art, New York; gift of D. and J. de Menil

way. Also of importance is the fact that in this first hallucination two of his visions were of birds. The importance of the bird as a personal totemic emblem for Ernst has already been established, but this choice takes on additional meaning when we realize that the bird also played a major role in the life of the shaman, a subject to which this study will subsequently return.

Ernst wrote that the night in 1906 when his pet bird died and his sister was born was his "first contact with occult, magic and witchcraft powers."[96] The event led to a series of mystical crises and the confusion between birds and humans, which, as he said, became evident in his later drawings and paintings. From this point of emotional crisis and mystical contact, Ernst described the next eight years of his life in a sentence that parallels the shamans' initiatory dream-experiences through which they meet animals, witches, and seers, and "travel" to forests, mountains, secluded places, and the spirit world in order to learn the secrets of their calling.[97] Ernst's discovery of the mystical experience is too similar to be coincidental, as he phrased it, "(1906-1914) Excursions into the world of marvels, chimeras, phantoms, poets, monsters, philosophers, birds, women, lunatics, magic, trees, eroticism, stones, insects, mountains, poisons, mathematics and so on."[98]

Immediately following this description Ernst wrote what is perhaps the strangest line of this very unorthodox autobiography:

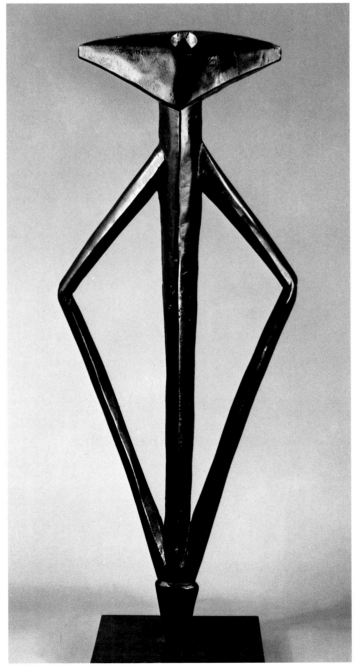

Kachina. Hopi. Arizona. Cottonwood root, paint, hide, and mixed media, 20¼" (51.4 cm) high. Estate of Jimmy Ernst. Formerly collection MAX ERNST

Whistle. Mossi. Upper Volta. Wood, 22⅜" (57 cm) high. Private collection

Max Ernst. *Head of a Man*. 1947. Oil on canvas, 20⅛ x 11⅞" (51 x 30 cm). Private collection, Paris

Head of equestrian figure. Senufo. Ivory Coast. Wood, 13½" (34.2 cm) high, overall. Private collection, New York. Full view reproduced page 585

(1914) Max Ernst died the 1st of August 1914. He resuscitated the 11th of November 1918 as a young man aspiring to become a magician and to find the myth of his time. Now and then he consulted the eagle who had hatched the egg of his pre-natal life. You may find the bird's advices in his work.[99]

The dates of this symbolic demise and resurrection are those of Ernst's entry into and dismissal from the German army during World War I. When Ernst wrote that he died and was resuscitated "as a young man aspiring to become a magician and to find the myth of his time," he was making a reference to his symbolic transformation into a shaman-artist. Ritual death

followed by rebirth is a process vital to all true shamanic initiations, for until the initiate dies and is reborn, he cannot have the knowledge of the spirit world, magic, and the special insight into hidden realities fundamental to the practice of his sacred profession.

Ernst's statement about consulting the eagle who brought him into the world is equally meaningful, because the ability to communicate with animals is one of the significant powers of a shaman. As Eliade pointed out, "All over the world learning the language of the animals, especially of birds, is equivalent to knowing the secrets of nature and hence being

Kono mask. Bambara. Mali. Wood, 18⅞″ (48 cm) high. Private collection, France

able to prophesy."[100] Material on shamanic phenomena even furnishes parallels to the unusual event involving this bird that Ernst cited in the last passage of his autobiography: "(1941) The bird followed the plane which brought Max to this country on the 14th of July and built his nest in a cloud on the East River."[101] Regarding the shaman's association with birds, Eliade wrote that being followed by a bird is symbolic of the spiritual journey to knowledge and power, that "being accompanied by a bird indicated the capacity, while still alive, to undertake the ecstatic journey to the sky and beyond."[102] This examination of Ernst's autobiography, then, has traced

the correspondences that exist between his highly unconventional and mysterious statements and the rituals and beliefs associated with the calling and initiation of the shaman in order to demonstrate the seriousness of his self-identification with this aspect of the Primitive.

Max Ernst's predilection for the bird as a personal shamanic emblem is further amplified by his own and others' tendency to represent him in the guise of his totem. Leonora Carrington's *Portrait of Max Ernst* of 1940 (p. 575) depicts him in a costume of bird feathers, and he appeared in an elaborate bird costume made by Dorothea Tanning at a 1958 costume ball

Max Ernst. *Capricorn.* 1948. Bronze (cast 1964), 94½ x 80⅝" (240 x 204.8 cm). Menil Foundation Collection, Houston

Mask. Kwakiutl. British Columbia. Painted wood, shell, and hair, 15" (38 cm) high. Collection Dorothea Tanning, New York. Formerly collection MAX ERNST

Max Ernst. *She Keeps It.* Collage from *La Femme 100 Têtes.* 1929

Mask. Yaka. Zaire. Painted wood, 8¾" (22.2 cm) high. Collection D. and J. de Menil, Houston

Max Ernst. *The Spirit of the Bastille*. 1960. Bronze (cast 1961), 123¼″ (313 cm) high. Menil Foundation Collection, Houston

Totem pole (memorial for Mungo Martin carved by Tony and Henry Hunt). Kwakiutl. Cemetery, Alert Bay, British Columbia. Painted wood.

Totem pole. Tlingit. Alaska. Painted wood. Saxman Totem Park, Alaska

Max Ernst. *Head*, from the series Miniature Masks. 1959. Gold (cast 1960), 3″ (7.5 cm) high. Private collection

Finger mask. Eskimo. Alaska. Wood and feathers, c. 3⅛″ (8 cm) high. Collection MATTA, Paris

Miniature mask. Eskimo. Alaska. Bone, 3¾″ (9.5 cm) high. Collection Dorothea Tanning, New York. Formerly collection MAX ERNST

Max Ernst in Bird Costume. Photograph by John Rewald. 1958. Collection Dorothea Tanning, New York

Max Ernst. *The Seer.* c. 1935. Oil on canvas, 9½ x 7½" (24 x 19 cm). Private collection

whose theme was "A Midsummer Night's Dream." His willful association with the bird again reflects affinities to shamanism, for shamans' costumes are an important aspect of their ritual practice, and of the three main creatures whose forms they imitate, the bird is the most common.[103]

Ernst once even described himself as a bird-headed figure, stating that "I saw myself with the head of a kite, a knife in my hand, in the attitude of *The Thinker* of Rodin. But it was actually the liberated attitude of Rimbaud's seer."[104] This passage refers to *The Seer,* a self-portrait of c. 1935 in which he combined elements of the Symbolist visionary and the Primitive mystic. Like the Primitive shaman, Ernst sought to utilize hallucinations and visions to become a seer, one capable of penetrating beyond appearances to give form to the surreal visions of his creative imagination. After describing the metamorphic visual process that initiated his collages, Ernst wrote, "Thus I obtained a faithful fixed image of my hallucinations and transformed into revealing dreams my most secret desires."[105] What he sought was not some literal communication with spirits and supernatural forces, but rather the ability to give material existence to the images that emerge from the primal recesses of man's creative consciousness.

During the early years of Surrealism Ernst was the artist most involved with primitivism and the imagery of Primitive art. However, his interest was shared in varying degrees by other Surrealists, Joan Miró as well as Masson. While Miró had no intellectual involvement in the subject, his images have close affinities to Primitive aesthetics in their basic principles. Moreover, like the Primitive artist, Miró sought to capture the vital motivating essence of things, a concern he articulated in

Opposite: Max Ernst. *Gay Dogs.* 1958. Painted wood and feathers, 32 x 7½" (81.3 x 19 cm), irregular. Collection Dorothea Tanning, New York

Leonora Carrington. *Portrait of Max Ernst.* 1940. Oil on canvas. Whereabouts unknown

Joan Miró. *Carnival of Harlequin*. 1924–25. Oil on canvas, 26 x 36⅝" (66 x 93 cm). Albright-Knox Art Gallery, Buffalo; Room of Contemporary Art Fund

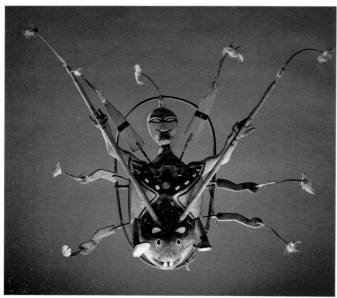

Mask. Eskimo. Kuskokwim River, Alaska. Painted wood, walrus tooth, feathers, and fiber, 35⅞" (91 cm) high. Hamburgisches Museum für Völkerkunde

a 1939 statement declaring that the artist must "try to discover the religious essence, the major sense of things...that of the primitive peoples."[106]

Elizabeth Cowling has proposed Eskimo masks as one of the earliest influences on Miró's work, especially *Carnival of Harlequin* of 1924–25.[107] Indeed, there are many affinities between his fancifully abstract figures and these masks; Cowling compares, for instance, the large round head of the figure in the left section of *Carnival of Harlequin* with a composite Eskimo mask from Nunivak Island. While the affinities of form and color are striking, it is impossible to show that the artist had access to such objects that early in his career. Indeed, Rubin's investigations have shown that Miró could not have seen Eskimo masks of this type until well after he painted *Carnival of Harlequin*.[108] Comparisons can also be made between this painting and many other Eskimo masks such as one with a bizarre face set into a teardrop body or the examples shown in the 1955 photograph of Breton's collection (p. 578), but the similarities can be considered only affinities, not influences.

Miró's work also reveals a strong relationship to prehistoric cave paintings;[109] he had a great enthusiasm for these images of animals and humans, about which *Cahiers d'art* alone had published five articles in 1929 and 1930. The impact of these cave paintings on Miró is often evident in his curvilinear figures of the 1930s and in his depictions of simplified animal

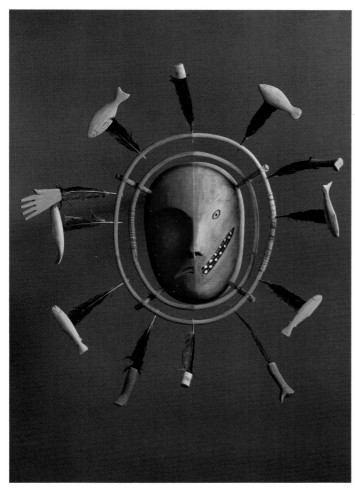

Mask. Eskimo. Nunivak Island, Alaska. Painted wood and feathers, 12⅝″ (32 cm) high. Thomas Burke Memorial Washington State Museum, Seattle

Mask. Eskimo. Alaska. Painted wood and feathers, 14″ (35.5 cm) high. Lowie Museum of Anthropology, University of California, Berkeley

forms placed on a wall-like surface. A striking example of this affinity to paleolithic imagery can be demonstrated by the gracefully stylized animals and horn shapes of his *Painting* of 1933 (p. 580), compared with an illustration of very similar forms arranged in the same overall composition, published in a 1930 *Cahiers d'art* article entitled "The Origins of Art and Culture."

Many other artists affiliated with Surrealism in the 1930s and 1940s were also interested in tribal art. Alberto Giacometti is treated elsewhere in this book, but among the others whose involvement was strong were Brauner, Matta, Paalen, and Lam, all of whom had very personal manners of assimilating Primitive influences.

Victor Brauner's art is pervaded by the same sense of mystery and iconic power found in many Primitive works. While many of his images only generally recall the forms of such prototypes as ancient Egyptian or pre-Columbian art, others reveal quite startlingly exact correspondences with specific types of Primitive objects. For example, in the *Force of Concentration of M. K.* of 1934 (p. 581), the nude protagonist whose body is crawling with miniature figures—literally attached to its surface—was inspired by the celebrated Austral Islands sculpture in the British Museum (p. 581), a sculpture that also fascinated Picasso (p. 330) and, later, Henry Moore.

Brauner was also interested in the two-dimensional

anthropomorphic animal figures common in the art of South America and Mexico and among the North American Indians. One of the best examples of his fascination with this imagery can be seen in his *Prelude to a Civilization* of 1954 (p. 584), which depicts the flattened profile of a giant animal whose surface is inscribed with a variety of stylized representations of horses and riders, warriors, animals, masks, and abstract symbols. Brauner based this concept on Plains Indian pictographic robes, which displayed a warrior's exploits on a hide whose form retains the overall shape of the animal. His mysterious figures also show strong affinities to prehistoric Southwestern petroglyphs and to ancient Mexican codex illustrations such as those in the Bibliothèque Nationale, Paris (p. 584).

Among the later Surrealists, the most dedicated and knowledgeable connoisseur of Primitive art has been Matta, who developed his large collection of tribal objects with a concern for invention as much as quality. Matta's relationship to tribal art is equally reflected in aesthetic affinities and general emotional impact as in direct visual borrowings. His assimilation of aspects of the Primitive is most evident in the monsterlike *personnages* in his paintings of the late 1940s and 1950s; signal examples of these are discussed by Rubin in the introductory chapter. During this period Matta created a variety of creatures whose bodies are often arranged along a vertical axis and joined with short, curving arms, as in *Being With* of 1946 (p.

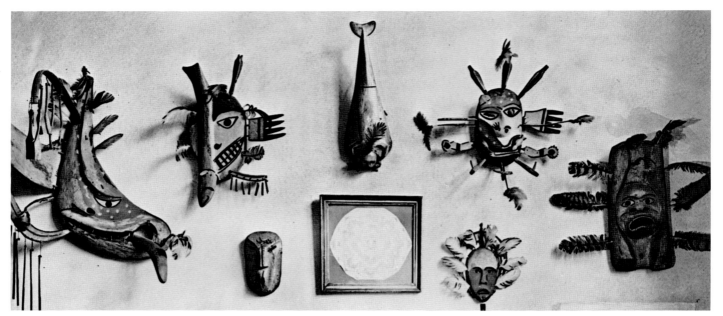

Eskimo masks, collection ANDRÉ BRETON, Paris, c. 1955

582). The figures in the right foreground and center that are vertically framed by polelike forms demonstrate strong resemblances to the Malanggan sculptures of New Ireland of which Matta owned a number and an excellent example of which was in Max Ernst's collection (p. 517). This relationship is especially apparent when the central figure of *Being With* is compared with a section of the Malanggan (p. 516), as both feature a figure enclosed within and holding onto a parallel set of flanking elements. These and a prominent sense of dramatic gesture are also prime elements of another sculpture that provided a model for this imagery: Alberto Giacometti's *Invisible Object*, the original plaster of which Matta owned (p. 504). Many of Matta's figures, as in *Wound Interrogation* of 1948 (p. 582), are also marked by an aggressiveness derived from their grasping gesture as well as the sharp pronglike elements

that form their open-work bodies and heads. One of his inspirations for this powerful imagery are the Karawari River figures of New Guinea. Matta has had a particular interest in these sculptures and has owned a number of them (p. 583).

Wolfgang Paalen also was an avid collector of Primitive art, although his approach to the subject was more academic than Matta's, and he devoted a great deal of his energies to its study. While his own work utilized forms of a generalized totemic nature, the major impact of his involvement with the Primitive can be seen in his writings. Concentrating on the artistic heritage of the Americas, Paalen was especially interested in the rich traditions of the Northwest Coast, and in 1945 his magazine *DYN* published several issues that featured articles on the arts of Mexico and North America.[110] Given his erudition and scholarly inclinations, Paalen became a spokesman for the Surrealists' appreciation of Primitive cultures and their art. In the introduction to the Amerindian issue of *DYN* he eloquently expressed the group's larger concerns at the end of World War II and emphasized America's new role as a cultural resource for war-ravaged Europe:

Until today the waves of cultural change have found their orientation only intuitively; thus occidental art by turns went through a certain osmosis with Asia, Africa, and Oceania; now it has become possible to understand why a universal osmosis is necessary, why this is the moment to integrate the enormous treasure of Amerindian forms into the consciousness of modern art....[111]

Surrealists such as Breton, Masson, Ernst, Tanguy, Paalen, and Lam sought political refuge in the Americas during World War II, and their experiences in the Caribbean, Cuba, Mexico, and the United States intensified their awareness of the importance of America's native cultures and contemporary artists.

In his 1941 article on the Cuban painter Wifredo Lam, Breton emphasized the bonds between Surrealism and the Primitive when he commented that "the modern eye has gradually taken in the endless variety of those objects of so-

Victor Brauner. *Revendication of the Symbol.* 1959. Oil on canvas, 21¼ x 25⅝" (54 x 65 cm). Private collection

Mask. Eskimo. Alaska. Painted wood and feathers, 18⅞″ (48 cm) high. Private collection. Formerly collection ANDRÉ BRETON

Joan Miró. *Painting.* 1933. Oil on canvas, 68½" x 6'5¼" (174 x 196.2 cm). The Museum of Modern Art, New York; gift of the Advisory Committee

Rock drawings. Taghtania, Algeria. Published in *Cahiers d'art,* no. 2, 1930

that was popular in Cuba and other Caribbean islands.[113] As a child he witnessed visions, trances, and animal sacrifices, developed a ritual awareness of the powers of the jungle and nature spirits, and became familiar with African or African-style objects used in magico-religious ceremonies.[114] Thus, to use Breton's words:

The rich resources of primitive vision are not lost on Wifredo Lam who, by virtue of his origin...has the unique opportunity of drawing on them instinctively, while at the same time remaining deeply involved emotionally in the social consciousness of this era, and after making himself master of the most highly developed technique.[115]

This was Lam's great synthesis as a Surrealist: He combined a close contact with tribal ritual with the cultural and artistic sophistication of the Western intellectual.

As an adult, Lam first became intrigued with African tribal sculpture while a student in Madrid in 1928.[116] And although he never studied the ethnographic basis of these cultures, he avidly and thoroughly assimilated their forms of figural abstraction. Lam acknowledged the nature of his debt to Primitive art when, referring to a Baule mask in his collection, he exclaimed, "You see—I have spontaneously recovered these forms! They have revived in me like an ancestral reminiscence!"[117]

called 'savage' origin...and aware at last of the incomparable resources of the primitive vision, has fallen so in love with this vision that it would wish to achieve the impossible and wed it."[112] In Breton's view Lam was the artist who could best achieve this assimilation of the visual and symbolic foundations of Primitive art. Michel Leiris, the Surrealist poet and leading French African ethnographer, has written extensively on Lam and, like Breton, has repeatedly commented on the painter's close ties with Primitive imagery and magic. Leiris pointed out that Lam's personal association with things Primitive stemmed from his childhood contact with his godmother, who was a "professional sorceress" in the voodoo cult

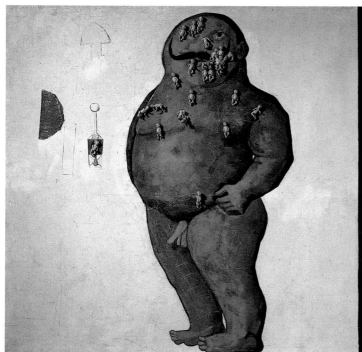

Above: Victor Brauner. *Force of Concentration of M.K.* 1934. Oil on canvas and objects, 59⅛ x 118⅛" (150 x 300 cm). Private collection, Paris

Right: Figure (God A'a). Rurutu, Austral Islands. Wood, 44" (111.7 cm) high. The Trustees of the British Museum, London. For another view of this work, see page 331.

In 1938 Lam moved to Paris, where he was soon befriended by Picasso, whose own "African"-style works of 1907–08 also influenced the young Cuban painter. In 1941 and 1942 a major change occurred in Lam's work. He replaced his earlier figures characterized by flat, oval faces with a more varied repertoire of forms and facial types newly intertwined with a lush jungle setting. This alteration of pictorial style can be attributed to Lam's return to his native Caribbean islands, to which he returned when the pressures of World War II forced him to leave France. Back in the Antilles, Lam was able to utilize the artistic lessons learned in Europe to express what he felt was a powerful sense of Primitive consciousness at the heart of his heritage. "After the many years spent far from the tropics," wrote Leiris, "the rediscovery of his homeland, occurring when the world was rife with a global war, was certainly a great shock to Lam. It incited him to re-evaluate everything, so that painting became a means not only of affirming himself, but of formulating by brilliant suggestive images what it is to be a man among men and a living being within the cosmic intensity."[118]

For Lam, the quintessential symbol of nature's power and presence became the lush foliage of the jungle and the dense fields of sugar cane, which are characteristics of the Cuban landscape as well as more general references to his affinities with Africa. The major example of this jungle imagery is *The Jungle*, 1943 (p. 534), executed in gouache, a fast-drying medium that permitted Lam to apply many thin, transparent washes of color so that multiple images could be read through one another. This technique not only created highly evo-

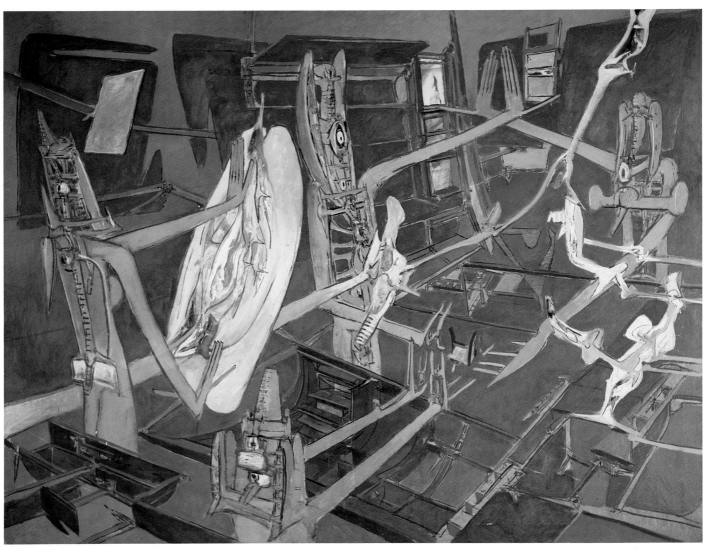

Matta. *Wound Interrogation*. 1948. Oil on canvas, 59 x 77" (149.8 x 195.6 cm). The Art Institute of Chicago; Mary and Earle Ludgin Collection

Matta. *Being With*. 1946. Oil on canvas, 7' 4" x 14' 11½" (223.5 x 456 cm). Collection of the artist

cative effects of transparency, but also suggested the "inter-penetration" of phenomena that is so significant an aspect of the Primitive vision of nature. *The Jungle* creates an impression of thick, impenetrable jungle vegetation, in the midst of which stand female figures whose tubular legs and rounded knees, buttocks, torsos, and breasts are conceived so as to be almost indistinguishable from the foliage surrounding them. Thus camouflaged, they are an integral element of the natural environment—a Primitive-inspired representation of humanity's union with nature. Lam himself described this synthesis when he wrote that in his jungle scenes we can witness "beings in their passage from the vegetal state to that of the animal still charged with the vestiges of the forest."[119]

The Jungle summarizes not only Lam's use of Primitive imagery but his debt to Picasso, whom he looked upon as both teacher and kindred spirit. Its dense foliage is peopled by four totemlike female figures who stand in the foreground of the typically shallow, nonillusionistic space, Lam's homage to both the common "reductiveness" of Primitive art and Picasso's *Les Demoiselles d'Avignon*. In both pictures, a standing female with an arm raised above her head is placed at the left-hand border to direct the eye toward the other figures on the right. A similar compositional relationship exists between the two women immediately to the right of the first figure, both of whom face the viewer with right arms held high and elbows pointing upward. There is a further correspondence between the two paintings in the large female at the extreme right of *The Jungle*, whose crescent-moon-shaped head Lam borrowed directly from the red crescent form in the still life located at the lower center of *Les Demoiselles*. Her body also recalls the figure in the upper right portion of Picasso's painting in that both have arms raised so that their elbows point back to the center of the composition.

Picasso's early response to Primitive sculpture is most clear in the faces of the two right-hand women of *Les Demoiselles*. But, as Rubin has observed, these are not identifiable with any particular tribal works that Picasso could have seen, as are the stylistic elements of Senufo sculpture adapted by Lam, as in the equestrian figure (p. 585). The forward-curving head and decorative facial scarification as well as the long nose and out-thrust mouth of the Senufo style are all reflected in the features of the seated and standing figures in the left section of *The Jungle*. The genitallike chin appendages of these faces are also commonly found in Lam's work and can be related, in addition, to the stylized beards of styles such as the Dogon or the Teke.[120] Other formal characteristics of African styles utilized by Lam in *The Jungle* include the emphatic treatment of buttocks and breasts and the simplified limbs, hands, and feet.

Still other sources for Lam's syncretistic use of Primitive imagery can be seen in *The Omen*, 1947 (p. 585), where the crowded forms of the tropical jungle have given way to a spare background that allows Lam's mythical creatures to hover menacingly. Their aura of mystery is in large part achieved through Lam's use of forms derived from two types of African mask he especially favored. The round head with staring eyes in the lower center of the painting derive from the Baule Goli mask (p. 585), an influence Lam himself acknowledged, as mentioned above. The heads in the upper right corner of *The Omen* are realized in an elongated angular facial style that derives from Kono Society masks of the Bambara (p. 571).

Yipwon figure. Alamblak. Karawari River. East Sepik Province, Papua New Guinea. Wood, hair, and canvas, 6'8¾" (205.1 cm) high. Private collection, New York

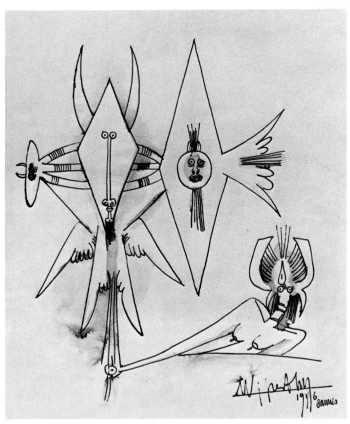

Victor Brauner. *Prelude to a Civilization.* 1954. Encaustic on composition board, 51¼ x 76¾" (130.1 x 194.9 cm). Private collection

Sun cult (Aubin Manuscript no. 20). Preconquest Mixtec. Mexico. Painted skin, 20⅛" (51 cm) high. Bibliothèque Nationale, Paris

Wifredo Lam. *Encounter.* 1946. Ink, 12 x 9½" (30.5 x 24.5 cm). Collection Mrs. Helena Benitez, Saarbrücken

Both individually and as a group, the Surrealists tried to apply their ideas to life as well as art—as Breton put it, "to transform the world, change life, remake from scratch human understanding."[121] In their effort to expand insight and perception, and to regenerate creative powers, they attempted to harness the common elemental resource of humanity: the unlimited potential of the unconscious, as manifested in dreams and myths. From the start the Surrealists were aware that these powerful forces so permeate the very fabric of Primitive societies that they obliterate any barriers between life and art; this realization explains the particular seductiveness for them of the Primitive model.

Although Breton was one of the earliest and most ardent Surrealist champions of primitivism, he eventually recognized the great difficulty Western society had relating effectively to tribal cultures. In 1955, eleven years before his death, Breton expressed his reservations about the state of primitivism, which he saw as suffering from lack of support from ethnographic research. Breton wrote:

Unfortunately, ethnography was not able to take sufficiently great strides to reduce, despite our impatience, the distance which separates us from ancient Maya or the contemporary Aboriginal culture of Australia, because we remain largely ignorant of their aspirations and have only a very partial knowledge of their customs. The inspiration we were able to draw from their art remained ultimately ineffective because of a lack of basic organic contact, leaving an impression of rootlessness.[122]

Although Breton despaired of the West's ability to re-create a spiritual integrity comparable to that of Primitive cultures and ultimately counseled a return to early European roots, Surrealist artists have continued to view them as a powerful source of inspiration.

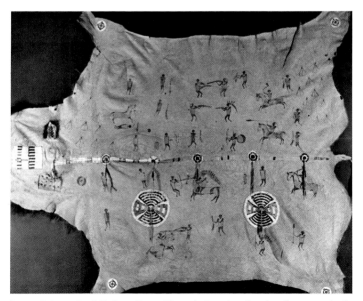

Robe. Hidatsa. North Dakota. Painted bison hide and quills, 9'10½" (300 cm) high. Linden-Museum, Stuttgart

Wifredo Lam. *The Omen*. 1947. Oil on canvas, 39⅜ x 41⅜" (100 x 105 cm). Collection R. Morone, Turin

Equestrian figure. Senufo. Ivory Coast. Wood, 13½" (34.2 cm) high. Private collection, New York

Goli mask. Baule. Ivory Coast. Wood, 39" (99 cm) high. Private collection

Figure. Lega or Bembe. Zaire. Wood, 8" (20.3 cm) high. Collection D. and J. de Menil, Houston

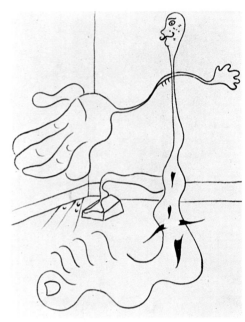

Joan Miró. *Statue*. 1926. Conté crayon on buff paper, 24½ x 18¾" (62.3 x 47.6 cm). The Museum of Modern Art, New York; purchase

Painting. Aborigine. Australia. Painted bark, 34" (86.4 cm) high. Friede Collection, New York

Joan Miró. *Man and Woman*. 1935. Oil on cardboard, 41¾ x 29½" (106 x 75 cm). Private collection

Loin cloth. Lake Sentani, Irian Jaya (formerly Netherlands New Guinea). Painted bark cloth, 22⅛" (56 cm) high. Tropenmuseum, Amsterdam

Head. New Britain. Painted wood, 61⅞" (157 cm) high. Musée Barbier-Müller, Geneva

Support for offerings. Mangareva, Gambier Islands. Wood, 70" (177.7 cm) high. Musée de l'Homme, Paris

Figure. Abelam. East Sepik Province, Papua New Guinea. Wood, 42½″ (108 cm) high. The Metropolitan Museum of Art, New York; The Michael C. Rockefeller Memorial Collection, gift of Nelson A. Rockefeller

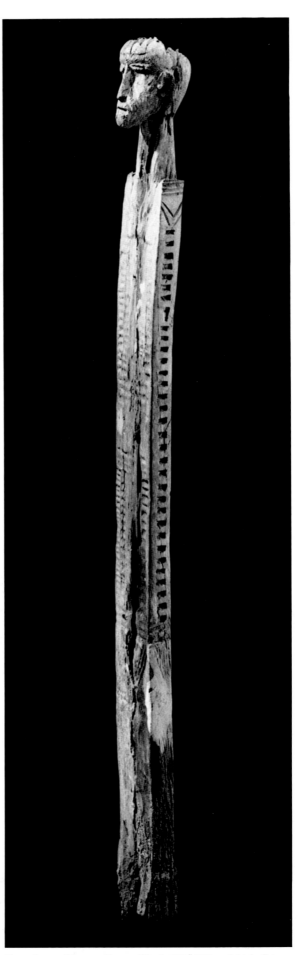

Grave figure. Kambe. Kenya. Wood, 7'2⅝" (220 cm) high. Private collection, Belgium

Grave figure. Giryama. Kenya. Wood, 59⅞" (152 cm) high. Private collection, Belgium

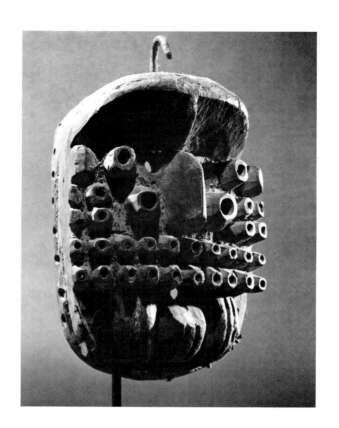

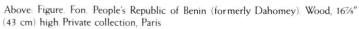

Above: Figure. Fon. People's Republic of Benin (formerly Dahomey). Wood, 16⅞" (43 cm) high. Private collection, Paris

Above right: Mask. Guere. Ivory Coast. Wood, 11" (28 cm) high. Private collection

Right: Mask. Grebo. Guiglo district, Ivory Coast. Wood and fiber, 16½" (42 cm) high. Musée d'Art Africain (I.F.A.N.), Dakar, Senegal, on extended loan to the Musée des Arts Africains et Océaniens, Paris

NOTES

1. Hans Richter, *Dada: Art and Anti-Art* (New York: McGraw-Hill, 1965), p. 16.

2. Ibid., p. 34.

3. Alfred Stieglitz's modern gallery at 291 Fifth Avenue in New York City presented the first commercial exhibitions of African and pre-Columbian art in the United States in 1914 and 1916. Also, the February 1916 issue of his magazine *291* featured a Bakota reliquary figure as the cover illustration and contained an article by Marius de Zayas entitled "Modern Art...Negro Art."

4. Gordon Frederick Browning, *Tristan Tzara: The Genesis of the Dada Poem, or From Dada to Aa* (Stuttgart: Akademischer Verlag Hans-Dieter Heinz, 1979), p. 11.

5. Alister Horne, *The Price of Glory: Verdun, 1916* (New York: St. Martin's Press, 1962), p. 328.

6. Francis M. Naumann, "Janco/Dada: An Interview with Marcel Janco," *Arts Magazine*, November 1982, p. 81.

7. Jean Arp, *Arp on Arp: Poems, Essays, Memories*, ed. Marcel Jean, trans. Joachim Neugroschel (New York: Viking, 1970), p. 39.

8. Arp, op. cit., p. 39.

9. Robert Motherwell, ed., *The Dada Painters and Poets: An Anthology* (New York: Wittenborn, 1967), p. xx.

10. Arp, op. cit., p. 338.

11. Richter, op. cit., pp. 20, 23, 77, 79.

12. Ibid., p. 20. Janco's masks also have affinities to the bark-cloth masks of the New Hebrides and New Britain as well as Marka and Bambara types.

13. Naumann, op. cit., p. 83.

14. Richter, op. cit., p. 23.

15. Paul German, "Das Plastisch-figürliche Kunstgewerbe im Graslande von Kamerun," *Jahrbuch der Museum für Völkerkunde, Leipzig* (Leipzig: 1911).

16. Man Ray's painting *Totem*, 1914, shares this Primitive minimalism.

17. Emmy Hennings, "Das Cabaret Voltaire und die Galerie Dada," *Als Dada Begann, Eine Dada Chronik* (Sanssouci Verlag, 1957), p. 42.

18. Tristan Tzara, "L'Art et l'Océanie," *Cahiers d'art* 1, 1929, pp. 59–60; "A propos de l'art précolumbien," *Cahiers d'art* 4, 1929, pp. 170–72.

19. Tristan Tzara, "Note sur l'art nègre," *SIC*, no. 21–22, September–October 1917.

20. Elmer Peterson, *Tristan Tzara: Dada and Surrational Theorist* (New Brunswick: Rutgers University Press, 1971), p. 46.

21. Tzara, "Note sur l'art nègre."

22. Peterson, op. cit., p. 11.

23. See "Chanson de cocadou," *Dada*, no. 1 (July 1917), and "Tribu Loritja," "La Chanson de Serpent," *Dada*, no. 2 (December 1917).

24. James George Frazer, *The New Golden Bough*, ed. Theodore H. Gaster (New York: Mentor, 1964), p. 196.

25. These theories were also developed by Andrew Lang and Wilhelm Wundt. See Evan M. Maurer, "In Quest of the Myth: An Investigation of the Relationships between Surrealism and Primitivism" (Ph.D. diss., University of Pennsylvania, 1969), pp. 28–30, 34–39.

26. Lucien Lévy-Bruhl, *Primitive Mentality*, trans. Lilian A. Clare (Boston: Beacon, 1966), p. 98.

27. Ibid., pp. 8–9.

28. André Breton, *Entretiens (1913–52)* (Paris: Gallimard, 1952), p. 245.

29. Sigmund Freud, *Totem and Taboo*, trans. James Strachey (New York: W.W. Norton, 1950), p. 1.

30. Ibid., p. 90.

31. Guillaume Apollinaire, *Alcools*, trans. Anne Hyde Greet (Berkeley: University of California Press, 1965), p. 12.

32. "Opinions sur l'art nègre," *Action 1* (April 1920).

33. See Maurer, "In Quest of the Myth," pp. 12–15.

34. *Sculptures d'Afrique, d'Amérique, d'Océanie* (Paris: Paul Guillaume, 1931).

35. Marcel Jean, *The History of Surrealist Painting*, trans. Simon Watson Taylor (New York: Grove, 1960), pp. 247–52. For the Surrealists' involvement with the native cultures of America and Oceania, see also José Pierre, *L'Univers surréaliste* (Paris: Somogy, 1983), pp. 67–77.

36. Paul C. Ray, *The Surrealist Movement in England* (Ithaca: Cornell University Press, 1971), p. 135.

37. Clifford H. Browder, *André Breton: Arbiter of Surrealism* (Geneva: Droz, 1967), p. 61.

38. Breton, op. cit., pp. 244–45.

39. André Breton, *L'Amour fou* (Paris: Gallimard, 1937), p. 106.

40. Michel Leiris and Georges Limbour, *André Masson et son univers* (Paris: Editions Trois Collines, 1947), pp. 127–28, and interview with André Masson by Evan M. Maurer, December 8, 1970.

41. *Iroquois Landscape* of 1942 is another example of Masson's use of native American themes.

42. Frazer, op. cit., pp. 120–24.

43. Adolf Basler, *L'Art chez les peuples primitifs* (Paris: Librarie de France, 1929), p. 9.

44. James George Frazer, *The Worship of Nature* (New York: Macmillan, 1926), pp. 316–440.

45. Ibid., p. 422.

46. Frazer, *The Worship of Nature*, pp. 378–80, 402–03, 427.

47. Interview with André Masson by Evan M. Maurer, December 8, 1970.

48. Masson, *Le Plaisir de peindre* ([Nice]: La Diane Française, 1950), p. 180.

49. Interview with André Masson by Evan M. Maurer, December 8, 1970.

50. Ibid.

51. Ibid. This type of "X-ray" image is also commonly found in the sculpture and painting of the American Indian tribes of the Northwest Coast, where it is specifically associated with the phenomenon of shamanism. See Evan M. Maurer, *The Native American Heritage* (Chicago: Art Institute of Chicago, 1977), pp. 290, 310.

52. Max Ernst, *Beyond Painting, and Other Writings by the Artist and His Friends*, ed. Robert Motherwell (New York: Wittenborn, Schultz, 1948), p. 194.

53. Patrick Waldberg, *Max Ernst* (Paris: Pauvert, 1958), p. 60.

54. Roland Penrose, *Max Ernst's Celebes* (University of Newcastle upon Tyne, 1972), pp. 14–15. Ernst's interest in ethnographic museums was characterized by the title of his 1965 sculpture *Le Musée de l'homme*, which represents a man seated on the ground with his arms across his knees—a pose taken directly from Ecuadoran and Costa Rican stone sculpture, c. 1000–1500 A.D. The same title was incorporated in a 1965 catalog done with the Alexandre Iolas Gallery.

55. Ernst, op. cit., p. 19.

56. Ibid., p. 27.

57. *Encyclopaedia Britannica*, 11th ed., s.v. "Pan."

58. Interview with Max Ernst by Evan M. Maurer, May 24, 1974.

59. Ernst, op. cit., p. 19. The nymph Echo also refers to Pan. Echo was an oread, a nymph of the forests and grottoes. She was said to have refused the love of Pan, who, in a fit of rage, had her torn apart by shepherds. Frazer also described Primitive rites in which men are symbolically married to personifications of nature. See *The New Golden Bough*, p. 110.

60. Ibid., p. 26.

61. Ibid., p. 28.

62. Waldberg, op. cit., p. 42. In 1973 Ernst produced *Standing Figure (Totem)*, a sculpture that is directly analogous to the argilite totems carved by the Haida of the Northwest Coast.

63. Freud, *Totem and Taboo*, p. 2.

64. See Maurer, "In Quest of the Myth," pp. 182–85.

65. Ibid., pp. 222–29.

66. Carlo Sala, *Max Ernst et la démarche onirique* (Paris: Klincksieck, 1970), p. 33.

67. Stephan-Chauvet, *L'Ile de Pâques et ses mystères* (Paris: Editions "Tel," 1935), pp. 83–86.

68. Interview with Max Ernst by Evan M. Maurer, May 24, 1974.

69. Ralph Linton and Paul S. Wingert, *Arts of the South Seas* (New York: Museum of Modern Art, 1946), pp. 42–43.

70. In 1938 Ernst created large cement figures of this type to decorate the walls of his home in Saint-Martin d'Ardèche.

71. Stephan-Chauvet, op. cit., pl. 28, fig. 66 and notes. The object was illustrated in Mrs. Scoresby Routledge, *The Mystery of Easter Island* (London: Sifton Praed, 1919).

72. Max Ernst, *Maximiliana ou l'exercice illégal d'astronomie* (Paris: Le Degré Quarante-et-un, 1964).

73. A copy of Fewkes's beautifully illustrated 1903 *Bulletin of American Ethnology* on Kachinas was in Ernst's library.

74. Peggy Guggenheim, *Out of This Century* (New York: Dial, 1946), p. 297.

75. John Russell, *Max Ernst* (New York: Abrams, 1967), p. 146.

76. Patrick Waldberg, "Max Ernst in Arizona," in *Homage to Max Ernst*, ed. G. di San Lazzaro (spec. issue of *XXe Siècle Review*; New York: Tudor, 1971), p. 57. (Ernst's library also contained a well-used paperback French edition of *Sun Chief*, by Don Talayesva. This moving autobiographical account of Hopi culture was so admired by Ernst that he had it specially bound in full leather.)

77. Lucy R. Lippard, "The Sculpture," *Max Ernst: Sculpture and Recent Painting* (New York: Jewish Museum, 1966), p. 44.

78. Julien Levy, "A Summer in Long Island," in *Homage to Max Ernst*, ed., G. di San Lazzaro (spec. issue of *XXe Siècle Review*; New York: Tudor, 1971), p. 61.

79. Frank Waters, *Book of the Hopi* (New York: Ballantine Books, 1966), p. 171.

80. Among Ernst's many other Kachina-inspired works are: *La Belle Allemande*, 1934–35; *Moonmad*, 1944; *Deux et deux font un*, 1956; *Homme*, 1960.

81. Waldberg, *Max Ernst*, p. 363.

82. Mircea Eliade, *Shamanism: Archaic Techniques of Ecstasy*, trans. Willard R. Trask (Princeton: Princeton University Press, 1972), pp. 518–69.

83. Lévy-Bruhl, op. cit., pp. 216–17.

84. Ibid., p. 269.

85. Ibid., p. 345.

86. Frazer, *The New Golden Bough*, p. 39.

87. Interview with Max Ernst by Evan M. Maurer, May 24, 1974.

88. Eliade, op. cit., p. 13.

89. Ernst, *Beyond Painting*, p. 26.

90. Eliade, op. cit., p. 38.

91. Ibid., pp. 157–58.

92. Ibid., pp. 121, 285, 602.

93. Ernst, *Beyond Painting*, p. 28.

94. Eliade, op. cit., p. 33.

95. Ibid., p. 35.

96. Ernst, loc. cit.

97. Eliade, op. cit., pp. 33–66.

98. Ernst, *Beyond Painting*, p. 29.

99. Ibid.

100. Eliade, op. cit., p. 98.

101. Ernst, *Beyond Painting*, p. 29.

102. Eliade, loc. cit.

103. Ibid., p. 156.

104. Ernst, *Beyond Painting*, p. 10.

105. Ibid., p. 14.

106. Georges Duthuit, "Enquête," *Cahiers d'art* 14, no. 1–4, 1939, p. 75.

107. Elizabeth Cowling, "The Eskimo, the American Indians and the Surrealists," *Art History* 1, no. 4, December 1978.

108. Cowling suggested that Miró could have seen composite Eskimo masks at the Musée de l'Homme, Paris, or the Pinart Collection, now at the Musée des Beaux-Arts et d'Archéologie in Boulogne-sur-Mer. However, William Rubin has

found that there were (and are) no Eskimo masks of this type in the Musée de l'Homme or in the Pinart Collection. He has ruled out the Barcelona Ethnographic Museum, sometimes considered as an early source, because it did not open until after World War II. In an interview with Masson, who was Miró's neighbor during the early 1920s, Masson confirmed that Miró did not see these masks until the 1930s.

109. William Rubin, *Miró in the Collection of the Museum of Modern Art* (New York: Museum of Modern Art, 1973), p. 60.

110. Wolfgang Paalen (ed.), *DYN* 4–5 (December 1945).

111. Ibid., introduction.

112. André Breton, *Surrealism and Painting*, trans. Simon Watson Taylor (New York: Harper and Row, 1972), p. 171.

113. Michel Leiris, *Wifredo Lam* (New York: Abrams, 1972), p. 7.

114. Ibid.

115. Breton, *Surrealism and Painting*, p. 78.

116. Jacques Charpier, *Lam* (Paris: Le Musée de Poche, 1960), p. 26.

117. Madeleine Rousseau, "Wifredo Lam—peintre cubain," *Présence africaine* 4 (1948), p. 591.

118. Leiris, *Lam*, pp. 9–10.

119. Wifredo Lam, "Oeuvres récentes de Wifredo Lam," *Cahiers d'art* 26, 1951, p. 186.

120. This particular feature also seems to relate to genital imagery used by Picasso in the late 1920s, as in the studies for his *Crucifixion*, of 1929. See also Robert Rosenblum, "Picasso and the Anatomy of Eroticism," *Studies in Erotic Art*, ed. Theodore Bowie and Cornelia V. Christenson (New York: Basic Books, 1970), pp. 339–93.

121. Anna Balakian, *Surrealism: The Road to the Absolute* (New York: Dutton, 1970), p. 49.

122. Breton, *Surrealism and Painting*, p. 333.

Ancestor figure. Geelvink Bay, Irian Jaya (formerly Netherlands New Guinea). Wood and skull, 17⅜" (44 cm) high. Museum voor Land- en Volkenkunde, Rotterdam

Henry Moore. *Maquette for King and Queen.* 1952. Bronze, 10½" (26.7 cm) high. Private collection

HENRY MOORE

Alan G. Wilkinson

Few twentieth-century sculptors have Henry Moore's encyclopedic knowledge of the history of sculpture, and few have written as perceptively as he on the nature of sculpture in general and on specific artists and subjects, including tribal art. In contrast to the scant documentary evidence of the specific examples of tribal art with which Modigliani, Epstein, Gaudier, and Lipchitz were familiar, Moore, especially in his sketchbooks of the 1920s, provides an invaluable record of the sculptures he knew.

Moore was born in 1898 in Castleford, Yorkshire, in the industrial north of England, the seventh child of a miner. At an early age he decided to become a sculptor and was fortunate in receiving much encouragement from his grammar-school art teacher, Miss Alice Gostick. In 1917 he joined the army and fought in the trenches on the Western Front. Unlike two other young sculptors, Gaudier-Brzeska and Duchamp-Villon, he survived, though he was gassed and spent some time in the hospital. Moore was already twenty-one when in 1919 he enrolled in a two-year course at the Leeds School of Art.

Moore's introduction to Primitive art was undoubtedly Roger Fry's *Vision and Design* (1920), which he read during his last year at the Leeds School of Art. Fry's chapter on "Negro Sculpture" opens with a condemnation of the academic tradition that was still the norm when Moore was a student:

What a right little, tight little, round little world it was when Greece was the only source of culture, when Greek art, even in Roman copies, was the only indisputable art, except for some Renaissance repetitions![1]

Both in the sarcastic remarks about the narrowness of the Greek tradition and in the praise for African and pre-Columbian sculpture, Fry's book was the initial catalyst for the most profound formative influence on Moore's development—his frequent visits to the British Museum in the 1920s.

I came on [*Vision and Design*] by chance while looking for another book in the Leeds Reference Library. Fry in his essay on Negro sculpture stressed the "three-dimensional realization" that characterized African art and its "truth to material." More, Fry opened the way to other books and to the realization of the British Museum. That was really the beginning.[2]

Moore arrived in London in the autumn of 1921, having been awarded, while at Leeds, a Royal Exhibition Scholarship to the Royal College of Art. Like Epstein before him, Moore was overwhelmed by the sculpture collections in the British Museum: "One room after another in the British Museum took my enthusiasm. The Royal College of Art meant nothing in comparison."[3] He has described in some detail the sculpture that particularly interested him: Egyptian, Assyrian, Sumerian, African, Oceanic, North and South American, Eskimo, and above all, the monumental pre-Columbian stone carving—Aztec, Mayan, and Toltec.[4] Moore's own broad definition of Primitive art—in the spirit of nineteenth- more than twentieth-century usages—encompasses works from all these periods and cultures:

The term "Primitive Art" is generally used to include the products of a great variety of races and periods in history, many different social and religious systems. In its widest sense it seems to cover most of these cultures which are outside European and the great Oriental civilizations.[5]

Henry Moore. *Standing Woman.* 1923. Wood, 12" (30.5 cm) high. City Art Gallery, Manchester

Moore's rejection of the Greek ideal and the academic tradition was a continuation of Gauguin's position in the 1890s when he wrote: "The great error is the Greek, however beautiful it may be."[6] Similarly, Moore recently recalled how consciously, during his formative years, he steered clear of the classical tradition: "There was a period when I tried to avoid looking at Greek sculpture of any kind. And Renaissance. When I thought that the Greek and Renaissance were the enemy, and that one had to throw all that over and start again from the beginning of primitive art."[7]

During the 1920s, Moore's interest embraced not only the tribal arts of Africa and Oceania, but many traditions, for the most part those of non-European sculpture. Later, in 1931, he discussed the global history of sculpture, emphasizing that Greek sculpture flourished only for a brief period, and that it was only one of many great sculptural traditions:

The world has been producing sculpture for at least some thirty thousand years. Through modern development of communication much of this we now know and the few sculptors of a hundred years or so of Greece no longer blot our eyes to the sculptural achievements of the rest of mankind. Palaeolithic and Neolithic sculpture, Sumerian, Babylonian and Egyptian, Early Greek, Chinese, Etruscan, Indian, Mayan, Mexican and Peruvian, Romanesque, Byzantine and Gothic, Negro, South Sea Island and North American Indian sculpture; actual examples or photographs of all are available, giving us a world view of sculpture never previously possible.[8]

That Moore made a comprehensive study of sculptures from many of these periods and cultures is revealed in his numerous notebook drawings of the 1920s. He made copies of some of the earliest known sculptures, such as the Palaeolithic "Venus of Grimaldi," which he had seen reproduced in Herbert Kühn's book *Die Kunst der Primitiven* (1923), as well as drawings of Sumerian, Egyptian, Etruscan, Indian, pre-Columbian, Gothic, and Eskimo art, and above all tribal sculpture from Africa and Oceania.[9]

Oceanic, particularly Marquesan, sculpture was the only tribal influence on Gauguin's work, visible primarily in his wood carvings. Picasso's interests, in 1907–08, lay more in African than in Oceanic art. For Moore, uniquely among major twentieth-century sculptors, these arts played a lesser role than pre-Columbian stone carving, both formally and in his choice of material, especially in his sculpture of the 1920s. The pre-Columbian influence culminated in the two stone carvings *Reclining Figure* of 1929, in the Leeds City Art Galleries, and the 1930 *Reclining Woman*, in the National Gallery of Canada.

In this book, however, we are focusing on tribal art, which today is generally the only art known as Primitive. In talking to Moore about his carvings of the 1920s we found only a few works that reflect the influence of African art. The most obvious examples are two of only three wood carvings of this period, *Head of a Girl* of 1922 and *Standing Woman* of 1923, both in the City Art Gallery, Manchester. Wood is the characteristic material of most African sculpture, and his choice of medium here is significant. Neither of these two works seems to relate to any particular tribal style, and, in the case of *Standing Woman*, the influence may have been second-hand. The short bent legs that merge into what is more of a base than feet could have been directly inspired by Gaudier's carving, *The Imp.* Moore must have seen this reproduced in Ezra Pound's *Gaudier-Brzeska: A Memoir* (1916), which he read in 1922 or 1923. Moore has written, "Another book that I found a great help and an excitement was Ezra Pound's book on Gaudier-Brzeska. This was written with a freshness and an insight, and Gaudier speaks as a young sculptor discovering things."[10] Even in his writings, Moore echoes several of Gaudier's statements published in Pound's memoir. Gaudier had commented, "The Indians felt the hamitic [African] influence through Greek spectacles."[11] Moore, in discussing his determination to reject the Greek ideal, wrote: "This removal

Henry Moore. *Relief Head.* 1923. Slate; 12½" (31.8 cm) high. Private collection

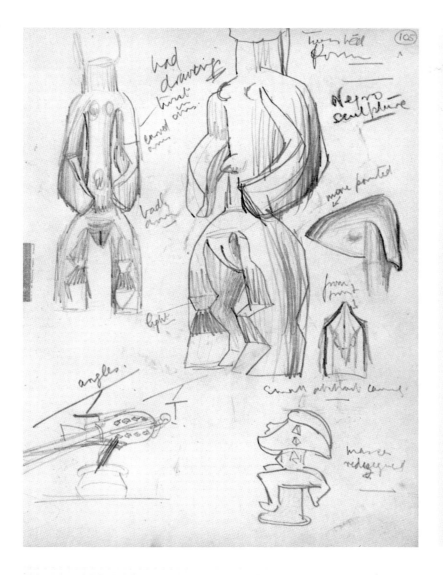

Above left: Henry Moore. *Page 105 from No. 3 Notebook.* 1922–24. Pencil, 8⅞ x 6¾" (22.5 x 17.1 cm). The Henry Moore Foundation, Much Hadham, England

Above right: Figure. Mumuye. Nigeria. Wood, 18⅞" (48 cm) high. The Trustees of the British Museum, London

Left: Head. Baga. Guinea. Wood, 24" (61 cm) high. The Trustees of the British Museum, London

of the Greek spectacles from the eyes of the modern sculptor (along with the direction given by the work of such painters as Cézanne and Seurat) has helped him to realize again the intrinsic emotional significance of shapes instead of seeing mainly a representation value…"[12] The intrinsic emotional significance of shapes—here in a nutshell is the potent alternative to the Greco-Roman tradition that tribal art offered. Tribal sculpture, with its astonishing freedom and variety of form invention, its intensity and directness of expression, and

its own internal logic, suggested to twentieth-century painters and sculptors boundless formal sources on which to draw in order to reshape the human figure. In a recent comment on two sculptures in the Museum of Mankind, London—a male and female wood figure from the Zande, southern Sudan—Moore wrote: "To discover, as a young student, that the African carvers could interpret the human figure to this degree but still keep and intensify the expression, encouraged me to be more adventurous and experimental."[13]

Moore has said that he had been exposed to the work of Gauguin while he was a student at Leeds (1919–21), although he was not particularly aware of his achievements as a sculptor. "I'd had the luck to know Michael Sadler, who was then Vice-Chancellor of Leeds University, a man who had bought Cézanne and Gauguin before 1914, and translated Kandinsky, and really knew what was going on in modern art."[14] In fact, Moore's only sketchbook drawings of European art of the late nineteenth and early twentieth centuries were sketches of works by Cézanne and Gauguin. The Henry Moore Foundation owns a pencil drawing based on three Cézanne Bather figures from *Les Grandes Baigneuses* of 1898–1905 (Philadelphia

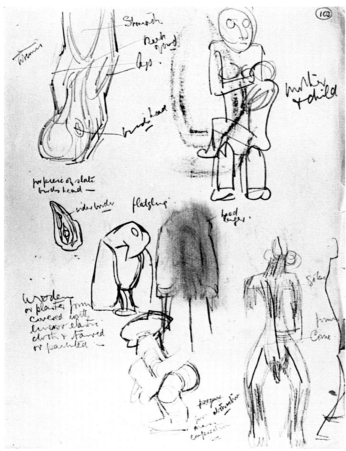

Above: Henry Moore. *Page 103 from No. 3 Notebook.* 1922–24. Pencil, 9 x 6¾" (23 x 17.2 cm). The Henry Moore Foundation, Much Hadham, England

Above right: Mother and child. Nootka. Vancouver Island, British Columbia. Wood, 10⅝" (27 cm) high. The Trustees of the British Museum, London

Right: Figure. Jukun. Nigeria. Wood, 34⅝" (88 cm) high. The Trustees of the British Museum, London

Museum of Art), which Moore had seen in the Pellerin Collection during his first visit to Paris in 1922.[15] On page 52 of No. 2 Notebook of 1921–22 is a pen-and-ink sketch, with the inscription "Gauguin," which was probably based on the charcoal drawing *Femme nue* of 1892.[16] This drawing, representing the Oriental pose that appears in many of Gauguin's paintings and works on paper, is reproduced in Charles Morice's *Paul Gauguin* (Paris, 1919, p. 172), the probable source of Moore's sketch. For Moore, as for Gauguin, books, reproductions, and photographs provided important source materials. Gauguin's drawing *Femme nue* had been, in turn, based on one of the figures in a photograph he took with him to Tahiti, a

Above: Head of a monkey. Ubangi (?). Central African Republic. Wood, c. 7¼" (18.4 cm) high. Private collection, New York. Published in Carl Einstein, *Negerplastik*, 1915

Left: Henry Moore. *Page 120 from No. 3 Notebook.* 1922–24. Pencil, pen and ink, 9 x 6¾" (23 x 17.2 cm). The Henry Moore Foundation, Much Hadham, England

photograph of the Javanese temple of Borobudur.[17] Moore's slate *Relief Head* of 1923 (p. 596) is probably his only work that reflects the influence of Gauguin's sculpture. In the early 1970s Moore described this work to the author as rather "Gauguin-esque," and recently he said to Ann Garrould, "I did not realize how much I'd been influenced by Gauguin when I carved that head."[18] The most likely source of inspiration was the painted plaster relief *Self-Portrait of Gauguin*, which is illustrated on page 78 in Charles Morice's book on the artist.

Another artist who influenced Moore in the 1920s was Epstein—not only the man and his work, but his collection, for Epstein was already on his way to amassing what was to become one of the finest private collections of tribal and exotic art.

In the 1920s the only practising sculptor in England for whom I had any respect was Epstein...After I had finished my student course and was appointed to the teaching staff of the Royal College [1924] I came to know Epstein quite well, and have never forgotten him taking me to his bedroom to see his collection of primitive carv-ings—it was so overflowing with negro sculptures etc., that I wondered how he got into bed without knocking something over.[19]

Moore made many drawings of African, Oceanic, Eskimo, Mexican, and Peruvian sculpture in the mid-1920s. His note-books from these years doubtless constitute the most com-prehensive record by any major twentieth-century artist of

specific works of tribal and Primitive art that attracted him. We not only have concrete evidence of many of the works that Moore particularly admired, but also, in a number of instances, his descriptions, made many years later, of the sculptures themselves. Drawings of African art outnumber those of works from Oceania, North America (Northwest Coast and Eskimo), and Peru. In the British Museum, exam-ples of African sculpture far outnumbered carvings from Oceania and North America (Northwest Coast and Eskimo), which may well account for the fact that Moore made many more drawings of African art than of works from the other geographical regions. (Surprisingly, there are few copies of the pre-Columbian sculpture that Moore so greatly admired in the 1920s.) For the most part, Moore's drawings of Primi-tive art were fairly straightforward and in some cases quite detailed studies of the works themselves. As the artist has often pointed out, drawing obviously makes one look at and analyze a subject far more intensely than merely observing it.

Moore made his drawings of tribal art either in the British Museum or from illustrations in books on Primitive sculpture. Almost certainly all the studies found on page 105 of No. 3 Notebook of 1922–24 are of works in the British Museum (p. 597): at lower left a Baga head;[20] at lower right a canoe-

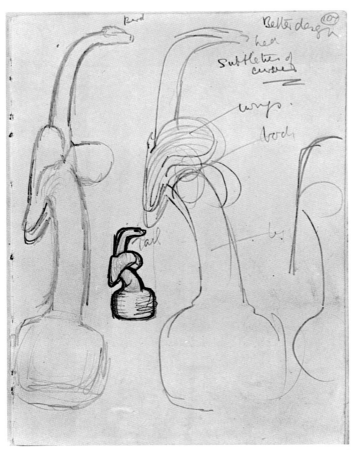

Henry Moore. *Page 107 from No. 3 Notebook.* 1922–24. Pencil, pen and ink, 9 x 6¾" (23 x 17.2 cm). The Henry Moore Foundation, Much Hadham, England

Henry Moore. *Page 106 from No. 3 Notebook.* 1922–24. Pencil, 9 x 6¾" (23 x 17.2 cm). The Henry Moore Foundation, Much Hadham, England

prow ornament from the Solomon Islands; at center right two studies of a club with the head in the form of a bird, from New Caledonia;[21] and two views of a Mumuye figure acquired by the British Museum in 1922. In 1951, during the Festival of Britain, the Colonial Office sponsored an important exhibition of tribal art, with the now quaint title "Traditional Art from the Colonies," which included this Mumuye carving. William Fagg persuaded Moore to visit the exhibition with him and to answer a series of questions about the nature of tribal art. Fagg asked Moore which of the sculptures he would select as showing the best use of the qualities of the wood. "The [Mumuye] seems to me one of the best from this point of view," Moore replied. "The carver has managed to make it 'spatial' by the way in which he has made the arms free and yet enveloping the central form of the body."[22]

On page 103 from the same 1922–24 Notebook (p. 598), the figure in profile at bottom center is based on a male figure from what had been (before World War I) the German-controlled area of New Guinea. It was copied from a reproduction on a loose page from an as-yet-unidentified German book or periodical which the author discovered among Moore's papers. To the right of this is a study of a Jukun male figure from Northern Nigeria, acquired by the British Museum in 1909 (p. 598). At upper right Moore has made a drawing of one of his two most important subjects—the mother and child—copied from what is in all likelihood a Nootka wood carving from Vancouver Island, British Columbia (p. 598). In 1981, Moore wrote of this carving and related Northwest Coast works that the mother-and-child theme

posed for the sculptor

the relationship of a large form to a small one, and the dependency of the small form on the larger. Its appeal lies particularly in its expression of two basic human experiences: to be a child and to be a parent. These...mother-and-child figures are remarkable. There is a great feeling of maternal protectiveness but they are not at all sentimental.[23]

Illustrations in two important early German publications on African art, Carl Einstein's *Negerplastik* (1915) and Ernst Fuhrmann's *Afrika* (1922), were the other principal sources for Moore's copies of tribal sculpture. On page 120 of No. 3 Notebook, the small head at right, just above center, was based on what is probably a head of a monkey reproduced in Einstein's book, plate 15 (p. 599).[24] To the left of this, the two heads are a free interpretation of the heads which appear on the neck of an Inca pot from Trujillo, which is reproduced in Ernst Fuhrmann's *Reich der Inka* (1922) as plate 15. The artist's copy of this book is inscribed on the flyleaf: "Henry Spencer Moore 1923." All the drawings on page 143 of No. 3 Notebook were based on illustrations in Fuhrmann's *Afrika*.[25]

A number of Moore's drawings reveal that certain works of tribal art were copied not simply for study purposes but with the intention of transforming them into ideas for sculpture. On page 107 of No. 3 Notebook of 1922–24, the two largest sketches are of the prehistoric stone pestle, in the form of a bird, North-East Papua New Guinea, in the British Museum (p. 354), which had probably also inspired Brancusi. The elongated proportions of the little bird seem to have presented problems for Moore, at this time a stone carver whose sculp-

Figure. Hawaiian Islands. Wood, 26½" (67 cm) long. The Trustees of the British Museum, London

Henry Moore. *Page 90 from No. 3 Notebook.* 1922–24. Pencil and chalk, 9 x 6¾" (23 x 17.2 cm). The Henry Moore Foundation, Much Hadham, England

ture was massive and blocklike. As he wrote of one of his own carvings, the 1924–25 Hornton stone *Mother and Child* (City Art Gallery, Manchester), "There is no neck simply because I was frightened to weaken the stone."[26] His smaller pencil, pen and ink sketch in the center of the page shows a much more compact, less elongated bird—and indicates that Moore was working out a less problematic form which he might translate into stone sculpture.

The studies on page 106 of the same notebook reveal the way in which the artist used the stone pestle as a point of departure, no longer making a straightforward copy of the original but, as the inscription on this sheet states, an "abstraction" from it. The four studies in the upper two-thirds of this page are reminiscent of Gaudier-Brzeska's 1914 carving *Birds Erect* (The Museum of Modern Art, New York).

The way in which Moore has altered the stone pestle in the studies on page 106 provides the key to our understanding of his working method. All the evidence is before us: the identified prehistoric sculpture and Moore's response to it—a rare occurrence in the study of the affinities between the tribal and the modern. In the four largest drawings in the upper two-thirds of page 106, he has not only created less elongated and more compact proportions than those of the pestle, but has radically transformed the smooth surfaces of the New Guinea carving, producing a complex series of planes and angles that owe an obvious debt to Vorticism and to the 1914 sculpture of Gaudier-Brzeska. Although these studies were not translated into sculpture, they are closely related to the angular surface of Moore's 1922 marble *Dog*.

Some of Moore's 1920s drawings of tribal art reflect, as we have seen, his description of the somewhat chaotic display in the ethnographical rooms of the British Museum, with its "inexhaustible wealth and variety of sculptural achievement (Negro, Oceanic Islands, and North and South America), but overcrowded and jumbled together like junk in a marine store, so that after hundreds of visits I would still find carvings not discovered there before."[27] In other drawings, such as those on page 90 of No. 3 Notebook (above), he focused his attention on one or two works. The crawling figure at the very top of the sheet is based on the Arawak (Dominican Republic) seat in the form of a male figure, in the British Museum.[28] Moore has recently recalled that during his student days, when this drawing was executed, the Caribbean sculptures in the British Museum were exhibited high up on a shelf and were somewhat difficult to view properly. Yet this Arawak carving had a special attraction for him: "I liked this partly because it was a reclining figure and partly for the freedom of the legs, they have so much life in them."[29] Here is a direct reference to the other major subject—the reclining figure—which, like the mother and child, has obsessed Moore from the late twenties to the present day.

The central and lower studies on this sheet were based on one of the most powerful and dynamic works of Oceanic art in the British Museum—the Hawaiian Islands crouching figure which probably represents a dancer. "This has been a favourite of mine ever since my student days," Moore has written. "It used to be exhibited in a large case with thirty or more other pieces but even then its amazing strength of form stood out

Henry Moore. *Studies of African and Eskimo Sculpture*. 1931. Pencil and chalk, 10¾ x 7⅛" (27.3 x 19.4 cm). Private collection

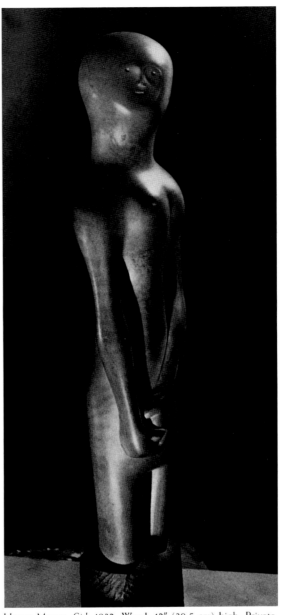

Henry Moore. *Girl*. 1932. Wood, 12" (30.5 cm) high. Private collection

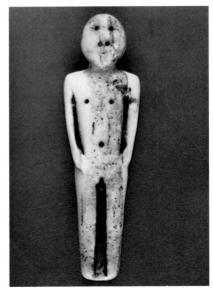

Figure. Eskimo. Alaska. Ivory, 3⅞" (9.8 cm) high. The Trustees of the British Museum, London

and I felt I had to sketch it. It has the flat back and powerful muscles of a gorilla, combined with the tension and strain of a wrestler."[30]

With hundreds of examples of Primitive art on exhibition at the British Museum, Moore singled out and drew a number of works which over the years have come to be considered among the finest examples of African and Oceanic art in the collection. The Mumuye, Jukun, Arawak, Nootka, and Hawaiian carvings discussed above were all included in William Fagg's 1970 exhibition at the British Museum, "The Tribal Image," whose criterion was sculptural quality. The sculptor's eye had recognized this quality in the mid-1920s.

The affinities between tribal and modern art were evident to Sidney Burney, London's most important and influential dealer in Eskimo, African, and Oceanic art during the 1920s and 1930s, whose gallery Moore certainly visited. In 1928 Burney organized a pioneering exhibition in which he showed African sculpture along with the work of contemporary artists: Zadkine, Epstein, Dobson, Hepworth, and Skeaping. An

Henry Moore. *Upright Motive: Maquette No. 11.* 1955. Bronze, 12¼" (31.1 cm) high. Private collection

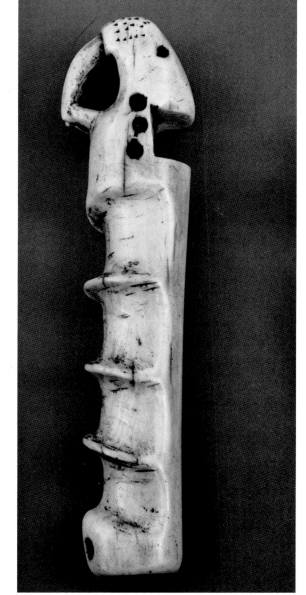

Drum handle. Eskimo. Alaska. Ivory, 6¼" (16 cm) high. The Trustees of the British Museum, London

enlightened review in *The Times* commented: "... what the exhibition brings out is the traditional character of all good sculpture, independent of place and period."[31] Four years later the English sculptor Leon Underwood[32] put together a similar but more ambitious exhibition at Burney's gallery, the purpose of which was to juxtapose works from Mexico, India, China, Egypt, Africa, Persia, and New Zealand with sculptures by Degas, Gaudier-Brzeska, Modigliani, Moore, and Hepworth, and two sculptures of his own.

During the 1930s, Moore's interest in tribal art continued, but its influence was more sporadic than in the previous decade. The radical change in direction in Moore's art, in carvings such as *Composition* of 1931, *Head and Ball* of 1934, and *Four-Piece Composition* from the same year, owes an enormous debt to the liberating influence of the sculpture of Picasso, Arp, and Giacometti—works such as Picasso's 1928 *Metamorphosis*, Arp's 1931 *Bell and Navel*, and Giacometti's 1934 *Woman with Her*

Throat Cut. Although he retained his own independence, Moore's sculpture and drawings of the 1930s were closely aligned to the work of the Surrealists, with whom he exhibited in the June 1936 "International Surrealist Exhibition" at the New Burlington Galleries, London. And, like the Surrealists, Moore turned to Oceanic and Eskimo sculpture for inspiration.

Moore had made few drawings of Eskimo sculpture, and its impact on his work, compared to that of Oceanic art, was minimal. On page 100 of No. 3 Notebook of 1922–24, the three studies just below center, with the inscriptions "fishtail" and "bore hole," are probably of Eskimo ivory harpoon heads, and between them is a sketch of an Eskimo needle case.[33] At upper right is a drawing of a Northwest Coast Indian pipe in the Christy Collection in the British Museum.

The 1931 drawing *Studies of African and Eskimo Sculpture* is of interest for several reasons. The inscription at the top of the sheet, "Remember Mexican mother and child at Burney's —simple power and intensity—and Negro figure for vitality

Malanggan figure. New Ireland. Painted wood and fiber, 41" (104.1 cm) high. The Trustees of the British Museum, London

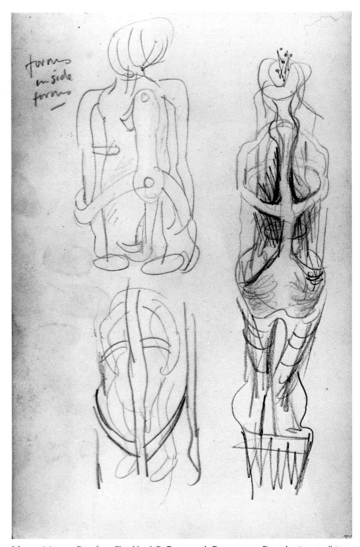

Henry Moore. *Page from Sketchbook B: Forms inside Forms.* 1935. Pencil, 8⅝ x 5½" (21.8 x 13.8 cm). The Henry Moore Foundation, Much Hadham, England

and pick of life ...," attests to the fact that Moore visited Burney's London gallery, where he exhibited his own work in Underwood's 1932 exhibition. That Moore was still in touch with Epstein and his collection is indicated by the continuing inscription: "and the figure belonging to Epstein—Negro mother and child for big primitive power." The two largest studies are of Dogon standing figures with bent legs. The two standing figures in the bottom half of the sheet are closely related to Eskimo bone and ivory figurative carvings, such as the human figure in the British Museum (p. 602). From these studies evolved Moore's 1932 boxwood *Girl* (p. 602), one of his few sculptures inspired by Eskimo art. In a much later sculpture, the 1955 *Upright Motive: Maquette No. 11* (p. 603), Moore blended organic forms with details probably borrowed from Eskimo art. The three single horizontal projections in the maquette are remarkably close to features found in Eskimo ivory drum handles.

Oceanic art was the dominant tribal influence on Moore's sculpture and drawings of the 1930s. He did not exploit as fully as did the Surrealists the highly charged, grotesque, and erotic imagery found in much of the art of the Pacific islands, but this is not to say that he was unaware of these characteristics. In 1941 he wrote:

The many islands of the Oceanic groups all produced their schools of sculpture with big differences in form-vision. New Guinea carvings, with drawn out spider-like extensions and bird-beak elongations, made a direct contrast with the featureless heads and plain surfaces of Nukuoro carvings; or the solid stone figures of the Marquesas Islands against the emasculated ribbed figures of Easter Island.[34]

Recently, Moore has compared the most obvious differences between African and Oceanic art:

Whereas African sculpture is bulky, powerful, and solid, seeming to reflect a down-to-earth attitude to life, the Oceanic peoples appear to me to have a more anxious, nervous, over-imaginative view of the world, expressing itself in fantastic, birdlike, beetlelike forms with a nightmarish quality about them.[35]

Moore's 1931 lead *Reclining Figure* was probably his first sculpture inspired by Oceanic art.[36] While the distorted, biomorphic forms of the figure are clearly indebted to the work of Picasso, the three parallel struts or ribs which cut across the hollowed-out torso were no doubt suggested by forms found in New Ireland sculpture such as the British Museum's Malanggan figure which Moore sketched in the mid-1930s. Of all Oceanic tribal styles, it was the sculpture

Henry Moore. *Study for Sculpture: Internal/External Forms*. 1950. Crayon, pencil, gouache, pen and red ink, 11½ x 9⅜" (29.2 x 23.8 cm). Private collection

Henry Moore. *Working Model for Upright Internal and External Forms*. 1951. Bronze, 25¼" (64 cm) high. Art Gallery of Ontario; gift from the Women's Committee Fund

from New Ireland which had the greatest formal influence on Moore's work of the 1930s.

Page from Sketchbook B: Forms inside Forms of 1935 leaves us in no doubt of Moore's fascination with New Ireland sculpture. The study at the lower left of the sheet shows a Malanggan's protective outer framework of vertical and curved struts; it was almost certainly based on a carving in the British Museum (page opposite).[37] The study at the top left of the sheet represents the figure inside the Malanggan. In the larger drawing to its right, Moore has transformed the tribal carving into an idea for sculpture. It is thus the point of departure for the many "internal/external form" drawings that Moore executed between 1935 and 1940. He has recently described a different New Ireland Malanggan carving in the British Museum as follows:

New Ireland carvings like this made a tremendous impression on me through their use of forms within a form. I realized what a sense of mystery could be achieved by having the inside partly hidden so that you have to move round the sculpture to understand it. I was also staggered by the craftsmanship needed to make these interior carvings.[38]

Moore's first internal/external form sculpture—*The Helmet*

of 1939–40—was not in fact related to Oceanic art but was based on an illustration he had seen in *Cahiers d'art* (1934) of two prehistoric Greek utensils or implements.[39] It was not until 1948–50, in drawings such as *Study for Sculpture: Internal/External Forms*, that he returned to the Oceanic-inspired motif, a continuation of the 1935–40 drawings. This drawing anticipates the definitive three-dimensional study for the first sculpture—the 1951 bronze *Working Model for Upright Internal and External Forms* (based on a maquette of the same year)—which thus has its ancestry in the New Ireland carving he had copied in his 1935 sketchbook.

One of Moore's finest wood carvings of the late 1930s, *Bird Basket* of 1939 (p. 606), also appears to reflect his continuing interest in Oceanic art. Whereas the strings in his work of the period were, according to the artist, suggested by mathematical models he had seen in the Science Museum (and also, in my opinion, by the work of Gabo), the vertical projecting forms of the carving, although spaced farther apart, are remarkably close to friction drums from New Ireland (p. 606). Even Moore's own title *Bird Basket* includes one of the words he used to describe the spatial sense of New Ireland carving: "a bird-in-a-cage form."[40]

Henry Moore. *Bird Basket.* 1939. Wood and string, 16½" (41.9 cm) long. Private collection

Friction drum. New Ireland. Painted wood, 18½" (47 cm) long. Private collection

Three Points of 1939–40 was one of the last sculptures Moore completed before concentrating for two years on his shelter and coal-mine drawings (1940–42). As with almost all his sculptures from 1921 to the early 1950s, this work was based on a preparatory drawing, one of the many studies in *Pointed Forms* of 1939, in the Albertina. *Three Points* is a problematic work in that extraordinarily disparate sources, including tribal art, have been discussed in connection with the sculpture. David Sylvester has suggested that Moore may have unconsciously derived the central spikelike form from the pointed, thrusting tongues of the horse and of the woman at left in Picasso's *Guernica* of 1937. Moore, however, apparently told Sylvester that the precise source of the sculpture was a painting in the Louvre, the sixteenth-century School of Fontainebleau double portrait of Gabrielle d'Estrées and her sister in the bath, showing the pinching of Gabrielle's nipple between her sister's forefinger and thumb—a somewhat unlikely source to say the least.[41] In fact when I discussed the Fontainebleau portrait with Moore, he rather whimsically dismissed the issue, and indicated that he was, one might say, leading Sylvester on a merry chase. Given Moore's obvious interest in Oceanic art, culminating in the middle and late 1930s in the New Ireland–inspired internal-external form drawings and in *Bird Basket* of 1939 (based on the form of friction drums), a much more plausible source may be found in tribal art. I am referring to the "hook" figures, or Yipwons, from the Karawari region of New Guinea, in which the penis is "protected" above and below by two pointed, riblike forms. If the penis and arched forms were removed from the New Guinea carving and seen in isolation, they could almost be mistaken for Moore's *Three Points*. Here again, his preparatory drawings for sculpture provide invaluable clues as to the way

in which Moore transformed his sources. In addition to the drawing in the Albertina, the 1939 *Seated Figure and Pointed Forms* also reveals Moore's brief obsession with pointed forms at the end of the 1930s. In the largest study at upper right, the two downward and two upward spikelike forms, practically touching, may have been inspired not by Oceanic art but by

Yipwon figure (detail). Alamblak. Karawari River, East Sepik Province, Papua New Guinea. Wood, 7' ½" (215 cm) high. Friede Collection, New York. Formerly collection MATTA. Complete figure reproduced in color page 73

Henry Moore. *Three Points.* 1939–40. Bronze, 7½" (19.1 cm) long. Private collection

Henry Moore. *Crowd Looking at a Tied-Up Object.* 1942. Pencil, black and colored chalks, wax crayon, and wash, 15¾ x 21⅝" (40 x 55 cm). Private collection

Nupe villagers, Nigeria, standing beside two veiled Dako cult dance costumes. Published in Leo Frobenius, *Kulturgeschichte Afrikas,* 1933

an African sculpture, such as the Pere figure in which the hollowed-out torso is composed of a series of upward- and downward-pointed forms (p. 8)—though it is highly unlikely that Moore saw one of these objects as early as 1939.

Between August 1940 and 1943, when he was commissioned to carve a Madonna and Child for St. Matthew's Church,

Northampton, Moore temporarily abandoned sculpture and, as an official war artist, concentrated first on the shelter and then on the coal-mine drawings. By the summer of 1942 he had completed the series of drawings of miners and begun filling a sketchbook with ideas for sculpture. In 1942 he also executed a number of larger, highly finished drawings of sculpture in outdoor settings, as well as the most famous of his pictorial drawings, as he calls them: *Crowd Looking at a Tied-Up Object.* With Surrealist overtones, it falls chronologically midway between Man Ray's *The Enigma of Isidore Ducasse* (cloth and rope hiding a sewing machine) of 1920 and Christo's *Lower Manhattan Packed Buildings* of 1964–66.

Moore suggested to the author that the idea of a tied-up object may have been suggested by a common practice in sculptors' studios. As a student in the modeling class at the Royal College of Art in the early 1920s, he remembered, he had kept clay moist by covering it with a damp cloth and tying string around it. He did not mention, however, the precise source for *Crowd Looking at a Tied-Up Object,* which was a photograph in Leo Frobenius' *Kulturgeschichte Afrikas* (1933), a copy of which Moore owned, showing Nupe tribesmen from Northern Nigeria standing around two veiled (but not tied-up) Dako cult dance costumes. In the history of primitivism, this is surely one of the few works inspired not by a work of art, but by a photograph of a tribal ceremony. Although Moore's drawing was unquestionably based on the photo-

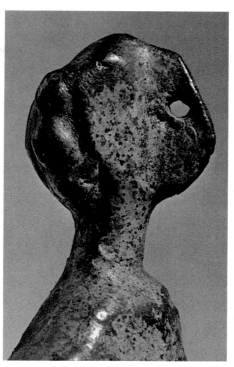

Henry Moore. *Maquette for King and Queen* (detail of King's head). 1952. Bronze, 10½" (26.7 cm) high. Private collection

Henry Moore. *Maquette for King and Queen* (detail of Queen's head). 1952. Bronze, 10½" (26.7 cm) high. Private collection

Headdress (detail). Igbo. Nigeria. Wood, 32⅞" (83.5 cm) high, overall. National Commission for Museums and Monuments, Lagos

graph, he has re-created the setting and the sense of drama and expectancy. Dwarfed by the enormous tied-up object, a crowd has gathered on a barren plain, as if waiting for the unveiling ceremony. The drawing is more enigmatic than the works by Man Ray and Christo, for in these we know what has been covered and tied up. The identity of the wrapped form in Moore's drawing remains a mystery.

Since 1942, Moore has created only a few works that show affinities with tribal art. In the *King and Queen* of 1952–53 (maquette illustrated p. 594), probably Moore's best known and most popular sculpture, he borrowed details from two African carvings. When he and William Fagg visited the exhibition "Traditional Art from the Colonies" in 1951 they looked in particular at the Igbo headdress from the Nigerian Museum. Fagg has written that Moore was greatly interested "to see how the [Igbo] artist had used this method of 'opening up' the human head. This seems to have led him to re-explore his own idea of 1930, and it appeared not only in the *King and Queen* of 1952 but in many of his major works throughout the 1950s."[42] This is a reference to the single hole through the thin heads of both the King and Queen. Fagg has also suggested that the King's crown may derive from another work in the 1951 exhibition, a Yoruba carving of a ram's head.[43] The pose of the *King and Queen* was inspired by Egyptian seated figures in the British Museum.

Moon Head of 1964 (p. 611) would appear to be the last Moore sculpture to have been inspired by tribal art. The two sections represent a "hand" (the view we show) and a "head," which in the earlier, smaller version was called *Head in Hand*. When he made the larger version he found that the "whole effect reminded me so strongly of the light and shape of the full moon that I have since called it *Moon Head*."[44] Although *Moon Head* has sometimes been compared to the thin forms of

Cycladic figurative sculpture, the exact source for the hand-shaped form, William Fagg told the author, was a Mama mask of a buffalo from Nigeria, which is illustrated in Fagg's 1963 book, *Nigerian Images* (p. 610). According to Fagg, the late Harry Fischer, Moore's friend and dealer, gave the sculptor a copy of this book soon after it was published. Moore has transformed the symmetrical Mama mask into something resembling an abstract horned head or a giant asymmetrical hand. Many years after Primitive art had ceased to be a dominant influence on his art, *Moon Head* shows Moore, in the mid-1960s, still receptive to the forms of tribal art that had such a profound influence on his development during the 1920s and 1930s.

That tribal art has been one of the major influences on Moore's sculpture and drawings is abundantly clear from the illustrations shown here of his work juxtaposed with African and Oceanic carvings. The cumulative influence of tribal, pre-Columbian, and Archaic and exotic court arts has probably had a more sustained impact on Moore's work than on the work of any other major twentieth-century sculptor or painter. The borrowings from tribal sculpture, so obvious in a number of Moore's carvings and bronzes discussed in this essay, clearly refute Goldwater's contention that its "direct formal adaptations have been few, and . . . very little modern sculpture even recalls the general proportions and rhythms of any specific primitive tribal style."[45] As we have seen, a number of Moore's sculptures not only recall tribal styles, but in some instances were directly inspired by specific works of tribal art which we have been able to identify.

That *Moon Head* of 1964 is, to date, Moore's last sculpture inspired by tribal art is not to say that during the past twenty years his interest in African and Oceanic art has waned. On the contrary, he has added to his modest collection of tribal sculpture, the most notable acquisitions being an important Luba mask, a Mumuye standing figure, two Mangbetu figures, and an eighteenth-century bronze Asante Kudo box. Moore's fascination with one of the greatest Oceanic carvings in the British Museum, the famed Rurutu Island figure (p. 331), was such that, like Picasso before him, he has recently had a bronze cast made from the original.

The 1981 publication *Henry Moore at the British Museum* marks the culmination of more than fifty years of intermittent writing about the art of sculpture, which began in 1920 with Moore's unpublished manuscript "History of Sculpture: Notes," now in The Henry Moore Centre for the Study of Sculpture, Leeds. Before this recent book, Moore's most important writing about tribal art was an article entitled "Primitive Art," which appeared in *The Listener*, August 24, 1941. In *Henry Moore at the British Museum*, the eighty-two-year-old artist discusses fifty sculptures in the collection, and rediscovers many works he had first seen as a student in the 1920s. Among the illustrations of tribal art, four are of carvings he had copied in his notebooks of the mid-1920s.

"The pieces illustrated are a very restricted personal selection," Moore wrote in the introduction to this book, "... but just as I would have been fascinated to know, say, what Picasso most liked in the Louvre and which works might have influ-

Mask. Mama. Nigeria. Wood, 19½" (49.5 cm) high. National Commission for Museums and Monuments, Lagos. Published in William Fagg, *Nigerian Images*, 1963

enced him, so I hope people will be interested to see what has excited and influenced me in the British Museum."[46] We would indeed like to know in far greater detail than we do what works of tribal art the other major artists of the twentieth century

Mask. Mama. Nigeria. Wood, 18⅛" (46 cm) high, overall. Collection Rita Reinhardt Bedford, New York

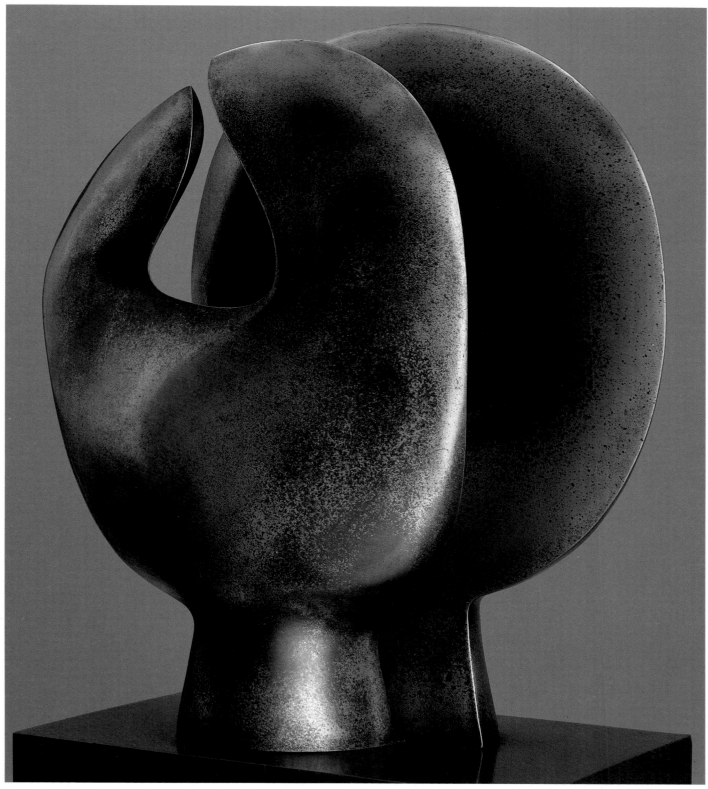

Henry Moore. *Moon Head*. 1964. Bronze, 22¾ x 17⅜ x 10" (57.8 x 44.1 x 25.4 cm). The Trustees of the Tate Gallery, London

saw and admired.

Moore's contribution to the history of twentieth-century primitivism is unique. His drawings of tribal sculpture present a fascinating record of particular works to which he responded. His sculpture reveals a wide range of affinities and interpretations of African and Oceanic art, from the African proportions of his 1923 *Standing Woman* to a work such as his 1964 *Moon Head* directly inspired by a Mama mask. With artists such as Modigliani and, to a lesser extent, Lipchitz, the discussion of tribal influences must be, by the nature of their work and by the lack of documentary evidence of the African sculptures with which they were familiar, somewhat speculative and generalized. Moore, on the other hand, in his writings, drawings, and sculpture has done much of the ground work for us, thereby augmenting both our understanding of his own assimilation of African and Oceanic sources and our appreciation of tribal sculpture as works of art in their own right.

NOTES

1. Roger Fry, *Vision and Design* (1920; reprint ed., Middlesex, England: Pelican, 1961), p. 85.
2. Henry Moore, *Henry Moore on Sculpture*, ed. with intro. by Philip James (London: MacDonald, 1966), p. 49. (In the following notes this book will be referred to as Moore.)
3. Ibid., p. 33.
4. Ibid., pp. 155–74.
5. Ibid., p. 155.
6. Robert Goldwater, *Primitivism in Modern Art* (New York: Vintage Books, 1967), p. 66.
7. Sandy Nairne and Nicholas Serota, eds., *British Sculpture in the Twentieth Century* (London: Whitechapel Art Gallery, 1981), p. 104.
8. Moore, p. 57.
9. For a detailed account of Moore drawings of tribal as well as other non-European sculpture, see Alan G. Wilkinson, *The Drawings of Henry Moore* (London: Tate Gallery/Art Gallery of Ontario, 1977), pp. 143–50. (In the following notes, this catalog will be referred to as Wilkinson.)
10. Moore, p. 49.
11. Ezra Pound, *Gaudier-Brzeska: A Memoir* (London: John Lane—The Bodley Head; New York: John Lane Co., 1916), p. 10.
12. Moore, p. 57.
13. Henry Moore, *Henry Moore at the British Museum*, photographs by David Finn (London: British Museum Publications, 1981), p. 96. (In the following notes this book will be referred to as *Henry Moore at the British Museum*.)
14. Moore, p. 32.

15. See Wilkinson, p. 67, no. 62, illus.
16. Ibid., p. 146, illus. figs. 112 and 115.
17. See above, p. 187, and Alan G. Wilkinson, *Gauguin to Moore: Primitivism in Modern Sculpture* (Toronto: Art Gallery of Ontario, 1981), p. 52, illus. fig. 15.
18. Quoted to the author by Ann Garrould (Moore's niece), June 1983.
19. *Henry Moore at the British Museum*, p. 10.
20. I am indebted to William Fagg for identifying this sketch as a copy of the Baga carving.
21. See B. A. L. Cranstone, *Melanesia: A Short Ethnography* (London: British Museum, 1961), p. 68, fig. 23. In fig. 23, the three clubs on the right are examples of the "bird-headed" type that Moore copied.
22. Moore, p. 173.
23. *Henry Moore at the British Museum*, p. 125.
24. William Fagg suggested to the author that this head was probably by the Ubangi.
25. See Wilkinson, p. 148, illus., fig. 120.
26. Henry Moore, *Henry Moore*, photographed and edited by John Hedgecoe (London: Thomas Nelson, 1968), p. 45.
27. Moore, p. 157.
28. See William Fagg, *The Tribal Image: Wooden Figure Sculpture of the World* (London: British Museum, 1970), no. 4, illus.
29. *Henry Moore at the British Museum*, p. 112.
30. Ibid., p. 86.
31. Nairne and Serota, p. 79.
32. Leon Underwood (1890–1975) was an artist whose reputation has suffered under the shadow of Moore and Hepworth, whom he taught life drawing in the early 1920s. His activities are relevant in the present context for a number of reasons. His own sculpture, oils, and engravings show the sporadic influence of tribal and Primitive art. He began collecting African sculpture in 1919 and over the years formed a substantial collection. Underwood's significant publications on African art include *Figures in Wood of West Africa* (1947), *Masks of West Africa* (1948), and *Bronzes of West Africa* (1949).
33. See Wilkinson, p. 150, fig. 131, for an illustration of page 100 from No. 3 Notebook.
34. Moore, p. 159.
35. *Henry Moore at the British Museum*, p. 91.
36. Nairne and Serota, p. 120. Anna Gruetzner has written: "Moore has recently said that the oddly juxtaposed strange shapes of the lead *Reclining Figure* (private collection) were directly inspired by Oceanic sculpture."
37. Christa Lichtenstern, in her article "Henry Moore and Surrealism" (*Burlington Magazine* 123, no. 944 [November 1981], pp. 645–58), was the first to point out that Moore's internal-external form drawings were based on New Ireland carvings.
38. *Henry Moore at the British Museum*, p. 81.
39. See Wilkinson, p. 144, figs. 93 and 94, for an illustration of the Greek bronzes and Moore's 1937 drawing of them.
40. Moore, p. 159.
41. David Sylvester, *Henry Moore* (London: The Arts Council of Great Britain, 1968), p. 36.
42. William Fagg and Margaret Plass, *African Sculpture: An Anthology* (London: Studio Vista, 1964), p. 30. The Igbo headdress (p. 609) is also illustrated on p. 30.
43. See Alan G. Wilkinson, *Gauguin to Moore: Primitivism in Modern Sculpture*, p. 298, fig. 112.
44. Henry Moore, *Henry Moore*, photographed and edited by John Hedgecoe (London: Thomas Nelson, 1968), p. 466.
45. Goldwater, p. 246.
46. *Henry Moore at the British Museum*, p. 7.

Helmet mask. Kota. Gabon. Wood, 24⅞" (63 cm) high. Musée des Arts Africains et Océaniens, Paris

Mask. Igbo. Nigeria. Wood, 15½" (39.4 cm) high. Collection John Rewald, New York

Figure. Eskimo. Alaska. Whalebone, 17¾″ (45 cm) high. Private collection. Formerly collection HENRY MOORE

Theodoros Stamos. *Sounds in the Rock.* 1946. Oil on composition board, 48⅛ x 28⅜″ (122.2 x 72.1 cm). The Museum of Modern Art, New York; gift of Edward W. Root

ABSTRACT EXPRESSIONISM

Kirk Varnedoe

For many American artists stalled at an impasse around 1940, primitivism, taken in a very broad sense, offered the solution to an entangling riddle: What basis could be found for a new art that was neither derivative nor provincial, that was individual yet universal, free from cant and canon yet absolute? A number of these artists found their answer in a form of the Primitive that was more an ambiance than a distinct style—a broad range of imagery and titles that less evoked tribal art than the origins of natural and human history.

This new tenor was already evident in the late 1930s, and became widespread in the early 1940s in pictures such as Adolph Gottlieb's *Pictograph* of 1942 (p. 616) and Jackson Pollock's *Guardians of the Secret* of 1943 (p. 617), with their suggestions of myth, archetype, and totemic signs. By mid-decade, such resonances had become the hallmark of much of advanced American art, in works as disparate as Mark Rothko's images of life's beginnings (e.g., *Primeval Landscape*, 1945, p. 617), and David Smith's fossil monsters (*Jurassic Bird*, 1945, p. 618), and in scores of other references to evolution and extinction, lost cultures and living ritual, in the works of Barnett Newman, Theodore Stamos, Mark Tobey, William Baziotes, Isamu Noguchi, and numerous others.

Some primitivizing notions had appeared in American art circles in the two decades before 1940, but in a very different form, often involved with a romanticization of local heritages and with a materialist political vision. For example, the Mexican muralists—Rivera, Orozco, Siqueiros, et al.—had been much admired for their revivification of the myths and forms of the ancient civilizations of their land, and for their use of this heritage as a focus for national unity and social renewal. In the late 1930s, however, disaffection with this kind of populist archaizing followed a general disenchantment with the Marxism that fostered it (a political shift made most decisive by reaction to the Hitler-Stalin pact of 1939). By 1940, when The Museum of Modern Art celebrated the melding of archaic and modern in the exhibition "Twenty Centuries of Mexican Art," the heyday of the muralists had already passed. Their rhetorically simplified naturalism, even in its most expressionistic moments, came to seem inadequate to the search for more cosmic universals in the 1940s.[1] The new, emergent form of primitivism was more thoroughgoing in its embrace of Primitive myths and signs, as matters not of collective sociology but of universal psychology, revealing the foundations of the modern mind. Also, the earlier affection for Mexican archaism in art had been symptomatic of a desire to buffer the dominance of European modernism, by the assertion of local elements of style and iconography. In the new primitivism that appeared around 1940, the recurrent invocation of the "universal" signaled, among other things, a more assertive engagement with the challenge of the modern art of Europe.

Specifically, the upwellings of references to the Prehistoric, the Primitive, and the Archaic coincided with increased attention to the works of the European Surrealists; and the Americans looked to Primitive art with an appreciation strongly conditioned by forms found in the recent work of Picasso, Klee, Miró, Ernst, Masson, and Matta. Surrealism affected not only the look of the American artists' primitivism, but also their insistence on a spiritual identification of contemporary artistic ideals with the motivating forces behind the creativity of early man.

Painters such as Gottlieb, Rothko, and Newman were at

615

Adolph Gottlieb. *Pictograph*. 1942. Oil on canvas, 48 x 36" (121.9 x 91.4 cm). Adolph and Esther Gottlieb Foundation, Inc., New York

John Graham in his studio. 1938. At left, a Fang reliquary figure. Photograph. Allan Stone Gallery, New York

odds with the kind of abstract painting they felt had become, especially in America, decorative or formal in a trivial sense. In their tentative steps toward the formulation of their own abstract styles, they thus insisted heavily on their concern for content. Identification with the Primitive was a way of claiming for themselves a less arbitrary, timelessly valid, vocabulary of nonrepresentational form—providing their primitivism could at the same time be distanced from what seemed to them a too superficial, merely formal appropriation of tribal art by some European modernists. In a rhetoric that often covered their tracks while it proclaimed their ideals, they thus castigated modern abstraction in order to lay claim to a more profound relationship with the Primitive artist. Gottlieb typified this need for self-differentiation when he said in 1943: "While modern art got its first impetus through discovering the forms of primitive art, we feel that its true significance lies not merely in formal arrangement, but in the spiritual meaning underlying all archaic works."[2] Though this pronouncement characteristically omits their debt to European predecessors (to whom it wrongly attributes a purely formal concern), it nonetheless reflects these artists' genuinely felt need for an approach that would be concerned with myth and the religious or magic force of Primitive expression. Such a concentration on general spirit, beyond specific styles or forms, typified their desire for elemental bases of human experience that would transcend regionalist, nationalist, and other boundaries of art/political polemic.

Gottlieb's use of the term "archaic" is moreover symptomatic of the way in which these artists' remarks often melded preclassical with prehistoric, or Incan with Inuit, in a synthetic concept of the Primitive, stressing universal common denominators of psyche over differing styles of art. For him and for fellow American artists, the evidence of innumerable articles in periodicals such as *Cahiers d'art* and *Documents* demonstrated—even to those who could not read the French texts and only studied the illustrations—that the Surrealists, at least, were concerned not so much with tribal styles per se as with a broad-based understanding of the spirit and meaning of Primitive art. To this quasi-ethnological ethos, and to the Surrealist emphasis on the special virtues of the Primitive mentality as a model for the modern creator, the Americans responded positively.

In other respects, however, the Surrealist spirit was alien, and the Surrealists' ideas about the Primitive failed to satisfy the aspirations of men like Gottlieb, Newman, and Pollock. The Surrealists' interests in parallels between the Primitive mind and the modern unconscious were predominantly tied to a Freudian concern with the pathologies of the individual psyche. Freud was, of course, important to the American artists of the early forties as well. But the Americans frequently invoked a notion of archetypes more characteristically associated with the concept of a "collective unconscious" found in the writings of Jung—that is, a belief in innate "racial memory" that made the contemporary unconscious a repository of form-symbols dating from earliest human experience. These vaguely "Jungian" ideas were implicit in the general vocabulary of American artists' references to the unconscious and to Primitive art. They owed their propagation, though, more to studio talk, and to self-styled theoreticians such as John Graham, than to any close study of Jung's own writings.

Above: Jackson Pollock. *Guardians of the Secret.* 1943. Oil on canvas, 48⅜ x 75⅜" (122.9 x 191.5 cm). San Francisco Museum of Modern Art; Albert M. Bender Bequest Fund Purchase

Right: Mark Rothko. *Primeval Landscape.* 1945. Oil on canvas, 54⅜ x 35" (138.9 x 88.9 cm). Collection Peter G. Peterson

Graham, a Russian émigré with firsthand knowledge of advanced European art, was a prominent figure on the New York art scene of the twenties and thirties as a painter and idiosyncratic aesthetician. He also owned, wrote about, and sold tribal art. Advising New York collectors, and in contact with major dealers in Europe, he was instrumental in acquainting David Smith, Gottlieb, Pollock, and others with Primitive objects of quality and in giving these artists a framework of ideas regarding the function and context of Primitive art. He insisted on the close similarities between prehistoric arts of all races and areas, and asserted that African sculptural styles equaled and likely preceded the achievements of the great early European civilizations. Moreover, he specifically insisted that the culture which produced these sculptures was a refined one, dedicated to "the expansion of the unconscious mind."[3] In his theoretical tract *System and Dialectics of Art* (1937), Graham held that a prime purpose of modern art should also be the exploration of the unconscious, in order to revivify contact "with the primordial racial past." The text defined creation as "the production of new authentic values by delving into the memories of the immemorial past and expressing them in pure form..."[4]

Such broad rhetoric concerning the Primitive and the unconscious did not by the late thirties require (and indeed Graham did not insist upon) the specific support of Jungian

David Smith. *Jurassic Bird*. 1945. Steel, 25⅜ x 35¼ x 7½" (64.5 x 89.5 x 19.1 cm). Private collection

doctrine. Moreover, the never-total American divergence from prior Freudianism rested primarily not on a bookish disagreement over psychoanalytic theory, but on changes in general attitudes toward style and ethos, in life as well as art. The Freudian idea of the mind and a Marxist-materialist view of society gave many of the Surrealists (as Irving Sandler has noted) a combination of metaphysical skepticism and radical political ideals that ill suited the quasi-religious, fatalistic tenor of the new American interest in myth and archetype.[5] Furthermore, Freudianism in the hands of the Surrealists led to amoral high spirits, obsession with *amour fou*, and urbane punning, and thus seemed part of the sophisticated European style of life for which most of the less well-to-do American artists had an (inevitably somewhat jealous) antipathy. Jung's ideas carried with them a solemn spirituality with which the Americans felt more comfortable, and which they found more appropriate to the circumstances of the war years[6]

These differences in approach were part of the broader fashion in which the specific factors of the American situation, and the events of the war years, demarcated the new primitivism of the 1940s from its European precedents. Whatever its formal or spiritual ancestry in Europe, this new American primitivism was recognizably the child of its time and place, responding to specific, immediate pressures. At a

basic level the new "regression" offered strategic escape for American artists buffeted by a decade of debate between nationalism and internationalism, and by strident argument over the sociopolitical responsibilities of art. The world of caves and tepees offered a repertory of abstract forms whose scope of meaning, beyond its obvious rebuttal of the hated parochialism of the American regionalist schools, seemed to transcend or at least circumvent virtually all the politics of the day. Within this aura of the elemental, many of the debates of the thirties could be addressed on loftier levels, with recourse to philosophical absolutes and a scientizing appeal to ultimate natural truths.

The American artists who adopted primitivizing styles, or who defended their emergent abstract styles by appealing to Primitive precedents, sought for example to outmaneuver the long-standing stalemate between the "masses" and the "unconscious." These two terms had been, as an editorial of 1943 asserted, the artistic watchwords of the previous twenty years.[7] In the thirties, the seemingly unbridgeable gulf between modernist originality keyed to inspiration in the "unconscious," and public responsibility (an art devoted to and comprehensible by the "masses"), had prompted a nostalgia for Primitive societies in which the artist's practical functions made him integrally essential to communal well-being.[8] The rhetoric of the vanguard artists of the forties, however, stressed the spiritual and psychological power of Primitive art rather than its social efficacy, and insisted on the ahistorical links that joined the modern and Primitive artist, rather than the historical factors that separated them.[9] This emphasis on collective truths that were timeless/psychic rather than historical/social matched and supported claims for a new, "apolitical" artistic individuality.[10] The modern artist's unconscious was held to be a direct link to a living well of collective memory; and difficult, apparently noncommunicative modernist abstraction was argued to be the true embodiment of eternal communal verities. By appeal to Primitive precedents, modernist individualism was thus defended as recovering a universality beyond matters of class or nation. Writing on the native-American art of the Northwest Coast in 1946, Barnett Newman argued: "There is an answer in these works to all those who assume that modern abstract art is the esoteric exercise of a snobbish elite, for among these simple peoples, abstract art was the normal, well-understood dominant tradition. Shall we say that modern man has lost the ability to think on so high a level?"[11]

Though Primitive forms had these qualities of seeming timelessness, many of the same artists saw them as especially appropriate for the historical moment of the 1940s. With the spread of fascism and the onset of global war, the modern world seemed to be marked on the one hand by the virulent resurgence of human irrationality, and on the other by new conditions of mechanized and (later) atomic terror that put twentieth-century man in a state of abject vulnerability analogous to that of precivilized man. It was argued that only an art based in deepest instinctual life, and concerned with emotions of primal distress, could provide appropriate expression for the age. Adolph Gottlieb put it thus:

If we profess kinship to the art of primitive man, it is because the feelings they expressed have a particular pertinence today. In times of violence, personal predilections for niceties of color and form seem irrelevant. All primitive expression reveals the constant awareness of powerful forces, the immediate presence of terror and fear, a recognition of the terror of the animal world as well as the eternal insecurities of life. That these feelings are being experienced by many people throughout the world today is an unfortunate fact and to us an art that glosses over or evades these feelings is superficial and meaningless.[12]

Such statements reveal a truth about the forties, embedded in a falsehood about the Primitive; for in affirming how the present resembles the prehistoric past, Gottlieb fabricated a past in the image of the present. His vision of affinity with the Primitive involves a common though erroneous projection of modern angst backward into the soul of early man (as discussed on pp. 35–38). In a corollary, more succinct statement, he added: "Today when our aspirations have been reduced to a desperate attempt to escape from evil, and times are out of joint, our obsessive, subterranean and pictographic images are the expression of the neurosis which is our reality."[13] Not only the sentiments, but also the language itself—geological, philological, and psychological in the same breath—typify the tone of the new primitivism.

In its earnestly solemn reaction against the flamboyant Freudianism of Surrealism, this tone might be criticized as evidencing not simply wartime concerns, but also—in conjunction with the corollary depoliticization—a provincial conservatism. Yet these attitudes had progressive consequences in art practice. The earnest rejection of Surrealist sophistication went hand in glove with a distaste for the polished finesse of technique evident in that side of Surrealism represented by Salvador Dali. This attitude gave a special impetus to the Americans' primitivist tendencies, and made

Robert Motherwell. *Indians*. 1944. Ink. Whereabouts unknown

Mark Tobey. *Eskimo Idiom.* 1946. Tempera on board, 43½ x 27¾" (110.5 x 70.5 cm). Seattle Art Museum; gift of Mr. and Mrs. Sam Rubinstein

them receptive to the influence of the rougher, more gestural aspects of the work of artists such as Picasso and Miró. While the Americans imposed a portentous and epic emotional tone, without a relieving playfulness or sensuous allure, they also sought an art that was raw and vital, free from "civilized" concerns for polished craftsmanship. In such a climate, the sense of inferiority previously felt by many American artists vis-a-vis Europe's achievements could be transmuted into rhetorical declarations of the positive virtues of the youthful "barbarism" of the Americas. Analyzing (and overgeneralizing) the ostensible limitations of European sensibility, Newman wrote in 1948: "Everything [there] is so highly civilized. The artist in America is, by comparison, like a barbarian. He does not have the super-fine sensibility toward the object that dominates European feeling. He does not even have the objects. This then is our opportunity, free of the ancient

paraphernalia, to come closer to the sources of the tragic emotion. Shall we not, as artists, search out the new objects for its image?"[14]

Seeking these "new objects," the new American primitivism further differentiated itself from antecedents in Europe in terms of sources of inspiration. Reviewing the evidence of the 1940s (in statements, articles, and titles, as well as in the works themselves), one is struck by the prominence of references to the art of the Americas, either in the tribal legacies of the Eskimos and Northwest Coast or American Indians or (to a lesser extent) in the great lost empires of Central and South America. With Europe cast into potentially permanent cultural eclipse by wartime chaos, there seemed to be a special impetus to locate other roots for a new beginning. Particular value resided in cultures untainted by association with the bankruptcy that seemed to have befallen Europe, and in forms

Mask. Eskimo. Alaska. Painted wood, 39" (99 cm) high. Collection George Terasaki, New York

that were independent of those Primitive sources (notably African) that had already been annexed to Europe's art.

In the 1930s, regionalists and Marxists alike had shared the credo that "only an autochthonous mythology, a mythology coming from the same soil, the same people," could be an effective basis for a responsible art.[15] With the advent of war and the heightened prestige of a psychologically based notion of art's creation and effect, such ideals were co-opted for a new blend of native-American admirations and modernist individualism. They were subsumed within the general notion that only by the deepest immersion in the local—one's own nation as well as one's own unconscious—could the elements of a truly universal art be found.[16] Ironically, this new American self-reliance literally "brought home" the roots of traditional European primitivist thought, which had been most intensively grounded—from Montaigne up to the discovery of

Polynesia in 1767—in an admiration for the newfound peoples of the Americas. Moreover, in these "new" and "native" emphases, the American artists were once again preceded by the Surrealists. André Breton, Max Ernst, and others had not only diverged from the Cubists' original focus on Africa in favor of attention to the South Seas, but had also been intensely enthusiastic about Northwest Coast and Eskimo art—long before it came to be fashionable among New York artists.

Like many aspects of the primitivism of the 1940s, the native-American "influence" existed more broadly on a conceptual level, in the artists' words, than in specific formal terms in their paintings and sculptures. Before it became a fully assimilated and fruitful impetus in the work of a few major artists, primi-

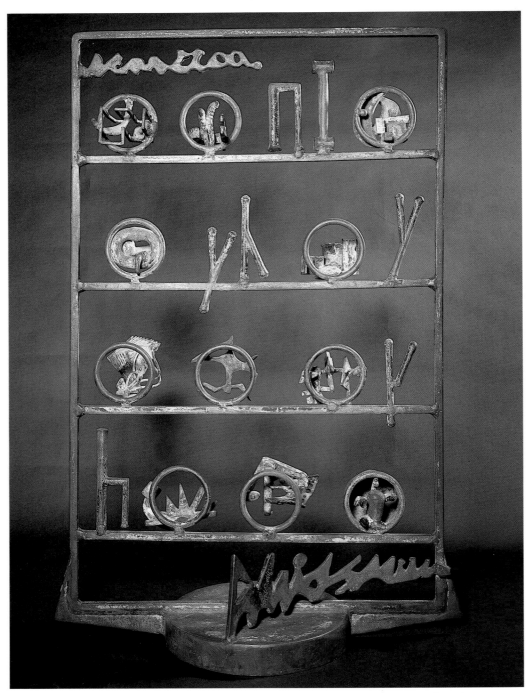

David Smith. *The Letter*. 1950. Welded steel, 37⅝" (95.6 cm) high x 11" (28 cm) diameter. Munson-Williams-Proctor Institute, Utica, N.Y.

tivism enjoyed several years of vogue in the mid-forties as a rationale and as a general "look"; it satisfied a wide range of needs, often relatively superficial, among artists of diverse talents and aims. In this general milieu, purely artistic concerns were often less important than secondary strategic advantages, in fostering the native-American emphasis.

As a foremost pragmatic advantage, indigenous cultures provided a heritage within which an American artist's desire to differentiate himself from European art could assert itself without risking association with the stifling regionalism of the 1930s. In this respect the 1940s witnessed not only a departure from immediate European precedents but also a transformed resurgence of a long-standing vein of American primitivist thought. Since World War I, modernism in American liter-

ature and the arts had recurrently intertwined with a celebration of native-American culture—a vanguard's ironic ancestral identification with the peoples that had been made the outsiders and victims of the nation's founding. The antiestablishment bridge between the "vanishing race," rooted in the land, and the avant-garde, bearer of the new spirit, had already been constructed before 1940, in the works of artists as diverse as Marsden Hartley, John Storrs, and George L. K. Morris (as Gail Levin observes in an earlier chapter of this book). Perhaps the most evident locale for a junction of internationalist-progressive and indigenous-American tendencies was the colony of artists and intellectuals in Taos, New Mexico. The dances created by Martha Graham in the 1930s, evoking the special mixture of tribal and colonial-Christian mysticism in

Headdress. Senufo. Ivory Coast. Wood, 57⅞" (142 cm) high. Museum für Völkerkunde, Berlin

the Southwest (e.g., *Primitive Mysteries,* 1931), linked this particular primitivist tradition to emerging developments in the visual arts in New York. Graham's career intertwined with the new primitivism not only in the darkly "archaic" Jungian/ mythic tenor of her choreography of the forties, and in certain of the sets Noguchi did for her (e.g., *Cave of the Heart,* 1946), but in the whole pattern of her confrontation throughout the thirties and forties with the conflicting demands of topicality and timelessness, internationalist modernism and the desire for roots in authentic, deeply personal experience.[18] Such issues, though characteristically masked in appeals to tribal lore and ancient myth, constituted a significant substructure of the primitivizing trends of the forties.

Obviously there are vast differences between the Aztecs and the Iroquois, between the ancient empires of Central and South America to which the Mexican muralists had looked for inspiration and the tribal societies of North America. In the context of American artistic primitivism of the 1940s, however, these diverse cultures had some common points of appeal. When the American artists sought an art to evoke the elemental truths they shared with immemorial ancestors, several factors favored the indigenous cultures, and not the least of these was racial. For the European nations, who had (despite their colonial policies) never developed internally an African slave population, "art nègre" lacked a problematic social aspect that it obviously possessed in the United States. Europeans, remote from both Africans and American blacks, tended to elide the two cultures. The fortunes of Africanizing

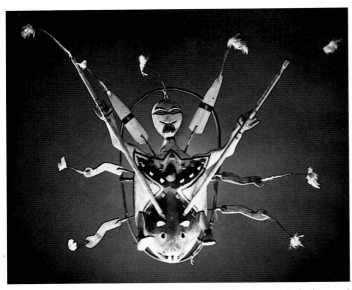

Mask. Eskimo. Kuskokwim River, Alaska. Painted wood, walrus tooth, feathers, and fiber, 35⅞" (91 cm) high. Hamburgisches Museum für Völkerkunde. Reproduced in color, page 576

David Smith. *Royal Incubator.* 1949. Steel, bronze, and silver, 37 x 38¾ x 9⅞" (94 x 97.5 x 25.1 cm). Collection Mr. and Mrs. Bagley Wright

primitivism in Europe had thus become associated with the chic of Negro blues and jazz (Josephine Baker et al.) in a fashion that was not exportable to pre–World War II America. Even though artists such as Gottlieb owned and admired African objects, it would have been quite a different matter for white painters in New York in 1940—as opposed to Picasso or Modigliani in Paris decades before—to evoke an ancestral linkage between their innovations and the art of Africa. While many American artists insistently called up general Primitive precedents as validation for their work, a specific linkage—via overt African sources—between an already beleaguered modernist minority and the far more seriously oppressed and populous black culture would have brushed too close to the specific social engagement that most of the artists were busy expunging from their art. Native Americans, constituting a

smaller and more comfortably folkloric social presence, were more easily available to Caucasian artists for annexation as an ancestral source.

American primitivism fed on a knowledgeable idealization of Primitive cultures, abandoning both the sense of raw wonder with which earlier European modernists first approached tribal art, and the shadowy glamour that had attended the more trivial primitivism of the 1920s. The associations of dark ferocity and libidinous indulgence long mistakenly attached to many "fétiches" of "art nègre" were displaced by a new, synthetic ideal of the Primitive, more readily applicable to those societies whose mythological and social structures were better-known locally. Gottlieb said: "That these demonic and brutal images fascinate us today is not because they are exotic, nor do they make us nostalgic for a past which seems enchanting because of its remoteness. On the contrary, it is the immediacy of their images that draws us irresistibly to the fancies and superstitions, the fables of savages and the strange beliefs that were so vividly articulated by primitive man."[19] (Ironically, "demonic" and "brutal" tend to reaffirm the old misreading of tribal art as expressionistic, even as the sentence denies the continued relevance of that appeal.) Such self-advertisements of a new seriousness should not be taken to mean that the artists of the forties became assiduous anthropologists; in fact the American artists were as a rule far less well-informed on anthropological matters than were Surrealist predecessors such as Ernst. The statement does point, though, to the more evident context of conscious mythological "packaging" that surrounded, and increasingly displaced, their concern for specific Primitive objects.

This emphasis on a more dispassionate awareness of the myths and practices surrounding tribal art reflects a transformation we have already observed at work on the American scene in these years. Again, the premises of a Marxist approach to art in the 1920s and 1930s laid the bases for the more antimaterialist approaches of the 1940s: in this case, a prior insistence on understanding all human productions in terms of their specific social contexts was transmuted into a "spiritual contextualism" centered on systems of belief rather than on economics. (This shift might interestingly be compared to the parallel changes, in these same years, in the styles of "contextual" and "aesthetic" display of Primitive objects by museums and galleries.)[20] Such an emphasis favored the native-American cultures, for their patterns of ceremony and cosmology were readily available in popular lore as well as in ethnological literature and provided the constant framework for appreciation of their art. Whether from the Primitive tribes of North America or the Archaic court cultures of Mesoamerica, indigenous art was associated with a ceremonial dignity, and with mythologies regarding the interreaction of man and cosmos, in a way that made it especially appealing to a new generation of primitivizing artists[21]

African art was less attractive to American artists of the forties, not just on sociopolitical grounds or because its mythologies were more obscure, but also in terms of its formal lessons. With its analytic opening-up of the plasticity of the human form (and either neutral or flatly simplified color), African sculpture had been crucially impressive to earlier modernists concerned with a Cézanne-derived faceting of volume and with the interlock of body and space. As William Rubin stresses (pp. 41, 55–58), the Surrealist generation had engendered a shift in emphasis toward a new appreciation of the more painterly, and seemingly more imaginative, aspects of South Seas art. Primitivizing American painters of the forties, however, were seeking definitive departures from figuration. They were inclined either to avoid the sculptural presence of the human body altogether, in favor of a more landscapelike space, or to substitute zoomorphic and other more abstract pseudobiological organisms in its place. The emblematic simplicity of native-American designs appealed to their concern for isolated, archetypal images. Moreover, the New York School painters' investigations into new possibilities inherent in the format and surface of a painting—notably in regard to allover activation of the pictorial field—led them toward two-dimensional rather than sculptural models. For these artists, the mural format of prehistoric and bushman wall drawings and the patterning of native-American textiles and totems were more immediately intriguing than African figures. Jackson Pollock said in 1944: "I have always been very impressed with the plastic qualities of American Indian art. The Indians have the true painter's approach in their capacity to get hold of appropriate images, and in their understanding of what constitutes painterly subject-matter. Their color is essentially Western, their vision has the basic universality of all real art."[22] Mark Tobey also paid explicit homage to the native-American heritage, in works such as *Eskimo Idiom* of 1946 (p. 620), which splays flat the layered complexities of Eskimo masks (p. 621) that combine faces and bodies, men and animals in ingenious systems of closure and disclosure. Tobey's *Drums, Indians, and the Word of God* of 1944—directly influenced by Northwest Coast objects in his own collection (p. 629)—typifies not only the interest in the patterned design of native Americans, but also the association between their art and matters of spirituality and ceremony.

Even in sculpture, artists like David Smith tended away from the articulated monolith and toward an open "drawing in space" less compatible with the more familiar African form-types. Only rarer types such as the helmet crests of the Senufo (which were available in New York by the 1940s, and which the artist could possibly have seen) bear affinities with the strongly pictorial nature of works such as Smith's *The Letter* (pp. 622, 623). Eskimo masks, however, showed a formal dispersal of parts and an incorporation of space that could have been attractive to the maker of *Royal Incubator* of 1949. Louise Bourgeois seems to have been exceptional, at least in works such as *Pregnant Woman* of the late 1940s (p. 631), in producing sculpture with affinities to African forms. Smith, and other artists such as Frederick Kiesler, saw the "stacking" principle of the Northwest Coast totem as a stronger model for assembled sculpture that would have the partly human but not traditionally figurative presence of the Surrealist *personnage*—as in Kiesler's *Totem for All Religions* of 1947. Isamu Noguchi drew on an even broader range of the native-American legacy. As did Barnett Newman, Noguchi admired Indian earthworks such as those of the mound-building peoples of Ohio and the Mississippi Valley (p. 626). They apparently figured among the inspirations for his landscape/sculpture projects, such as *Contoured Playground* of 1941 (p. 626) and *Monument to the Plow. This Tortured Earth* of 1943 (p. 627), though most directly inspired by an aerial photo of war damage in Africa, also reflects the study of the Indian mounds. Noguchi's response to the Indian earthworks typifies

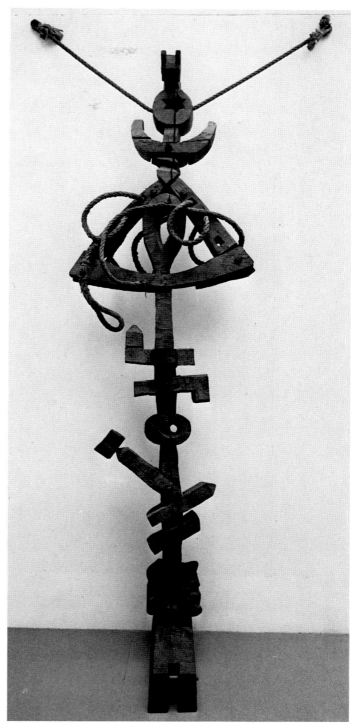

Frederick J. Kiesler. *Totem for All Religions.* 1947. Wood and rope, 9'4¼" x 34⅛" x 30⅞" (285.1 x 86.6 x 78.4 cm); upper rope extensions: left, 34¼" (87 cm), and right, 33¼" (84.4 cm). The Museum of Modern Art, New York; gift of Mr. and Mrs. Armand P. Bartos

the intertwining of artistic primitivism and scientizing natural-history interests among the progressive artists of his generation; for this response blends his nostalgia/respect for the communal art labor of earlier societies with a geological fascination regarding the timeless natural artistry of erosion.[23] Moreover, in the embrace of tribal earth monuments as antidotes to both the sterility of modern memorials and the depletion of art's power by gallery commerce, Noguchi's primitivism of the thirties and forties also anticipates the concerns of the earthworks artists of the 1970s.

All these references to native-American art did not, how-

Isamu Noguchi. *Contoured Playground.* 1941. Plaster, 3 x 26 x 26" (7.6 x 66 x 66 cm). Collection Isamu Noguchi Foundation, Inc., New York

The Great Serpent Mound, Adams County, Ohio. c. 20 x 5 x 737' (6 x 1.5 x 225 m)

Isamu Noguchi. *This Tortured Earth*. 1943. Bronze, 28 x 28 x 4" (71.1 x 71.1 x 10.2 cm). Collection Isamu Noguchi Foundation, Inc., New York

ever, add up to a specific stylistic "influence." The spirit of the new primitivism was one of synthesis, and it sought out elemental forms of quasi-anonymous archetypal universality—banishing in the process the culture-specific inflections that had often accompanied earlier primitivizing art (such as Marsden Hartley's "Indian" style, p. 452). Given their stated aims of shedding inherited conventions, these painters looked to Primitive art not primarily as a repertory of style, but as evidence of form-giving energies that superseded aesthetic consideration. In their initial primitivizing works, the American artists made more direct iconographic reference to Primitive lore and signs; but such references steadily gave way to a stronger concern with artistic process, in which the spirit of the Primitive was translated into modern creation in ways both less specific and more profound.

Though the vanguard American artists of the forties may at the outset have occasionally borrowed formal devices or signs from tribal arts, ultimately their primitivism was an ethos of elimination, an impetus to sweeping away all received inflections of style. Their search was for configurations with an air of inevitability that belonged to the forms of natural history and elemental communication more than to the realm of aesthetics. Accordingly the inspirations they drew from the forms of Primitive art were often assimilated, along with other sources in the domains of linguistic signs and the natural sciences, into images with broad, culturally nonspecific overtones of the atavistic. Frequently these images suggest a

metaphor of the geological and/or the archaeological—the simultaneous exhuming of deep strata of both biological and spiritual existence, where the ultimate pressures of necessity, rather than any culturally determined conceits, were the shapers of form. The catalog text for a Gottlieb exhibition of 1947 chose its terms of praise appropriately: "The fragments which he has unearthed in his excavations of our common underworld—an underworld which unites Mayan, Oceanic, Paleolithic and Atomic man—he has synthesized into a powerful and remarkable signature."[24]

This archaeological metaphor in the primitivizing art of the 1940s divides into two complementary lineages. On the one hand, a variety of imagery evokes genetic beginnings, prehistoric forms of evolutionary growth or destruction, and cellular-level biology. Rothko's work from 1940 to 1946 is the prime example (e.g., *Ritual*, 1944, *Slow Swirl by the Edge of the Sea*, 1944, p. 628, and numerous untitled paintings and watercolors), but Newman's initial seed/amoeba drawings and paintings of 1944–45 are equally apt (e.g., *Gea*, 1945), and the references to fossil creatures and geological stratigraphy in the works of David Smith, Theodoros Stamos, and William Baziotes are just as certainly bound to natural history.[25] On the other hand, and occasionally overlapping, one finds a repertory of cipher-forms and schematic picture-signs that evoke unknown alphabets, original geometry, and primitive methods of writing. Gottlieb's Pictographs and David Smith's *The Letter* are prominent instances. There are also evocations of cavewriting in Pollock's painting (e.g., *Wounded Animal*, 1943, p. 643, and *Guardians of the Secret*, 1943), as well as an evident

Mark Rothko. *Slow Swirl by the Edge of the Sea.* 1944. Oil on canvas, 75⅜ x 84¾" (191.4 x 215.2 cm). The Museum of Modern Art, New York; bequest of Mrs. Mark Rothko

fascination with calligraphic signs in Smith's drawings, in the later work of Gottlieb, and in the paintings of Franz Kline and Mark Tobey.

An idea central to the primitivist "regressions" of the 1940s would seem to be the rapprochement of these two kinds of form—the primal sign inscribed upon the surface and the natural record embedded in the earth—as a metaphoric reunion of the human mind with the processes of nature. Such imagery or metaphor is neither secondary to nor dissociated from the more obvious talk of Primitive art that accompanied it. Probing for the fundaments of man's modes of representation and their connections to natural law was central to the whole endeavor of advanced American art in the forties. And it is here, in the imagery rather than in the rhetoric, and on this deeper level of meanings, that the new American primitivism connected most forcefully to a larger set of issues. Here it reaches beyond its roots in Surrealism, and beyond the particular pragmatic or political concerns of its own day, to attach itself most significantly to basic currents ongoing in modernist primitivism since Gauguin, and to the larger issues of primitivism as a pursuit of Western artists and intellectuals since the eighteenth century.

In immediate terms, the reunion of the mind and nature at

the level of ultimate beginnings was an ideal that found support in ethnological theories of the Primitive mentality, familiar to the Surrealists and broadly influential between the two World Wars. The French anthropologist Lévy-Bruhl had early in the century described the mind of the "savage" as lacking the systems of clear distinction that characterized the logical thought of civilized man.[26] This view would later be refuted by Lévi-Strauss's insistence on the logical structure of Primitive thought, opposed but equal to the rationality of Western science (see my discussion of this shift in the idea of the Primitive, in the final chapter of this book); but before the 1950s it was a notion widely held, and ascribed to by Jung and numerous other writers on anthropology. In Lévy-Bruhl's account, Primitive man experienced the world in a less divided fashion. For him the boundaries between the animate and the inanimate, between animals, plants, and men, were permeable and freely crossed. This state of "participation," where meaning and form were bonded involuntarily and without hindrance, presented for the modern artist a dream of escape from the alienating effects of rationality. In praising Stamos's work in 1947, Barnett Newman argued that the modern artist, too, had transcended the attitude of "sensibility" that had set man apart from nature, isolating him and

Totem pole. Haida. British Columbia. Painted wood, 43⅝" (110.8 cm) high. Private collection. Formerly collection MARK TOBEY

Mark Tobey. *Drums, Indians, and the Word of God.* 1944. Tempera on wood, 18½ x 13⅞" (47 x 35.2 cm). Whereabouts unknown

making nature only an object of contemplation. Speaking of paintings such as Stamos's *Sounds in the Rock* of 1946 (p. 614), he said that they "reveal an attitude towards nature that is closer to true communion. His ideographs capture the moment of totemic affinity with the rock and the mushroom...In this Stamos is on the same fundamental ground as the primitive artist who...portrayed the phenomenon... always as an expression of the original noumenistic mystery in which rock and man are equal."[27]

Inevitably such claims bring to mind Jackson Pollock's famous dismissal of the question of working from nature: "I am nature." William Rubin has rightly associated this bravado remark (which echoes in the words of other artists of Pollock's generation) with a Romantic tradition of the natural or naive poet,[28] a tradition long joined to a primitivist spirit in literary and philosophical domains. This connection in turn opens the way for us to see the deeper linkages of the ideals of the American artists of the forties, not just to Lévy-Bruhl and Jung, but to the core historical issues of Western primitivism.

The triadic association between "untutored" forms of expression, the innermost sources of creation, and the basic forces of nature is a constellation going back at least to the writings of Herder. The dovetailing by artists of the forties of simultaneous interests in prehistoric writing, scientizing natural history, and tribal art is another formulation of this recurrent nexus. In this view, Primitive arts—the unselfconscious poetry of tribal song, or the configurations of the bushman's design—are seen as shaped by a suprapersonal emotional/ psychological necessity, and as destined for an integral role in collective life. Their forms are thus identified with the dream, central to modern nonrepresentational art, of universal signs: representations simultaneously cultural (of the human mind, not slavishly imitative of nature's appearances) and natural (linked directly to universal meanings in a way that escapes contingency). Such signs would rise from and address levels of consciousness at which the problematic barriers between body and mind, between self and society, between the laws of nature and the productions of men, are permeable if not dissolved. Primitivism has thus been recurrently joined, throughout its existence as a mode of Western thought, with speculation on the origins of language and the nature of signs, and with the search for an absolute or "natural" art in harmony with immutable, universal forms of meaning. (See further discussion of this issue, pp. 192, 208.)

This will toward the intermingling of cultural and natural fundaments is manifest in the 1940s not only in the widespread

Adolph Gottlieb. *Pictograph-Symbol*. 1942. Oil on canvas, 54 x 40" (137.1 x 101.6 cm). Private collection, New York

fascination with ancient alphabets and fossils, but also in the interplay between titles and images—notably in the work of Rothko, where images born from the union of Surrealist fantasy and microscopic biology were baptized with titles evocative of Greek mythology (*Sacrifice of Iphigenia*, 1942), Christian mysteries (*Gethsemane*, 1945), and Jewish demonology (*Rites of Lilith*, 1945). To his thinly brushed, delicately billowing forms, Rothko thus attached associations of intense traditional gravity; and the great themes of human thought were linked to the deepest moments of natural generation. Rothko's dramatic redirection of his art away from the contemporary social scene (e.g., his series of New York subway scenes) to such a fusion of the epic and the elemental appears to have had little to do with inspiration from non-Western art, and a good deal to do with formal models in André Masson or still earlier in Odilon Redon, and in the science he learned at Yale.[29] Yet this shift from the proletarian to the protozoic traveled under the rhetoric and apparent spiritual guidance of an ideal of the Primitive. Rothko spoke with envy of the "archaic" artist's privilege of living in a society where transcendent art could find its expression in communally valid hybrids of human and animal form. The modern artist's task was to create equivalents for these "monsters and gods" in new forms, free from any residual association with familiar things.[30]

Various scholars have found among the shapes of Rothko's works of the mid-1940s suggestions of native-American sand paintings, or of costumes and implements of Primitive ritual.[31] His art seems a prime example, however, of the ways in which Primitivism operated in the art of the 1940s on levels that lay beyond whatever specific stylistic influences appeared, and in domains of meaning rarely touched on in direct primitivizing rhetoric. Without citing Jung directly, Rothko argued for a timeless validity of art derived from the unconscious.[32] Moreover, the aqueous character of pictures such as *Slow Swirl by the Edge of the Sea* (p. 628) and *Figure in Archaic Sea* may be in harmony with Jung's observation that "water is the commonest symbol for the unconscious."[33] The delicate ciliated organisms that hover in these canvases use the fragile yet irresistible stirrings of primal evolution as equivalents for the generative power of the most basic levels of consciousness. They move vertically across banded strata that define breached horizons between rootedness and ascension, potential and blossoming, preconscious thought and higher development. Typically, the cutaway vision of these images emphasizes continuity above and below such divisions, and the organic integrity of a transformation that binds diverse forms to a single driving energy. These shapes were, Rothko said, "organisms with volition and a passion for self-assertion," his modern equivalents for the "monsters and gods" without which "art cannot enact our drama."[34] Suggested here are metaphors for thought, for the primal archetypes Rothko felt should guide his work, emerging from the depths of consciousness with indeterminate potential yet with a preordained, "natural" inner impulse to self-definition. "Our unconscious mind," John Graham had written at the end of the thirties, "contains the record of all our past experiences individual and racial, from the first cell germination..."[35]

Adolph Gottlieb shared Rothko's concern for myth and his sense of identification with the Primitive; the two painters' interests in common are suggested by the related titles of their works of the period 1943–45. Yet the form in which Gottlieb chose to express these interests is sharply different. Where Rothko's regression conjured a primitive state of fluid biotic metamorphosis, Gottlieb's yielded, in his Pictographs of 1941–51 (pp. 616, 633), a field of linguistic fragments, a kind of primal printer's type-tray of sign imagery. The sources for these linear scaffoldings and schematic signs are diverse. Though we may well disagree, the artist himself insisted that the compartmentalization of Christian narratives in early Renaissance predella paintings and fresco cycles were more important sources than the precedents he could have seen (already transformed from prior sources in Primitive scripts and textiles) in the art of Paul Klee (p. 496) and Joaquin Torres-García.[36] In any event, modern European artistic models informed the style as certainly as did the resembling

Louise Bourgeois. *Pregnant Woman.* c. 1947–49. Painted wood and plaster, 52⅜ x 7¼ x 9⅝" (133 x 18.5 x 24.5 cm). Collection A. M. B.

Blanket. Tlingit. Alaska. Dyed wool and cedar-bark fibers, 69" (175.2 cm) high. Collection Esther Gottlieb, New York. Formerly collection ADOLPH GOTTLIEB

structure in the Tlingit blankets of the Northwest Coast Indians. Yet, when Gottlieb exhibited a Pictograph for the first time (*Pictograph–Symbol*, shown in a group show of 1942; p. 630), critics immediately asserted an Indian, and specifically a Northwest Coast, origin for the design.[37] Though Gottlieb had indeed been attracted to American Indian art well before this (at least as early as 1937, when he admired the display of the State Museum in Tucson, Arizona), he did not acquire his own Tlingit blanket until after these initial reviews.[38] Its presence in his collection may have informed the structure of some of the artist's subsequent works, such as *Night Forms* of c. 1949–50.

The primitivist interests of the Pictographs, however, go beyond such matters of specific style to general matters of substance, concerning the structure of the deepest levels of the human mind as revealed in the earliest forms of writing. Gottlieb attempted to associate his work with an early period in the evolution of human signs, when the nugget elements of communication have yet to be yoked under a conventional grammar and maintain a raw independence—units of thought originating in nature and cohering as new meaning only in the

prelogical mind. The titles of the Pictographs, such as *Eyes of Oedipus*, explicitly associate this notion of early language formation with the central myths of the Western tradition, in a manner that parallels the tenets of contemporary publications by the philosopher Ernst Cassirer. Cassirer's work of the 1940s, such as the essay *Language and Myth*, investigated the origins of religious thought and of language as linked phenomena, and further asserted, in a fashion highly congenial to the expressed sentiments of the New York painters, that "art, like language, is originally bound up entirely with myth. Myth, language and art begin as a concrete, undivided unity, which is only gradually resolved into a triad of independent modes of spiritual creativity."[39]

The basic attraction to the structures of Primitive writing is at least as old as modernist primitivism itself, stretching back to Gauguin's fascination with and use of the Rongorongo symbols of Easter Island (p. 189). Of more immediate relevance to Gottlieb and his generation, however, were the numerous works of Joan Miró and Paul Klee that manifested a deep interest in prehistoric pictograms for their apparent fusion of representation and writing.[40] The essentially Cubist

Adolph Gottlieb. *Night Forms.* c. 1949–50. Mixed media on masonite, 24 x 30" (60 x 76 cm). Adolph and Esther Gottlieb Foundation, Inc., New York

compartmentalization and fragmentation of the Pictographs is more particular to Gottlieb, however. Gottlieb's Pictographs insist on a prominently divided field of signs in a way that rejects the cursiveness of automatist "writing" and evokes not the spontaneous eruption of a deep-level flow of consciousness, but a primal ordering impulse and the Primitive mind's ability to hold its elements of meaning in suspension rather than dissolve them in seamless flux. The insistence on an overall grid in Gottlieb's "language" also differentiates his formal interests from those of Miró and Klee, with their concern for open-field patterns of marking. "Like those early painters who placed their images on the grounds of rectangular components," he said in 1944, "I juxtaposed my pictographic images, each self-contained within the painter's rectangle, to be ultimately fused within the mind of the beholder."[41] This arrangement was intended to de-center and disperse the viewer's response in a fashion that Gottlieb found commensurate with the spirit of the earliest, most basic forms of perception and self-expression. "When I say I am reaching for a totality of vision," he said, "I mean that I take things I know—hand, nose, arm—and use them in my paintings after

separating them from their associations or anatomy. I use them as a totality of what they mean to me. It's a primitive method, and a primitive necessity of expressing, without learning how to do so by conventional ways....It puts us at the beginning of seeing."[42] As this latter statement testifies, Gottlieb sought to use the deep past to achieve a greater immediacy of experience in his art, moving through borrowed symbols of the Primitive toward basic strata of human perception. But in his work, and especially in the Pictographs, the allegiance to acquired formats and overtly primitivizing form seems to have impeded rather than encouraged arrival at "the beginning of seeing" and the establishment of a powerfully original abstract style. Indeed, for all the persuasiveness of his comments on Primitive art, Gottlieb seems to embody a rule of paradox broadly applicable in American art of his time: the more evident and conscious the pictorial attention to Primitive forms, the less ultimately successful the work became. Only when he had subsumed the primitivizing impulse more deeply into his work, in the later 1940s, did the Pictographs reach their highest level of achievement.

Though more evidently tied to automatist biomorphism,

Rothko paralleled Gottlieb in diverging from his Surrealist sources. He strongly modified the corporeal and visceral references of Surrealist and Picassoid imagery, in favor of a more complete break with the visible and sensual world—a regression to a subhuman realm that has closer affinities with the (microscopically inspired) world of Redon, and particularly with the photographic and diagrammatic imagery of biological science.[43] This avoidance of anatomical referents paralleled the rejection of the Freudian bent of Surrealism; it emptied out suggestions of the sexual-pathological or oneiric for more neutral, universal connotations of organic life.

Despite these parallels, there is an implied argument in the differing imagery of Rothko and Gottlieb—between an idea of organic consciousness rooted in the earliest germination and thus essentially sensual and seamless, and an idea of thought's dependence on a primal separation and rearrangement of experience into a constructed edifice of language. It should not be surprising, then, that while Gottlieb's art continued to depend to some degree on cognitive references (e.g., reduced signs for landscape space, calligraphy), Rothko's work evolved toward a virtual annulment of form-reference and more purified appeal to sensory experience—thus moving beyond a primitivizing look, and assimilating the notion of a "primitive" reduction to more basic levels of visual experience, in more decisive and fruitful fashion. The contrast between their works of the mid-forties is, however, more than just a matter of their own talents and temperaments. Essentially the same confrontation of opposing "natural" and "mental" fundaments occurs within the early imagery of the artist who joined with Rothko and Gottlieb in their famous letter to the *New York Times* of 1943,[44] Barnett Newman.

Somewhat paradoxically, Barnett Newman is central to an understanding of primitivism in the New York School—paradoxically, for while he was the most articulate, knowledgeable, and prolific spokesman for the new attention to Primitive art, he did not actually begin painting until rather

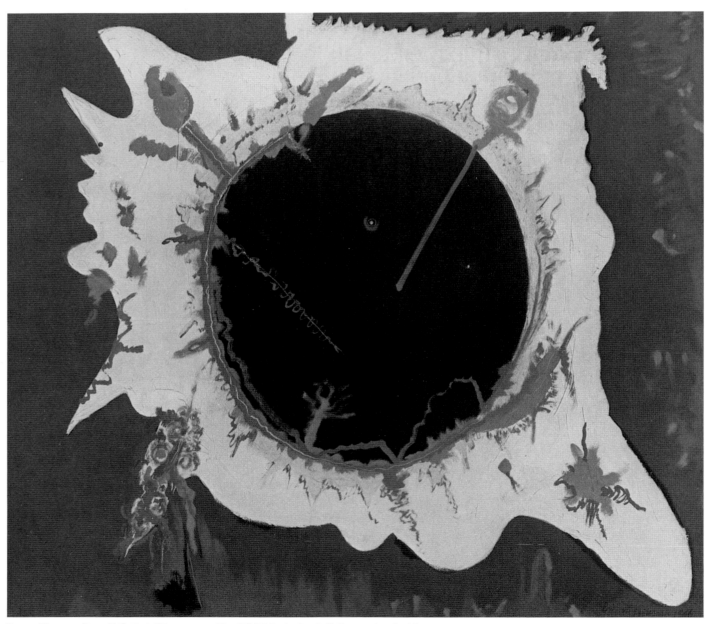

Barnett Newman. *Pagan Void.* 1946. Oil on canvas, 33 x 38" (83.8 x 96.5 cm). Collection Annalee Newman

late (c. 1945–46), and his own painting and sculpture show no overt connection with any Primitive style, tribal or pre-historic. He spoke often, and with great admiration, of such tribal artists as the native-American mound-builders. As an ardent propagandist, he wrote several essays and man-ifestolike statements that used the evidence of Primitive art as a validating defense for new abstraction; and, more specifi-cally than others of his generation, he hewed closely to a precise and informed appreciation of tribal styles. Yet primi-tivism functioned in his early work (1945–47) not as a set of references to specific tribal art, but only as a generalized evocation of the primordial, suggestive of the techniques and style of Max Ernst (e.g., *Genetic Moment*) and in general iconographic terms, as a confrontation between basic emblematic signs of the genetic and the geometric (e.g., *Euclidian Abyss*). After 1947 a "primitive" element in his work could only be identified in broad conceptual terms, as an ethos of reductive purification.[45] The case of Newman thus raises pointedly a set of issues that have been implicit in everything we have been discussing regarding Gottlieb, Rothko, and others: issues of the gap between words and work in American primitivism, and of the various levels at which primitivism operated in the forties: as formal quotation, as synthetic metaphor, and finally as invisible, assimilated ideal.

Along with floating linear signs that recall Rothko's gos-samer organisms, Newman's early drawings and paintings (c. 1945–46) show kernel or seed forms, emblems of enclosed potential (e.g., *Gea*, 1945); later these erupt into more

Barnett Newman. *Euclidian Abyss*. 1946–47. Oil and gouache on canvas board, 28 x 22" (71.1 x 55.9 cm). Collection Mr. and Mrs. Burton Tremaine, Meriden, Conn.

Barnett Newman. *Genetic Moment*. 1947. Oil on canvas, 38 x 28" (96.5 x 71.1 cm). Collection Annalee Newman

explosive forms that suggest simultaneously events both cos-mic and cellular (*Pagan Void*, 1946). On the other hand, many of the same works include angled or rectilinear elements that refer to the ideal, geometric products of the mind. Titles such as *The Death of Euclid* and *Euclidian Abyss* are emblems of Newman's dissatisfaction with the sterility of a secularized geometry he associated with the Grecian tradition, and of his reverence for forms more closely connected to irrational and primal mysteries in the natural world.[46] It is not surprising that his studies in the natural sciences should have led him (through the encouragement of his friend Tony Smith) toward a synthesis of these mind-nature oppositions, in the form of quasi-mystical geometries ostensibly rooted in the laws of natural growth.[47] The synthesis he sought, and which he admired in Egyptian and in certain Primitive arts, was that of a formal system of uncompromising abstract purity, fused in spiritual contact with the awe of the natural world, and directly linked to its underlying order. Such purified universal forms were, he felt with Rothko and others, the appropriate modern vehicles for an experience associated with the great mythological and religious themes.

It has been suggested that the trademark "zip" of Newman's later work ultimately derives from the sharp vertical divisions in the designs of the Northwest Coast Indians.[48] Yet when the artist was asked on one occasion to speak of these "zips," he said that they were like the cry of a gull in the vastness of the Northern tundra.[49] Surely an adequate account of the role of primitivism in Newman's work must lie somewhere between such overly specific formal attributions on the one hand and

Mask. Ramu River, Madang Province, Papua New Guinea. Wood, shell, and fibrous mud, 13½" (34.3 cm) high. Friede Collection, New York

Helmet mask. Witoto. Colombia. Mixed media, 11" (28 cm) high. Museum für Völkerkunde, Berlin

his own poetic embroidery on the other. More completely than any other artist of the day, Newman presents us with both a highly developed rhetoric of admiration for the Primitive and a major artistic achievement. But there seems no evident bridge between the two, and we must proceed by indirection. The evocation of the desolate gull's cry is in fact consistent with a central aspect of Newman's conception of the Primitive: the experience of primal terror, of isolation against nature, that he insisted gave rise to the thoroughgoing spiritualization of what he took to be the Primitive world view.[50] As a sign of sheer vertical ascent in a vast open field, the "zip" has appropriately parallel connotations. It replaces the metamorphosing organismic energies of Rothko's protozoa with a distilled vector of mystically uncorrupted and undifferentiated energy, divorced from associations of evolutionary change. This is entirely in keeping with Newman's rigorously ahistorical idea of Primitive spirituality, an idea in turn essential to the anti-Marxist and existentialist positions he supported as the bases for modern art.

Newman's various writings on Primitive art represent a dramatic reversal of notions current elsewhere in the 1930s and earlier 1940s. Socially conscious writers of the thirties had stressed the efficacy of Primitive art as an element of practical and/or magic collective utility; and, as we have seen, primitivizing artists of the early and middle forties tended to defend their abstractions by referring to the larger collective validity of myth. In texts such as "The First Man Was an Artist,"

however, Newman argued for the primal nonutility of art and dissociated the beginnings of art even from (*pace* Gottlieb's linguistic signs) the original urge to communicate. Choosing a position with a long history in anthropological thought, Newman asserted the fundamentally nonimitative nature of man's initial representations. He described the essentially solipsistic and spiritual urges that led man to make sculpture before pottery, art before language. Such arguments flew directly in the face of Marxist theories of the origins, purposes, and determining forces of artistic production, and set up in their stead an imagined ancestral artist whose combination of volitional freedom and one-to-one confrontation with awesome forces beyond his control made him the legitimizing father of existential abstraction. The tribal artist, Newman said, was moved neither by "social realities" nor by any mere sense of design; his shape-content was "dictated by a ritualistic will towards metaphysical understanding."[51]

As an extreme of one position, Newman suggests a telling contrast between primitivism as it defined itself in the American avant-garde immediately after World War II and primitivism as it reappeared at the same moment in Europe, in the art of Jean Dubuffet. Newman looked to the Primitive artist as a model of purified spirituality, creator of abstractions that embodied the basic underlying order of nature. Dubuffet insisted instead on the aggressively deforming, obsessive, and fetishistic character of Primitive thought, and on the intensive physical involvement of the Primitive with the rough and irregular surface materials of the natural world. His statements on Primitive art stressed the radical challenge posed to Western mores by the "values of savagery" he admired as superior: "instinct, passion, mood, violence, madness."[52] Accordingly Dubuffet acted on the premise that the modern artist should approach the "savage" spirit by an aggressive embrace of daily life in all its energy, by an assimilation of objects regardless of any discriminating norms of beauty, rather than by reductive aesthetic simplification. He opposed not only the analytic, sculptural concerns of much earlier primitivism, but also the increasing tendency of contemporary American art to use a primitivizing ethos as the point of departure for a steadily more exclusive emphasis on abstract form. The encrusted surfaces of his canvases (e.g., *The Cellarman*, 1946) suggestively echo the caked-on application of mud and pebbles in the objects and ornaments of diverse tribal cultures (such as a Witoto mask from the Amazon region). The raw admixtures of his fetishistic objects, as in *The Magician* of 1954, with its rough melding of roots and slag, conjure grotesque physiognomies in a fashion that has distinct affinities not only with the material processes of tribal art, but also with Primitive imaginative response to anthropomorphic forms in nature. In such works, Dubuffet's literal *nostalgie de la boue* sought to fuse the untempered physical and emotive aggressivity he sensed

in tribal objects with the unpoliced force found in the graffiti and in the trashiness of the modern city. Directly contrary to Newman's aloofness, he held that the Primitive spirit was recoverable within Western culture, not via the "dead language" of a desiccated high humanism, but in the marginal and the vernacular, the "language spoken in the streets." Dubuffet thus anticipates today's graffiti artists even as he echoes the primitivist tastes of Gauguin, who similarly identified the urban marginals of modern society as embodying the most significant residue of the Primitive, and thus the greatest powers of creation. (In a characteristic use of linguistic metaphor, Gauguin had praised the spontaneity of criminal slang over tradition-burdened high civilized expression, arguing that "It's in Mazas [a notorious Parisian prison] that you still find the genius of a language; there a new word is created and understood once and for all. At the academy one can only proceed by etymology and it takes a century to adopt a new expression.")[53]

Below left: Jean Dubuffet. *The Cellarman*. 1946. Oil and mixed media on canvas, 18⅛ x 15" (46 x 38 cm). Private collection, Switzerland

Below right: Jean Dubuffet. *The Magician*. 1954. Slag and roots, 43½" (109.8 cm) high, including slag base. The Museum of Modern Art, New York; gift of Mr. and Mrs. N. Richard Miller and Mr. and Mrs. Alex L. Hillman and Samuel Girard Funds

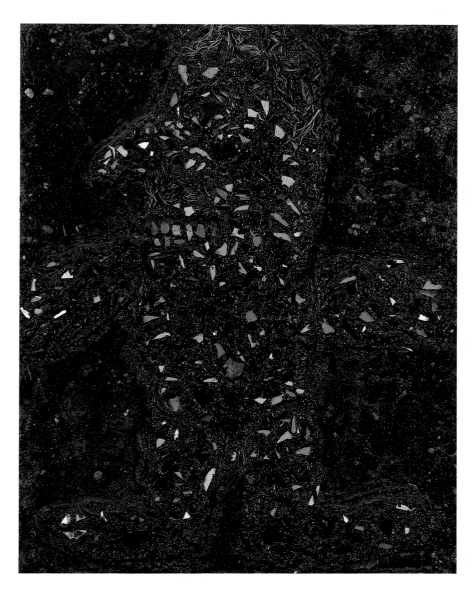

Figure. Wapo Creek, Gulf Province, Papua New Guinea. Painted wood and shell, 25″ (63.5 cm) high. Friede Collection, New York

Jean Dubuffet. *The Reveler.* 1964. Oil on base of black acrylic, 76¾ x 51¼" (195 x 130 cm). Dallas Museum of Art; gift of Mr. and Mrs. James H. Clark

Dubuffet's notion of primitivism sees the modern artist and his tribal forebear as spiritually kin to madmen, children, and other marginals and heretics. In this view the function of the artist's primitivizing work is necessarily antagonistic, running disruptively against the grain of conformist, repressive Western society in order to revivify the anarchic energies of primal man. This contrasts sharply with the ideal implied in much of the rhetoric of American artists of the forties, of the modern artist as heir to the role of tribal priest or shaman, involved in giving form to the communal myths of his time. The Americans held out the prospect that the artist's exploration of his unconscious, and his corollary recovery of the Primitive, would be a redemptive rather than a revolutionary act. Nowhere is this notion of the artist as myth-giver or shaman more evident, or more richly problematic, than in the enshrinement of Jackson Pollock as the most telling representative of the new American aesthetic. On the one hand, Pollock undertook a genuine engagement with the Primitive, intensely felt and of serious consequence for the production of powerful art. On the other hand, much of what has been said about Pollock's primitivism, and about Pollock as modern Primitive, seems inaccurate and contrary to an adequate understanding of his work.

Pollock's interest in native-American art is evident in a general color sense (particularly the strong use of yellow, red, and black) in some works of the later 1930s, in the shamanic overtones of *Naked Man*, and occasionally in more specifically suggestive forms such as the exceptional shield shape and snakelike forms of *Circle*. In the forties, such references recur in instances such as the feathered headdress of the right-hand personage in *The Moon-Woman Cuts the Circle* of 1943 (p. 643).[54] This affinity apparently stemmed in a general fashion from his youth in the West. His involvement with modernist primitivism, however, received its crucial stimulus from Pollock's working-through of the lessons of European artists, especially Picasso and Masson, and from the enthusiastic, eccentric primitivist ideals of John Graham. We know of Pollock's interest in Graham's 1937 article on "Primitive Art and Picasso," and Irving Sandler has underlined the importance of this connection by pointing to the strong resemblance between the Eskimo mask there reproduced by Graham and the torsion-wracked forms of the central head in Pollock's *Birth* of 1939–40 (p. 642).[55] The linkage is on the one hand extraordinary, for it represents one of the few instances of Pollock's borrowing more or less directly from a specific tribal form. On the other hand it is tellingly characteristic, as Pollock here associates a tribal design with an image of procreation in a fashion typical of his primitivist imagery's recurrent concern with psychomachia between the primal forces of male and female, death and fecundity.

Pollock's evocations of myth and archetype in the period from 1942 to 1946 bore a personal psychological intensity that

Jackson Pollock. *Circle*. c. 1938–41. Oil on composition board, 12¾ x 12" (32.2 x 30.5 cm); image, 11¾ x 11" (30 x 28 cm) diameter, irregular. The Museum of Modern Art, New York; gift of Lee Krasner in memory of Jackson Pollock

is as self-evident to any observer as it is problematic and fraught with controversy for those who would interpret the works in terms of the psychological theories of Freud and Jung. Pollock underwent psychoanalytic therapy from 1939 to 1941, in an attempt to overcome a problem of recurrent depression and accompanying alcoholism; his doctors were of Jungian persuasion. In the 1970s, several art historians cited this psychoanalysis, and the artist's friendship with people knowledgeable about Jung's ideas, in order to support specifically Jungian iconographic interpretations of his works of the early 1940s.[56] It is indeed likely that Pollock became familiar, one way or another, with general notions of archetypal form

Jackson Pollock. *Naked Man.* c. 1938–41. Oil on canvas mounted on board, 50 x 24" (127 x 60.9 cm). Private collection, New Jersey

as bridge between the personal imagination and more global dimensions of human experience. However, Donald Gordon has shown that Pollock's psychiatric treatment did not touch on any specific considerations of Jungian theory.[57] William Rubin has also correctly insisted on the limitations of the artist's involvement with the specifics of Jung, and on the limited usefulness of that involvement as a pretext for interpretation of the artist's paintings.[58] Specific readings of Jungian iconography in Pollock's primitivism are perhaps no more inconclusive than other interpretations; but they have virtually no external evidential support, and risk imposing a particularly skewed view of the painter as quasi-illustrator.

Nonetheless, it does in general terms seem justifiable to see Pollock's involvement with mythic themes and prehistoricizing or tribal signs as parallel to, and involved with, his "archaeology of the self," his search for self-definition as both man and painter. Rubin himself associates both the form and content of the primitivizing *Birth* with this effort at self-establishment, specifically in regard to Pollock's confrontation with Picasso. Rubin feels that the mask Graham had reproduced in 1937 became an appropriate and useful focus for Pollock's attempt, in 1939, to "go beyond" Picasso—specifically to challenge Picasso's *Demoiselles d'Avignon,* which had gone on view in New York in May of that year, and whose impact Rubin identifies, along with traces of Picasso's work of the 1930s, in *Birth.* Considerably more distorted than the most extreme of the masklike faces in Picasso's *Demoiselles,* and providentially North American, the mask Graham had wished to associate with the European master became, as Rubin analyzes, the device appropriated by Pollock in his battle with Picasso for the emergence of his own style. The mask was furthermore an ideal vehicle for imaging the pain of childbirth (a trauma that Rubin sees as playing an important role in Pollock's fantasy life, connected to his often painful and problematic relationship to his mother).[59]

Paradoxically, it is perhaps Picasso himself whom Pollock most closely resembled in the intense, personally obsessed tenor of his association of Primitive art with primal energies of sexuality, fertility, and creativity—associations nowhere more evident than in the violent life force that erupts from *Birth.* Here, as in the *Demoiselles,* we sense an engagement with tribal sources that goes beyond matters of unconventional form to touch on intuitions of propitious magic attending the making of a new artistic self. This personal investment gave Pollock's primitivizing phase an intensity unrivaled among his peers. Yet his most dramatic fusion of Primitive and modern activities of art-making occurred not in this sequence of archetypal images and mythic themes from 1942 to 1946, but in the great poured abstractions that were made afterward. There we find a less evident, more deeply seated assimilation of tribal art, on broader formal and spiritual terms.

The nature of Pollock's ambitions in painting made him receptive to the possibilities implicit in cave drawings and wall paintings, not only in terms of mural scale, but also in terms of Primitive artists' disregard for internal divisions of the field, their penchant for layered palimpsests of signs, and their inspired sensitivity to the changing nature of the working surface. Pollock's poured paintings suggest an affinity for all these general aspects of native-American practice. However, it would be wrong to draw the connections too tightly. It has seemed intriguing to some writers, for example, to associate

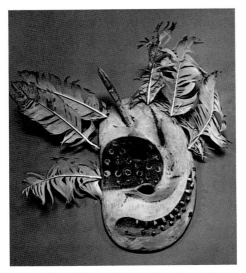

Above: Mask. Eskimo. Hooper Bay, Alaska. Painted wood and feathers, 8½" (21.5 cm) high. The University Museum, University of Pennsylvania, Philadelphia. As published in John D. Graham, "Primitive Art and Picasso," *Magazine of Art*, April 1937

Left: Jackson Pollock. *Birth*. 1939–40. Oil on canvas mounted on plywood, 46 x 21¾" (116.8 x 55.2 cm). Collection Lee Krasner Pollock, New York

Pollock's innovative way of pouring paint directly onto a canvas placed face-up on the floor with the pouring technique of Navaho sand painters, and further to add this to the roster of influences the artist garnered from his upbringing in the West.[60] Pollock doubtless knew of the Indian sand painters, though he almost certainly never saw such work in process until The Museum of Modern Art provided demonstrations by native-American artists in the context of its exhibition of Indian art in 1941. Moreover, these artists created rigidly prescribed, dominantly geometric designs, antithetical to the look and the spirit of Pollock's own poured canvases.

If Pollock was impressed by sand paintings, his appreciation likely involved a general sympathy with the "choreography" of their art-making ritual and with the notion—which would be championed by John Cage in the later 1940s—of the viability of ephemeral, activity-oriented art as a central concept in tribal and other non-Western societies.[61] He had a strong feeling for nature and for proximity to the earth, and an equally intense involvement with the careful, ritualistic building-up of his surfaces in the poured paintings—qualities Rubin has referred to as Pollock's "telluric" instinct and his engagement in "gardening" the canvases.[62] It is on such deeper, less direct but more consequential levels that the affinities between Pollock and the Primitive are most suggestive. A painting such as *Wounded Animal* of 1943 already demonstrates Pollock's interest in Primitive mark-making, in whatever format, as an activity of magic intent, bridging the gulf between representation and reality, between depicting and doing. The slashed marks and the arrow-form here echo similar markings on animal imagery in prehistoric caves like Altamira, markings thought to evidence prehistoric man's belief that strokes made against the image would be efficacious blows against the living creature, object of the hunt. Such paintings point to a concept in harmony with Pollock's emergent redefinition of modernist painting: the ideal of an artist deeply grounded in collective myth but equally fixated on the physical experience of the work at hand, engaged in a ritually intense activity of marking an open-ended surface, creating his image with a sense of physical and psychological as well as aesthetic satisfaction.[63]

As if in affirmation of this model of physical and psychic engagement Pollock impressed his handprint among the skeins of paint in some of the poured paintings, such as *Number 1, 1948* (p. 645). He further multiplied this mark in a fashion that reinforces its connection with such prehistoric patterns of hands as those on the walls of the Castillo cave in Spain (p. 645). With arresting spontaneity and without the baggage of inherited mythic symbolism, Pollock here asserted, as Miró and others had before him (p. 646), perhaps the most elemental emblem of kinship with the Primitive artist, personal and of the moment, yet universally recognizable and timeless.[64] The handprint affirms a primitivism that goes beyond matters of stylistic reformation of the visual world, moving closer to the fundamental core of the mythic.

There is, however, a cautionary note to consider with regard to Pollock's internalization of a tribal persona. From the earliest phases of his primitivizing work, Pollock indicated his identification with the primitive myth-giver and bearer of the mysteries, the shaman. *Naked Man*, c. 1938–41 (p. 641),

Jackson Pollock. *Wounded Animal.* 1943. Oil on plaster on canvas, 38 x 30" (96.5 x 76.2 cm). Private collection

Jackson Pollock. *The Moon-Woman Cuts the Circle.* 1943. Oil on canvas, 43⅛ x 41" (109.5 x 104 cm). Musée National d'Art Moderne, Centre National d'Art et de Culture Georges Pompidou, Paris; gift of Frank Lloyd

Jackson Pollock. *Number 1, 1948.* 1948. Oil on canvas, 68" x 8'8" (172.7 x 264.2 cm). The Museum of Modern Art, New York; purchase

shows such a personage, with the attributes both of man and totemic beast. Yet if it was the poured paintings rather than the earlier primitivizing canvases that most deeply engaged and assimilated such affinities, it was also their misguided interpretation that was ultimately most successful, in a problematic and inadvertent way, in providing a myth for their time. This took place through the popularization of the image of Pollock at work and through the critical construction of a Pollock persona—instinctually flailing the gestures of an alienated freedom, in an existential void—adapted to the intellectual temper of post–World War II America.[65]

Through overheated critical "appreciations" such as that of Harold Rosenberg and also through Hans Namuth's extraordinary photos of the poured paintings in process, Pollock came to stand for the man of lonely and compulsive action and to be identified with a sense of scale, energy, and anxiety-of-freedom that were held to be quintessentially modern and specifically American.[66] Particularly with his violent death, he seemed to represent the Jungian hero who had passed through the dark period of the investigations of the unconscious to emerge triumphant, superior yet tormented and marginal—the artist as exemplary sufferer, a shaman for our time.

Evocative as it is, we should be aware of the distortions of this kind of myth of Pollock as modern Primitive. Too often it proposes to us a caricatured cowboy existentialist, and imposes on Pollock's work from 1947 to 1950—the wonderfully soaring, lyrical ribbons of paint that are literally danced

onto the canvas—a dour conception of agonized psyche that carries over from the very different, overtly tormented, primitivizing work of the period 1939–46.[67] It was in a far more positive and fulfilled way—in the liberating consequence of the primacy of action and in the model of an intense engagement with art as process—that Pollock's deep assimilation of a spirit of primitivism in the poured paintings was genuine, fruitful for himself and for posterity. In this latter sense, Pollock's legacy may legitimately be seen not only in the achievements of painters like Morris Louis and Frank Stella, but also in the subsequent vogue of Happenings and in the ritual-oriented performance art of the 1970s.

It is in any event primarily on such conceptual levels rather than in any evident formal citations or suggestive titling that the primitivism of the 1940s carried over, when it carried over at all, into the most mature work of the artists who had been its champions around 1946. In general, by the early 1950s, it seemed as if primitivism had been part of an episode of engagement with Surrealism, a necessary rite of passage toward the achievement of a more independent abstract style in progressive American painting. A similar pattern, furthermore, characterized the development of the sculpture of the period. There had been isolated instances of primitivism in American sculpture prior to 1940, in works such as John Storrs's hybrids of skyscrapers and totems (p. 465) or in pieces such as Alexander Calder's exceptional *Apple Monster*—which is, as William Rubin has noted, a near-direct match for New Guinea Imumus (p. 58). But, as with American painting,

Jackson Pollock. *Number 1, 1948* (detail). 1948. Oil on canvas, 68" x 8'8" (172.7 x 264.2 cm), overall. The Museum of Modern Art, New York; purchase

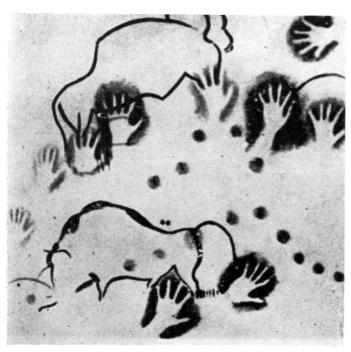

Detail of cave painting, Castillo, Spain. Published in G. Baldwin Brown, *The Art of the Cave Dweller*, 1928. This book was in Pollock's library.

sculpture's most intense period of engagement with myth and with evocations of the primal came around 1946–47, then gave way to more abstract, expressively more reserved, forms in the fifties.

In the late 1930s and early 1940s, parallel with several painters of their generation (such as Rothko), American sculptors such as Herbert Ferber and Seymour Lipton passed from an early involvement with naturalist style and subjects of social contemporaneity to a more abstract formal vocabulary focused on mythic themes. And, as it did in painting, Surrealism figured prominently in the transformation of sculpture's look. To some sculptors, this came as a logical and gradual development; for others it involved a drastic self-reformation, not only in response to European models and to the demands of world events, but also in reaction to accelerating changes in American painting. David Hare was consistently in dialogue with European influences, and produced work in the 1940s that showed a personal adaptation of the lessons of Surrealism to new themes of myth and magic (see, for example, *Magician's Game*, 1944, p. 647). By the mid-1940s and largely as a response to war and the atomic bomb, even sculptors such as Theodore Roszak, whose constructivist-inspired work of the thirties had celebrated technological modernity, looked to the more expressive, process-oriented aspects of Surrealist art and to a rough, often grotesque repertory of Surrealist-inspired form, to give shape to primal distress. In this climate many of

Joan Miró. *Woman Dreaming of Escape*. 1942. Oil on canvas, 51¼ x 76¾" (130 x 195 cm). Collection Mr. and Mrs. Morton Neumann, Chicago

the dream-forms of Surrealism (especially the visceral and often sadistic images of Giacometti's sculptures of the early 1930s) were transformed into aggressive nightmares. Bones and birds became spiky skeletal monsters and horrific airborne predators, while the simple process of metal welding became a vehicle for tortured, twisted shapes of anguish (for example, Lipton's *Moloch* of 1946 or Roszak's *Spectre of Kitty Hawk* of 1946–47)—to the point that a "regressive" disregard for finish and an "archaic" evocation of mythic horror became predictable, even formulaic aspects of much of American metal sculpture around 1950. The scarred dignity of a work such as Ferber's *He Is Not a Man*, 1950 (p. 648), looks backward to the insistent violence of this archaizing period, even as it participates in the less corporeal vocabulary of iconic natural forms

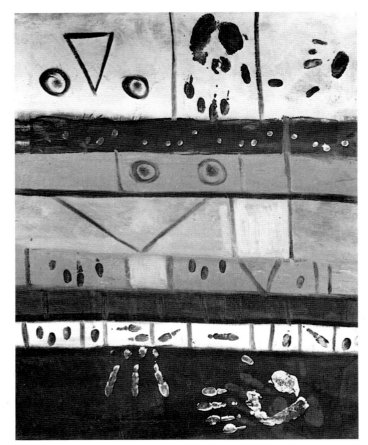

Above: Theodoros Stamos with petroglyphs, Sandia, New Mexico, 1947

Left: Adolph Gottlieb. *Black Hand*. 1943. Oil on linen, 30 x 24" (76.2 x 61 cm). Private collection, New York

seen in the works of painters such as Stamos (p. 614) and announces a new, more reserved emotive tone and clarified formal presence. Lipton had earlier confirmed his own absorption in this general sense of things Primitive. While denying that he consciously sought "universal analogies of form trying to parallel prehistoric sculpture, primitive sculpture, or other modern plastic ideas," he maintained that in his exploration of instinctive, subconscious realms he had found "the Paleozoic in man. The dinosaur and its bones have come alive to me. The bud, the core, the spring, the darkness of earth, the deep animal fountainhead of man's forces are what interest me most as the main genesis of artistic substance."[68] Lipton's rhetoric is symptomatic of the ways in which the idea of the Primitive became especially intertwined with the evolutionary idea of the prehistoric in the sculpture of the day. In this regard as well as in other aspects of primitivism in American sculpture of the forties, however, the paradigmatic career was that of David Smith. In his development we find restated, with significant modifications, many of the issues of meaning we have been considering in pictorial primitivism.

The first indications of primitivist interests in Smith's career were coincident with his first efforts in sculpture. He and Dorothy Dehner spent eight months in the Virgin Islands in 1931 because, as she later recalled, they "wanted to be Gauguin";[69] and there Smith began fashioning small objects from wire and natural materials such as coral. His awareness of tribal art dates from this same period, for he became a friend of John Graham's in the late 1920s or early 1930s. In 1933, Graham arranged for Smith to fashion bases for the African objects in the Crowninshield Collection, a collection Graham had helped form as advisor/dealer.[70] The Crowninshield collection was with Smith while he made the bases, and four carved wooden sculptures of that year (e.g., Untitled, p. 649) reflect his study of the lessons of the African sculptors' methods and vocabulary. These are, however, notably inexpressive objects, with little relation to the kind of primitivism that emerges in Smith's work in the 1940s.

The major surge of primitivizing inflections in Smith's sculpture began in the very late 1930s, when he added to his repertory of modern form (especially his command of the lessons of Picasso and Gonzalez) a vocabulary of formats and signs influenced by the great Archaic civilizations of Egypt, Babylonia, and preclassical Greece. These archaizing tastes supported his attraction to ideographic, narrative relief-style work (especially in the *Medals for Dishonor* of 1939–40) and at the same time offered a check on the biomorphic grotesquerie for which, in his personal version of Surrealism, he had an affinity. Smith's sculpture of the forties was often violent in theme and feeling; in this his work aligns with that of Pollock in the same years, in contradistinction to the more passive, neo-Symbolist *poésie* of Rothko, Stamos, Baziotes, et al. Yet he seems never to have looked to tribal art as a source-model for expressive deformities, or to have been interested in the corrugated surfaces or obsessive accumulations of fetish objects. If the *Medals for Dishonor* reflect one side of his interest in the Archaic—the narrative, pictographic side—*The Hero–1952* of 1951–52 (p. 649) reflects the other: his admiration for the iconic, monumentally restrained dignity and clarity of preclassical sculpture such as that of the Cyclades. Each of these in turn dovetailed with his interests in European modernism—the former with his more expressive, discursive

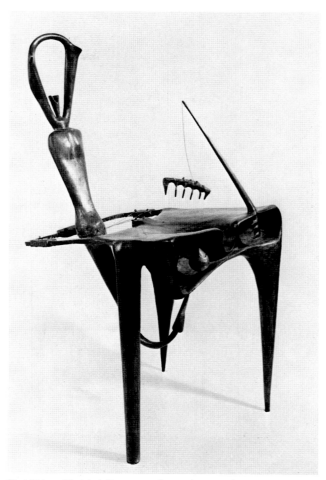

David Hare. *Magician's Game.* 1944. Bronze (cast 1946), 40¼ x 18½ x 25¼" (102.2 x 47 x 64.1 cm). The Museum of Modern Art, New York; given anonymously

Theodore J. Roszak. *Spectre of Kitty Hawk.* 1946–47. Welded and hammered steel brazed with bronze and brass, 40¼" (102.2 cm) high, at base 18 x 15" (45.7 x 38.1 cm). The Museum of Modern Art, New York; purchase

Herbert Ferber. *He Is Not a Man*. 1950. Bronze with welded metal rods (unique cast, from original in lead), 67¼ x 19½ x 13⅜" (170.9 x 49.4 x 33.9 cm). The Museum of Modern Art, New York; gift of William Rubin

interpretations of Picasso and the early Giacometti, the latter with his less obvious attention to aspects of Brancusi and the later Giacometti.

Smith was a voraciously inquisitive autodidact, and there can be little doubt that he familiarized himself with a broad range of non-Western art of all kinds. Like others of his generation, he borrowed notably from a native-American source. Of all the tribal forms that may have attracted Smith, the most evident is that of the Northwest Coast totem — perhaps precisely because it combined a modular-assembly principle of accommodating diverse parts, in a way that satisfied his more discursive, improvisational side, with a nonspecific but monumental and restrained figural presence. The idea of a personal totem, a regular formal system wedded to a more improvisational accumulation of quasi-automatist signs of autobiographical reference, appears in *Pillar of Sunday* of 1945 (p. 650)—an ironic juncture of tribal religious form with his own fantasy-representation of his church-going mother.[71] (On a preparatory drawing for this work, p. 650, Smith inscribed "totem.") By the time of the Tanktotem series, the formal reference to the stacking of images in the native-American pole had been muted. Only the generic associations of tribal ritual and sacred presence remain to affect, via the title, our reading of the standing pieces.[72] In general, too, Smith's primitivism was a synthetic "regression" that existed more in the realm of themes and on the level of invisible inspiration than in evident dependence on artistic models in tribal or Archaic sculpture. We find in his work much the same blends discussed earlier in the work of his painter cohorts, of elementalism and the unconscious, and of natural history and "linguistic" concern for early signs—but with markedly different inflections of meaning.

Not only in works like *Jurassic Bird* (p. 618) and *Landscape with Strata* of 1946, but in countless references and drawings in his notebooks, Smith reveals himself to be, like Rothko and Newman, an assiduous student of the natural sciences. As did many of the painters of his generation, he frequently haunted the American Museum of Natural History. The museum displays—not of ethnology but of biology—strongly impressed his imagination, and he kept photos of them to inform his work (p. 652). He showed a keen curiosity for specifics in the domains of animal morphology, embryology, and paleontology. But where Newman's and Rothko's concerns were with the microbic levels of life, or with the seed, Smith's art was more often based on the fossil—the reduced remnant and pared-away schema rather than the purist bud of undifferentiated potential. While all three looked to evolution as a metaphor for unconscious processes, Smith's evolutionary interests had pointedly to do not with aqueous genetic transformation, but with the struggle for dominance, the battle of life and extinction among the differing species. His lumbering ancient predators, such as *Royal Bird* (p. 653) and *Jurassic Bird*, evoke a time of elemental violence and competition that is matched by the modern world referred to in the brutal *Spectres of war*, such as the *Race for Survival (Spectre of Profit)*.[73]

Rather than seek the common elements of ancient, tribal, and modern man in the "inner universals" of myth and the natural laws of generation, Smith looked with more jaundiced eye at the conditions of inhuman competition and violence that related his society to its prehistoric counterpart. His monstrous avians and other skeleton forms served different

David Smith. Untitled. 1933. Wood, 12¼ x 3½ x 1½" (31.1 x 8.9 x 3.8 cm). Estate of the artist

David Smith. *The Hero—1952.* 1951–52. Painted steel, 73¾ x 25½ x 11¾" (187.3 x 64.7 x 29.8 cm). The Brooklyn Museum, New York; Dick S. Ramsay Fund

purposes from those of the frequent bone-forms and occasional fossils of Surrealism (notably the pterodactyllike creature in Giacometti's *Palace at 4 A.M.*, a sculpture Smith had already studied with profit in the later 1930s). Formally, they freed him from the constraints of anthropomorphism and thus encouraged experiments in a more boldly dispersed open-work graphism. In avoiding essentialist genetic metaphors of thought, these creatures also pointed away from the notion of an enclosed unconscious of eternally invariant symbols. His conflation of evolutionary struggle and contemporary woes—capitalist exploitation, fascist totalitarianism—offered an implicit critique of that primitivizing idealism which sought a "natural/universal," rather than a sociopolitical and materialist, essence of mankind. Instead of retreating beyond matters of politics into a hypothetical primal past, Smith's monsters projected the conflicts of the present back into the deepest history of life on earth, and by extension proposed a less solemnly quiescent and archetypally determined imagery of the modern unconscious.

In the area of language and interest in the primal sign, manifest in *The Letter* (p. 622), *Letter to Australia, The Banquet,* and numerous other sculptures, drawings, and notes, Smith's "regressions" were similarly politically tinged. On one level, his interest in a hypothetical early period when meaning and sign were inextricably joined in picture-images was fueled by a simple distrust of words, grounded in a dislike for verbal "explanations" of art. But this was extended to a broader principle of seeking out forms that bespoke a purity as yet undominated by an ideological control and debasement of communication. In a prose-poem accompanying his sculpture

Above: David Smith. Sketches for *Pillar of Sunday*. 1945. Graphite, pen and blue and black inks, and black tempera, 10 x 7¼" (25.4 x 18.4 cm). Fogg Art Museum, Harvard University, Cambridge; gift of David Smith

Right: David Smith. *Pillar of Sunday*. 1945. Painted steel, 29¼ x 17½ x 9½" (74.3 x 44.4 x 24.1 cm). Indiana University Art Museum, Bloomington

based on the letters *y* and *h* he evoked "the return to origins, before purities were befouled by words," when artists created letters as "object symbols," "before words were made to be degenerated by moralists pragmatists, money changers, and rut [sic] educators."[74]

From such remarks, we can adduce another level, of content rather than only of structure, at which Smith's *The Letter* could be seen as reflecting his admiration for tribal forms such as the part-figural, part-ideographic Senufo headdress (pp. 622, 623). In broader terms, this attitude toward language also provides a bridge between Smith's primitivist and modern admirations. It underlies his deep admiration for James Joyce, as a creator who liberated the word from its conventional restraining controls and restored the free creative play to communication. Later, in the text "The Language Is Image" of 1952, Smith restated and expanded the same line of thought, in which an original unity of vision and meaning has been dismembered, and creative potential imprisoned, by modern

Western culture. "Judging from Cuneiform, Chinese and other ancient texts, the object symbols formed identities upon which letters and words were later developed. Their business and exploitation use has become dominant over their poetic-communicative use, which explains one facet of their inadequateness. Thirty or forty thousand years ago Primitive man did not have the word picture, nor this demand for limited vision. His relationship to the object was with all its parts and function, by selection, or the eidetic image.... The cave man from Altamira to Rhodesia had produced true reality by the eidetic image."[75]

Smith's references to the perceptual-psychological phenomenon of the eidetic image, which recur throughout his writing and in his notebooks as well, were linked to his ideal of the bond between the Primitive and the modern artist. Eidetic images are forms of waking hallucination, in which normal boundaries between the productions of the mind and the evidence of the senses are broken down, and a subject *sees* an image of extraordinary completeness and impact, without the person or object in question actually being present to the eye. In writings on perception and in anthropological texts of the 1920s and 1930s, this power of image-ing was ascribed particularly to children, "savages," and artists.[76] The eidetic ability elevated the "mind's eye" to co-equality with visual sensation, dissolving the boundaries between imagination and perception, myth and reality. It produced representations that were held to be medians between subjectivity and objectivity, between the racial unconscious and the individual experience. It is intriguing that Smith should thus return us, in the psychological parlance of his time, to the very same admiration for the Primitive mind as the seat of superior, transperceptual representation (and therefore as the locus of primal creativity) that moved Gauguin in his fascination with the superstitious imaginings of the Breton women and Tahitian natives (pp. 182, 200). In Smith's case, the interest is one with an added social dimension, as he stresses that the power of his work operates, like the eidetic image, on a preverbal level of representation, in a domain of perception which is "open to any man, in any status, ignores the language barrier."[77] Here is the venerable common dream of linguists as well as artists, of an Adamic language, a system of noumenal signs which unites rather than divides humankind, and embraces an unequivocal fullness of meaning.

Significantly, Smith does not suggest, either in these words or in his work, that such a system of signs is to be regained simply by the exhuming of archaic form or the mimicry of tribal design. In the recurrent appeal to eidetic experience as in the development of his formal choices, Smith sought out a "universality" based less on the latently conservative, semi-Jungian precepts of shared eternal symbols than on a more neurological ideal of universal visual capacities. His idea of visual perception as a classless, timeless human faculty moves away from symbol toward sight as the basis of interest in the Primitive mind, and as the basis for a modern art—a movement consonant with the goal of *tabula rasa* stripping-away that by the late forties had supplanted the search for archetypal symbol which first spurred the new American primitivism. In this regard, Smith's work of the period c. 1949–50 recapitulates the same absorption and transcendence of primitivism that we observed in Pollock, Newman, and Rothko.

The primitivism of the forties was at its best a self-consuming enterprise. For those artists who reflected most tellingly on the Primitive artist as a model, the borrowing of tribal forms and the pointed evocation of ancient myth came themselves to be recognized as falsifications of the hunger for absolutes and the drive to universality that were the most challenging bases of the primitivizing movement. A new kind of primitivist tone, superseding the gloomy heavy-handedness of the war years, appears in the works and the words of the New York school around 1948. Barnett Newman expressed it most forcefully:

We are reasserting man's natural desire for the exalted, for a concern with our relationship to the absolute emotions. We do not need the obsolete props of an outmoded and antiquated legend. We are creating images whose reality is self-evident and which are devoid of the props and crutches that evoke associations with outmoded images... We are freeing ourselves of the impediments of memory,

association, nostalgia, legend, myth....[78]

This shift in attitude may help to explain why Clyfford Still, whose work of the late thirties and forties had the emotional valence and sometimes the evident signs of the primitivizing interests of the time, should have later disavowed all responsibility for titles such as *Totemic Fantasy* that had been attached to his early paintings[79]—despite the fact that he invented, or at the very least concurred in, these appellations when the works were first shown or sold. There was a general tendency among all these painters, by 1950, to abandon the portentous (and sometimes rather arbitrarily applied) titles characteristic of the forties, in favor of simple numbers, generic titles, or no titles at all. New nomenclature reflected new content. The neutralization of titles accompanied the elimination of borrowed forms and signs; and this in turn signaled a disenchantment with the ideal of an archetype or primal cipher as vehicle for universal meaning.

These changes manifested a broad-based move away from the vestiges of Surrealism, and specifically away from a concept of the symbol-laden unconscious as the fount of artistic experience and the ground of the viewer's response. A more stringent empiricism displaced the debates over *ur*-forms of ultimate cognition and human tradition that had characterized the forties. At the same time, Rothko, Newman, Gottlieb, and to a lesser extent Pollock began producing closely related works in apparent or self-declared series—another instance of the new air of the universal or even clinical that came to be associated with the "experiments" of the new abstraction.

The symbolic and mythic phase of primitivism had not been a necessary prelude to advanced abstraction in the New York School; for, as the examples of Gorky and de Kooning prove, some artists were able to work directly from the European tradition toward new art of high originality and impact. (Gorky was in fact explicit in his rejection of primitivism as self-deluding escapism, and of Primitive art as an insufficient model for a creativity attuned to the dynamic complexity of modern experience.)[80] But for a great many artists primitivism was a necessary means to the full realization of their own originality, and a theater of confrontation with some of the most pressing concerns of this decade. It would be too easy simply to dismiss the phenomenon as a transitional concern of immature or less-talented artists, or to identify its significance too exclusively in terms of the personal psychological developments of a few key creators.

The episode of primitivism in American art of the forties should instead be seen in its broad cultural implications, in the context of the contemporary struggle between fascism and Marxism on the world stage, and especially in juxtaposition to the challenge of fascism. In a very general sense, we find here a recurrence of the situation examined earlier in relation to Gauguin (see pp. 181–83): a modernist primitivism concerned with the universal bases of culture opposes an ideology of human evolution based on a historicist, racist misapplication of natural science. As Gauguin's admiration for Primitive creativity responded to the dominance of a misapplied Darwinism, so the primitivist interests of the Abstract Expressionists were formulated, to a very significant degree, as alternatives to the latter-day Darwinist ideas of racially determined history favored by the Nazis.

It is worth re-stressing that there was more than one form of appeal to the Primitive abroad in the world in the 1940s, and that more was at issue than matters of artistic style. Of all the Primitive forms that have captured the imagination of twentieth-century man, certainly the swastika was among the most potent. This ancient cosmological symbol, on the banners of Hitler's Germany, testified to a frighteningly successful revivification of the power of archaic myth. For any thinking person in Western civilization in the late 1930s and 1940s, the fascists' assertion of collective social integration as a bastion against the alienating uncertainties of modern life, and their apparent reconciliation of Primitive racial myth with aggressive science and technology, presented a challenge of the most disturbing kind. As Erich Kahler proposed in a special issue on myth in *Chimera* just after the war: "Fascism exposed a basic need of the human psyche, one that the age of rationalism refused to recognize."[81]

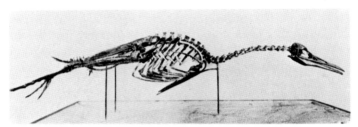

Fossil skeleton of the prehistoric birdlike creature *Hesperornis regalis* from the collection of the American Museum of Natural History, New York. Photograph. Archives of David Smith

The debate surrounding the nature of myth as a subject for art, so central to the shifts in American art around 1940, echoed the concerns for the Nazi challenge. Marxist materialism, as the unbending foe of mystification and the transcendental, denigrated all myth. But the economically determined "scientific" ideal of society the Marxists offered in opposition seemed, for many artists and intellectuals, inadequate to the age, in the face of the demonstrated power of irrational atavism to threaten the world order. As Kahler put it later, "We do not meet the dangers inherent in this human propensity by denying it, regarding it as overcome or to be overcome, or as the residue of ancient superstition, but only by recognizing it and taking it into account."[82] The primitivism of the early New York School, in its urge to create a mythic form of expression appropriate to the time, should be seen as engaged in a program of abandoning materialism in order to take into account the challenge of the Nazis, and to counter it *on its own terms*. Against the fascist fusion of bad myth and bad science, the primitivist ideals of the American artists proposed a union of good myth and good science.

Where the Nazis appealed to archaic myth as an enduring ground of tribal unity and basis for the classification of cultures, the New York artists emphasized a syncretist spirit of myth that would touch on universal bases of all human experience. Their admiration for tribal art was an assertion of antiracist cultural relativism, the nonhierarchical celebration of all human creativity, as opposed to the culture-specific, exclusively Aryan regression of the Germans. Similarly, the Germans looked to revived myth and ritual as a way of achieving the suppression of individuality in the modern collective state. The American ideals of recuperation of archetypes were founded on a more complex psychoanalytic

model, of analogy between the healthy integration of the individual personality and the solidarity of the society.[83] In both the individual and the culture, the living awareness of enduring symbols in the unconscious was to foster not mere submission to the tyranny of genetic memory, but a liberating capacity for immediate, spontaneous experience. Primitivism as a precondition for individuality, archetype as the catalyst of creativity—these combinations of atavism and aggressive experiment, as we examined them in the case of Pollock's development, for example, constituted a specific alternative to totalitarian primitivism.

In Nazi Germany, the bad version of the tyranny of human tradition was supported by a bad version of natural science which asserted the ironclad dominance of racial laws. The countering primitivism of the Americans sought to link their vision of tradition to an opposed notion of science, as the seat of inquiring wonder rather than enslaving rules. American primitivism of the forties was linked with the ideal of science as a model of nonsectarian collectivism in the service of truth, and as a route of access to the mysteries and awesome, humbling forces of nature. The biological and evolutionary imagery of Rothko, Smith, Newman, and others evoked not only a life force prior to racial differentiation, opposed to the teleological elitism of Nazi genetic theory, but also a specifically scientizing vision of archaeological, paleontological, and microbiological investigation. (Indeed, in a general sense of analogy, the implicit combinations of fossils and cells, of ideographs and amoebae in these works of art are restatements on other levels of the same concerns for synthesis between genetic transformation and social competition that marked the most advanced concerns of scientific speculation on evolution in the forties.)[84]

Wolfgang Paalen, a Surrealist and primitivist writer and artist of the forties, wrote in 1945 that "To a science already universal but by definition incapable of doing justice to our emotional needs, there must be added its complement, a universal art; these two will help in the reshaping of the new, the indispensable world consciousness."[85] This stress on scientific endeavor as a model for new transcultural forms of expression had already been present in Pollock's response to an inquiry about the emergence of a new American art, in 1944: "The idea of an isolated American painting, so popular in this country during the thirties, seems absurd to me, just as the idea of creating a purely American mathematics or physics would seem absurd."[86] To this principle of universality, so in harmony with the thrust of the American search for ultimate original absolutes of myth and language, was joined the feeling that modern science further dovetailed with the urge to primitivism in its confrontation with the unknown. The general feeling for a new age of myth, as well as the specific primitivist interests of Rothko (organic energies as bases of life), Newman (abstract form as higher truth), Pollock (merger with nature), Smith (eidetic perception), and others, is implicit in this idea of science's most advanced reach. One text of the period makes the connections especially clear. In his examination of "The Persistence of Myth" in 1946, Erich Kahler argued that "even at the most advanced front of human knowledge a situation has been reached where an extreme expansion of man's power at the same time brings him to realize anew the extent of his ancient powerlessness to resolve the cosmos."

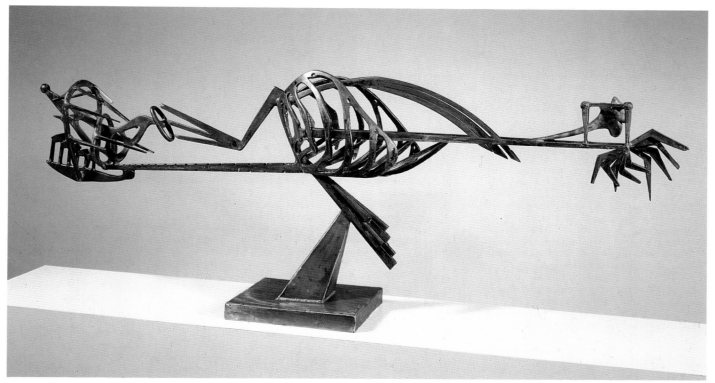

David Smith. *Royal Bird*. 1947–48. Welded stainless steel, 21¾ x 59 x 9" (55.2 x 149.8 x 22.9 cm). Walker Art Center, Minneapolis; gift of the T. B. Walker Foundation

The boundaries of our reason become more and more clear, and the rationalistic overconfidence in an unlimited dominion of nature by reason has been discouraged by natural science itself. In its recent stupendous advances, physics has arrived at a border region that seems to refuse itself to rational penetration. It has pushed forward into the realms of the submicroscopic, where phenomena can no longer be pictured, but only schematized, that is, symbolized; so deep into the innermost structure of the elements that it has discovered their modes of transformation one into the other and so has come to recognize the elements themselves as being only specific arrangements, linkages of general energies...

Physics, at a new level, merges the inner and outer world, postulates on epistemological grounds a unity that was taken for granted in early, religious periods...The findings of research, by completely dissolving the object into a complex of relations, have led the physicist ever farther away from the sphere of sense perceptions into one of abstract conceptions...In this, physics, starting with the external, curiously corresponds with the preceding theory of psychoanalysis, which, starting with the internal, has effected a merging of the inner and outer world by seeing reactions that are directed outward as projections of inner situations. Physics has, by its very triumph, stirred in man the primeval shudder in the face of the impenetrable reaches re-emerging at the borders of the outer world; psychoanalysis has revealed man's disguised dread of his inner depths. But physics, as well as psychoanalysis, has shown that these anxieties are functions of each other, that they are one and the same dread of the unknown, which is the true source of myth.[87]

Myth and science, the most Primitive and the most modern, were held to be mirrors one of the other; and one senses in the primitivizing of the New York artists a desire for art to act as the reconciling bond between such apparent opposites: first as the embodiment of ancient signs and myths, and subsequently as the theater of confrontation with universal abstract truths and fundamental energies. Just as it was felt that the darkness of the war period was a throwback to primal

vulnerability, so many writers in the later forties expressed feelings that the findings of advanced science seemed to be returning man to a condition of mythic awe before the cosmos. This correlation became especially evident in the wake of the atomic bomb. The rhetoric surrounding the opening of this fearful door onto a new unknown domain sounded quite suggestively like the rhetoric of Newman and other artists on the modern experience as a spiritual echo of the Primitive.[88]

The idea that the lessons appropriate to the future lie in an understanding of the deep past is of course not unique to art; and the desire to recover an earlier integration of knowledge and intuition, art and science, forms a deeply pervasive theme in Western thought. In the twentieth century, though, these issues seem especially close to the endeavor of vanguard artists, both in their deep fascination with the art of Primitive man and in their love-hate relationship with the progress of science. In these terms as in others we have discussed earlier, the primitivist phase of New York School painting seems not only to have been joined to some of the broadest and most pressing issues of Western culture in the forties, but also to have represented a symptomatic confrontation with questions of the role of art in society and in history that have consistently attended the development of twentieth-century art. The investigation of the subconscious roots of human representations, the fascination with the ideal of the universal sign, and the matter of linkage between the deep irrational past of man and his present science-dominated culture are hardly passing infatuations or unworthy concerns for art. Assimilated in one form by the various abstract styles that supplanted evident Primitive references in American art at the end of the forties, these broader recurrent aspects of modernist primitivism persisted as challenges endemic to modern culture, challenges that artists would be drawn to confront again in a subsequent generation.

NOTES

For a vast amount of valuable research assistance that contributed substantially to the preparation of this essay, the author is indebted to Joan Pachner.

1. See the discussion of Pollock's involvement with, and debt to, the Mexican muralists, in Irving Sandler, *The Triumph of American Painting* (New York: Harper and Row, 1971), pp. 103–04. The importance of the Mexicans for Pollock and others is also stressed by Robert Carleton Hobbs, in "Early Abstract Expressionism: A Concern with the Unknown Within," in R. C. Hobbs and Gail Levin, *Abstract Expressionism: The Formative Years* (Ithaca: Cornell University Press, 1978), p. 14.

2. Adolph Gottlieb, from "The Portrait and the Modern Artist," typescript of a broadcast on "Art in New York," WNYC, October 13, 1943, cited in Mary Davis MacNaughton, "Adolph Gottlieb: His Life and Art," in *Adolph Gottlieb, A Retrospective* (New York: The Arts Publisher, in association with the Adolph and Esther Gottlieb Foundation, 1981), p. 42. Barnett Newman also critiqued the misunderstanding of Primitive art by earlier European modernists and associated this misunderstanding with the deficiencies of abstract painting in Europe. His comments appear in "The Plasmic Image," a manuscript he worked on from 1943 to 1945. See the large excerpts from this text, and Thomas Hess's comments, in Thomas B. Hess, *Barnett Newman* (New York: Museum of Modern Art, 1971), esp. pp. 37, 39.

3. John Graham, "Introduction" to *Exhibition of Sculptures of Old African Civilizations* (New York: Jacques Seligmann Gallery, 1936), p. 3.

4. John Graham, *System and Dialectics of Art* (New York: Delphic Studios, 1937), p. 15. On John Graham and his importance for the New York School artists, see Irving Sandler, "John D. Graham: The Painter as Esthetician and Connoisseur," *Artforum*, October 1968, pp. 50–53; and Sandler's discussion of Graham's impact on Pollock, in *Triumph*, pp. 105–06.

5. See the analysis by Irving Sandler of the split between the Surrealists and the New York painters, in Sandler, *Triumph*, pp. 63–64.

6. On the psychological tenor of the early works of the Abstract Expressionists, see Hobbs, "Early Abstract Expressionism: A Concern with the Unknown Within," loc. cit., pp. 8–40.

7. Editorial, *View*, series 3, no. 1, 1943; cited by Dore Ashton in *The New York School: A Cultural Reckoning* (New York: Penguin, 1980), p. 20.

8. Alfred Barr, in "Preface and Acknowledgment" in Leo Frobenius and Douglas C. Fox, *Prehistoric Rock Pictures in Europe and Africa* (New York: Museum of Modern Art, 1937), said "technical and esthetic qualities are enviable but no more so than the unquestioned sense of social usefulness which these prehistoric pictures suggest....Today walls are painted so that the artist may eat, but in prehistoric times walls were painted so that the community might eat."

9. On the move away from history and into the mythically charged psyche, see Hobbs, loc. cit.; and Sandler, *Triuimph*, pp. 63–64. The most pointed rejection of a materialist picture of tribal life was Barnett Newman's "The First Man Was an Artist," *Tiger's Eye*, no. 1, 1947, pp. 57–60. But the anti-Marxist aspects of Newman's position were already implicit in the comments of Wolfgang Paalen in "The New Image," *DYN*, no. 1, April/May 1942, p. 7: "Engels was in error when he wrote 'Men must eat, drink, be clothed and sheltered before they are able to concern themselves with politics, art, science, or religion...' The irrefutable evidence of anthropology and psychology is that art, science, and religion are inseparable interpreta-

tions of the external world, as the beginnings of thought." Paalen's remarks are characteristic not only of the expanding rejection of Marxism, but of the tendency to look to the authority of science for confirmation of the newly prized, ahistorical universals of human experience.

The idea of art's nonpractical origins had already existed in the work of writers such as G. H. Luquet. In *L'Art et la religion des hommes fossiles*, 1926, translated as *The Art and Religion of Fossil Man*, trans. J. Townsend Russell (New Haven: Yale University Press, 1930), Luquet says (pp. 111–12) that "I consider it impossible for figured art to have been anything but a disinterested activity in its initial phase. As writes Breuil [l'Abbé Breuil, earliest and foremost authority on cave painting]: 'If art for art's sake had not come into being, magical or religious art would never have existed...'" Luquet's image of the first artist as creating primarily for the pleasure of doing so is in turn an echo of the primitivist attitude of Coleridge toward the origins of science; Coleridge (as cited by Peter Medawar in *Pluto's Republic* [New York: Oxford University Press, 1982], p. 31) held that "The first man of science was he who looked into a thing, not to learn whether it could furnish him with food, or shelter, or weapons, or tools, or ornaments, or *play-withs*, but who sought to know it for the gratification of knowing."

10. For an analysis of the idea of an "apolitical" individualist position in the political thought of the 1940s, see Serge Guilbaut, *How New York Stole the Idea of Modern Art*, trans. Arthur Goldhammer (Chicago: University of Chicago Press, 1983), e.g., pp. 75–79.

11. Barnett Newman, "Northwest Coast Indian Painting" (New York: Betty Parsons Gallery, 1946).

12. Gottlieb in "The Portrait and the Modern Artist," loc. cit., cited by Sandler, *Triumph*, p. 64; and by MacNaughton, loc. cit., p. 42.

13. Gottlieb, in *Tiger's Eye*, no. 2, December 1947, p. 43; cited by MacNaughton, p. 44.

14. Newman, "The Object and the Image," *Tiger's Eye*, no. 3, March 1948.

15. "Only an autochthonous mythology, a mythology coming from the same soil, the same people, the same cultural superstructure of the same economic order can be an effective intermediary between art and material production...." A. L. Lloyd, "Modern Art and Modern Society," *Art Front*, October 1937; cited by Ashton, op. cit. p. 71.

16. In 1937, reviewing the "consciousness of country" that characterized her earlier work, Martha Graham called it "a temporary but inevitable isolation necessary to find something akin to a folk condition of truth from which to begin." See "Affirmations 1926–37," in Merle Armitage, ed., *Martha Graham* (1937). The dispute between the local and the universal is one that was joined to modern art from the moment of its origins in late nineteenth-century Symbolism, especially with regard to the opposition between a regionalist/naturalist concentration on the peasantry and a Symbolist concentration on the broader *volkisch* spiritual mysticism of the same "Primitives." The notion that true universality could only be attained by an artist deeply rooted in his own land was especially evident in the 1890s, in a resurgent form of Northern Romanticism. See my essay on "Nationalism, Internationalism, and the Progress of Scandinavian Art," in *Northern Light: Realism and Symbolism in Scandinavian Painting, 1880–1910* (New York: Brooklyn Museum, 1982), and the comments of Marcia Vetrocq (with specific reference to parallels in the New York School) in her review, "Souls on Ice," *Art in America*, September 1983, pp. 116–23.

17. See the remarks of Evan Maurer on the Surrealists and the American Indians, in this volume, pp. 561–75; also the map of the Surrealist worldview, which gives an enormously prominent scale to Alaska (p. 556). A prominent promoter of Northwest Coast art and culture was the Surrealist

Wolfgang Paalen; see his articles on "Paysage Totemique," *DYN*, no. 1, April–May 1942; no. 2, July–August 1942; and no. 3, Fall 1942. See also his "Totem Art," *DYN*, special Amerindian number, no. 4–5, 1943–44.

18. On Graham and the New York School, see Ashton, op. cit., p. 143. Ashton cites Graham's remarks on the dance *Dark Meadow*, quoted by Margaret Lloyd, *The Borzoi Book of Modern Dance*, 1949: "It stems back to our remote ancestry, going into the barbaric, the primitive, the roots of life, coming out of racial memory. It is concerned with the psychological background of mankind."

19. Gottlieb, "The Portrait and the Modern Artist," cited by Sandler in *Triumph*, p. 63.

20. There is a need for a full account of the shifting treatment of tribal arts in displays of the 1920s, 1930s, and 1940s. The role played by dealers in their isolating concentration on tribal objects as aesthetic objects—beginning with Stieglitz in 1914 (pp. 454 ff.)—was crucial in disseminating the kind of nonethnological formal approach implicit in, for example, many Cubists' appreciation of tribal art. In New York, the exhibitions of prehistoric and tribal art mounted by The Museum of Modern Art were crucial arenas; and in this respect René d'Harnoncourt stands as a decisive figure in formulating a new installation aesthetic for tribal art. A key account of changes in museology appears in Trevor Thomas, "Artists, Africans, and Installation," *Parnassus* 12, nos. 1 and 4, January and April 1940. Thomas notes: "With the more fashionable swing to an appreciation of native art, the formation of private collections and the consequent soaring of market evaluations for specimens, the museums have set about re-arranging their collections with an eye to their display as rare treasures. The motive of the display conception tends to be in terms which are aesthetic and away from the ethnological viewpoint." Thomas then predicts: "On the swing of the pendulum the next stage in the display fashion for native art will probably revert in part to something not unlike the old ethnological attitude but incorporating much of the aesthetic appreciation." Commenting on The Museum of Modern Art's installation of the exhibition "Twenty Centuries of Mexican Art," Nicolas Calas found that it "does sometimes make the art treasures...look like goods in an elegant Fifth Avenue shop window. When the visitor of the exhibition leaves the ground floor and the Azteques statues for the Spanish rooms or the modern section of Mexican art he feels less like passing through ten or twenty centuries and more like going to another department of Saks or Macy's..." ("Mexico Brings Us Art," *View* 1, no. 1 [September 1940], p. 2). Greater debate circulated, however, around The Museum of Modern Art's exhibition of South Seas objects in 1946. In a review in the *Art Bulletin* 28, no. 2 (June 1946), the anthropologist Gregory Bateson closely examined the premises of this installation as a work of art itself. Bateson examines the pacing, lighting, and sequence of d'Harnoncourt's display in connection with changes in recent anthropological theory, especially with regard to d'Harnoncourt's "mood" evocations, seen in correspondence with current thinking regarding psychology in Primitive societies. The article makes clear, and generally commends, d'Harnoncourt's substitution of a generalized setting of light, changing color, etc. to evoke the spirit of the different tribal arts of the South Seas. Such a shift from strict ethnological contextualism toward abstract symbolism seems perfectly in tune with the modern painting of d'Harnoncourt's contemporaries. In another, less specialized review of the same exhibition, in *View*, series V–VI, 1945–46, Leon Kochnitzky directly linked the Museum's installation decisions not only to the aesthetic lessons of modernist appreciations of tribal arts, but also to the rejection of an earlier positivist

anthropology in favor of a more myth-conscious emphasis on magic and psychology in the approach to tribal man.

21. A good example of the interrelationship between South American, Mesoamerican, and American Indian admirations can be found in the collection of articles in the special Amerindian issue of *DYN*, no. 4–5, 1943–44. Note especially the concentration on matters of cosmology, mythology, astronomy, etc., in articles such as "Totem Art," "The Enigma of Maya Astronomy," and "New Discoveries in the Temple of the Sun in Palenque." On the changing image of the American Indian and the increasing interest in shamanism and mysticism in the period of the 1930s and 1940s, see Aldona Jonaitis, "Creations of Mystics and Philosophers: The White Man's Perception of Northwest Coast Indian Art from the 1930s to the Present," *American Indian Culture and Research Journal* 5, no. 1, 1981, pp. 1–45.

Another instance of concentration on native American art in the 1940s is discussed by Ann Gibson, in "Painting outside the Paradigm: Indian Space," *Arts*, February 1983, pp. 96–103. This instance involved the group known as "Semeiology" or "Indian Space," in which the participating artists (Steve Wheeler et al.) combined a devotion to Northwest Coast Indian design with an admiring notion of a new kind of space revealed from within the twentieth-century theories of physics. This kind of linkage between primitivist interests and modern physics is echoed by other writers and artists of the time, as seen in the text cited in note 87 below.

22. Jackson Pollock, "Jackson Pollock," *Arts and Architecture*, February 1944, p. 14; cited by Sandler in *Triumph*, p. 65.

23. See Thomas Hess, "Isamu Noguchi '46," *Art News*, September 1946, pp. 34 ff.

24. Victor Wolfson, catalog for Kootz Gallery, New York City, January 1947; cited by Guilbaut, op. cit., p. 148.

25. On Stamos, see Ralph Pomeroy, *Stamos* (New York: Abrams, n.d.). On Baziotes, see Mona Hadler, "The Art of William Baziotes," Ph.D. diss., Columbia University, 1977; also *William Baziotes: A Retrospective Exhibition* (Newport Beach: Newport Harbor Art Museum, 1978), with essays by Barbara Cavaliere and Mona Hadler; and two articles: Barbara Cavaliere, "An Introduction to the Method of William Baziotes," *Arts*, April 1977, pp. 28–29; and Mona Hadler, "William Baziotes: A Contemporary Poet-Painter," *Arts*, June 1977, pp. 102–10. Another of the Abstract Expressionist group who flirted with primitivism in his early work was Richard Pousette-Dart; see the discussion of his primitivist interests, and reproductions of his early masklike images, in Gail Levin, "Richard Pousette-Dart's Emergence as an Abstract Expressionist," *Arts*, March 1980, pp. 125–29.

26. Lucien Lévy-Bruhl, *Les Fonctions mentales dans les sociétés inférieures*, 1910, translated by Lilian Clare as *How Natives Think* (London: George Allen and Unwin, 1926). This view is a refutation of positivist theories of the nineteenth century, especially that of Tylor, which held that tribal practices were motivated by a need for explanation or by practical demands. Taking as his point of departure Durkheim's insistence on the importance of "collective representations," Lévy-Bruhl asserted that "myths, funeral rites, agrarian practices and the exercise of magic... are the primitive's response to collective needs and sentiments which are profound and mighty and of compulsive force" (p. 25). Lévy-Bruhl explains that "their mental activity is too little differentiated for it to be possible to consider ideas or images of objects by themselves apart from the emotions and passions which evoke these ideas or are evoked by them" (p. 36). Thus, since "the reality surrounding the primitives is itself mystical" (p. 37), "the difference between animate and inanimate things is not of the same interest to

primitive mentality as it is to ours" (p. 40). "It is not a question of *association*. The mystic properties with which things and beings are imbued form an integral part of the idea to the primitive, who views it as a synthetic whole" (pp. 44–45). See especially the chapter on "The Law of Participation," pp. 68 ff. For Jung's related ideas of undifferentiated Primitive thought, see "The Psychology of the Child Archetype," in *The Collected Works of C. G. Jung*, vol. 9, part I, trans. R. F. C. Hull (New York: Bollingen, 1959), esp. pp. 153–54. Reflections of this conception of the Primitive mentality appear virtually everywhere in the rhetoric of the artists of the 1940s. For example, Frederick Kiesler spoke of his design for Peggy Guggenheim's "Art of This Century" gallery as reaching backward in time "to break down the physical and mental barriers which separate people from the art they live with, working toward a unity of vision and fact as prevailed in primitive times, when seemingly conflicting experiences existed in complete harmony, when the God and the representation of the God, the demon and the image of the demon were equally immediate and real..." (*VVV*, no. 2–3, 1943, p. 76). For more on Kiesler's ideal of "primordial unity" in this space, see Cynthia Goodman, "Frederick Kiesler: Designs for Peggy Guggenheim's Art of This Century Gallery," *Arts*, June 1977, pp. 90–95; and Melvin Paul Lader, "Peggy Guggenheim's Art of This Century: The Surrealist Milieu and the American Avant-Garde, 1942–1947," Ph.D. diss., University of Delaware, 1983, esp. p. 114.

27. Barnett Newman, introductory essay for *Stamos* (New York: Betty Parsons Gallery, 1947); cited by Hobbs, p. 26, note 5.

28. William Rubin, "Pollock as Jungian Illustrator: The Limits of Psychological Criticism," *Art in America*, December 1979, p. 86. On the idea of relationship between art and nature, a series of epigrams in *DYN*, no. 1, April–May 1942, under the title "Seeing and Showing" (p. 27), advanced the principle Pollock espoused: "Not to paint *after* nature, but to work according to its great rhythms; not to follow its fortuitous aspects, but to grasp its universal procedures." David Smith, in "Second Thoughts on Sculpture," in *College Art Journal* 13, no. 3 (Spring 1954), pp. 203–07, continued and expanded the line of thinking apparent both in Pollock's dictum and in the Newman description of Stamos cited in note 27 above: "The artist is now his own nature, the work is the total art. There is no intermediary object...This represents a closer position to the total or ultimate degree. His new position is somewhat that of primitive man. He is not the scientific viewer of nature. He is a part of nature. He is the nature in the work of art" (cited in Barbara Rose, *Readings in American Art since 1900* [New York: Praeger, 1975], p. 250).

29. For consideration of Rothko's formative sources, see especially Stephen Polcari, "The Intellectual Roots of Abstract Expressionism: Mark Rothko," *Arts*, September 1979, pp. 124–34; Robert Rosenblum, "Notes on Rothko's Surrealist Years," in *Mark Rothko* (New York: Pace Gallery, 1981); and James Ward, "The Function of Science as Myth in the Evolution of Mark Rothko's Abstract Style," unpublished qualifying paper, Institute of Fine Arts, New York University, 1977. Ward examines the particular curriculum and texts of Rothko's years at Yale and considers the possibilities of correlation between specific text illustrations and Rothko's imagery.

30. Rothko, "The Romantics Were Prompted...," *Possibilities* I, no. 1 (Winter 1947–48), p. 84.

31. Rosenblum, op. cit., p. 8, compares *Slow Swirl at the Edge of the Sea* with a Navaho sand painting from The Museum of Modern Art's 1941 exhibition of "Indian Art of the United States." Sandler, in *Triumph*, p. 179, holds that "Although the hybrids in Rothko's myth-inspired pictures are abstract, they do allude to observable phenomena—underwater

organisms or the paraphernalia used in primitive rituals." Sandler, in a note appended to this comment, refers to the similar association of Rothko's images with "shields, arrows, and other objects associated with primitive rites," made by William Seitz in his Princeton Ph.D. dissertation of 1955, "Abstract Expressionist Painting in America."

32. In the joint interview "The Portrait and the Modern Artist," already cited with regard to Gottlieb (see note 2 above), Rothko argued that the myths of antiquity were "the symbols of man's primitive fears and motivations, no matter in which land or what time, changing only in detail but never in substance, be they Greek, Aztec, Icelandic or Egyptian. And our modern psychology finds them persisting still in our dreams, our vernacular and our art, for all the changes in the outward conditions of life" (cited in Sandler, *Triumph*, p. 63).

33. See the discussion of water as symbol in mythology, in C. G. Jung, "Archetypes of the Collective Unconscious," 1934, in *The Collected Works of C. G. Jung*, vol. 9, part I, pp. 17–22.

34. In "The Romantics Were Prompted...," Rothko included a broader reference to the connotations of his forms:

On shapes:
They are unique elements in a unique situation.
They are organisms with volition and a passion for self-assertion.
They move with internal freedom, and without need to conform with or violate what is probable in the familiar world.
They have no direct association with any particular visible experience, but in them one recognizes the principle and passion of organisms.

35. Graham, *System and Dialectics of Art*, p. 19. This idea may derive partly from Freud. In his *Introductory Lecture* on the interpretation of dreams, Freud had written: "The [archaic] prehistory into which the dream-work leads us back is of two kinds—on the one hand, into the individual's prehistory, his childhood, and on the other, in so far as each individual somehow recapitulates in an abbreviated form the entire development of the human race, into phylogenetic prehistory too...It seems to me, for instance, that symbolic connections, which the individual has never acquired by learning, may justly claim to be regarded as a phylogenetic heritage." This passage, from *The Standard Edition of the Complete Psychological Works of Sigmund Freud*, vol. 15, p. 199, is cited by Frank J. Sulloway in *Freud, Biologist of the Mind* (New York: Basic Books, 1979), p. 338. This reference, as well as much other valuable information on the background of association between microbiology and the symbolization of the unconscious, was made available to me in an unpublished paper by Jeffrey Weiss, "Microbiology in Art: Symbolism to Biomorphism," Institute of Fine Arts, New York University, 1983.

36. For an extended consideration of the sources of the Pictograph compositions, see MacNaughton, pp. 32–35. On the question of Klee particularly, see Andrew Kagan, "Paul Klee's Influence on American Painting: New York School," *Arts*, June 1975, pp. 54–59; and *Arts*, September 1975, pp. 84–90. Gottlieb affirmed his position that the compositional divisions of the Pictographs reflected his love of early Italian painting, in an interview with Martin Friedman in August 1962 (p. 5 of the typescript in the archives of the Adolph and Esther Gottlieb Foundation, New York City). Torres-García's concern for sources in the ancient indigenous cultures of the Americas is explained in his book *Metafisica de la Prehistoria Indoamericana* (Montevideo: Publicaciones de la Asociacion de Arte Constructivo, 1939).

37. Reviewing the exhibition at Wildenstein (in which George L. K. Morris also showed a work entitled *Indian Composition*, which contained actual birch bark and nails), A. Z. Kruse of the *Brooklyn Eagle*

Enrico Baj. *Angry General with Decorations.* 1961. Oil and collage on canvas, 51 x 38" (129.5 x 96.5 cm). Museum of Contemporary Art, Chicago; promised gift of Joseph and Jory Shapiro

reported on May 24, 1942: "Adolph Gottlieb tenders a direct compliment to modern French symbolism and American Indian themes in his carefully premeditated combination of both." In an unidentified clipping of a review of the same exhibition—a clipping now in the archive of the Gottlieb Foundation—Carlyle Burrows, on May 31, 1942, commented that of the abstractions in the show "The richest in symbolical invention, suggesting the American Indian culture, is Adolph Gottlieb's Alaskan motive..." I am grateful to Sanford Hirsch for bringing these clippings to my attention and for helping my research in the Gottlieb Foundation archive.

38. On the acquisition of the blanket, see Mac-Naughton, p. 38. The key document with regard to Gottlieb's earlier appreciation of native American arts, during his stay in the Southwest, is a letter from Gottlieb to a Paul Bodin, written in March of 1938 and now preserved in the Gottlieb Foundation archive; there the artist describes the "State Museum here which has a marvellous collection of Indian things."

39. Ernst Cassirer, *Language and Myth,* trans. Suzanne Langer (New York: Harper and Brothers, 1946, republication by Dover, 1953), p. 98.

40. For Miró's interest in Primitive sign systems, see especially Sidra Stitch, *Joan Miró: The Development of a Sign Language* (St. Louis: Washington University Gallery of Art, 1980); also Gail Levin on "Miró, Kandinsky, and the Genesis of Abstract Expressionism," in Hobbs and Levin, op. cit., pp. 27–40. On Klee see James Smith Pierce, *Paul Klee and Primitive Art* (New York: Garland, 1976); also Andrew Kagan, "Paul Klee's Influence on American Painting," loc. cit.

Gottlieb's interest in primitive forms of writing is explored by Karen Wilkin in *Adolph Gottlieb: Pictographs* (Edmonton: Edmonton Art Gallery, 1977). Wilkin cites in her Appendix a June 1935 article in *The American Magazine of Art,* entitled "Phases of Calligraphy," in which modern European art was juxtaposed with petroglyphs, hieroglyphs, and pictographs.

41. Gottlieb, in Sidney Janis, *Abstract and Surrealist Art in America* (New York: Reynal and Hitchcock, 1944), p. 119.

42. Gottlieb, *Untitled Edition—MKR's Art Outlook,* no. 6, December 1945, pp. 4,6; cited by Sandler, *Triumph,* p. 196, and by MacNaughton, p. 34.

43. Rosenblum, loc. cit., p. 9, discusses connections between Rothko and Symbolism, not only in regard to Redon but more broadly. See also the discussion by Ward, loc. cit., of microbial imagery in Rothko's works.

44. See MacNaughton's discussion of this letter, signed jointly by Gottlieb, Rothko, and Newman, loc. cit., pp. 40–41. MacNaughton reprints the letter completely in an appendix to her article, p. 169. In defending their work against the incomprehension of the *Times* critic, Edward Alden Jewell, the artists affirmed their belief in the timeless validity of "archaic" symbols and stressed their "spiritual kinship with primitive and archaic art."

45. On the idea of primitivism and its connection with the impetus to reductive purification, see Ann Gibson, "Regression and Color in Abstract Expressionism: Barnett Newman, Mark Rothko, and Clyfford Still," *Arts,* March 1981, pp. 144–53.

46. See Newman's comparison between Egyptian and Greek understandings of form, in Hess, p. 42.

47. For the evidence of Newman's specific interest in golden-section geometry and for the relevant bibliography of works by Cook, Hambridge, Ghyka, et al. that supported this line of thought, see Barbara Cavaliere, "Barnett Newman's *Vir Heroicus Sublimis:* Building the Idea Complex," *Arts,* January 1981, pp. 144–52. On Tony Smith's involvement with such theories of proportion and numerology, Margi Cohen Conrads has given a paper, "Mathematical Systems in Tony Smith's Sculpture," at the Goodson

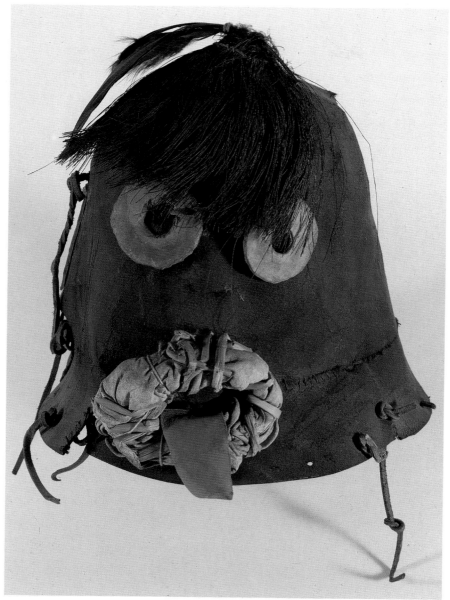

Mask. Pueblo. Arizona or New Mexico. Leather and mixed media, 11⅜" (29 cm) high. Lebel Collection, Paris

Symposium, Whitney Museum of American Art, 1977. Such theories were surveyed and criticized by Milton Brown precisely at the time when Smith and Newman were attracted to them; see "Twentieth-Century Nostrums: Pseudo-Scientific Theory in American Painting," *Magazine of Art* 41, no. 3 (March 1948), pp. 98–101.

48. Brenda Richardson, *Barnett Newman: The Complete Drawings, 1944–1969* (Baltimore: The Baltimore Museum of Art, 1979), pp. 20–22.

49. Personal recollection of Herbert Ferber, communication with author of November 1983.

50. The belief that culture originates in Primitive man's profound fear is one with a long history (see my discussion of Gauguin's interest in Tahitian superstition, p. 199). Newman made a special point of insisting that "All primitive art...was based on terror." See the discussion of this by Hess, p. 43. See also Hess, *passim*, for a sensitive discussion of this estimation of Primitive mentality in the larger context of Newman's interest in mysticism.

51. Newman, "The First Man Was an Artist," loc. cit.; cited by Sandler, *Triumph*, p. 187. For some background to Newman's antimaterialist idea of the primacy of the art impulse in early man, see note 9 above.

52. Jean Dubuffet, "Anticultural Positions," notes for a lecture given at the Arts Club of Chicago, December 20, 1951, in Andreas Franzke, ed., *Jean Dubuffet*, trans. Joachim Neugroschel (Basel: Editions Beyeler, 1976). I am grateful to Phyllis Hattis for providing me with this particular translation.

53. Paul Gauguin, *Cahier pour Aline* (Paris: Société des Amis de la Bibliothèque d'Art et d'Archéologie de l'Université de Paris, 1963): "C'est encore à Mazas où se trouve le génie d'une langue; là un mot nouveau est créé et compris à tout jamais. A l'Académie on ne peut procéder que par étymologie et il faut un siècle pour adopter une nouvelle expression."

54. See the review of discussion of this picture by authors such as Robertson, Alloway, Read, and Langhorne, in Rubin, "Pollock as Jungian Illustrator: The Limits of Psychological Criticism," *Art in America*, November 1979, pp. 104–05. As to whether the headdress in question denotes a male or female personage, see also the response to Rubin by Elizabeth Langhorne in *Art in America*, October 1980, p. 62.

55. On the importance of John Graham for Pollock's primitivism, see Irving Sandler's letter to *Art in America*, October 1980, pp. 57–58. See also note 4 above.

56. For a full review and analysis of theses and articles offering Jungian interpretations of Pollock's iconography, see Rubin, "Pollock as Jungian Illustrator...," two parts, loc. cit.; and the responses to Rubin listed in notes 54 and 55 above.

57. Donald Gordon, "Pollock's 'Bird,' or How Jung Did Not Offer Much Help in Myth-Making," *Art in America*, October 1980, pp. 43–53.

58. Rubin, "Pollock as Jungian Illustrator...," parts 1 and 2, loc. cit.; see also Rubin's response to Langhorne et al. in *Art in America*, October 1980, pp. 65-67.

59. These ideas on Pollock, Picasso, and primitivism were generously communicated to me by William Rubin, in advance of their inclusion in his forthcoming monograph on Pollock.

60. See for example the discussion by Bryan Robertson in *Jackson Pollock* (New York: Abrams, 1960), pp. 82–83.

61. Sandler, in *Triumph*, p. 113, suggests: "Perhaps the Navajo Indians did influence Pollock, but not because they taught him the 'drip' technique, but rather because they obliterated their pictures at the close of their ritualistic ceremony. To them, the act of painting was more important as magic than as picture-making. Their attitude may have given Pollock the confidence to take liberties with conventional approaches to painting."

62. See Rubin on Pollock in "Pollock as Jungian Illustrator...," parts 1 and 2, loc. cit.

63. Sandler, in *Triumph*, p. 106, cites a long passage from Graham's *System and Dialectics of Art* which contains the notion of the Primitive artist as combining a particular blend of mythic involvement and spontaneity.

64. Pollock's use of the handprint has numerous precedents in modern art. In discussing one of these, Gottlieb's *Black Hand* of 1943 (p. 646), MacNaughton, p. 39, points to a Picasso aquatint of 1936 with handprint. Hobbs, p. 10 and p. 25, note 3, also cites the Gottlieb, and mentions other possible models for Pollock in the work of Miró (cover for Miró's 1936 exhibition catalog at the Pierre Matisse Gallery) and Hans Hofmann (*The Third Hand*, 1947). Meyer Schapiro discussed Pollock's handprints in a British radio broadcast, published as "Younger American Painters of Today," in *The Listener*, January 26, 1956, pp. 146–47. Charles Stuckey also considers Pollock's handprints and their possible sources, in "Another Side of Jackson Pollock," *Art in America*, December 1977, pp. 80–91. The particular illustration reproduced here (p. 645), from a book on cave art listed in the inventory of Pollock's library, was brought to my attention in a seminar report on Pollock and primitivism by Claude Cernuschi, Institute of Fine Arts, New York University. The handprint offers a unique blend of fate and liberty, in its dual possible references to occult symbolism, via the palmistry lore with which the Surrealists were at times infatuated; and to process, especially in regard to automatism and the instinctive expression of the individual without system of representation.

65. On the construction of the myth of Pollock, see William Rubin on "The Myths and the Paintings," in "Jackson Pollock and the Modern Tradition," part I, *Artforum*, February 1967, pp. 14–22; and on the larger intellectual and political contexts for such rhetoric, see Guilbaut, esp. chaps. 3 and 4.

66. Barbara Rose, "Hans Namuth's Photographs and the Jackson Pollock Myth—Part One: Media Impact and the Failure of Criticism," *Arts*, March 1979, pp. 112–16.

67. See Sandler on the "ecstasy" and "anxiety" in the "drip" paintings, in *Triumph*, p. 112. Rubin also asserts the "whole spectrum of emotions" in Pollock's dripped paintings, "containing far more of passion, joy, exuberance, ecstasy, delight, gravity, tenderness, suffering, grace, fragility, and at moments even charm," in "Jackson Pollock and the Modern Tradition," loc. cit., p. 17.

68. Seymour Lipton, "Some Notes on My Work," *Magazine of Art* 40, no. 7, November 1947, p. 264, cited by Robert S. Lubar in "Prehistoricism in Sculpture, 1940–1955: David Smith, Theodore Roszak, Seymour Lipton," unpublished paper, Institute of Fine Arts, New York University, 1983.

69. Dorothy Dehner quoted by Karen Wilkin in *David Smith: The Formative Years* (Edmonton: The Edmonton Art Gallery, 1981), p. 9.

70. Rosalind Krauss, *The Sculpture of David Smith: A Catalogue Raisonné* (New York: Garland, 1977), p. 4.

71. See the discussions in *Pillar of Sunday* in Edward Fry, *David Smith* (New York: Solomon R. Guggenheim Foundation, 1969), p. 43; and in Wilkin, op. cit., p. 14. For a suggestively similar configuration and theme, see the Wolfgang Paalen *Paysage totémique de mon enfance*, 1937, reproduced in *DYN*, no. 3, Fall 1942, p. 29. Both works likely owe something to the structure of winged protrusions on Northwest Coast totem poles.

72. See Rosalind Krauss, *Terminal Iron Works* (Cambridge: MIT Press, 1971), for an ambitious argument situating the concept of totemism (especially as per Freud's *Totem and Taboo*) as the bridge between the sexual iconography of Smith's early work and an ongoing formal-cum-epistemological question of "possession" she sees as central to Smith's engagement with modernist

sculpture. Krauss's argument derives largely from her own reading of the issues at stake in modernist sculpture and from her own formal analyses of the relation of the viewer to Smith's sculptures. Though Smith referred to the Primitive on several occasions in his comments on his work, none of his comments suggest the kind of specific psychoanalytic and anthropological thinking about the role of the totem that would buttress Krauss's theory. Moreover, some of his associations of the Primitive world view with eidetic vision (see note 75 below) suggest he did not see the Primitive as experiencing a world constrained and kept divided by taboo systems. Instead he looked to the Primitive mentality as the seat of a superior form of perception, involving more complete rather than more limited acts of "possession" of the world through cognition, and as the locus of an unalienated communion with nature (see note 28 above).

73. On the associations of primeval struggle, see Fry, op. cit., p. 63; Rosalind Krauss in *Terminal Iron Works*, p. 126; and Karen Wilkin, op. cit., pp. 14–15. I am also indebted to an unpublished paper by Robert S. Lubar, cited in note 68 above.

74. This page of notes is reproduced as "Page from a Willard Gallery exhibition announcement," in Garnett McCoy, ed., *David Smith* (New York: Praeger, 1973), p. 71.

75. David Smith, "The Language Is Image," *Arts and Architecture*, February 1952, p. 21.

76. On eidetic imagery, see E. R. Jaensch, *Die Eidetik und die typologische Forschungsmethode*, translated as *Eidetic Imagery and Typological Methods of Investigation* (New York: Harcourt, Brace, 1930); and Jaensch, *Eidetische Anlage und Kindliches Seelenleben* (Leipzig: Verlag von Johann Ambrosius, 1934). In the former work, Jaensch specified: "The eidetic investigations have already shown that the closest resemblance to the mind of the child is not the mental structure of the logician, but that of the artist. In fact there are to be found among artists numerous personalities that permanently keep the characteristics of the youthful phase of development" (p. 47). The work of Jaensch and others is referred to by Charles Robert Aldrich in his *The Primitive Mind and Modern Civilization* (orig. 1931, republished New York: AMS, 1969). One of Aldrich's evocations of Primitive mental life brings together many of the notions recurrent in the remarks of such disparate primitivizing artists as Gauguin, Newman, and Smith:

The primitive society always and inevitably feels itself to be in danger....The savage is like a child who has been fed from infancy on ghost-stories, and who knows that he lives in a haunted house. The world of the savage is really haunted in solemn fact; for he has not lost contact with his unconscious to anything like the extent that civilized man has lost it. Hence when he meditates intently upon his dead mother he is likely to see her memory-image so vividly that it appears before him as an illusion of a vision, a ghost. It may be that this is a form of l'*image eidetique* that has recently engaged the attention of psychologists. [Pp. 98–99.]

Aldrich further cites the work of E. Tripp on the experimental production of eidetic afterimages by visual concentration on objects against neutral grounds (p. 99). (Smith referred to eidetic images and afterimages in virtually the same breath as identical phenomena; see "The Artist and Nature," in Garnett McCoy, ed., *David Smith*, p. 117. It is justifiable to speculate that Smith's practice, apparent in studio photos of the 1950s, of studying his sculptures as silhouettes against specially devised neutral grounds, may have been encouraged by his notions of interraction between eidetic and afterimage perception.) Aldrich goes on to connect the eidetic phenomenon to Jungian ideas of inborn racial memory, and to cite "the similarity of these products [i.e., hallucinations of eidetic perception] the world over and among people of the most diverse cultures" as "evidence that below a certain depth, below mere personal experience, the funda-

mental psyche is the same in all mankind. The eidetic phenomena indicate a primordial stage far less evolved than any savagery now existing, when our ancestors had not yet become able to discriminate the actually seen from the well-remembered" (p. 102). The connections of such ideas to those that motivated Gauguin in works like *Spirit of the Dead Watching* (see discussion p. 199) are quite direct. In the interest in the eidetic image, many of the same issues that engaged Gauguin—of the independence of mind from enslavement to received sensation, and the origins of representation in inner-generated projection—are restated. Just prior to the chapter on "Representations" in which eidetic phenomena are discussed, Aldrich sets the stage by stating: "The question of whether a perception is simply a quasi-mechanical reaction to a sense stimulus, or whether it may be full of subjective elements such as value and meaning is highly important. It is obvious that the more subjective human perceptions are, the more is the external world of objects in which we live a world of our own creating" (p. 57). Smith's interest in the eidetic phenomena may have had more to do, however, with the Surrealist concern for this form of hallucination as a way of simultaneously incorporating and transforming the world. In an article on "Le Message automatique" in *Minotaure* of December 1933, André Breton referred to the work of Jaensch and others on eidetic phenomena. These experiments tended to prove, he said, that "perception and representation—which seem to the ordinary adult to be so radically opposed—should only be taken as the dissociated products of a *single, original, faculty*, of which the eidetic image makes us aware and of which we recover the traces in the primitive and the child" (p. 65). Automatism, Breton argued, provided the way back to this lost "state of grace" where subjectivity and objectivity merged. I am grateful to Jeffrey Weiss for bringing the Breton article to my attention.

77. Smith, "The Language Is Image," p. 33.

78. Newman, "The Sublime Is Now," *Tiger's Eye*, no. 6, December 1948, p. 53; cited in Sandler, *Triumph*, p. 149.

79. Stephen Polcari, "The Intellectual Roots of Abstract Expressionism: Clyfford Still," *Art International*, May–June 1982.

80. In a letter of November 24, 1940, to his sister Vartoosh, Gorky said: "Aesthetic or highest art is that which responds sensitively to complexity and thereby enables man to better understand that complexity. For that reason I do not consider primitive art great art but instead interesting art. For me great art derives from complexity, from the clash of many new and opposing ideas. Primitive art results largely from isolation and isolation cannot produce aesthetic or high art because it lacks all-encompassing experience. Advanced societies have the greatest potential for great art because of their complex confrontations." Karlen Mooradian, ed. and trans., *The Armenian Correspondence of Arshile Gorky: 1937–1948* (Chicago: Gilgamesh Press, 1978), p. 265.

81. Erich Kahler, "The Persistence of Myth," *Chimera* IV, no. 6, Spring 1946, p. 9.

82. Ibid.; also, on the debate surrounding the appropriateness of myth in modern art, see the Lloyd editorial in *Art Front* cited in note 15 above, and Harold Rosenberg, "Breton—A Dialogue," *View*, series 2, no. 2, May 1942.

83. The idea of analogy between personality and culture, specifically with reference to the notion of integration as a standard of health, was one of the central aspects of Ruth Benedict's influential anthropological work, *Patterns of Culture*, of 1934 (reprinted with a Preface by Margaret Mead, Boston: Houghton Mifflin, 1959). The specifically antiracist tenor of the anthropology of Franz Boas and his students here seems pointedly directed against the racist ideals of culture then emergent in

Germany. In this regard, see also Franz Boas, *Anthropology and Modern Life* (New York: Norton, 1928), where a skimming of the chapter titles will suffice to show the level of concern with ideologies of racism.

84. On the neo-Darwinist synthesis of Mendelian genetics with social-competitive models of natural selection, see Ernst Mayr, *The Growth of Biological Thought* (Cambridge: The Belknap Press of Harvard University Press, 1982), pp. 566–70.

85. Wolfgang Paalen, from his introduction to the special Amerindian issue of *DYN*, nos. 4–5, 1943–44; cited by Evan Maurer in his Ph.D. dissertation "In Quest of the Myth: An Investigation of the Relationships between Surrealism and Primitivism," University of Pennsylvania, 1974, p. 327.

86. Jackson Pollock, from an interview in *Arts and Architecture*, February 1944, p. 14; reprinted in Maurice Tuchman, *The New York School: The First Generation* (New York: New York Graphic Society,

n.d.), p. 117.

87. Kahler, loc. cit., pp. 9–10.

88. On the post-bomb rhetoric in relation to the New York School's idea of the Primitive, and also on the merger of primitivist and scientizing interests within these artists' appreciation of the American Museum of Natural History, see Jeffrey Weiss, "Science and Primitivism: A Fearful Symmetry in the Early New York School," *Arts*, March 1983, pp. 81–87.

Bird figure. Senufo. Ivory Coast. Wood, 53¼" (135.3 cm) high. Collection Erle Loran, Berkeley

Walter De Maria. *Lightning Field.* Quemado, New Mexico. 1971–77. 1 mile x 1 kilometer; 400 stainless-steel poles averaging 20'7" high, arranged in a rectangular grid. This vast grid of poles articulates the rolling desert terrain and serves as a theater for spectacular meteorological displays. The measured grid is characteristic of contemporary rationalized aesthetics, but the sense of place engendered, and especially the earth-to-sky relationship of the work, has affinities with Primitive sites and systems of nature worship.

CONTEMPORARY EXPLORATIONS

Kirk Varnedoe

Since World War II, the balance between ideas and objects in artistic primitivism has shifted. For Picasso, Miró, Ernst, and the other leading artists of prewar Europe, notions of the Primitive began with, or found their primary focus in, concrete examples of tribal art. The generation of the Abstract Expressionists, however, favored a broader synthetic idea of the Primitive. Their view (as discussed in the preceding chapter) centered on the spirit of myth and magic more than on specific forms, and found mature expression in types of abstraction that showed no evident links to tribal styles. An even more marked tendency to see the Primitive in conceptual rather than concrete terms has been evident since the later 1960s. Earthworks such as Robert Smithson's *Spiral Jetty* of 1970 (p. 663), performance art such as the rituals of Joseph Beuys (p. 681), and countless other contemporary works have modeled themselves not on Primitive painting or sculpture but on the organizational patterns of tribal and prehistoric societies, on ideas about the structures of Primitive thought and belief, or on collective expressions such as architecture and dance. Lost religious systems, new concepts of the Primitive mind, and enigmatic monuments such as Stonehenge (p. 662) have largely displaced discrete objects as the dominant source of inspiration for primitivizing artists today.[1]

This shift does not seem to have diminished the affinities between contemporary and Primitive art. On the contrary, the connections appear to be more diverse, and may in some ways seem more thoroughgoing, than in earlier modernism—but they are very different in form and meaning. Early modern artists pulled tribal art, figuratively, out of the ethnological and natural-history museums; the new primitivists have

pushed Western art back into those same domains. Smithson, Beuys, Nancy Graves (p. 678), Charles Simonds (p. 680), and many other artists of the past two decades have in fact produced art that refers directly to the displays of natural-history museums, and that speaks of both the methods and the subjects of anthropological and paleontological research.[2] In such works, primitivism seems to have come full circle, from object without context to context without object. Simonds's little civilizations, appearing as misplaced instructional dioramas, provide the converse bookend to Picasso's initial excision of African sculptures from their didactic display in the Trocadéro.

Central to these changes have been a new kind of artist and an expanded idea of modern art. In the sixties, a new generation of predominantly middle-class, college-trained artists, sophisticated and self-conscious in art-historical awareness, began producing systems and process art, conceptual art, performance art, earth art, and other unorthodox work that rejected many of the premises of earlier modernism. In one sense, the intention of these artists was to make art that was newly shocking and difficult to accept, thereby reviving the avant-garde combativeness they felt had been smothered by the broad acceptance of abstract painting in the 1950s. However, much of the rhetoric of the day spoke of closing, rather than widening, the gap between art and its public. In denying what were seen as limiting, ultimately market-serving ideals of individual "touch" (in the connoisseur's sense) and self-contained objects, this new work aspired to overcome a perceived alienation between modern art and society at large. Appropriately, it was described by its makers and admirers in terms that were less those of the fine arts than of

Stonehenge. Salisbury Plain, Wiltshire, England. c. 1800–1400 B.C. 97' diameter, stones above ground 13½' high

anthropology. Echoing traditional (if inaccurate) descriptions of tribal artists as indifferent to aesthetic concerns, the new artists and their critical supporters spoke of future art becoming, as Primitive art had been, more integrally engaged with broader systems of nature, magic, ritual, and social organization.

This changed notion of modern art in turn encountered an altered picture of the Primitive. In the sixties and seventies, the paperback bookstore—rather than the curio shop, the gallery, or the ethnological museum—became the prime locus of many artists' contact with tribal cultures. There the artist encountered an ethnological vision newly shaped by structuralism, in works such as Claude Lévi-Strauss's *Tristes Tropiques* (1955), *The Savage Mind* (1962), and *The Raw and the Cooked* (1964). These writings were influential in both style and substance. They framed a strongly felt critique of the pretensions of modern technological society, and a countervailing appreciation of Primitive life and thought, in a tone of intellectual rigor free from sentiment or taint of romance. Lévi-Strauss's structuralist anthropology held Western culture no further "advanced" than, but only different from and even in significant ways inferior to, that of tribal societies. It furthermore depicted the Primitive mind not as the domain of magic and hallucination previously evoked by writers such as Lévy-Bruhl (see pp. 542–43) and venerated by the Surrealists, but as the seat of powerful forms of logic, separate from but comparable to scientific thought. The critical rationalism of such views both demystified and ennobled the Primitive for those artists who came to maturity after 1960, and who reacted against the ideals of the Abstract Expressionists. The latter had still associated myth with mystery and cherished an

ideal of preliterate man's alogical imagination and spontaneity. But the structuralist view suggested a different kind of Primitive mentality—one which, as the generator of a strict binomial order in all matters material and spiritual, could be appropriated as a forebear of Minimalist and systems art. The global overview employed by structuralism, in which fetishes and fishhooks, totems and table manners were equally meaningful expressions of this collective ordering, was also congenial to the aims of artists seeking to deny established ways of categorizing and valuing modern art.[3]

All this has yielded a primitivism that declares itself, for better and worse, more knowing, and in the process begs the question whether its frequently bookish results are more truly radical or authentic than the allegedly "merely formal" incorporations of tribal art by early modernists such as Picasso. The aesthetic and ideological sources underlying the recent attraction to Primitive cultures are certainly rich enough to sustain artistic achievements of depth and power—but biased and formulaic enough to encourage a lot of banal, bad, and sometimes sinister work. To sort it all out, we must examine more critically where recent primitivism came from, what it promised and what it has delivered, and what it might mean. Why Stonehenge in the space age?

A seemingly obvious answer would be that primitivism came as a 1970s backlash to the high-tech, sharp-focus aesthetics of the 1960s (Pop Art, Minimalism, and hard-edge abstract painting), rejecting impersonal rationality in favor of new ideals of artistic, personal, and political liberation that involved closer contact with nature both earthly and universal. For all the truth such a scenario might hold, however, it seems unpromisingly pat in its correlation to the clichés of

Robert Smithson. *Spiral Jetty.* Great Salt Lake, Utah. 1970. Black rock, salt crystals, earth, and red water, coil 1,500' long, c. 15' wide

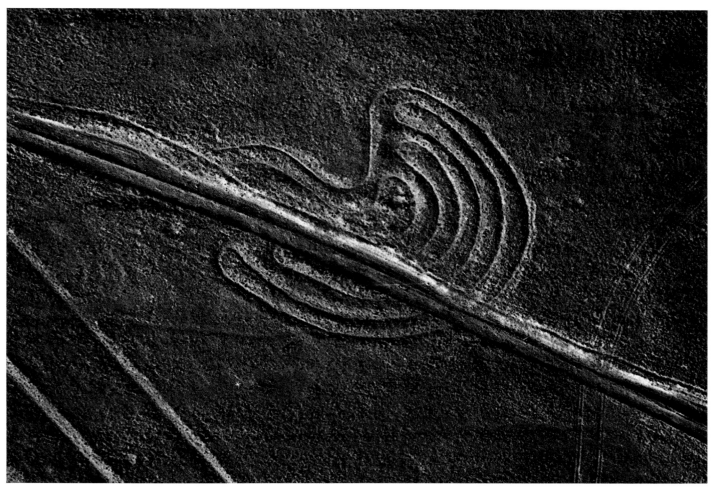

Ground drawing: half-maze. Nazca. Pompa Ingenio, Peru. c. 300 B.C.–700 A.D.

Michael Heizer. *Double Negative* (Second Displacement). Virginia River Mesa, Nevada. 1969–70. 1,600 x 50 x 30'

Michael Heizer. *Double Negative* (Second Displacement) (aerial view). Virginia River Mesa, Nevada. 1969–70. 1,600 x 50 x 30'

Michael Heizer. *Complex One/City.* Near Hiko in south-central Nevada. 1972–76. Cement, steel, and earth. 23½ x 110 x 140'

recent cultural history—and wrong on several counts. Major aspects and artists of the new primitivism were formed in the sixties, and a legacy of rationalized aesthetics has played an important role. Moreover, a strict opposition between cold modern rationalism and shaggy Primitive instinct is as unhelpful in understanding contemporary art as it is in approaching tribal societies. Recent primitivism's richest and most troubling aspects need characterizing in terms of a more complex blend of the scientific and the sensual, the fettered and the free. Earthworks, as the splashiest instance of affinity between new art and the Primitive, seem a good place to start.

The reductivist aesthetics of the early 1960s, with their talk of basic forms of perception and elemental systems of organization, already contained a notion of the *primitif*—in the French philosophical sense of the term, suggesting both germinal origins and irreducible essences of experience. The Minimalist ideal of neutral forms at the base-level of cognition set up an implicit bond between reduction and regression, between hard-edged geometry and the *ur*-forms of the mind, a juncture of the pristine and the primal popularized by Stanley Kubrick's choice of a Minimalist slab to embody the origin of all human achievement in the opening scenes of the film *2001* (1968). It was then but a short step from the monolithic to the neolithic, from such stark blankness to forms of more explicitly archaizing severity. Robert Smithson (who had already established himself as a Minimalist sculptor)

and Michael Heizer took that step in their early earthworks. Heizer's *Double Negative* of 1969–70 and *Complex One/City* of 1972–76 brought to mind the monumental geometries of Mesoamerican ruins, and Smithson's *Spiral Jetty* (1970, p. 663) similarly recalled prehistoric land drawings (p. 663). In these works a concern with process focused on geological action, and an interest in "real-time" systems embraced a scale of millennial endurance. Minimalist absolutism became fused with associations of ultimate survival and extinction that conflated the drama of man's past with the basic forces of natural history.

With their implications of soaring escape from mundane concerns (especially those of the art market) and of confrontation with the elemental, these works focused many of the anti-urban dissatisfactions of the day. Embodying anew the ideals of wide-open spaces and titanic gestural freedom that had marked the critical mythification of the Abstract Expressionists, the early earthworks exhilaratingly suggested a new kind of Wild West artist hero and a spectacular way to tap the larger spirit of pretechnological societies. In retrospect, however, they project a romantically bombastic pessimism as well. Not only freedom but echoes of Ozymandias ring across these lunar settings. Heizer's work ruled inhuman scales of desert space and geological time with a broodingly insentient authority, and Smithson's *Jetty* was even more self-consciously (in its accompanying rhetoric and film) a showplace of inexorable decay.[4] Their archaeological imagery referred not to the creative handwork of tribal artists but to vestiges of lost societies that embodied vast collective labor and ambitions to cosmic knowledge—on a scale that suggested the freeway builder, rather than the painter or sculptor, as the modern counterpart. Such imagery melded hubris and *vanitas*, transcendent aspiration and entropic fate, as it projected contemporary ideas of overweening power and ecological despair backward into time.

The epic portentousness of these pioneer earthworks reverberates the rhetorical tone of the late years of the Vietnam war (though their romance of the wasteland may have had other sources both personal and societal)[5] In outdoor projects of the later 1970s, the settling of this artistic territory brought an undeniable diminution of energy but also a steadier focus on Primitive man's experience of time and nature in anti-epic, explicitly personal terms. Later works such as Richard Fleischner's *Sod Maze*, Richard Long's stone arrangements, or Martin Puryear's bound structures (p. 671) refer to prehistoric and tribal sources in less chest-thumpingly monumental terms. They suggest, more than what might first appear to be only a domestication of scale, a quite different spirit of the Primitive as their inspiration.

The concept of orientation or alignment is critical to many of these earthworks and other outdoor pieces of the sixties and seventies, and can focus our understanding of the issues at stake. Stonehenge (p. 662), or more especially the vast designs on the Nazca plains in Peru (p. 668), are key cases in point. On the one hand, especially when seen from the air,

such monuments give one kind of thrill, of utopian, virtually scaleless power—and a shiver of timeless conceptual enigma in their marking-out of the order of the universe for religious purposes that presage modern science. Yet when experienced firsthand, at ground level, these structures have a different kind of impact, strongly subjective and kinesthetic, evoking the heightened personal sensation of place in nature both proximate and global. Beginning with Smithson and Heizer, and continuing through outdoor works by Walter De Maria (p. 669), Robert Morris (p. 670), Nancy Holt (p. 670), Michelle Stuart (p. 671), Richard Long (p. 668), and others, we can see a recurrent concern for such structures of alignment, a concern that oscillates between the math of astronomy and the immediacy of experience, maps of knowledge and fields of perception, the cosmic and the chthonic. For these artists, the geomancy of ancient sites, and Primitive systems of order that align stars and stones together, are often crucial inspirations[6]

Such models can, of course, inspire imitation as well as innovation. Indeed, mazes for wandering and homemade "observatories" dealing with astral alignments had both become overfamiliar strategies by the end of the seventies. The best work in this vein, though, has gone beyond mere druidic exoticism of form to embrace the alignments of Primitive sites in a fuller way. It has been concerned to stimulate an experience in which the two senses of orientation merge—by structuring the kinesthetic experience of physical place while

Richard Fleischner. *Sod Maze*. Permanent installation, Newport, Rhode Island. 1974. Sod over earth. 18″ x 142′ diameter

humanizing and making immediate a sense of position in a larger map of space and time. Assimilations of these aims may leave behind all but the broadest, and deepest, correlation with Primitive antecedents. In James Turrell's *Roden Crater Project* in Arizona (p. 672)—in which the whole volcanic dish will be shaped into a seamless, object-free visual field opening onto the sky in razor-rimmed regularity—the essential premises of merger between earth and heavens, and between individual sensory perception and global spiritual awareness, are reformulated in nonimitative, modern ways that create all the more powerfully the simultaneously self-locating and self-dissolving sensations of primal awe.[7]

Within these differing responses to Archaic and tribal systems of alignment, we can begin to see a fundamental ambivalence in the concept of the Primitive. On the one hand, recent artists have paid homage to forms of prehistoric and Archaic construction that were apparently too impersonally scaled or too mathematically determined to appeal to earlier modernists. And the admiration for vast collective feats (such as those of the mound builders, the people of Stonehenge, and the pre-Columbian societies of South and Central America) has been accompanied, implicitly and explicitly, by a fascination for the massive social integration, ritualized behavior, and will to cosmic determinism that seem to lie behind such remnants. Yet at the same time the model of Primitive societies, often in some of the same aspects, has equally been invoked as the source for artistic liberation and

personal self-fulfillment, prompting a rejection of basic conventions earlier modernists still generally respected (e.g., discrete objects, individual "touch") and a concern with immediate private experience, especially seen as irrational, intuitive, and anti-authoritarian. This volatility of the collective and the personal, reason and instinct, high order and childlike spontaneity lies near the center of the particular character of contemporary primitivism.

It might seem axiomatic that rigid social patterning and huge collective geometries are the vehicles and signs of inhibiting repression, and that the informality of assembled mud and twigs is a better arena for the release of the improvisatory, innovative energies that have generally been primitivism's most potent yield. Yet much of contemporary art has argued that these opposed readings of the spirit of the Primitive need not be either/or choices. In fact, the two aspects frequently seem intertwined—in the double sense of the ideal of alignment, for example, but also within the basic methods of much recent work. On the one hand prescriptive ritual and strict patterns of organization appear; on the other the manifest goal seems to be a keener, more supple responsiveness to materials and environment and a consequently more immediate, personal psychic engagement. Such blending refers us not only to an enriched idea of the Primitive but also—beyond the fairly direct connections of earthworks to Minimalism—to a more complex legacy of the aesthetics of the sixties.

Richard Long. *Stones in Iceland.* 1974

Richard Long. *Walking a Line in Peru.* 1972

Ground drawing: triangle. Nazca. Pompa Ingenio, Peru. c. 300 B.C.–700 A.D.

Walter De Maria. *Mile Long Drawing* (detail). Mohave Desert. 1968. 2 parallel 4"-wide chalk lines, 12' apart and 1 mile long

Robert Morris. *Observatory.* Oostelijk Flevoland, Netherlands. 1970–77, enlarged and reconstructed at a different site, 1977. Earth, wood, and granite, outer ring 300' diameter

Nancy Holt. *Sun Tunnels.* Near Lucin, Utah, in the Great Salt Lake Desert. 1973–76. Four concrete pipes, each 18' long, 9'½" diameter; "X" configuration 86' from end to end across axis. The tunnels are aligned with the sun on the horizon (sunrises and sunsets) on the solstices.

Nancy Holt. *Sun Tunnels.* 1973–76. View through the northwest tunnel. Holes cut in the pipe project the pattern of the constellation Draco in the darkened interior.

Michelle Stuart. *Stone Alignments/Solstice Cairns.* Rowena Dell Plateau, Columbia River Gorge, Oregon. 1979

In specific and functional terms, the art of the early 1960s licensed primitivism in at least two major areas. The general concern that works express the process of their making, and the advent of mathematical systems as generating formulas for art, opened the way to new rule-bound methods of creating— methods in which clinical repetition easily shaded over into evident ritual. Also, especially in sculpture, the denial of metaphor in favor of immediately perceived qualities of weight, scale, shape, and orientation helped promote a puri- fied poetry of raw materials and bodily awareness. In both areas a purging reduction to basics in the intellectual structure and the physical experience of art redefined simplicity and set the preconditions for new ways of engaging the spirit and forms of Primitive creativity. Here we locate the common ground shared by artists of quite different persuasions, such as Richard Long and Carl Andre. Smart art and dumb art, computer grids and kids' games, the arch and the archaic often formed strange bedfellows in this important breeding-ground of the new primitivism. Two artists whose works embody especially clearly such a mix of interests, and who serve as bridge figures between different aesthetics, are the late Eva Hesse and Jackie Winsor.

In the heyday of Minimalism and Pop, Hesse evolved an outsider's vocabulary of malleable materials and structures that had specifically visceral, sexual associations. Within the

Martin Puryear. *Installation.* 1977. Corcoran Gallery of Art, Washington, D.C. Cedar, fir, and rawhide, 18x16½'. Puryear's wood-and-hide works frequently evoke tribal dwellings, shrines, and implements.

James Turrell, *Roden Crater Project*. Currently in progress. A volcanic crater near the Painted Desert in Arizona, to be partially reworked by the artist. Underground chambers will be created within the volcano rim, oriented to daily and yearly astronomical cycles, as well as to singular events such as eclipses (calculated as much as 12,000 years in advance). The bowl of the crater will be shaped into a parabolic dish from within which the whole vaulting of the heavens will be experienced with exceptional immediacy. The view from the rim will join this experience to that of the curving horizon, and to awareness of the undisturbed primal geology of the region.

grids and serial sequences of early sixties art, on the other hand, she found not just alien clinical logic but an auto-biographical, poetic voice with which to shape her preoccupations. Seen in conjunction with creepily tactile surfaces and stringy or warped forms, Hesse's acts of repetition seemed more compulsive or therapeutic than merely mechanical.[8] Similarly, in the slightly later structures of Jackie Winsor, patterned procedures and geometric forms also became the vehicle for work that projected ritualistic obsessiveness of process and willfully crude physicality. Particularly in her early log-and-twine pieces (p. 674), Winsor articulated the basic experiences of weight and scale in blunt, awkwardly sensual terms and showed how simple rule-bound tasks could by dint of gritty insistence express a personal cathechism of toil.[9] Here, as with Hesse, math shaded into mantra: Aesthetic strategies designed to shut down the Zenlike gestural liberties of Abstract Expressionism wound up serving as ways to recover, in altered and newly acceptable form, the release of psychic energies through surrender to artistic process. In the work of these and other artists of the late sixties and early seventies, the syntax of Minimalism served both as ground and as foil for the articulation of work that, without specific reference to tribal or prehistoric cultures, nonetheless set the terms of a new allusive primitivism.

Not only in the fascination with ancient feats of engineering such as Stonehenge or Avebury, but also in the basic means and methods of Hesse, Winsor, and a broad spectrum of other recent work, instinct and physicality have been pointedly joined to intelligence and conceptual schema in ways that are fruitful rather than fatal. Artists such as Richard Long and Michelle Stuart, for example, involve themselves with the earth, and with raw materials, in the most physically immediate fashion. Long's country walks and his stone arrangements express the simplicity of a child's rhyme and the freedom of unparceled topography (pp. 667, 668), and his gallery pieces carry this feeling over into elementary placements of rocks and sticks (p. 675) and finger-paintings of mud (p. 675). Stuart's imprinting of stones and rubbing of local earth similarly engage her body with the Archaic and prehistoric sites she visits (p. 676). In each artist's work primal contact replaces anything that could traditionally be called technique. Yet in the organization and presentation of their art they show an equal concern for systems of charting, cataloging, and counting—Long in the measuring correlations of distance and time that determine his movements and markers (p. 676) and Stuart in the grid systems and book forms that stratify her paper memories. In Michael Singer's work, too, the ghost of a guiding pattern, often a buried grid, governs ephemeral weaves of sticks and branches (p. 677). The air of ritualistic prescription surrounds his response to found properties of weight and shape, and the final air of balance is not only that of pebble and twig but also that between the rough necessity of a bird's nest and the refined sparseness of Shinto ceremony. In the work of Long, Stuart, and Singer, Primitive

Eva Hesse. *Vinculum, II.* 1969. 23 rubberized wire-mesh plaques stapled to shielded wire, 19'5" x 3" (591.7 x 7.6 cm), with 23 hanging extruded rubber wires, knotted, ranging in size from 7" (17.9 cm) to 62" (157.6 cm). Size installed, 9'9" x 2½" x 9'7½" (297.2 x 5.8 x 293.5 cm). The Museum of Modern Art, New York; The Gilman Foundation Fund

Though Hesse's materials were often industrial, her use of them evoked associations with the body, and with the rough or ritualistic look of tribal artifacts. These overtones, and the personal psychological charge of her work, shaped a vocabulary that would be widely used by primitivizing artists in the 1970s.

Eva Hesse. *Ishtar.* 1965. Wood, cork, paint, and rubber, 36 x 7½ x 2½" (91.4 x 19 x 6.3 cm). Private collection

Eva Hesse. Untitled. 1970. Fiberglass over polyethylene over aluminum wire, seven units, each 7'2" to 9'3" high. Collection Mr. and Mrs. Victor W. Ganz, New York

Jackie Winsor. *Bound Square.* 1972. Wood and twine, 6'3½" x 6'4" x 14½" (191.8 x 193 x 36.8 cm). The Museum of Modern Art, New York; purchase

Jackie Winsor. *Four Corners.* 1972. Wood and hemp, 30 x 48 x 48" (76.2 x 121.9 x 121.9 cm). Allen Memorial Art Museum, Oberlin College, Oberlin, Ohio; gift of Donald Droll in memory of Eva Hesse

Richard Long. *River Avon Mud Circle.* 1982. Mud on white wall (destroyed). 10'10" (279.4 cm) diameter. Sperone Westwater, New York

Richard Long. *Marble Stone Circle.* Marble, c. 8' diameter. Jean Bernier Gallery, Athens

Michelle Stuart. *Nazca Lines Star Chart*. 1981–82. Earth from Nazca, Peru, on paper, 120 x 168″ (304.8 x 426.7 cm). Private collection

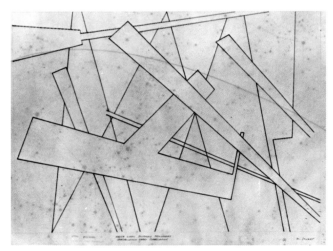

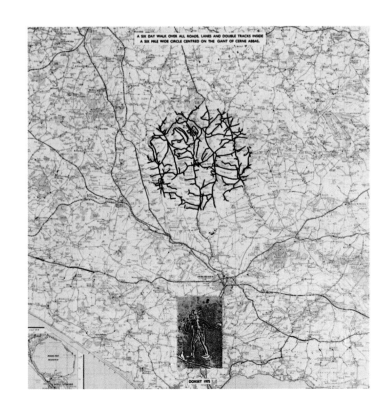

Above: Michelle Stuart. *Nazca Lines Southern Hemisphere Constellation Chart Correlation*. 1981. India ink on vellum, 17 x 22″ (43.2 x 55.9 cm). Private collection

Right: Richard Long. *Cerne Abbas Walk (A six day walk over all roads, lanes and double tracks inside a six mile wide circle centered on the Giant of Cerne Abbas)* (detail). 1975. Two parts: ink and photograph on Ordinance Survey map (scale 1″= 1 mile), 28½ x 29″ (72.5 x 73.6 cm), and black-and-white photograph, 14⅛ x 21⅛″ (36 x 53.5 cm). The Tate Gallery, London

Michael Singer. *First Gate Ritual Series 10/78*. 1978. White pine, stones, and marsh reeds, 8'4" x 14' x 19'10" (254 x 426.7 x 604.5 cm). The Fort Worth Art Museum; purchased with funds from Mr. and Mrs. Lewis Kornfeld and Nancy O'Boyle and matching funds from the National Endowment for the Arts Museum Purchase plan

Michael Singer. *First Gate Ritual Series 4/79*. Dayton, Ohio. 1979. Destroyed

experience is internalized as a mutually reinforcing combination of patterned behavior and responsive sensual awareness. And here, in the personal deep structure of the activities more than in any formal references to prehistoric or tribal sites and monuments, a distinctively contemporary poetry of primitivism emerges, one in which frames of logic and documentation restrain and distance, yet focus and enhance, the emotive associations of the deep past.

These artists seem "knowing" in a productive rather than an inhibiting way. The changed parameters of recent art and new ideas of Primitive culture promote not just a different kind of quotation but a newly complex sense of identification across cultural barriers. Such work evidently belies simplistic divisions between rationalist and primitivist aesthetics. But by extension it also suggests larger ways in which recent primitivism may represent something more than simple escape from, or opposition to, modern Western culture. A possible derivation from its particular hybrid character is the premise that the Primitive and the modern are less antagonistic than mutually nourishing. This premise, moreover, is not art's alone. It belongs to broad intellectual currents of the recent past: currents that, connected to all we have been considering, can help us close in on the basic question of primitivism's contemporary relevance.

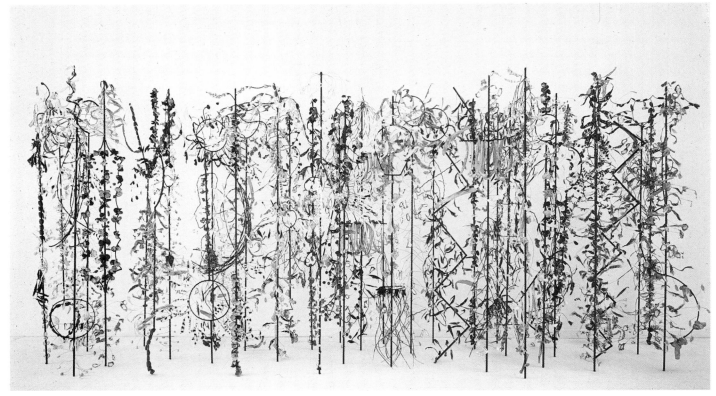

Nancy Graves. *Variability and Repetition of Variable Forms.* 1971. Steel, wax, marble dust, acrylic, plaster gauze, and latex, 38 units, 10 x 15 x 35' (305 x 457.5 x 1,067.5 cm), overall. National Gallery of Canada, Ottawa. The imagery of natural forms in this piece—twigs, vines, berries, beetles, and cowrie shells—reflects the artist's experience of the artifacts of Primitive cultures of the South Pacific islands. The work is closely related to another, *Shaman,* 1972, in the Wallraf-Richartz Collection, Cologne, which was inspired by Northwest Coast Indian cultures.

However paradoxical it may seem, a recurrent modern idea has held that advances in technology bring us closer, for better and worse, to our Primitive counterparts. The negative version of this view compares the anxiety of modern times with the presumed picture of Primitive man consumed by fear. Or, in a variant of the same pessimism, contemporary conflict and destruction are seen as recurrences of the brutality of a violent state of nature, with modern weapons recapitulating Darwinian struggle. Both of these depressing connections were abroad in the 1940s (see the chapter on Abstract Expressionism, pp. 619, 648–49), and they have been extended since. Smithson's *Spiral Jetty* film was on the same wavelength, with its equations between dinosaurs and bulldozers and its

larger metaphor of cultural doom linked to the entropy of nature in an eternal spiral of history.[10] We have all become inured, too, to the notion that our latest technologies put us ever closer to the threshold of a new Stone Age in ultimate cataclysmic terms.

But there has been a brighter side as well to such images of correlation, stressing a mutual give-and-take between the Primitive past and the technological present. Certainly few new ideas enjoyed a wider vogue in the 1960s than Marshall McLuhan's vision of the "global village," in which triumphant telecommunications would literally return us to our senses, restoring a Primitive fullness of consciousness and tribal intimacy on a worldwide scale.[11] In practical terms as well as in popular imagination, it has also been demonstrated that advances in electronic intelligence bring us closer to the Primitive mind rather than distancing us from it. The metaphor of Stonehenge as a computer is the monument of this correlation, in which the smarter we get the smarter we realize they—or we—always were.[12] As it extends toward silliness, this optimism passes the belief that the Hopi language is better equipped to deal with the quantum universe, to arrive eventually at Atlantis updated to encompass ancient spacemen building megalithic runways. There is, however, something quite important at work here, and it seems to work directly on a great deal of recent primitivist art. It serves to explain the recurrent connection between new primitivism and science and the frequent evocation of the Primitive as scientist. The phenomenon is evident in revived archaeoastronomy and geomancy, in methods that display the archaeologist's grid and the anthropologist's structures, and also in unlikely combinations of interests, such as appear in the work of Nancy

Nancy Graves. *Fossils.* 1970. Wax, gauze, marble dust, acrylic, and steel, 36" x 25' x 25' (91.4 x 762 x 762 cm). Collection of the artist

Nancy Graves. *Totem*. 1970. Animal skin, steel, gauze, wax, oil paint, latex, and acrylic, 8'6" x 3' x 3' (259.1 x 91.4 x 91.4 cm). Collection of the artist

Graves: the world of shamanism and skin-painting run-on with that of Muybridge and moon maps.[13] The common denominator is a fascination for man's ways of ordering, seen in dialogue with the order of nature he seeks to embrace in his systems. The new languages of science are celebrated as another way of knowing, one that does not alienate us from nature but increases our wonder as it brings more nature, and more mystery, into our understanding, thereby establishing ways of recovery, new avenues of communion with separate and lost cultures. Such work seemingly proposes that one of art's roles in an age of high science is to humanize this underlying universal spirit of inquiry, to isolate and communicate in immediately accessible form a basic sense of wonder and a mental reach that links contemporary man to his seemingly most distant human counterparts. If we want the happy answer to the question posed earlier, Why Stonehenge in the space age? this is getting toward the point.

But there is a dark side to this issue as well, and it has to do with more than just bad art or even overtly pessimistic art. It has to do with primitivism per se, and it involves politics. All the questions we considered a moment ago, of collectivity versus individual experience, of controlling order versus instinctual liberty, translate eventually into larger political implications. Inasmuch as it has been by definition a critique of modern Western society, all primitivism has always had such implications, and they reverberate through good and sensitive art as certainly as through the broad range of neo-tribal agitprop that the last two decades have witnessed. The latter work, in which political concerns have been aggressively self-conscious and specific, most quickly forces to the fore uncomfortable questions about the ultimate content of all ideals that propose escape from the Western tradition into a Primitive state.

Throughout the past two decades, at least since hippies adopted Indian wear, a loose alliance of ideological interests—feminism, ecology, anti-imperialism, antinuclear movements, and racial minority consciousness—has contributed to the allure of primitivizing styles and trappings. Simultaneously, Third World nations have intensified their concern for the integrity of their own tribal arts. This new climate of awareness has fruitfully opened the way for many artists to reestablish contact with their own heritages, as in Romare Bearden's homage to African culture, and has sensitized Western artists to the racial and historical issues involved in references to foreign cultures (which may in part account for the vogue of more "neutral" prehistoric, rather than African or other tribal, sources). The resultant reform in consciousness has produced a highly variable yield in art. At its most banal, self-styled political primitivism has yielded harmless role-playing, conjurings of Atlantean fantasies, and astrological or alchemical mysticism. In other manifestations, however, it has been the arena for iconographies of regression that give more serious pause and that need examining in regard to the politics of primitivism old and new.

From a very early date, Western appreciations of Primitive man have had a built-in ambivalence about freedom and determinism. For example, Primitive expressions have been seen as closer to original structures of communication and thought, and thus as shaped by an underlying necessity that transcends the vagaries of stylistic change. This notion of necessity imagines equally an unselfconscious spontaneity and an involuntary bonding to deep structures of the mind or of nature. Admiration for the apparently fixed and unchanging communal styles of tribal and prehistoric man may thus have the paradoxical aim of liberation of modern spontaneity (as in the case of Pollock, for example, see pp. 640–44) or the more direct appeal of nostalgia for the security of suprapersonal absolutes.[14] Often, as was the case with the Abstract Expressionists, modern artists have pursued the two appeals at

Romare Bearden. *The Prevalence of Ritual: Baptism*. 1964. Photomechanical reproduction, synthetic polymer, and pencil on paperboard, 9⅛ x 12" (23.2 x 30.5 cm). Hirshhorn Museum and Sculpture Garden, Smithsonian Institution, Washington, D.C.

Charles Simonds. *People Who Live in a Circle. They Excavate Their Past and Rebuild It Into Their Present. Their Dwelling Functions as a Personal and Cosmological Clock, Seasonal, Harmonic, Obsessive.* 1972. Clay on wood base. Clay portion: 8⅜ x 26¼ x 26⅛" (22.2 x 66.7 x 66.4 cm); base: 32⅛ x 32⅛ x 32⅛" (81.6 x 81.6 x 81.6 cm). The Museum of Modern Art, New York; Kay Sage Tanguy Fund

once, imagining that a universal language, a "myth for our time," was to be found in the most liberated and deep-seated realization of the self. In a broad range of ideologically tinged recent primitivism, the same ideal is reconstrued to equate personal psychodrama with broad political concern, on the ostensible model of the Primitive priest or shaman as both marginal madman and communal healer.[15] Of course, the crucial ingredient missing in a modern pluralist society is the shared consensus that gives the shaman his stature and power of communication. And to an unsettling degree, as if in response to this isolating lack of cult unity, some of the most prominent manifestations of this art have inclined toward the nostalgia of collectivism, or primal determinism, as a remedy for modern woes.

In several instances of feminist primitivism, for example, the simpler and suppressed truth called back from Primitive societies has seemed to involve a reduction of identity to gender and of culture to biology. An iconography of blood, hair, and organs, reacting against an earlier formalism associated with male hegemony, has marked countless recent works that express feminist consciousness as integral with bodily awareness. Womblike spaces and visceral symbols that would be equally at home in the oneiric male sadism of Surrealism are incorporated in objects and rites that—frequently in explicit insistence on their linkage to tribal or

prehistoric cults and arts—celebrate a "natural" order of tribal life yoked to the imperium of blood and soil.[16]

Such imagery is not the exclusive preserve of one kind of politics. Charles Simonds's initial demonstrations of primal earth-body-architecture connections were personal and direct; and his "little people" at first seemed to combine a kind of Tolkienian charm with liberating political ideals of an ephemeral, community-oriented art. But the Spenglerian cycles subsequently constructed for them, and the relentlessly explanatory documentation that has bricked them in, have made the humor grimmer as the fantasies of totalitarian social solidity and biological determinism that pervade their sexualized anthropology become more insistently evident.[17]

Nowhere is the political problematic of recent primitivizing art as explicit, however, as in the singular work of the German Joseph Beuys. Through his idiosyncratic production of talk and tallow runs a self-proclaimed program of social renewal, as well as a less-remarked-upon strain of symbolism that harks back to German chthonic mythology. Beuys's own personal myth of survival and rebirth (centering on the 1943 crash of the Luftwaffe plane he was piloting and his rescue by nomad Tartars) is the ghost in his metaphoric machine, an unwieldy apparatus of padded hardware, turn-of-the-century vitrines, and mad diagrams, running on a pseudoalchemical breviary of primal substances, especially felt, fat, and honey.

Joseph Beuys. *Object from Eurasia, 32. Movement from Siberian Symphony 1963.* 1966. Chalk on blackboard, felt, fat, and hare carcass, 70⅞ x 90⅝ x 21⅝" (180 x 230 x 55 cm). Collection L. Schirmer, Munich

His performances with (totemic?) animals dead and alive are only the most evident instances of his self-conscious orchestration of the shaman's role, in this case both intended and proclaimed as that of redemptive focus for a reawakened German national consciousness. Voice of the new left and advocate of liberation, Beuys and his myth are nonetheless

uncomfortably reminiscent of older appeals to a Northern sense of self-in-nature, which were exploited to dark effect by National Socialism.[18]

Just as it was made clear earlier that geometric order and binding pattern need not necessarily spell repression, so it should be clear that biology is not liberty and that the ideal of regression closer to nature is dangerously loaded. But this is virtually a truism and still does not get at a deeper aspect of what is sinister in recent primitivism. Beyond admiration for the monuments of crushingly authoritarian collective societies (more often Archaic than tribal) or sociobiological atavism—both of them fairly obvious warning flags—there are subtler, deeper currents in new primitivist art that suggest disturbing precedents.

As we said at the outset, work that has styled itself as postmodern has looked to anthropological models of tribal and prehistoric integration of art and society as curatives for the separation or alienation of art from its viewers and for the consequent undermining of art's relevance and power. The desire behind many earthworks and site sculptures, as we analyzed it, was precisely to overcome this barrier, to involve a fuller range of the viewer's experience, and to instill a sense of alignment that heightened awareness of place and moment. In conjunction with astral and earth orientations and references to menhirs or megalithic monuments, many of these works were intended furthermore to yield on a personal, self-

Joseph Beuys. *"I Like America and America Likes Me."* 1974. A week-long performance at the René Block Gallery in New York. Beuys (here wrapped in a cloak) lived in a cage with coyote, who was specially chosen as an animal of importance to American Indians but despised by the American white man.

dissolving level the sense of community with immemorial rhythms of natural order and human tradition. These latter conditions seem laudable enough, and yet they are virtually the same terms Albert Speer had in mind in his design for the ceremonial zeppelin fields and parade grounds of the Third Reich. Indeed, one of the German monuments most admired by the Nazis was a great circle of monoliths consciously modeled on Stonehenge, intentionally kept devoid of independent sculpted figures and slated for use especially on solstice festivals, where the alienating atomism of modern society would be dissolved in a reaffirming merger of *Blut und Boden*, of the folk with the cycle of the seasons and the soil.[19]

While total art and totalitarian art may start out from very different places, they share enemies and can wind up approaching each other. To the extent that primitivism presents itself—as many of its recent advocates have presented it—as the righteous foe of the modern, it falls into perilous fellowship with other such foes and begs unflattering comparisons. If we want an unhappy answer to why a modern Stonehenge, this is at least in the vicinity.

However, it is richer and more in keeping with everything this book has been about to see primitivism, modern or postmodern, not only as a symptom of cultural disaffection but as a sign of life. Only in its least creative moments and only for the conventionally minded or uninformed can the twentieth-century fascination with the tribal be seen as a wholly negative—or wholly affirmative—response to modernity. It has been, as primitivist thought has always been, a dialogue of self-projection, discovery, and self-criticism, in which modern life provides both the need for alternatives and the means for uncovering and understanding them. Daumier and folk prints gave Gauguin his points of affinity with Hokusai and the Marquesans, and they in turn reinvigorated Giotto for him (p. 185). Gauguin then, with Cézanne, led Picasso toward his crucial connection with tribal sculpture, and that helped him elevate to greater effect his admiration for Rousseau and his own caricatural power.[20] Amid all that is familiar in the latest neoprimitivist painting, both in the nationalist rhetoric that boosts it and in the revivalist look (e.g., A. R. Penck), what is most happily recognized is the restatement, however slight, of this kind of dialogue, in the new infatuation with graffiti.

A. R. Penck. *Defense.* 1983. Resin on linen, 8'1½" x 11'4½" (247.6 x 346.7 cm). Mary Boone Gallery/Michael Werner Gallery

Keith Haring. Untitled (Totem). 1983. Enamel on wood, 9' x 43" (262 x 109.2 cm). Collection of the artist

Here the sophisticated devices of modern international signage blend with cartoon conventions and streetwise inventions in alternatively upbeat and ominous subterranean pictographs of modern life (e.g., Keith Haring). Communication theory and cave painting meet in the South Bronx. More deeply and richly, this essential interchange is manifest in the best of the art we have been discussing. Minimalism, structuralism, and modern technology have not simply provided the antitheses from which recent primitivism has fled, nor only encouraged the bookish smothering of instinctual originality. They have opened up as well new ways of access to Primitive thought and society, new levels of affinity that in turn reform and redirect our art and point to the recovery of neglected inspirations among our own resources.

The idea of primitivism as flight from civilization, or of Primitive art as a wholly "outsider" challenge, is an offshoot of the Romantic notion that true progress, true revolution, indeed truth in its most irreducible sense is only accessible when we step outside the enchaining confines of culture.[21] Modern ideas of the mind and of the constraints of language suggest that this fantasy of escape is never to be realized. Yet this need not mean that the power of primitivism lies only in delusion, or that we are prisoners of conventions that bar us from contact with anything beyond our ken, or kin. Modern thought and style are not only blinders but also powerful lenses. The history of modernist primitivism and the character of its best recent examples speak directly to the point. This is a process of revolution that begins and ends in modern culture, and because of that—not in spite of it—can continually expand and deepen our contact with that which is remote and different from us, and continually threaten, challenge, and reform our sense of self.

NOTES

The author wishes to thank Elyn Zimmerman and Adam Gopnik for many valuable discussions that helped give form to this essay.

1. The shift referred to here has had its parallels in other fields as well, as primitivist tendencies have appeared, in transformed and newly energized fashions, in dance, poetry, and music of the last two decades. For some relevant material regarding poetry, see Jerome Rothenberg and Diane Rothenberg, *Symposium of the Whole: A Range of Discourse toward an Ethnopoetics* (Berkeley: University of California Press, 1983), especially the chapter on "Contemporary Moves." For a key instance in music, see Steve Reich, "Postscript to a Brief Study of Balinese and African Music" and "Notes on Music and Dance," in *Steve Reich: Writings about Music* (Halifax, N.S.: The Press of the Nova Scotia College of Art and Design, 1974). Reich's differentiation (p. 40) between former incorporations of the *sound* of tribal instruments and current efforts to assimilate the *structure* of such music is exemplified by his own *Drumming* (based on his researches in Africa). His ideas exemplify the opposition to superficial exoticism and the urge to more knowing probes of Primitive cultures that have motivated much recent primitivism.

2. Museums of natural history have been, of course, an ongoing source of inspiration for modern artists, in part because they often combine displays of natural science with those of ethnology. See Jeffrey Weiss, "Science and Primitivism: A Fearful Symmetry in the Early New York School," *Arts*, March 1983. The American Museum of Natural History has been a particularly rich ground for art since 1945. In the 1940s, the fascination with both ethnological and biological displays there was attested to by David Smith's sculpture (see pp. 652, 653) and also by Claude Lévi-Strauss (see Lévi-Strauss, "The Art of the Northwest Coast at the American Museum of Natural History," *Gazette des Beaux-Arts*, 1943, p. 75). Robert Smithson continued this tradition by featuring the Hall of the Dinosaurs in his *Spiral Jetty* film; see Elizabeth C. Childs, "Robert Smithson and Film: The *Spiral Jetty* Reconsidered," *Arts*, October 1981, pp. 68–81. On Nancy Graves's work with bones in a different spirit of comparative morphology, see *Nancy Graves: Sculpture, Drawings, Films, 1969–1971* (Aachen: Neue Galerie im Alten Kurhaus, 1971); and Linda Cathcart, *Nancy Graves: A Survey, 1969/1980* (Buffalo: Albright-Knox Art Gallery, 1980). On Beuys, see Caroline Tisdall, *Joseph Beuys* (New York: Solomon R. Guggenheim Museum, 1979)—though this catalog does not do justice in its reproductions to Beuys's practice of installing his work in heavy glass vitrines of the type associated with older museological practice in the natural sciences (see especially the large installation of his work at the Hessisches Landesmuseum, Darmstadt). For Charles Simonds, see John Neff et al., *Charles Simonds* (Chicago: Museum of Contemporary Art, 1982). There Neff says (p. 10) of Simonds that "As this catalogue goes to press, he is exploring the possibilities of a visionary, environmental museum of natural history."

3. Lévi-Strauss's relationship to modern art is a subject worthy of examination in itself. It seems clear that his admiration for Picasso strongly intertwined with his response to tribal arts (see his remarks on Northwest Coast art, cited in note 2, above). Indeed, his influential model of Primitive thought, as proposed in "The Science of the Concrete" in *The Savage Mind* (1962), seems to involve an image of creativity—that of the *bricoleur*—formed on the model of Picasso's collages and on Surrealist thought, projected onto tribal man. Lévi-Strauss's debts to earlier modernist aesthetics, seen in conjunction with his impact on the thinking of more recent artists, offer a rich model of primitivism as modernism's self-projection and self-reforming critique. Unfortunately, Lévi-Strauss's personal response to more recent art has been far less rewarding.

Also important in this regard was George Kubler's *The Shape of Time* (New Haven: Yale University Press, 1962). Kubler's antiorganic model of historical development in formal sequences, and his concern for families of objects regardless of traditional notions of artistic merit, reverberated through the Minimalist aesthetics of the sixties. The coincidence of Kubler's own concentration on pre-Columbian Art and the contemporary resurgence of artistic interest in sites such as Nazca, Chichén Itzá, and Tikal provides another point of contact between this archaeological/historical thinking and the aesthetics of the present.

4. On Smithson and the iconography of crystallization, extinction, and decay, see Childs, "Robert Smithson and Film," loc. cit.; and Adam Gopnik, "Basic Stuff: Robert Smithson, Science, and Primitivism," *Arts Magazine*, March 1983. The basic texts in this regard are in Nancy Holt, ed., *The Writings of Robert Smithson* (New York: New York University Press, 1979). On earthworks more generally see John Beardsley, *Probing the Earth: Contemporary Land Projects* (Washington: Smithsonian Institution Press, 1978); and Beardsley's forthcoming book, *Earthworks and Beyond* (New York: Abbeville, 1984). Specifically on the affinities between recent and Primitive earthworks, see the special issue of the *Art Journal* edited by Robert Hobbs, on "Earthworks: Past and Present," Fall 1982.

5. The negative tone of parts of Minimalism and some earthworks may stem from a love-hate relationship with bleak urban settings, such as is also evident in aspects of Richard Serra's work. In this regard Smithson's early article on "Entropy and the New Monuments" (see Holt, ed., *The Writings of Robert Smithson*) is revealing. In an unpublished paper at the Institute of Fine Arts, New York University, Robert Knafo has also analyzed Smithson's imagery of pollution, wasteland, and decay as connected to his earlier gory crucifixions, in light of Smithson's involvement with failed Catholicism and his related attraction to the bleaker visions of T. S. Eliot.

The idea of decay and dereliction presents an interesting juxtaposition to more "pure" Minimalist notions of antihistorical time, with their attention to synchrony over diachrony. The role played by George Kubler's antihistorical, anti-individual theory of the patterns of development of objects in past civilizations (see note 3, above) needs more thorough examination in relation to such questions of aesthetics in the sixties.

6. For a key examination of concepts of viewer relation to, and interaction with, contemporary sculpture—seen in specific connection with the model of prehistoric sites—see Robert Morris, "Aligned With Nazca," *Artforum*, October 1975.

7. On the work of Turrell, see Barbara Haskell, *James Turrell: Light and Space* (New York: Whitney Museum of American Art, 1980).

8. On Hesse, see Lucy Lippard, *Eva Hesse* (New York: New York University Press, 1976).

9. On Winsor, see Ellen H. Johnson, *Jackie Winsor* (New York: The Museum of Modern Art, 1979).

10. See Childs, "Smithson and Film," and Gopnik, "Basic Stuff."

11. See especially McLuhan, *Understanding Media: The Extensions of Man*, 1964; and *War and Peace in the Global Village*, 1968.

12. See Gerald S. Hawkins, *Stonehenge Decoded* (Garden City, N.Y.: Doubleday, 1965).

13. See Cathcart, *Nancy Graves*, for the artist's fascination with the photographic analysis of movement by Eadweard Muybridge and for her series of works based on NASA maps of the moon, as well as her series of work concerned with prehistoric art (e.g., *Paleo-Indian Cave Painting*, 1971, p. 16).

14. These two tendencies in primitivist thought coincide roughly with two long-standing philosophical notions of the accessibility of truth, discussed by Karl Popper as optimistic and pessimistic epistemology. "Each of them forms the basis of one of the two diametrically opposed philosophies of the state and of society: on the one hand, an anti-traditionalist, anti-authoritarian, revolutionary and Utopian rationalism of the Cartesian kind, and on the other an authoritarian traditionalism" (see Popper, "Sources of Knowledge and Ignorance" in *Conjectures and Refutations* [New York: Harper and Row, 1968], p. 11). Popper's distinction, and his identification of the radical strain of rationalism, also bears on my earlier remarks regarding Gauguin's rationalism and its separation from Romantic traditions (see pp. 201–02).

15. For an examination of recent self-manipulation and shamanistic practice in art, see Thomas McEvilley, "Art in the Dark," *Artforum*, Summer 1983; also the catalog by Erika Billeter, *Mythos und Ritual in der Kunst der 70er Jahre* (Zurich: Kunsthalle, 1981). The developing modern interest in shamanism is traced by Aldona Jonaitis in "Creations of Mystics and Philosophers: The White Man's Perceptions of Northwest Coast Indian Art from the 1930s to the Present," *American Indian Culture and Research Journal* 5, 1 (1981). See also "Stones, Bones, and Skin: Ritual and Shamanic Art," a special issue of *Artscanada*, December 1973/January 1974; and *The Coming and Going of the Shaman: Eskimo Shamanism and Art* (Winnipeg: The Winnipeg Art Gallery, 1978).

16. See Lucy Lippard on "Feminism and Prehistory" in *Overlay: Contemporary Art and the Art of Prehistory* (New York: Pantheon, 1983). On the larger issues of connection between biology and sociological polemic, see two volumes under the auspices of the Dialectics of Biology Group, Steven Rose, ed., *Against Biological Determinism* and *Toward a Liberatory Biology* (London: Allison and Busby, 1982).

17. See Neff et al., *Charles Simonds*, especially for Simonds's own texts concerning the varieties of his "little people."

18. On shamanism in his work, Beuys has remarked: "I take this form of ancient behaviour as the idea of transformation through concrete processes of life, nature and history. My intention is obviously not to return to such earlier cultures but to stress the idea of transformation and of substance. That is precisely what the shaman does in order to bring about change and development: his nature is therapeutic.

"Of course the shaman can operate genuinely only in a society that is still intact because it lies in an earlier stage of development. Our society is far from intact, but this too is a necessary stage. It's the point of crisis that sets in at every stage of history and which we can observe in the past. Once the intactness has gone, a kind of metamorphosis begins. So while shamanism marks a point in the past, it also indicates a possibility for historical development. It could be described as the deepest root of the idea of spiritual life, deeper even than the mythological level of the later stages of Greek or Egyptian cultures for example....

"When we consider our own stage of historical materialism and all the things we experience as negative in our current crisis, we have to admit that this stage too is a historical necessity. I experienced it in the war and I feel it now every day: this state of decay that comes with a one-sided understanding of the idea of materialism. When people say that shamanistic practice is atavistic and irrational, one might answer that the attitude of contemporary scientists is equally old-fashioned and atavistic, because we should by now be at another stage of development in our relationship to material.

"So when I appear as a kind of shamanistic figure, or allude to it, I do it to stress my belief in other priorities and the need to come up with a completely different plan for working with substances.

For instance, in places like universities, where everyone speaks so rationally, it is necessary for a kind of enchanter to appear" (Tisdall, p. 23.)

On the myth of Beuys, see especially Benjamin Buchloh, "Beuys: The Twilight of the Idol; Preliminary Notes for a Critique," *Artforum*, January 1980, pp. 35–43.

19. The monument in question is the 1927 Tannenberg Memorial, designed by Johannes and Walter Kruger. Its place in a reorientation of the German monument, as well as its relation to subsequent Nazi ideals, is discussed by George Mosse in *The Nationalization of the Masses* (New York: New American Library, 1977), esp. pp. 68–71.

20. On Gauguin and Picasso, see my chapter and that of William Rubin, earlier in this book. On Picasso and the interchange between caricature, African art, and Cubism, see Adam Gopnik, "High and Low: Primitivism, Caricature, and the Cubist Portrait," *Art Journal*, Winter 1984.

21. One writer on the nature of discovery and invention who has always stressed this formative and sustaining role of culture is Stephen Jay Gould. See, for example, his discussion of Darwin's discoveries regarding Galápagos finches, in "Darwin at Sea," *Natural History*, September 1983. On the ratifying role of society in discovery, see also Augustin Brannigan, *The Social Basis of Scientific*

Discoveries (New York: Cambridge University Press, 1981).

For further considerations on the above material, see also the catalog *Primitive Presence in the '70s* (Poughkeepsie, N.Y.: Vassar College Art Gallery, 1975), and the review by Carter Ratcliff, "On Contemporary Primitivism," *Artforum*, November 1975; and Janet Kardon, "The Ethnographic Model," in *Masks, Tents, Vessels, Talismans* (Philadelphia: Institute of Contemporary Art, University of Pennsylvania, 1979).

Robert Smithson. *Circle.* 1973. Fossilized shale, 18 x 11" (45.7 x 27.9 cm). Collection Mr. and Mrs. Harris Weston, Cincinnati

Ground drawing: spiral and zigzag. Nazca. Pompa Ingenio, Peru. c. 300 B.C.–700 A.D.

PHOTO CREDITS

Photographs reproduced in these volumes have been provided, in the majority of cases, by the owners or custodians of the works, indicated in the captions. The following list, keyed to page numbers, applies to photographs for which an additional acknowledgment is due. Individual works of art appearing here may be additionally protected by copyright in the United States of America or abroad, and may not be reproduced in any form or medium without the permission of the copyright owners.

Frontispiece: © The Detroit Institute of Arts (Dirk Bakker)
Opposite 1: Creative Photography Ltd., Parnell, New Zealand
2: Margit Baumann, Bern
4: Top right, © Foto Wettstein and Kauf, Museum Rietberg, Zurich; bottom left, courtesy Museum Rietberg, Zurich; bottom right, courtesy Museum Rietberg, Zurich
5: Top, Ken Cohen, New York; bottom, Ken Cohen, New York
6: Hubert Josse, Paris
8: Speltdoorn, Brussels
9: © Colorphoto Hans Hinz, Allschwil-Basel
10: Left, Studio Contact, Paris
11: Left, Jerry L. Thompson, Amenia, N.Y.
12: Right, Larousse, Paris
13: © Malcolm Varon, New York, 1983
15: Top left, Ken Cohen, New York; top right, © the Trustees of the British Museum, London; bottom left, Ken Cohen, New York; bottom right, André Koti, Paris
16: © Malcolm Varon, New York, 1983
18: Jean-Luc Mabit, Paris
20: Left, André Koti, Paris; right, MoMA (Kate Keller)
21: Lee Boltin, Croton-on-Hudson, N.Y.
22: MoMA (Mali Olatunji)
24: Left, eeva-inkeri, New York; right, courtesy Forum Gallery, New York
28: © the Trustees of the British Museum, London
30: Museum für Völkerkunde, Berlin (Dietrich Graf)
31: MoMA (Mali Olatunji)
32: Museum für Völkerkunde, Basel (Peter Horner)
33: Musée de l'Homme, Paris (J. Oster)
34: Top left, © Colorphoto Hans Hinz, Allschwil-Basel; top right, © Museum für Völkerkunde, Basel; bottom left, © Museum für Völkerkunde, Basel (Peter Horner)
35: © Colorphoto Hans Hinz, Allschwil-Basel
36: Roger Asselberghs, Brussels
37: Top left, Indiana University Art Museum, Bloomington (Ken Strothman and Harvey Osterhoudt); bottom left, Igor Delmas, Paris; bottom right, James Mathews, New York
38: Roger Asselberghs, Brussels
39: Left, Musée de l'Homme, Paris (J. Oster); Ken Cohen, New York
40: Jerry L. Thompson, Amenia, N.Y.
44: Mario Carrieri, Milan
45: Top, courtesy M. Knoedler and Co., New York
46: André Morain, Paris
47: Top, Igor Delmas, Paris; bottom left, Poro, Milan
48: André Koti, Paris
49: Musée Barbier-Müller, Geneva (Pierre-Alain Ferrazzini)
50: Courtesy Art Gallery of Ontario, Toronto
51: Eric Pollitzer, New York
53: Right, Soichi Sunami

55: André Koti, Paris
56: © Malcolm Varon, New York, 1983
58: Left, MoMA (Mali Olatunji); right, A.S.C. Rower, New York, © A.S.C. Rower, New York, 1984
59: Right, courtesy The Metropolitan Museum of Art, New York
60: Top, Soichi Sunami; bottom, © Appollot Photographie, Grasse
61: Left, Hubert Josse, Paris; right, Indiana University Art Museum, Bloomington (Ken Strothman and Harvey Osterhoudt)
63: Little Bobby Hanson, New York
64: Top, Musée de l'Homme, Paris (P. Destable); bottom, all rights reserved The Metropolitan Museum of Art, New York
65: Left, MoMA (Kate Keller); right, © Speltdoorn, Brussels
66: Top, Museum für Völkerkunde, Berlin (Dietrich Graf); bottom left, Michael Arthur, San Diego; bottom right, MoMA (Mali Olatunji)
67: Top, Musée de l'Homme, Paris (J. Oster); bottom right, David Reynolds, New York
68: Jerry L. Thompson, Amenia, N.Y.
69: Left, Robert Griffin, Los Angeles; right, Igor Delmas, Paris
70: Left, A. C. Cooper Ltd., London; right, Eric Pollitzer, New York
71: A. C. Cooper Ltd., London
72: © Speltdoorn, Brussels
73: A. C. Cooper Ltd., London
75: © the Trustees of the British Museum
77: Appollot Photographie, Grasse
79: O. E. Nelson, New York
80: Top and bottom left, courtesy Perls Gallery, New York
81: Courtesy Archives Denyse Durand-Ruel, Rueil-Buzenval, France
84: © The Metropolitan Museum of Art, New York, 1984
86: Top, courtesy Museum für Völkerkunde, Vienna; bottom, courtesy Museum für Völkerkunde, Vienna
87: Courtesy Museum für Völkerkunde, Vienna
88: Top left, courtesy Museum für Völkerkunde, Vienna; bottom, © the Trustees of the British Museum, London
89: The National Museum of Denmark, Copenhagen (Lennart Larsen)
90: Courtesy Museum für Völkerkunde, Vienna
92: Museum of the American Indian, Heye Foundation, New York (Carmelo Guadagno)
93: Courtesy Museum für Völkerkunde, Vienna
95: © American Museum of Natural History, 1984 (R. P. Sheridan)
96: Top, Eric Pollitzer, New York; bottom left and right, The National Museum of Denmark, Copenhagen (Lennart Larsen)
97: Bottom left, Dennis Barna, Brooklyn, N.Y.
101: Bibliothèque Nationale, Paris
102: Bibliothèque Nationale, Paris
103: © The Metropolitan Museum of Art, New York, 1984
104: Hubert Josse, Paris
105: Musée de l'Homme, Paris
106: Bibliothèque Nationale, Paris
107: Bibliothèque d'Art et d'Archéologie, Fondation Jacques Doucet, Paris
108: Little Bobby Hanson, New York
109: Top, Musée de l'Homme, Paris (D. Ponsard)
110: Bibliothèque Nationale, Paris
111: Courtesy Galerie Albert Loeb, Paris
112: Musée de l'Homme, Paris (Jacques Viot)
113: Hubert Josse, Paris
114: Top, Hubert Josse, Paris; bottom, Eric Pollitzer, New York
115: Top, courtesy Pierre Matisse Gallery, New York; bottom, Musée de l'Homme, Paris (van de Broek)
116: Rheinlander Photoatelier, Hamburg
119: Top right, Peter Moore, New York

122: Denise Colomb, Paris
124: In Focus Production, Tucson
126: Musée de l'Homme, Paris
127: Roger Asselberghs, Brussels
129: Jerry L. Thompson, Amenia, N.Y.
130: A. C. Cooper Ltd., London
131: Barnes and Bradforth, London
134: Speltdoorn, Brussels
135: Speltdoorn, Brussels
136: Igor Delmas, Paris
137: Musée Royal de l'Afrique Centrale, Tervuren
140: Igor Delmas, Paris
141: Berriet, Paris
142: Berriet, Paris
143: Courtesy Kunstmuseum, Basel
144: René-Jacques, Paris
145: Poro, Milan
146: Igor Delmas, Paris
147: Bob Kolbrener, St. Louis
148: Hungarian National Gallery, Budapest
150: Vladimir Markov (V. I. Matrei)
152: Bottom, Alfred Stieglitz
154: Top, Poro, Milan
155: Courtesy The Minneapolis Institute of Arts
156: Hubert Josse, Paris
158: MoMA (Mali Olatunji)
159: André Koti, Paris
161: Roger Asselberghs, Brussels
164: Soichi Sunami
165: Poro, Milan
170: Right, Musées Nationaux, Paris
173: Bottom right, Speltdoorn, Brussels
175: Ray Manley, Tucson
176–77: Courtesy The Sterling and Francine Clark Art Institute, Williamstown, Mass.
178: © The Metropolitan Museum of Art, New York, 1983
184: Tom Scott, Edinburgh
186: Top, Fotograf Ole Woldbye, Copenhagen; bottom, all rights reserved The Metropolitan Museum of Art, New York
187: © The Metropolitan Museum of Art, New York, 1983
190: © Colorphoto Hans Hinz, Allschwil-Basel
192: Left, courtesy Musée Gauguin, Tahiti (Dominique Charnay)
195: Right, A. C. Cooper Ltd., London
196: Left, A. C. Cooper Ltd., London; right, courtesy The Art Gallery of Ontario, Toronto
197: Right, A. C. Cooper Ltd., London
198: Top left, courtesy The Art Gallery of Ontario, Toronto; bottom right, Jan and John F. Thomson, Los Angeles
199: Right, Musée Barbier-Müller, Geneva (Pierre-Alain Ferrazzini)
202: Speltdoorn, Brussels
203: Left, all rights reserved The Metropolitan Museum of Art, New York
204: John Webb, Cheam, Surrey, England
209: © Museum für Völkerkunde, Basel
210: Courtesy M. Knoedler and Co., New York
214: Right, Hubert Josse, Paris
221: Top, Bruce C. Jones, Rocky Point, N.Y.
222: Left, all rights reserved The Metropolitan Museum of Art, New York
223: Ray Manley, Tucson
225: Top, courtesy The National Museum of African Art, Eliot Elisofon Archives, Smithsonian Institution (Eliot Elisofon); bottom courtesy Michel Kellerman
228: Top, André Koti, Paris; bottom, Larry Ostrom
229: Left, Larry Ostrom; right, André Koti, Paris
230: Left, courtesy M. Knoedler and Co., New York
231: Left, André Koti, Paris; center, Eric Pollitzer, New York
232: Left, MoMA (Kate Keller); right, Ken Cohen, New York
233: Right, courtesy Bern Historical Museum
234: Left, © The National Museum of Ireland
235: Bottom, Hubert Josse, Paris
240: MoMA (Kate Keller)

531: Right, Igor Delmas, Paris
536: Bottom, courtesy Francis M. Naumann, New York
539: Top, Richard di Liberto, Fresh Meadows, N.Y.
540: Hubert Josse, Paris
541: © the Trustees of the British Museum, London
542: Little Bobby Hanson, New York
543: Eric Pollitzer, New York
546: Courtesy Charles Ratton, Paris
547: Hamburgisches Museum für Völkerkunde (Brigitte Claassen)
549: All rights reserved The Metropolitan Museum of Art, New York
554: Soichi Sunami
556: Top right, The American Museum of Natural History, New York (Rota)
559: Top, © Städelsches Kunstinstitut, Frankfurt am Main (Ursula Edelmann, Frankfurt am Main)
560: Top right, © The Denver Art Museum
562: © Arnold Newman
563: Ray Manley, Tucson
564: Left, Soichi Sunami
565: Right, Eric Pollitzer, New York
567: Left, © Malcolm Varon, New York; right, Eric Pollitzer, New York
568: MoMA (Mali Olatunji)
569: Left, Glenbow Photograph, Calgary, Alberta
570: Left, Mme Sabine Weiss, Paris; right, MoMA (Kate Keller)
571: André Koti, Paris
572: Top, Hickey-Robertson, Houston; bottom left, Eric Pollitzer, New York
573: Left, Taylor and Dull; center, Bill Holm, Seattle
574: Top right, © Malcolm Varon, New York; bottom, Eric Pollitzer, New York
576: Bottom, Hamburgisches Museum für Völkerkunde (Brigitte Claassen)
578: Top, courtesy L'Oeil, Lausanne; bottom, courtesy Richard L. Feigen and Co., New York
579: André Koti, Paris
580: Top, Soichi Sunami
581: Top left, Studio Marion-Valentine, Paris; bottom, © the Trustees of the British Museum, London
584: Top left, Walter J. Russell, New York; top right, courtesy The Pierre Matisse Gallery, New York (Eric Pollitzer, New York); bottom left, Linden-Museum, Stuttgart (Ursula Didoni)
585: Bottom left, MoMA (Kate Keller)
586: Top right, Soichi Sunami; bottom right, courtesy The Pierre Matisse Gallery, New York (Oliver Baker)
588: Left, Musée Barbier-Müller, Geneva (Pierre-Alain Ferrazzini)
589: All rights reserved The Metropolitan Museum of Art, New York

590: Left and right, Roger Asselberghs, Brussels
591: Left, Igor Delmas, Paris; top right, courtesy Henri Kamer Gallery, New York; bottom right, courtesy Musée des Arts Africains et Océaniens, Paris
596: Top, © City Art Gallery, Manchester; bottom, courtesy Marlborough Fine Art Ltd., London
597: Top right and bottom left, © the Trustees of the British Museum, London
598: Top and bottom right, © the Trustees of the British Museum, London
601: Top left, © the Trustees of the British Museum, London
602: Top right, courtesy the Henry Moore Foundation, Much Hadham, England; bottom, © the Trustees of the British Museum, London
603: Left, courtesy the Henry Moore Foundation, Much Hadham, England; right, © the Trustees of the British Museum, London
604: Left, A. C. Cooper Ltd., London
606: Bottom, Jean-Luc Mabit, Paris
607: Top, A. C. Cooper Ltd., London
609: Right, courtesy The Art Gallery of Ontario, Toronto
610: Bottom, Ken Cohen, New York
612: Left, Musées Nationaux, Paris
614: MoMA (Mali Olatunji)
616: Top, © Adolph and Esther Gottlieb Foundation, New York, 1980 (Robert Emates, New York)
617: Top, Don Myer; bottom, courtesy Pace Gallery, New York, © estate of Mark Rothko
618: Courtesy Christie, Manson and Woods International, New York
621: © Justin Kerr, New York, 1983
624: Top, Hamburgisches Museum für Völkerkunde (Brigitte Claassen); bottom, courtesy Smithsonian Institution, Washington, D.C.
625: James Mathews, New York
626: Top, Rudolph Burckhardt, New York
627: Eric Pollitzer, New York
628: MoMA (Mali Olatunji)
629: Right, Adolph Studly
630: © Adolph and Esther Gottlieb Foundation, New York, 1980 (O. E. Nelson, New York)
631: Rudolph Burckhardt, New York
632: Courtesy Adolph and Esther Gottlieb Foundation, New York
633: © Adolph and Esther Gottlieb Foundation, New York, 1979 (O. E. Nelson, New York)
634: Malcolm Varon, New York
635: Right, courtesy Wadsworth Atheneum, Hartford; left, Malcolm Varon, New York
636: Left, Little Bobby Hanson, New York
637: Left, Pierre-Alain Ferrazzini, Geneva; right, MoMA (Mali Olatunji)

639: David Wharton
640: MoMA (Kate Keller)
641: Courtesy Richebourg/McCoy Gallery, New York
642: Left, courtesy The Tate Gallery, London
643: Top, courtesy E. V. Thaw, New York
644: MoMA (Kate Keller)
645: Top, MoMA (Kate Keller)
646: Top, Michael Tropea, Chicago; bottom left, © Adolph and Esther Gottlieb Foundation, New York, 1979 (O. E. Nelson, New York)
647: Top, Geoffrey Clements, New York; bottom, Soichi Sunami
648: Eric Pollitzer, New York
650: Right, University of Indiana Art Museum, Bloomington (Ken Strothman and Harvey Osterhoudt)
656: Tom van Eynde, Berkeley, Ill.
657: D.A.D./R. W. Dreyfus, Paris
660: © Dia Art Foundation, 1980 (John Cliett)
663: Bottom, © Marilyn Bridges, 1979
665: Courtesy Xavier Fourcade, Inc., New York
666: Courtesy of the artist
668: © Marilyn Bridges, 1979
669: © Walter De Maria, 1968
670: Top, © Pieter Boersma GFK, Amsterdam, courtesy Leo Castelli Gallery, New York
671: Top, courtesy of the artist; bottom, courtesy of the artist (Maryanne Caruthers-Akin, Portland, Oregon)
673: Bottom right, Cristos Gianakos, New York
676: Bottom left, courtesy of the artist (Leslie Harns)
678: Top, Joe Schopplein, San Francisco; bottom, Peter Moore, New York
679: Bottom, Lee Stalsworth
680: Rudolph Burckhardt, New York
681: Bottom, courtesy Ronald Feldman Fine Arts, New York (Caroline Tisdall)
682: Right, courtesy Mary Boone Gallery, New York (Alan Zindman/Lucy Fremont, New York); left, Ivan Dalla-Tana, New York
684: Courtesy John Weber Gallery, New York (J. Ferrari)
685: © Marilyn Bridges 1979